Henry Scott, Third Duke of Buccleuch

Tim Hurlocker

Published by Tim Hurlocker, 2024.

While every precaution has been taken in the preparation of this book, the publisher assumes no responsibility for errors or omissions, or for damages resulting from the use of the information contained herein.

HENRY SCOTT, THIRD DUKE OF BUCCLEUCH

First edition. November 5, 2024.

Copyright © 2024 Tim Hurlocker.

ISBN: 979-8230886426

Written by Tim Hurlocker.

to Russ Roberts

author of *How Adam Smith Can Change Your Life*

Avarice and injustice are always short-sighted.

-- Adam Smith

CHAPTER 1

P ROFESSOR OF MORAL PHILOSOPHY *June 1759*
The June sun rises early in Glasgow, Scotland, and on that summer day it shone warmly through his windows as Adam Smith sat down to breakfast. As the Professor of Moral Philosophy at the University of Glasgow, he started his days early. Adam stirred sugar into his tea, and taking a tentative slurp, unfolded a letter in a shaft of sunlight.

Robert Reid, Adam's house servant, bustled into the room bearing bread and butter on a small plate, saying "Eggs in a moment sir. Sadly, no strawberries today."

"None at all? It's June, Robert, high time for strawberries." Adam's tastes were plain, but strawberries were his favorite.

"Wagon never arrived at market yesterday, I'll check again today." Robert was a big man, yet surprisingly graceful in the small dining room. Adam appreciated the optimistic tone Robert unfailingly kept, strawberries or no. He paid Robert well to keep him in his service.

"Is Thomas up?" Adam maintained a student boarder named Thomas Fitzmaurice, second son of Lord Shelbourne. Robert turned to the stairway, prepared to shout for the lad.

"Here I am, Robert. Tea please." Thomas, age fourteen, entered the room and slid into a chair across from Adam, who poured him a cup from the pot on the table. Robert disappeared into the kitchen, re-appearing in a moment with two plates of eggs. Thomas dove in with the eagerness of his age.

Adam pondered his student as he ate. Gangly and awkward as he was, Thomas was a bright lad with a bright outlook, unlike the sullen demeanors of some of the other entitled youths Adam had taught. As the boy paused his breakfast onslaught for a sip of tea, Adam noticed a wrinkle cross his otherwise smooth brow. "Any news from brother William?" he gently inquired.

Thomas paused a moment before his reply. "No letter, I'm worried Mr. Smith. Last he wrote, he expected a battle near a place called Minden. I think that's in Austria." Thomas' brother, William Petty, was an officer in the British Army.

"Well, that's a worry. Be brave Thomas, your brother is a resourceful fellow." Adam sought to change the subject. "Tell me again why William's last name is Petty, and you are a Fitzmaurice?

Diverted, Thomas shrugged and took another gulp of tea. "Father changed our name for some reason, more titles I suppose. Doesn't matter really, William will someday replace Father as Lord Shelbourne. I never understood why our title can't be the same as our name."

"We are all more than names and titles, Thomas." replied Adam. "What matters are heart, mind, and character. Speaking of which, can you show me your expense accounts this afternoon? I must assure the current Lord Shelbourne that his son knows the proper value of a schilling."

Thomas' eggs had disappeared. Robert returned with a bowl of steaming porridge; setting it in front of Thomas he admonished, "Keep it off your shirt young man. Tidy gentlemen get respect." Thomas nodded, his mouth already full. He was still young enough to see adults, even servants, as figures of authority. Adam took pride in treating all serving people with dignity and respect. Not only did that comport with the Golden Rule, but it was invariably true that happy servants served best. Robert was an easy man to like, and he was reliable.

Thomas paused again, slurped his tea, and added moodily, "If William gets killed in Austria, then I'll have to be Lord Shelburne." Adam gave the lad his full attention at this doleful remark, and Thomas added, "Not sure I want that, sir." Although such titles came with great wealth and social position, they implied great responsibility as well.

Adam pondered his young student with sympathy. "You are Thomas Fitzmaurice to me, and in my eyes, that will always be enough. Now, walk to class with me or we'll both be late."

As they strode across the sunlit square at the center of the University of Glasgow, the warm morning sun lifted all spirits. Thomas' natural exuberance returned as he kept stride with Adam, greeting classmates as he saw them. Jumping ahead, he pulled the heavy door open for Adam to precede him into the building. The only person in the anteroom was Dr. Joseph Black, Adam's close friend, and the current Professor of Natural Philosophy. Black would later discover carbon dioxide, and his further discovery of latent heat began the study of thermodynamics. In 1759, he was already widely acclaimed for his teaching ability.

"Good morning, Dr. Black, here is your pupil Thomas in the nick of time. If *you* are still here, *he* is not tardy," Adam said jovially.

"Good morning, Dr. Black," said Thomas respectfully.

"Greetings to you Thomas, I hope you brought your thinking cap today," said Dr. Black, smiling; it was obvious that Thomas was one of his favorites.

"Please go easy on us sir!" protested Thomas with a grin. Dr. Black opened a door, holding it for the boy as they both left the room. Adam, alone in the anteroom, momentarily pondered his reflection in the window. In his prime at age 36, his neat wig firmly in place, Adam brushed an imaginary speck off his coat. Turning, he opened a third door into a large lecture hall. A sea of student faces awaited him there.

"Good morning, gentlemen!" announced Adam as he closed the door and strode to his lectern.

"Good morning Mr. Smith!" chorused the class. He always had their eager attention as his lectures were popular. Adam would begin a topic slowly, asking many questions, framing the issue. At times, early on, he would seem unsure, almost absent-minded. But as he warmed to his subject he grew more animated, his speech came faster and with more assurance, until he was rolling towards a conclusion that seemed utterly inescapable. Adam's reputation had spread wide, so notables from across Europe sent their sons.

• • • •

SEVERAL BLOCKS AWAY, a tall, handsome man stood before a tall mirror in his lodgings as his valet put the finishing touches on his appearance. Charles Townshend, age 34, second son to his brother George, was particular about how he looked. George was a general fighting in Canada, and in 1767 would become Lord Lieutenant of Ireland. Charles, gifted with a wit barbed for ready ridicule, was born for politics. Seeking to improve his financial position, he'd traveled up from London to take an important step in that direction. His butler, Cook, a tall, angular man with thinning hair and a dour expression, hovered nearby.

"What time does Smith's class begin?" asked Charles.

"In five minutes. Would you like to walk, or shall I call a carriage?" replied Cook.

Charles looked nonplused. "So, we'll be late either way?"

"I thought you wished to speak to the professor after his class?" Cook raised an eyebrow, wondering if he'd made a mistake. Whatever could be said of the man, he was attentive to his duty.

Charles glanced at him but kept most of his attention on the fine figure he cut in the looking glass. "Yes, that is my intention. He's rumored to be the best lecturer in Europe, and I want to see for myself. It's a lovely day, we'll walk." Charles' valet placed the powdered wig carefully on Charles' head, but Charles invariably made the final adjustments himself.

"Very well, sir," said Cook. Turning to the valet, he dismissed him curtly, "Leave us." The valet complied promptly without a word.

"I want to look impressive. Do I?" Charles' request sounded more like an instruction.

"Undoubtedly. You bring an air of Parliament to Glasgow, if I may." Cook knew his role perfectly.

Cook led the way down the street, a step or so in front of Charles, clearing the way through the pedestrians. Cook was deferential to the well-dressed tobacco lords and prosperous tradespeople, but preemptory towards the laboring classes. Cook considered his station considerably above the common man, living as he did in the orbit and reflected glory of Charles Townshend.

· · · ·

INSIDE THE LECTURE hall, Adam warmed to his subject. "We are apt to imagine that slavery is almost gone, because we know little of it in this part of the world. But at present slavery is still almost universal. I will now show that slave labor is less productive than paid labor; that avarice and injustice are always short-sighted."

Charles and Cook entered the University grounds and walked through the inner courtyard. Cook asked for directions to Smith's class, and a willing student led them inside and up a stairway. Their purposeful steps echoed in the deserted upper hallway as the lecture hour was in full swing. The student pointed towards a door, bowed, and left; Cook seized the handle and opened it for Charles. Charles swept past and into the back of Adam's class. His regal presence stopped Adam Smith mid-sentence, and Charles saw a sea of student faces turn as one to look at him. Charles was used to this, and indeed it was his constant intention to present himself as an important man. Yet he was taken aback; the sea of faces seemed decidedly unfriendly. One brash student even put his finger to his lips as if to shush him! They clearly thought him less important than their professor.

Adam called out, "Good day sir, what can I do for you?"

Charles replied, "I'm sorry to interrupt you Mr. Smith, I am Charles Townshend."

Adam gave him a short bow from the front of the class. "It's a pleasure to see you in Glasgow, sir. Please find a seat while I continue."

Since empty seats were few and far between, Cook gestured to the two closest students to relinquish theirs. They complied, not too happily, and stood near the door while Charles and Cook took their seats. In his bright blue coat, Charles Townshend sat in stark contrast among the drab students.

Adam continued, "Last month, I met in Edinburgh a remarkable American named Ben Franklin. He is the man famous for flying a kite in a thunderstorm and proving that lightning is electrical. We discussed trade and finance. Mr. Franklin believes the best unit of value is not a pound sterling or an ounce of gold, but an hour of human labor. Labor, says Franklin, is the root of all wealth. It is only by labor that anything of value is created at all. Labor includes both physical work and the product of our intellect. Land produces cattle and corn only when the farmer applies his intelligent effort."

Adam paused, shooting a swift glance at his new guests, but he saw no reaction. He was not at all sure if Charles Townshend would agree with his lecture, but with the implacable trust Adam placed in his own good sense, he continued unabashed.

"Labor, not gold or silver, *is* the root of all wealth." Adam paused for effect. "Gold and silver are just money; the real wealth of a nation is found in the fruits of its labor. So then, is Franklin right? Should an hour of honest labor replace the pound sterling? How about a bank note worth One Pound Labor?"

Adam paused again, looking expectantly at his audience. He could see that Townshend was engrossed; Cook was looking about the room. Slowly, a student raised his hand. "Some people work faster than others?" he began tentatively.

"Exactly!" Adam confirmed, "An hour of labor varies too much to be a good standard of value. Last summer I watched some villagers race to harvest their hay, as the threatening sky promised rain. A hard rain could spoil the crop, so they worked like the very devil. People work hard when the possible benefit is great."

Adam paused again for a point of contrast. "Now consider slave labor. The slave gets no benefit; his situation is hopeless. Justifiably, he works as little as possible and has no incentive to improve his work. Why should he, when his owner reaps all the reward? Slavery is the least efficient form of labor, precisely because it is so inhuman, so demotivating. Would Franklin's proposed unit of labor be an hour of the oppressed slave, or of the frantic haymaker? The industrious blacksmith, or the lazy loafer? Or perhaps the spectacular value of an hour's time with Ben Franklin?"

After the lecture, Adam and Charles crossed the university courtyard with Cook hovering behind them. "You are impressed with Mr. Franklin, Professor Smith?" asked Charles.

"Franklin is a remarkable man, very engaging. But please, just call me Mr. Smith." Adam was not overly impressed with titles, since doctorates could be bought for the price of an impressive certificate. Just then Adam spied Thomas and hailed him. When the boy approached, Adam gestured towards Charles in all his magnificence.

"Thomas, meet my distinguished guest, Charles Townshend of London. Mr. Townshend, this is Thomas Fitzmaurice, the second son of Lord Shelburne. Thomas boards at my house so I can tutor him directly." Adam was pleased that Thomas, despite his youth, presented himself so well. He wondered if Lord Shelburne knew what a fine son he had.

"An honor to meet you sir," said Thomas, with a bow.

"And you, young man. I know your father well from Parliament. Do you enjoy Mr. Smith's tutelage?" Charles could be very charming, although rarely to the young or otherwise unimportant.

"Indeed sir." Thomas shot a glance at Adam, wondering at the question.

"Don't embarrass the lad, Mr. Townshend," Adam said with a smile. "Thomas, remember your accounts later today." After Thomas had run off, the three proceeded with their walk in the sunshine.

"Shelburne, hmmm?" mused Charles. "If Lord Shelburne trusts you with even his second son, that is high praise. Your reputation seems well-earned."

"Reputation?" asked Adam with raised eyebrows.

Soon they were in Adam's office, with Adam sitting behind his desk and Charles in a chair opposite. Cook stood unobtrusively by the door. "So, Mr. Townshend, to what do I owe the pleasure of your visit?" Adam asked pleasantly.

"Your skeptical friend David Hume gave me this in London," began Charles, sliding a copy of Smith's new book, '*The Theory of Moral Sentiments*,' across the desk towards him. "Would you be so kind as to sign my copy?"

Adam, visibly pleased, turned the book, opened the cover, and dipped a quill in ink. He signed neatly, in a slow, round hand, simply, "Adam Smith." Looking down as he signed, careful to avoid messy ink spots, he said, "Mr. Hume is skeptical about many things. I am indebted to him. Have you read much of it then?" He blew on the ink softly.

"All of it," replied Charles, "It's a remarkable effort, challenging in subject yet easy to comprehend. It is well-received in London. I found especially interesting your discussion of merits and demerits; of rewards and punishments."

"You honor me sir," Adam humbly replied. This was more than could be expected, although Charles Townshend had a reputation of being a well-read and erudite man.

Charles continued, "I've heard people say you are the best lecturer in all Europe. From what I just observed, I can see why."

Adam colored slightly. "Now you flatter me sir."

"Which brings me to the purpose of my visit," Charles straightened his back and laced his fingers in front of him. "Four years ago, I wed the lovely Caroline Scott, widow of the heir to the Buccleuch estate. Are you familiar?"

"Of course. The Buccleuch estate is the largest landholding in lowland Scotland," replied Adam.

"Just so," Charles affirmed with a nod. "Caroline was left with three children. The oldest, Henry Scott, became the Third Duke of Buccleuch at age five, when his grandfather died. His father died of smallpox when the poor lad was only four." Charles feigned sadness for the plight of the future Duke. After a moment, he continued. "Henry is currently at Eton, age 13, and will finish there in four years. He has a brother, Hew Campbell Scott, and a sister, Frances."

Adam took this in for a moment, nodding. "I understand the family lives in London?" Adam knew more than he showed, as the famous were discussed widely. Both the Buccleuch and Townshend names carried weight. Just that year, Charles' brother George had accepted the surrender of Quebec, after General Wolfe died on the Plains of Abraham. That thrilled the entire nation.

"Our estate is at Adderbury, just north of Oxford. The children were all born there. Are you familiar?" Charles asked.

Adam smiled slightly. "I was a student at Oxford for six years. But I don't travel often, except to Edinburgh."

"I see. Well, I have a proposition for you, which brought me all the way to Glasgow." Charles paused for what he hoped was a dramatic effect. "I'd like you to be Henry Scott's tutor. Travel with him to Europe, including France, when he graduates from Eton. How does that strike you?"

Here was a spectacular, once-in-a-lifetime opportunity for any teacher, especially one from poor Scotland. Charles felt pleased that he could offer such benevolence to this humble professor, even if Smith's book was currently all the rage in intellectual London. Benevolent, even though he planned to pay Smith with young Henry's money. He'd make himself Henry's guardian within a year, giving him the financial authority to make this excellent offer to the trendy, though plain, Scottish intellectual. Yes, Charles was pleased with himself.

"Assuming the war is over by then?" asked Adam calmly.

Charles was surprised that this question came first. Henry would graduate in 1764. "Of course, the war will be over by then," he stated flatly. "It is already three years duration. Wars are too expensive to last much longer. Not only do I expect peace with France, but I hope to include Paris in young Henry's Grand Tour of Europe." Charles paused, seeing Adam nodding to this, but saying nothing. "With you, hopefully," he added lamely. "I imagine it will be a grand opportunity for you to see the wider world."

The two men looked at each other across the desk for a pause that seemed to Charles about two seconds too long. Adam leaned forward and put his folded hands on the desk. "Mr. Townshend, you do me great honor. Let me consider for a moment. I would have to resign my position as professor to take such an extended assignment abroad."

Charles turned in his chair and waved Cook out of the room. Cook complied attentively, as he'd been listening to every word and knew the financial offer was forthcoming. Charles turned back to Adam. "I offer a salary of 300 pounds per year, plus expenses."

Adam gulped, as that was an enormous salary for the times. It was twice his current income as a professor, and professors were responsible for their own expenses. His income would effectively triple. He replied slowly, "I... am also Dean of Faculty here."

"What does that mean? That you're the Head Professor?" asked Charles, slightly bewildered as to why that might matter when he'd just offered 300 pounds per annum.

"I am the chief administrator for the University. I keep most of the accounts, run the committees, hire staff, and so on." Adam replied evenly.

Outside, Cook stood near the door. He leaned towards the crack slightly, listening intently. Although Charles Townshend excused his butler when discussing substantial deals, Cook was a calculating man keenly interested in the actual amounts at stake. He failed to hear anything useful this time.

Inside, Charles nodded to Adam with apparent understanding. "Not just a cloistered professor after all, Mr. Smith? You have a substantial position here, one that would be difficult to fill in your absence. But your administrative skill makes you even more desirable as Henry's tutor. Henry Scott will, God willing, take his place in government once he reaches the age of majority. He will help lead this great nation. His proper education and good judgement are important to this country's welfare."

Charles paused, surprised that he'd drawn himself to full height despite remaining seated in his chair. Softening his tone, he added, "That is why I want the best teacher in the kingdom for my stepson. I will add a pension of 300 per year for the rest of your life. You could write books to the end of your days. How much do you earn here, might I ask, for all your duties? Including what Lord Shelburne pays you to board his lad?" Charles knew he was being rather forward, but he threw caution to the wind as his offer was now fabulous.

Adam remained calm. "Rather less. Tell me more about young Henry."

Charles relaxed. "With pleasure. Henry is a fine, robust lad in good health, not too different than Shelburne's lad really. Henry is a bright boy, eager to learn, and with good discipline for such a young age. Other boys like him. I'm sure you'll have little difficulty with him."

"What of his personality, his nature? How is he about the house?" Adam inquired.

"As I mentioned, he is at Eton currently. He comes home on holidays." Charles replied, thinking this Smith fellow was the very opposite of absent-minded. That was a keen question, uncomfortable even.

"He must have just started at Eton...? Adam persisted.

"Well, yes. Before that he was at various boarding schools for much of his upbringing. All good reports from the school headmasters, I assure you," said Charles. He felt like he was parrying thrusts from the gentle professor.

Adam paused thoughtfully, recognizing that Charles probably didn't know his stepson very well. He dropped that line of inquiry, noting what it implied about Townshend's motives. They were likely more financial, and perhaps political, than they were fatherly. "Is he learning Latin, Greek? Much of my assigned reading would be in the original. So much is lost in bad translation," asked Adam, changing direction.

"Certainly. I am also recommending French," Charles said crisply.

Adam nodded and said, "Language is the means of both arts and science, and important discoveries are happening in many countries. A young man in this university is teaching himself German, just so he can read the latest advances in his field." Adam checked himself from going further.

"I wasn't thinking of German too..." said Charles doubtfully.

Adam was quick to reassure him. "Oh no, a boy can only learn so much! French would be valuable. I can read and write the language but speaking it in France would require practice. Assuming the war is over by then," he added.

"Of course, it will be over by then. All treasuries would be empty long before. Now, as first born, Henry is not destined for the military. He is born for Parliament." Rather than press Adam for an immediate decision, Charles stood suddenly. "Can you show me your fine university?" he asked. Cook instinctively stepped back into the room, unbidden, at the sound of the chair being pushed back.

Adam rose with an obliging smile. "Gladly. After you Mr. Townshend."

Charles turned to Cook and dismissed him. "Return to our rooms, Cook, and make sure I'm ready to depart in the morning." Cook nodded and disappeared.

Wisely, Adam led Charles across the commons and away from the faculty room or the President's office. They would fawn over the distinguished guest, that would drag on, drinks would be drunk, and Charles wouldn't see a thing. They entered a building and wound towards the back, passing shelves filled with natural curiosities, samples, instruments, and other evidence of natural philosophers at work. They entered a cluttered workshop, where sat Dr. Black with a young man in his early twenties. Both looked up from their close collaboration, surprised.

"Dr. Black, Mr. Watt, allow me to introduce Mr. Charles Townshend, member of Parliament. Mr. Townshend, this is Dr. Black, our Professor of Natural Philosophy." Adam said rather formally. Dr. Black stood quickly and gave a short bow.

"It's a pleasure to meet you, Professor," said Charles politely.

"Likewise, sir," said Dr. Black.

"This is Mr. Watt, an ingenious lad who repairs navigation instruments, musical instruments, and just about everything else," said Adam with a smile. James was as popular with the professors as he was handy with tools.

"Honored to meet you sir," said James, standing.

Charles nodded cursorily at James, but he looked at Adam when he responded, "You have tradesmen working in the University?"

James' face fell, his mouth opened to speak, then shut quickly.

Adam, seeing Charles slight James, said hastily, "Mr. Watt is the only person in Glasgow who can repair navigation instruments for our ship captains. He is also conducting experiments with steam, working with Dr. Black here." Adam kept an even, informational tone, as if Charles' condescension was simply due to a misunderstanding. He added, "How is your German coming along, Mr. Watt?" but received no answer as Dr. Black was speaking.

Dr. Black said, "James does what we like to call 'applied science,' Mr. Townshend. He is invaluable."

"Inside the University? What guild does your workman belong to?" Charles believed that only tradesmen worked with tools, and that tradesmen didn't belong in a university. He was oblivious that James was increasingly nettled by his imperious manner. To Charles, what a tradesman thought of anything was unimportant.

Despite his headstrong youth, James kept a civil tongue. Although he was only 23, he knew how lucky he was to have a place inside the University where he could work, tinker, and experiment. "That's just the problem," he said, "there is no guild for instrument repair. It's too specialized. But they wouldn't let me set up shop without serving seven years in a guild. They decided I must be in the Hammersmith Guild."

Charles was looking about the cluttered room, seeing violins, teakettles, sextants, clarinets; he gave only glancing looks at this Watt fellow as he spoke. Tradesmen were beneath his station, that should be clear to all. Yet he listened to what James was saying. However arrogant, manipulative, or cold-hearted Charles Townshend might be, no one ever doubted his intelligence. He could adjust to any situation as needed.

"Remind me what the Hammersmiths do?" asked Charles, contemplating a flute hung on the wall while rubbing his chin.

"Mostly they make pots and pans, kitchen utensils, and the like," answered Adam, helpfully.

"I see. Your man has his workshop here to escape the guild apprenticeship. What else can Mr. Watt do, shoe horses?" Charles couldn't help himself.

Adam winced, but Dr. Black and James Watt took the blow with more grace than could be expected. Both knew that it never paid to offend the powerful. Black spoke up, repeating "We conduct experiments, Mr. Townshend." James looked gratefully at his friend and mentor. If the Professor could keep his temper, so could he.

"Actually, I *can* shoe a horse," said James. "But that's not why they set me up in this shop. We think we can improve the steam engine that pumps water out of the mines. I daresay that's a mite tougher than hammering a horseshoe," James added. He couldn't help himself either.

James boldly caught Charles' eye and held it; Charles met his gaze for a long moment before dismissively turning back to Adam and Dr. Black. "Fascinating," said Charles with a flat tone, "What else have you to show me Mr. Smith?" Looking only at Dr. Black, Charles added, "Pleasure to meet you gentlemen."

James rolled his eyes at Dr. Black as Charles followed Adam out of the workshop. He felt thoroughly insulted by the arrogant Englishman, but he didn't let on to save Mr. Smith any embarrassment. Once they were gone, James looked at Dr. Black as he sat down to resume their previous discussion. "There goes someone too high and mighty for me! What do you say, Dr. Black?"

"He'd mind his manners if he knew what you can do, James. I'm not sure of Townshend's interest here, but I'm sure it involves our valuable Mr. Smith." He put a sympathetic hand on the young inventor's shoulder. "Thanks for keeping a lid on your teakettle!"

Adam and Charles left the university grounds to visit Glasgow's booming commercial center. Ships bringing tobacco from America would sail up the Clyde and unload at Glasgow, closer and more accessible to ships from the west than was London on the Thames. Enterprising merchants and tradesmen would fill the returning tobacco ships with leather goods and manufactured items favored in the Colonies. They visited tanneries, warehouses for ship stores, and a pin factory.

After a long afternoon, the late day sun was still high in the summer sky as they found themselves back at the university entrance. A fancy carriage pulled up, and Cook popped out. He held the carriage door open, awaiting Charles. "Well, Mr. Smith, I thank you for your time and the tour. Glasgow appears to be thriving; I had no idea so much building was going on here." Charles beamed at Adam, turning on his political charm.

"The colonial tobacco trade has been a boon to us poor Scots," replied Adam, "It's a brisk trade that benefits all."

"Most interesting. Now Mr. Smith, before I go, can you give me a clue about traveling with the young Duke when the time comes?" Charles looked at Adam for his reply, but also for clues as to what the polite professor might really be thinking.

"I am interested, Mr. Townshend, and I accept your fine offer. I will mention your proposal to no one, until I hear from you when he graduates." Adam was smiling, calm and reserved as always. Inside it felt like he was galloping uncontrollably away from his predictable, satisfying life.

Charles beamed and shook Adam's hand with real warmth. "Excellent, Mr. Smith, excellent!" Charles was nearly likeable in his obvious satisfaction; his trip was successful, his prize secured. "You will hear from me," he promised. He turned and climbed carefully into the carriage, and Cook closed the door behind him. Cook stepped around the carriage to enter by the opposite door. Charles leaned out the window, holding his signed copy of *The Theory of Moral Sentiments*. "Your book is what brought me here, Mr. Smith. Do you plan to write again?"

"I hope to, Mr. Townshend. My duties as Dean take much of my time." Adam spoke up to be heard over the jangling harness and snorting horses.

As the carriage pulled away, Charles called out, "Write what you can, Mr. Smith, the world needs you!" With a wave of his hand he was gone, leaving Adam wondering how many of Townshend's lavish promises might come true. Time would tell.

CHAPTER 2

ADDERBURY *December 1763*

Darkness overtook the fancy carriage as it splashed along the wet road to Oxford behind a four-horse team. Their breath formed clouds of vapor that wreathed their fine black heads. By the time the carriage reached the Buccleuch estate at Adderbury the cold rain had turned into big wet flakes of snow. Henry and Hew were coming home for Christmas.

They were eagerly expected. As the carriage clattered into the courtyard, liveried servants emerged with torches that wavered fitfully in the winter wind. A hostler caught the horses and held them steady. Before a servant could reach the carriage door, it opened from inside and Cook stepped out. He stood aside, holding the door for the more important occupants. "Home, young gentlemen! Your mother will be so pleased to see you both." Cook could be charmingly unctuous when he tried.

Henry, seventeen, climbed out first, dressed in an expensive wool overcoat. He was followed by Hew, almost two years younger and similarly dressed. They stretched and stamped their feet, as it was a long cold ride from London. Snowflakes stood in stark torchlight relief against their dark coats and dark, wavy hair. Cook himself held open the large, ornate door to the manor house, and the boys swept inside. Servants took their coats, shaking free a cascade of sparkling droplets. For a moment, it was just them and Cook in the entry hallway.

Henry clapped his brother on the shoulder. "Home for Christmas, brother! But only you return to school in January. I'm off to Paris!" His broad smile showed beautiful teeth, rare in those times.

Hew smirked at his brother, not without envy. "Better you than me, Henry. The guns are hardly cold yet and you're off to see the enemy."

"The war is over, and I shall be perfectly safe," countered Henry. "Wars aren't fought by the rich anyway. They're fought by the peasants."

"And second sons," said Hew, before they were interrupted by a squeal of delight from their sister Frances, age 14, who came running towards them at top speed.

"You're here, you're here! Happy Christmas Henry! Happy Christmas Hew!" Frances' run ended abruptly in Henry's big hug.

"It's good to see you, Frances!" Henry laughed, genuinely happy to see his exuberant sister. "You're growing up!

Frances switched hugs to Hew. Henry noticed that Frances was only a few inches shorter than Hew; Hew in turn was two inches shorter than Henry, who stood an inch or so less than six feet.

Hew held Frances at arm's length. "Frances, you're taller by the minute! I can almost see you growing, sister!"

Caroline Townshend swept into the room, both arms wide in welcome. "My sons!" she exclaimed, sweeping them both into her arms, shunting Frances aside without a look. Each son kissed her cheek dutifully, then she released them. "I'm sure you're both cold and hungry from your travels," Caroline led them towards the drawing room where a cheerful fire burned bright in the huge fireplace. "Come warm yourselves and I'll ring for some nice hot tea." Over her shoulder, she ordered, "Frances, have the maid see to it."

"Yes, Mother," said Frances. She saw the maid already turning to comply, while giving Frances a quick, friendly wink. Her aunt, Lady Mary Coke, would later write about Frances in her diary, noting that her sister Caroline was, "insensitive to her merits." Her mother's severity hurt Frances, but her natural childish exuberance found its reward. All the servants loved her.

"Hot tea sounds wonderful. I smell something delicious cooking and I'm famished," said Henry.

"Your appetite is only half of mine, big brother. I hope there's plenty," added Hew, who had never gone hungry in his life in the formal sense. Yet at age sixteen he was always hungry.

"Charles will be home shortly, and we eat at six," announced Caroline. "Cook, see that the boys have all they need to dress for supper, including lots of hot water."

"Yes, my lady," Cook murmured.

At that moment the door opened again, and Charles Townshend entered the hall, casting his coat and hat to a servant. Charles beamed at his family as they all re-entered the entry hall from the drawing room. "I'm home! Here's the whole family!" Charles exclaimed as he swept Frances into a big hug that was obviously sincere; she was his favorite. "Hooray, Christmas is nigh!" Releasing Frances, he clapped the boys on their shoulders. "The boys are home; the holidays can begin." He left his hands on their shoulders while looking them up and down with satisfaction. "You both look hale and healthy. Did you travel well?" As usual, Charles' larger-than-life personality filled the room.

"Six hours in the cold wet gloom, Father, but it's all right now. We're home!" smiled Hew.

"It's good to see you, Charles," said Henry, more reserved than his younger brother.

"How do you feel now that Eton is behind you?" inquired Charles, looking Henry in the eye and giving him his full attention. "Are you ready for your next adventure?" Charles and

Henry were about the same height, although Charles was growing stout on the fine meals he ate while in London.

"Not yet, Charles. First, I'll eat and have Christmas!" Henry laughed, unwilling to discuss his future in the hallway.

"Who would have thought the damn war would last seven years?" responded Charles, relieved that Henry seemed to be in a good mood. Henry could be prickly, and much of his plan depended on maintaining a good relationship with the duke, even though he was Henry's legal guardian. Charles was planning for September 2, 1767, the day Henry turned 21 and inherited everything, both the Scotland estates and their English estate at Adderbury. The family returned to the warm drawing room, where the maid was ready to pour tea.

An hour later, at six o'clock, the head of the serving crew rang a little bell, calling everyone to dinner in the richly furnished formal dining room. Charles and Caroline entered and took seats at opposite ends of the table. Hew and Henry, dressed for dinner in jackets and cravats, sat next to each other on one side; Frances entered unaccompanied, and took the seat opposite Hew. An empty place setting sat unoccupied opposite Henry, who announced, "I invited James MacDonald of Sleat to dine with us. Apparently, he is delayed."

Charles raised his eyebrows. "MacDonald of Sleat?" he asked, "Do you mean the Highlander family?"

"Yes, James is heir to the Lord of the Isles. Such a violent heritage for such a good-natured fellow," said Henry.

Cook entered the dining room immediately after the servants brought the soup, announcing, "May I present James MacDonald of Sleat."

James MacDonald stood in the doorway, bowing, looking nothing like the frightful Highlanders of old. He was a stylish, handsome young man about Hew's height; well-educated, well-dressed, and some thought, too glib. Born in Scotland, his Catholic mother had been forced to flee to France for sheltering Bonnie Prince Charlie after his defeat at Culloden in 1746. Fluent in both French and English, he could even imitate a Scottish brogue from his mother. James was wealthy, educated, handsome, and he knew it. He strode forward and took the empty place at the table.

"Greetings everyone! I am so sorry to be late. Have I missed a course or two?" said James with a smile. Because he was so genuinely charming, James knew to expect every indulgence for his minor errors, such as tardiness. Even Caroline was smiling at him; Frances looked almost frightened of being so close to such a handsome fellow.

"Not at all, James! We just sat down. Pray settle there next to my sister Frances. You know Hew; this is my mother, Caroline, and my stepfather, Charles." Henry gestured at each in turn, but since soup had already been served, no one stood to greet him, and no one seemed to mind the informality.

"It's a great honor to meet you, Lady Caroline, and you, Mr. Townshend," said James with due gravitas, shaking a napkin into his lap. He turned to Frances with a slightly exaggerated formality. "It's a particular pleasure to meet *you*, young lady. I'm a good friend of your brothers; they talk about you incessantly." A twitch at the corner of his mouth gave him away to Henry and Hew, but Frances was both pleased and flustered.

"Ah, um, it's a pleasure to meet you as well. I'm sure my brothers barely mention me, but your words are kind." Frances recovered her poise, and her words ended well.

"Oh, but you must call me James! I know all about you, Frances. Henry confides in me, but he doesn't share much with the other students," James half-turned in his seat to address Frances and she blushed again. Charles and Caroline watched, amused. It pleased Charles to see Frances become the center of attention.

"Hew, on the other hand..." says James, with perfect timing. He gave Hew a mischievous wink; Hew caught on.

"Yes, everyone at school knows about my sweet sister Frances. But I assure you, only with the greatest respect," intoned Hew, though his slow smile gave him away.

Frances, blushing and confused, blurted out, "Hew, I am sure you are a liar!" Belatedly, she saw everyone laughing and grinned sheepishly. James had that effect on people; so remarkable even Caroline seemed happy and at ease. It was good to have guests at Adderbury, and weren't her sons handsome? With his brash and humorous entry James had diffused much tension. It was his gift.

Between soup and entrée, Henry asked, "James, where will your Grand Tour begin? France, Germany, Rome?" Most young men went on Tour to have fun, particularly with women who wouldn't affect inheritances back in England should their youthful indiscretions result in inconvenient children.

"I am destined for Rome, but the first leg of my journey is Paris. You?" responded James.

Charles interjected, "Paris as well. Henry, I have your beginning itinerary already prepared."

Henry nodded, then suggested, "Why don't we travel to Paris together James? Have you made your arrangements?"

James answered with a big smile of delight, "No, I haven't. It's settled then!"

"Very well James, I believe you sail in just under a fortnight. I will have Cook send you the particulars. Will you have a tutor with you?" Charles asked.

"Not as yet," James answered, "My father is arranging for my contacts in Rome, but not before then. Henry, who is your tutor?" Often chosen for academic prestige, tutors sometimes became little more than chaperones and travel companions for their charges. Many privileged students studying abroad, at great expense, spent most of their time gambling, drinking, and whoring; the tutor provided a veneer of respectability.

Henry glanced at Charles for confirmation, but said, "I suppose it will be my current man, John Hallem..."

Charles cut in smoothly, "Henry, I have secured the best tutor in all of Europe. He is Adam Smith, a well-regarded professor at Glasgow University. I sent his book to you."

Henry was stunned. John Hallem had been his personal tutor at Eton; both had developed an unspoken assumption that Hallem would go with Henry on his Grand Tour. How could Charles have decided this without consulting him? A well-educated and attentive teacher, John Hallem was a mild-mannered, religious man who imposed little or no discipline.

"So," began Henry slowly, "Mr. Smith *and* Mr. Hallem, or...?"

"Just Mr. Smith." Charles said bluntly. "I'm sending Cook to help manage your affairs while you study. I'm sorry if Mr. Hallem thought he was going, as I made no such offer."

"I get along very well with Mr. Hallem," replied Henry, calmly but with a noticeable edge on his tone, "I wish you had asked me first." He struggled to suppress his rising irritation at his domineering stepfather, especially since he'd invited James.

The happy supper atmosphere drained quickly; no one else spoke. Hew wolfed his food, Caroline took a deliberate sip of her wine, and Frances kept her head down while rearranging food on her plate. James, impossible to embarrass and involved in the conversation anyway, eyed both Charles and Henry while slowly lifting a fork to his mouth.

Charles remained in charge of the deteriorating situation. "Actually, I made these plans five years ago Henry, when I first read Mr. Smith's book. It made quite a splash in London at the time, and I found it had great merit. I hired him before others could." Charles calmly looked at Henry, who was clearly nettled but had not raised his voice. Both were conscious of James, and didn't want to air family disagreements. "Did you read it?" Charles had to see this through.

Henry shook his head, but answered, "I don't recall. What was the title again?"

"*The Theory of Moral Sentiments*," said Charles.

Henry nodded, then his nod turned to a shake. "I remember the book, but I haven't opened it."

The long quiet moment following prompted Frances to attempt a diversion, saying brightly, "James, will you be in Oxford through Christmas?"

Caroline, releasing her own tension, barked, "Hush Frances, don't interrupt. Please mind your manners."

Frances, chagrined and deflated, hung her head and said quietly, "Yes, Mother."

Into the awkward family tension sailed irrepressible James. He leaned sideways towards Frances, not looking at her, and whispered conspiratorially, "Yes!" Frances fell in love with James at that moment, in the crush-like devotion that happens with teen girls. Caroline seemed not to notice, so Frances snuck a small smile at James, and he winked.

Charles was grateful for the momentary distraction, as it allowed him to collect his thoughts. "My copy is in the study. If you start on it over the holiday, you'll know why I chose Mr. Smith for you. I hired the best."

"I was so anxious for the holidays, so I could read another schoolbook!" snapped Henry, giving vent to his anger. "So, John Hallem is no longer employed? We must look after him."

Charles sighed inwardly, beginning to regret the huge offer he'd made to secure Smith. "Perhaps we can offer Mr. Hallem a modest pension," he replied, remaining calm. Charles Townshend was already famous for his debate skills in Parliament, so he felt confident he could see this one through. The stakes were high.

The table fell silent as Henry and Charles locked eyes. Charles broke first, sensing he was being a tad preemptory in tone. He softened and began again, "Henry, your future is bright. When you return from your Tour, I'll have a borough lined up and you can stand for Parliament. That is a big responsibility; you must prepare."

"I see you have my future all planned, Charles," Henry said bitterly. Caroline brought her head up at his tone, alarmed.

"You are still young," said Charles, "I am looking out for your future as Duke. You were given much by birth, but from such high-born men, much is asked." Charles softened, leaned back, and rested his arms on his chair. His posture was thus disarmed as he changed tone and added, "You'll like Mr. Smith, I found him very perceptive and quite charming. He is about the same age as your Mr. Hallem."

Henry was silent for a moment, pretending he was preparing a bite, then dropped his fork and glared at his mother. "Were you aware of this five-year plan for my enlightenment?"

"Oh Henry, you know I leave such arrangements entirely to Charles. I'm sure he knows best. And just hear yourself complaining about being in Parliament! That seems like quite a nice problem to have." Caroline was satisfied with her answer and folded her hands, inviting no further inquiry into her role in his education.

James MacDonald leaned towards Frances and whispered, "The difficulties of the rich," making her snort. Caroline noticed but didn't take the bait, keeping her hands folded and her mouth shut. The problem with irrepressible people is they don't always know when to stop, and James was no exception. He got away with it this time, by looking at his grim-faced friend and observing, "Henry, I have heard that Mr. Smith's book is very sensible once you get going."

"Have you read it?" asked Henry.

"No, I was hoping I could borrow yours," deadpanned James.

Henry laughed despite his irritation. James was dangerous, but he sure was fun. John Hallem was inoffensive, but not much fun at all. Perhaps Charles' plan, though imperious and irritating, would work fine, especially the part travelling with James. Professor Smith couldn't prevent him from having a good time. Perhaps he could practice his French on the legendary Parisian women. Henry resigned himself to his fate. James was right, these were silly problems, and he could only laugh at himself.

He took a deep breath, keeping a smile off his face as he asked Charles, "Will we meet Smith here, or when we board ship for the crossing?"

"I expect him here at Adderbury just after the New Year," Charles replied, pleased.

• • • •

ON A BLUSTERY AFTERNOON, days later, Charles stood in the warm drawing room near the crackling fireplace. Caroline sat in an upholstered chair nearby. Outside the snow had turned back to rain, but it remained an indoor winter day. "Here we are at his graduation, and he still calls me Charles," he said suddenly. "Hew and Frances call me Father."

"He's the oldest. Henry can remember his own father. Have you asked him to call you Charles?" she asked.

"No, I've kept our agreement. Though I'm not sure what the lad could remember about him, at age four." They'd discussed this before, as Henry had rarely called Charles Father, even when he was a small boy.

Caroline rose, hands clasped to control her sudden agitation. "He remembers the funeral. He cried and cried. I'm not sure why, as his father was rarely home and scarcely seemed to notice him."

"I will keep our agreement dear. He can call me Charles," he reassured her, frowning.

Caroline wasn't agitated about what Henry called Charles. "This trip to France... I suspect these tours corrupt young men more than educate them. I'll not have Henry fall in his father's footsteps." Caroline had started pacing but stopped to look at Charles to emphasize her last sentence.

"Be calm, Caroline. I've thought of that. I agree that Paris is too much temptation for the boy, so they'll stay in Toulouse. A nice, quiet town where the archbishop lives," Charles replied. "Second, I've arranged to have a nice, quiet professor go with him. Third, Cook will be our eyes and ears throughout. Does that ease your mind somewhat?"

"I like the part about the archbishop," she answered, "I do fear the morals of any young man in Paris. Especially if that dashing James MacDonald is along. A pair of young dukes will be irresistible to both the gamblers and the ladies."

"They'll only visit Paris a fortnight. After a stop at the Embassy to meet Lord Hertford, Henry will be on his way to Toulouse." Charles reached out as if to touch her shoulder, but she was over two feet from his outstretched hand. Caroline made no move to close the distance.

"A lot can happen in a fortnight, Charles," she replied sternly. "I'm counting on you to keep a tight leash on Henry."

The door opened and Hew entered, followed by Henry. Hew gave Caroline a peck while Henry flopped onto a sofa. Charles plastered a big smile on his face and said, "Well, here are the two fine examples of English manhood we were just discussing, Caroline!"

"I thought we were Scots," said Henry dryly.

"Yes, sure, your lands and ancestors are in Scotland. Just a slip of the tongue, you fellows look splendid," Charles recovered easily from his gaffe. It was an easy one to make as no Duke of Buccleuch had resided in Scotland for over one hundred years. Most wealthy Scots lived in England, where the weather was better. The Scotts of Buccleuch were no exception.

"Henry, we have never even been to Scotland. How Scottish can we be?" remarked Hew.

Henry smirked at Hew. "You have a point there. I'll visit France before I visit Scotland." He turned to Charles. "Any word from Mr. Smith?"

"We expect him any day. Slow roads at this time of year," replied Charles.

Hew sat down on the other end of Henry's sofa. A moment passed in silence. "I tried to read his book," said Henry, at last.

"And?" Charles asked, eyebrow raised.

"The first sentence has forty-two words in it! What does holiday mean to you?" Henry tone was unexpected, and scathing; his resentments evidently unmollified.

Charles was taken aback, but after a brief pause, persisted, "Did you understand that first sentence?"

"Yes, Smith supposes that we humans care about one another as part of our nature. I thought holidays were about eating, drinking, and dancing," Henry added, sarcastically.

Charles remained in control of himself. "I understand, Henry, but Mr. Smith will arrive at any time."

"Did you promise him I'd read his book?" demanded Henry.

"No, but he might presume it. I wrote him that I'd given you a copy." Charles stood his ground. Henry was still his responsibility, though he obviously had a mind of his own.

Changing the subject, Henry asked, "Am I to understand that our time in Paris will be short?"

Caroline spoke up. "The shorter the better Henry, your Tour is to further your education. Paris is too much temptation for study. It appears Oxford hasn't been much better." Caroline added the barb as she resented that Henry and Hew had spent their last two evenings in the pubs instead of at home.

"What does the word holiday mean to you, Mother?" snapped Henry.

Caroline was caught short by his insolence. "Hew, can you leave us?" she said tersely. Hew, surprised, stood and walked out, closing the door behind him. Henry watched him go, wondering if he should follow, rankled by the expectations placed on him without his input.

"Henry, you are old enough to hear the truth about your father," began Caroline.

"Caroline don't..." protested Charles.

"Before he sees Paris he must know the danger. Henry, your father fell prey to the bottle and loose women," Caroline announced.

Henry looked at her blankly. "I thought he died of smallpox here at Adderbury. I remember everyone wearing black at his funeral."

"Yes, he came home to die. Whatever he caught, he caught it at the brothel. He lived there most of the time," spat Caroline bitterly.

Left unsaid was why Henry's father had found so little solace at home. Nine years older than Charles, Caroline was not known for her warmth or kindness. She was first and foremost the privileged daughter of the Duke of Argyll; she remained bitter about her first husband's manifest character flaws. Everyone had considered it a fortuitous match, bonding the estates of Argyll with those of Buccleuch. It was good for everyone but her, she thought. Henry's father never even became Duke, as Henry's grandfather survived his son by a year. The title skipped a generation; the fall of a favored son was a sad tale but not unique. There was a long silence as Henry looked at his mother, then his shoes, and then Charles. No one spoke.

Finally, Henry said, "I take it Hew and Frances...?"

"They don't know, and you must never tell them," said Caroline flatly.

"So, you worry that I'll go to Paris and succumb to women and drink?" asked Henry.

"And gambling," said Caroline.

"Gambling too?" Henry was overwhelmed by dirty laundry. He had little recollection of his father, but the ugly news hit him hard, nevertheless.

Charles gathered himself and added, "Gambling is how your father lost nearly all the Buccleuch estate in England. Your home here at Adderbury was barely saved. All the remaining lands are in Scotland, Henry."

CHAPTER 3

H IGHWAYMEN *December 1763*
Dawn had barely appeared on that late December morning in Glasgow, the very opposite of the warm June day four years earlier when Adam and Charles had struck their agreement. Misty and wet, gloomy and cold, Joseph Black and James Watt stood cloaked and hatted in the University courtyard as a rickety carriage pulled by a two-horse team came to a stop before them. Robert Reid jumped down from the driver's seat just as his passenger emerged from the building. Adam Smith, for twelve years Glasgow's esteemed Professor of Moral Philosophy, was venturing out into the wider world.

A letter from Charles had arrived some months before, confirming the terms of their contract for the further education of Henry Scott. On such an inauspicious morning, the plan was finally in motion, and nothing would be as it had been before. Adam Smith would never live in Glasgow again.

Robert double-checked the two large trunks lashed to the bed of the battered carriage. Adam faced his friends, Joseph and James, although he always addressed the eminent chemist as Dr. Black. A look of fond regret showed in their somber countenances. Bundled as they were, their pale faces offered the only clues to their sentiments.

"Safe travels my friend," said Dr. Black, "I know you well enough not to expect many letters, but if you send an address, I'll write."

"Goodbye, Dr. Black. You know me as well as anyone. I will surely write," replied Adam, who then turned to the young Mr. Watt. "Goodbye James, good luck with your experiments."

"I'll miss you Mr. Smith," said James plainly, emotion in his voice. He looked at the carriage and put a hand on the sideboard.

"Is this old cart the best you can do? It seems like you should travel in finer style!" The carriage was indeed a humble vehicle, with the driver uncovered and only a small awning for the passengers in the back. But talk about the carriage quelled the lump in his throat; Mr. Smith and Dr. Black had changed his life. James Watt was only two years from his momentous discovery of the steam condenser, which would in turn lead to a practical steam engine. Watt's revolutionary invention would not have been possible without the patronage of Dr. Black and Mr. Smith. Yet on that cold wet morning, he was just an emotional young man who felt he was losing an essential friend.

"The carriage I usually rent is in repair. This is all I could find on short notice. I'm sorry, Mr. Smith," said Robert.

Adam laughed. "It will do, Robert, I'm not a fancy man. I hope this rain won't last, or you'll be wet. It's three long days to Oxford." Adam extended his hand to Dr. Black, and then to James, in turn. They shook solemnly, each for longer than the standard handclasp. Three titans of human knowledge stood in the courtyard that dismal gray morning, all already accomplished, but all too young to know how brilliant their futures would be.

"Farewell," said Adam as he climbed into the carriage behind Robert, who took up the reins. As the carriage lurched into motion, Joseph and James waved silently to their friend. He waved back. Then they were gone, closing one chapter as another began.

All morning, they lurched along the bad road. Adam had brought a small book, but between the damp and the jolting carriage, he couldn't read. He watched the muddy fields crawl by, lost in his thoughts. Occasionally he'd offer a comment to Robert, but from the back seat it was difficult to make himself heard. Adam lapsed into reverie, thinking of his warm kitchen at the university, his colleagues, and the many faces of his students. He was trading all that to help educate one man, just one. Was it worth it, at any price?

Adam smiled, checking his nostalgia. Was he really the expert on human nature that the success of his book implied? If so, he needed to see more of the world. He needed to see Europe, especially France. Here he was, on his way to do so. Adam suspected he would learn at least as much as his student. Three hundred pounds per year! Contented, he made himself as comfortable as possible in the rocking carriage and tried to doze.

Robert stopped to rest the horses when the rain let up just past noon. He'd packed bread, cheese, and ham for their dinner, and as they ate the sun struggled to break through the low clouds. It succeeded just as they finished, and the brightness was so gratifying that Adam climbed up on the driver's seat beside Robert. The trip resumed in exhilarating sunshine, and they both pulled their hoods back. Thus liberated, they could converse.

Sitting high up beside Robert, Adam reveled in the transformation that sunshine made upon the winter countryside. Grays became green and water sparkled everywhere. Adam felt his spirits rising, this was a fine adventure indeed. He glanced at Robert; the pleased expression on his plain face suggested he felt the same. Adam rubbed his bare head with his hand, combing the short curls with his fingers, enjoying the absence of his wig. Sitting on the driver's seat made Adam feel more like a comrade than master and servant. Yet that had been his daily relationship with Robert for many years. At the end of this journey, it would end.

Adam considered what he knew of Robert. He was always at work before Adam rose, and he left after Adam's mother had eaten supper. In the middle of the day, Robert had several hours to himself. He was literate, as most Scots were, spoke clearly, and could keep his temper. In fact, Adam reflected, he had never seen Robert become angry, except once with a stubborn horse.

"You have a fine temper, Robert, you never seem to lose it," remarked Adam, breaking the comfortable silence as they bounced along the rutted path.

"Not while I'm working for you, Mr. Smith," said Robert with a grateful smile at Adam's compliment. "I'll get angry on my own time."

"I appreciate that about you, Robert, and so does Mother." Adam's compliment was sincere; he was never gushing in his praise so when he gave it there was real meaning. He was going to miss Robert.

"She's a fine lady," stated Robert, "and I'm pleased to serve your household, Mr. Smith."

"What, may I ask, do you do with your spare time Robert?" inquired Adam, pushing the natural boundaries between men of different social orders. Adam spent his evenings drinking claret with tobacco merchants and ship captains in Glasgow. Robert spent his evenings serving Margaret Smith. Adam didn't even know if Robert had a wife. "Are you married?" The boundaries were loosening as their relationship wound towards its end. Adam almost regretted asking it, but he was interested. This man had served him breakfast for almost six years.

"Ah, no," blushed Robert. "I, ah, have a lady friend." He looked at Adam sheepishly, then added, "She's an honorable woman, no whore, Mr. Smith."

"Oh, of course not! I don't sit in judgement, Robert. I just realized that after all our years together I don't know much about you. I'm sorry if I embarrassed you. Your relationship is safe with me."

"It's all right, Mr. Smith," said Robert easily, sliding past the old restrictions with good humor. "She's a ship captain's wife."

He grinned broadly, and Adam had to laugh. Ship captains could be gone for years at a time. "How about you, Mr. Smith? Will you ever marry? I get asked about you sometimes."

"Asked about me? By whom?" Adam hadn't expected Robert to ask the same question.

"No offense," answered Robert, "but it isn't your good looks. The widows know a professor makes a tolerable salary, and you're not a violent man. They'd line up to make your acquaintance, they would."

"Not my looks, then?" smiled Adam.

"You are a neat and tidy person, Mr. Smith," Robert laughed, "That counts for something."

Adam laughed. The sun shone, almost warm at this point, and despite the huge changes in his life he felt happy. Perhaps it was *because* he was making huge changes.

"I don't marry because of Mother," Adam said frankly. "Father died before I was born, so I've always known I'd have to look after her. She never remarried, and I couldn't bear the thought of her growing old alone."

"Lots of married folks live with their parents," stated Robert plainly.

"Not without conflict, my good man!" Adam laughed again but changed the subject. "Looks like our sunshine is leaving us," he said, looking at the sky critically. Robert, watching him, saw a small nervous glance cast his way. Robert was a simple man, but not a dumb one. He suspected how Adam managed, and it probably wasn't with a captain's wife. There were plenty of very respectable ladies who would do the deed for one pound sterling and never say a word. Cash was king in poor Scotland.

When the rain returned sometime later, Adam retreated under the awning and their conversation ended. Robert huddled under his cloak until they found an inn just before dusk. Adam watched him as he secured rooms, stabled the horses, and managed their luggage. His motions were purposeful and efficient; Robert could certainly do much more than make eggs for breakfast. Adam sought his room gratefully. It was a humble abode, but after supper and a pint, Adam fell asleep the moment his head hit the rough pillow.

The weather worsened overnight. Rain, heavier than the day before, but also wind. While tightening down the awning to prevent it from tearing away, the canvas tore anyway because it was old. While Adam sipped tea by the fire, Robert miraculously found a spare canvas and fashioned a repair. Although they were delayed two hours, his new awning was an improvement over the original. With Adam bundled into the back under his heavy cloak, they finally departed in continuous heavy rain.

It was a long, miserable wet day for them both. Worse for Robert, as he sat on the high seat under a huge, hooded cloak. They didn't even stop for dinner. By the middle of the gloomy afternoon Robert was looking for the next inn, but all he passed were the occasional farmer cottages.

The dark day was getting darker as the afternoon wore on. The patient horses pulled the old carriage up a small slope, where the road passed through a stand of trees. A hooded rider stepped his horse into the middle of the path, sideways. He stayed there, blocking, so Robert stopped. "What is the trouble, sir?" bellowed Robert in a loud voice.

With a crash of brush, a second hooded horseman appeared suddenly to the right of the carriage. Adam's heart leaped into his throat; they had driven into a trap. Fierce eyes glinted over a rough beard as the highwayman pointed a pistol directly at Robert. Less than ten feet separated Robert from his mortal peril.

"Your money or I'll fire!" snarled the man.

Perhaps three agonizing heartbeats passed before Robert's answer. Adam was petrified. "Not a farthing for the likes of you!" snapped Robert.

Adam started violently at this, as the outlaw was instantly infuriated. What was Robert thinking? "Right now, or this is your last day," replied the man, dead earnest.

"Not a farthing," replied Robert slowly. Adam couldn't understand how Robert could appear so calm while inviting death to them both. But he remained petrified, mute, with the rain pouring down.

As if in slow motion, Adam watched the man pull the trigger of his pistol. Amazingly, it misfired. The scowl on his bearded face showed his unhappy surprise.

"Haw, wet powder!" cried Robert, "mine's dry!" He pulled a pistol from beneath his cloak, pointed and fired in one smooth motion. At the sight of Robert's gun, the outlaw jumped his horse, and it was just enough for the ball to miss. He vanished into the trees, as Robert cursed, "Missed him, by God!" and seizing the reins, violently started his own team. As the horses surged forward the first rider bolted his horse into the trees and disappeared.

Robert whipped the reins relentlessly as the team thundered down the path. The old cart bounced so badly he feared it would fly apart. Adam, in shock, was tumbled about in the back seat. When he managed to right himself, Robert tossed the pistol, still slightly smoking, into Adam's lap. "Can you reload?" demanded Robert.

"No," Adam gasped, "I've never even held a gun!" Robert raced on for several minutes, then slowed the team to a trot. The horses couldn't run like that forever, and he decided there was no pursuit. The old carriage was holding together. Still, he was rather eager to get his pistol reloaded.

Around the next bend they saw a large inn, a sight for Adam's frightened eyes. Robert pulled to a stop, got down, and helped Adam step down. He took the pistol from Adam's shaking hand and concealed it beneath his cloak. A man came out, and Robert arranged for the care of the horses, and themselves. Adam followed Robert into the common room where they found a table near the fire. A few men sat at table on the far side, out of hearing.

"Where did that pistol come from?" blurted Adam.

Robert looked more smug than frightened, but Adam felt the opposite. "It's my prize possession, Mr. Smith," he beamed.

"You could have been killed!" Adam's whisper sounded fierce, venting his anxiety.

"Not hardly. I could see his powder was wet in the pan. These guns don't work good in the rain," said Robert as if he was discussing burnt eggs at breakfast.

"The other rider may have been armed," insisted Adam.

"I could tell he was only a boy, Mr. Smith." Robert waved at the serving woman, "Claret?"

She set down two glasses, opened the bottle, and served Adam. Before she could fill Robert's, Adam's glass was empty. She refilled it.

Adam looked at him over the rim as he gulped his second glass. Robert said sympathetically, "I can see you've had a fright, sir." He waved again, "Lass, bring that bottle back, will you? Mr. Smith, I wouldn't think of driving you halfway across England unarmed. You are a trusting soul, God bless you, but some men just can't be trusted. But I'm sorry it happened."

"I'd like to say all's well that ends well, but when you fired, I.... nearly wet myself," confessed Adam.

Robert suppressed a guffaw, he thought that was fine humor from the Professor, a man he truly admired but one not known for jokes. He didn't want to embarrass him, however. "Just between you and me, Mr. Smith."

"I still hear a ringing in my ears," said Adam, pushing on them experimentally with both fingers.

"Sorry the bugger was on your side of the carriage," said Robert contritely.

"You have served in our house for many years. We see each other every day. And now you see that I am just a timid fellow," said Adam. At that moment their roles seemed reversed, and Robert was the worthwhile man.

"You've had a fright, sir. Timid isn't the word I'd use," said Robert.

"You are... kind. I, you... we're all equal when the gun fires, so to speak," Adam said hesitantly. He paused, looking at his remarkable servant. Robert met his gaze but was uncomfortable with where the conversation was going. Fortunately, the woman brought hot bowls of mutton stew at that moment. Robert refilled Adam's glass, then raised his own to his lips.

"Do you ever resent being a servant in our house?" asked Adam suddenly.

Robert set his glass down firmly. "No. Stop right there, Mr. Smith. You've had a fright. I am very happy serving you."

Adam didn't let it go. "You don't... I don't know, regret your position?"

"We can't change the world, Mr. Smith. It's bigger than any of us. My friends envy me," Robert replied gravely.

"Envy you? How so?" asked Adam.

Robert ticked them off on his fingers, "I work inside, you never yell, you respect my dignity. I learn things by listening to you. My friends say to me, 'Robert, you got it so easy working for the Professor.'"

Adam was drunk, sentimental but not sloppy, and failed to note that none of Robert's fingers counted "pay" as one of the benefits. Money was why he worked, but not necessarily what made him happy.

"I see. Yes, the world changes slowly, if at all," he said thickly, "but then, it can change suddenly. You surprise me, Robert. You have a pistol, for God's sake!" Adam drained his glass, set it down. "I am in your debt."

"A reloaded pistol, I might add," said Robert. "Sir, your mutton is getting cold."

CHAPTER 4

M EET THE TOWNSHENDS *New Years 1764*
Early on a gray afternoon two days later, Robert drove the dilapidated Glasgow carriage down the long avenue leading to Adderbury's grand entrance. As he pulled the tired team to a halt in the courtyard, Cook emerged from the front door, followed by two liveried servants. Cook eyed the humble carriage dubiously. It looked like one of the farm hay carts, not suitable conveyance for an eminent professor. The carriage door opened before a servant could grasp the handle, and Adam climbed out, somewhat stiffly.

"Mr. Smith, we are honored to welcome you to Adderbury. Wonderful to see you again, sir, after five years' time," greeted Cook.

"I'm glad to arrive, Mr. Cook! It's been a long trip. I place myself in your hands," replied Adam, as the servants unloaded the two large trunks from the back of the carriage. Robert remained in the driver's seat.

Cook called up to him, "You there. Pull your cart through that gate and stable your horses. Someone will show you the kitchen if you need to eat." He spoke to Robert as he did to his own serving staff, imperious, peremptory.

Robert nodded and picked up the reins. Adam stepped over and looked up at him. "Thank you, Robert. I'll find you."

"Don't worry about me, Mr. Smith. Good luck," said Robert as he started the team.

Cook waited at the door, holding it open for Adam. The servants disappeared ahead of him, one on each end of the first heavy trunk.

"Please follow me, Mr. Smith, the family is anxious to meet you," Cook said with the same unctuous tone Adam remembered from their first meeting in Glasgow. "Is the cart driver your only attendant?"

"We typically have but one in Scotland," replied Adam as he followed Cook inside.

The entrance was elegant, with rich furnishings and subdued paintings, small canvases but in large, ornate carved frames. Adam glimpsed the drawing room just off the entrance, empty, as Cook led him down a long hallway with polished wood floors. Their heels clicked off their steps in the quiet. A door at the end of the hall opened, and a young man emerged. He was remarkably handsome, well-dressed, but quite young, Adam thought. "Excuse me, are you Mr. Smith?" asked Hew, before Cook could say anything.

"Yes, it's a pleasure to meet you Henry," said Adam, and he bowed.

Hew laughed boyishly. "I'm Hew, Henry's brother. Pleased to meet you Mr. Smith," as gracefully, charmingly, the lad bowed back. "They're waiting through the door there," he said, pointing.

"Honored to meet you, Hew," replied Adam in a formal tone, but with a smile. Hew was instantly likable.

"And you, sir," said Hew, and he continued down the hall. Adam turned to see Cook holding the door open. Adam was still in the hallway when Cook announced him.

"Sir, Madam, may I announce the arrival of Mr. Adam Smith," intoned Cook. Adam sped up his last few steps to catch up with Cook's words, and thus found himself stepping quickly into the room as if he'd been running to get there. He stopped short and absorbed the scene.

The drawing room was large, with a fire burning opposite Adam. Straight ahead, Charles Townshend posed with this left elbow on the mantle. To Adam's right, a middle-aged woman rose from her chair as he entered. Seated on a richly upholstered sofa to the left, Adam first glimpsed Henry Scott, Third Duke of Buccleuch. Henry remained seated.

"Greetings, Mr. Smith!" boomed Charles, "I hope your travels were uneventful?"

"It's good to see you again, Mr. Townshend," said Adam, "My travels were quite eventful, but they are of little consequence. It's good to be here."

Charles extended his arm towards Caroline. "May I present my wife, Lady Caroline Townshend."

Adam bowed low. "An honor and a pleasure to meet you, my Lady." Adam took in the natural set of Caroline's mouth, even as she tried to look pleasant at their introduction. Her dress was dark, with little ornamentation, though rich. She wore her hair pulled back in a tight coif. Adam found her severe in all respects, although he could see that she once had beauty. She looked matronly at her forty-six years.

"Welcome to our home, Mr. Smith," said Caroline cordially. "Cook, please see to refreshments."

Charles' arm swept to his right, and Adam's eyes followed. "This is Henry Scott, Third Duke of Buccleuch."

Henry rose as he was introduced; he was taller than Hew, young, dashing, handsome, but with a small air of haughty unfriendliness. Here was the heir to the richest estate in Scotland, and he looked the part, with aquiline nose, high forehead, generous mouth.

"I'm pleased to meet you, Henry," said Adam.

"The pleasure is mine, Mr. Smith. I'm glad you arrived safe and sound." Henry's diction was crisp and formal, almost stiff; but with poise that belied his seventeen years. Henry had known he would be Duke for as long as he could remember. He did not smile.

Adam smiled and said disarmingly, "All I can say is that I'm here in one piece and ready for adventure!" There was an awkward pause. Adam noted painfully that he was the only one smiling. There was tension here, but he was not sure of the source. Was it himself?

"Yes, it will be an adventure!" said Charles, knowing how to move along from an uncomfortable moment. He'd caused many such moments in Parliament; it was almost his stock in trade. "Mr. Smith, you must need refreshment from your journey. Dinner at six?"

Adam sensed he was being dismissed, just as Cook arrived with tea service. They were uncomfortable with him, but he didn't know why.

"Cook! Show Mr. Smith to his room. Make sure he has all he needs," directed Charles. "See you at six, Mr. Smith."

"You must be tired," added Caroline.

Cook, exasperated, turned the service about and motioned for another servant to take it. Adam turned to follow Cook out the door. In the doorway, Adam turned back towards Henry, who was still standing.

"Henry, a good way to become acquainted is to visit the booksellers together. Are you free tomorrow?" Adam was the teacher, and he would not be cowed.

Henry was taken aback. After a moment he said, "Well, yes. That seems fine. Say, mid-morning, after breakfast?"

"I look forward to it," said Adam, "There are some excellent shops in Oxford; if there are any titles we miss we can find them in London."

He turned towards Charles. "Mr. Townshend, I have prepared a list of books that I plan to assign. I can review them with you if there is a concern about the expense," stated Adam.

"I'd like to see your list, but only to understand your plan of education. Don't worry about the expense; buy what you think best for Henry," said Charles. "Cook, make the arrangements."

"Thank you," said Adam. "I am once again in your hands, Mr. Cook."

Adam followed Cook as they wound down hallways for some time. The house was enormous, with no part unfurnished. The expense must be staggering, thought Adam. How could so few people fill all this space? How could they heat it all?

Finally Cook stopped and opened a door, standing aside for Adam to enter.

"I hope you find your room comfortable, Mr. Smith," said Cook.

"Thank you, Mr. Cook. Could you send for my servant, Robert?" asked Adam. "Only after he's finished eating."

Cook turned to a servant who had just deposited Adam's second trunk in his room. "Go find Mr. Smith's servant and tell him he's wanted."

Adam called after him, "Only when he's done eating!"

"Is there anything else you need?" asked Cook solicitously.

"No, thank you Mr. Cook," Adam replied. He was suddenly, keenly aware of a pressing need to use the chamber pot.

"Supper is at six then. Good day, Mr. Smith," said Cook, then he turned on his heel and departed. Adam found himself slightly nettled at Cook's supercilious manner, but he had more pressing issues. Within a half hour, Robert knocked, and Adam opened the door to admit him.

"I trust your accommodations are acceptable?" asked Adam.

"And then some, this place is right fancy," said Robert, looking around at Adam's plush room.

"Adderbury has been the English home of the Dukes of Buccleuch for one hundred years. This house represents the height of good fortune," said Adam.

"Perhaps sir, but good fortune is different for every man," observed Robert.

Adam, a bit surprised, gestured with both hands at the spacious, beautiful room that surrounded them. "Rich lodgings are a good indicator of richness, Robert. Isn't this lavish?"

Robert shifted his weight uneasily, sensing he was suddenly discussing philosophy with a philosopher. He was a plain man, but like many Scots, a thoughtful one. "Good fortune is more than just things, I suppose," offered Robert, humble enough to know that even the richest camel wouldn't pass through the eye of a needle.

Adam smiled at him. "Indeed, Robert, indeed. All that glitters is not gold." Adam gestured Robert to an upholstered chair, with fancy embroidery decorating the seat. Robert perched carefully on the very edge. Adam took a seat opposite. "I'd like you to return to Glasgow and help my mother move back to Kirkaldy. The University has graciously allowed her to stay thirty days, but I don't want to presume upon them," said Adam. The University had provided his home for twelve years; now he must yield his domicile to the person who would replace him as Professor of Moral Philosophy. Kirkaldy is where Margaret Smith raised Adam, a small town across the Firth of Forth north of Edinburgh.

"I will Mr. Smith, depend on it," replied Robert firmly. "Would you like me to leave right away?"

"I would," nodded Adam. "As you can see, here in the duke's orbit I have everything I need."

"I'll leave tomorrow then," said Robert. "How long d'ya think you'll be in France?"

"Two years or more, I expect," answered Adam. "Mr. Townshend will share his expectations with me." Robert looked uncomfortable; he clearly had something to say. Adam suspected that despite their different stations in life, they would miss each other.

"Two years...," Robert began, then paused. He took a deep breath and bravely plunged ahead. "Then, sir, begging your pardon, I may not be here when you get back. I've made up my mind to go to Canada."

Adam was surprised. This was as unexpected as the encounter with the highwayman.

"Canada? Is this just a reckless impulse? Have you fired your imagination like you fired your pistol?" asked Adam, sounding a bit theatrical in his own ears.

"I'm going, Mr. Smith," said Robert resolutely. I'll see your dear mother to Kirkaldy first, don't you worry. You've both been very kind to me."

Adam and Robert sat looking at each other for a long moment. The moment suddenly seemed even more momentous than their pending separation had made it.

"What made you decide on Canada?" asked Adam.

Robert took a moment to compose his thoughts, then replied, "I've been thinking about it ever since I heard you talk about General Wolfe capturing Quebec. How the good general died on the Plains of Abraham taking the city from the French. It just stuck in my head."

"That was several years ago, Robert. Have you been thinking about it all that time?" Adam inquired.

Robert nodded. "Pretty much, sir. Never thought I'd have a proper chance, not wanting to leave your employ. Your trip to France seems a likely time."

Adam sat nodding for several long moments. Robert sat waiting, knowing how Adam looked when he marshalled his thoughts. At last Adam stopped nodding. He took from his pocket a leather purse, heavy with coins. After another pause of decision, Adam shook three coins into his palm. He weighed them there, looking at them, and then he extended the purse to Robert.

"Let this be the start of your Canada fund. If you decide not to go, you can return it to me. You must know you always have a place with me, Robert."

He held the purse, arm extended, but Robert didn't take it. "I can't accept that, sir, gracious as it is," said Robert. "Thank you, Mr. Smith, that's a right kind gesture."

Adam left his arm extended. "It's more than a gesture, Robert. Take it."

"I can't," he said. "No one would believe how I came to the money. They'd think me dishonest."

Adam scoffed, but he placed the purse on the writing desk. Seating himself, he prepared quill, ink, and paper. "Canada will be richer for having you, Robert. I'm going to write up this investment. These are funds for an expedition led by you. It will put all minds at ease," Adam stated as he scratched the quill across the heavy stationery. Everything about Adderbury was high quality, even the paper, he thought.

Robert sat watching him write, as Adam always wrote slowly. His plain round script was very legible, but his slowness meant he typically used an amanuensis. It took him several minutes to finish, then he held it carefully while he blew the ink dry. He handed it to Robert for inspection. Robert read it slowly, and then read it again. He looked up at Adam with tears in his eyes. "God bless you, Mr. Smith," he said.

Supper at six found the family in their established dining positions. James MacDonald's empty seat awaited Adam.

"May I announce Mr. Smith," said Cook at the door. Everyone stood as Adam entered and took his place at the table. A servant poured a glass of claret.

"So glad to have you here, Mr. Smith!" greeted Charles, as everyone resumed their seats.

"Thank you, Mr. Townshend, I appreciate your splendid hospitality," said Adam in a formal tone.

"We are so honored to have such a distinguished scholar in our home, Doctor Smith," said Caroline.

"Thank you, Lady Caroline, but 'Mr. Smith' suffices. Doctors are healers; I am but a teacher," replied Adam courteously.

"Perhaps Mr. Smith, but your fame is your best credential. Your book on sentiments made quite a stir here in London," replied Caroline pleasantly, who of course hadn't read a word of it.

"Thank you, Madam," nodded Adam, pleased. He was keenly aware, suddenly, that he was the only one there with a Scottish accent.

Charles and Henry exchanged glances; Charles arching his eyebrows and Henry shifted uncomfortably. He'd barely cracked Smith's book. "I found the book most excellent," said Charles. "Mr. Smith, Cook tells me there was some excitement on your journey?" Henry saw that Charles had covered for him, but he felt irritated anyway.

"Excitement?" Adam hadn't told anyone of their scrape; it must have come from Robert.

"Apparently your man was telling tales about an attempted robbery?" suggested Charles.

Adam laughed it off. "Oh, yes, but Robert saw them off. All's well that ends well."

"Saw them off?" inquired Charles. "Cook said no one believed your man's story as he wouldn't show them his pistol. I was shocked a gun might have been involved!" Charles' voice went up, with a hint of the theatrical. His oratory skill was legendary.

"Robert has the good sense to hide his gun around strangers," said Adam. "I didn't even know he had it."

"My God was anyone shot?" Henry asked eagerly, breaking his planned stoic reserve. This was too interesting to feign indifference.

"Oh no, no injuries," reassured Adam. "The robber's gun misfired in the rain, and Robert missed his aim."

"Shots fired!" interjected Hew excitedly, "Tell us how it happened!"

"Yes, we want details!" Frances clapped her hands. This Mr. Smith was so different from most who visited Adderbury.

"Oh, the less said, the better," replied Adam. "But Robert was very brave." At that moment the soup was served, causing a break in the conversation. As the servants filed back out past Cook, Adam turned in his chair.

"Mr. Cook, please tell your staff that Robert was telling the truth. Also, could you see that Robert has provisions for his ride back to Glasgow? He plans to leave first thing tomorrow," instructed Adam. If he was going to travel with this Cook fellow, he must establish proper footing from the very start. Cook looked startled, and then looked at Charles. Charles' nod was just perceptible.

"Of course, Mr. Smith," Cook's unctuous tone slid back into place. "There seems to be more to this Robert person than we supposed."

Adam turned back to the table, where everyone awaited his next words eagerly. "Yes, there is," confirmed Adam. "Two men waylaid us on a rainy evening two nights ago. One blocked the road and the other accosted us with a pistol. His powder was wet; Robert's was not. Although he missed his shot, the robbers fled." He deliberately kept the theatrics out of his voice.

"Were you scared, Mr. Smith?" asked Frances in an awed voice.

"Terrified, actually," Adam admitted with a rue smile. "It all happened very quickly. I have no experience with weapons of any kind."

"That is quite a story, Mr. Smith," said Charles, who was unused to being upstaged at his own table but had enjoyed Smith's brevity. "It might have turned out differently had the robber's gun not misfired. We are glad you made it through safe and sound. Ah, here's the next course."

Servants took soup bowls and replaced them with plates of lamb and gravy. They retreated and the conversation resumed amidst the clack and clatter of the silver as they ate.

"That is certainly more excitement than we typically see around here," said Caroline. "Do you suppose there are highwaymen in France?"

"Never fear, my dear, Cook will have authority to hire servants, guards, coachmen, as needed," Charles replied confidently. "Henry, speak up if you find Cook's arrangements insufficient in any way. Same goes for you, Mr. Smith."

"I will," said Henry. "Charles, who will be deciding the particulars of our travel schedule, Cook or Mr. Smith?"

Adam noted that Henry called his stepfather Charles. He also noticed that Henry's question put Charles on his guard; he made a show of putting down his fork and wiping his mouth with a napkin, stalling for time to consider his answer.

"I've given general instruction to Cook, and he will manage expenses," replied Charles when he was ready. "Mr. Smith decides where you will go, and when. You are to meet as many eminent persons as you can; government officials of course, but also intellectuals, military men, perhaps even an artist or two. I'd like you to see how other societies order their affairs."

"Will the French receive us civilly, seeing how they just lost the war?" asked Henry.

Charles gave a dismissive wave of his hand. "I have little concern about that. The fighting did not come to France itself, so the common people did not suffer. Only the soldiers suffered, but that is the way of things."

"The people suffered from their taxes being spent for war, instead of improvement," said Adam.

"Hah!" snorted Charles. "Any money saved would be wasted by the French nobility, as it usually is. But yes, seven years of war surely depleted the French treasury just as it depleted ours." He forked some lamb into his mouth but continued with a grin. "Avoid gloating, as a courtesy." The Seven Year's War was the first world war; the North American theater was called the French-Indian War. The war finally ended in 1763 and was considered a defeat for France.

Frances offered a dish to Adam. "Mr. Smith, you missed this pudding. Do you care for some?

"It looks delightful, Frances, I certainly do," said Adam, helping himself before a servant could arrive. "Hew, when do you return to Eton?"

"Tomorrow morning, alas!" replied Hew.

Caroline frowned at her son. "Tut tut, you are good at your studies. You'd just spend your time skylarking if you lingered here."

"I'd rather be going to France to skylark," said Hew.

"Continue your studies, Hew, and we'll discuss that. Perhaps next year you can join Henry," Charles announced.

"Really?" asked Hew, happy at the news. He imagined himself telling his school chums.

"By tomorrow afternoon I'll be missing you, Hew," said Frances plainly.

"You warm my heart dear sister," returned Hew, sincerely. He didn't see his sister often, but she sparkled even though Mother was stern.

"Frances, do you go off to school?" asked Adam.

"No, I have tutors who come here to Adderbury," said Frances. She wrapped a napkin over her head like a scarf, adopting the look of a sad-eyed waif. "I'm just a poor shut-in, with no chance of skylarking like Hew." Adam and the boys laughed.

Caroline missed her daughter's comic affectation entirely. "Nonsense, Frances, you do carry on so. Your penmanship is excellent, and you have several friends here."

Charles picked up his ears at that. "I say, Frances, I could use you as my amanuensis. Could you scribble quick enough to keep up with me?"

"No one writes as fast as you talk, Father, but I can try," sassed Frances.

Henry finished his plate, drank deeply, and put his glass down. "When do we leave for London? When do we sail to France?" He looked at Charles for this, not Cook.

"To London the day after tomorrow," replied Charles. "You sail for Calais on the first of February."

"James MacDonald is in London waiting for us," reminded Henry.

"Henry, you watch out for that James MacDonald," warned Caroline. "He'll have you in trouble or drunk under a table somewhere."

Henry laughed, causing his mother to frown. He said, "James is a Highlander so there's really no answering for him," causing his brother to snort with suppressed laughter. "If we're lucky he'll leave his kilt and claymore at home."

"Listen to your mother, Henry," said Charles seriously. "Too much time in either London or Paris will lead you astray. I didn't ask Mr. Smith to be your party chaperone."

"I suppose that will be Cook's job?" was Henry's sarcastic retort, but he wondered what Mr. Smith knew about his father's demise.

CHAPTER 5

CROSSING THE SAME RIVER TWICE *January 1764*
A fancy carriage pulled by a two-horse team waited on a cloudy, cool morning as Adam and Henry emerged from the house. A servant held the carriage door open.

"After you, Mr. Smith," said Henry courteously.

"Thank you, Henry," said Adam as he scanned the sky before climbing in. "Perhaps we'll avoid the rain today." Henry followed Adam into the carriage.

"I'm sure the book shops will be dry," responded Henry.

"Dry, but not boring," quipped Adam. Henry had to roll his eyes as puns were the worst. "Books are the keys to the universe," Adam added, unaware of Henry's reaction. The carriage seats faced each other, so they could converse easily as the carriage rolled down the lane towards Oxford, only a few miles away. "I prepared a list of books we should buy," said Adam. "First, how confident are you reading Latin and Greek?"

Henry didn't like admitting his weaknesses. "Confident in Latin, weak in Greek," he replied guardedly.

Adam shook his head at Henry's inadvertent rhyme, then smiled. "You know, they say the pun is the lowest form of humor."

Henry had to laugh. Maybe Mr. Smith would be a tolerable fellow after all. "Don't mention my Greek to Charles," he said.

"Of course not," said Adam casually, as he consulted his list. "Some translations are terrible, so we must avoid those. Are you familiar with the ancient Greek, Heraclitus?"

"I can never keep those ancients straight in my head," said Henry. "The name sounds familiar, but I'm not."

"Heraclitus held that the only constant is change," Adam explained. "No man crosses the same river twice."

Henry was puzzled. "How can that be? We'll cross the Thames twice today ourselves." The Thames was a small river as far north as Oxford, but it flowed right past the universities.

"The rest of his saying is 'but it's not the same river, and you're not the same man," responded Adam.

Henry grinned. "Will you fill my head with such nonsense all the way to France?"

Adam grinned back and explained, "The river changes, and the man changes. So, it's a different river and a different man every time. The river rises and falls, and you, hopefully, will grow ever wiser."

A bell rang when they opened the bookshop door, and the comforting smell of books absorbed Adam. When he attended Oxford as a student, his refuge was the library. That positive association with books would never leave him; late in life he made a careful list of the many volumes in his personal library. Oxford was a great center of learning, and thus the bookshop appeared prosperous and featured a wide selection of subjects and authors. Adam was in his element. The bookseller approached, a stooped, elderly man with a pinched and bespectacled face. Judging by the clothes and manner of these two customers, he sensed a big sale. "How may I help you gentlemen?" he said, hands folded as if in supplication.

"Good day sir," replied Adam. "We have a list of books in mind, how about we start at the top? Do you have Plutarch's Parallel Lives? The bookseller saw the list in Adam's hand and bent his head as if to read it. Adam smiled and gave it to him.

"In English, or Greek?" asked the bookseller.

"Can you recommend the latest English translation?" asked Adam, glancing at Henry.

Henry followed Adam and the bookseller about the store for the next half hour, listening to their discussions with one ear and watching the other patrons of the store with a roving eye. A few students, a professor or two, and a fetching lass in a green cloak. Her hood was thrown back, revealing clean, wavy brown hair.

One by one, a stack of books grew on the counter. Henry noticed two were books he'd been assigned at Eton, which pleased him as his study effort would be less. The girl glanced at Henry and smiled as she went out the door, pleasing him even more. His attention reluctantly returned to Adam as he sensed they were almost done.

"Lastly, do you have the History of England, in four volumes, by David Hume?" asked Adam.

The bookseller's face darkened at the mention of Hume's name. His unctuous manner disappeared. "No sir, we do not carry books by the infidel Hume. This is Oxford, after all. We don't sell such radicalism!" he said, his nose rising higher with his assumed moral righteousness.

"The History of England is radical?" asked Adam, taken aback.

"If it's written by that unbeliever David Hume it is," stated the bookseller with finality. Henry was surprised by the man's vehemence; this Hume fellow must be quite the rogue.

Adam paused. Henry imagined he was counting to ten, but he didn't know Adam well enough to read the tight expression on his scholarly face. Adam looked at Henry. "I'm sure we can find Hume's History in London." Adam said tersely, at last.

"Let me add the total for these books, then," said the bookseller, his solicitous manner slipping back into place as he took up a quill.

"No, thank you, I'm sure we can find all these books in London as well," said Adam with an even tone. "Come, we'll cross the Thames again," he said with a wink at Henry, but with his mouth a tight line.

As they moved towards the door, the bookseller shouted angrily, "David Hume is an infidel!" Henry followed Adam out the door, puzzled, and the bell rang again as they left.

As the carriage clattered away, Henry saw Adam express anger for the first time. He could tell that anger didn't come naturally to such a calm man. Adam's face was flushed, and he struggled with his composure. "Oxford dogma! They haven't changed a whit since I was a student here. Heaven forbid that anyone have a thought of his own."

"Mr. Smith, please explain," said Henry. "Who is this Hume fellow and why are we leaving with no books?"

"David Hume is my close friend from Edinburgh," replied Adam, forcing himself to answer calmly. What outburst there had been was over.

"That's understandable then, the man called your friend an infidel," said Henry. "I'd be mad too. What makes him say that?"

"Hume is a philosopher. He has written the finest English history there is, and I'll assign no other," stated Adam.

"That man lost a big sale," said Henry. "He felt strongly against your friend."

"Hume is a religious skeptic," answered Adam. "Here in Oxford, skepticism is not allowed." The angry edge crept back into Adam's voice.

"Are you angry because they should be more tolerant of your friend?" asked Henry. "Or because you're a skeptic too?"

Adam looked levelly at Henry for several seconds before answering. "Mr. Hume, despite his prodigious talents and knowledge, was twice denied a university chair because he dared to question Church doctrine. He was deemed a threat to the young."

Adam carefully avoided revealing his own theology to Henry. It was too soon, if ever. He also omitted the fact that while a student at Oxford in the 1740's, he'd been disciplined for reading Hume's "Treatise of Human Nature." This was several years before he met Hume in person, in Edinburgh in 1751, when a young Adam was charging a schilling per head for his lectures on jurisprudence. Because he was always circumspect, Adam Smith did get a university professorship and kept it for twelve years. In his writings, Adam would often refer to God as "the Author of Nature."

"So, you stay discreet," said Henry, nodding. "I understand. This Mr. Hume sounds interesting."

"You'll meet him in Paris," replied Adam. "Hume is Embassy Secretary to the new British ambassador, Lord Hertford."

Two days later they assembled in the driveway for departure. Charles would accompany Adam and Henry to London; later, Adam, Henry, Cook, and James would travel on to Dover, a port on the English Channel. From there they'd be off to foreign lands, an exciting prospect for Henry and Adam both. James MacDonald, having been born in Scotland, raised in France, and educated at Eton, was the only one of the four who had ever crossed the Channel.

The largest and most expensive carriage the Townshends owned, a magnificent eight-seat coach and six, painted shiny black and polished to a high shine, waited before Adderbury's door. The well-groomed team of matched black horses stood quiet in their traces. There would be two drivers and one footman serving them, plus Cook. Caroline and Frances stood in front of the house door, flanked by a crowd of Adderbury servants including the head cook and most of the kitchen staff. They had received permission to see the young duke depart, as two or three years was a long time. None could be sure they'd ever see Henry again.

As they assembled, Caroline placed herself in front of Henry and put both hands on his lapels. She pulled him down to kiss him, and he could see her eyes were moist.

"I love you Henry," Caroline said with a quaver in her voice. "Please, please promise you won't fall in with bad company. Your future is so bright if you don't, if you don't…" Caroline buried her face in his coat as Henry put his arms around her.

"I'll be good, Mother," comforted Henry. "Mr. Smith and Cook will see me straight."

"It's not Mr. Smith who will lead you astray. Don't be too proud to learn, Henry," pleaded Caroline. "You are a duke, but still a very young one."

Henry patted her back, then held her at arm's length. "Don't worry, and don't be too hard on Frances here." Releasing his mother, he turned to his sister and Frances jumped into his big hug.

"I'm going to miss you so!" cried Frances.

"I expect letters from you dear sister. Write long and often, and if Mr. Smith allows me a single moment's rest, I'll write you back!" Henry tried for humor as his eyes were moist too.

"It will be lonely with you and Hew both gone," wailed Frances plaintively. She clung to Henry.

"Shush, Frances, you do carry on so," said Caroline. "Let Henry go so they can be off."

Charles stepped towards Caroline and gave her a perfunctory peck. "Indeed, let's be underway," he said. He was back and forth to London all the time, so his leaving was routine. But first he turned to Frances.

"Come Frances, a hug for Father!" He spread his arms wide, and Frances hugged him close. Charles was the only father she ever had, as her father had died before she was born. In that way Frances was like Adam.

"Goodbye Father!" Frances released him and he climbed into the carriage. "Goodbye Henry!" she added as Henry climbed in after. "Goodbye Mr. Smith!" she added after a moment, as he took his seat. Adam nodded and smiled at the young girl from his window. Cook climbed in last, and the footman closed the door. The driver cracked his whip, and the team stepped forward. Frances ran after them a few steps, then waved again. "Goodbye Cook!" she called out. Cook, surprised but pleased, gave her a little wave. Then they were gone.

Inside the carriage, they settled into their seats. The road between Adderbury and London was a good one, so they'd make good time.

Charles looked at his companions with satisfaction. "We are off, good!" he beamed. "Mr. Smith, may I see your list of books? Henry, how is your Greek?"

CHAPTER 6

BEN FRANKLIN IN LONDON *January 1764*

The common room at the distinguished London boarding house was warm; the huge fireplace held a roaring fire. The sofas and chairs were finely upholstered; the dark wood of the carved tables shone with polish. Soft late afternoon light shone through the many windows, though muted by winter overcast. The room was magnificent; the room was empty.

Cook swung open the door, and Charles strode through followed closely by Adam and Henry. A servant appeared instantly to take their coats and hats. Charles was chagrined but didn't let on. He was in London, and he liked to make a grand entrance wherever he was. But there was no audience sitting in the great room to receive him.

"Cook! See our luggage to our rooms, and make sure Mr. Smith and Henry have all they need. Supper at six, everyone?" said Charles. His instructions and his question were said in the same tone of voice.

"I am quite fatigued, Mr. Townshend, and will take supper in my room," said Adam politely.

"Henry, you rogue!" said James MacDonald of Sleat, who entered the room by the opposite door. The refugee Highlander was resplendent, dressed in a deep blue jacket, spotless shirt and waistcoat, snug breeches, and polished black boots. His left hand held a sparkling glass of champagne, his right was extended towards Henry as he strode across the room. Henry clasped his hand warmly, then clapped his friend on his back. It was always a pleasure to see James.

"I was hoping to get a good night's sleep before I met up with you," grinned Henry.

"Not a chance! We have wine to drink, and women to woo!" laughed James.

"I was afraid of that," smiled Henry, his spirits lifting. In their years at Eton, James was always the one who wanted to do it more, do it faster, do it now. He was the impetus for their adventures, and for the same reasons, their misadventures. Henry thought James bordered on recklessness, but he wouldn't have had it any other way. Life was livelier with James in it.

"Afraid?" James put his hand on Henry's shoulder and looked him in the eye. He pretended to look earnest. "It's good to face your fears, Henry."

"Lead away James, it's good to be in London," Henry assented, still smiling. He spun on his heel and followed James out the door without even seeing his room. He didn't acknowledge the servant who stood there expectantly, ready for the coat and hat Henry never relinquished.

Charles accepted a glass from a servant, turned, and found himself alone. Disappointed, he made his own way to his room, unescorted. They were early. He knew from long experience that the luxurious common room would soon fill with distinguished men, and sometimes elegant women, smoking and drinking before supper. After supper, there would be cards, conversation, and more smoking and drinking. All would be his audience. Charles was in London, his element.

Henry and James lived in rarefied air, and they knew it. All eyes turned when they entered a room, and they felt it. Wealth, power and opportunity came from hereditary titles, and they had them. James and Henry walked out on that first night in London and started taking advantage as only teenage boys can.

That first night they just ended up drunk. The next night was far different; they went to a ball, with dancing and ladies and some truly delightful punch. Henry and James separated when each sought shadowy nooks with their willing partners. The lovely brunette with Henry, whose name he struggled to recall the next day, offered her breast so easily. But as young and drunk as he might be, Henry knew that his sons would inherit. He could not tempt such a monumental fate so early in life, with a girl whose name escaped him. A secret reason young nobles studied abroad was to let their youthful indiscretions play out on foreign soil. Inconvenient heirs were more easily denied patrimony that way. Thus, Henry slept alone, hot-blooded, and dreaming of France.

On the third night they first had a staid dinner with Adam and Charles. Afterwards, James led them to a roaring gambling hall. James was at his peak with the fawning young ladies, telling jokes, laughing, liking it when they touched him. James gambled extensively and ended the night winning a small amount after some rather frightful swings of fortune. Henry just watched, remembering his father's failures and the blunt conversation with his mother back at Adderbury. It was a sobering thing to contemplate, so he made up for it by drinking more. Alcohol didn't let him escape the truth but added to his resentment.

At a quarter to ten the next morning, Charles spied Adam reading a broadsheet in the common room. Charles looked his best on his way to Parliament, with Cook attending closely as usual.

"Good morning, Mr. Smith, what is your plan for today? Is Henry about?" Charles called out.

"I wait for him now, Mr. Townshend. We'll complete our book purchases today," replied Adam.

"Excellent! It's nearly ten, do you suppose the lad is still in bed?" Charles craned his neck to look towards the stairs, as if Henry's appearance was imminent.

Adam stood. "I'm sure he's just moments away. Good day to you, Mr. Townshend."

"Good day," returned Charles as he strode towards the door followed by Cook.

Adam climbed the stairs and knocked on Henry's door. "Henry?"

He heard nothing. Adam knocked again. "Henry, are you up?"

Henry groaned and rolled over. He was half-dressed from the night before and sprawled on his rumpled bed. An empty wine bottle sat on the nightstand, disgustingly. He was so dry he ached. He reached gratefully for the pitcher of fresh water the servants had left for him.

"I'm up," Henry grunted. "Give me an hour or two, Mr. Smith?" he called through the door. His dry throat cracked, and he took a drink of water straight from the pitcher.

"I arranged for us to meet someone at the book shop. If we hurry, we won't be late," Adam said, raising his voice to be heard through the panel.

"Who? Can't it wait? I am unwell this morning," said Henry, sitting on the edge of his bed holding the water pitcher with both hands. He lifted it to his mouth again. Water never tasted so good, but his head ached terribly.

"Not really," Adam said, keeping his voice calm as he grew irritated by having to talk through the door. "We're meeting my friend, Ben Franklin. You know, the kite-flying American. I would hate to miss him while we're here in London."

The door flung open, and a bleary and disheveled Henry stood in the doorway. "Give me fifteen minutes," he said, and closed the door again before Adam could say another word.

In the carriage enroute, Adam gave Henry a slab of buttered bread. Eating made his head feel considerably better; by the time they arrived he felt his thoughts coming into order. They were only fifteen minutes late, which Adam considered fortunate, all things considered. Henry had even managed to pull himself together, with the frantic help of his valet. Only his puffy red eyes gave him away.

"Good morning, Mr. Franklin!" Adam hailed his friend as they entered the bookseller's shop. "We are almost punctual, but not quite." Henry saw a neatly dressed rotund man of middle height, gray, in his mid-fifties, clasp Adam by the hand.

"Mr. Smith, I knew you'd be here as promised," said Franklin good-naturedly. "So good to see you again." The American turned towards Henry. "And who is this impressive youngster?"

"May I present Henry Scott, Third Duke of Buccleuch," said Adam formally. "Henry, this is Ben Franklin, the American colonial representative in London."

Henry didn't feel impressive, and he sensed that Franklin's keen, but kindly eyes saw exactly how he felt; tired, rumpled, thick. Henry straightened, then bowed. "Pleased to meet you, Mr. Franklin. We learned of your electricity experiments at Eton. You are rather famous," said Henry.

"Or infamous, depending on who's asking," replied Franklin with a twinkle in his eye. "It's an honor to meet you, Henry. So, you are the young duke Charles Townshend has been raving about?" He smiled as he looked him up and down. There was something in Franklin's manner that was very informal but also ingratiating; a good person to represent colonial interests in London.

"Raving?" Henry said. "Do you mean raving mad?

"Raving as in boasting, actually. He is quite proud of you," said Franklin with a bemused smile.

"Do you know Charles well?" asked Henry.

"As the American representative, I know him as I lobby Parliament," replied Franklin. "He is ambitious, he is eloquent, and I suspect he harbors dreams of being Prime Minister."

"Yes, that sounds like Charles," replied Henry. Although he wanted to remain dignified, he couldn't help but smile when he said it. There was something about Franklin's open, frank manner that drew him in.

"Charles mentioned once that you'll have a seat in Parliament one day. Are you ready for that?" asked Franklin.

Henry was startled by such a direct question from a man he'd just met, yet he never thought to avoid answering. "Well, I suppose that's why I'm traveling abroad with Mr. Smith here." Adam had been observing the introduction with a small smile on his face.

"A finer tutor could not be imagined, Henry," said Franklin. "Who would imagine that there could be a *theory* of morals? A *science* of human nature?"

"I don't follow sir. A theory of morals?" Henry's head was still clouded.

"The science of how we behave; why we feel, think, and act the way we do. Have you read Mr. Smith's book?" asked Franklin.

The light finally penetrated; Henry glanced at Adam and sheepishly admitted, "I tried to, but the first sentence had forty-two words in it." His words sounded lame in his ears.

"Ben, you embarrass the lad," protested Adam with a smile. "Henry will have plenty of time to read it in France. That's why we're here, to buy books for his trip."

Franklin smiled with delight. "What a wonderful way to spend the day, with books!"

"The more time you can spend with us, the better," said Adam. "Can the colonies spare you?"

The bookseller approached, and Adam asked him, "Do you have the History of England by David Hume?"

"Yes," the man replied, "All four volumes. Mr. Hume's history sells very well. The controversy helps, I suspect." Adam, Franklin, and Henry followed the bookseller as he collected the volumes of Hume's History. "What else?" the man inquired.

"I have a list," replied Adam, and Franklin moved close to inspect it with the bookseller. Henry stood back, watching three grown men grow happily animated as they pointed to which books they liked best. The bookseller led Adam towards the next items on the list, but Franklin didn't follow. He put his hand on Henry's shoulder; a gesture that would normally be overly familiar, with Franklin seemed grandfatherly.

"Henry, in your travels among the great, you might find that your tutor is perhaps the greatest," said Franklin.

"He seems like a fine fellow," replied Henry tentatively.

"Take advantage of your time with Mr. Smith. Lost time is never found again," counseled Franklin.

"Do you know David Hume?" asked Henry.

Franklin smiled broadly. "I do indeed, and Mr. Hume is good friends with Mr. Smith." They watched as Adam and the bookseller added to the stack of books growing on a table.

"Mr. Smith was upset they didn't sell Hume's books in Oxford, said Henry. "The bookseller there called Hume an infidel."

Franklin raised a finger as if quoting someone, and intoned, "He that would live in peace and ease, must not show all he knows, or judge all he sees." Henry did not know that Franklin was quoting himself. Franklin continued, "Hume, alas, just says his thoughts out loud, devil be damned. And he pays for it, as you saw. Somehow, through it all, Hume remains a most amiable fellow. Not a bitter bone in his body."

"So is Hume really such an unbeliever?" asked Henry skeptically.

"I suppose, although much less than is the fashion in Paris these days," said Franklin. "But you should ask him yourself, Henry."

Henry pondered a moment, then said, "I like to know where a man is coming from."

"Even better, where a woman is coming from," deadpanned Franklin.

Henry laughed; Franklin was open, engaging and humorous which made him immediately likable. "What other good advice can you offer, Mr. Franklin? You are a fountain of wit."

"Beware what you ask, young duke," replied Franklin. "My trade is printing, which I learned as a young man here in London. In Philadelphia, I published a sheet called Poor Richard's Almanac. I sold wit by the penny, wit by the pound."

"For example?" encouraged Henry.

"A penny saved is a penny earned," offered Franklin. "No gains without pains." He looked at Henry over his spectacles. "Haste makes waste. Little strokes fell great oaks."

"Very good," replied Henry with a grin, his headache forgotten. "Have you more such quips?"

"Fish and visitors stink in three days," said Franklin. "A man in a passion rides a mad horse." He looked Henry in the eye and added, "When you are good to others, you're best to yourself."

Henry was nodding along, but this last comment struck him as unexpectedly deep. "Yes, I suppose that's true. Doing someone a kindness makes me feel better."

Franklin stopped near a table, apparently at random, and turned to face the young duke. "That's a moral sentiment Henry. I know an excellent book on that very subject!" Henry saw that

Ben had picked up a copy of Smith's *Theory of Moral Sentiments* from the tabletop, where it had been prominently on display.

"Point taken, Mr. Franklin. I'll read his book. At least it's not in Greek," nodded Henry.

"You already know the meaning of that long first sentence, Henry," replied Franklin earnestly. "There is something in our natures that favors human kindness."

When the carriage returned Adam and Henry to the boarding house, Cook met them in the drive and opened the carriage door. He said, "Henry, your Father is looking for you. He's inside."

Henry hopped out and went straight inside; Adam climbed out more slowly. He turned to Cook. "Mr. Cook, these books will go with us to France. Can you see that they're packed in a stout crate for shipping? They must not be exposed to damp."

"Assuredly, Mr. Smith," replied Cook.

"There you are!" said Charles as he rose from his chair in the common room as Henry entered. "I didn't expect you to be so late. Mr. Gainsborough is waiting to continue your portrait."

"Has he been waiting long?" Henry asked, belatedly remembering the agreement he made with the painter when they'd ended their session the previous afternoon with the work incomplete.

"An hour or so, but we fed him dinner," said Charles.

"I suppose I'd better," responded Henry. "I promised Mother my portrait before we sail."

Charles was not given to gestures of affection towards Henry, but now his hand went to his shoulder. "We want something to remember you by. You'll be gone for three years, after all."

"Mother is afraid I'll meet with accident or other misfortune." Henry's tone implied that her concerns were misguided; the young thought themselves invincible and Henry was no exception.

"Life has risks, of course. Humor your mother, Henry. She loves you very much." Charles' tone was sincere, so Henry met his eye and nodded.

Henry passed through the common room and entered the room beyond, where sat Thomas Gainsborough, portrait painter, age thirty-five. Gainsborough vied with Joshua Reynolds for the title of best portrait artist in London. Wealthy patrons paid handsomely for such excellent portraiture; polite Gainsborough worked very quickly, while the humorous Reynolds would have his subjects laughing. Both skills were valuable for the market they served.

"Good afternoon, Mr. Gainsborough, my apologies for making you wait," said Henry.

Gainsborough smiled. "I had a most satisfactory dinner while waiting. So you are just in time."

Henry changed into the coat he wore during the sitting the day before and adjusted himself in the portrait chair to match the same portrait angle. He asked, "Where is the dog today?"

"I left him at home," replied Gainsborough. "That part of the portrait is complete." He picked up his brush, dabbed his palette, and addressed the unfinished portrait. Only Henry's head and face were incomplete. He looked at Henry, set down his brush carefully, and rose to adjust Henry's head with gentle hands to better illuminate his face with light from the window. Returning to his chair, he picked up his brush.

"Just hold that pillow like you held the dog, with your fingers laced. Keep your face turned and chin lifted. Lift just a bit less," instructed the painter, and then he began. Henry hoped his tired features had returned to normal, and his hangover not captured for eternity.

"I became quite attached to that dog," joked Henry. "This pillow is a rather poor substitute. Now my painting will show me with a melancholy frown." He felt witty after his enjoyable conversation with Franklin that morning.

Gainsborough smiled, and Charles entered the salon. He slid over behind the painter and assessed the work with a hand on his chin. "That is excellent of the dog," observed Charles.

Gainsborough turned around to address Charles, "Sir, may I remind you that Henry has not seen the unfinished painting. Be sure not to spoil his surprise."

"Oh, of course not. My apologies," said Charles.

Gainsborough remained turned in his seat, brush paused in mid-air, looking at him. Finally, Charles caught the hint and moved back towards the door. "Thank you, sir," said Gainsborough as he resumed his work. His brush moved swiftly, as he looked from the canvas to Henry and back again.

Charles observed for a few moments, and then spoke from the doorway as he leaned against the jamb. "It's important to finish this up, Henry. You leave for Dover tomorrow."

"So soon? James and I have hardly explored London yet," replied Henry, while continuing to look towards the window with his chin just so.

"The weather is fair in the Channel. You won't enjoy the crossing if the weather changes," stated Charles flatly. "Dukes and farmers alike will line the rail in misery."

"Do you mean seasickness?" asked Henry, concerned.

Charles laughed. "That's exactly what I mean. In good weather you can make Calais in a day."

James appeared in the doorway behind Charles, who yielded so James could step inside. He grinned at Henry. "It's the end of January in England, Mr. Townshend, how bad can it be?"

"Hullo James," said Henry without moving his head. "You've been to sea. How bad is it?"

"I never get seasick, and this will be my seventh crossing," replied James.

"That's reassuring," said Henry in relief.

"But you should see the rest of the passengers," continued James with a wicked look in his eye. "My advice to you is 'puke downwind.'"

"So, you see that haste is warranted," interposed Charles as he turned to go. "I will see you at supper."

Gainsborough continued his brisk work as James stepped further into the room. "You have a fine reputation in London, Mr. Gainsborough. I've seen your work. I'm James MacDonald of Sleat."

Gainsborough glanced up at him, then looked back to his painting. "Thank you, sir. Can I paint your portrait sometime?" He was always looking to drum up business.

"Excellent idea, James, here you hold the dog," said Henry, holding out the pillow.

"I'm working on your face, Henry, and I need the shadows just so. Please keep your face turned towards the window," admonished the painter, politely.

Henry reverted to his pose. "Yes, sorry. Dogs don't like James because they smell the Highlander in him." Henry knew he could poke fun at James because his confidence was unassailable. It was the weak boys who couldn't take a joke.

"Plenty of time to have my portrait made; I am a young man," laughed James. "I'll wait until the warm Italian sun tans my skin, so you can paint me with a ruddy glow."

Adam approached the common room down the back hallway. He noticed three young maids clustered behind a screen, peering into the salon. Their backs were to Adam, blocking passage, as they tittered at something in the room beyond.

"Greetings, ladies, may I pass?" asked Adam politely.

The maids jumped, surprised by Adam's voice. They murmured their apologies and scurried off, giggling. Adam entered to find the objects of their attention—two handsome, rich young dukes.

"Mr. Smith, are you ready to sail?" asked James brightly.

"Have you ever had your portrait painted, Mr. Smith?" asked Henry at the same time, angling his eyes without turning his head.

"No, no, not yet," replied Adam. "Maybe never."

"How will posterity remember you if there is no portrait?" asked Henry.

"With imagination as they read my books, I suppose," answered Adam. "Humble professors don't strike heroic poses. That's for kings, ministers, generals....and dukes."

Gainsborough looked up. "I'll paint anyone, Mr. Smith. Keep that in mind when you return to London."

The painter made the final few touches to Henry's portrait and announced, "There, finished. I'll make some background touches, and framing. You can look."

Henry rose from his portrait chair, shrugged off the portrait coat, and joined Adam and James on the other side of the portrait easel as they nodded with appreciation. It was a fine portrait, although Henry quietly thought his nose wasn't quite that long.

"That *is* a good rendering of the dog, don't you think?" said Henry.

CHAPTER 7

ROAD TO DOVER *February 1764*

Charles slept fitfully, with disjointed dreams oddly peopled by those he knew slightly or had once known. He awoke the morning of Henry's departure unable to recollect any person or plot, other than he knew his dream had taken place in France. So many of his plans depended upon Henry's success.

Cook was absent this morning as he made the final preparations for their journey. Charles' valet served him alone as he dressed. The trip to France was an epic journey for Cook, thought Charles as he peered at his reflection in the mirror. The valet placed his wig on his head, and then Charles adjusted it. He beamed back at himself. Today was the first step of something very big indeed. Was Cook up to the job?

Charles had waited until the very morning of departure to give Adam and Cook their final instructions. He had considered telling them earlier, and he'd considered telling them each by letter. Finally, however, he'd decided that it was too risky that they might share their assignments with each other. Charles wanted both Smith and Cook to report on each other. Henry's future required such prudence, he reasoned.

He found Cook supervising the loading of the trunks onto the big carriage. "Cook, step aside with me for a moment," said Charles in a low tone, hooking his butler by the elbow.

"Continue, I'll be right back," called Cook over his shoulder, "keep loading." He followed as Charles drew him around a corner and out of sight.

"Are there any problems or delays?" asked Charles.

"No sir, we will leave within the hour," replied Cook.

"Cook, you're my eyes and ears in France," said Charles, looking Cook squarely in the eye. "I'll expect weekly letters, no less."

"Weekly letters, of course," nodded Cook.

"Watch his expenses like a hawk. Henry knows who he is, and I'm afraid he'll not respect the value of money," Charles said intently. "He'll spend like a drunken sailor."

Cook nodded, warmed by the importance of this great mission for Charles. Cook was nervous himself, traveling abroad, but he had proven himself long ago as a man who could get things organized, get things done. Charles was counting on him. "I will sir," Cook said as he bobbed his head. "But how should I tell him no?"

"With tact and suggestion, and then a weekly report to me. Try to delay impulsive things he might want to do," instructed Charles. "I want to know what he is doing, where he is going, and how much he is spending."

"Do I understand Mr. Smith will be setting Henry's agenda?" asked Cook.

"Yes," Charles said definitively. In your letters, include what Mr. Smith is doing, and if it seems like Henry enjoys his lessons."

"I will sir," said Cook obediently.

"Most importantly," said Charles, leaning close and putting his hand on Cook's shoulder, "let me know if Henry gets into trouble with women. We can't have him leaving sons and daughters across France. I'm not concerned about serving girls, but if Henry has an interest in the daughter of someone important, I'll need particulars. Remember, Cook, you are my eyes and ears."

Cook almost trembled at the hand on his shoulder. Charles was putting his trust in him, and he would not let Charles down. "You can count on me, sir," he said loyally.

"Thank you Cook," said Charles, extending his hand for a rare handshake. "Safe travels to you."

After Cook returned to the carriage loading with a glow of self-importance, Charles returned to the common room. He spied Adam sitting alone drinking a cup of tea. He pulled up a chair and sat on the edge, leaning towards Adam. "Today is the big day, Mr. Smith," said Charles, feigning excitement in his tone. "Do you have any concerns before departure?"

"None, Mr. Townshend, we are ready to go," said Adam, calmly taking another slurp of the hot tea. He nibbled on some toast. Inside his placid exterior he felt quite nervous, but he couldn't show it to Charles. "Do you have any instructions for me?"

"Call me Charles," he told Adam disarmingly. "May I call you Adam?" Charles wanted to make the conversation more personal, and less contractual.

Adam looked at him blankly, then smiled charmingly. "I prefer Mr. Smith, Mr. Townshend, but I deeply appreciate the familiarity. You see, I don't pretend to any titles or credentials, so professionally I go by Mr. Smith. It is all I have that preserves the teacher-student relationship."

A master rhetorician himself, Charles had to marvel at Mr. Smith's artful decline. "Why don't you want to be called Doctor, or Professor?" he asked.

"Professorships can be bought and sold just like doctorates," replied Adam. He took another sip.

"Or seats in Parliament," snorted Charles. "I see your point. I will call you Mr. Smith, even though I am not your student."

"You are the father of the student, which is nearly as important, Mr. Townshend," said Adam.

"Indeed. Indeed." Charles took a deep breath while nodding in agreement. "Well, Mr. Smith, you have complete authority over Henry's tour. Much depends on his success, and yours." Adam nodded, but said nothing, waiting. Charles continued, "Cook will make arrangements as you require, and manage expenses. Should you have any need, or difficulty, write me."

Adam dipped his head in acknowledgement. "I will, thank you Mr. Townshend. Does Mr. Cook know my role?"

"Yes. Cook will do what you ask," said Charles. "I do have one concern I'd like to discuss."

"Concern?" asked Adam with a lifted eyebrow.

"I worry about wine, women, and song Mr. Smith," said Charles earnestly. "Henry is young, handsome, and full of himself. We need him to study, meet important people, learn how to conduct himself. He'll be in Parliament by the time he is twenty-five. He must be ready."

"I understand your point, but not my role, exactly," said Adam, setting his cup down.

"You are not his chaperone," assured Charles, "but let me know if he strays excessively. Boys will be boys, but there must be a limit. His mother worries."

"Yes," Adam nodded, "I'll write if I become alarmed."

"Good," replied Charles with a sigh of relief, "thank you Mr. Smith. It's an awkward thing to discuss. His unfortunate father, God rest his soul, fell prey to those temptations."

"I thought his father died of smallpox?" Adam's eyebrow was arched again.

"That's what finished him, yes. Henry's father spent most nights out of the house, if you understand my meaning." Charles paused a long moment, looking at Adam, then added, "and gambling."

"Say no more," said Adam with a somber tone, "I'll stay aware."

Charles beamed and sat back in his chair. "That's why you'll spend only a week or two in Paris, before moving south towards Toulouse. Paris would be too much temptation, I'm afraid, at least at the beginning."

Adam nodded, finished his tea, and stood. "Spring in southern France sounds delightful," he said pleasantly, "my only apprehension is the voyage." Charles laughed, and then accompanied Adam to the door.

The magnificent coach and six stood in front of the boarding house, ready for departure. Charles stood with Henry and Adam as James appeared, looking dashing as always. Cook was discussing the route with the coach drivers.

"Good morning, James, here we go!" Henry was excited but also slightly nervous.

"Lovely gloomy day in London," replied James. "I can hardly wait for balmy France."

"It's eighty miles to Dover, so you'll spend the night and sail tomorrow," said Charles. "Godspeed, Henry, and good luck." They shook hands; it was a long moment before Charles let go with a nod.

"I will. Take good care of Mother, Charles," said Henry in a cool and formal tone, and then he turned towards the coach.

"Write often, Henry," said Charles to Henry's back as he climbed in. He turned next to Adam. "Good luck Mr. Smith, I leave Henry in your capable hands. Prepare him to serve England well. Write me."

"I will," replied Adam, shaking Charles' proffered hand. "Give my regards to Lady Caroline."

Adam climbed in, followed by Cook, who closed the door. The driver snapped his reins, and the polished coach pulled away, with six trunks stacked behind. Charles waved, and called out,

"Godspeed! Good luck!" as the receding coach took the whole situation out of his hands.

The passengers settled into the upholstered seats of the coach as it rattled down the Adderbury drive, and then turned onto the lane. Henry and James sat on one seat, facing Adam and Cook on the other.

"All right, we're off!" exclaimed James. "Have you ever traveled abroad, Mr. Smith?"

"This is my first time, James," replied Adam. Since meeting James MacDonald at the boarding house, Adam had been impressed by his keen intelligence and his quick wit, and especially his ebullient nature. Combined with his good looks and devil-may-care attitude, Adam wondered not whether James would lead Henry astray, but how, and when. It was near-impossible not to like the handsome lad and want to be around him. Therein lay danger, for James knew no limits.

Henry asked Adam, "Do you expect to be seasick?"

"Fully," replied Adam. "I once became ill sailing across the Firth of Forth."

"Great," said Henry with a grimace. "So should we wear old clothes aboard?"

James enjoyed being the experienced one despite being the youngest. "You'll be wearing a greatcoat because of the cold. Stay downwind of me!" he laughed.

"I can see why so few venture abroad," said Henry.

"Nonsense, Henry, the world is our oyster, and we must ready ourselves to shuck it!" James' happy confidence was infectious, even Cook smiled. James changed his voice as if he was orating on stage. "If a captain's aim is to preserve his ship, he would keep it in port forever!"

"James quotes Thomas Aquinas, very good," nodded Adam appreciatively. James was one of the best students at Eton and could write nearly as well as he spoke.

"Who?" said Henry.

"You never did pay attention in Divinity class, Henry," mocked James.

"James, tell me how you came to be raised in France," inquired Adam. He knew his family were refugees after the Battle of Culloden in 1746, but he wanted to hear it from James directly.

"When I was just a wee tot, my mother harbored Bonnie Prince Charlie himself after his defeat," said James. "Naturally, Mother had to flee the country and our titles were forfeit. We came to France like so many others. Eventually, passions cooled enough for her to send me to Eton."

"In your opinion, which is the richer country, England or France?" asked Adam.

James pondered that for just a moment. "Oh, England I imagine. But France seems richer when you see the farmland."

"I propose an experiment," announced Adam. "Each of us estimate how many of the people we see are wearing shoes. We'll compare notes on the English percentage when we arrive in Dover. Then we can do the same thing on the road to Paris."

"So, shoes as a measure of a nation's wealth?" asked Henry.

"Perhaps," replied Adam. "Only through observation might we find out. Since it's February, we may presume that everyone who has shoes would be wearing them. Mr. Cook, please join us if you please."

Everyone turned to look out the coach windows. As it happened, there were several people on the road at that moment, some booted, some with shoes, and some barefoot. James said, "I see a fellow with his feet wrapped in burlap, does that count as shod?"

"Stockings are not shoes, James," said Adam, who had seen the same pitiful fellow.

"Do we count the wee ones?" Henry asked a while later as they passed a line of children being marched along by a young woman.

"Children are people too, Henry," confirmed Adam. Although the woman had shoes, none of the children did.

They continued their observations throughout the day, including when they stopped for a cold dinner at a roadside inn. As the rich passengers watched the feet of the pedestrians, those on foot marveled in turn at the expensive coach and its beautiful matched black team as it rumbled past. They could only imagine a life of such ease and comfort.

Cook said very little throughout the day, although Adam could see that he was listening. In the afternoon, Adam was the only passenger who didn't doze occasionally. Near dusk they stopped at the inn where they would spend the night. All got out and stretched, happy to be done traveling despite the high style of their conveyance. Cook, back in his element, promptly arranged things with the inn keeper. The drivers began uncoupling the sweaty horses, who had done the real work of the day and would need their oats, water, and rubdowns. The trunks stayed lashed to the back of the coach.

"Join us for dinner, Mr. Cook?" asked Adam, during a pause in the flurry of instructions Cook was giving to the servants. Cook had been almost entirely silent during their long coach ride.

Cook looked towards Henry, but he had just followed James inside. Cook nodded to Adam. "I'd be pleased, Mr. Smith."

In less than an hour, Henry, James, and Adam were seated in the tavern around a stout, plain table in the corner. It was a roadside inn, frequented by travelers of any class. Teamsters, tradespeople, and seamen filled the other tables, the din of their rough voices and the clattering cutlery filled the close, warm room. Night had fallen, and everything was ruddy orange in the light of the fire and lanterns. A single candle burned on the tabletop before them.

A serving girl set two tankards of ale in front of Henry and James, then pulled a glass from her apron pocket and poured claret for Adam. The girl departed, and all three took a long pull from their drinks. "So, what percent were shoeless, Henry?" asked Adam.

"I'd say one in four," replied Henry thoughtfully. "I couldn't keep an accurate count of all the people we saw."

"And you, James?" Adam queried.

"Perhaps two in ten?" said James with arched eyebrows. "I'd never really focused on footwear before, it was a bit melancholy. What did you see, Mr. Smith?"

"I saw three in ten," said Adam. "Perhaps I was looking most at the children."

Cook arrived at the table, and Adam gestured to the seat next to him. Cook sat down as Adam caught the eye of the serving girl and pantomimed drinking an ale while he pointed at Cook. She nodded from across the room.

"Mr. Cook, you are just in time," said Adam. "What was your estimate of shoes today?"

"Er, I'm not sure. I only glanced occasionally. I'm sure Henry's count is accurate," said Cook.

"Did you hear Henry's estimate?" asked Adam.

"No, but I saw that he was being very observant," Cook said, sounding a bit like a proud parent of a schoolchild.

"Well then, we total and divide by three," said Adam. "That result, coincidentally, matches Henry's estimate of one in four, without shoes, on the road to Dover. Mr. Cook, you were right without realizing it."

Cook wasn't sure if that was a compliment, as he couldn't follow Adam's mental mathematics. The girl arrived with his ale at that moment with a well-timed diversion. "Food's coming, gentlemen!" said the girl, and within moments she set a steaming plate of fried fish in front of them. Another girl arrived with soup, diverting everyone for several moments as they ate hungrily.

When Henry came up for air, he asked, "Cook, when does the ship sail tomorrow?"

Cook finished his bite hastily and wiped his mouth before answering. "We leave with the tide at eight in the morning, Henry. The ship is about five miles from here, so we'll leave by six."

Adam, Henry, and James all nodded, their mouths full. Henry swallowed and then asked, "Should we eat breakfast that early?"

"I advise against it," said James. "Perhaps a bit of bread, and some tea." He pushed back his chair and began to load his pipe. He gestured with his pipe towards Henry with a questioning look.

"No, thanks. You know I never dabbled much with tobacco," said Henry, shaking his head and remembering how much he'd hacked and coughed that time he'd tried to smoke.

"Ah," said James, lighting the bowl with the candle and puffing a cloud of smoke over the table, "tobacco is best just after supper."

"Glasgow has profited handsomely from the growing tobacco trade with the colonies," observed Adam, who smoked rarely but knew many of the Glasgow tobacco merchants personally.

"Cook," said Henry, I'm a bit worried about our luggage. If you are finished, can you check it? And please confirm that our transportation to the ship will not delay us."

Cook saw that he was dismissed. The seeming camaraderie of the tavern dinner did not blur the social distinctions, so he stood to go. "Of course," he said, "Good night, gentlemen, I will knock at your door at half before six."

Only Adam acknowledged his departure. "Good night, Mr. Cook," he said, and Cook gave a small nod and a glance as he passed out of the room. Adam's intent was to do everything in his power to get along with Cook, and thus keep Charles Townshend mollified.

Henry decided to try a small draw on James' pipe and puffed it awkwardly. He exhaled blue smoke, and then coughed once. Adam was strangely pleased to see Henry unused to tobacco, as if it were a sign of restraint and good character. Most personal vices appeared early in the lives of the rich.

The voices at a table behind them grew louder as the men drank more ale. One teamster was holding forth in a loud, clear voice, and without turning, Adam, Henry, and James all stopped talking and tuned in to what the man was saying.

"I tell ye, the French can't drink like we English," said the teamster, "They sip their sweet wine while we guzzle good English ale!" His companions hailed this as great wisdom, lifted their mugs to the center of the table in a laughing toast, and then proved his point with a long drink.

Wiping his mouth, a second man jeered, "We ain't dainty like the Frogs!"

The group rewarded him with more laughter, and raised their mugs again shouting, "Hear, Hear!"

A third fellow, a seaman by the look of him, added, "Frenchie can't handle a full ration of grog!" As if to prove himself superior to all Frenchmen, he raised his mug and drank it empty. He looked at his companions triumphantly as they cheered him on.

There was a call for more ale, and much loud drunken laughter. A fourth man lifted his glass for attention, as if his contribution was to be the supreme national insult, topping all his tavern fellows. "The French slurp slimy oysters *raw!*" he declared.

Silence at this from his mates. Dumbfounded and chagrined, the man sank down and hid his face in his ale. He expected approbation and saw disapproval instead.

After a moment the second man said, "Raw oysters be delightful."

The third man said, "I once et two score at a single supper."

The first man volunteered, "I like the little tender ones, not the big meaty ones you have to chew."

CHAPTER 8

A CROSS THE CHANNEL *February 1764*
The party boarded a three-masted sloop in Dover harbor early the next morning, bound for Calais. Adam had imagined that he'd step aboard a docked vessel, but instead they were rowed to the ship at anchor. The oarsmen deftly kept the stout rowboat close alongside as cargo nets were lowered for their luggage. Laughing, Henry and James swarmed up the short rope ladder with the agility of youth. Adam and Cook, apprehensive and less nimble than the boys, accomplished the task without incident. Their trunks were swung aboard and swiftly stowed by the sloop's crew, who then prepared to raise anchor.

Henry was smiling ear to ear, as this was a great adventure. "Our first trip abroad, Mr. Smith! Are you ready?"

"As ready as I'll ever be," returned Adam cautiously, his fears abated a trifle by his young student's ebullience.

Fascinated, everyone but James watched the seamen swarm to their tasks. The anchor came up slowly, clanking, and some of the sails were unfurled. The fog surrounded them in fits, sometimes quite dense, then torn with huge rents that revealed the early morning sky. The ship began slowly, drifting outwards with the tide. The chill breeze struck them as they approached the Channel proper, so Cook appeared promptly with greatcoats as they all found places to sit on deck. The sails filled, the sloop leaned with the freshening breeze, and they were on their way to France.

The wind was favorable, and the fog shredded away to nothing as the sloop shouldered into the first waves of the open Channel. Sunlight sparkled on the ocean spray, beautiful; then the bow of the ship plunged downward from the wave crest.

Within moments, Adam was heaving over the side of the lee rail. Nothing seemed beautiful after that; he hung there, one arm draped over the rail, in the abject misery that is seasickness.

"Well, that didn't take long," laughed James, standing with Henry, feet braced with one hand on the windward rail.

"Poor Mr. Smith. The wind is bracing, is it not?" shouted Henry.

"How are you feeling?" asked James, shouting close into Henry's ear to be heard over the wind whipping through the shrouds.

Henry nodded, as the ship made its sickening drop into the trough of the next wave. "It feels like a bucking horse, but I'm catching the rhythm of it," he shouted back.

"Not queasy at all?" probed James.

"Yes, actually, a little queasy," admitted Henry. "Not bad, though."

James pointed towards the ship's cabin and made his way to the door. Henry stayed where he was and noticed Cook hanging over the far rail. Poor man, Henry thought, and resolved not to ask him for anything during the voyage. As the ship plunged again, Henry wondered if he was not far from seeking his own spot on the lee rail. His stomach churned.

James appeared, smoking a fat cigar. "Here Henry," he shouted, smoke this. It helps with seasickness."

Henry took the cylinder of tobacco from James and inspected it. He could smell it burning even in the stiff wind. "What is this? Where is your pipe?" he asked.

"Hard to keep a pipe lit in this wind," replied James, speaking close to his ear. "This is a cigar, from the West Indies. I predict cigars will replace pipes someday."

Henry took a tentative puff and coughed. "That's harsh. I don't see the charm of tobacco."

"Give it a chance Henry, try it again," advised James, as the ship plunged into the next trough.

Henry took another, bigger puff, and slowly exhaled. He nodded at James and looked at the glowing cigar as the ship climbed the next wave. "I think I'm getting the hang of it," said Henry.

"More is better," said James.

Adam hung grimly to the rail; his stomach had emptied but the illness remained. Green spots swam in his vision, and his head spun. He'd clawed his wig off his head and stuffed it inside his greatcoat to avoid losing it overboard. Adam's brown curls were wet and plastered to his forehead. He heard someone else being violently sick behind him. Turning his head in misery, he saw that it was Henry. There was no dignity in seasickness, none.

James was laughing when Henry came up for air. "Curse you, James!" sputtered Henry, "You are a bad man." James' answer went unheard as Henry heaved over the rail once more. Henry ended up in the same position as Adam as they sat on deck with one arm over the rail.

"I find it helps to stare at the horizon. All else is motion," said Adam grimly.

"How can I be so sick when I ate so little?" gasped Henry, coming up for air again.

"I suspect the stomach upset is not the cause, but the consequence of our dizziness. Keep your eye on the horizon," Adam advised again, and this time Henry took note. Eventually they reached a stable form of misery, both staring out to sea. As the waves and wind grew less, they could converse while keeping their eyes locked desperately on the stable horizon.

"Charles warned me of this," said Henry.

Without turning, Adam said, "You call him Charles, but your sister calls him Father."

"Frances was born after our father died," Henry replied. "Charles is the only father she knows. I was nine when Charles married Mother."

"Frances and I share that unhappy distinction," said Adam.

"Your father died when your mother was, er, with child? With you?" Henry struggled to find the proper words while his head spun.

"Yes. I am all my mother has," said Adam in a flat tone.

"Is that why you haven't married?" asked Henry bluntly, all delicacy lost as they hung there on the rail.

"I suspect. I always knew I had to look after her. Yet off I sail to France," Adam answered.

"To better support her, Mr. Smith," said Henry. "I know Charles gave you a pension."

"Yes." Adam grimly kept his eye on the horizon.

Several minutes passed in silence, then Adam said, "I've been a professor over twelve years. It's time to learn more. We'll do that together." He turned and caught Henry's eye, briefly, before both snapped their gaze back. Henry agreed with Adam; the horizon was surely his friend in this awful seasick misadventure.

"Funny how I'm a Scot who is going to France before I've ever been to Scotland," offered Henry minutes later.

"Never?" Adam's head turned again. "You will be the largest landowner in Scotland without...?"

"I'll go there for the first time when I reach Majority, in September '67," said Henry. "Then I'll live at Adderbury, I suppose."

"Will you represent Scotland in Parliament," asked Adam, "or a borough in England?"

"Charles will buy me a borough in England," snorted Henry, "With my money!"

"Is Charles your legal guardian?" asked Adam, keeping his head turned away. Neither of them had heaved for the past half hour, and for that they were grateful. They both wanted to keep it that way, and the lack of eye contact allowed franker talk.

"Yes," Henry said. "Charles decides everything until I turn twenty-one."

Crossing the Channel took just under six hours, a good time, but by the time the rowboats had ferried them ashore in Calais it was nearly dusk. Henry assumed the seasickness would end the moment he stepped ashore, but he was wrong. He and Adam trudged with uncertain steps up a hill from the water's edge, following Cook. James led the way, although the youngest he was the only experienced man among them, and certainly the best groomed after their nauseating journey.

"Whether England or France, it's a joy to be on land," said Adam.

"I'm not much of a sailor," Henry replied. "Not much for tobacco either. I thought James was my friend."

"He's just a mischievous one," Adam replied. "Are you hungry?"

"Oh God, no," said Henry fervently.

Henry hardly cared that he was on French soil, but he was very grateful to lie on a stationary French bed. As soon as the darkened room quit spinning, he slept for hours.

It was nearly ten the following morning when the four of them assembled next to the hired coach that would take them to Paris. The journey would take over three days, but James was familiar with the trip. The coach was a far cry from the elegant Adderbury coach that bore them to Dover, but the team of four horses, although shaggy and mis-matched, appeared up to the task.

It helped that James spoke fluent French. Cook, also, could speak well enough to order the servants to be careful when loading their trucks on board. At first, Henry couldn't make out a word that was being spoken around him, but soon his ear began to match the speech cadences with the French he'd learned at school. By the end of breakfast, he could understand much of the casual conversation around him. By the puzzled look on Adam's face, Henry guessed he was still struggling to match the sounds to the words. Adam could read and write French well, but in Glasgow French was seldom heard.

They climbed into the carriage and sat facing each other again, this time with Cook and James on one side, and Henry and Adam on the other.

"Judging by the enormous breakfast you just ate, I'd say seasickness isn't a terminal disease," said James to Henry.

"Damn you, James," replied Henry, but he couldn't help smiling. He was happy that his seasickness hadn't survived the night.

"As we travel," said Adam, "remember to watch for shoes. We'll compare notes when we approach Paris."

The carriage lurched forward, and their journey to Paris began. After rattling about for ten minutes, there was a severe jolt as one wheel bounced through a hole in the road. Cook unexpectedly broke the silence. "We already know that English roads are better than French ones!" Everyone laughed, and Cook looked pleased but said no more. Adam recalled what James had said, and it matched his first impression of France; the land looked better, but the people seemed poorer.

Three days later, the coach clattered into the outskirts of Paris. The tired travelers were in various stages of dozing, but they perked up with the rising traffic around the great city. "How long will we stay in Paris, again?" asked Henry.

"Only about ten days," Adam answered, "Charles insisted we leave for Toulouse right away." He didn't want to appear critical, so he added, "He gave me a letter of introduction to the archbishop, who is expecting us."

James shook his head. "Not much time to sample the charms of Paris, Henry."

Henry laughed. "I'm sure that was his main concern, James. He knows you and your wayward ways."

"Life is short my friend, enjoy it while you can," cajoled James. "Especially Paris!"

Adam changed the subject, saying, "What is our conclusion on shoes?"

"I'd say half the people are barefoot," volunteered Henry. "James?"

"I concur, about half," declared James.

"Mr. Cook?" inquired Adam.

"Again, I must apologize, I was not paying much attention to shoes," said Cook.

"I also estimate about half," Adam agreed. "So, by this single observation about shoes, can we presume that England is twice as wealthy as France? They have twice the rate of bare feet as England."

Something rang false about this, but Henry wasn't sure. He and James exchanged glances. James answered with confidence, "No, only half again as wealthy. Rates are not totals. Three-quarters in England wear shoes; one-half in France."

"Excellent, James," nodded Adam. "Shoes are but one measure of wealth, of course." He looked out the window at a group of French peasants walking along the busy road, and added, "Every child barefoot in February tugs at the heart."

"I agree, Mr. Smith," said James seriously, "your science is melancholy, is it not?"

CHAPTER 9

TEN DAYS IN PARIS *February 1764*

A wan sun broke free in the late afternoon as the carriage rolled into Paris. Henry, Adam, and Cook stared in rapt wonder at the magnificent buildings that lined the avenue. James watched them gawk with a bemused smile. After days of February overcast, the sun on the building facades was beautiful even to James, who had seen the sights before. Where London was drab, Paris was light.

The carriage crossed the Seine and came to a stop in front of the Parc Royale hotel in the Faubourg de St. Germain, in the very heart of elite Paris. Henry and James led the way through the ornate doors, held for them by French servants in colorful livery. Cook and Adam entered behind them, followed by more servants toting their trunks. It seemed that servants were bustling everywhere.

James spread his arms with a wide smile. "Ah, Henry, only ten days! I'm here for a glorious month!" James turned in a circle and then stopped, noticing that several well-dressed Frenchmen were watching their entrance, as well as some lovely Parisian ladies.

"Mother warned me about you," said Henry. "This is one time she might be right."

"Life is short, and we are rich," said James, putting his arm around Henry's shoulder and pulling him close. "Be a shame to waste a single moment."

Adam approached and interrupted politely. "Henry, James, I told Mr. Hume that we would call upon him as soon as we arrived. We might also meet the new ambassador, Lord Hertford. Meet right here tomorrow morning at ten?"

James looked at Henry, who was nodding, then turned back to Adam. "That early?"

"Ten is fine, Mr. Smith," replied Henry firmly, "we'll be here."

Adam departed to find his room, escorted by a servant, as Cook approached. "All your luggage has been sent to your rooms. I have already tipped the staff, so please don't give them extra," he advised.

"Have them draw me a hot bath," instructed Henry, and Cook nodded and left. He turned back to James, who had caught the eye of an elegant young lady and was thus distracted. Henry waited a moment, then poked his friend with his finger to gain his reluctant attention.

"Be quick with your bath. We have business to attend to my friend," said James.

Henry shook his head. "You should hunt alone, James. I plan to glory long in my bath, and then stretch out on a wonderful soft bed. It feels like I've been jostled in carriages for weeks on end."

"You have ten precious nights in Paris, and you spend the first one in bed," said James. "Alone. So, I must carry the fight until the dawn's early light." He looked back at the woman and smiled.

"No James," said Henry flatly. "You will be here promptly at ten, presentable to meet the ambassador."

"Both propositions can be true, as I am young!" James said over his shoulder as he left him.

At ten-thirty the following morning an elegant French carriage rolled to a stop before the rowhouse that now served as the new British Embassy in Paris. The Seven Years War had ended just a year before, so much of the embassy business involved prisoner exchanges and the settlement of claims. Lord Hertford had persuaded the philosopher David Hume to be his

Embassy Secretary; one, because Hume could write beautifully and skillfully, and two, because Hume was an amiable fellow and much-loved in Paris.

Inside the carriage, Adam and Henry waited for James, as his eyes were closed and his head rested on the seat. After a moment, Henry poked him and said, "James, we're here. Look sharp man,"

James awakened with a snort. "Yes, of course, I was just resting my eyes for a moment."

"When did you get in?" asked Henry.

"Early," replied James. "It was still dark out. I'm not sure."

James took a deep breath as he stood with Henry outside the carriage, then they followed Adam through the door. Inside, a male receptionist stood to greet them.

"Good morning," said Adam, "We are here to see Mr. Hume."

At the sound of Adam's Scottish brogue, the large frame of David Hume filled the doorway behind the receptionist. Over six feet tall, at fifty-three years he was also growing quite stout. Dressed in the British scarlet uniform, he was a mountain of red. Hume smiled broadly and spread his arms in wide welcome.

"Mr. Smith!" he boomed, "You have finally arrived!"

"Yes, my dear Hume, hello!" said Adam as he clasped hands with the Embassy Secretary, his friend. "We arrived last night and came right away. So good to see you."

"Likewise, likewise," Hume replied, "and who are these fine young gentlemen?"

"May I introduce Henry Scott, Third Duke of Buccleuch," said Adam, "and this likely fellow is James MacDonald of Sleat." Henry and James both bowed formally, but Hume barely dipped back. He was an informal man, though very courteous in speech.

"It's a pleasure to meet you Henry, and you, James," said Hume. Henry heard the Scottish burr in Hume's voice. He recalled Adam's story of how he'd met Hume in Edinburgh over ten years before, and how they'd become fast friends even though Adam lived in Glasgow.

"And you sir," answered Henry. "Mr. Smith speaks of you highly."

"I should hope so!" Hume beamed, "He has yet to best me in argument!"

They all laughed, and then Hume added, "Though we seldom disagree."

"Is Lord Hertford in?" asked Adam.

"Unfortunately, no," said Hume. "He should return in two or three days; he would hate to miss you." Hume gestured towards his office, and they entered to find three chairs. Hume motioned the receptionist for a fourth, and soon they were all seated comfortably.

"Young and old, rich and famous, I've a premonition that this little meeting holds bold portent," said Hume grandly.

"How so," asked Adam.

"The future of Scotland adventures abroad," answered Hume, shaking his head as if he were amazed at the question, and gesturing with his broad hands. "No where in Paris is there a room filled with such eminent Scots!" Hume's manner was so light-hearted and gregarious that they all laughed again. Plus, his comment was true.

"What you learn in France will help you manage your estates back home," Hume continued, looking at Henry. "But also remember that we've just ended seven years of war. We must step gently; avoid appearing too...triumphant." He raised his eyebrows as if in admonition, but then his grin betrayed his mock seriousness.

"So, you'd like us to behave as proper Englishmen?" asked Henry.

"Well, personally, as proper Scots," deadpanned Hume, then he continued, "As Embassy Secretary, I serve the Ambassador. The French know my Scottish accent. Henry, they'll hear you as English."

"I've always considered myself English," said Henry. "I was born and raised in England. I have never seen my lands in Scotland."

Hume pondered that for a long moment, with a blank look on his face. Adam knew the look; it meant Hume was processing something in his mind. But this placid look could rattle some, especially nervous individuals, although Hume was always kind to everyone. Finally, he answered, "As do so many Scottish landowners." Hume turned and asked, "Were you born in Scotland, James?"

"Yes," replied James, "then smuggled into France as a babe after the Rebellion."

"My dear Hume, we hear your concern," said Adam, smiling. "We'll be on our best behavior. Our every step will nobly advance England's reputation."

"Well, I do serve the British Ambassador," replied Hume in mock seriousness. "Our reputation is my official business. As Alexander Pope said, 'act well your part, there all the honor lies.'"

"Do you hear, James?" Henry elbowed James with a smirk. This large, polished, and witty Hume was the very opposite of the stiff British functionary he'd expected.

"But to err is human, forgive divine," replied James.

Henry laughed, but he saw Hume give Adam a meaningful look. Hume turned back to James. "I see you know some Pope, James. He's the most quoted Englishman since Shakespeare." He turned and asked, "Adam, what is your favorite Pope line?"

"Hope springs eternal in the human breast," answered Adam promptly.

"Henry, any Pope in your pocket?" asked Hume.

A perfect quote popped into Henry's head, and he said it out loud even though he wasn't sure if it was by Alexander Pope. "A little learning is a dangerous thing!" he nearly shouted. He laughed, and saw Hume look at him placidly and smile.

"Beautiful! You can both quote Pope," said Hume. "There is hope for mankind yet. Do you know any more?"

James answered, "Nope, fresh out of Pope."

"Blessed is he who expects nothing, for he shall never be disappointed," said Adam with a smile while looking at his student. All eyes turned towards Henry to see if he could respond.

"My gun has but one shot, apparently," said Henry.

James looked puzzled. "That doesn't sound like Alexander Pope..."

"Charms strike the heart, but merit wins the soul," Hume volunteered.

"The eternal sunshine of a spotless mind," countered Adam.

"Fools rush in where angels fear to tread," responded Hume.

"What reason weaves is by passion undone," dueled Adam.

Hume placed his hand over his heart and looked at Henry as he said, "To wake the soul by tender strokes of art; to raise the genius and mend the heart."

At such sincere eloquence by the ungainly philosopher, the room went silent. "Was all that Alexander Pope?" asked Henry finally.

"Indeed," answered Hume. "We're just pausing for breath. I hope you respect your tutor."

"Tut, Hume," said Adam, "we just read a lot. Alexander Pope is such a pleasure; I regard him as the best poet in the world. I was twenty when he died."

"Where do you travel next?" asked Hume.

"Toulouse," said Adam. "James here goes to Rome."

Hume drew a sheet from his desk and dipped a quill. "In Toulouse, you must see my cousin, the Abbe Colbert d' Castlehill. I will also prepare a letter of introduction to Marshal Richelieu in Bordeaux."

"You never mentioned a French cousin," remarked Adam with raised eyebrow.

"I have a Scottish cousin living in France," replied Hume. "Colbert joined the Gallican Church after the Rebellion. He's been here since he was fourteen. The Scottish Cuthbert is 'Colbert' in French. You will find him very helpful, and he'll introduce you to the archbishop." Hume's quill went back to the ink well, then continued scratching across the page. He wrote quickly with a bold, legible script.

"That would please Charles Townshend," said Adam. "He wants Henry to mingle with the great."

Hume turned to look at Henry and regarded him kindly. "Your title and wealth will dazzle some, and they will fawn over you," he said seriously, looking him in the eye. "But in the salons of Paris, you'll find your unassuming Mr. Smith is the famous one."

"I'm beginning to see why," answered Henry, taking Hume seriously in turn. "I'm part way through his book." Henry had hardly made it through twenty pages yet, but he noted how earnestly both Ben Franklin and David Hume had praised the mild-mannered philosopher, as if they both sensed that Henry didn't take Adam seriously. "I think I'll like his philosophy," he finished lamely.

Hume gazed at him for a long moment before responding. "Philosophy is good," he said as he raised a finger to Henry. "But in all your philosophizing, be still a man."

"More Alexander Pope?" Henry raised an eyebrow as they rose to leave.

"No, Henry," said Hume, putting a hand on his shoulder. "That is my advice to you."

After supper at the hotel that night, Adam bid them goodnight and went to his room. Cook turned to Henry and inquired, "Will you need me again today, Henry?"

Henry shook his head. "No, good night, Cook." Ten minutes later, he met James in the lobby and set aside all thoughts of philosophy. "Let's walk, it's not raining," said James and they ventured out. Cook, nobody's fool, watched them go from his upstairs window. He thought of following them, but then remembered he was in Paris and would likely make a mess of things. Instead, he began a letter to Charles.

Hours later, drunk, Henry and James gambled in a crowded gaming salon. Henry placed a ten-pound bet on the green felt table and picked up the dice. The sea of shiny faces, most as drunk as he, cheered him on. The pretty girl in green, who had stayed close to him the whole evening, pressed her breast into his back. Henry cast the dice, and the crowd roared.

"Winner," said the croupier, and he matched Henry's wager on the table.

"Let it ride, Henry!" cried James, "Let it ride!"

Flushed and excited, Henry nodded and cast the dice again, feeling the soft press of the girl.

"Winner," said the man; now there were forty pounds on the felt. The crowd around the table was packed in tight, watching the two handsome boys who had quickly become the highlight of their evening. "Let it ride!" cheered the crowd lustily.

Henry picked up the dice again, tossed them in the air and caught them, and then threw them smartly across the table. They bounced in the corner; drunk as he was, he wasn't sure he could see them properly.

"Winner!" said the croupier; even he was impressed by Henry's run of luck. "Let it ride!" shouted the crowd excitedly. Eighty pounds! Excitedly, with all eyes on him, Henry eagerly cast the dice again.

Snake eyes, Henry could see them clearly this time. The crowd deflated with a loud "oh;" the run was over. James cried, "Double or nothing!" and the crowd erupted with more cheers. "Double or nothing!" they clapped and shouted. Henry snatched up the dice and shook them in his hand. He looked at the ring of perspiring, excited, intoxicated faces watching him. Flushed with the excitement of the crowd, James shouted "Roll, Henry!" The girl in green cried and clapped her hands, "Yes, roll, Henri!" in her lovely French voice. He could feel her soft hand on his arm.

Henry looked at the dice in his hand, his head spinning. Something deep inside him made him stop. He slowly set the dice down on the green felt. Drunk as he was, he was not going to tell Charles and Cook that he'd lost 160 pounds gambling on his first full day in Paris.

"No, I've lost my winnings, that's enough," said Henry thickly, then he turned and plunged through the crowd, suddenly feeling sick. He emerged into the cold air outside, soon joined by James.

"You're right, Henry," James slurred as he put a hand on his shoulder. "You are prudent. But come, the night is not over yet. That lovely lass in green has her eye on you…" smirked James as he led Henry back inside. Reading his friend's expression, James added, "No more gambling tonight."

Much later, Cook awakened to a loud voice in the street outside his window. Out of his bed in an instant, he confirmed that it was Henry and James returning; the loud voice had been a drunken exclamation of James'.

As they entered the hotel, James said, "Then it's agreed, a brisk ride at dawn."

"I'll be here James," replied Henry, "promise me you will too."

"At dawn!" said James in a loud whisper, as they were already inside.

At half past dawn the next morning, Adam stepped out for a morning walk. He was surprised to see Henry across the street, holding two saddled horses. Adam crossed over to him, and said, "Good morning. You're up early."

"Good morning, Mr. Smith," replied Henry. Adam noticed he looked rumpled and tired. "Did you happen to spy James inside? He is late for a promised ride."

"No sign of James, I'm afraid," replied Adam, as he stroked the nose of the closest horse.

"Carousing at night, sleeping till noon," said Henry shaking his head slowly. "Yet he promised me a morning ride." He watched as Adam switched to pet the other horse. "Do you ride, Mr. Smith?" Henry asked.

"Not often," replied Adam, "but horses are noble beasts."

"I suspect James has left me holding the horses," said Henry. "Here is your chance to ride again."

Adam continued to pet the horses; one a handsome chestnut, the other a gray mare. "You know," he said, "a horse is much bigger and stronger than we are. Yet we ride it, guide it, care for it. Do you suppose it knows that our intelligence is superior to its own?"

"I've seen them broken for the saddle," replied Henry, "they are not born to submit to us. They buck and roll and bite until they are tamed. Horses are smart, and they know their riders."

Adam was impressed by this. He gestured to the mare and asked, "How tame is this one?"

Henry laughed. "I assure you this one is fully domesticated. I'm told her name is 'Passion." He saw Adam move to the mare's side. "Do you need help to mount?"

Adam placed his left foot in the stirrup and mounted easily in one smooth motion. Gathering the reins, he said, "When I was a lad of fourteen, I rode from Glasgow to Oxford by myself. It took eight days; my buttocks remember it still."

"So, you can command this beast?" grinned Henry.

"Can any man truly control his Passion?" questioned Adam philosophically as he cantered off.

Henry mounted swiftly and followed. Although the morning was brisk, it was dry, so they rode for over an hour, conversing and observing the Paris architecture. After a few wrong turns, they found their way back to the Parc Royale. Dismounting, Henry handed the chestnut to a servant. "I shouldn't have doubted your horsemanship, you ride well for a professor!" he complimented Adam as the professor slowly dismounted the mare, landing on his feet with a grunt.

"I feel like day seven on the road to Oxford," Adam groaned, rubbing his sore posterior.

"So, there you are, Henry," called James jovially as he emerged from the hotel. "I arrive bright and early, and no Henry as agreed. But I see you rode with Mr. Smith instead."

"No James," said Henry, shaking his head. "You have just arrived and are making a bold show of it. When Mr. Smith stepped out this morning, you were already a half hour late."

"To your great credit, Henry, you are excessively punctual," observed James sardonically. "I can only hope to catch a small ray of your orderly brilliance."

Henry grinned. "Thank you, James, I'll take that as a compliment! Now, to breakfast!"

The three re-entered the hotel and found a table. Soon they were served a hot breakfast, including a fried sausage that smelled intoxicating. James noticed how attractive the serving girl was, while Adam and Henry ate ravenously. "James, what was your impression of Mr. Hume yesterday?" asked Henry, drawing his attention back to his table mates.

"If ever a man mismatched his reputation, it's Mr. Hume," declared James.

"Because he looks like a farmer?" Henry smiled.

"That, yes," replied James, "but for such a famous infidel he is entirely likeable. Not a cloven hoof or forked tail in evidence."

Interested, Adam asked, "What is Hume's reputation here in Paris? Do they accept him despite his religious skepticism?"

"Accept him? I dare say the Paris crowd is more atheist than he is. Poor Hume, on your side of the water he has too little religion; here he is thought to have too much!" said James.

"Too much?" Adam was puzzled. "How so?"

James put down his fork, took a drink of water, then explained. "Most of France is Catholic, and just as religious as Scotland. Toulouse, for example, is the seat of the archbishop. But the aristocracy here in Paris think Reason and Science have made religion obsolete."

"They are open atheists, do you mean?" pursued Adam.

"Yes, but only with each other," James replied. "They shoo the servants away when they discuss philosophy. Otherwise, the servants would be outraged and betray them to the bishops."

"And the bishops would in turn speak to the King?" Adam wanted to know how power and authority worked in France.

"Not necessarily, but the bishops have enough authority even in Paris to cause mischief," said James with his mouth full.

"What are your views on religion, Mr. Smith?" asked Henry bluntly, hoping he'd answer now that they were in France.

Adam put down his fork and wiped his mouth with his napkin. He took a long pull on his water glass before answering carefully. "The universities would not let Hume teach because of his skeptical views. So perhaps the less said, the better."

Henry and James nodded at this, understanding Adam's reticence. It made Henry even more interested, but he didn't pursue the subject. Instead, he asked, "So, you don't plan any religious texts in my course of study?"

"Not I," said Adam, "but you'll be enrolled in the Toulouse University, so you'll see plenty I imagine."

CHAPTER 10

ROAD TO BORDEAUX *February 1764*
By the end of their week in Paris, Adam and Cook grew concerned about Henry and James. The boys were out until all hours, often drunk, and exhibited no discipline whatsoever. Adam had planned to begin Henry's formal course of study upon their arrival in Toulouse and had left the crate of books unopened. He began to question that judgement. By Cook's fretful manner, Adam could tell that he shared his worries, but their relationship was still too distant to discuss it frankly. Both could see the wisdom of Charles' instruction to keep their Paris stay short. Neither could bring themselves to chastise Henry for fear of jeopardizing their relationship so early in the expedition. So, they worried but said nothing.

Hume asked Adam to accompany him to the famous Parisian salons, where the foremost intellects of France discussed philosophy, science, and art. The Parisian sophisticates lionized Hume for his kind manners, good humor, and especially for his daring religious skepticism. They accepted Hume where his English brethren thought him the devil incarnate. Hume loved them in return; what a coup it would be if he could manage introductions to the famous Mr. Smith. *The Theory of Moral Sentiments* had been translated into French, though so poorly that most of them read it in the original English. Champions of reason and science, the French intellectuals were open to Smith's theory of human nature. They would welcome the Glasgow professor with open arms, but Adam refused Hume each time.

The problem was language. Adam Smith was an expert on language, able to read and write Latin, Greek, French, and Italian. In 1761 he penned "A Dissertation on the Formation of Languages," and early in his career he critiqued Samuel Johnson's dictionary. His lectures were famous, not just for their keen insights but for how compellingly he could deliver them. Yet he struggled to understand the spoken French that flowed musically all around him. He could speak French well enough for the patient servants to eventually understand what he wanted, but his ear was too slow to follow the rapid native French of the Parisians. Adam had no desire to cross wits with the best of France without first mastering their spoken language, although Hume reassured him that they would gladly speak with him in English. Adam remained adamant, knowing they would return to Paris at the end of the Tour. He would not go into verbal battle until he felt properly armed.

At the end of the week, Hume informed Adam that the ambassador wouldn't return for another fortnight. Unwilling to wait for Lord Hertford, Adam and Cook decided it was best to leave Paris the very next day. Henry seemed subdued and hung over when they broke the news, and he didn't object. Accordingly, a coach and four arrived outside the Parc Royale at first light the next morning. As Cook oversaw the loading of their trunks and luggage, Adam noted ruefully that Cook's French was considerably better than his.

Hume appeared, mountainous in his greatcoat, holding two sealed letters in his hand. At that same moment Henry emerged, dressed for travel.

"Your letter of introduction to Abbe Colbert," said Hume as he handed the first sealed envelope to Adam, "although he knows you are coming as I sent him a letter the day you arrived. He'll help you find suitable lodgings in Toulouse."

"Thank you, Mr. Hume," said Henry. "We won't misbehave." Adam noted that Henry did not look hung over this morning, which was a hopeful sign.

James appeared, disheveled, as if he'd just rolled out of bed and stuffed bare feet into his boots. He had a blanket around his shoulders as he stood bareheaded in the chill morning air.

"The Embassy has little fear on your account, Henry," replied Hume cordially, then turned to Adam with the second letter. "Here is a letter of introduction to Marshal Richelieu in Bordeaux. Charles Townshend will be quite impressed if you can introduce Henry to the wily old general."

"Goodbye, and thank you," said Adam as he took the second letter from Hume. "I will write when we arrive in Toulouse."

"Safe travels, Henry," said James as Henry climbed into the carriage, "I'll tell my tales of Rome when we meet again."

The carriage Cook had engaged had two bench seats, both facing forward. Adam and Henry were in the back, so Cook climbed in the front. As the carriage rolled south through Paris, each looked out their window and little was said. The magnificent Paris architecture soon faded away, replaced by rolling farmland. Cook's head was bowed as he reviewed some papers in his lap.

"I'm going to miss James," said Henry to no one in particular.

Cook turned in his seat to look at Henry. He raised a bill of particulars in his left hand as his right arm draped across his seat. "Mr. MacDonald is a rare delight," he said, "but we will not miss his influence on our budget. I paid the Parc Royale twenty-three pounds sterling for your gambling debts, Henry."

Henry sat up uncomfortably and looked at Cook, who met his gaze with a serious look of his own. Adam sat silent, observing. He could sympathize with Cook's delicate position; Charles had given him responsibility for finances but as butler, Cook had little personal authority over Henry. Cook was both Henry's servant and Charles' manager, and Adam watched with interest how Cook would balance his tasks. Once Henry started his course of study, Adam knew he might have similar problems.

"Yes," replied Henry stiffly. "We needn't mention it to Charles. I'm sure that small sum can be buried in your expense reports?"

"Charles' instructions were explicit, Henry," said Cook firmly. "I posted a letter to Charles from the hotel his morning."

"Saying what, exactly?" Henry glared at Cook, anger rising.

Cook met his gaze and did not waver. Adam felt a new-found respect for Cook's fortitude, as this could not be easy for him. Adam knew the success or failure of Henry's Grand Tour might depend on the outcome of this one terse discussion. Otherwise, they would both end up failed custodians of a pampered son as he dissipated both himself and his family fortune.

Cook kept his voice level. "Mr. Townshend specifically asked that I report on any gambling debts. That's why he wanted our stay in Paris to be brief."

"Charles doesn't trust his wayward stepson, I see," said Henry bitterly.

Cook said nothing, but stayed turned around in his seat facing Henry. He glanced at Adam but found little relief in his reserved expression.

"Does he think I'll gamble away the fortune?" Henry spat. "And with it, his political future?"

Adam could see that Cook was flushed, but he remained calm and his tone level. Adam realized that he had underestimated Cook's merit because he didn't like the man personally.

"Mr. Townshend's instructions were explicit. He worries about your youth, your inexperience Henry. He fears the worldly and unscrupulous will take advantage," Cook said evenly, as any temperate parent might reason with their wayward teen.

Henry snorted sarcastically, "Because I associate with a wild spendthrift Highlander like James?"

"Mr. Townshend rather likes James," replied Cook. "He's worried about your title, Henry. You are a Duke, and the sweet smell of money attracts flies. He fears the Siren's call of wine, women, ...and gambling."

"I am not my father, Cook," said Henry tersely. He looked at Adam, but his reserved look offered little to either. There was a long tense silence, as each knew the conversation wasn't over. Cook reversed himself in his seat so that he looked over his left shoulder, as his neck was cramped.

"My father had a gambling problem," Henry said to Adam. "Charles is worried that I'll follow in his footsteps and lose the family estate." Adam nodded at this but said nothing.

"It's my responsibility to manage expenses and keep Mr. Townshend closely advised," said Cook, before taking one step too many. "He means the best for you Henry."

"Damn it, Cook!" Henry exploded. "I am not my father! Charles is not my father!" He took a breath and added petulantly, "You both treat me like a damn child."

Cook was wise enough not to stoke Henry's fire and remained silent. Adam found himself rooting for Cook's success in the tense parley.

"At the end of this Tour I'll turn twenty-one," said Henry fiercely. "I'll decide things for myself!" He glared at Cook, then added meaningfully, "Including who will serve me."

Cook's neck flamed red, but to Adam's silent admiration he stood by his guns.

"Yes, Henry, that is clear," responded Cook, "but until then I am employed to look after your affairs. Part of that is managing your expenses." Cook took a deep breath and kept his composure. He looked at Adam and added, "And Mr. Smith's, of course."

"We appreciate what you do, Mr. Cook," acknowledged Adam with sincerity. "Henry, Mr. Townshend asked similar things of me; not financial so much as educational." With a nod to Cook, he added, "Mr. Cook and I both serve you." Adam's tone was level and pleasant, and Cook looked relieved by Adam's unexpected support.

Henry crossed his arms and turned away from them, staring out the window at the winter fields. To Cook's further relief, Adam changed the subject. He took one of Hume's envelopes from his pocket, bearing the bright red Embassy wax seal, and waved it.

"I have here a letter of introduction to the most famous retired general in France, Marshal Richelieu. I suggest we detour through Bordeaux to see him. He must be nearing seventy years," said Adam.

"Before Toulouse?" asked Cook with quizzical eyebrows.

"Yes," replied Adam, "it seems easier to go there on the way, rather than make a separate trip. We'll also see Bordeaux, an important trading town."

"Why must we go out of our way to meet an old general?" pouted Henry.

"I was asked to seek introductions to the leading statesmen and intellects of France," replied Adam simply.

Cook turned back, happy to have Adam's support in whatever form it might take. "Yes, yes," he said eagerly, his instructions were explicit..."

"Explicit?" shouted Henry, startling them both. "Charles is the least explicit person in all of England! He changes his meanings to suit the moment." Henry crossed his arms again, sat back in his seat, and frowned. "He is perfect for Parliament; I'm much less sure of his skill as a parent," he added morosely before lapsing into silence. Two hours passed before anyone ventured another word.

· · · ·

THREE DAYS LATER FOUND them deep in the heart of France. The sun was warm on their faces when they stopped for a bite of dinner, so Adam and Henry decided to saddle and mount the spare horses and ride in front of the team. The advent of spring, coming early as they headed south, brightened their spirits.

"Tell me more about this old general we're going to see," said Henry as they rode side by side.

"Marshal Richelieu was the best military mind in France during our recent war. Only a few years ago, the Marshal was our archenemy," replied Adam. "If we want to know how France thinks militarily, then he's the man."

"France lost the war, Mr. Smith!" Henry said with an unexpected laugh.

"Yes, thankfully," said Adam with a rueful grin. "The Marshal had an invasion army assembled but lacked a suitable fleet to get him across the Channel. The war lasted seven years because of minds like his."

"Does he still have the ear of the king?" asked Henry.

"Hume says he does," Adam answered, "but that he stays away from Paris to avoid palace intrigue. Which is why we'll find him in Bordeaux."

Although the three of them conversed in English, French was everywhere around them. Adam was beginning to understand broad snatches of the conversations, and Henry was adapting like a native. One afternoon while Henry dozed in the back seat, Adam and Cook made a sport of interpreting the conversation of the drivers, sharing a laugh when translating the curse words. He observed that Cook was less commandeering in tone when speaking to the French servants than he was prone to be in England. Cook was keenly observant and could adapt to a changing situation, like being in a foreign land. He was Charles Townshend's trusted man for a reason, decided Adam, and he was determined to forge an alliance with the difficult man. The success of Henry's education, and his pension, might depend on it.

Traveling through the heart of France showed without doubt that the country was poorer than England in many ways beyond shoes. While they saw the farmland at its late winter worst, they noted most readily the poverty of the clothes, livestock, and dwellings. Yet after a week, with the weather growing warmer, Adam and Henry trotted the spare horses into the outskirts of Bordeaux. "I see a rising number of shoes, Mr. Smith," observed Henry. "Is Bordeaux a prosperous city?"

"Yes, because it's a trading town," answered Adam. "Bordeaux is the Atlantic port for the farm products that travel down the Gironde, wine, wheat, linen. They grow rich on the trade."

"But trade doesn't create more wheat or wine," challenged Henry. "Are the merchants getting rich on the backs of the farmers?" Adam knew that when Henry said 'farmers,' he wasn't referring to the peasants who tilled the soil, but to the entitled landowners.

"That's a good question, Henry," Adam said, "but remember the value of the unseen thing." At Henry's puzzled look, he continued, "Trade creates value by putting the goods in the right hands, at the right time. Ask a man with a wagon full of ripe strawberries who looks desperately for a buyer, because the sun is hot. The product of all his labor could be lost, but for a merchant willing to trade with him."

Henry nodded thoughtfully as they continued into the heart of the bustling town. "So, the unseen thing is something that doesn't happen? The strawberry sale not made?"

"The thing we didn't choose, the path we didn't take," said Adam, "the opportunity we trade for something else. Without the opportunity to trade, we can't improve our position. We can't prevent the loss of our strawberries. A trade benefits both sides or it won't be made."

As they rode near the wharves, the bustle and activity increased. Men with wheelbarrows full of rope, wagons loading and unloading, well-dressed merchants deep in conversation over a barge cargo. Messenger boys dashed about between the horses, wagons, and carts. Even the horses looked healthier in busy Bordeaux. "It reminds me of Glasgow on the Clyde," said Adam, "The tobacco ships from the American colonies, and all the leather goods and small manufactures we send them."

"It's hard to see the unseen thing," Henry observed. "I just see speculators grabbing a share of what they didn't make."

"Yes," laughed Adam, "they certainly grab a share. But without shipping a farmer's market is very small. Serving a big market allows for specialization and efficiency."

"Specialization?" asked Henry.

Adam nodded. "One farmer can concentrate on turnips and let another grow corn, or wheat. The local market might never use a whole crop of turnips; his price would be low and some likely wasted. Instead, he barges them down the Gironde and can sell them all at a good price."

"Wouldn't it be better if every man were self-sufficient, and could grow everything?" Henry asked.

"Are you equally skilled at Latin and Greek, Henry?" asked Adam.

"You know I'm not," said Henry, puzzlement tugged down the corners of his mouth and wrinkled his forehead.

"Then you wouldn't advertise yourself as a tutor of Greek," Adam smiled, "you'd leave that to some other fellow. Here's another example. One man working by himself might make a few pins a day. He must heat the forge, pull the wire, attach the head, sharpen the point. Several men, each doing but one part of the task efficiently, can make several thousand pins per day."

Henry threw another look at Adam, trying not to be nettled. "As a professor how do you know about making pins?"

"There is a pin factory in Glasgow," Adam replied simply. "I asked."

CHAPTER 11

MARSHAL RICHELIEU *March 1764*
At two o'clock in the afternoon, a French servant in colorful livery announced them formally into the presence of Marshal Richelieu.

"Presenting Mr. Henry Scott, Third Duke of Buccleuch in Scotland. Also Mr. Adam Smith, Professor of Moral Philosophy at the University of Glasgow." The man stood ramrod straight, spoke clearly, and gave the impression of a former soldier.

Adam was thankful he could understand their introductions. Cook remained at the inn where they had spent the previous night, with Adam and Henry riding to the Marshal's estate on horseback. They were unsure of their reception, but the ex-soldier had conveyed their letter inside and shortly after, ushered them into a massive high-ceiling room, gloomy with closed drapes, where a small fire burned in a massive stone fireplace. Beside the mantel stood Marshal Richelieu, lion-maned and still an impressive figure at age sixty-eight.

"Come in, come in, young Duke," invited the Marshal in a deep, cordial voice, in English. He motioned towards the servant, "Open that drape and let in a bit of light." The broad shaft of sunlight illuminated rich furnishings and large oil paintings. Henry and Adam trekked across the large room towards Richelieu, with Adam lifting his feet consciously to avoid an unseemly stumble on the thick carpets. They both bowed low.

"Hume speaks highly of you, Duke Henry. I am Richelieu." The Marshal's manner had a gravitas born of a long life of confidence and command.

"It's an honor to meet you sir. This is Mr. Smith, my tutor. He's a close friend of Hume," said Henry, wondering why the Marshal hadn't acknowledged him yet.

Richelieu nodded towards Adam, but said bluntly, "I never had much use for philosophers Mr. Smith. I am a man of action."

"If ever there was one, sir," replied Adam graciously, bowing again. "Thank you for giving us an audience." Henry was impressed by Adam's calm response to the Marshal's brusque words.

"I respect Hume, although he is a blasted infidel," grumbled Richelieu. That may be in vogue in Paris, but not throughout France. But his history of England is excellent."

"Agreed, sir," replied Adam, glancing at Henry. The crate of books was still unopened.

"I have my doubts about you, Mr. Smith, after I read your book," said the Marshal, surprising Adam and Henry both. After a moment he added, "But it is sensible." He turned his keen eyes on Henry. "What do you think of it, young Duke?"

Surprised, Henry stammered his reply. "I, I.... I've started it, and it does seem, well...sensible."

"Hah! I suspect you haven't read more than a few pages," said Richelieu. "Your answer would be different if you had."

Henry was abashed. There was no hiding from the Marshal. "True, sir," he admitted, then added lamely, "it deals with Man, a complicated subject."

"Not so complicated as all that," replied Richelieu. "In war for example. There is strategy, yes, but mostly it's terrible and bloody and elemental. Do you fence, young Duke?"

"Yes," Henry replied, further taken aback, "I had some instruction at my school, at Eton."

"Eton, eh?" said the Marshal, and one corner of his stern mouth twitched. "Had I ships enough I might have rudely interrupted your fencing lessons at Eton." He lifted his head and called loudly to the servant standing at the far door, "Bring swords!"

In a twinkling the servant delivered two fine swords in elaborate scabbards. Richelieu handed one to Henry and drew the other. He inspected his closely, lovingly, then moved into the center of the shaft of light streaming through the tall window. "Show me your swordsmanship, young Duke!"

"Surely you jest, sir," replied a startled Henry. Adam was speechless with surprise.

"Not at all," growled the Marshal. "I am almost seventy; you are young and robust. I trust you won't wound an old man." He stood with his tip down and adopted a fencing stance. "Remove your coat, unsheathe that blade, and touch tips."

Henry obeyed, shucking his coat and drawing the sword, which was without doubt the finest blade he'd ever held in his hand. He moved into the light opposite Richelieu, and self-consciously adopted his fencing stance. Henry felt ill at ease, even ridiculous, to be fencing with an old man he'd just met. He raised the blade and touched tips with the general.

"Let's hope you don't accidentally cut yourself," said Richelieu, and then smiled broadly for the first time since they'd arrived. "Although I'd enjoy telling Hume that it was the will of God!" He laughed at his own joke; Adam had to laugh as well. The Marshal had a sense of humor.

Richelieu suddenly attacked with a one, two, three stroke combination that Henry successfully parried. It was obvious that that the attack was deliberately slow, but Henry felt pleased that he hadn't embarrassed himself. He couldn't suppress a brief smile. "It's been a while since Eton," he said.

"Of course," said the Marshal, sword up with his other hand behind his back. "Now, you come at me." Henry intended to attack similarly, but at his first stroke Richelieu parried so aggressively that Henry's sword flew out of his hand and clattered across the stone floor. Adam jumped out of the way in fright. Richelieu laughed heartily.

"Every block is a strike," he said, "that is your first lesson."

"Every block is a strike?" wondered Henry, both embarrassed and bewildered.

"The young Duke can hear!" mocked Richelieu, then in a serious tone he explained. "When a man attacks you with a sword, he means to kill you. He will slash with all his might. Your block must be as strong as his attack. Stronger even!"

Henry retrieved the sword and while bringing it back, stumbled on the edge of a carpet. Further embarrassed by his lack of grace he said sarcastically, "Or perhaps just dodge?"

Richelieu laughed and said, "Yes, dodge your way to victory, young duke! Come, try again. This time use your muscles. Grab the hilt!"

Henry stepped forward resolutely, touched tips, and then swiftly attacked. He was not unskilled; at Eton he had been one of the better fencing students, but his steps and approach showed practice but not experience. The ring of swords was much louder, but Richelieu disarmed Henry again on his third stroke. The sword flew out of his grasp; the hilt guard scraping his knuckles on the way. He inspected his hand for blood in consternation.

"You embarrass me sir," said Henry in a respectful tone despite his wounded pride. "I have little experience outside the studio."

"I'd say no experience at all," said the Marshal brusquely. Then in a softer tone, added, "Which is a good thing, young duke. Spilled blood is not soon forgot. I should know."

"As a general, did you actually come to blows with the foe?" asked Henry. "With Englishmen?"

"And Scots, and Germans, and Austrians," said Richelieu gravely. "I have killed men with both these swords."

Henry reluctantly picked up the sword and resumed his stance, painfully aware that the old warrior was playing with him. "What is the second lesson, sir?" he asked bravely.

The Marshal stood with his tip down while he answered. "The knowledge that an unlikely foe can beat you. In this case, a man fifty years your senior." With that, Richelieu attacked again. The sword strokes rang through the cavernous room. Watching spellbound, Adam considered how he might describe this unusual fencing lesson in his letter to Charles. It continued for a quarter hour more, with the Marshal stopping at times to describe a finer point of footwork or arm angle. Henry was earnest; the Marshal was smiling. Finally, he stepped back and dropped his point.

"Humility, young duke, is a lesson best learned early," Richelieu said. "I've seen many eager boys dead on the battlefield, bright with blood." He stepped closer to Henry and took back the sword. Standing with both swords point down, he added, "Know your limits, and your strengths, so when you act it's decisive and with effect."

"How do I know my limits when I am untested?" Henry asked.

Richelieu smiled, looked at Adam, and then back at Henry. "You don't. That is the beginning of wisdom, young Duke. You don't." He moved towards the fireplace and returned the blades to their scabbards. "Confidence is not something you think, it's something you believe. Practice and preparation give you hope, then you make a leap of faith. You follow your instinct."

Richelieu turned towards Adam, and added, "Not that far from your theory on sentiments, Mr. Smith, if your science can tolerate the faith." Hearing this, Adam suddenly wondered if the fencing lesson had been as much for his benefit as Henry's.

The Marshal clapped his hands and called, "Refreshments!" He turned to his guests and put one hand on each of their shoulders in an unexpected gesture of intimacy. "You must stay the night!"

After coffee, served by a very comely lass, Richelieu gave them a tour of his home. They emerged into the late afternoon sun and strolled the enormous garden, exquisitely cultivated with flowers of all kinds. At the far end of the lawn, he turned and gestured towards the massive stone structure. "They say a man's home is his castle," he smiled, "Mine is an actual castle. I had the moat filled and turned into flower beds." He caught Henry's eye, and added, "Swords into plowshares, you see."

They rode horses about his estate until dusk. The ex-soldier in servant livery rode behind them at a discreet distance. Other than this one man, Henry noticed that nearly all the household servants were attractive women. At supper that evening, they met another handsome woman, with dark hair and dark eyes, about forty years old.

"This is Louise, my head of household," is all Marshal Richelieu said as he introduced her. "I invited her to join us." Adam and Henry bowed before they were seated at the sides of the table, with their hosts at the ends. Two attractive younger women attended them; one caught Henry's eye every time she served the table.

"Welcome, monsieur," demurred Louise.

"Louise speaks little English, but she can understand some," said the Marshal, effectively excusing her from participating in the dinner discussion, as he continued to speak in English.

Henry saw Adam take several furtive glances at Louise, which amused him.

"So, Duke Henry, tell me how you came to acquire such an illustrious tutor," began Richelieu, and Adam, surprised, saw the old man wink at him.

"My stepfather, Charles Townshend, hired Mr. Smith five years ago while I was still at Eton," replied Henry.

"Charles Townshend, eh?" muttered the old general, and Henry was afraid that the Marshal might question him about Parliament, and how would he answer? But then he turned his head towards Adam. "Because of the book he wrote?" Richelieu looked back towards Henry.

"My stepfather was impressed with it, yes," said Henry.

"Mr. Smith, your book is a challenge to me. Your optimistic view of human nature is admirable, but perhaps naïve. As a soldier, I am less sanguine about the goodness of men."

Adam gave a courteous nod towards Louise and replied, "Perhaps women secure the balance of our good natures."

"Ha!" Richelieu slapped his hand on the table at this. "You make an artful point there Mr. Smith." He beamed at Louise, and then added, "That is certainly true in this house."

Henry noticed that Louise wore no rings on her fingers. He wasn't sure what her relationship to the Marshal really was, but he could guess. She was attractive even to Henry, twenty years younger. Henry flushed when the serving girl bent low over the table to refill his glass. As he brought the glass to his lips, he saw Adam steal another glance at Louise. She seemed to follow their conversation closely but said almost nothing.

"Mr. Smith, are you a skeptic like your friend Hume?" asked the Marshal bluntly.

"Mr. Hume gave us the letter of recommendation; you must find him of some merit?" replied Adam cautiously.

"Artfully dodged again," Richelieu acknowledged, but didn't pursue the question. "As Embassy Secretary, Hume helped forge the Treaty of Paris. He secured the return of Minorca to the British."

"In exchange for Guadalupe in the West Indies, as I understand," replied Adam.

"Yes, and Guadalupe's sugar is more valuable to France than the island of Minorca," Richelieu mused, then added, "Still, it galls me."

Henry spoke up. "We learned about your victory at Minorca in school, sir. They executed Admiral Byng for it, shot him on the deck of his own flagship. May I ask your thoughts on that?"

Richelieu put down his fork and took a sip of wine before answering. "I was commander of the land forces laying siege to Fort Phillips. We had already overrun the island; the fort was the last holdout. Byng led a fleet of a dozen ships against our Toulon fleet, evidently to relieve the fort, which was impossible." He took another drink of wine before continuing.

"Byng started with the wind behind him but bungled the approach." The Marshal placed the pot of boiled greens on the table to indicate Minorca, and then used the salt, the pepper, and the butter dish to show the approach of the British fleet. "The first of his ships," he explained pointing to the butter, was pounded by several of ours." He arranged a fork, a spoon, and the butter knife to show the French ships. "Byng was never able to bring all his guns to bear." He slapped the table with his hand again, making the ships jump. "It was a decisive French victory, and Byng slunk off to Gibraltar for repairs."

"In class they said his mission was to relieve Fort Phillips," said Henry, "and it fell shortly after he retreated."

"It would have fallen anyway!" exclaimed Richelieu. "I had already captured the island! Byng could have pounded our ships to splinters and still not landed enough men to relieve the fort. Your Admiralty sent him on a fool's errand, and he paid for it."

Henry had no response to this as Eton had only taught him the official British view, which was that Byng was executed for cowardice and failure to do his duty. His mouth opened; he thought better of saying anything and shut it again.

Adam confirmed the Marshal's view. "Admiral Byng was made a scapegoat. Losing Minorca was too great a blow for British prestige."

Henry was stunned by the news that Admiral Byng died to salve the Admiralty's reputation. He finally recovered to say, "It's an honor to hear the story from such an eminent authority, sir."

"The British in the fort fought with great tenacity," Richelieu acknowledged. "They earned my respect. After the surrender, I let them all go." He leaned towards Henry for emphasis. "*With their weapons*, mind you, that is how much I respected them."

"Thank you, sir, for Britain's sake," answered Henry, somewhat awkwardly.

Richelieu looked at Adam and said, "See, you are turning the young Duke into a statesman!" He thumped the table with the heel of his dinner knife for emphasis. "Charles Townshend will be pleased."

Dessert was served by the beautiful serving girl, and Henry took a bite of the delicate confection. "This is delightful!" he blurted.

"Yes, delightful," answered the Marshal, winking at the serving girl.

"Do you know Charles Townshend?" asked Adam.

"I know of him," conceded Richelieu, "Forgive us for keeping an eye on British politics." He eyed Henry keenly. "Townshend married well."

Henry flushed red; embarrassed and tongue-tied, he had no response. The old warrior had cut to the heart of the matter, and there was no parry or riposte.

Adam intervened to rescue him, asking, "Marshal, I understand Minorca wasn't your only activity in the war?"

"Indeed not," snorted Richelieu. "I had an invasion army assembled in Normandy in 1757. Oh, for the lack of boats!"

"It would have taken a mighty armada, sir," replied Adam calmly. "We were beaten in the Mediterranean, but the Royal Navy rules the Channel."

Richelieu frowned at this and stared long at Adam. "Perhaps," he grudgingly admitted at last.

After supper they retired to a warm den, lit by firelight and candles, walls decorated with ancient shields and arms. They drank wine and conversed for two hours more, but soon the conversation was entirely between Adam and the old Marshal. Finally, they stood to find their beds.

"Felicity will show you to your room, Henry," said the Marshal, indicating the girl who had captured Henry's eye throughout the evening.

Felicity led him down a long hallway, then opened a door that revealed a large bedroom lit by several candles. He followed her inside as she walked around the far side of the bed. She looked at Henry with lowered lashes. "Would you like me to prepare the bed for you, monsieur?" she asked seductively, deliberately leaning low over the bed so that her blouse fell open.

"Yes, please, Felicity" replied Henry as a wide grin spread across his face.

Adam had been in his room just minutes before he heard a soft knock at his door. He opened it to admit Louise, who had towels and a pitcher of water. His heart beat dangerously fast as

Louise turned down his bed. He noticed she'd let down her hair and had changed into a deep blue night dress.

Louise stood across the bed from Adam and smiled. She pulled the laces on the front of her dress, slowly, seductively. Adam stood stock-still, entranced. "Is there anything else, Monsieur Smith?" she asked in perfect English.

. . . .

HENRY AND ADAM TOOK their leave of Marshal Richelieu early the next morning and trotted back towards the inn in bright sunshine. Henry was whistling, but he had to stop each time his memory of the night before caused him to grin broadly. "I'm really beginning to enjoy France, Mr. Smith!" said Henry, brightly.

"Yes, it's lovely today," replied Adam, who also seemed to be in a good mood. "It sure beats the English rain."

"My whole childhood we were at war with France. It is good to see they are people, just like us," said Henry.

"People are much the same everywhere," replied Adam, nodding. "Most differences are cultural, and often superficial."

"Like eating frogs?" said Henry, laughing.

"Frogs, yes," smiled Adam. "Haggis."

Henry laughed out loud, as he and his Eton pals loathed haggis, a Scottish sausage made of sheep guts. "Point made!" he exclaimed. The sun was warm on his face, and he felt happy. They rode for several minutes without speaking.

"Do you suppose the Marshal keeps a harem?" asked Henry suddenly. Adam flushed red, and seeing it, a delighted grin of understanding spread across Henry's face. No wonder his tutor was in a good mood! Adam was spared having to answer as they passed a group of peasants on the road, herding cows.

The poverty of the humble peasants, their clothes ragged and carefully patched, sobered them both. They'd seen worse in Central France, far from the economic benefit of the river traffic. But the average French peasant lived worse than his English counterpart, Henry was sure. He wondered how the French compared to the Scots. He'd heard it was so cold in Scotland that surely everyone would have shoes. "I notice the French nobility treats their peasants worse than we do our commoners," said Henry, as they walked their horses for a shady stretch beneath budding trees.

"Generations of peasants serving generations of nobles," replied Adam somewhat cryptically.

"Do you suppose it's by divine right," asked Henry, "are social classes determined by God?

"I hesitate to speak for God, Henry, and I suspect those who presume to," said Adam carefully.

"Do you mean priests and bishops?" Henry sensed he was getting close to Adam's view on religion, which he guarded closely.

"Sometimes," agreed Adam, "but we know where the priests and bishops are coming from. It's their job to speak for God. I'm suspicious of those who pursue their own interests in the name of God."

Henry nodded, and they trotted along for almost a minute before he added, "How about the divine right of kings?"

"Charles wants you to learn statecraft, Henry," replied Adam, "Like knowing which ideas can get you thrown in prison. We fought the English Civil War over religious questions, but the French did not. Some authority we best not question."

CHAPTER 12

TOULOUSE *March 1764*

They boarded their carriage for Toulouse at ten the next morning in pouring rain. Despite the inclement weather, Cook noted Henry's lingering good mood. Last night he'd been ebullient. He was glad Henry's meeting with the old general had gone so well. Mustering a pleasant tone, he called back over his shoulder, "Well, quite the weather change today!"

"Luckily, Brits are waterproof," laughed Henry.

"Scots must be both waterproof and windproof," added Adam. "The farther north one travels, the tougher one becomes."

"Is that why we fell prey to the Saxons?" replied Henry. "They have worse weather?"

Adam laughed. "I doubt it. The French have good weather, and they ruled Britain for 200 years after the Battle of Hastings."

"1066," smirked Henry, pre-empting his teacher. "Ancient history."

Adam smiled, and Cook laughed in the front seat, rare for him. Henry was happy, and that pleased him. He'd make a comment in his next letter to Charles. Adam said, "French influence endures. Although we are often at war with France, we are not so different as people."

The carriage splashed along at a good pace on the fine road. The further they traveled from the prosperous region of Bordeaux, the worse the roads would become.

"Tell me about this man we are to meet in Toulouse," said Henry.

"Abbe Colbert," said Adam, "is Hume's cousin, an ex-Scot who fled here after the Rebellion. Jacobite Scots are sprinkled about France."

"Like James' mother," nodded Henry. "Is Abbe Colbert the reason we're staying in Toulouse, instead of Paris?"

"Toulouse in the seat of the archbishop, and the University," replied Adam. "You will attend school for a term here and meet Archbishop Brienne."

"Charles doesn't trust me in Paris," Henry observed flatly. After a comic moment, he innocently asked "What is the nightlife like in Toulouse?"

"I don't know if the archbishop likes a good party," laughed Adam again. "By reputation, Toulouse is much quieter than Paris. Charles sent us here to study, Henry. Not to visit Hume's cousin."

"Where will we be staying?" asked Henry.

Cook spoke from the front seat, "Yes, I'm anxious to know our accommodations and expenses."

"Hume said the Abbe would direct us, as he knows Toulouse intimately," replied Adam.

As they rolled towards Toulouse over the next two days, the traffic diminished, the roads worsened, and the people looked poor. The bustle of Bordeaux faded into listlessness; people walked with less urgency. It was late afternoon when they approached the outskirts of Toulouse. Steering towards the largest church steeple, they wondered why so few people were about. The streets seemed oddly quiet. As the magnificent church came into view, they saw a solitary figure in a black cassock standing in the street before the main entrance. The carriage pulled abreast and came to a stop. The second driver dismounted and opened the door for the passengers.

"Welcome, welcome, I am Abbe Colbert," said the robed man. "Who are you?"

The Abbe spoke an English that made Henry remember James. Abbe Colbert arrived in France at fourteen, joined the

Catholic Church in France, and now at thirty ran the church at Toulouse. His superior, Archbishop Brienne, oversaw the entire region.

Adam bowed and replied, "I am Adam Smith, and this young man is Henry Scott, Third Duke of Buccleuch."

"Welcome," said the Abbe. "David's letter arrived just yesterday so I was hoping I hadn't missed you. Safe travels, I hope?"

"Yes, very pleasant," replied Adam politely.

The driver and coachman awaited instructions. No servants emerged from the church.

Henry bowed formally. "It is a pleasure to meet you, Abbe Colbert."

The Abbe smiled. "Likewise, monsieur. I hope my black robes don't scare you! David's letter said you were coming for education?"

"Yes," replied Henry, "he spoke highly of you, Abbe."

"David said you were coming *here* to learn, but that you could say prayers *anywhere*," replied Abbe Colbert good-naturedly, "David's humor gets the best of him sometimes." Everyone laughed. Adam and Henry were pleasantly surprised by the friendly, engaging manner of the Abbe. Cook climbed out of the carriage and stood quietly behind them. No one introduced him.

"Abbe Colbert," asked Adam politely, "could you direct us to lodging for this evening?"

Colbert looked at him blankly, then laughed. "Mercy, I'm not sure. I've only just arrived myself, a month ago. I live here at the church."

"Just an inn for the night," said Adam pleasantly. "We'll find better quarters tomorrow."

"Yes, yes," replied the Abbe, "an inn. Just the thing. Now, where might one be?" he asked himself with his hand to his chin.

. . . .

WITHIN TWO WEEKS THEIR habitation worries were resolved to their great satisfaction. With the Abbe's assistance, Cook found a big house quite near the church. It seemed ideal to Adam and Henry, featuring an inner courtyard and garden, spacious, well-furnished rooms, and a household staff eager to have a tenant to serve. The previous owner was a dead French naval captain whose widow couldn't maintain the place. Desperate to sell, she gratefully accepted a year's lease at a very reasonable sum. The woman almost wept when Adam told her they'd like to retain the servants, including a cook, hostler, and maid. Cook was elated when he discovered how little it would cost, many times less than if they'd been in Paris.

Abbe Colbert visited often, both for their company and to work with Adam at his French pronunciations. Abbe had the patience for it, and he'd been born and raised in Scotland so he could understand Adam's difficulty much better than a native French tutor. Henry found a horse and made riding a daily routine, and he was enrolled in the local university. The crate of books was cracked open, and reading assigned. Henry spoke French quite well, but neither of them made many contacts or friends during the first two months they were in Toulouse. Abbe Colbert had very few local contacts as he was so new to the parish, but he was a friendly, optimistic, intelligent man who they grew to like immensely.

On a warm drowsy afternoon in May, Abbe Colbert let himself through the gate and passed through the garden towards the door. He spied Henry sitting in the shade in a far corner of the courtyard reading a book. In fact, he had dozed off.

"Hello Henry!" greeted the Abbe, "you are the very picture of studious repose!"

Startled, Henry awakened with a jerk. "Huh! Oh, hello Abbe." He made to stand but Colbert waved him down with a laugh.

"I'll tell Adam I found you deep in prayer," he said with a smile as he passed through the door. Abbe Colbert was welcome anytime and came whenever he had a moment or was bored. He found Mr. Smith intellectually stimulating, and he felt nostalgic appreciation for fellow Scots, however far removed. There was never a lack of interesting conversation.

As Abbe approached the small, sunlight room that Adam used for his study, he could hear the professor trying to work with a French amanuensis. The scribe labored with his quill at a small desk near Adam's.

"Labor in all its forms is the ultimate source of wealth," he heard Adam say, and as he appeared in the doorway, Adam was saying, "Oui, ul-ti-mate..." Adam looked up to see the Abbe laughing in the doorway.

"Your diction improves every week, Mr. Smith!" said Colbert, hearing the progress of his pupil. It tickled him that he was the tutor of Henry's tutor.

"Hello Abbe," said Adam, bemused. "You are too kind."

"Are you working Mr. Smith?" he asked. "I mean, more than with Henry?"

"Well, I'm trying. It's very quiet here and I have little to do otherwise," Adam said, trying to avoid sounding like he was complaining about the slow pace of life in Toulouse.

"It's a church town," smiled Colbert, lifting the tasseled end of his cassock belt.

"I'm not complaining, Abbe," Adam said ruefully. "If I can tame my Scots accent perhaps this worthy fellow could understand my words. I have the slowest pen in the Union."

"What task have you set for yourself?" asked Colbert.

"An inquiry into why some nations are wealthy, and some are not," Adam replied.

Abbe Colbert nodded agreeably. "They who have the most gold wins, I suppose?"

"I suspect there's more to it than meets the eye," said Adam.

Henry entered behind the Abbe and they crowded the small room. Adam dismissed the amanuensis with a nod, and Colbert took the seat just vacated.

"I have news," he announced. "It appears that the archbishop won't return until the fall. He remains anxious to meet you both."

Adam sighed. "A disappointment. I will advise Mr. Townshend in my next letter."

Cook suddenly appeared at the door. "Forgive me, but I have already advised Mr. Townshend in my last letter. I heard it from a servant who knows the church cook."

The Abbe looked nonplussed for a moment, then said, "There are few secrets in the world. My news is older than it seemed a moment ago."

"Henry knows no Frenchmen whatsoever," said Adam with a hint of frustration, "and we've been here two months." Henry knew the servants by then, but Adam meant important people that Charles would appreciate. He neglected to recall Marshal Richelieu, but their single visit was not a relationship.

"I've been reading your Theory, Mr. Smith," said Henry.

"Our expenses remain admirably low here in Toulouse," added Cook.

"Good, Henry. Good, Mr. Cook. We'll just have to entertain ourselves at present," Adam said resignedly.

"I have a question for both of you," said Henry. Cook arched an eyebrow, so Henry added, "No, not you Cook. You can go." Cook nodded and vanished, but of course he remained outside the door, listening. He took no offence at Henry's brusque tone; he knew his place.

Adam and the Abbe gave their attention to Henry as he asked, "How can you have a *theory* about *moral* sentiments?"

"Well, I found a good publisher in London," replied Adam dryly.

Henry had to laugh, but only for a moment. He'd thought about this question for awhile, and he wanted to discuss it with both his tutor and the Abbe at the same time. "What I mean is that, well, a theory means it's rational, like science."

Adam was impressed with the quality of the question. "Indeed, it's a theory about why people act the way they do."

Henry turned towards the Abbe. "But isn't morality determined by God? How can our sentiments be moral without reference to holy scripture?"

He turned back to Adam. "Yet your theory mentions God only in passing."

Adam and Colbert exchanged a long look. Colbert raised his eyebrows and invited Adam to respond by pointing his finger at him, as if to say, "you handle this one!"

"My theory holds that morals arise from our social natures," replied Adam, "God made us sociable, and the proper rules for sociability arise from there."

"Social rules? I thought morality comes from God, that He determines what is right and what is wrong," objected Henry.

"Everything is the province of God, Henry," said Abbe Colbert, "He makes us who we are, but does not decide how we will behave. That is left up to us."

"God sends his moral lessons written on the faces of the people around us," added Adam helpfully. "Their expressions are a mirror for us."

"Mr. Smith, that's the most I've heard about God from you since we met," said Henry. "Abbe, do you agree?"

"I do, Henry, I do," replied the cleric, "God rarely speaks to us directly. We can't all be saints. He sends his messages through events, through people."

"Would your cousin Hume agree?" asked Henry.

The Abbe paused with surprise, but then smiled as he thought of his answer. "David proves that even a religious skeptic can be a moral person." He shook his finger at Henry in mock anger. "But eternal salvation is another thing entirely!"

After Henry left, Adam and the Abbe looked at each other gratefully for the mutual support each had offered. Colbert had wondered whether his new friend Mr. Smith was as radical as his amiable cousin Hume, but Adam's words reassured him. His science didn't necessarily conflict with his faith, so different from the view of the Paris atheists. Yet he also observed that Adam tended to call God, 'the Author of Nature' in his writings. Still, Abbe Colbert had learned much from Henry's deep and unexpected questions.

Another month went by, and some of the house servants found permanent employment and were replaced. For a while, several new servants were tried but not all were satisfactory to Cook. Their mistakes cost them their potential employment, but for Adam and Henry life was unaffected other than seeing a series of new faces. Adam was generally pleased with the progress of Henry's studies, but he noticed that his student's enthusiasm waned. Henry grew increasingly bored with the slow pace of life in religious Toulouse, compounded by his lack of friends and suitable amusements. He was pleased to see that without James' influence, Henry drank little.

Arriving home from university one day, Henry spied Adam reading in the courtyard. Adam looked up and closed his book. "How were classes today, Henry?" His routine greeting garnered a serious expression from Henry as he sat down next to Adam in the shade of an ornamental tree.

"Boring, Mr. Smith," he said frankly. "Almost nodded off again. They drone like bumblebees."

"Don't snore in class or you'll besmirch our Scottish reputation," Adam deadpanned.

"When I speak my classmates must think I'm as English as they come," returned Henry with a chuckle. He turned serious again. "They look at me like I'm wearing the scarlet uniform of an English soldier, complete with fixed bayonet."

"Have a care about your English reputation then," said Adam with a smile, hoping to divert him. "Have you finished Plutarch's Lives?"

"I have a few Lives left yet," replied Henry, smiling belatedly at his own witticism, which had been unintended.

Adam smiled back at Henry. In Toulouse, he'd found it easy to maintain a good relationship with his student. Granted, they were in a church town, but that had been his biggest worry, and it was much relieved by Henry's good character and pleasant demeanor. Adam Smith the famous professor wasn't failing in his teaching. Henry was an excellent student by nature, despite knowing that his future was financially easy regardless of what he did or did not do. Someone had instilled values in the entitled boy, and it was a huge comfort and relief to Adam.

"Mr. Townshend expects a report from me soon," said Adam, grinning. "I'll say you sleep through class and that you aren't really sure why Alexander was Great."

"Tell him I finished your book and that you are now filling my head with skeptical French philosophy," laughed Henry.

Adam noticed a new servant, a man who appeared to be in his twenties, appear at the door. He'd never seen the man, who withdrew when he saw Adam looking at him. Adam thought nothing of it and returned his attention to Henry.

"Little of that skepticism here in Toulouse," said Adam, "as I'm sure you've already discovered. The Catholic Church frowns on it."

"Perhaps that's what makes things so frightfully dull," mused Henry.

"It was the same at Oxford in my youth," nodded Adam sympathetically. "Books were my best friends. See you at supper, Henry."

As Adam was leaving, a very lovely serving girl entered, carrying a tray of food for Henry. He nodded at her, noticing that she seemed flushed. A very pretty girl indeed, he thought to himself. Perhaps this maid would remain, he thought idly as he walked away.

Henry noticed the beautiful girl coming with her tray and saw an angel rescuing him from his boring existence. As she leaned to set down the tray, the inviting view of her decolletage drew Henry's eyes like magnets. Her raven hair framed a face that featured large, liquid dark eyes.

"Something to eat, monsieur?" she purred.

"Yes, please," stammered Henry, "merci."

She took a moment to place his napkin and utensils next to the plate. She saw that Henry couldn't take his eyes off her.

"Anything else, monsieur?" she asked in a low voice, suggestively. She pointed to herself and added, "Collette."

"I'll ring if I think of anything, Collette" was all he could manage to say, kicking himself.

She walked slowly towards the door, then turned her head and caught his lingering eye. An enticing smile as she left gave Henry little doubt that her invitation was real. She was gone just seconds before he stood to follow. Reaching the door, he saw her waiting at the far end of the hall. Then she vanished with a low laugh, so he started after her.

Midway down the hall Adam stepped through a side door, directly into Henry's path. "Oh, excuse me, Henry, but about that letter to Charles...," Adam began, standing in the middle of the hall. Henry braked to a halt.

"Can we discuss it later, Mr. Smith?" said Henry impatiently, turning to edge past him.

Adam put his hand to his chin as if in contemplation. "It's rather important," he said, "Are you engaged with something right now?"

"Er, yes, actually," said Henry, as he began to step around his oblivious tutor.

Adam stopped him with his hand as he began to move by. "It will take but a minute. Let's return to your dinner."

Reluctantly, Henry followed Adam back to the room where his food lay untouched. Adam pulled up a chair. "Eat, eat, while I talk," gestured Adam, so Henry sat down and ate a grape.

"Is it so urgent that you report to Charles today?" asked Henry. He meant to sound less terse than he did.

"Not really," answered Adam, "I'm thinking about future reports that I must write." Out of the corner of his eye he glimpsed Cook pass an open doorway. "Or that Cook may write," he added.

"Cook spies on me for Charles, I know," said Henry in a low voice as he ate more grapes.

"This is less about Charles and more about you," Adam replied, looking at Henry in his usual calm, self-assured manner.

"How so," said Henry warily.

"Well, it's about affairs of the heart," said Adam.

"So, you spy on me as well, Mr. Smith?" Henry responded with a smirk.

"I observe. I noticed the pretty girl, for example," Adam replied, maintaining his even tone. "I must caution you."

"What good is being young, rich, and titled if I can't woo a pretty girl?" Henry demanded.

"Not just any pretty girl, Henry," answered Adam, remaining perfectly calm. "She is not of your social class."

"That doesn't make her less pretty," Henry replied.

"Of course not," said Adam, "In many ways it makes her lovelier. I'm sure your wealthy Duke-ish charms would sweep her off her feet. But consider the harm you might do her."

"So now you are the defender of French chastity?" Henry snorted, nettled by his embarrassment.

Adam smiled broadly. "That would be a tall order indeed. I'm thinking of this girl, in this place."

Henry put down his fork, sat back with folded his arms, and frowned. He gave his tutor his full attention. "I'm listening, Mr. Smith."

"You see her as a moment's delight but would never consider marriage. Is that so?" asked Adam in that same level, calm voice.

"Yes, of course," answered Henry uncomfortably, "but she seems willing."

"Let's say that the chance of you falling in love and proposing marriage is, oh, perhaps one in a thousand," started Adam, ever the scientist.

"More like one in a million," said Henry, "but we'll assume long odds."

"You see one in a thousand odds as no chance at all then," confirmed Adam.

"Agreed," said Henry with an emphatic nod, "You can assure Charles that I won't marry this girl." Henry fought down a rising tide of resentment of both Mr. Smith and Cook and their stifling ways.

Adam continued, "She sees you as the chance of a lifetime, Henry. How many rich young dukes will cross her path?"

Henry had to grin, but he kept his arms crossed. "It's good to be a duke then!"

Adam's tone never changed, always staying thoughtful and reasonable. "If you notice her charms, do you suppose others don't? I'm sure half the men in Toulouse are aware of such a young pretty woman."

"Must I apologize for my good fortune?" asked Henry archly, "Good luck to those other fellows, she is free to choose."

Adam leaned forward to deliver his lesson. "Yes, she might risk all for the slim chance of snaring a duke. When she fails, as you admit she must, her reputation will suffer. Toulouse is not Paris, Henry. Men who might have courted her will now spurn her. Those men will *certainly* resent the rich duke."

Henry shifted uncomfortably in his chair. Adam paused to see if he wanted to respond, but Henry took a bite of bread and said nothing. He tried to swallow his own resentment.

"We might even lose our welcome here," continued Adam meaningfully. "All that, even if no child results, no illegitimate heir for the house of Buccleuch. A moment of pleasure can cause a lifetime of pain, Henry."

Henry finished his bite and took a drink before he responded to Adam's calm lecture. "You sure can spoil a good time, Mr. Smith."

CHAPTER 13

RETURN OF JAMES MACDONALD *August 1764* Dawn was Henry's favorite time of day, although being young, he often slept through it. The sun was just up as he saddled the big chestnut gelding that had become his favorite horse in the stable. Henry rubbed noses with the handsome animal and gave it a stub of carrot.

"Pyrenees, I love you," cooed Henry, as he nuzzled the beast. The stable hands knew the horse and saw that the affection was mutual. Henry led Pyrenees out of the barn, placed his boot in the stirrup, and swung easily into the saddle. An early shaft of sunlight warmed his face; the eager horse pranced with expectation. It was good to be alive.

Entering the lane behind the barn, Henry cantered off. The countryside around Toulouse was golden, and the harvest had commenced. Hay wagons were already out as Henry rode by. The wagon teamsters knew him by sight and waved. Henry waved back; he felt a natural appreciation for servants who worked with horses in any capacity. Henry knew the love of a good horse, and he liked anyone who could feel the same.

For an hour Henry reveled in his ride with Pyrenees. As they entered the head of the long, straight lane that returned them home, he spurred his horse to a dead run. The scenery flashed by, faster and faster, until it was a mere blur. Henry rode with exhilaration, matching his body motion with that of the big horse, bent low over the neck like a jockey. Finally, Henry slowed to a gallop, and then a canter. Pyrenees was magnificent; Henry wondered again if he should buy the horse and take it back to England with him.

Far ahead he spotted a solitary horseman awaiting by the side of the lane, not far from their house and barn. As he drew closer, he could see it was a man riding a jet-black horse. Although he sat motionless, there was something familiar about him. A huge smile split Henry's face as he came close enough to recognize his friend James MacDonald. James was grinning too. "James!" exclaimed Henry as he pulled Pyrenees to a stop. "I supposed you in Rome these many months."

"Hello, Henry!" answered James as they clasped hands, both still mounted. "My tutor is unwell, so my departure from Paris was much delayed. So much so that Mr. Smith's letter found me."

"What letter?" asked Henry.

James pulled a letter from his pocket, unfolded it with a flourish, and pretended to read from it. "It says, 'Our mutual friend is bored and grows listless. Please come and cheer him up in Toulouse.'"

Henry couldn't tell if James was joking. "Did Mr. Smith really write to you?"

"Indeed, he did," answered James, more seriously. "I was surprised."

"Me too," said Henry as he inspected the letter James handed him. "I thought he liked my academic seclusion here."

"I thought Smith considered me a bad influence," said James, "Your situation must be dire."

"How long are you here?" asked Henry, smiling again.

"Until I receive word that my tutor is enroute to Rome," James replied, "My schedule is thus deliciously vague."

"Will you stay with us?" inquired Henry.

"Is there breakfast?" James asked with a laugh.

They cantered their horses into the courtyard and dismounted, handing the reins to the new hostler, the man Adam had seen the day he'd interrupted Henry's amours. They paid the man no attention and strode inside to find Adam and

Cook seated at breakfast. Both stood to greet the smiling young gallants, and both were genuinely pleased to see Henry so happy.

"James MacDonald, what a surprise!" greeted Adam.

"Surprised, Mr. Smith?" said Henry, smiling but doubtful. "James showed me your letter."

"I supposed we were in confidence, James, but no matter," said Adam, not evidencing any embarrassment over his minor duplicity. His gambit had been successful. Looking at Henry, he added, "All work and no play makes Henry a dull boy."

"Sit, sit, both of you," said Cook. "We are just awaiting breakfast. I'll have them bring more."

Henry and James pulled up chairs on either side of Adam. They both grabbed bread from a covered basket on the table. Henry poured them both a cup of tea. "What does one do for fun in Toulouse?" asked James after his first bite. "I've never been."

"Well, it's been mostly study," answered Henry.

"I've been writing some," Adam volunteered.

James looked at them, one to the other, while chewing his second bite. Swallowing, he said dryly, "I see that I've come in the nick of time."

Cook returned, followed by Collette loaded with dishes. She sat them down, glanced at James ever so briefly, and then departed for more.

"How lovely," said James, watching her leave. "I thought you said it was dull around here?"

"No James," said Henry, shaking his head. He looked at Adam reassuringly. "I'll give him the talk, Mr. Smith."

Before James could respond Collette returned with their breakfast, ham, eggs, and sliced fruit. James gazed in wonder at the pretty serving girl, but Henry noticed that she was far more reserved and proper than when she had served him alone. She avoided meeting his eye, but he noticed that James couldn't catch her eye either. They dug in, and for a few minutes no one spoke.

"Pass the salt," Adam asked Henry, breaking the silence. The boys ate in silence for several more minutes as Adam watched, bemused. Finally, James came up for air.

"That horse you rode is splendid, Henry," he said, taking a sip of tea. "Tell me."

"A three-year-old gelding named Pyrenees," returned Henry, "Runs like the wind."

James raised an eyebrow. "Have you raced him?"

"No," said Henry, "In fact, we haven't seen any horse racing here in Toulouse."

"I suspect the Church frowns on the gambling aspect of horse racing," said Adam.

"Something to do!" said James expansively. "Let's organize a horse race. No betting allowed."

"No betting?" scoffed Henry, "Isn't that the point of racing?"

"Of course it is," laughed James. "I meant no *open* betting. We won't invite clergy to wager."

Adam smiled uncomfortably as he rose to go. "I presume you boys are in jest. We must not embarrass Abbe Colbert."

After Adam was away, James asked, "Who is Abbe Colbert?"

"You'll meet him soon," replied Henry, he's the head of the local church."

"He sounds like a wet blanket, Henry," said James.

"Not at all," replied Henry firmly, shaking his head. "He's a fine former Scot and he's our friend and benefactor here." He looked at James seriously, making sure he caught his friend's eye. Satisfied, he continued, "How do you propose to begin James?"

James leaned forward and rested his arms on the table. "With an exhibition, Henry. We'll race each other, just for sport." He took another drink of tea. "We'll pass the word that two Scottish dukes will race for the honor of Scotland in France. Perhaps we'll draw a small crowd."

"Did you see my horse, James? Pyrenees will demolish you," said Henry with certainty.

"Excellent," James responded, "I love over-confidence in my opponent. I'll remind you of that when we set the betting odds." He sat back with a broad smile, and added, "Privately, of course."

At that moment the hostler led James' black horse past the window where they sat. Henry nodded his appreciation for the splendid animal. "Although you ride a fine horse, my friend. What is his name?"

"Blanco," replied James.

"Spanish?" Henry asked.

"Not that I know of," James shrugged, "I bought him in Paris. His Spanish name gives him an air of foreign mystery, which can be helpful when laying odds."

Henry nodded, suspecting more flash than substance, not recognizing that very illusion was James' goal. "So, when should we have this race with Blanco, the international horse of mystery?"

"Sunday afternoon, of course," replied James promptly, "Best time to draw a crowd." He pushed back his chair and stood. "Since it's only an exhibition, I give you even odds."

Noon Sunday found Henry and James in the barn, getting Pyrenees and Blanco ready. Both men performed these tasks themselves, for each saw the animal as more of a partner than mere beast. Good horsemen formed a bond with their mounts; horses, like dogs, are capable of loyalty. Saddle blanket smoothed; saddle, cinched just so; the riders carefully prepared their mounts and then led the horses out of the barn and into the yard. They were dressed elegantly, like gentlemen, but the fine horses needed no additional ornamentation.

The large barn was built on the side of a hill and thus had two levels. The stables were on the ground floor, with the upper structure used to store hay. A large trapdoor allowed hay to be loaded or unloaded directly from wagons parked below. As they walked their horses through the courtyard, workers were unloading hay from a wagon through the open trapdoor. The men were nearly finished and worked furiously for fear of missing the horse race. Henry thought it unusual for them to be working on Sunday, but it was haying season.

"A fine day for sporting, eh Henry?" James was grinning ear to ear.

"Indeed, James," replied Henry with pretend formality, "Who will the crowd favor?"

"Me, of course," James said simply.

"Are you sure?" doubted Henry with raised eyebrow.

"I let slip that I was Catholic, and I live in France," confided James. "You, sadly, are a Protestant who's just passing through."

"Jacobite," Henry laughed as they approached the gate. "Five pounds, even odds, as agreed?"

James nodded, but said, "Hush, Henry. Gambling is wrong. Especially for such a pittance as five pounds."

"More than that I'd have to report to Cook," admitted Henry as the hostler opened the high gate ahead of them. As they rode through, the large crowd outside cheered loudly. Over three hundred people thronged the gate, and the crowd extended down the lane.

James stood in his stirrups and waved to the crowd with a wide smile, and the cheer redoubled.

"See Henry, they've come to watch us battle for the honor of Scotland," James said proudly.

"So many!" exclaimed Henry, "I'd never have thought..."

"Remember," laughed James, "I speak French like a native."

The crowd parted and formed a path to the head of the lane, which was their starting point. As they walked their horses through, James leaned close to Henry and in English said, "They want to be us, Henry. They dream of the life we live."

"They hope to see one of us fall off," smirked Henry, but as they rode through the cheering crowd, he could see that James was right. Toulouse was a dull town, and everyone needed entertainment. That was James' specialty. Henry knew he had likely found the best horse in all Toulouse in Pyrenees, and James' horse Blanco, although a hand shorter in height, was a splendid animal. Henry and James themselves, turned out in their finest, completed the spectacle.

"Mostly peasants, but quite a number of the gentry as well," observed James, still in English. "I predict a profitable season of horse-racing ahead of us!"

"The French love their horsemanship," said Henry as they reached the head of the lane. He was surprised to see Adam and Abbe Colbert standing at the fencepost. If the Abbe was here, it meant the event was effectively sanctioned and thus safe for the crowd to attend without worry. Henry looked at James as they aligned their eager mounts side-by-side. The long, straight lane was fenced on both sides, so the crowd was safely beyond the rails. Henry felt confident in both himself and in James, as they'd practiced their horsemanship together on the fields of Eton. He reached over and shook James' hand.

Adam stepped forward to start the race, smiling up at Henry, who felt a pang of embarrassment as he hadn't even mentioned their race to him or the Abbe. James had done all the talking, apparently. Behind Adam stood Collette, and behind her, the hostler. Collette wasn't looking at Henry, but he noticed the hostler looking at Collette.

"The race is one half mile! Keep the course clear! Ready, gentlemen?" called Adam in his loudest lecture voice, but in his Scots-accented French. The crowd stilled expectantly.

"Ready!" called James.

"Ready!" said Henry, just as Blanco snorted and bucked suddenly and Pyrenees shied sideways.

"Go!" shouted Adam.

Blanco burst forward and was two strides ahead before the startled chestnut even began. Henry felt the powerful horse recover and launch forward, and the race was on in earnest. The crowd quickly blurred beside them as they thundered down the lane. As the horses reached their full running stride, Henry remained behind by a horse's length. Slowly, the gap began to close as the bigger horse began to assert itself. James was riding flawlessly, low over Blanco's neck with his body rocking to the horse's motion. Pyrenees edged forward, bit by bit, and Henry was every ounce the horseman James was. A throng of spectators marked the finish line; at their great speed it rushed up to greet them. The horses flashed past the post neck-and-neck to the roar of the crowd.

Henry and James slowed their plunging mounts, exhilarated. "I think you beat me, James!" exclaimed Henry breathlessly.

"Yes, yes I did!" shouted James happily. Pyrenees had never quite closed the gap.

As they walked the proud horses back towards the finish, the spectators roared their approval, soon joined by those who had watched at the starting line. They lionized James, as they were Catholics, they loved their horsemanship, and they loved a good entertainment.

Henry and James dismounted inside the barnyard gate, and servants closed it to the crowd. The wagon was gone, the trapdoors closed. Household servants milled about in happy agitation; they parted as Adam and Abbe Colbert approached.

"What an exciting race!" exclaimed the Abbe, showing himself as more man than cleric.

"Thank you, Abbe, it was as good a losing effort as I can imagine," said Henry wryly.

"Noble effort, Henry!" said James happily, clapping him on the back. "You just couldn't beat Blanco's mysterious foreign talent."

"Nervous foreign talent," noted Henry dryly, "Blanco startled Pyrenees at the start."

James shook his head, but he couldn't help from smiling while he returned, "There is always an excuse for losing." He laughed and looked at Henry, rubbing his fingers briefly in a way that meant bank notes. Both Adam and the Abbe noticed James' gesture.

"Er, I hope there is no gambling involved in this horse racing?" ventured Abbe Colbert, "That would displease the archbishop."

"Of course not, Abbe!" reassured James with a broad smile, "Henry needed new horseshoes, so I lent him the price." James laughed, then looked at Henry and chortled, "Too bad they were made of lead!"

James gave Blanco over to the hostler and followed Adam and Abbe Colbert inside the house. Henry walked Pyrenees into the barn, as he enjoyed caring for any horse that cared for him. He pulled the saddle and blanket and rubbed him down, then brushed him, freshened his water, filled the oat bag. After forty minutes, he stabled Pyrenees and gave him an apple before he left.

Inside, Henry could hear the others at dinner, laughing boisterously. He felt drowsy, his post-race excitement had left him fatigued. Rather than join them in the dining room, he sought his bed for a brief rest. Pulling his boots off, he laid his head down and immediately plunged into a dream. He felt the world rushing by in a blur, as it had while racing, but in his dream, he was standing stock still. Amidst the rush he saw Collette, serving him, bent low over her tray, beautiful. Then imaginary horses were upon him, and Henry awakened with a start, disoriented. The house was quiet but judging by the light it was still mid-afternoon. He sat up, rubbed his eyes, and pulled on his boots.

Taking coins from his purse, he went in search of the victor. Despite James' post-race gesture, Henry didn't settle small debts with banknotes, especially here in southern France. Illiterate folks were often suspicious of unfamiliar paper, but coins they accepted happily. Henry realized that he wasn't sure exactly how Cook settled the expenses of his Tour.

He stepped into the hallway and shouted, "Cook! Have you seen James?"

In ten seconds, at the far end of the hallway, Cook appeared. "No," he called out, "perhaps he's attending to his horse."

A short path connected the upper floor of the house with the upper level of the barn. Henry opened the side door and stepped inside and found himself surrounded by saddles and horse tack equipment. "James!" he called out, "are you here?" Hearing nothing, he passed through the tack room and into the barn loft. At the far end stood the mountain of hay already harvested.

"James?" said Henry, and he heard a scuffling as James stepped out from behind the stacks, brushing straw off his rumpled shirt.

"Henry," answered James as he tucked in his shirt, grinning sheepishly. Glancing back into the hay, he strode towards Henry to intercept him.

"I've come to pay my debt," said Henry, starting towards his friend.

Suddenly James vanished from sight, falling headfirst through the open trapdoor. A sickening crunch filled Henry with horror. He rushed forward, screaming, "James!"

Looking down he saw James lay crumpled, with his head at an impossible angle. With overwhelming dread, Henry flung himself over the floor edge, hung by his fingers, and then dropped the remaining three feet, scraping his chin unnoticed on the rough trapdoor. Tumbling over backwards, he recovered his feet and rushed to James' side. Turning James by his shoulder, he saw the head roll back, neck broken. James had died instantly, right in front of Henry.

Henry cried out again, "James!" and pulled the body close. Collette looked down from the loft, face terrified. She screamed as she saw James' body, then clamped a hand over her mouth and fled. In his growing shock, Henry dumbly noticed that Collette had straw in her hair.

Cook crossed the barnyard at a dead run, followed by Adam.

"James is dead!" cried Henry in anguish.

CHAPTER 14

B EAUDRIGUE *August 1764*
It was past five o'clock, an hour before sunset, and the light streamed into the far end of the long sitting room through a single open drape. The rest were closed, and Henry, sitting in the shadowy end of the room with Cook and Adam, recalled his sword practice in the shaft of sunlight that had lit the great hall of Marshal Richelieu. Cook poured drinks for each of them. Adam gulped his, so Cook refilled his glass. Henry lifted his glass. "To James," he toasted solemnly.

"To James," said Cook and Adam, and all drank. Several minutes passed in silence, each absorbed in their own dark melancholy. Henry was no stranger to death, having lost his father at age four, his sister Caroline at seven, and then his brother, also named James, when Henry was twelve. All had died of illness; James, heartbreakingly, at age eight. Henry remembered the somber black funerals, distantly, as he'd been at boarding schools and only saw his siblings when home on holiday. James MacDonald's accident had been so different; sudden and right before his eyes. Henry buried his head in his hands and sobbed.

Adam shuddered as he recalled how James' head had rolled on his shoulders when the servants removed his body from the barn. He felt a stab of remorse for writing the letter that had brought him to his doom, but then shook his head, remembering how happy Henry had looked when he strode into breakfast after his friend's arrival. Adam took another drink and wondered with apprehension how Henry would recover from such a shocking blow.

Cook's stomach roiled as he sipped his drink while watching Henry's grief. Noticing Adam's glass was empty again, he refilled it unasked. Returning his gaze to Henry, he recalled the boy's brave stoicism at the death of his brother six years before. Charles had been overly solicitous, trying to comfort the lad but only making him retreat further into his stony silence. With a pang of insight, Cook realized that was when Henry called his stepfather Charles, and never again Father.

Minutes ticked by. Henry raised his head, took a drink, and set his glass firmly down on the polished table beside him. At the clink, Cook and Adam raised their heads and looked at him.

"This was no accident," declared Henry.

"Careful, Henry," cautioned Adam, "What makes you say that?" He worried that a servant might overhear and gossip.

"The trap door was closed when we stabled our horses after the race," said Henry, "Someone knew James was in the loft, and with whom, no doubt."

"No doubt?" asked Adam gently. "Who was he with, Henry?"

"Collette," answered Henry flatly.

Adam nodded thoughtfully, but said nothing, wondering how to keep Henry from lashing out destructively with his blame. It was the most natural reaction in the world to feel that an accident must have been someone's fault, but such accusations could easily harm innocents.

Keeping his voice calm and level, Adam pointed out, "It might still have been an accident."

Henry stood, looking at Adam, strong feeling battling in his breast in the face of Adam's calm reason. He diverted by instructing Cook, "Can you see to James' body? Make sure it's treated with respect, and prepared for transportation to his mother in Paris?"

"Yes, Henry," replied Cook, "I've already taken steps in that regard."

"If you could check on it now, please," directed Henry, and Cook knew he was dismissed. As he turned towards the door, it flew open, and Abbe Colbert rushed in. Cook lingered.

"Oh, dear me, Henry," lamented the Abbe, "I'm so sorry about James." He wrung Henry's hand, and then held on to it.

"A shocking loss, Abbe," said Henry in a low voice, "I am not yet recovered."

"Understandable, understandable," nodded Abbe Colbert, releasing his hand. "However, the magistrate is here and questioning the servants."

Adam put his glass down while looking at Henry. "Here, now?" asked Adam, "He has not announced himself?"

"Unusual, indeed," fretted Colbert, "He has four gendarmes with him. He was inspecting the barn when I came in."

"And here he comes," said Cook, standing back from the door.

A well-dressed man of middle height strode through the door with an air of absolute authority. His clothes were immaculate, his posture and grooming impeccable, his stare, icy. He was dressed like a prosperous Bordeaux trader, with no uniform or robes to denote his power. Yet he held it in the palm of his hand. "Greetings gentlemen, I am David Beaudrigue, Chief Magistrate of Toulouse," he announced imperiously. Looking at Henry, he added, "I regret the loss of your friend."

"Thank you, sir," said Henry.

Beaudrigue glanced at Adam, Abbe Colbert, and then Cook, then back to Henry. "Monsieur Scott, I must ask you a sensitive question. Are you comfortable answering it with these men in the room?"

"Yes," replied Henry promptly. "This is Adam Smith, my tutor, and this is Mr. Cook, my butler and guardian."

Cook, to his credit, met the Magistrate's doubtful glance firmly; he was prim and pinched, but he was also proper. There was never a thread misplaced with Cook, who had long served the polished Charles Townshend.

Stepping to the door, Beaudrigue closed it. Turning to Henry, he stated in a policeman's voice, "There was a horserace with the deceased earlier today. Did you bet on the outcome?"

Startled, Henry stammered "No," as a cold sweat erupted at the Magistrate's blunt question. Guiltily, he added, "It was just a race between friends."

"No wager, no debt owed to the winner?" leveled Beaudrigue, never taking his eyes off Henry.

"No, we did not wager," lied Henry, heart pounding.

"You watched him fall through the hay door?" asked Beaudrigue.

Henry blanched at the memory, composed himself, then answered, "Yes."

"You did not speak of a debt?" Beaudrigue persisted.

"Yes, yes, I did speak of a debt," replied Henry, remembering his last words to his friend, "but it was not a wager. I owed James five pounds."

"For what," asked Beaudrigue, introducing a casual tone into his voice. For the first time he looked away by glancing at Adam.

"Er, horseshoes, sir," stammered Henry.

"Yes!" said Abbe Colbert with evident relief, "I heard them discuss horseshoes earlier today, Monsieur Beaudrigue." His eager tone trailed off as he remembered, "much earlier..."

The magistrate addressed Henry formally, "Thank you, Monsieur Scott. Your word as a gentleman settles the question; the Abbe puts it beyond doubt." He then turned to Cook, who had remained by the door during the exchange. "Please call my men, Mr. Cook."

Cook promptly opened the door and saw four gendarmes in the hallway beyond. At his gesture they marched in; the first pair holding the arms of the hostler, the second pair holding Collette, tear-stained and very frightened.

"I questioned these two servants," said Beaudrigue coolly, factually, "This one opened the hay loft door, and the woman was in the loft with the deceased." He paused for effect and saw that Henry was glaring at the hostler, who in turn stared determinedly at the floor. Despite the many times he'd handed the reins to this man when returning from a ride on Pyrenees, he had never learned his name. Beaudrigue could see that Henry suspected the man.

"So," he continued, "let's look at the possibilities. Perhaps they were working together to rob their victim?"

"No!" cried Collette.

"Or perhaps the man was jealous?" Beaudrigue never lost his policeman's tone, despite the raw fear of his captives. The hostler stared at the floor and said nothing, but Collette flashed a hateful look at him.

"Or this was all just a tragic accident," Beaudrigue concluded innocently, looking at Henry.

"Why did you open the hay door?" Henry burst out at the stoic hostler, making Adam, who was somewhat drunk, jump.

Bemused, Beaudrigue answered for the man, "He claims he opened the door and then went to get the hay wagon."

The hostler finally erupted, saying fiercely, "I didn't know anyone was in the loft!" Then he returned his stare to the floor, unwilling to meet anyone's eye, especially Beaudrigue's.

"Why did you open the door before the wagon was in place?" followed Henry, still glaring at the man.

"He claims there isn't enough clearance for the doors to open, due to the high sides of the hay wagon. This is true, we checked," said Beaudrigue casually. He could see that Henry suspected the man, and he further suspected that jealousy was involved considering Collette's rare beauty. "But it does not answer the question, does it?"

There was a long pregnant pause, and Beaudrigue looked at each of them in turn. Finally, he turned back to Henry and said conversationally, "Monsieur Scott, if you suspect this man, I can put him to torture. We'll find the truth soon enough."

"Torture?" said Henry, not believing what he'd heard.

"We will find the truth, sir," replied the magistrate in his cold, level voice. "Perhaps we should torture both, to find if they were partners in crime?"

"God, no!" Henry exclaimed, realizing that Beaudrigue was deadly serious despite his casual tone.

The magistrate paused, satisfied with his work. "So, you approve that my official report will say this was just a... tragic accident?"

All eyes turned to Henry, even the baleful glare of the hostler. Collette sobbed; Adam and Cook waited for Henry to reply with bated breath. Henry grimly pondered the situation, his heart throbbing painfully in his breast.

"My word alone is sufficient for you to torture this man?" Henry finally asked.

"Yes," said Beaudrigue matter-of-factly, "Or the woman, or both. You are a gentleman, and these are just servants. Just speak the word and we will find the truth."

"No, please," sobbed Collette.

Henry looked at Adam, then Cook, then at the blank faces of the gendarmes holding the servants whose fate he held in his hands. He suspected the hostler, he knew he was jealous of Collette, but he couldn't say for sure he'd known James was in the hay loft with her. Could his strong feeling alone justify torture for the man? Henry shuddered at the responsibility.

Taking a deep breath, he straightened and faced Beaudrigue, who seemed to be enjoying his role in this tragedy. Henry would not make it worse. "Sir, I thank you for your prompt attention to this dreadful accident," Henry said formally, "Let these people go."

Adam and Cook breathed separate sighs of relief, both already wondering how they'd report this dark eventful day to Charles.

• • • •

THREE WEEKS LATER AND five hundred miles north, Charles stood in the Adderbury garden in warm September sunshine, composing a speech. Frances, acting as his amanuensis, sat scribbling at a small garden table surrounded by paper, quills, and ink.

"Therefore, let us resolve to *never*...., no, wait, strike that," said Charles as he paused, chin in hand, to ponder his direction. "Therefore, we resolve to *always*...."

A servant appeared in the garden with a packet of letters, saying, "The post, sir."

Charles welcomed the distraction and plucked at the bundle. "One moment dear, let me see what has arrived."

"I will re-copy the last paragraph," said Frances, "It's a complete mess."

Charles lifted a brow at Frances but returned to the letters. "Please do. There is a letter here from Mr. Smith," and after a moment more added, "and one from Cook. Good."

Charles opened the thin envelope, and suspecting nothing began to read out loud. "Dear Mr. Townshend, I write to tell you that Henry is doing well and in good health. But I regret to inform you that young James MacDonald was killed in a tragic accident."

"No!" cried Frances in alarm, covering her open mouth with her hand as she jumped to her feet.

Charles had little choice but to continue, "Henry saw it happen, and was understandably much affected." Charles looked up from the page with a grimace. "Good God, that's terrible," he muttered, as Frances began to wail.

"As were we all," he continued reading, "Henry behaved admirably despite his shock and sadness, especially when questioned by the local magistrate." Charles tried to comfort Frances. "Well, now dear, that is such a tragedy."

Caroline swiftly appeared as Frances buried her face in her hands, crying uncontrollably. "Frances, you do carry on so! What is this?"

Charles, exasperated at his wife's cruelly inappropriate timing, informed her quickly, "James MacDonald is dead. Killed in an accident right in front of Henry."

"Oh God, that is awful news!" exclaimed Caroline, "How is Henry?"

"Fine, apparently, though deeply sad I'm sure," replied Charles, "let me continue the letter."

Charles read silently, as Hew joined them in the garden. They all waited for Charles to finish.

"What's going on?" asked Hew.

"James is dead, Hew," sobbed Frances. "Accident."

"No! How dreadful!" Hew gasped, then Charles raised his hand.

"Smith says James broke his neck and died instantly," Charles reported, "so he didn't suffer. He fell from a hay loft through an open loading door. The magistrate investigated that same day, and Henry behaved admirably despite his grief."

"What an awful thing to lose his friend before his very eyes!" lamented Caroline, wringing her hands.

"Oh, poor James!" Frances wailed, "poor Henry!"

"Frances, compose yourself," said Caroline, "We must face anguish with dignity."

Frances fled the room in tears, making Charles wince. "Caroline, dear, we all feel terrible," he reproached his wife gently.

"Yes, well, I'm thinking about Henry," replied Caroline, daubing her eyes with a handkerchief, "He must be devastated."

"I can't even imagine," said Hew. "James was so full of life. Now he's not," he finished lamely.

"Yes, Caroline," said Charles in a comforting tone, "we must think of Henry. But first let me read Cook's report. Smith's was brief, but Cook's envelope is fat."

They all found chairs, and for several minutes Caroline and Hew watched Charles read Cook's letter page by page. Finally, he looked up. "Hew, can you give your mother and I a moment alone?" Hew was disappointed, but departed without a word, wondering. Caroline looked at Charles with apprehension.

"Cook says there was a horse race between Henry and James on the day of the accident," said Charles, "It drew quite a crowd, apparently, with James winning a close race."

"Yes?" Caroline prompted.

"The magistrate asked Henry if there was a wager placed," said Charles, "It appeared he suspected foul play."

"Oh Henry, gambling!" Caroline's hand flew to her mouth in dismay.

"Not so, apparently," replied Charles, "Cook says the magistrate was satisfied on that account. There was no bet, so no motive."

"How could there be a motive for an accident?" asked Caroline, not quite following.

Charles continued, "Cook says the questioning turned on who left the hay door open for James to fall through. The magistrate suspected the local servants, but Henry defended them, saying it was an accident."

Caroline took a deep breath and regained her composure. "It sounds like Henry behaved honorably, despite the awful shock. Still, how horrible for him."

Charles wondered if he should stop there, but decided Caroline was composed enough to hear. "Cook says Henry suspected one of the servants but declined the magistrate's offer to *torture* the man. Good God."

Caroline and Charles exchanged a long grim glance, saying nothing, with neither reaching for the other. Finally, Charles said, "Perhaps we should send Hew to join him."

CHAPTER 15

D EATH OF JEAN CALAS *October 1764*
Henry rode Pyrenees in the late October sun, part of his daily routine. Sometimes he rode Blanco, as he'd bought both horses after James' death. He would decide later whether to take them home to England; in the meantime, he couldn't bear to part with either of them. Cantering into the courtyard, Henry dismounted and led the horse into the barn. Henry took care of both horses personally, which he privately enjoyed, as both the hostler and Collette had been discharged. It had been very difficult to hire new servants since James' death.

Cook emerged from the house and found Henry in the barn, brushing Pyrenees. "Mr. Townshend sent a letter," he announced. "He asked me to meet Hew in Paris and bring him here to study with you."

A smile, rare in the past month, creased Henry's smudged face. "Hew? Well, good! I could use a friendly face around here."

Cook was glad to see Henry show any sign of humor. "Mr. Smith says you don't plan to travel soon?

"No, I'm enrolled for another term at the University," replied Henry as he filled the oat bag. "Has the landlord been paid?"

"Yes, I took the liberty of paying two months in advance to calm her fears," nodded Cook, "Your accounts are in order. I plan to leave tomorrow."

"Good," said Henry absently as he returned to his brushing, "It will be good to see Hew."

Adam met him as he returned to the house a half hour later. "Ah, there you are Henry. The Abbe will arrive shortly with news. He asked if you'd be here."

"News?" asked Henry.

"It's a mystery," said Adam. "Oh, there is the Abbe now. Speak of the devil and he appears." Adam frowned at his poor choice of words but changed to a smile as the cleric entered.

"Good day, Mr. Smith, greetings Henry," said Abbe Colbert. It had become everyone's unspoken goal to cheer Henry whenever possible.

"Let us sit and hear your news," invited Adam, gesturing to the chairs. "It may be a few moments before we can offer refreshments. We are short of servants at the moment."

Once seated, the Abbe began, "I think I know why the archbishop has remained away from Toulouse." He paused for dramatic effect, but Adam and Henry looked at him blankly, so he continued. "His Eminence fears the Calas verdict." Colbert paused, but again he saw blank looks from Adam and Henry. The case of Jean Calas was all the rage in Toulouse, but Adam and Henry seemed disconnected. In fact, few of the locals shared much with either, especially after the visit by David Beaudrigue over a month earlier.

"Calas?" ventured Adam, trying to be helpful. "I've heard of it; can you review the particulars?"

"You are perhaps too secluded here," said the Abbe, shaking his head. "I'll be brief, the facts are these. A merchant in Toulouse, Jean Calas, a Protestant, found his son Marc-Antoine dead in his house, with marks that indicated hanging."

"Suicide?" asked Henry.

"Apparently," returned Colbert, "but to avoid the stigma of such a calamity, Jean Calas claimed his son was murdered."

"That is a serious charge," said Adam, "Why would he say such a thing and compound the tragedy?"

Abbe Colbert shifted uncomfortably; as a Scot it was hard to explain this to his compatriots. "In France, life can be very hard."

He paused a long moment before continuing, "To discourage suicide, there are awful consequences."

Adam looked at Henry, then back to the Abbe. "Consequences?" he asked with apprehension.

"The unfortunate body is dragged naked through the streets and mutilated," said the Abbe in a low voice, "the poor family suffers additional humiliation and disgrace."

After a long pause, Adam muttered, "Good God." Henry sat silent, mouth agape at such barbarism.

"It gets worse," said the Abbe, "David Beaudrigue didn't believe Jean Calas."

"Beaudrigue!" said Adam, startled.

"He is the chief magistrate," replied Abbe, "Beaudrigue accused Jean Calas of murdering his son, and sentenced him to death."

"Murdering his son!" blurted Henry, "on what evidence?"

"Jean Calas is Protestant," explained Abbe Colbert, "and France is a Catholic country. Marc-Antoine wanted to renounce his father's faith to be eligible for a position in law or government, as these positions are not open to Protestants. He and his father argued, strenuously."

Adam shook his head and said, "But Abbe, an argument does not prove murder."

"No," Colbert agreed, "there was much hearsay evidence but little actual proof. Beaudrigue decided to make an example of Jean Calas. He declared that if the son was indeed murdered, then the main suspect was his father, and the alleged motive was religion."

"I don't like the sound of that," said Henry.

"Beaudrigue doesn't really care if it was suicide," continued the Abbe, "He turned poor Marc-Antoine into a Catholic martyr. He was buried as a Catholic while his father was in jail. The magistrate inflamed the people with half-truths and omissions."

"What was omitted?" asked Adam.

"Antoine's gambling debts, for example," answered Abbe Colbert.

"I can see why the archbishop might want to avoid such a spectacle," said Adam, "So, what is the fate of Jean Calas?"

"He is to be executed tomorrow, after public torture to force his confession," said the Abbe matter-of-factly. "Will you go?"

Henry looked at Adam, shaking his head, but neither answered. "You are here to observe the French justice system, no?" asked the Abbe.

• • • •

AT TEN THE FOLLOWING morning a crowd began to fill the town square in bright sunshine. On a raised platform in the center of the square was mounted a large wheel. A priest with a large red cross on his robes raised his arms and exhorted the crowd to pray for sinners. Abbe Colbert led Adam and Henry to a second-floor balcony where they had a good view down on both the wheel and the crowd. Although mostly peasants filled the square, tradespeople and the local gentry crowded each other for the best spots. A festival atmosphere prevailed.

"Abbe Colbert," protested Henry, "as a man of the cloth, how can you sanction this?"

"I don't, Henry, I don't," he replied, "I am not the law. We must obey the King, even when he acts through his local authorities."

Henry pointed to the priest on the platform and arched his questioning eyebrows, but kept his mouth closed. "A priest attends all executions, Henry," explained the Abbe patiently.

The square was now packed, with a row of gendarmes surrounding the platform to keep it clear of spectators. A murmur swept the crowd, and it parted to admit David Beaudrigue, flanked by two soldiers in uniform, as he approached the platform. They stood at the steps as he ascended and then turned with arms raised to quiet the crowd.

"Let it be known to the citizens of Toulouse," he began in a loud, clear, authoritarian voice, "the merchant Jean Calas is found guilty of murdering his son, Marc-Antoine."

The crowd roared at this, and it sounded ugly to Adam and Henry, who looked at each other with growing apprehension. Beaudrigue continued his oratory, "The unfortunate and beloved Marc-Antoine Calas, who simply wanted to be Catholic!" Another roar rose from the crowd, as the soldiers stood their positions impassively. Executions were a regular duty, but they didn't always draw this many people.

"The sentence of Jean Calas has been upheld," Beaudrigue shouted, "The sentence is death!"

With shouts and catcalls, the crowd parted as two gendarmes escorted Jean Calas, sixty-four years old, through the square and up the platform steps. He was followed to the foot of the steps by his wife and remaining son, and his daughter, all of whom were crying openly. Henry noticed that a minority of the spectators, mostly women, were weeping instead of cheering. As he watched, he saw the discharged hostler in the crowd near the platform. He was cheering, not weeping. A black fury swept over Henry, but then Beaudrigue drew his attention back.

"Bind him to the wheel!" commanded the magistrate in a loud voice.

Two gendarmes stood Jean Calas with his back to the wheel and bound his feet to blocks nailed into the platform. Bending the old man backwards, they tied his hands over his head and stretched him face up along the circumference of the wheel. A silence came over the crowd.

"Jean Calas," said Beaudrigue in a dramatic voice, "do you confess to killing your son?"

"No!" shouted Calas hoarsely, as his wife wailed plaintively.

Beaudrigue stalked the platform like an actor. "I'll ask you once more," he shouted, his voice ringing clear throughout the square, "Do you confess willingly and accept a quick and merciful death?"

The crowd hushed to hear his answer. Mustering his voice, Calas called out, "I die innocent!"

The spectators remained very quiet, and the crying of the family could be heard. Calas' answer meant torture, and Beaudrigue nodded to a black-hooded man standing to the rear of the platform. He seized the handle of the geared wheel and pushed it opposite the direction of the victim's feet. Adam could see the muscles stand out on the executioner's bare arms, and in the relative quiet, he heard both of Calas' arms pop out of their shoulder sockets. Calas screamed and the crowd roared again.

"Jean Calas, here is a priest," called Beaudrigue in his loud stage voice, as the cleric bowed his head close to Jean Calas, as if listening. Henry was repulsed seeing the priest taking part in the macabre show that the magistrate was conducting. He glanced at the Abbe, whose face was locked into a frown that gave little hint of what he might be feeling.

"Confess to this man of God and repent your sin!" shouted Beaudrigue. Calas said nothing, keeping his mouth clenched shut to avoid screaming. Beaudrigue nodded again to the executioner, who stepped forward and turned the crank forward until more ruptured ligaments tore another cry from the elderly victim. The gear in the crank clicked into its new position, and convulsions rippled along the man's limbs. Henry felt sick; he looked at Adam who was watching grimly, lips pressed closed, with white knuckles as he gripped the balcony rail.

Beaudrigue raised his hand again, and the crowd fell silent. "We'll let him think about it. Please, everyone, refresh yourselves," said Beaudrigue as if inviting them to a picnic. The crowd began to line up at tables where food and drink was offered. Soon, they were eating and conversing around the platform where Jean Calas remained in agony. His wife, son, and daughter hugged each other at the foot of the steps. Henry was appalled. His heart nearly broke when he heard Jean Calas' wife cry out, "I love you husband!" Clearly, the wife didn't blame her husband for the death of her eldest son.

A servant appeared with a platter of delicacies for the grandees on the balcony. Adam and Henry waved him away with revulsion. For nearly a half-hour, Jean Calas suffered silently in the noontime sun. Henry imagined pain in his arms and shoulders, in sympathy to the victim's suffering perhaps, but also because he was gripping the balcony with clenched hands.

Beaudrigue raised his hand again to regain the crowd's attention. "Jean Calas, did you murder your son?" he called out again.

"Father!" croaked Calas, and the spectators grew very quiet.

The priest bent his ear close to the victim, and called out, "Confess to me, Jean Calas," putting a hand to his ear theatrically, "Did you kill your son?"

"Father, how could you believe it?" cried Calas, in a surprisingly loud, clear voice. In the silence, it seemed to Henry that the crowd's blood lust deflated. Beaudrigue and the priest both looked discomfited; the point was to whip the crowd into a frenzy of retribution, not make them wonder if perhaps the victim was innocent.

Beaudrigue nodded to the executioner, who stepped forward for the last time. Instead of turning the wheel further, he slipped a garrote around the prisoner's neck and finished him. When Calas was dead, the executioner gave a nod to the magistrate. The spectators seemed cowed by the departure of life and remained silent.

Beaudrigue raised both arms and shouted triumphantly, "Behold the fate of murderers!"

The crowd found its voice again, although Adam thought their roar was somewhat less fulsome than before. A cart full of straw was wheeled into the square. The gendarmes moved the people back, while others helped the executioner cut free the corpse. Together they pitched the body from the platform and onto the cart, which was wheeled back, doused with oil, and lit with a torch. As the body began to burn, the ugly smell caused the crowd to stream out of the square.

"How can these people applaud such barbarism?" Henry asked Adam in horror. Adam shook his head, saying nothing, but pointed grimly at Beaudrigue still standing on the platform, arms crossed, with a smile tugging at the corners of his mouth as he watched the pyre of the man he destroyed.

Emotionally shocked, Adam and Henry moved out of the square with the last of the crowd. Abbe Colbert had left immediately for his church, where a large number were making their way to pray. As the Abbe had provided the carriage that morning, Adam and Henry were left without transportation. Fearing for Henry's health after two successive traumas, Adam impulsively pulled him into a drinking establishment. Soon, they were sitting on opposite sides of a small table with heads bent over flagons of red wine. They did not discuss what they had just seen, but instead listened to the crowd around them. To a man, the patrons thought Jean Calas guilty of murdering his son to prevent him from turning Catholic. They had no doubt about it, none, and they were celebrating the public murder and torture that compounded the tragedy of a man who seemed innocent.

As they drank and listened, saying nothing to each other, Adam weighed how long this terrible lesson in public passions should continue. He was ever more worried about the effect on his student. Adam had never seen war in his life, but he could now see clearly how terrible passions could infect people like contagion. He tilted his head towards the door questioningly, but Henry shook his head no. They sat and drank, listened and wondered, but it hardened them. Adam found himself wondering who was closer to an understanding of human nature, him or the old warrior Marshal Richelieu.

After an hour they decided to walk back to the house. It was a full three mile hike in the warm late afternoon sun. The light was fading as fast as their waning energy when they entered the shadowy, quiet house. Nothing stirred, no servant greeted them. "The house seems empty," said Henry.

"Cook has gone to fetch Hew," said Adam, "perhaps the servants have been sent away."

"I'm not that hungry," said Henry glumly.

"I could use a bottle of claret," said Adam, "Come, let us start our search in the kitchen." He didn't want Henry to be alone just yet. They walked the shadowed hall towards the kitchen, which was located far back in the house. In all the time of their long stay, their food had always been brought to them. They knew where the kitchen was but were not familiar with it.

"We must leave Toulouse," Henry said as they walked.

"I agree," Adam found himself saying, "As soon as Mr. Cook arrives with Hew, we will travel to Montpelier." Adam had already planned that trip, but now they wouldn't be returning to Toulouse.

They found the kitchen lit by the low glow of the banked fire. "Hello," called out Henry, "is there anyone in this house?" A plump middle-aged woman appeared, tying a clean apron around herself.

"Looking for a bite to eat, monsieur?" she asked pleasantly.

"And a bottle of claret," answered Henry, "if you have it. Are you the only one here?"

"I'm the only one you need to get fed," she said with a smile, "I have fresh chicken, roast carrots, and bread."

"That sounds splendid. Where should we sit?" asked Adam, feeling relief that here, at last, was a normal, warm human being.

"Sit at the kitchen table here, both of you," she said, "I'll fetch the bottle."

Adam and Henry took seats on simple wood chairs and slumped over their arms folded on the table. The woman set glasses down, uncorked the bottle, and filled them. Seeing their tired body postures and haggard expressions, she took the bottle with her. Adam and Henry both drained their glass while watching each other, then looked for more.

"I'll bring the bottle back when you've eaten," said the woman as she lit an oil lamp and some candles with a brand from the fire. The room brightened, and she bustled about like she owned the place.

"I'm not sure I have an appetite," said Henry morosely.

"We'll see about that when we put some food in front of you," she said wisely.

"Horror and anguish are hard work," observed Adam while watching Henry's glum face, "Fear and revulsion take a lot out of a man."

The woman set cups of fresh water before each of them, watched them drained immediately by the parched men, and then refilled them from her pitcher. She placed a plate of bread and butter on the table; both set themselves to buttering and eating. Neither could believe how good simple bread and butter could be. In a twinkling she placed warm plates of chicken and carrots before them. For several minutes they ate in silence while the woman tidied the kitchen.

Henry took another drink of water, wiped his mouth, and sat back. He caught Adam's eye and said, "I believe that man died innocent."

"We may never know," said Adam, "but it seemed he was tortured because of his religion. Murder alone usually means hanging."

Adam and Henry both resumed eating. As they finished, the cook returned with the bottle of claret. She refilled their glasses and then surprised them by pulling up a chair and sitting down with them.

"Marc-Antoine killed himself and ruined his family," she said firmly. Her guests gaped at her.

"How do you know?" asked Adam.

"Antoine was a vain, pompous fool, always putting on airs," said the woman, "Thirty years old and he could not keep a job." She jabbed a finger at them knowingly, "*then* he started gambling."

Henry, surprised by the woman's familiar frankness, said with disbelief, "Surely you can't know for sure if he killed himself?"

"He was a strong man," she replied, "Jean Calas and all his family couldn't have hung him if he didn't want to be hung."

"He killed himself knowing what would happen to his body, to his family?" doubted Henry.

"Antoine was resentful and always blaming others," she persisted, "including his father. It might have been spite." Both men were glued to her every word, and she enjoyed the attention. She had the natural confidence of someone who knows they are good at their job. She continued, "He wanted to turn Catholic so he could work for the government. Those jobs are easier to keep, if you can get them."

"Was Marc-Antoine a devout person?" inquired Adam.

She scoffed, "Not hardly, he rarely went to either church. He needed a job to pay his debts."

His father, Jean Calas, disagreed?" probed Adam.

The woman shrugged. "I suspect Jean Calas thought God more important than Mammon."

"Did you attend... the death today," Adam asked haltingly, unable to say the word *torture*.

"I never go," she said simply, "they disturb my sleep."

Adam nodded and looked at Henry, who was nodding emphatically at this. He asked her, "How often do executions occur?"

"About once a month, usually a simple beheading or a hanging, if the person is poor," she answered, refilling their empty glasses.

"Not a public torture, like today?" asked Henry.

She shook her head. "Not often. The magistrate was putting the fear of God into the Protestants; making an example of poor Jean Calas."

"Did you know him well?" asked Henry, who shuddered at the memory of the horrible popping sounds when the wheel had dislocated the man's shoulders.

"Only by slight acquaintance," she said, "as I am Catholic myself. I kept quiet to be sure I wouldn't have to testify. Jean Calas was honorable, perhaps a bit too pious. Not much humor," she said, summing up.

Adam pondered the remarkable woman they'd found in the kitchen. He felt better with the food, the bottle, and especially, with the local insight she shared. "Madam, what is your name?" he asked.

"Julia," she said with a smile, and then spread her arms and added, "and this is my kitchen. I've been cooking most of your food since you've been here." Adam and Henry were humbled by the thought that neither, in all the time they'd occupied this house, had met the cook. That wasn't surprising in many respects, but it seemed they had been terribly remiss as they sat in her kitchen being revived.

"I could not imagine a better place to be right now than in your kitchen, Julia," said Adam thankfully, and she beamed.

"Blessed are the hands that prepare the food," added Henry, and she couldn't resist placing her hand on his for a moment. That momentary human touch sparked something in him, pushing back against his black mood.

"Merci, monsieur," nodded Julia gratefully.

"Julia, please fetch another glass and join us if you would," invited Adam. Henry glanced at him, wondering at this breach of social protocol, as it wouldn't do to blur the distinction between the served and the servants. But he did not object; he found that he considered Adam's unusual gesture entirely fitting.

Blushing some, she brought a glass back and accepted a pour from Adam, who then raised his own. "To Julia," he toasted, and then spread his arms and added, "and to Julia's kitchen."

"To Julia," toasted Henry, and he found himself smiling. Such is the effect of angels in dark times.

CHAPTER 16

L EAVING TOULOUSE *November 1764*
Cook was not due back from Paris for at least three weeks after the death of Jean Calas. When most of the servants quit, neither Adam nor Henry cared to seek replacements for such a short duration. Julia was there, and she saw that a man tended the fires as the nights were growing cold. Henry spent much of his time with Pyrenees and Blanco, either riding them or caring for them. He wasn't communicative so Adam worked on his book and worried. Abbe Colbert hadn't come by since the execution; Adam suspected that he feared Henry's outrage.

Henry and Adam took their meals in the kitchen with Julia, and these became the bright spots in their somber last days in Toulouse. Henry found himself helping Julia with her tasks, like bringing the kindling, feeding scraps to the hogs, and clearing the table. These little moments puzzled Adam, as entitled persons such as Henry never performed menial tasks, but he was delighted that Henry's despondency seemed less acute in the kitchen. Julia remained the positive, steadfast cook that had won their hearts with bread and chicken and claret.

One afternoon as Adam neared the kitchen, he heard Henry and Julia talking. Before entering, he listened outside the door. They seemed to be discussing bread, and Adam envied Henry's fluent command of the French language. When he opened the door, he was shocked to see Henry, in an apron, kneading bread dough!

Henry raised a well-floured finger and pointed it at Adam in mock severity. "Tell no one, Mr. Smith!"

Julia laughed and clapped her hands, raising a cloud of flour dust. It occurred to Adam that Julia, with her comforting motherly manner, was the very opposite of Henry's own mother

Caroline. He felt a wave of relief at the break in Henry's dark mood and credited the matronly French cook. The severe shortage of servants meant they did most tasks for themselves, but they found those daily chores had become a welcome diversion to their melancholy. Still, it surprised Adam to see Henry baking bread. In an apron, no less.

Henry had talked to Adam about his revulsion at the Toulouse crowd's bloodlust; not just how they cheered torture, but how afterwards they all congratulated each other that justice was served. How could that be justice? How could they surrender their natural skepticism to a demagogue like Beaudrigue? Was it religious intolerance alone, or something far darker buried in human nature?

Adam was impressed by the quality of Henry's questions, but regretted they came from such a horrible lesson, and so soon after he witnessed James' tragic fall. He suggested that what motivated the crowd even more than Beaudrigue was the confirmation and approval of the people around them. Perhaps the approval of others was a greater persuasion than their confidence in their own rational thoughts. Perhaps they should have skipped the execution, Adam thought for the thousandth time. Some lessons seemed too hard to bear.

The next day Adam found Henry in the barn, preparing Pyrenees for his daily ride. "May I join you?" he asked, trying to sound casual.

"Sure, I'll saddle Blanco, Mr. Smith," agreed Henry in a neutral tone. Adam wasn't sure if he was pleased at the prospect or not. As Henry saddled the handsome black horse it was apparent to Adam how much he loved the beasts. The horses and the cook seemed to be helping with Henry's trauma recovery.

They mounted and walked the horses out the gate and into the lane. A pang struck Adam as they passed the gatepost where he had started the race between these same two horses. So much tragedy had struck since then. "You seem to enjoy Julia's kitchen," ventured Adam, keeping his voice upbeat.

"I do," Henry nodded, and almost smiled. "She reminds me of Mrs. Lewis."

"Who?" Adam didn't recognize the name.

"Mrs. Lewis," Henry explained, "the cook at Buckingham School for Boys, my boarding school."

"You were fond of this Mrs. Lewis?" probed Adam, interested in any possible glimpse of what had made Henry the boy he was.

"Very fond," said Henry frankly, "she was like a mother to me."

"Ah," nodded Adam, "and when were you at this school?"

"Ages, oh, eight to thirteen, before I went to Eton," responded Henry. "Mrs. Lewis had a son my age, William. We were fast friends." Henry laughed at the memory and waved his hand over his head and added, "William had this big mop of straw-colored hair."

"I see the connection," said Adam, "God bless the cooks!"

Henry nodded and replied wistfully, "William and I would visit the kitchen, and his mother would slip us warm biscuits. We had to eat them on the spot, or all the other boys would want one."

"Did William know you were a duke?" asked Adam.

"Sure, all the boys knew," Henry answered as his smile turned down. "The headmaster would parade me in front of potential customers. Most of the boys were afraid of me, not because I might thrash them, but because I could get them in trouble if they thrashed me."

"But not William?" he asked as the horses reached the end of the lane.

"No, not William, even though he was a cook's son," replied Henry thoughtfully as they came to a stop. "Charles always seemed annoyed when he'd come to fetch me to Adderbury and find my clothes a mess because I was playing with the servants. Those were my happiest times, Mr. Smith."

Three days later Henry sold Pyrenees and Blanco to a horse merchant in Toulouse. They reminded him too much of James. The horses fetched a good price, as they were so well known. The merchant was knowledgeable of his trade, so he understood when he saw the young Englishman sobbing as he said goodbye to the big chestnut gelding. Henry walked back to the house in a cold wind that matched his mood.

Cook arrived with Hew just two days before the planned departure to Montpelier, the site of the Languedoc assembly, which lies to the southeast on the Mediterranean coast. Despite his long travels, Cook immediately began arranging details with Adam, outraged that the servants had quit but understanding why they had to abandon their prepaid rent. Cook shuddered when Adam told him about the torture Henry had witnessed in his absence.

Hew slept most of the day after their arrival, sore from a week's journey in a rattling carriage. Henry embraced him, welcomed him, but to Hew, something seemed wrong. He could see his brother was injured, but could hardly imagine how, or how much. Hew was dismayed that he'd have to continue traveling.

The morning of their departure, Cook stood in the house driveway surrounded by several trunks. A freight wagon pulled up, and the driver got down from his high seat. He and Cook pondered the task before them. "Is there no one who can help us load this baggage?" asked Cook.

"Sorry, they drafted my helper to work on the roads," shrugged the driver.

"The house servants have been let go," said Cook, "I suppose it's just us." The driver and Cook struggled to lift the first trunk to the back of the wagon, but they just managed. A carriage pulled into the driveway behind the freight wagon.

"You there!" Cook shouted at the carriage driver, "Can you help us load this luggage?"

"Not me, monsieur," replied the man, "I've a bad back from fighting the Austrians. I can barely put my boots on."

Hew emerged, oblivious to the situation. "Cook, can you see to my trunk? It's in my room."

Cook tried to hide his exasperation. "Certainly, Hew. It will be just a moment, as we appear short-handed this morning."

"I'll catch a bite to eat then," responded Hew and he disappeared back inside, passing Adam as he emerged.

"Ah, Mr. Cook," greeted Adam, "I appreciate your help with my luggage." Pointing to one of the trunks on the ground, he added, "Watch out for that one, it's full of books."

Cook's smile was more like a grimace. "Certainly, Mr. Smith."

"I'll see about breakfast," said Adam, passing Henry coming out.

"Cook, my trunk is ready to go," said Henry.

Cook set down his end of the next trunk, causing the driver to do the same. "Henry, we have very little help this morning. Why don't you see to some breakfast?" he said, with superhuman restraint. He and the wagon driver hoisted the next trunk with a grunt.

Henry caught on, belatedly. "Thank you, Cook," he said, as he eyed the two drivers and the task at hand, "We missed your assistance while you were gone to Paris. Hew and I will carry our own trunks."

Cook was surprised and grateful, as Henry's offer was nigh unprecedented. "Thank you, Henry, I'm concerned we will miss the boat."

"Boat?" asked Henry, "We're not taking the carriage?"

"We're taking this carriage to the boat," replied Cook, preparing to lift the next trunk. "Mr. Smith made your arrangements while you were gone." He and the driver groaned, trying to lift Adam's books, but they just made it.

Henry found Adam and Hew in the kitchen being served eggs, bread, and jam by Julia. "Sit down, sit down, Henry! I'll have you a plate in a minute."

"Thanks, Julia," replied Henry, pouring himself a glass of milk from the pitcher.

"First name basis with the cook?" Hew inquired as Henry drained the glass.

"Yes," answered Henry archly, "her name is Julia." His arm swept the room, "And this is her kitchen."

"A fine place it is," agreed Hew, "but no house staff for normal dining?"

Julia brought a plate for Henry. "I'm sorry this is the last plate of food I'll be serving you, Duke Henry. Your appetite makes me feel appreciated."

"I'll miss you, Julia." Henry said, simply, and she had to turn to hide sudden tears.

"We are only five miles from where we board the canal boat," said Adam.

"Tell us about this boat," said Hew, setting down his glass. "Do we plan to row upriver? I thought the Gironde flowed into the Atlantic."

"It does," nodded Adam, "that's why they built the Royal Canal. It will take us nearly the entire distance to Montpelier."

"That reminds me, Hew. Cook needs us to bring our trunks out by ourselves," said Henry.

"What's the world coming to?" replied Hew with a chuckle, "We must haul our own trunks, we must row our own boat, what else must we do?"

"More eggs?" offered Julia.

"Sure," nodded Hew eagerly.

"Well Hew," smirked Henry, "Charles wants us to become self-reliant men."

"So, when you're in Parliament you can make your own tea? Black your own boots? Brush your own jacket?" mocked Hew.

"Astonishing what one man can accomplish if he puts his mind to it," returned Henry, but his brother's words made him ponder his own evolving thoughts regarding servants. There was a world of difference between Julia, Collette, and the hostler, and the three were found in a single house in Toulouse. Henry found it increasingly difficult to see them as mere servants instead of as individuals.

Cook and the driver had the baggage loaded on the wagon when Henry and Hew carried the last trunk out of the house. Henry waved Cook away and the boys hoisted the trunk by themselves. The driver completed the lashings.

"That's the last, we're ready," said Henry to the assembled group. Julia appeared, wiping her hands on her apron, to say goodbye.

"Goodbye Julia, you are a lifesaver," said Adam sincerely.

"Goodbye!" said Julia, beginning to cry. Impulsively, she put her arms around Henry and hugged him tight. "Safe travels, young Duke."

Henry was embarrassed by the sudden warm gesture, but he hugged her back. He held Julia at arm's length. "You are a wonderful cook, Julia, and I will miss your fine meals." Hew and Henry joined Adam in the carriage, with Cook sitting next to the carriage driver. They waved to a weeping Julia as they left the Toulouse house behind.

Inside the carriage, Henry and Hew faced forward while Adam sat facing them in the forward seat, his back to the horses. "I'll miss Julia, but I won't miss Toulouse," stated Henry in a downbeat tone.

"You sure made an impression on the cook, Henry," said Hew.

"She made an impression on us," Henry replied, "Julia reminded me of the cook at my London boarding school."

"She did seem... motherly," ventured Hew.

"Henry looked at Hew blankly. "Yes," is all he offered with a neutral expression. Hew caught another glimpse of Henry's darkness.

Adam jumped into the sudden awkward pause, saying, "A fine woman who lightened a dark moment, we won't forget Julia." Adam paused, but the boys were still looking at him, so he continued, "Let me tell you about Montpelier. It's on the Mediterranean, so it should be pleasant weather."

"Southern France has all been pleasant weather, compared to England," observed Henry, but then added darkly, "that hasn't made it a better place."

Adam tried again for a diversion. "Scotland has worse weather than England, and I am a Scot who actually lives in Scotland," said Adam lightly, "Do you know, it is possible to grow grapes in Scotland, using glass hothouses? You can make a tolerable wine in Scotland."

Sitting side by side, Henry and Hew gave Adam the same blank look, not following.

"At about thirty times the cost as can be grown naturally in the south of France," Adam completed his thought.

"Everyone knows you can't grow grapes in Scotland, Mr. Smith," said Hew, shaking his head.

"Mr. Smith is talking about advantages," offered Henry, "Due to a better climate, the French are thirty times better than Scotland at winemaking."

"But the cool temperatures make Scottish wool much finer than that in France," said Adam, "There can be profit in the trade of fine wines for fine woolens."

"Unless we're at war with France, often as not," replied Henry, downbeat again.

"True, war makes everyone poorer," agreed Adam.

Hew looked at each of them and shook his head. "Father sent me here to cheer you up, Henry, not to discuss boring things like trade."

"Actually, Hew," interjected Adam, "a letter from Mr. Townshend came with Mr. Cook. I am to tutor you under the same agreement as we have to instruct Henry."

Henry laughed suddenly, "Yes, Hew, you must know *why* Alexander was Great!"

"It's good to see you smile, brother," said Hew.

"We're going to Montpelier to attend the Languedoc Estates parliament session," said Adam getting back on track.

"France doesn't have a parliament," Henry observed. Again, there was that downbeat tone, slipping back every time a laugh might drive it away, thought Adam. Hew had arrived just in time; both for their canal trip and for Henry's sake.

"This regional assembly is the closest they have," continued Adam, "This is a rare chance, Henry. Abbe Colbert invited us as his guests."

"Abbe Colbert!" cried Henry, "Look at what they did to that man! Because he wasn't Catholic! How can the Abbe live with that?"

Adam was taken aback but Hew jumped into the breach. "Whoa, Henry, I haven't met this priest. Is he really that terrible?"

"No, no, not at all," hastened Adam to smooth things, "Abbe Colbert is horrified at the execution, as are we all. You can ask him when we meet him at the boat."

"We're sailing with him?" asked Henry, incredulous.

"Not sail, exactly, but yes, we are his guests," Adam replied, and then admonished them both. "Henry, Hew, remember that we are in France. Catholicism is the official religion here. England fought a civil war over religion a hundred years ago. It cost us King Charles, but it also established Parliament." Adam paused, but he could see that both boys were listening to him. He took a deep breath and continued, "The king rules by divine right, and that divinity is Catholic. This assembly in Montpelier is the only partial exception to the King's direct rule in all of France."

Henry had mastered himself during Adam's cautionary speech. "I understand, Mr. Smith. We will behave."

"You'll meet many important people there, including the archbishop, finally," said Adam, "Charles will be pleased."

"Yes, pleased," replied Henry sarcastically.

"These are affairs of state, this experience will help when you serve in Parliament, Henry," said Adam, worried that Henry might skip the sessions he'd gone to great lengths to arrange.

"You act as if there is an open seat waiting for me," said Henry sardonically.

"I suspect that is true; seats in Parliament are bought and sold," said Adam matter-of-factly.

CHAPTER 17

R IDING THE ROYAL CANAL *December 1764*
Henry, Adam, and Hew stood on the quay next to a long canal boat. Toulouse was the western end of the Royal Canal, completed some eighty years before during the reign of the Sun King, Louis XIV. An engineering marvel, the canal linked the Mediterranean with Toulouse, which in turn connected to the Atlantic via the Garonne and Gironde rivers through Bordeaux. The Languedoc region flourished with the growing export trade; but without the shipping risks posed by pirates and Spaniards on the route through the Strait of Gibraltar. Barges of wheat and wine replaced wagons on poor roads in the French interior, reducing both the transport cost and spoilage during transit.

The long barges also carried passengers; some with fancy painted cabins, others, like the one before them, were rigged with awnings so they could be used for freight as needed. Cook stood a few feet away, anxiously overseeing their many trunks loaded in the stern. The passenger seats were forward, and the awning was down as the weather was fine that crisp December morning. A stout pole in the bow connected a pull rope to the team of two horses standing ready on the raised path that ran along the canal edge. A tillerman onboard, and another walking the path with the horses, composed the entire crew; both were currently wrestling the heavy trunks onto the skinny boat.

Abbe Colbert approached, flanked by two robed priests. Greetings were pleasant, which was a relief to Adam as he was nervous about how Henry might react. Adam and the Abbe boarded first and took the most forward bench; Henry and Hew were next, then Cook, sitting alone. The last bench was taken by the two priests that accompanied Abbe Colbert. Everyone faced forward as the man took his position at the tiller, and the other started the team. The long, narrow boat swung out into the placid water, and they were underway. Their speed matched that of the plodding horses.

"Not exactly sailing, is it?" was Henry's dry first comment.

Abbe Colbert turned in his seat and said enthusiastically, "The Royal Canal is a great accomplishment, it connects the Atlantic to the Mediterranean!"

"It seems we're going slower than a carriage would," said Henry dubiously.

"But by a more direct route," replied the Abbe positively, "the shortest distance between two points is a straight line. And I must say, a boat is a better ride than a carriage on poor roads."

"It seems a far better way to move freight," observed Adam, as he watched a barge full of cargo swing into the canal behind them.

Henry made Adam's stomach sink by saying, "Abbe, you are a man of the Catholic Church..."

"Gallican Church, actually," interjected the cleric.

"Is that different?" asked Henry.

"It's the French branch of Catholicism, approved by the King," answered the Abbe.

"How could any man of God witness the torture of Calas and know that it was done in the Lord's name?" asked Henry bluntly.

"Oh, my goodness, Henry, that wasn't done in the Lord's name," replied the Abbe, raising a hand, palm out, as if to stop him. "A flawed, power-drunk man took the Lord's name in vain."

"Obviously and hideously, yes," replied an unsmiling Henry. Adam turned in his seat to look at Henry, listening intently but remaining silent. He could see Hew and Cook doing the same.

"Unfortunately," continued Abbe Colbert, "that man is the Magistrate, David Beaudrigue. He holds a lifetime appointment from the King himself."

"It looked like enforced religion to me," said Henry simply, "the priest was part of the show."

"Scoundrels often cloak themselves in the clothes of moral righteousness," agreed the Abbe. "Beaudrigue is the magistrate, which is separate from the Church. At the Estates du Languedoc, the magistrates sit for the people, as their protector."

"We agree on the scoundrel part," is all Henry said in reply, but his tone was bitter.

Abbe Colbert was up to the task and remained engaged to win back his friend. "We are all fallen angels, Henry. There are bad people outside the Church, and sometimes even inside. The Church, the King, and the landed nobility are the three pillars of the Kingdom. It is the established order, and we live within it. It's not perfect, as man is imperfect."

"No where near perfect," retorted Henry, "judging by the injustice we saw in Toulouse."

"Yes, I admit that was horrible," conceded the Abbe patiently, "but does that one injustice call into question the whole order of things? It is easy to tear down, much harder to build anew."

"Do you suppose this is the only injustice Beaudrigue will commit?" asked Henry.

"We change what we can, and we live with what we can't," replied Abbe Colbert, with a shrug. "We don't see God's whole plan, just our part in it."

"Perhaps wisdom is choosing the course that best suits the purpose at hand," interjected Adam cryptically. Both Henry and the Abbe wrinkled their foreheads in puzzlement, but Adam's banal comment served his purpose of ending the debate before acrimony. The boat drifted slowly down the canal behind the walking horses.

The languid pace lulled the boys to sleep. They awoke to find the boat stopped behind several other boats and barges. "What is the delay, oarsman?" asked Cook.

"This is a tiller," said the man, pointing at the tiller, which did indeed look like a long oar, "We're stopped to pay a toll."

"How long?" asked Cook, peeved at his dry insolence.

"Depends on Pierre's dinnertime," replied the man, nonplussed.

"Who is Pierre?" asked Cook.

"Pierre collects the toll," he said, "everyone passing must pay Pierre."

Cook was defeated by this answer, and they all sat quietly for a moment.

"We're drawing a pretty slow line here, Abbe," commented Henry dryly, and everyone laughed excessively, pleased to relieve the tension remaining from the theological debate.

"Yes, the canal is run by tolls," said Abbe Colbert, smiling.

"There are more to come?" inquired Adam.

"Yes, each town takes their share," replied the Abbe, "hopefully quicker than Pierre seems to be." After a half hour, the man tending the horses on the path paid the toll and they were underway, albeit slower than before because the boats were bunched up behind each other.

"Underway at last," said Adam. Two hours later, they repeated the experience at the next toll stop.

"There has to be a better way to run a canal," said Henry, "I could walk there faster than this."

"Can we get out of the boat?" asked Hew, "I have to pee."

"I'll join you," said Henry, and both boys leapt the short distance between the boat and the raised canal berm. The boat rocked as they departed, and the boys disappeared beyond the path.

"I don't think I can make that jump," observed Adam to Cook, who agreed by shaking his head.

Henry and Hew stood side-by-side under a tree, urinating. "I never told you how sorry I was to hear about James," said Hew.

"Thanks. I remember when father died, but barely," said Henry, "Do you?"

"Not at all," Hew replied, "Charles is the only father I remember."

Henry nodded somberly and said, "Death changes a man," thinking of himself.

"For the worse, I imagine," deadpanned Hew.

Henry had to laugh, mostly at himself. "You have a dark and irreverent soul, brother."

They returned to the track to find themselves about fifty yards behind their boat.

"Well, consider my family," retorted Hew. "Race?"

"Nah," started Henry, but when Hew burst forward he instinctively started after him. Hew's lead proved just sufficient to reach the horses a step ahead Henry. Both were flushed and laughing.

"Cheater!" gasped Henry.

"Says the loser!" laughed Hew.

Henry put his arm around Hew as they trudged behind the horses, waiting for an opportunity to jump back aboard. In the boat, Adam and the Abbe watched the boys walk the path just ahead of them. "It's good that his brother is here," ventured the Abbe.

"Yes," replied Adam, "Death is the hardest lesson of all, and Henry just learned it twice."

"He holds me accountable for everything done in the name of Catholicism, I'm afraid," said Colbert.

"He'll learn there are allies amongst his enemies, and enemies among his allies," offered Adam, "Not easy for a young man to see which are which."

Abbe turned to Adam and said earnestly, "I'll always be his ally, Adam. He has the makings of a good man."

"He knows, Abbe. Your robes frighten him." Adam smiled at the gentle cleric and added, "I don't think you do, particularly."

Abbe Colbert laughed self-deprecatingly. "Let's hope he sees a better view of France at the Estates du Languedoc."

The boat remained too far from the bank, so the brothers walked on. Henry pulled a letter from his pocket and opened it. "Charles sent me a letter," he said, "towards the end it gets very interesting." He read Charles words, "If you go much into mixed company, as I suppose you will, let me warn you against any female attachment."

"Hmmm," mused Hew, "define 'attachment' Father?"

Henry continued to read, "Your rank and fortune will attract women of subtle character. You should not be the dupe of their projects," Henry dug his elbow into Hew and continued, "for such connections make a young man both ridiculous and unhappy."

Where are these women of subtle character, might I ask?" inquired Hew innocently.

"Wait for this, Hew," said Henry as he read on, 'Gallantry is one thing, attachment is another.' I know what he means by gallantry!"

"I do too, Henry!" laughed Hew.

"Lastly," Henry grinned as he read, 'A man should manifest spirit and decorum, and preserve his mind free in *less* as well as great things."

"I think gallantry is a greater thing, not a lesser," observed Hew.

"The key words here are 'decorum,' and 'ridiculous," said Henry, "Charles says we can gallivant as long as we don't embarrass the noble estate of Buccleuch."

"So, we should gallivant discreetly," nodded Hew, taking the letter from Henry and inspecting it closely. "Hey, this isn't Father's handwriting," Hew noted, "this is Frances!"

"Frances!" said Henry in disbelief, taking the letter back. "I can't believe Charles would use Frances to pen *this* letter!"

"Something to keep in mind when I next see dear sister," said Hew.

Henry pointed ahead of the plodding team, "Look, the boats ahead are letting off passengers. We must be stopping for the night." They waited on the bank for the rest of the party to disembark.

"Board tomorrow before eight, below the locks!" called the tillerman.

"Are there lodgings nearby?" Cook asked the man.

"Over the rise is a hamlet with an inn or two. Best hurry as they'll be full," he said. Another canal boat pulled up and began to disgorge passengers, and another was close behind that one.

Cook and Abbe Colbert hastened away to secure their arrangements for the night. Adam led the boys as they joined other passengers walking over the rise to the inn.

"Duke Henry!" called a stentorian voice behind them. Marshal Richelieu, flanked by servants, was dressed in his traveling clothes but still resplendent. They stepped off the path to greet him.

"An honor to see you again, Marshal Richelieu," said Henry with a bow, "May I present my brother, the Honorable Hew Campbell Scott."

"A pleasure," replied the Marshal to Hew, who bowed as Henry had done. "It appears that you are the younger brother?"

Hew recognized that he was meeting someone important, although he wasn't sure where he'd heard that name before. "Yes, sir. Two years younger."

"Second sons go to the military," said the old Marshal gruffly, "Are you practiced with the sword?"

"Just fencing at Eton, sir," replied Hew.

Marshal Richelieu winked at Henry and said to Hew, "Have Henry here give you a lesson."

Henry grinned broadly and said, "I'll find the first opportunity, sir."

"Practice, yes, but a career in the military is not for me," volunteered Hew.

"You don't always get to choose when you must fight," replied the Marshal, "Confidence comes from being ready."

"Yes, sir," replied Hew, impressed by the Marshal's gravitas and bearing.

"And how is the philosopher, Mr. Smith?" Marshal Richelieu turned his attention to Adam.

"I think I am learning more than my students, Marshal Richelieu," replied Adam with a smile, remembering Louise.

"Have you read his book yet?" Richelieu was looking at Henry.

"Indeed, I have," replied Henry, "I must admit some of the finer points are still sinking in."

"Have you read it?" Richelieu asked Hew suddenly.

"Er, was it assigned?" asked Hew, not sure what book they were talking about.

"Mr. Smith is famous," the Marshal was blunt, "My friend Voltaire has read his book. Don't you know who you are traveling with?"

"Mr. Smith, my apologies," said Hew contritely.

"None required, Hew, none required," Adam reassured him, "You've only just arrived. We'll settle on your course of study on the boat tomorrow."

Cook approached. "I have secured two small rooms. Food is ordered but may be delayed."

"If I may excuse myself, I will go find this room," said Adam and he left them.

Marshal Richelieu nodded towards Cook without looking at him, and asked Henry, "Is this your man?"

"Yes, Mr. Cook," Henry replied.

"Is he all the help you have?" inquired the Marshal.

"Yes, but Mr. Cook is very efficient," answered Henry loyally.

Richelieu turned to one of his assistants and whispered in his ear for a long moment. The servant hastened off, and the Marshal turned back to them.

"I will have a small pavilion ready shortly, and you are welcome to stop by for supper," he said. "Don't count on the inn, it will be crowded and dirty." The Marshal left them, and the boys entered the inn. It was packed with travelers and their servants, all calling for service. The smell of kitchen smoke and pressed humanity thickened the air inside. The boys backed out to regroup with Cook, who was behind them.

"I'll try for some food, but finding a suitable table may be difficult," Cook warned.

"See what you can do, Cook, we'll wait out here in the fresh air," Henry responded, and Cook plunged into the crowed inn. The Marshal's attendant touched his shoulder, and Henry turned to see Felicity and another beautiful young woman standing behind him.

"Monsieur, Marshal Richelieu offers Felicity and Lucy to assist you this evening, with his compliments," presented the attendant formally, adding, "He said you were short-staffed."

Henry and Hew couldn't contain their broad smiles. "Please give our warm thanks to the Marshal for this very timely kindness," said Henry gratefully.

Henry looked at Felicity, remembering their night in Bordeaux. "Felicity," he smiled at her, and she smiled back.

"Lucy," said Hew, surprised as well as grateful. He looked at Henry, "We are no longer short-staffed!"

• • • •

EARLY THE NEXT MORNING, Cook emerged from the inn with Adam and Abbe Colbert. He cast about, looking for Henry and Hew.

"I'll find them," promised Cook, "I suggest you go ahead, and we'll meet you at the boat." Adam and the Abbe walked in that direction, joined by the two priests who looked as if they'd slept outside. Cook looked for the boys, and not seeing them, headed towards a large hay barn.

"Henry? Hew?" called Cook, but he heard no response.

Cook stuck his head inside the barn door, and called again, loudly, "Henry?"

He stood outside the barn, perplexed and uncertain. Most of the other travelers had already made their way to the boats as it was almost eight. Finally, Cook threw propriety to the wind, cupped his hands and shouted at the top of his lungs, "Henry! Hew!"

Inside the barn, up in the hay loft, both boys sat up suddenly some distance from each other. They had straw in their disheveled hair and their clothes were rumpled. Both looked next to them and confirmed they were alone. Henry called out, "Here, Cook!"

Springing from the hay, the boys emerged from the barn trying to brush their clothes with their hands. "We're late for the boat, we must hurry," urged Cook, relieved but exasperated.

"First, I must pee," said Henry adamantly, "We'll be right behind you Cook."

Cook headed for the boats, and the brothers again stood side-by-side, peeing in the shadow of the barn. "I like this gallantry thing," said Hew, grinning.

"Yes," smirked a rumpled Henry, "I feel very gallant right now."

"We read about Marshal Richelieu at school," said Hew, "He almost invaded England once."

"God bless the British Navy," nodded Henry.

"Aside from that," said Hew with a big grin as he fastened his trousers, "the Marshal's a capital fellow!"

Henry and Hew were the last on board and took the rearmost seats. They noticed the two priests weren't in their boat, but the Abbe was, with two other well-dressed men they didn't recognize occupying the forward two seats. Cook gave them each a roll of bread and a piece of ham, which they consumed in minutes. Within a half-hour of launch, both boys were sprawled sleeping in their seats as the boat resumed its slow passage south.

Two hours later, Hew sat up with a snort, awakening Henry as well. "Where are we?" he asked to no one in particular.

"What time is it?" asked Henry.

"I like to rise early as well," Adam said bemusedly, "usually, before noon."

"I'm thirsty," said Hew, seeking the water barrel and raising a dipper full. He eyed it dubiously, then sniffed it, before drinking it. He refilled the dipper and handed it to Henry, who drank the tepid water without hesitation.

Adam said, "Hew, I've been working on your reading list. Is now a good time?"

It was obvious to all of them that Hew was hung over and reviewing a reading list was not among the things he wanted to do. "Sure, Mr. Smith," he replied bravely. Adam handed him two folded pages, and Henry looked over Hew's shoulder as he reviewed them.

"Hew, *The Theory of Moral Sentiments* should be first on your list," advised Henry, warming Adam's heart although he said nothing.

"Oh?" said Hew, "Who wrote that one?"

Henry looked at Adam with embarrassment. "Mr. Smith, of course."

"I'm sorry again, Mr. Smith," said Hew, chagrined, "Here it is, you put it last on the list."

One of the two strangers in the front seat stood up and made his way back and sat in the unoccupied seat beside Cook. He was a short, well-dressed man of plain round features, stout but not fat. "Please forgive my interruption, but are you Adam Smith?" he asked, addressing Adam, not Cook.

"Yes," said Adam pleasantly.

"Allow me to introduce myself," the man said, "I am Anne Robert Turgot, the Farmer General of Limoges. Abbe Colbert, here, knows me."

"Good to see you, Turgot," said the Abbe with a nod. Henry wondered how a man could be named Anne, but it didn't matter as everyone addressed Turgot by his surname, which was pronounced 'tur-go.'

"I'm pleased to make your acquaintance, Monsieur Turgot," said Adam, "These are my students, the Honorable Henry Scott,

Third Duke of Buccleuch in Scotland, and Hew Campbell Scott, his brother."

Turgot bowed to the boys, who both straightened up as if to deserve it despite their scruffiness. "An honor, Monsieurs Scott," he said formally. Turgot's manners were impeccable, and his sharp eyes missed nothing. "Mr. Smith, do you have time for a question?"

"Certainly, Monsieur Turgot," replied Adam graciously, seeing as they had the whole afternoon.

"Just Turgot, Mr. Smith," he said kindly. "I have read your *Theory of Moral Sentiments*, my compliments to you."

"Thank you, Turgot," nodded Adam, pleased again. Henry pointed discreetly at Turgot and raised his eyebrows to Hew as if to say, "See, I told you!"

Turgot asked, "You use the phrase "invisible hand" when you discuss how wealth may be distributed through society. How is this invisible hand different from the Hand of God, or from chance fate?"

"As each person buys or sells for their own interest," replied Adam, "they benefit others even though that is not their intent. Trade doesn't happen unless both sides think it benefits them. A natural order of value develops through exchange, which shows others how they might apply their human capital to the best advantage. Prices and costs rise and fall with the particulars of production and demand, with no authority needed to set a price. That is the invisible hand."

"Thank you, Monsieur Smith, it is an honor to hear you explain it," said Turgot. "Are you attending the Estates?" Adam understood that Turgot used the word 'estates' to refer to the Montpelier meeting of the landed estate noblemen with the Church and Royal authorities.

Abbe Colbert spoke up, "Yes, as my guests."

"Excellent," Turgot answered, "after the drama of last year, I wasn't sure the King would allow another such meeting."

"Drama?" inquired Adam, interested.

"The King's representative, Duke Fitz James, insisted that the provinces implement the royal taxes. The Parliament refused, as their advice had not been sought on the merits of the tax increases. Fitz James tried to have the Parliament arrested. All of them! In turn, the Parliament ordered the arrest of Fitz James!" Turgot grew almost animated with his explanation, although he was by nature a steady, calculating man.

"Luckily, calmer heads prevailed," interjected Abbe Colbert.

"Why didn't Parliament think the King's taxes had merit?" asked Henry.

"The provinces know their situation better than Paris," responded Turgot, "The King has little local knowledge, which leads to unreasonable and unpopular edicts."

"Like burdensome taxation?" asked Adam.

"Yes," nodded Turgot, "but also the official prices for wheat and other grains."

"What goes to Paris rarely comes back," opined Abbe Colbert.

"It's more than that," said Turgot, "as the tax collector, I know that *how* we tax can be as important as the *amount* of tax."

"Like the inefficient method of collecting the canal tolls?" ventured Adam.

"Exactly!" exclaimed the reserved Turgot, happy that Adam put his finger on a primary example. "We should collect the entire toll at once, and then distribute the proceeds to each landowner and the canal operator. Less delay means more profit for all, but such coordination requires trust."

Henry glanced at Hew, who was dozing again so he poked him discreetly with his elbow.

"Will canal tolls be discussed at the Estates?" asked Adam.

"Yes," Turgot replied, "I will propose a common canal fee. The agenda is set in advance, approved by the King."

"Will they discuss the Calas case?" asked Henry unexpectedly, making Adam freeze and putting the Abbe's teeth on edge.

Abbe Colbert answered for Turgot, "No, the King does not involve himself in local justice."

"Turgot, you said you were the tax collector but earlier you said you were a General Farmer..." started Hew, sitting up suddenly and surprising them all.

Turgot laughed, which made his rather serious demeanor vanish as his face lit up. They all immediately liked him more because of it. "The Farmer General collects the taxes from the farmers; in other words, from the landed estates."

"They reap the King's share of the harvest," added Colbert, trying to be helpful.

"After the Estates I travel to Paris to meet my friend and mentor Dr. Quesnay," informed Turgot, turning to Adam. "Will your travels take you to Paris? We would enjoy discussing trade at greater length."

"Geneva, first, to see Voltaire," replied Adam, "then we go to Paris."

Turgot nodded, "Give Voltaire my sincere regards, Monsieur Smith."

CHAPTER 18

E STATES DU LANGUEDOC December 1764
"Tell me again why we're attending this meeting?" asked Henry, eyes closed, as their carriage entered the city of Montpelier, six miles from the Mediterranean. He found himself wishing they didn't have to go, as it sounded boring.

"The Estates du Languedoc is one of the few regional parliaments still allowed by the King, as it is also the oldest," said Abbe Colbert."

Adam interjected, "Charles was particularly interested that we attend. Unlike in England, here the parliaments serve at the pleasure of the King."

"All the important people in southern France will be here," added the Abbe eagerly, "including Archbishop Brienne, at last."

"Your boss?" asked Henry.

"I am his vicar, yes," replied the Abbe, "The Archbishop is a fine man, liberal in his thinking."

"What does he think of the execution?" asked Henry coldly. In his mind's eye, he remembered the priest putting his hand to his ear, playing his part in Beaudrigue's hateful spectacle.

"He was appalled, I assure you," replied the Abbe in a much cooler tone, concerned that Henry was still so surly about the unfortunate Calas. They lapsed into an uncomfortable silence; Adam and the Abbe sitting across from Henry and Hew, with everyone looking anywhere but into the eyes of each other.

The carriage slowed to a halt and the Abbe leaned out the window to see they were in a long line of carriages conveying meeting attendees.

"It appears everyone is punctual," said the Abbe, "I suggest we walk from here." They disembarked and began walking alongside the line of carriages, most of which were also disgorging well-dressed passengers. They walked two abreast, with Henry and Hew leading Adam and the Abbe. The boys paused as a carriage door opened in front of them, and when it closed, they were suddenly face to face with David Beaudrigue. Henry's heart raced with both anger and fear seeing the polished but brutal man.

"Well, if it isn't the young Duke," said Beaudrigue, "a pleasure to see you again." Looking Hew up and down, he added, "Who is this similar-looking young man?"

"Magistrate," said Henry stiffly, his face a mask, "this is my brother, the Honorable Hew Campbell Scott."

"An honor to make your acquaintance," said Beaudrigue amicably, "Your brother conducted himself admirably after his friend's unfortunate accident. I am the Toulouse magistrate, David Beaudrigue."

Hew was impressed, and replied, "Thank you for the kind words, Magistrate." Hew impulsively joked, "When I grow up, I want to be just like him," digging an elbow at Henry.

"You could do worse," smiled Beaudrigue, who stepped aside and tipped his hat to Adam and Abbe Colbert, who had watched the exchange with bated breath. The group continued walking with the other meeting participants who were streaming towards the conference hall.

"Well," said Hew brightly, "that chap seems nice enough."

"Not hardly, Hew," Henry hissed, his face rigid. "That's the torturer, Beaudrigue!"

"Sorry Henry, he didn't seem so evil when he was complimenting you," retorted Hew.

"Watch him torture someone to get the picture," snapped Henry with a scowl.

Dignitaries thronged the entrance to the large hall, bishops, nobles, merchants, and magistrates clustered thickly, with servants hovering everywhere for last minute assistance. The meeting participants steadily funneled in towards the huge carved double doors, open and guarded on each side by a resplendent soldier in arms.

Abbe Colbert spotted his superior in the crowd, so he called out while waving a hand, "Archbishop Brienne, Archbishop!"

A distinguished man in bishop's robes turned at the vicar's call and stepped away from the throng at the door. Not quite forty years, Archbishop Etienne Charles de Lomenie de Brienne was in his second year as head prelate for the Languedoc region, the richest in France. His long face featured an aquiline nose over a small mouth, a handsome man with quick, intelligent eyes. His meteoric rise in the church hierarchy was in full swing during the 1764 Estates du Languedoc. Brienne would eventually become Finance Minister for King Louis XVI and die in prison at the hands of the Revolution in 1794, age 66.

"Abbe Colbert, there you are at last," said Brienne, smiling at his vicar.

"Let us step aside for a moment," said Colbert, shepherding the group another step from the crush of attendees, "so I can introduce my friends." Henry pulled Hew aside so the Abbe and Dr. Smith could greet the archbishop first.

"May I introduce Mr. Adam Smith," said the Abbe with a hand on Adam's shoulder.

"It's a pleasure to meet you, Mr. Smith," said Brienne cordially, "I read your book and found it interesting."

"It's an honor to meet you, Archbishop," replied Adam formally.

Archbishop Brienne smiled broadly and said, "Not enough God in it, I'd say, but a lot of common sense."

"Here is Henry Scott, Third Duke of Buccleuch in Scotland, and his brother, Hew Campbell Scott," introduced the Abbe. Both boys bowed to the prelate.

"It's an honor to meet you finally, Archbishop," said Henry in a brittle tone that sent a shiver of alarm down Adam's back, "although oddly, not in Toulouse."

"Yes, I missed you there," replied Brienne.

"You also missed the execution of an innocent man," said Henry coldly, to the sinking despair of both Adam and the Abbe. The warm smile disappeared from the face of the archbishop, and an awkward silence ensued.

Abbe Colbert jumped in hurriedly, anxiously, "Henry was much affected by the Calas execution, Archbishop. It was a truly awful thing to witness."

"So I've heard," replied the archbishop in a level tone, "I share your dismay, Duke Henry."

"Will this injustice be discussed in the meeting?" asked Henry bluntly, making Adam's heart race faster.

"No, the agenda is set," answered the archbishop coolly, "I hope, as my guests, you will not disrupt the assembly in any way?" He met Henry's fierce gaze and held it.

"We'll be quiet as mice," interjected Adam in a pleasant tone, "We appreciate the invitation, Archbishop."

Brienne nodded, then turned on his heel and made his way towards the door, nettled by Henry's outburst but maintaining his dignified composure the entire time.

Hew broke their tense silence in an awed voice, saying "That was just an archbishop, Henry, what would you have said if it was the Pope?"

"Henry, Archbishop Brienne is very much on our side," cautioned the Abbe, relieved for the moment but still anxious about what would come next with the volatile young duke, and whether it would harm his ecclesiastical career.

"I'm sorry, Abbe," said Henry, "I expect that was less respectful than what he's used to."

"I'll survive, and so will the archbishop," said the Abbe, "provided that's the end of it!" he added with a nervous laugh as they all followed Brienne through the large doors of the assembly hall. Adam went last, shaking his head and wondering what would come next with Henry. If he was this outraged at injustice in France, how would he deal with the inevitable injustice he would find back home?

Once inside, Abbe Colbert led the way to a spectator balcony overlooking the main floor of the large hall. The assembly area was arranged as a three-sided rectangle, with the chairman's place at the open end. On the left side, twenty bishops filed in, followed by three archbishops, including Brienne. They took their seats and were followed on the right side by twenty-three nobles, the entitled lords of the large estates that formed the Languedoc region. This group included the stately Marshal Richelieu, who nodded when he saw them on the balcony as he made his way to his seat.

"No music or ceremony," whispered Hew, "such a plain hall for such fancy people."

"That's on purpose," confirmed Abbe Colbert in a low tone, "Too fancy and the King might suspect we're pretending to be royal." He pointed to the group filing in after the nobles, "Here comes the Third Estate, forty-six who represent the people, balancing the Church and the Nobility."

As the largest group filed in, Henry wondered how both Beaudrigue and Turgot, the magistrate and the tax collector, were in the group representing the people. He asked this of the Abbe.

"The Farmers General make sure that the nobles are paying their share of the public burden," answered Colbert, "and the Magistrate protects the people from criminals."

Henry pondered that answer, but did not reply as he watched Archbishop Brienne stand to call the assembly to order. "Attention please! Our chairman, Archbishop Dillon of Narbonne!"

Archbishop Dillon entered and took his place in the presiding chair at the center of the assembly. A stout man in his mid-forties, Dillon was born and raised in France but was the son of an Irish Jacobite colonel. Dillon preceded Brienne as the archbishop of Toulouse, moving to Narbonne in 1763 to become the head prelate for southern France. The archbishop stood in front of his chair and in a loud voice announced, "Stand to recognize the King's representative!" The entire assembly rose to their feet, and it struck Adam that there were virtually no servants or attendants in evidence. The whole arrangement of the meeting, while plain and relatively unceremonious, seemed designed to show the balance and equality of French society. Yet their travels through France had revealed a social stratification greater even than England.

"Charles Martel speaks for the King!" called Archbishop Dillon, and a small dapper man in exquisite dress entered and took his place with the nobility.

Adam whispered to Abbe Colbert, "He looks less robust than his namesake," and the cleric hid his smile with his hand. Charles Martel, nicknamed Charles the Hammer, was the legendary Frankish warrior who defeated the invading Moslems at the Battle of Tours in 732, over one thousand years earlier. Grandfather to Charlemagne, Charles Martel began the unification of the Frankish kingdoms. The King's Representative was the physical opposite of the legend.

"The Estates du Languedoc will now begin," announced Archbishop Dillon.

As the various speakers were introduced and the long list of topics were discussed, Henry and Hew grew disinterested in following the particulars. Instead, they watched the various participants; some attentive, some bored, some apparently napping. Although each attendee represented a substantial interest, here in the assembly they were just well-dressed or well-robed Frenchmen sitting in rows. Henry's eye kept returning to Beaudrigue, and one time he was sure the magistrate returned his glance despite the distance that separated them. Abbe Colbert finally relaxed, accepting that his young guest wasn't going to cause another disruption over the fate of Jean Calas.

As the day progressed and the speakers droned on, Henry only paid attention to snatches of the discussion. He leaned forward and poked Hew when Turgot rose to speak.

"Tolls for the Royal Canal should be collected at the beginning of each journey, and the proceeds distributed equitably to the landowners and the Canal operator," declared Turgot in a clear voice.

"We'll never see the money!" called out the representative of the Riquet family, who held the Royal monopoly on Canal maintenance and operation and sat with the nobles.

"Efficiency comes with trust," replied Turgot calmly, "Less delay raises the revenues shared by all. Our trip from Toulouse was almost a day longer than it needed to be, because of the many tolls!"

Later, King's Representative Charles Martel rose, and in a thin reedy voice announced, "I present the King's revenue requirements for the Languedoc region." The spectators in the balcony could see that the ear of every attendee paid close attention as the diminutive man read a long list of tonnages and fees. The numbers meant little to Henry and Hew, but they could feel the tension between the demands of the King in Paris, and the men from the richest region in the country. The nobles owed their titles to the King, but never wanted to send King Louis XV all that he desired.

Charles Martel finished his list to a discontented murmur from the assembly; from that Adam presumed that the King's request was higher than they thought it should be. Would the Estates reject the King's request, as they had the previous year when they and Fitz James tried to arrest each other?

Marshal Richelieu rose to speak, and such was his stature that all voices quieted to hear him. "To show our allegiance to the King, I propose that we build a new ship for his Majesty's navy," announced the Marshal, "a seventy-four-gun ship of the line named *Languedoc*." A murmur of approval swept those assembled, despite the cost of such a ship it was a symbolic gesture of unity that would mollify the King. "Perhaps we can win a battle or two," concluded the Marshal as he resumed his seat. The ship was completed in 1766 and took part in the Battle of Chesapeake in 1781, where the British squadron was blocked from relieving Cornwallis at Yorktown, thus effectively ending the American Revolutionary War.

"They go out of their way to please the King," Abbe Colbert whispered to Adam, "The old Marshal is crafty."

Turgot stood to speak again, as he was apparently the unspoken leader of the tax collectors. "Taxes should be paid after the harvest, as a percentage of value, and paid in money, not merchandise."

Charles Martel rose to say with finality, "They won't declare their whole harvest!" His voice seemed like a pipsqueak compared to Turgot's clear tones.

"It's my job to see that they do," replied Turgot firmly, "What we have now is more delay, more spoilage, more thievery, and less profit."

A prosperous merchant rose at this and said, "We must know the King's wheat prices *before* we contract for shipping and export. Late prices make our profit pure guesswork!"

"How can we insure our ships without knowing his prices?" added a trader from Bordeaux.

The first merchant continued boldly, "How about a free trade in wheat and wine? Let us set prices according to the harvest, and the market."

"You would abandon all control!" shouted Charles Martel, "Tell me, what would you have the King do?"

"Laissez faire!" said the merchant stoutly, "Leave us alone!"

In a noisy tavern that night, Adam, Henry, Hew, and Cook sat at table holding their cups. They leaned inward to hear each other over the boisterous drinking going on around them.

"I know we are distinguished guests," ventured Hew, "but how am I to stay awake tomorrow? I fought the drowsy devil all afternoon."

Henry nodded but said, "Some parts were pretty dry, but Turgot and the Marshal caught my ear."

"Yes, where is the Marshal?" said Hew with a smirk, looking about as if it might be possible for the Marshal to be slumming in a common tavern, "I'm feeling a bit short-staffed."

"Mind yourself, Hew," said Henry, but he couldn't suppress a grin.

Adam consulted a page of notes he'd taken that day, and answered, "Tomorrow's agenda discusses riverbank maintenance, canal operation rates, and road levies. Just the things Charles wants you to know."

"Oh God," said Hew in mock despair.

"Adam, would it be possible to skip tomorrow?" asked Henry, agreeing whole-heartedly with Hew's sentiment.

"But they'll discuss canal maintenance!" replied Adam in a shocked tone, "We can't miss that."

Henry and Hew looked at Adam for a long moment, and finally Adam broke into a slow smile that showed that yes, he was kidding. Cook listened attentively for possible inclusion in his next letter to Charles but missed Adam's humor entirely.

"If I can take notes for Charles," replied Adam, "I suppose I can take them for you. Mr. Cook, we won't mention this to Mr. Townshend, will we?"

Before Cook could answer, Henry asked him excitedly, "Cook, can you get us to the waterfront and find us a sailboat?"

"Yes, I think so," stammered Cook, taken off guard. "When?"

"First thing tomorrow," answered Hew eagerly, "sailing on the Mediterranean!"

"Er, must I go?" asked Cook apprehensively, "I get queasy..."

"We learned how to sail at school," replied Henry, "Just get us a boat!"

Cook proved his administrative worth and by noon the next day they were standing dockside on the E'tang du Mejean, a large lagoon off the Mediterranean Sea. He'd arranged their carriage departure at first light that morning, found a man with a twelve-foot single-sail open boat, and here they were, rigged and ready. As Henry and Hew set off slowly, picking up a small breeze, Cook watched apprehensively. Here were the last two male heirs of the Buccleuch line, setting off in a small boat alone. The water was very calm, easing his concerns. They would have doubled had Cook known the boy's only previous sailing experience was with small punts on the calm lakes between Eton and London.

Henry manned the rudder and Hew stood in the bow, forward of the sail and with one hand on the mast. The sun sparkled off the clear blue water, although it wasn't hot due to the season. For a long while they just enjoyed the sensations of slipping through the water on the gentle breeze, warmed by the temperate weather and the quiet freedom. Henry began to tack the boat, and their speed through the water dropped as they changed angles to the wind. Hew sat amidships.

"Do you think we'll see those girls again?" he asked Henry.

"Felicity and Lucy?" asked Henry with a grin, knowing exactly who he meant.

"Lucy was as lovely as can be," said Hew dreamily, then looked at Henry, "so was Felicity, of course."

"First time, Hew?" smiled Henry.

Hew reflexively brought a finger to his lips to shush Henry, then recognized they were at least a mile from shore. "Yes. Don't tell anyone." he said, trying to sound stern.

Henry laughed. "Charles prefers that we make our youthful mistakes abroad, less risk of inheritance claims."

"That's for you to worry about, Sir Duke," mocked Hew with a grin.

"If I die, you'll be the duke, Hew," replied Henry, seriously.

"You'll live to a ripe old proper dukedom," said Hew, staying light-hearted, "As the second son, am I allowed more of these so-called youthful mistakes?"

Henry smiled, but then it faded. "I wonder if James didn't make that mistake, Hew."

"How so?" said Hew, puzzled.

"James was in the hay loft with one of the servant girls when the trap door was left open," Henry answered.

"You mean it wasn't an accident?" asked Hew, shocked.

"I'll never know for sure," his brother replied, "Adam warned me about upsetting the household. He stopped me from pursuing that same girl, saying the local men would be watching her like hawks."

Henry paused but Hew hung on his next word, so he continued, "I took his advice, but James.... didn't."

"Was she pretty?" Hew asked, but he knew the answer before Henry confirmed it.

"Very. Very pretty," he confirmed, nodding. "I thought Adam was being foolish, but now I can see his point."

"I liked James," said Hew wistfully, "Frances cried and cried when she heard the news."

"I cried too," nodded Henry, "We were friends all through Eton." After a long pause, he added, "I miss him."

"If it wasn't an accident, you should have told the magistrate." blundered Hew, forgetting.

"The magistrate was Beaudrigue! He offered to torture them for me!" Henry grew agitated with the recollection.

"The same man we just met?" asked Hew.

"*You* just met. I think you said he was *nice*," replied Henry sarcastically. His face clouded with a frown.

They didn't speak again for a long while, and then only to navigate back towards the dock where Cook was scanning the horizon for them, hand shading his eyes from the westerly sun. The craft glided in smoothly and Hew jumped out. He handed the painter to the man waiting with Cook, then helped hold the boat while Henry climbed out. They both headed up the slope behind Cook without another backward glance at the man who had provided the boat.

"Here's an advantage of being the second son," said Hew, "I can marry for love. You, brother, must marry for title."

"What?" Henry said disbelieving, "I can certainly marry for love!"

"If she has the right title, sure you can," replied Hew, "I heard Mother and Father talking about it before I left Adderbury."

"What, exactly?" demanded Henry under scowling brows as they trudged up the hill.

"Just a snatch of, 'get him married to the right family' sort of thing," said Hew.

"Oh great," sighed Henry.

"And then you get elected to Parliament," Hew continued, "They clammed up the minute they saw me."

"I wonder if it's my future they're talking about," said Henry grimly, "or theirs."

"Father means well, Henry," defended Hew, but then he added, "I just hope he doesn't have me lead a regiment somewhere."

CHAPTER 19

T HE ROAD TO FERNEY *Spring 1765*

The Estates du Languedoc lasted another two weeks; Adam and Abbe Colbert attended daily but Henry and Hew took several days to explore, ride, and sail. Yet Henry absorbed some key lessons from watching the French elite discuss taxation and spending. While he couldn't evaluate the quantities and prices, it became apparent who the reformers were and who were not. Surprisingly, Archbishops Brienne and Dillon turned out to be reform-minded, as was Turgot and the old warrior Marshal Richelieu. The representatives from Bordeaux were practical and business-minded; those from Toulouse less so, which made the relative liberalism of Brienne and Dillon even more remarkable. Suppertime discussions with Adam and the Abbe were often more interesting than the Estates themselves. Hew was less engaged and often bored, but never lost his good cheer. Adam thought Hew was slowly restoring Henry's good nature and resolved to tell Charles the good news in his next letter.

To avoid congestion on the roads, they decided to leave Montpelier two days before the formal end of the Estates. Early in the morning of their departure, Henry bridled and saddled one of their hired horses and led it out of the barn. As he fed it an apple, two mounted horsemen entered the square. With a start he saw that it was Abbe Colbert and Archbishop Brienne dressed in riding clothes and not their clerical robes.

"Good morning, Archbishop, good morning, Abbe," greeted Henry cordially, "It took me a moment to recognize you."

Brienne nodded with a smile, "You're up early, young duke. I apologize, church robes are not the best for riding."

"Actually, it makes you seem more approachable," responded Henry, "for I owe you an apology." He said it impulsively; he had certainly not planned to apologize to anyone. Seeing the clerics in normal clothes made them seem like men, and not representatives of the church.

"For what, Henry?" asked the archbishop gently.

"I spoke rudely the day we met," said Henry, looking up at them, "My passions got the best of me, and I blamed you for the actions of others. Please forgive me."

"Of course," said the archbishop, his features softening, "Your passion shows you care about justice. No need to apologize for that, Henry."

"I had some hard words for the Abbe as well, and I regret them," Henry continued, running with his unexpected rush of sentiment. "Abbe Colbert has been a wonderful host in Toulouse." He felt a flood of relief hearing himself apologize, as if he was shedding a weight that he didn't know he'd been carrying.

Brienne laughed and said, "What would I do without the capable Abbe Colbert? You might not know this about me Henry, but both of my parents were Irish. Passions run deep, which is why faith and truth are so important."

"You are a good man, Henry," said Abbe Colbert, "Are you leaving Montpelier today?"

"Yes, we leave in a few hours," Henry nodded.

"Then we take our leave of you here," the Abbe replied, "Unless you care to join us on our ride this morning?"

"I'd like that very much Abbe," said Henry, and he mounted his horse. Together they trotted out of the yard and down the street, three abreast.

· · · ·

AFTER LEAVING MONTPELIER, the group travelled in a rather leisurely manner towards Marseilles, where they stayed for two months because the weather was so fine. Christmas was a low-key affair, mostly a dinner with the four of them wishing for traditional English yuletide fare but instead eating fish fresh from the Mediterranean. Which they all agreed was a fine substitute considering the quality of the French cook. Henry impulsively spent the colossal sum of 150 pounds on an elegant set of porcelain dishes and had them carefully packaged and shipped to Adderbury. Cook argued against this purchase, finally yielding when Henry promised to write to Charles directly and absolve him of any blame in the extravagance. Adam thought the purchase unusual but was not too alarmed given that Henry had since Paris demonstrated remarkable financial prudence for a young man of means. When the dishes arrived at Adderbury, Caroline was so pleased with the quality that nothing more was ever said about the expense.

Marseilles offered the finest winter weather any of them had ever experienced, so Adam assigned a relaxed reading schedule that both boys enjoyed. Sitting in the warm sun with a book, reading and napping interchangeably, was as restorative as it was educational. Finally, in mid-March, they turned their eyes north.

Henry began the trip on horseback, with Adam, Cook, and Hew riding in the carriage. After two hours of this, a hard rain forced Henry to tie the horse to the back of the carriage and take refuge inside. He shrugged off his overcoat and handed it to Cook as his breath fogged the rain-streaked windows.

"Well, that was fun until it wasn't," said Henry ruefully, "I wish someone could predict the weather."

"All we have is the barometer, which measures the pressure of the atmosphere," said Adam, assuming his teacher role. "A rising barometer means clear weather. I'm sure the weather operates on scientific principles, someday we'll discover more of them."

"Do you have a barometer with you?" asked Hew.

"Of course not," replied Adam with a smile. "They are scientific instruments. A Frenchman, Blaise Pascal, used a barometer to find that air pressure is less at high altitude."

"Take lightning," Henry said, "What we used to think was the wrath of God is now captured in a jar by Ben Franklin."

"Yes!" said Adam, delighted to see his student engaged, "or the rainbow. Before Newton explained the spectrum of light, what were we to imagine about rainbows?"

"It means that the rain is passing, and some sun is shining through," contributed Hew.

"We know that because Isaac Newton existed," said Adam, "otherwise, we'd still attribute rainbows to God."

Cook rarely participated in Adam's speculative discussions, but suddenly he burst out with, "Rainbows, lightening, rain, all of these are God's creation! God's will! We attribute everything to him!" Cook then fell silent, knotting his hands anxiously in his lap.

Surprised by Cook's rare outburst, there was a moment of awkward silence as the carriage splashed along the muddy road. Adam recovered first. "Dear Mr. Cook," he said calmly, "indeed they are. As *we* are, and the world around us. Explaining what causes a rainbow doesn't make it any less wonderous. To me, it becomes even more profound."

Cook nodded, recognizing that he'd overstepped his bounds, and that Adam was offering a safe exit to the situation. "Indeed," he said restrainedly, "thank you, Mr. Smith. I apologize, Henry and Hew."

"No need, Cook, no need," shrugged Henry.

"You always figure things out for us, Cook," added Hew, "I'll hear you speak your mind anytime."

"Speak up, Cook, as long as it's not in front of anyone else," added Henry, remembering how firmly Cook had opposed the porcelain purchase. But expenses were Cook's province, while science was Adam's.

After a half hour of silence in the swaying carriage, Henry asked, "Mr. Smith, say again why we're traveling all the way to Geneva?"

"Geneva has no king," Adam replied, "only a republic of sorts. A republic of landowners, though not a democracy necessarily. Charles would like us to investigate."

"Will it be more interesting than Montpelier?" asked Hew.

"I doubt it," answered Adam shaking his head, "Geneva is full of Calvinists. They frown on fun. But Ferney is right across the border."

"What is Ferney?" asked Henry.

"Ferney is the home of Voltaire," said Adam simply.

The carriage rolled to a stop, and they heard voices outside. Henry looked out and saw a large wagon blocking the road as workers unloaded the last gravel from its bed. The rain had let up but it was wet and muddy, and the workers looked filthy and miserable as they moved slowly and sullenly. A mounted overseer sat on his horse holding a short, knotted whip. Hew frowned as he watched from the carriage window. "Those fellows don't look happy. Is this a prison work gang?"

Adam leaned out and asked the carriage driver, "Corvee?"

"Oui, monsieur," he replied with a nod.

"These men are paying the labor tax by working on the road," explained Adam.

"So not a tax on labor, but a tax paid in labor?" asked Henry.

"Yes," Adam said, "it's a form of conscription. Turgot said it is very unpopular, and he hates to enforce it."

Henry eyed the overseer and commented, "It must be unpopular if it's enforced with a whip."

"That looks like slavery to me, Mr. Smith," observed Hew, "Thank God we don't have slavery in England."

"Well," replied Adam dubiously, "the Navy does press men for service. Instead of a week's work on the roads, a man might be at sea for years against his will. Subject to Naval discipline!"

"But only sailors in seaports get pressed," objected Henry, "and here we are in the middle of farmland."

"Slavery is worse because it's permanent," said Adam, "But it feels like bondage to these poor fellows. Turgot would do away with the corvee if he could."

At length, the wagon was emptied and pulled away. As the carriage passed the workers, one bold fellow made eye contact with Henry, and for his temerity he received a lash from the overseer. The worker recoiled, stung, but the whip left a different kind of mark on Henry.

Ever since Henry had finished Adam's *Theory of Moral Sentiments*, he found its lessons penetrating his consciousness, unevenly, prompted by the examples he saw in daily life. Wherever they went, he now noticed people's shoes. He could see when people adopted pompous airs, or an assumed tone of authority, in vain attempts to elevate themselves over their peers. In deciding what to do, folks watched the people around them, taking cues from their fellows. Henry knew that all eyes were on him when he passed, that his fine clothes and expensive harness made him the envy of every peasant they encountered. Should he respond with kindness, or contempt? There was no changing the social order that made him a duke; some things were set in stone, and he was the natural beneficiary. The social order meant stability. Yet, somehow, he knew it was wrong when that muddy French peasant felt the lash.

• • • •

AFTER MANY DAYS OF travel, the group arrived in the city of Lyon, where they stayed another month. Adam explained that Geneva could be cold until April, so he was in no hurry. The boys read, rode horses, and wandered the streets of the ancient city. Lyon had been the capital of Gaul during Roman times, strategically located at the confluence of the Rhone and Saone rivers, so there was much to see of both history and commerce. Roman roads were still much in use. When not roaming the city, Adam continued to work on his book, which he'd tentatively decided to call *An Inquiry into the Wealth of Nations*. Cook stayed busy managing their expenses, plus acting as valet to Henry and Hew. Other than his outburst over rainbows, Cook artfully straddled his responsibilities as both manager of their trip and as ostensible servant to the boys. Yet his prickly manner and formality kept him personally distant from Henry, Hew, and Adam, even after a year in France together.

In mid-April they set out for Geneva through blossoming trees and fields. The distance between Lyon and Geneva was just under 100 miles, so on the afternoon of the fourth day they rolled down the long, well-groomed lane that led to Ferney, the home of Voltaire. Adam found himself getting nervous, rare for him, at the thought of meeting the best-known writer in all of France. In Lyon, he'd assigned Henry and Hew to read Voltaire's satire *Candide*, published in 1759, the same year as Adam's book. Adam recalled reading it in the original French; he'd been both delighted in the wit and disturbed by the cynicism.

The courtyard was empty in the mid-afternoon sun as the carriage rolled to a stop before the door of the large house. A few chickens scratched about, and two dogs started to bark, but there was no sign of anyone. Henry and Hew tumbled out, eager to stretch their legs, followed by Adam and Cook. A servant poked his head out the door, saw them, and then withdrew before they had a chance to hail him. Two full minutes passed before a tall man emerged and strode towards them, over sixty but in evident health and dressed in a dark frock coat.

Hew was closest to the door, so he asked, "Hello! Are you Voltaire?"

"No, young master, I am Tronchin, his physician," replied the tall man, who Adam estimated at just over six feet. "Are any of you the philosopher Adam Smith?"

Adam stepped forward, "I am here, Dr. Tronchin, and well met indeed." He gave a short bow, but Tronchin met him with hand extended. Adam straightened and shook his hand.

"I've been loitering about hoping to meet you, Mr. Smith. My son speaks highly of your teaching," said Tronchin, pumping the professor's hand.

"Allow me to introduce my students," said Adam, gesturing to each in turn, "Henry Scott, Third Duke of Buccleuch, and the Honorable Hew Campbell Scott, his brother." Cook, standing behind them and to the side, was not introduced.

Tronchin's manner was both distinguished and warm, impressing them all. "My pleasure, Brothers Scott. My son traveled all the way to Glasgow to learn from Mr. Smith. And here you've brought him along with you!"

"How is Francois?" asked Adam.

"He just left Glasgow, so I won't see him for a month or two," replied Tronchin, "Says it wasn't the same without his favorite professor."

"He didn't leave on my account, did he?" Adam asked fretfully, not understanding Tronchin's mild joke.

"No," Tronchin chuckled, "he finished his course of study. Your replacement was adequate, apparently."

Adam smiled, relieved. "Francois' discipline is exemplary. I hope he makes you very proud as a father."

"He always has," acknowledged Tronchin with a somber nod, "That's why I sent him all the way to you."

"Can you guide our next steps, Dr. Tronchin?" asked Adam, "Should we unload our baggage?" He turned to see that servants had appeared and were already unloading the carriage behind him. Cook fluttered about, unsure of the plan, but seeing that the servants clearly had one.

"Your accommodations await," said Tronchin, "please follow me." The group fell in behind the tall Genevan, with Adam first and Cook last, as they passed through the doors and down a long hallway.

"Is Voltaire at home?" inquired Adam at the broad back walking in front of him.

Tronchin turned his head but kept walking while he responded. "Yes, but he is very strict about his time. At any moment there are a dozen or more visitors here. You may see him at dinner tonight." Tronchin stopped abruptly and turned, and his visitors stacked up short behind him. "Or maybe you won't," he declared, "Voltaire works continuously. He likes to have people about him, but not if they interfere with his work. Today he is not feeling his best. Don't be offended if you don't see him at supper. Voltaire is a gracious and generous man, and he wants to meet you, Mr. Smith."

True to his warning, Voltaire's place sat empty at dinner that night, although twenty or so guests dined around his table. Dr. Tronchin hosted, the food was excellent, they were glad for their safe arrival, and that no carriage ride beckoned on the morrow.

Up early the next morning, Henry walked through the extensive gardens of Ferney. In the morning light everything was quiet and peaceful, green and pastoral. The spring bloom was upon the wide variety of plants, all meticulously tended. After walking for a half hour, he turned the corner of a hedge and discovered an elderly gardener potting a plant at a workbench, dressed in a neat smock and a soft hat. The man looked up at him and smiled.

"Good morning, monsieur," said the gardener.

"And you," nodded Henry, "These gardens are exquisite. Are they in your care?"

"Yes, thank you for the compliment," said the old man, "Appreciation is a wonderful thing."

"Yes," nodded Henry, guessing that the gardener probably didn't get many compliments.

"It makes what is excellent in others belong to us as well," continued the gardener, patting the dirt around a cutting in a small pot.

Henry looked at the man, surprised by such a deep thought coming from such a humble gardener. The wisdom of age, he thought, but he said, "That is nicely put. What is your name?"

"Francois, the gardener," said the man, "and yours?"

"I'm Henry, here visiting," he responded, pleased by the old man's easy familiarity. Most servants couldn't see past his title of Duke and were either silent or overly obsequious. Not this fellow, but Henry omitted his title anyway. He didn't want to sound haughty since they had only just arrived, and he was drawn to the open and intelligent charm of the elderly man. Frankly, Henry seldom acknowledged servants of any kind, Cook and Julia excepted.

"It's very peaceful here," offered Henry, "a good place to be alone."

"Yes," replied the gardener placidly, "we are rarely proud when we are alone. My garden expects little of me." He began potting another cutting and glanced sideways at Henry. "I choose to be happy as it's good for my health."

"An optimistic outlook, monsieur," replied Henry, nodding, as the old man certainly had the look of good health about him.

A sharp cryptic glance from the man was followed by a small smile that crept across his face before he answered, "Yes, it's the best of all possible worlds. Life may be a shipwreck, but we must not forget to sing in the lifeboats!" The gardener raised his index finger to give his point emphasis.

Henry burst out laughing. "Laugh in the face of misfortune, I agree!" he said, lifting two more pots to the table for the old man as he saw the number of cuttings he was potting. Henry wondered if the gardener had read *Candide,* if in fact he could read at all.

"The longer we dwell on our misfortunes the greater their power to harm us," added the man, pleased at Henry's gesture, and with a broad smile that unexpectedly showed good teeth. "The most important decision we make is to be in a good mood."

"You are the most philosophical gardener I have ever met," said Henry, "you almost make me want to take up farming."

"Almost?" smiled the gardener, clearly pleased, "Keep your feet on the ground and your hands in the earth, Henry. God gave us the gift of life; it's up to us to live it well."

"If you can't be happy in your garden, where can you be?" asked Henry rhetorically with raised palms.

A short, stout serving woman appeared at the nearby door, about twenty feet away. She scowled and called out, "I won't keep your breakfast hot forever old man!"

The gardener seemed unaffected by the brusque words of the woman, but he smiled at her and lifted his hand to acknowledge her warning. He turned to Henry and said with a grin, "I don't know where I am going, but I am on my way!" He followed the woman through the door and left Henry laughing.

When Henry returned to the main house, he found Hew and Adam sitting at breakfast, attended by Cook. He pulled up a chair as Cook put a plate in front of him.

"You look happy, brother," said Hew with his mouth full. "Is there good news?"

"Beautiful gardens here," replied Henry, "and I met the most amusing old gardener."

"It's my job to amuse you Henry," said Hew, "what can I learn from this gardener?"

"Well, first, how to grow a really beautiful garden," said Henry.

"Hmmm, this getting harder by the minute," said Hew, chewing but with a hand on his chin, "I guess you're on your own, brother."

Henry laughed, and Adam smiled at him. "It's good to see you laughing, Henry," he said simply.

"It is good, Henry," said Cook haltingly, "to see you happy, if I may." Cook flushed and diverted himself by pouring him a glass of juice from a pitcher. The food was excellent, as was the supper the night before.

"Thank you, Cook," replied Henry, and added with exaggerated sentimentality, "this breakfast makes me feel, well, *just so happy!*"

Everyone laughed, even Cook, and then a knock at the door announced Tronchin, who towered over the table.

"Good morning," he said, "Voltaire will meet with you at two o'clock this afternoon. He is particularly interested in your account of the Calas execution."

The laughter went out of everyone, but they nodded. "Wonderful," returned Adam, "We'll be ready at two."

"In the meantime," added Tronchin, "may I interest you in some pistol practice? There is a noted expert here, Monsieur Dumond, and he has volunteered to assist you."

"We accept," said Henry, "that sounds fun."

"Do we have any pistols in our luggage?" asked Hew doubtfully.

Tronchin shook his head, "No need, Dumond has several. Mr. Smith, have you any interest?"

Adam paused, remembering his fright when Robert had fired a pistol at the highwayman. "No, it's safest for everyone if I remain unarmed," he replied with a smile and shake of his head.

Later that morning Henry and Hew met Dumond, an ex-soldier nearing fifty with a significant facial scar along his cheek that made him look particularly fierce. They stood on a cropped lawn, behind a folding table where four pistols, balls, powder, and other equipment were laid out carefully. Dumond didn't smile beneath his huge mustache, which Henry suspected hid another scar. But he spoke clearly and carefully as he walked them through the parts of the pistol. Although both boys had fired pistols before, they'd never had such formal instruction, and they listened carefully.

"Lastly, is the flint," explained Dumond, pointing to the small chip held firmly in its clip near the hammer, "When the hammer strikes the flint, the spark ignites the powder in the pan. That flash in turn ignites the powder in the barrel, which fires the shot. Any questions?"

"Have you ever killed anyone with a pistol?" asked Hew, wide-eyed.

Dumond raised an eyebrow but saw that the insensitive question came from an inexperienced and unchastised teen of nobility. He dipped his head and replied, "Oui, monsieur."

"During war?" asked Hew.

"Oui, monsieur," nodded Dumond.

"What country were you fighting?" asked Hew, fascinated.

Dumond paused before asking politely, "What nationality are you?"

Henry and Hew answered simultaneously but differently.

"English," said Hew.

"Scottish," said Henry.

Dumond squinted quizzically at this odd answer to a simple question, but answered diplomatically, "Then the man I killed was a Prussian."

They fired the various pistols for over an hour, learning how to reload each pistol and understanding the differences of each. The targets were blocks of wood placed on several poles planted at various distances, by which they learned the critical lesson of not firing too soon if they were being charged by an antagonist. A target had to be within ten yards before they had a reasonable chance to hit it; not just because they were inexperienced but because the guns were not that reliable and there wouldn't be time to reload before a man would be upon them with sword or bayonet. But when they asked Dumond to hit a target on the farthest pole, he hit it on the first shot on four successive tries, one from each pistol. The boys had to conclude that it was mostly their inexperience, and they resolved to practice every chance they got.

Presently, Dumond produced two sheathed swords. "Practice with the blade?" For nearly fifteen minutes Dumond spoke of nothing but how they should place their feet.

"We swordfight with our feet?" asked Hew finally, impatient. Henry saw just a hint of a smile beneath the moustache at this; even the fierce old soldier found Hew amusing. Then he had Henry advance upon his brother and Hew parried his slow strokes just like they had practiced at Eton. Dumond motioned for Hew to advance upon Henry; when he attempted his first stroke Henry blocked so hard that the sword flew out of Hew's surprised hand. Dumond smirked, as he'd seen that move before.

"Ow, Henry," exclaimed Hew, sucking on his scraped knuckle as he retrieved the sword from the grass.

"Now square off again. Say, fight till first blood?" deadpanned the old soldier.

"What?" asked Henry, shocked.

"I lose already," said Hew, "Look, my knuckle is bleeding."

Finally, Dumond smiled. "I jest. You are brothers, not antagonists." He looked at Hew and added, "Are you, the youngest son, destined for war?"

"You're not the first to ask that," replied Hew, "Lucky the war was over before I got old enough to fight."

"War is part of man," replied Dumond seriously, "Men fight and die, always. I think that it is better to fight than to die."

Across the lawn they could see Tronchin approaching in his staid black Calvinist frock coat. "Come gentlemen, it's time to meet Voltaire," he said, "He's a very punctual man."

CHAPTER 20

VOLTAIRE *April 1765*

Henry and Hew followed Tronchin into the house and through the door of a large, ornate, and brightly lit sitting room. Adam was already there, seated by himself in one of the straight-backed chairs. Tronchin bade the boys take a seat, and they had hardly done so when Francois the gardener entered the room, although the smock had been replaced by clothes considerably more elegant. They stood again, Henry with a broad smile of recognition.

Voltaire smiled at Henry but greeted Adam first, saying, "Ah, Scotland, where we look for all our ideas of civilization! You have put the world on notice, Mr. Smith."

"It's an honor to meet you, Voltaire," said Adam with a bow, feeling ridiculously pleased at his host's unabashed compliment.

"Hello, Henry, we meet again," said Voltaire.

Henry bowed low, then straightened and said, "You are a most amusing gardener monsieur!"

"And who is this young man?" asked Voltaire, looking at Hew.

"This is my younger brother, the Honorable Hew Campbell Scott," replied Henry as Hew bowed.

"A pleasure to meet you, Honorable Hew," said Voltaire, "As the second son are you then destined for war?"

"I hope not," replied Hew, "I'd make quite the target sitting on a horse in a bright red uniform." It was dawning on Hew that Voltaire was indeed the amusing gardener Henry had met that morning.

"The beginnings of wisdom, young man!" Voltaire clapped his hands in delight. "Common sense is not so common, I'm afraid. I'd question any man who thinks that I should die for his glory."

They all took a seat, including Tronchin, and the same stout serving woman brought tea. While cups were being poured, Voltaire turned to Adam again. "Mr. Smith, I have read your Theory. Few can raise themselves above the ideas of their time. You, monsieur, have done so. With books as with men, a very small number play a great part."

"Thank you for reading my book, monsieur," said Adam humbly, heart warmed to the point of embarrassment at such accolades from a writer he respected so much.

"Don't call me monsieur, call me Voltaire," he replied, then he turned to Henry and added, "Although my real name *is* Francois."

Francois-Marie Arouet, seventy, adopted the name Voltaire after his 1717 imprisonment in the Bastille for a year for the crime of writing a satirical verse that was unappreciated by Regent Philippe II, Duke of Orleans. The name Voltaire was taken from the word *volontaire*, which means determined and self-willed in French. In 1726 he offended the powerful Rohan family and was sentenced again to the Bastille, but instead spent over two years in exile in England. There he continued to write, met Alexander Pope and Isaac Newton's niece, and was deeply affected by the relative freedom he found compared to his native land. When he was allowed to return to France, he published in 1733 the complimentary *Letters Concerning the English Nation*, which caused another huge scandal and Voltaire was forced to flee Paris once again. Eventually he settled in Ferney, very near the border with Geneva, where he could easily escape should the authorities come to arrest him. Voltaire never stopped speaking his mind, and advocating for freedom of thought, religion, and speech. He loved both the arts and sciences and became good friends with Marshal Richelieu, who also chose to live outside of the Paris intrigues.

"Merci, Bella," said Voltaire to the serving woman, "perhaps some sweet cakes as well?"

"I only have two hands," the woman replied brusquely, "I'll bring them next."

"I would be helpless without you, Bella," said Voltaire as she turned to fetch the cakes.

"Finally, some real truth from the great philosopher!" she barked on the way out.

"Bella keeps me humble," is all he would say before asking, "I understand you witnessed the execution of Jean Calas?"

"Yes, it was horrible," said Henry, feeling the stir of now-familiar anguish at the memory.

"May I ask you about it?" inquired Voltaire, "If I do not find anything pleasant, at least perhaps I will find something new."

"Please do, although I get a sinking feeling every time I think about it," said Adam.

"Me too," said Henry.

"I have already heard much from my dear friend Marshal Richelieu," began Voltaire, "I also recently interviewed Pierre Calas, the brother, who confirms suicide and not murder. Is that your view as well?"

"We only saw the execution," replied Adam, "so we know the details only by hearsay."

"I came away thinking him innocent," volunteered Henry, "by the firm way he withstood the torture. And what he said to the priest when asked for his dying confession."

"Which was?" asked Voltaire with a raised eyebrow.

"Jean Calas asked the priest how he could believe such an awful thing," Henry answered soberly.

Bella entered again and placed a tray of cakes before them without comment, and then withdrew. Hungry, Hew immediately took three.

"My talk with Pierre was most heartbreaking," said Voltaire, "He was banished to a monastery but escaped to Geneva."

"Geneva is Calvinist, and skeptical of the Toulouse charges. We welcomed him," Tronchin said approvingly.

"For taking their father's side, the family was narrowly spared a similar fate," said Adam, "His daughters were sent to a convent, even though they are Protestant."

"Was there a large crowd in attendance?" inquired Voltaire.

"Yes," Henry shuddered, "Their bloodlust was horrible."

"No opinion is worth burning your neighbor for," said Voltaire, shaking his head. "Better to risk saving a guilty person than to convict an innocent one. Did the crowd cheer the torture?"

"Yes," nodded Henry, "the magistrate David Beaudrigue claimed Calas killed his son over religion."

"People run with the herd, and find safety in it," Voltaire replied sadly, "No snowflake in an avalanche ever feels responsible."

"Another dark mark against France," intoned Tronchin.

"Yes, but it can happen anywhere," replied Voltaire, "In England it appears necessary to put an admiral to death occasionally as encouragement to the rest."

"You refer to Admiral Byng?" asked Adam.

"Yes, I had the full account from Richelieu, who should know," he replied, "But I am being unfair. When I lived in England, I found that people could mostly say what they wished."

Hew swallowed his cake and said, "You lived in England?"

"I was a refugee in England for two years to avoid the Bastille," the writer replied. "You see why I live close to the border even now, always prepared to flee. Liberty of thought is the very life of the soul. But speaking your mind is risky in France."

"You defend free speech even if you find it hateful?" asked Henry.

"I may not agree with what you say, but I'll defend to the death your right to say it," Voltaire answered firmly.

"Let's hope it doesn't come to that!" said Adam.

"But the magistrate told lies that caused a man's death," said Henry, thinking Beaudrigue's false words were as hateful as could be imagined.

"The wicked will use anything as a pretext," Voltaire explained, "The more often stupidity gets repeated, the more it appears as wisdom. Those who can make you believe absurdities can make you commit atrocities. The only antidote to official lies is the free expression of contrary thoughts."

"Why didn't someone publish the truth of the matter, for all to understand?" wondered Hew.

"Because so few can read and write, Hew," replied Voltaire, "Dark superstition leads weak souls to blame crimes on anyone who doesn't think like them."

"Beaudrigue will go unpunished!" Henry exclaimed, "He inflamed the crowd with vile falsehoods."

Voltaire looked at Henry sympathetically, seeing how the young man was still deeply troubled by what he had witnessed. Voltaire's reply was gentle in tone, but blunt; "Clever tyrants are never punished, Henry. We live in a tyrannical world."

"So there seems to be little that we can do," summed up Adam.

"Wait," said Voltaire, holding up his palm face outwards, "every man is guilty of all the good he did not do. Come, let us ponder. No problem can withstand the assault of sustained thinking."

Tronchin suggested in a firm voice, "The power of the pen—perhaps some of your famous letters, Voltaire?"

"Hmmm, a letter-writing campaign?" mused Voltaire, "let me give it thought. Not a letter, perhaps, but a Treatise on Tolerance for you to take to the King. Discord is the great ill of mankind, and tolerance is the only remedy!" He ended with a flourish, raising his hand to punctuate the idea.

"To the King? Of France?" said Adam, not sure he'd heard correctly.

"Of course!" responded Voltaire with enthusiasm, "You are going to Paris, are you not? I assure you, the King and his ministers can all read."

Tronchin stood, signaling the interview was over. After taking their leave of Voltaire, they didn't see him again for nearly a week. The boys enjoyed Ferney in springtime, riding and shooting and attending plays held in Voltaire's private playhouse, where they also had several dance lessons. Adam met with the other guests, ate with them, and attended the plays with the boys.

One night at dinner they met Duke Rochefoucald, a young enthusiastic man about Henry's age, who was a devoted admirer of Adam Smith. Hew was seated next to him and listened patiently as the young duke praised *The Theory of Moral Sentiments*. Henry laughed at this, knowing Hew was struggling to make much progress in his tutor's book. Adam was seated next to Voltaire's place, across from Tronchin. Henry sat next to Adam and across from Hew, with another dozen guests, including Monsieur Dumond, filling out the long table. Voltaire's place sat empty.

The head servant, a tall, thin man in fine livery, rang a small bell. "Be seated, everyone! The first plates will be out shortly."

Bella entered carrying a large tureen, followed by several servants holding the rest of the first course. The soup was served, and everyone picked up their spoons. Tronchin folded his hands and bowed his head in prayer. Seeing this, both Hew and Henry put down their spoons and bowed their heads until the Calvinist finally raised his head.

"Is Voltaire working on the treatise?" asked Adam, blowing on his spoon to cool the hot soup.

"He works like a man possessed," replied Tronchin, "Intolerance excites his sense of justice."

"Did Voltaire really get thrown in prison?" asked Henry.

"Indeed. And when he returned from exile in England, he still couldn't risk living in Paris," said Tronchin, "That's why all the world comes to Ferney."

"As we have, gratefully," nodded Adam.

The soup was consumed in short order, and the servants swept in to remove the soup bowls. Then they returned with the main course, a rich dish made of chicken. In the bustle of the servants, Voltaire entered and without announcement took his place at the head of the table. "There you are!" said Tronchin.

Adam started to rise, but Voltaire waved him down, saying, "Sit, sit, continue!" Bella appeared out of nowhere and put a plate with a small salad in front of Voltaire. He looked at her inquiringly, "What kind of dressing?"

"Whatever it is, it's already on there," replied Bella. Voltaire forked a leaf and sniffed it tentatively before putting it in his mouth.

"He rarely eats what his guests eat," explained Tronchin.

Voltaire gestured to the loaded table. "If I ate like this every day, I wouldn't have made seventy years. Tronchin has me on a very healthful program."

"Program?" prompted Adam.

Tronchin answered, wiping his mouth with his napkin, "Exercise, fresh air, drink clean water, wholesome foods, alcohol in moderation. It's no secret, prevention is better than a cure."

"In other words," said Voltaire, "the art of medicine consists of amusing the patient while nature cures the disease. I sometimes think doctors do more harm than good. Tronchin, here, excepted of course."

"Apology accepted," said Tronchin with a smile as he took another bite.

"Doctors put drugs of which they know little, into bodies which they know less, for diseases which they know nothing at all!" joked Voltaire.

Tronchin took no offense, knowing his friend too well, but added, "For a healthy body there is nothing solid but virtue and clean living. Bloodletting does nothing but weaken the patient."

Voltaire said, "Men will always be mad, and those who think they can cure them are the maddest of all." Henry, Hew, and the other guests were listening intently, straining to hear over the dinner table din.

"Voltaire, can you tell us how you were sent to the Bastille?" asked Hew boldly. All eyes turned to their host for his answer, which came after a long pause.

"No," Voltaire said flatly. Hew looked chastised, and the guests were embarrassed for him. Tronchin looked at their host disapprovingly, so after a moment Voltaire relented, and replied to Hew, "If you want to know who controls you, look at who you are not allowed to criticize."

"My question was insensitive," apologized Hew.

"Not at all, young man," said Voltaire, shaking his head, "We judge a man by his questions as much as his answers. But the Bastille is a place I'd rather forget. Even today I must always be ready to run because I dare to speak openly. God is a comedian playing to an audience that is too afraid to laugh."

"It's risky to speak out," agreed Adam, "as my skeptical friend Hume well understands."

"I presume upon my English freedoms," said Henry, "I've always thought I could say whatever I wanted."

Voltaire nodded in agreement. "Despite your bloody history, there is some measure of tolerance in England. People are full of weakness and errors; let us pardon each other our follies – it is the first law of nature!"

"Let the person without sin cast the first stone," added Tronchin.

Voltaire turned to his old friend in admiration. "Do you see how a religious man like Tronchin can reach the same place as I, the rational philosopher?" Everyone smiled at this; then with deft comic timing Voltaire added, "There is no God, but don't tell my servant lest he murder me at night!"

Everyone was shocked by this scandalous joke, but there were several snorts of suppressed laughter. "My Treatise on Tolerance is nearly complete," Voltaire continued, "But I have thought twice about who should deliver it to the King. It must come from a Frenchman; one he already trusts." He reassured Adam by adding, "I'll have a copy made so you can see how I defend poor Jean Calas."

Voltaire stood and lifted his glass in a toast. Voices fell silent and everyone raised a glass. In a loud voice he said, "Intolerance – we must crush the infamous thing!"

• • • •

THREE DAYS LATER, HENRY woke early and knocked gently at Hew's door. "Hew, are you there?" After a moment, he knocked again. "Hew?"

Beyond the door he heard a muffled voice, "No."

"No ride, or no, you're not there?" said Henry, smiling beyond the door.

"Too much wine," said Hew sleepily, "go away."

Henry found the kitchen, where Bella was already up and beginning to assemble breakfast. "Good morning, Bella, is there a spot of tea?" he said brightly, half-expecting a curt response.

"Tea is an English drink," she said matter-of-factly, "I can make it, but I have coffee hot."

"I prefer coffee, thank you," replied Henry, pleased. He was developing a real taste for coffee.

Bella set a cup in front of him and poured black coffee from a pot. He sipped it cautiously.

"My God, this is superb," he gushed, "what makes it so good?"

"I made it that way, Monsieur Duke," she replied crisply.

Laughing, Henry said, "I can see how you've earned Voltaire's confidence."

"We are what we eat," she responded, "the old man's health passes through my kitchen."

"This is a very clean kitchen," agreed Henry.

"Cleanliness is next to Godliness, you know," she answered.

"I notice Voltaire is very informal with his servants," ventured Henry, "Why do you call him 'old man?'"

Bella eyed him for a moment, then decided to answer frankly. "He's old because he eats proper. We all want him to live as long as possible."

"How long have you cooked for him?" asked Henry.

"Ever since he came here, near ten years," she answered, adding, "He is a kind, generous man who needs a firm hand sometimes."

"Judging by this coffee, he's found the right person in you, Bella." Warmed by the drink, Henry went to the stable to pick a horse for his habitual morning ride. He stopped at the stall of a likely mare, a handsome gray with a white blaze on her forehead. Seeing the hostler at the far end of the barn, he called, "Hey there, is this horse ready to go?" The elderly man walked towards him as quickly as he could.

"Good morning, monsieur, a horse?" the hostler asked.

"Can I take this one?" asked Henry, pointing to the mare.

"Oui, she's ready," he nodded, "Her name's Saucy."

"Saucy, like for food?" asked Henry, not sure if he'd heard correctly.

"Oui," said the garrulous old man, "Reminds me of something I heard the master tell a guest once." Henry raised an eyebrow at him, so emboldened, the man continued, "He said the English have only one sauce, melted butter." The man smiled, showing several missing teeth, "Well, Saucy rides smooth, like melted butter."

Henry laughed as the hostler led Saucy out of the stall. Henry helped saddle and bridle the beautiful animal. "Have you been here a long time?" asked Henry as he combed Saucy's mane.

"Since he arrived," said the man, adding, "It was tough times before he came."

Henry cantered out of the courtyard and through the garden lane. He spied a neat, elderly gardener in the distance. He trotted over and dismounted, leading Saucy along the garden edge. "I hoped I would see you here again, Francois," greeted Henry cheekily, "We're leaving tomorrow for Paris."

Voltaire smiled broadly at the familiarity. "So, the lesson continues for the young English duke."

"Actually, my lands are mostly in Scotland," Henry said.

"Our country is that spot to which our heart is bound," Voltaire replied, then asked, "Is that England or Scotland?"

"A good question," nodded Henry, "England, until I met Mr. Smith. Now I'm less sure."

"You are fortunate in your tutor," acknowledged Voltaire, "Tronchin greatly admires Mr. Smith, as do I. What do you like best about Scotland?"

"I've never been there," Henry admitted.

"You must go and hear what your heart has to say about it," advised Voltaire.

"I'll go when I inherit my estates," answered Henry.

Voltaire fixed him with a keen look. "They may resent your coming, Henry. It's not enough to conquer, you must learn to seduce. Don't let your triumphs be loveless."

"Loveless? How so?" asked Henry, pulling on Saucy's bridle to keep her from cropping the garden plants.

"In marriage, in career, in everything, dare to think for yourself," said Voltaire earnestly, looking him in the eye, "Only then can you hear your own heart when it tells you what to do."

"What if my head and heart argue?" wondered Henry, "That's as often as not."

"They always argue," responded Voltaire, "but your head and heart are partners, not enemies. Paradise was made for tender hearts; hell for loveless hearts."

"My heart makes mistakes, I'm afraid," said Henry ruefully.

"Don't let the perfect be the enemy of the good," said the elderly philosopher, "We're neither pure, nor wise, nor good; we do the best we know."

Henry nodded, understanding good advice when he heard it, then asked, "So we fumble our way towards truth, by trial and error?"

"Yes," agreed Voltaire, "Lots of errors. So, love truth and pardon error, as we are all imperfect creatures. Cherish those who seek the truth but beware those who say they find it. Doubt is an uncomfortable condition, but certainty is a ridiculous one."

Henry wondered about this comment, but at that moment a horse approached behind them. Turning, they saw it carried Adam. "Good morning to you both," he greeted them. "Henry, are you coming or going?"

"A question we should all ask ourselves daily!" laughed Voltaire.

"Going, Mr. Smith," responded Henry with a grin, "Care for company?"

"Enjoy!" said Voltaire happily, "Remember Henry, wherever your travels may lead, *paradise is where you are*!"

CHAPTER 21

THUNDERSTRUCK IN PARIS *Summer 1765*

On a warm summer Saturday Charles Townshend returned to Adderbury in the late afternoon, tossed his hat to his attentive valet, who then held the door as he swept inside. Caroline greeted him by extending her hands and offering her cheek for a peck, but they did not embrace.

"So good to have you home from the Parliamentary Wars!" Caroline said sincerely, as she found Adderbury frightfully dull in his absence. Despite their limited intimacy, Charles brought energy everywhere he went.

"Good to be home," Charles replied, smiling, "there's been a lull in the fighting."

Frances ran in and jumped into his arms. "Hello Father, I missed you!"

Charles hugged Frances tightly. "I missed you too dear. I should be home for several days."

Caroline felt slightly miffed by the warmth that Charles showed Frances, though she rarely showed warmth towards either. Instead, she said, "Now Frances, don't smother him. Run and get ready for supper."

"Yes, mother," replied Frances, skipping out unchastised.

"We received letters from France today," Caroline said excitedly, putting a hand on Charles' arm.

"Excellent! Where?" he responded, then followed Caroline into the drawing room. She pulled a drape, letting a broad band of sunlight illuminate the shaded room. Charles sat in his favorite armchair and Caroline presented him with the bundle of letters. He rifled through them quickly, then used a letter opener to open the first one, from Henry.

"Henry, Smith, and Cook sent letters," he said as he unfolded Henry's, "Wait, Hew included a sheet with Henry's ...."

Caroline pulled a chair close and sat while Charles read Henry's letter silently, narrating bits to Caroline as he absorbed them.

"Met Voltaire!" he exclaimed, "quite a lot about him ... met the archbishop in Montpelier, and someone named Turgot... will be in Paris within two weeks, wonderful!"

"Does he mention that dreadful execution?" asked Caroline, "His last letter was so dark."

"Only that Voltaire asked him about it. Dear, Henry is meeting with the great!" said Charles happily as he handed Henry's letter to his wife. "Here, see for yourself."

"I'm glad he's safe and in good spirits," she said, taking the folded sheets as Charles quickly read Hew's single page.

"Hew seems his usual irrepressible self," commented Charles, handing Caroline the sheet as he opened Adam's envelope.

After reading both her son's missives, Caroline said with satisfaction, "Sending Hew was good for Henry. Those boys always got along."

Charles took several minutes to read Adam's letter carefully, before dropping it to his lap and saying thoughtfully, "Smith is meeting my every expectation. Says that Voltaire wrote a Treatise on Tolerance to send to the King of France." He leaned towards Caroline and exulted, "*While* they were there, and *after* talking with Henry!"

"The King of France!" Caroline clapped her hands with delight. "Perhaps this Voltaire fellow mentioned Henry in his treatise to the King!" She added, "Mr. Smith seems like a very nice man, although perhaps a bit absent."

"Well, our absent-minded professor has Henry meeting all the right people so far," agreed Charles, happy to see Caroline pleased at the good news from her sons.

"Henry will be Duke, but what arrangements can be made for Hew?" she asked.

Charles hastened to reassure her that he had not been idle regarding Hew. "I have already inquired about buying him a regimental command. He says he's been practicing with the sword."

Frances returned, wearing a different dress, and asked, "What news from France, Father?"

Charles smiled at her and replied, "The boys are almost to Paris, Frances."

"Paris!" exclaimed Frances, "they can practice their gallantry there!"

· · · ·

RELIEVED OF THE DUTY to carry Voltaire's Treatise to the King, Adam and the boys took their time wending their way towards Paris. They stopped for a week in Orleans, where Joan of Arc had helped break the siege that eventually led to the end of the Hundred Year's War some three hundred years before. Her help was not as a warrior, but as divine inspiration as she claimed to have seen heavenly visions. The modern nations of France and England emerged in the aftermath, ending the long mix of kings and their claims tying southern England to northern France that had begun with the French victory in England at the Battle of Hastings in 1066.

It was full summer when their carriage finally rolled up to the same hotel they'd stayed in previously, the Parc Royale, which would be their home for the remainder of their time abroad. Neither Adam nor Cook felt Paris was an undue risk to Henry's discipline any longer, and any concern was outweighed by the lure of the elite luminaries they might meet. Adam was privately pleased by this development, as he was ready to match wits and words with the best of France. But they would have to keep an eye on Hew.

Tired of their long carriage ride, everyone retired early that evening with supper sent to their rooms. Henry loved stretching out on a good bed after so many hours in a rattling wagon over dubious roads. He lay on his bed, boots off, musing on Paris. In the next room Hew lay musing also, snoring gently. Henry dozed and dreamed uncomfortably of his dead friend James.

Promptly at nine the next morning, Embassy Secretary David Hume found his friend Adam Smith at his breakfast table in the Parc Royale. Hume was huge and resplendent in the scarlet uniform of his Majesty's government as he spread his arms wide and boomed, "It's good to be a Scot!" Hume was famous for saying intemperate things, but he was so charming when he did so that even his enemies liked him. Adam stood to greet the gentle giant, clasping both his arms.

"David, so good to see you my friend," greeted Adam, "please join me, I'm just setting down to breakfast."

Hume eyed the dainty French chair dubiously. "Attendant, can you provide a stouter chair?"

The head clerk snapped his fingers at a small serving boy, who returned in a moment pushing a large drawing room chair almost too big for him. Hume gave the lad a coin for his heroic labors, then seated himself gracefully. In his mid-fifties, Hume was growing quite stout, but he handled himself with grace and dignity. Hume was the perfect diplomat; civilized, literate, perceptive, eloquent, and humorous.

"It is my duty as Secretary to be as stout as I can manage," Hume said, "I represent a veritable mountain of Scottish success at the British Embassy."

The small attendant brought Adam's breakfast on a tray, then looked at Hume inquiringly.

"Coffee, and a pastry," said Hume, "perhaps two pastries." He beamed while waiting impatiently for Adam to take a bite of eggs, then chew, swallow, and take a sip of his tea. "You are the world's worst letter-writer my friend," stated Hume, "but your adventures have arrived in Paris ahead of you."

"How so, Hume?" asked Adam as he took another bite.

"Is it true that Voltaire wrote his treatise about the Calas affair while you were visiting him?" Hume asked in a rush of pent-up enthusiasm.

"Yes," nodded Adam, taking another drink of tea, "He asked what we'd seen. He had already interviewed Pierre Calas, the exiled son of the, er, deceased."

Hume leaned forward in his excitement. "Voltaire's treatise is all the rage in the salons. It's said the King has already read it. I hope to have a copy soon."

"You can read my copy," said Adam as he spread jam on toast.

"Your copy?" Hume asked with raised eyebrows.

"The copy Voltaire gave me," Adam replied, "He said he'd already sent a copy to Paris."

Hume sat back in stupefied satisfaction as his coffee and pastries were served. He took a drink of coffee, set the cup down carefully, then said, "I don't know if I'm prouder that I'm *your* friend, or that you are apparently *Voltaire's* friend, or as Embassy Secretary discovering an important foreign message. By Jove, all three!

"I'll need my copy back," laughed Adam, "Don't send it to London or we'll never see it again."

Hume used his knife and fork with the tender pastries, as he was a thoroughly civilized man and would not be seen licking his fingers. "I was very sorry to hear about poor James MacDonald. We could not possibly have suffered a greater loss than in that valuable young man."

"Such a tragedy," nodded Adam, "Very hard on Henry."

They ate without speaking for a few minutes, then Hume said, "Now, to the future. The salons beckon, and I will be your guide."

"I heard of these salons," said Adam warily, "warned, rather."

"Nonsense," said Hume, "the salons offer the finest of entertainment. Lovely women, educated men, charming palaces, good food."

"How about educated women?" asked Adam.

"Touche, I am easily distracted by beauty," agreed Hume, "I surely don't mean to slight the very formidable women who host the salons. They are well-educated indeed, as you'll see this afternoon."

"We've only just arrived, Hume. Already I have an appointment?" protested Adam.

"You, and young Duke Henry," affirmed Hume, "I promised Comtesse Boufflers that I would deliver both of you promptly at two."

"Who is this Comtesse?" asked Adam, taking his last bite of eggs.

Hume finished his pastry, wiped his mouth and took a drink of coffee before he responded. "Comtesse Boufflers is mistress to the Prince de Conti, one of the highest-ranking officials in the kingdom. Former mistress, I suppose, as the Prince favors younger women these days. But I assure you that the Comtesse has lost none of her beauty."

"Why are these salons so interesting?" asked Adam. "You never liked small talk, Hume."

"Small talk?" snorted Hume, pretending to be indignant, "These are the most intellectual discussions in all Europe. More importantly, they love me here. In England, I'm a rude infidel Scotsman. Here, I feed on ambrosia, drink nothing but nectar, breathe only incense, and walk on flowers. The Parisians champion reason, and love even me, a large ungainly philosopher. I may decide to live here permanently," he concluded archly.

"That would be a great loss to the English-speaking world, my friend," replied Adam, laughing at Hume's exaggerations but wondering if Hume was serious. They finished eating and Hume waited while Adam ascended the ornate open staircase to retrieve Voltaire's treatise from his room. Coming down were Henry and Hew, and they stopped mid-stair.

"Did you already eat, Mr. Smith?" asked Hew.

"Yes, with Hume," replied Adam, who then looked at Henry and added, "We are invited to a salon at two o'clock."

From the stair Henry waved at Hume, who waved back at the boys. Henry asked Adam, "A salon? Do you mean, like, drinks and chit chat?"

"Pretty much," nodded Adam, "but with famous French people. Hume says Voltaire's treatise has landed with a splash, and everyone is discussing the affaire d'Calas."

"My first day in Paris and I must listen to old people chit-chat?" whined Hew.

Shaking his head, Adam said a smile, "You are welcome to come, Hew, but I don't think your attendance is required."

"But mine is?" asked Henry.

"Yes," said Adam, still smiling, but now he was nodding.

Downstairs, Henry and Hew greeted Hume warmly and then emerged into the warm bright sunlight. "Look out Paris, here I come!" said Hew, ebullient.

Henry grabbed Hew by the arm and looked him in the eye before laying down the law, "No gambling, Hew."

"Aww, what's the fun in that?" complained Hew, "I won't bet the estate. Or embarrass Father."

"No gambling," maintained Henry in a serious tone, "It's nothing but trouble. A simple bet I made with James, on a horse race, was questioned as cause for murder when he died. *By Beaudrigue*. I'll never gamble again." Henry felt relieved that he could finally tell someone, especially his younger brother who needed the lesson.

"I hear you brother," nodded Hew soberly, before raising his eyebrows and deadpanning, "How do you feel about wine, women, and song?"

At half-past one, Hume arrived at the Parc Royale to pick up Adam and Henry, although the distance was at most two miles. The carriage delivered them in short order to the Palace of the Prince, where liveried servants opened the carriage doors for them, opened the Palace doors for them, and escorted them into the large, ornate, well-lighted wing where the Comtesse held her salon. A string quartet played music in one corner, and a well-dressed crowd of about forty turned as one when the servant announced them at the door.

"May I announce Monsieur David Hume, Monsieur Adam Smith, and Henry Scott, Third Duke of Buccleuch."

Instantly they were thronged by the crowd, mostly men but several women, greeting Hume and pressing to meet the new visitors. Two handclaps and a commanding but pleasant voice cut the din, "Please, everyone! Make a path to the punch for our illustrious guests!"

The throng parted to create an aisle, at the head of which stepped Comtesse Boufflers. At a distance of thirty feet, Adam was thunderstruck by her calm beauty and elegance. Three abreast they approached up the aisle of smiling, applauding faces, but those faces were a blur, dazzled into bright obscurity by the lovely blaze of the Comtesse. They stood before her as the crowd gathered behind them.

"Hume, please introduce your famous guests," invited the Comtesse graciously, "As you can see, they've attracted quite a crowd."

"Comtesse, it is my honor to present Henry Scott, Third Duke of Buccleuch," said Hume in his cultured but unmistakable Scot's brogue.

"It's a pleasure to be here, Comtesse," said Henry, bowing low, his voice marking himself as English to everyone. He'd heard Hume pronounce her name "Boo-flay" but he wasn't sure enough to risk it.

"Thank you for coming," smiled the Comtesse, "I hope you don't find us old and boring."

"And this is my close friend, the philosopher and professor Adam Smith," announced Hume with an air of triumph.

Comtesse Boufflers smiled charmingly at Adam as he rose from his deep bow, and surprisingly, she reached out and took his hand. "It is a great pleasure to meet such a good friend of David's. You are always welcome here, Mr. Smith."

Adam decided he had never heard such music as the sound of her voice. Although the Comtesse was about forty, Hume had been right about her beauty, charm, and elegance. Adam was utterly transfixed.

"Ah, yes, it's a pleasure madam, merci," he stammered, finding his mouth suddenly dry as cotton, but his accent confirmed to all that Smith was indeed a Scot. A servant handed him a glass of claret, which he gratefully sipped to restore himself. Hume established himself next to Adam and Henry as the Comtesse organized her guests into a reception line.

A rapid succession of faces passed in front of Adam, each with a pleasant introduction perhaps supplemented by a comment from Hume or the Comtesse. Then each moved on to greet Henry, and the next person stepped up. Adam was so keenly aware of the Comtesse standing so close to him, that the names blurred with the new faces as he met each one. Diderot, d'Alembert, and so many others sounded familiar, but none of them made a clear mark on his consciousness as he mindlessly repeated pleasantries with each. Only the Comtesse mattered to Adam Smith, the famous Scottish intellectual but a man like any other.

Henry knew none of the guests, even by reputation, as he greeted each one formally. He was pleased to find none of the initial frostiness he'd seen in Toulouse and elsewhere in France. In the carriage on the ride over, Hume had characterized Comtesse Boufflers as an 'anglophile,' and it appeared most of her guests felt the same. Once they had met everyone, servants refilled their glasses, and they began to mingle.

"Mr. Smith's book was recently translated into French," said the Comtesse.

"Badly, much was lost in the translation," replied Hume.

"The translator claims his errors are because each language expresses abstract thoughts differently!" laughed the Comtesse.

A guest asked Adam, "Have you read Voltaire's Treatise? I heard you paid him a visit."

Adam nodded and said, "He makes a compelling case for the innocence of poor Jean Calas."

The guest followed with, "Was it well composed?"

"Clear, concise, cogent," said Adam, nodding, "The words of Voltaire are meant for all, to be read by all."

"I daresay, Mr. Smith was with Voltaire when he wrote his masterpiece for the king. Rubbing elbows!" said Hume animatedly, extending his elbows and inadvertently poking Henry.

"Ah, no," Adam replied, "Voltaire writes alone in his studio."

Another guest, a portly man not nearly so tall as Hume, spoke up. "I hear an Italian, Beccaria, has just published an essay, "On Crimes and Punishments.""

Adam wasn't familiar, so Comtesse Boufflers smoothly intercepted the question by saying, "It's being translated. Beccaria argues that torture is always wrong, and public torture especially so."

Again, Adam was transfixed. He recalled Hume's words at breakfast and could better understand why it was difficult to rank the woman's many evident charms.

"A little torture puts the fear of God into people!" said the rotund guest.

"Or fear of the magistrate," said Adam, catching Henry's glance.

Henry soon realized that he was more ornament than participant, as every guest wanted to talk first to Adam. The elite Parisians were less awed by a duke than by an eminent philosopher; soon Henry was standing on the sidelines drinking another glass of the excellent fruit punch. After several minutes, the Comtesse appeared next to him as he watched the guests revolve around Adam and Hume.

"Tell me Henry, how did you come to have such an illustrious tutor?" she asked.

"My stepfather engaged Mr. Smith years ago, after reading his book," Henry replied, "I was still a schoolboy."

"Charles Townshend, I believe?" inquired Comtesse Boufflers.

"Yes, I'm surprised you know of him," replied Henry, especially since all the salon's interest seemed focused on the philosophers.

"It's rumored that Charles Townshend has his eye on being Prime Minister," she said.

"What? Charles?" replied Henry, surprised.

"He is Chancellor of the Exchequer, is he not?" asked the Comtesse.

"He is? Charles?" replied a stupefied Henry. It seemed he'd been away too long, but Charles' letters were all full of instructions for Henry, and little about his role in government.

Comtesse Boufflers gave him a dazzling smile, and then laughed disarmingly. "You should write to your stepfather more often, Henry. We pay close attention to who is leading England, as you might imagine." She laughed and put her hand on his and disarmingly added, "You should too!"

"I am at your disadvantage, Comtesse," said a chagrined Henry, conscious of her soft hand, "We only arrived yesterday, and I have yet to read my mail."

"All the best news passes through my salon," said the satisfied hostess.

"Charles has been busy, it seems," Henry replied.

They stood side-by-side, holding glasses of punch, as they watched Adam Smith hold court for the first time in Paris. The circle of guests listened attentively as Adam lectured at some length. Too far away to hear the particulars, Henry could see that Adam spoke confidently, standing in his plain black coat amongst the elegant and colorfully dressed French intellectuals.

"Charles said Mr. Smith is the best lecturer in all Europe, but I have never heard him lecture," observed Henry. "He is so modest and unassuming by nature. Look at him now."

"Have you read his *Theory of Moral Sentiments*?" she asked.

"Yes, have you?" he said, remembering his embarrassment when Marshal Richelieu had asked the same question a year before.

"What a lovely idea, a science of sentiments," she replied, "I have begun to read it in English. I am not very far advanced yet, but I think it will please me."

CHAPTER 22

I NTERVIEW WITH THE KING *Summer 1765*
Henry and Hew stood before full-length mirrors in Henry's large room at the Parc Royale, with Cook fussing over the finishing touches of their elegant dress as they prepared for their first visit to the Paris Theater. Neither wore a wig, but both were dressed at the very height of current English fashion. Cook finished brushing their shoulders and adjusting their collars as they admired their reflections.

"Paris is a far cry from Toulouse," said Hew, "Not exactly a church town, is it?"

"You forget the Cathedral of Notre Dame?" answered Henry.

"It seems more of a tourist attraction," observed Hew, "But have you seen the ladies?"

"The ladies of London are just as pretty," said Henry stoutly, "Have some patriotism, man."

"God Bless King George," smirked Hew, "but remember Father's words about gallantry. I think it's our duty." It tickled Hew that they could speak in code without Cook catching on. But then again, little got past the keen eye of Cook.

Henry looked away from his reflection and turned to his brother. "The Comtesse knew of Charles' promotion before I did, Hew," he said soberly, "so beware those women of subtle character."

"Well, Saint Henry," responded Hew, "I will say the same to you."

Cook rode with Adam, Henry, and Hew to the theater, where they disembarked amid a crowd of well-dressed Parisian elite. Cook stayed in the carriage. It was easy to find Hume in his Embassy uniform, and he led them to box seats. The walls and columns were painted gold, and the chairs were richly upholstered. Adam's heart fluttered when he saw Comtesse Boufflers in the adjoining box with an older man so resplendent he knew it must be the Prince d'Conti himself. She smiled and waved at him, which he returned, keenly aware of his relative frumpiness dressed in his plain black frock coat.

"A full house," observed Hume, "I hope the King attends; he comes seldom since the death of his son."

"Tragic to lose his only son to consumption," Adam nodded, looking across the theater at the ornate first box, reserved for the King whether he attended or not.

Hume pointed to a handsome woman, dressed less ostentatiously than most, sitting in a box with a distinguished man. "There is Julie Espinasse. We'll attend her salon later this week. Next to her is Jean d'Alembert, the mathematician." Adam recognized d'Alembert from Comtesse Boufflers salon but had not spoken to him directly.

"Look, there is Turgot!" said Henry, pointing. At his gesture, Turgot looked up towards their box and waved.

"He just arrived in Paris," said Hume.

"This is spectacle!" exclaimed Hew, "London is drab."

"Patriotism, Hew," admonished Henry with a laugh.

"Listen to your brother, Hew," Hume agreed with a smile, "It's my Embassy duty to tell you that. Look, the King!"

King Louis XV entered his box, dazzling in gold and white, draped with ermine. A tall, handsome man in his mid-fifties, he was without a queen or consort since the death of Madame Pompadour. He stood alone in his box as he waved to the crowd; everyone stood and applauded until he took his seat. Two servants sat discreetly behind him.

The heavy gold curtain opened to reveal an elaborately dressed man standing on the stage. He held up his hand to quiet the crowd. "Attention, please! We have special guests in the house this evening, May I present the famous Glasgow philosopher, Mr. Adam Smith!"

Adam was stunned to see the man pointing right at him, and all eyes turned his way. Hume nudged his elbow, so he stood to sustained applause. He waved awkwardly, self-consciously, aware that he was the most humbly dressed person in the entire building. He saw the King himself applauding, and a glance at the Comtesse showed her clapping energetically and beaming at him. With a gulp, he quickly resumed his seat.

"With Mr. Smith is Henry Scott, Third Duke of Buccleuch in Scotland!"

Henry stood briefly and waved to polite applause, then he quickly resumed his seat. Dukes took second place to philosophers apparently, but he took no offense.

Hew got ready to stand but forgot that he was the second son. Unannounced, he tried to look nonchalant as the announcer said, "Your Majesty, our guests, our audience, please enjoy the performance!"

The curtain closed, and Hume whispered to Henry, "I told him to say Scotland. The French like the Scots better than the English."

"But I have an English accent," said Henry quietly.

"Yes," Hume whispered back dryly, "I suggest that you don't mention the war."

The curtain opened to show the players in position for the first act, and the orchestra began.

• • • •

TEN O'CLOCK THE NEXT morning found Adam, Cook, Henry, and Hew eating a late breakfast together in the Parc Royale. The door opened to reveal a driving rain, and Hume strode in streaming. The same boy attendant came to take Hume's raincoat and held out his arms for it. Hume smiled, and walked to the cloak rack and hung it himself to keep it from being inevitably drug on the floor by the lad. He gave him a coin and a pat on the head regardless, then approached the table where everyone was watching him with pleasure, except perhaps Cook.

Hume spread his arms wide and announced in a booming voice, "The King requests the pleasure of your presence! Today!" Mouths full, they all gaped at him. Yet at two o'clock in the afternoon an exquisite white coach and six delivered them to the broad driveway of the Palace. Liveried attendants opened the carriage door, and they were greeted by a smartly turned major domo who escorted them into the vast marble Palace. Two soldiers fell into step behind them as they walked a long gilt hallway, with a ceiling that Henry thought impossibly high. Two attendants swept open the large carved doors at the end of the hall, and the major domo stepped aside so they could enter. The room was vast, ornate, golden; but the throne stood empty at the far end.

Hume, Adam, Henry, and Hew stood close together, wondering what they should do. In a moment, a side door opened, and the King entered, dressed elegantly but without robes, crown, or other extravagance. Known as Louis the Beloved, King since the age of five, he was still a man like any other.

Louis XV approached, greeting them informally, "Welcome, Hume. Welcome, Mr. Smith, Welcome, Duke Henry." Everyone bowed low, but he waved them up with his hands.

"Informal, informal, my guests," he said, "I want to talk of Toulouse. But first, who is this young man?"

"This is my brother, Hew Campbell Scott, Your Majesty," said Henry in a clear voice.

"Welcome Hew Campbell," said the King, smiling briefly but charmingly. "Please, sit," he gestured to a heavy, ancient table standing to one side of the room. The King sat at the head of the table, and they arranged themselves on either side. From another door, two ministers came in and took seats, one with a quill and paper as if to take notes. They were not introduced, so all eyes turned to King Louis XV.

"I have read the Treatise of Voltaire, and the sad story of Jean Calas," he said, looking at Adam. "I understand you were there."

"Only the execution, Your Majesty," replied Adam, "not the trial."

"I see," said the King, "It appears there was an injustice done. Do you agree?"

"I do, Your Majesty," stated Adam, "I agree with Voltaire's excellent words on the subject."

The King looked at Henry. He tried to speak in as firm a manner as Adam had. "I do agree, Your Majesty. I watched Jean Calas die. He died with honor, and I believe he died innocent."

The King pondered Henry for a long moment, seeing the tension this brought to the young man's face. Doubtless the Englishman had witnessed a terrible thing. He looked at Hew.

"I wasn't there, Your Majesty," said Hew, "I came later to cheer up Henry."

The King smiled and replied, "I hope you succeed." Turning to Adam and Henry, he added somberly, "I am sorry you witnessed such a spectacle in France. We are usually an enlightened nation."

Hume was attentive and saved them from trying to formulate a proper answer for this unexpected royal apology.

"I certainly find enlightenment here in Paris, Your Majesty," he volunteered diplomatically.

"Thank you, Hume," replied the King, "As an official representative of England, I want you to know how seriously we take this unfortunate incident, even though it is entirely an internal French matter."

"Yes, Your Majesty, thank you for including me," replied Hume gravely. Hume really was the ideal diplomat, although history in hindsight would say he was underemployed at the task. Similarly, Adam Smith puzzled historians by spending his last valuable years superintending Scottish customs instead of finishing his third book, a promised volume on jurisprudence.

"Voltaire's treatise is compelling," said the King, "I am reviewing the case of the Calas family. Duke Henry, what is your view of the magistrate's actions, David Beaudrigue?

Henry gulped and tried to formulate a calm answer to this direct and poignant question from the King. He wrestled with the bitterness he felt and won. "Your Majesty," he replied calmly, "I did not see the trial. But his performance at the torture and execution was shocking in the extreme." Henry took a deep breath to steady himself.

"How so?" asked the King.

"He whipped up the crowd... by mocking the victim during his torment." Henry found himself shaking and gripped the arms of his chair.

"But Jean Calas remained firm throughout his torture?" pressed the King in a gentle tone.

"It brought tears to my eyes, Your Majesty. Jean Calas convinced me of his innocence while broken on the wheel," replied Henry. Adam detected a small quaver in Henry's voice but was bursting with pride at his steady performance before the King.

Again, the King pondered Henry for a long moment; Henry could hear the rapid scratching of quill on paper, but he kept the eye of the King until he finally turned to Adam.

"And you, Mr. Smith?" he asked, "What is your view of the Magistrate Beaudrigue?"

"I stood next to Henry, and saw what he did, Your Majesty," replied Adam, "It appeared that the Magistrate was trying to turn the crowd against the Protestants, who have lived peaceably amongst them."

"Both England and France have had their share of religious bloodshed," said the King, "Let's hope those days are behind us. How long are you in Paris?"

"I expect at least a year, Your Majesty," Adam replied.

"Excellent!" smiled the King, "You must join us at our hunt next summer. We vacation at Compiegne for two weeks. Do you ride, Henry?" Gone was the somber tone of religious torture and executions, and relief swept Henry.

"I love horses, Your Majesty," replied Henry, smiling, "We'd be honored."

"Splendid," said the King. He turned to Hew, "As second son, do you have your regiment yet?"

"Er, no, Your Majesty, not yet." stammered Hew.

"Should you ever lead men into battle against France," said the King seriously, "remember our meeting here today. We are men just as you."

• • • •

WEEKS LATER, NEWS OF their meeting with King Louis XV reached Adderbury. As Charles read the letter silently, his face reflected a rising tide of pleasure and excitement. "Caroline, Caroline, come quickly," he shouted, grinning uncontrollably.

She rushed into the drawing room, expecting disaster. "What? Are the boys safe?"

Instead, Charles swept his wife into a rare embrace and danced her around the drawing room. "Safe? Why yes, they are!" he exclaimed as he spun her around, "They met the King of France!"

"Oh Charles, you do carry on so!" said Caroline, genuinely pleased. "That is wonderful news." Imagine what she'd say to the ladies at cards!

Charles took her on another turn around the room, skipping and singing, "The King of France! The King of France!" in an entirely undignified expression of his giddy happiness. Even Caroline had to smile at his infectious excitement.

Frances rushed in, saying "What news, Father?"

Charles let go of Caroline and waltzed Frances around the room. "The boys have met the King of France! He's invited them to go hunting with him!"

"How exciting for them!" exclaimed Frances happily as Charles spun his stepdaughter into an upholstered chair.

"Smith is paying off handsomely," Charles said to Caroline, "I'm off to London a day early." He shouted "Carriage" to the servants outside the room, then grabbed Caroline by both arms excitedly and added, "I want to brag about Henry at the club!"

• • • •

THE MORNING AFTER THEIR meeting with the King, Cook knocked on Henry's door at the Parc Royale. He balanced a tray with tea on one hand like a waiter. "Henry? I have your tea," Cook called through the door.

The next door opened and a rumpled Hew stepped out. "Morning, tea sounds great."

"Here, take this and I'll fetch more for Henry," replied Cook, handing him the tray.

Henry opened his door in time to see Hew take his first sip. "What? Only one cup, Cook?"

"I'll be back in a moment with more," said Cook, hurrying off.

"How often are you up before me, Hew?" accused Henry.

"You are a tough act to follow, brother," replied Hew, taking another satisfying drink of Henry's tea, "Rise at dawn, no gambling, hob-nobbing with the King, what have you."

"You have to be up early if you're commanding a regiment," replied Henry tartly.

"Yes, and as commanding officer I get first crack at hot tea and hot shaving water," Hew fired back, grinning, "You Parliamentarians can drink lukewarm tea in complete safety!"

Adam was in his apartment dressing himself. He hadn't acquired a valet in Paris, and he hated to ask Cook to perform such a personal service. He'd caught the tail of his coat in his trousers, and his shirt collar rode outside his coat collar in back. Missing both these sartorial faux pas while inspecting himself in the mirror, Adam adjusted his wig and stepped out of his room. He passed Cook in the hall as he returned with Henry's tea, and at the head of the stairs he spotted Hume in the lobby.

"Good morning, Hume!" he waved.

"Good morning, my friend," said Hume, "I just sent the boy for coffee. Interested?"

"Tea, yes," said Adam, arriving at the bottom of the stairs. Hume spotted Adam's coat mishap and reached out unobtrusively to correct them.

"I'm surprised you remembered your breeches, Mr. Smith," he said with a grin, "You are a bit disheveled."

"Oh, thank you," said Adam, embarrassed, "I don't want to ask Cook."

"I thought so," nodded Hume, who turned and snapped his fingers and called, "St. Jean!"

A smartly dressed young man, of middle height and whose café au lait skin indicated Caribbean ancestry, appeared promptly at Hume's side. "Oui, monsieur?"

"Mr. Smith, I present St. Jean, your new valet," announced Hume, "I have found him most satisfactory during my time in Paris. He will assist you."

"I'm pleased to meet you, St. Jean," replied Adam pleasantly as the valet bowed. Turning to Hume, he asked, "What might Charles say to the expense, I wonder? Cook may take it as an affront."

"I'm sure Charles assumes you have a valet, Mr. Smith," Hume said, "After meeting the King himself, I suspect you have wide latitude."

"I accept your service, St. Jean, gratefully," smiled Adam, nodding at the man. "Why are you willing to give him up?" he asked Hume as they were seated.

"I have news," Hume replied, "Lord Hertford has been recalled to London, and me with him. We depart as soon as his replacement arrives."

"Who will be the new ambassador?" asked Adam.

"Unsure. Lord Hertford asked to be relieved, so it was no reflection on his performance," said Hume.

"And you, Hume?" inquired Adam, "what are your plans? London? Edinburgh?"

"London, I'm sure," Hume answered, "I may be offered a Secretary of State post in the Chatham administration. I imagine I'll be here at least another month; it could be more."

"Hmmm, the philosopher as statesman?" Adam mused, hand on chin while smiling up at his tall, uniformed friend. Hume was a mountain of scarlet wherever he went.

"Yes, the philosopher," replied Hume with satisfaction, "and don't forget *historian*. I'm sure my History of England was read far more than my Treatise on Human Nature."

"Henry has read all through your History, and is puzzling through your Treatise," nodded Adam.

"Puzzling?" asked Hume with raised eyebrows.

Adam turned to find a kitchen servant, but St. Jean anticipated him. "What can I get you, monsieur?

"Sugar, if you please," said Adam, and St. Jean disappeared.

"He seems attentive enough," said Adam to Hume agreeably.

"He is the best servant I've ever had," replied Hume, "You don't have to rely on Mr. Cook. You know he spies for Townshend, don't you?"

I'd expect nothing less," answered Adam, "Charles has much riding on Henry's success."

"That's the open joke in London," replied Hume.

"Joke?" Adam's eyebrows went up at this.

"That Charles married into his wealth, and will use it to become Prime Minister," said Hume seriously, blowing on his coffee to cool it, "Ambitious chap, to say the least. He must make his move before Henry reaches his majority. Then it becomes Henry's money instead of Charles'.

St. Jean returned with the sugar and spooned some into Adam's cup until he raised his hand to stop him.

"Another thing," said Hume, "I've arranged for St. Jean to take you to a clothier today. We must update your wardrobe if you're to mingle with the King's Court."

"My wardrobe?" asked Adam, raising his eyebrows again.

Later that day, their carriage pulled up to a fancy storefront and St. Jean popped out. He held the door for Adam and then led the way inside, where the merchant welcomed them. "Monsieur, we are ready for you," he said, "please follow me."

"We?" thought Adam, but they followed; the man pulled aside a thick velvet curtain to reveal a large fitting room with several tall mirrors. Hume and Comtesse Boufflers rose from their chairs, surprising Adam completely.

"I hope you don't mind some help, Mr. Smith," said Hume, "The Comtesse is a foremost fashion authority." She certainly looked fashionable to Adam as she stood there, radiant, and his tongue failed him for a moment.

"I see," Adam stammered, "Comtesse, it's a pleasure, although somewhat embarrassing."

"Oh, don't be embarrassed, Mr. Smith!" she smiled disarmingly, "I will only offer my opinion, not help you dress."

The clothier, assisted by St. Jean, removed Adam's coat and measured him carefully. Pleased that his customer was a normal sized person, he began fitting Adam to the latest French fashion. Adam felt ridiculous, but he knew it was for his own good and the Comtesse was completely and utterly mesmerizing. As he stepped out for inspection after donning each suit behind another curtain, the Comtesse would offer her critical assessment. After she had accepted one outfit and rejected two, Adam stepped out in a red velvet suit lined with golden embroidery.

"I look like a court jester in this one," said Adam ruefully.

"That's redder than a regiment of redcoats!" laughed Hume, who was not wearing his uniform for this occasion.

"Would you two Scots feel more comfortable in tartan plaid?" inquired the Comtesse archly, "I declare it excellent, and you must wear it to Court."

"Ouch, Comtesse, that barb strikes deep!" protested Hume with a grin, "Tartan is still taboo, such is the fear the Young Pretender struck into London twenty years ago."

The Comtesse laughed, "I know, that's why I said it! Still, Mr. Smith, take my advice and buy that suit. I will find you a suitable occasion to show it off."

CHAPTER 23

E LOISE *August 1765*
Attended by St. Jean, Adam stood in front of a tall mirror in his room at the Parc Royale, admiring himself in one of his new suits. He knew his appearance was much improved, but still felt slightly ridiculous as he was so used to his traditional Scottish dress. Throughout their journey so far, his clothes had never been an issue, but now he was in Paris. There was a knock on the door; St. Jean opened it to reveal Cook.

"Who might you be?" asked Cook of St. Jean in a cool voice.

"Mr. Cook, this is St. Jean, my new valet," introduced Adam, "Hume recommended him."

"Bonjour, Monsieur Cook," said St. Jean respectfully, with a small bow.

Cook didn't respond to him other than a slight nod, then looked back to Adam. He noticed the new clothes but didn't comment on them, instead asking, "Will you require anything of me this afternoon? You and Henry are going out?"

"Yes, we're meeting Hume," Adam replied, "Unless Henry says otherwise, I don't need you today, Mr. Cook."

"Understood, thank you Mr. Smith," said Cook. He gave another long, cool look at St. Jean, and then closed the door behind him as he left.

St. Jean brushed an imaginary speck off Adam's shoulder and said, "Your carriage will arrive at three o'clock monsieur."

Precisely at three, a coach and four pulled up in front of the Parc Royale. St. Jean opened the hotel door for Adam, and he stepped out a bit self-consciously in his new clothes. As St. Jean opened the carriage door for him, another carriage pulled up behind them and Cook stepped out of it. Henry appeared behind Adam.

"Are we not riding together Mr. Smith?" asked Henry, puzzled by the two vehicles.

"I assumed we were, Henry," replied Adam, looking questioningly at St. Jean.

Henry asked Cook, "Is there a mix-up?"

"Yes, there is," replied Cook in a tart voice, "Mr. Smith's new valet took it upon himself to order a coach without consulting me."

"Oh, no harm, Mr. Cook, said Adam cheerfully, "Give your driver a coin for his effort, and we'll take this one."

"Mr. Smith, I am responsible for expenses. I arrange transportation," said Cook frostily.

"Oh, come now, Cook," said Henry, "Tip your man and let him go. We'll take Adam's coach."

"As you wish, Henry," Cook answered, as his eyes shot daggers at St. Jean. Adam's valet noticed Cook's ire but said nothing as he climbed into the carriage behind Adam and Henry. Cook remained behind as the driver snapped his whip and the horses pulled away.

"St. Jean, in the future please coordinate with Mr. Cook when Henry and I travel together," said Adam in a neutral tone.

"Oui, monsieur," nodded St. Jean, and he said no more.

"So, we're off to another salon," smiled Henry, "I see you've dressed for the occasion."

"Yes, I had assistance as you might suspect," answered Adam.

"Who?" asked Henry.

"St. Jean here, plus sartorial advice from Hume, and Comtesse Boufflers." Adam felt his heart flutter when he mentioned her name, but he gave no outward sign.

"The Comtesse was pleased to have you in her salon, she told me so," smiled Henry, guessing at his tutor's infatuation. Of all the famous people they'd met so far, she was the only one who appeared to make Adam nervous.

"We're the shiny new object, I suspect," replied Adam.

"You are, Mr. Smith," laughed Henry, "I'm just another well-dressed bystander."

"Hardly, Henry, they know you, and they know Charles," responded Adam.

"The Comtesse knew more about Charles than I did!" agreed Henry, "Did you know that he is Chancellor of the Exchequer?"

"I heard that just yesterday," nodded Adam.

"Still, I feel a bit out of place at these salons," said Henry.

"Don't be, they enjoy a distinguished audience," said Adam, "They love to talk; you're here to listen. A better classroom I couldn't imagine."

"Better to be seen than heard, you say?" smirked Henry.

"Not at all," replied Adam seriously, "In fact, be ready for their questions."

"We go to a different salon today?" Henry asked.

"Yes, Madame Espinasse," nodded Adam, "We'll meet Hume there."

The carriage pulled to a stop in front of an attractive but not ostentatious house located within walking distance of the Palace. Despite being in a nice neighborhood, they followed the house servant up a narrow flight of wooden stairs to a very plain door, where they clustered on a tiny landing while the servant knocked once. The door immediately opened, and they were ushered inside.

Julie Espinasse hosted a formidable salon, in the elite ranks of all salons in Paris, but it was the near opposite of the ornate setting at the Prince d'Conti's palace where Comtesse Boufflers operated. Although well-maintained and pleasantly furnished, there was no gilt, no marble, no glittering high ceilings. The room was plain, although the eighteen to twenty guests who filled it, all looking at them with cups in their hands, were well-dressed indeed. Adam's first impression was that his new suit matched the occasion, and then Hume in his scarlet Embassy uniform loomed before him. A greeting formed on Hume's lips but then he remembered his manners, clamped his mouth shut, and stepped aside to reveal Madame Espinasse, their hostess.

"Welcome, Mr. Smith! Welcome, Henry Scott!" she said graciously, with a short curtsey, as they bowed. "You honor us, please come in." Julie Espinasse, who they would always address as Madame, was exceptional in many ways. She was not a rich man's mistress, although it was rumored that she and Jean d'Alembert were more than friends. Raised and educated in a convent, by virtue of intelligence and beauty, she managed to gain sufficient means to operate her salon autonomously. She was a small woman, about five foot three, in her mid-thirties, conservative in her dress and with a keen wit sparkling behind her large, dark eyes. Most remarkable, Madame Espinasse was successful despite her lack of noble blood.

Since she didn't give her name, Hume jumped in to complete the introduction. "This is Madame Espinasse, hostess of the most intellectual salon in Paris," he said, and she smiled at him.

"I suspect Baron d'Holbach would argue that point," she smiled, "but thank you, Hume."

"Thank you for inviting us, Madame Espinasse, the honor is ours," Adam responded.

"Indeed, Madame," added Henry, "Hume speaks highly."

"Yes, yes, my dear Hume," agreed Madame Espinasse, putting her arm on his scarlet uniform sleeve and looking up at him, "He towers over us in more ways than one."

"Kind words for such a large philosopher, I am in your debt Madame," deadpanned Hume.

She kept her hold on Hume's arm, and said, "He's a large and lovable man, whether we consider his philosophy, his history, or his British diplomacy."

"You can see why I come here," smiled Hume, "the flattery is exquisite."

"Tea, coffee, claret?" she asked them, as a servant appeared at her elbow.

"Claret," both Adam and Henry answered simultaneously, and the servant vanished.

"Mr. Smith, I see someone has taken you shopping since I saw you at the theater," observed Madame Espinasse with a twinkle in her eye.

"Indeed, Madame, quite a change from what I'm used to," Adam replied, a bit self-conscious as the guests were beginning to crowd close behind his hostess and Hume. "How do I look, if I may be so bold as to ask?" Adam smiled and spread his arms.

"Like a perfect French gentleman," laughed Madame, but then she added, "But you don't have to be beautiful to attend my salon. We discuss serious things here, which is why you are so *particularly* welcome. We have read your Theory, monsieur."

Releasing Hume's arm and taking Adam's, she turned and began introducing Adam and Henry to the guests, who formed themselves into a line. Again, Henry realized that they were mostly interested in his humble tutor and after a while he drifted to the side of the room and took a refill of his glass from an attentive servant. He watched as the guests milled about Adam, attended closely by Hume. A young woman appeared at his side, holding a cup of tea.

"Such an honor to travel with a famous philosopher, is it not?" she asked, taking a sip. Henry turned to look, and her beauty struck him like a wave. She was elegantly dressed, with fine features and a generous mouth, and only a few inches shorter than himself.

"Yes, it is," he answered readily, "More than that, actually. Mr. Smith is a fine person. In the whole time I've been with him, we've never had a cool word between us."

"My first impression is of a warm and kindly man," she said as they watched Adam mingle, "Have you read his Theory?"

"Yes, and you?" Henry replied, absorbing with rising excitement that this beauty was close to his age, and obviously well-educated.

"I must wait for a proper French translation, I'm afraid," she said ruefully, "It seems a contradiction, a theory about sentiments. Thinking about feeling, no?"

"Exactly," answered Henry, nodding, wanting to be agreeable, "but not really. Hmmm..." and he ended by shaking his head. She waited, looking at him with calm eyes that he noticed were green, matching the auburn tone of her lustrous hair, arranged in a becoming but simple coiffure. "Sentiments aren't just feelings," he continued, earnestly, "they are more like... judgments we feel to be true. Does that make sense?"

"Oui, monsieur," she smiled at him, plainly, simply, bewitchingly.

"Call me Henry," he said, returning her smile.

"I'm Eloise, Henry," she replied, offering him a hand, which he took and bowed low over before releasing it. The skin on her hand was smooth, nails perfect, but the hand itself was rather large, with long, strong fingers.

"Most of his book seems like common sense," said Henry, suddenly voluble, "People care what others think of them, and we want to be liked. But then, somehow, it's deeper."

"How so, deeper?" she asked, with a tilt of her head.

"We see how others behave, but it's much deeper to think of how we behave," he said, "How others see us, and then, what we think of ourselves. That part is much more unsettling."

"I must read Mr. Smith's book as soon as I can," Eloise replied, "It seems it would apply to every single person in the world."

"Did you attend University, Eloise?" Henry asked, foolishly, but charmed by her elegant diction and obvious learning.

"Of course not, I am a woman," she laughed, "I was taught by private tutors."

"It's pleasing to discuss philosophy with a woman," said Henry, "It is usually a man's preserve."

"And whose fault is that monsieur?" Eloise asked with an elegantly raised eyebrow, "Girls are rarely educated in France. We are half the population. If our country is a bird, it flies with one wing only. This salon is one of the few places where ladies can discuss philosophy in all of France."

At that moment Madame Espinasse rang a small bell to announce two new arrivals. "Everyone!" she called out, here are Doctor Quesnay and Turgot!"

Henry was thankful for the distraction, as he'd sensed he'd said the wrong thing. They watched as Madame Espinasse took Quesnay and Turgot straight to Adam, and the group surrounding them parted in deference to the old physician and his student, Turgot. Too far away to hear their greetings, Henry noticed servants arranging chairs in a large oval.

Inside the cluster of guests, Madame Espinasse made introductions. "Quesnay, Turgot, may I present Mr. Adam Smith, the Scottish philosopher," she said, adding, "Dr. Quesnay is the King's physician, and the leading expert on the wealth of our country."

"We met on the canal boat, Mr. Smith," said Turgot pleasantly, "it's good to see you again."

"Likewise, Turgot," replied Adam, "An honor to meet you, Dr. Quesnay. I'll introduce you to Duke Henry when I get a chance."

"Monsieur Smith, your reputation precedes you," said Quesnay, "Your young student seems occupied with Eloise," he gestured towards the youngsters standing apart from the group. "He impressed the King, by the way."

"The King!" replied Adam, pleasantly surprised, "How so?"

"The King thought him very manly when they spoke of the Calas affair. 'Passionate but restrained' is how he put it. Admirable for such a young man," said Quesnay.

"He liked the cut of his jib, so to speak," offered Hume.

"Let's take seats so we can continue our discussion without fatigue," suggested Madame Espinasse. Henry and Eloise stood behind the oval of chairs as the others were seated, including Hume, Adam, Quesnay, Turgot, Madame Espinasse, and several others. The remaining guests stood or pulled up additional chairs to sit close enough to hear. Although quite informal, for the first time the leading French Physiocrats met with the stars of the Scottish Enlightenment, yet to the casual eye it was just a group of well-dressed people sitting in a circle of chairs.

Madame Espinasse started things off by asking Adam, "Mr. Smith, are you preparing Duke Henry for prosperity, politics, or pleasure? I understand he will be the largest landowner in Scotland?"

Henry felt all eyes upon him, including Eloise, who gave him an appreciative look.

"I can only help him make his own choices well," replied Adam, "I am fortunate in the quality of my student."

"Madame," said Henry, "rest assured that I pay close attention to everything Mr. Smith says."

"That's always been my policy as well," added Hume looking at his friend, "despite his youth." Hume was twelve years older than Smith.

Quesnay cleared his throat and began their discussion. "The war is over, and France is in debt. We must improve the yield of our farms. Turgot wants to simplify taxes, which will help. But since wealth ultimately comes from the land, that is where our focus lies."

"The wealth of the land is undeniable," agreed Smith, "but labor is the real measure of the value of all commodities. The price of everything is the toil and trouble of acquiring it."

"I agree with Mr. Smith," added Hume, "everything in the world is purchased by labor."

Quesnay and Turgot exchanged looks, and Quesnay nodded to him as if to say, "you take this."

"The peasants go with the land," said Turgot, "their labor is presumed. Their work embellishes the natural productivity of the fields."

"In Scotland," returned Adam, "the land would yield little without the work of the farmer. France is far more fertile than Scotland, but I suspect the farmer is just as important here."

"The peasants come and go, but the land endures," said Quesnay.

"But what motivates the people to farm diligently?" asked Hume.

"Hunger!" said a wag standing behind the chairs, and a ripple of laughter swept the room, but the key participants stayed serious.

"Or hope," said Adam. "Consumption is the sole end and purpose of all production. People aspire to more than just survival. Raising a family, and providing them comfort, for instance. What is prudence in the conduct of every private family can scarce be folly in that of a great kingdom.”

“Some of that production must be saved, must it not?” inquired Madame Espinasse, “To add to a nation’s wealth? How can a nation grow rich without a large store of gold?”

“A nation is not made wealthy by the accumulation of shiny metal; it’s enriched by the economic prosperity of its people,” replied Adam, “Labor, not gold and silver, is how all the wealth of the world was originally created.”

Eloise spoke up, asking, “But Monsieur Smith, gold and silver are permanent, while consumption is fleeting. How can a nation accumulate wealth by consuming all the product of its lands?” Impressed, Henry looked sidelong at Eloise with a growing infatuation as she spoke. She was as smart as she was pretty.

“A good question Mademoiselle,” answered Adam, “Not all production is consumed immediately. Some money is spent on things that last, like furniture, pots and pans, ships, houses. But if permanence was the measure of wealth, could not a nation become rich by accumulating durable pots and pans?” Everyone laughed at this, including Eloise, demonstrating confidence and a fine temper to go with wit and beauty. As young as she was, she was not intimidated by the crowd of eminent people surrounding her. Adam continued, “The wages of labor encourage industry, if the worker can keep some of the gains. Individual ambition can thus serve the common good.”

“Avarice, the spur of industry!” joked Hume and got another laugh. Henry thought Eloise looked angelic when she smiled.

“Increasing the wages of labor increases the price of the goods, does it not?” countered Turgot.

"It also increases the workers' ability to buy them," returned Adam, "Is this improvement in the lives of the lowest ranks of people to be regarded as an advantage, or inconvenience, to society?"

At that moment the door opened without a knock, and King Louis XV stepped into the room. Madame Espinasse sprang to her feet and curtsied deep. "Your Majesty," she said gravely.

"Ah, there you are Quesnay," said the King, "I have a boil on my..." He pointed at his ass to spare the word.

Quesnay rose and said, "Of course, Your Majesty," and followed the King out the door. Everyone resumed their seats and Madame Espinasse beamed.

"Surely, the leading men of France are found in my salon!" she said with satisfaction.

Later, Eloise approached Madame Espinasse as she was talking in a small group with Henry, Adam and Hume. "I must be going, Madame," said Eloise, pulling on her gloves, "thank you for your hospitality."

Madame Espinasse turned and took both of Eloise's gloved hands in hers. "You are always welcome here my dear Eloise!"

Eloise turned to Henry and said formally, "It was a pleasure to meet you, Duke Henry."

"The pleasure is mine, Eloise," Henry returned, "May I escort you to your carriage?"

"Yes, thank you," she smiled demurely.

Henry offered his arm, and they walked out the door. Madame Espinasse passed a knowing smile to Adam and Hume, as the attraction between Henry and Eloise seemed obvious to all.

Henry walked her down the narrow stairs and out into the evening sunshine. Smiling, Henry turned and took both her hands in his. Eloise was flushed and radiant. "When may I see you again, Eloise?" he asked, trying to sound calm while his heart beat furiously.

She didn't answer immediately, and he helped her step up into her open carriage. He closed the carriage door as she was seated, and then she looked down at him standing in the driveway. Through lowered lashes she asked invitingly, "Will you be attending the Harvest Ball, Henry?"

CHAPTER 24

R OUSSEAU *August 1765*
The orchestra played a sprightly tune, and the colorful dancers swirled across the broad dance floor, surrounded by a ring of spectators, with everyone dressed in their finest. Henry and Eloise had eyes only for each other, but the onlookers kept an eye on them; Eloise because of her graceful beauty, and Henry because of his handsome and alluring wealth. Hew danced past them, a smile plastered on his face, but Henry didn't have time to focus on Hew. He was dazzled by Eloise.

The dance ended and they stepped to the side to catch their breath. "Henry, that was delightful!" said Eloise, clutching his arm close.

"You dance beautifully, Eloise, I can only hope to keep up," replied Henry, looking at her and putting his hand over hers. He was slightly flushed and damp from his exertions, and she was glowing.

"Excuse me for a moment, Henry. Don't run off with anyone!" said Eloise and she left for the ladies' room. Hew appeared at his side the moment she left.

"Hew, the lessons paid off!" said Henry, putting his arm around his perspiring brother. They'd spent considerable time at dance lessons at Ferney.

"Yes brother," panted Hew, "I'm trying to avoid embarrassment in front of all this beauty." Hew pointed towards a pretty girl across the room; she noticed and gave him a small wave of her hand as encouragement. "Eloise seems lovely?" he noted, seeing that his brother was head over heels.

"And smart," replied Henry nodding his head, "you should have heard her at Madame Espinasse's salon."

"You're quite the intellectual, Henry, but don't talk her to death," advised Hew with a grin.

Henry raised his eyebrows and answered him archly, "Am I to take advice from my younger brother?"

"Yes," replied Hew promptly, "Perhaps I *am* born to command."

"Or perhaps not," said Henry, "You should attend a salon with me. It's more than just chit-chat."

"Just put me up on a horse, in a bright red uniform, and give me a noble and glorious end with a musket ball right between the eyes," said Hew, suddenly fierce, "Spared the chit-chat, by God!" Amidst the gayety, Hew let a dark note creep into his voice, making Henry wonder. "Father would approve," muttered Hew.

Henry looked at his brother with concern, and said, "I'd rather chit-chat, Hew."

Just then the girl crossed the room to claim Hew, and they joined the dancers on the floor. Henry was relieved to see Hew smiling again as he danced. Eloise appeared at his elbow, with two cups of punch. They stood close, side-by-side, as they watched the others dance. Henry pointed to where Comtesse Boufflers was gently trying to get Adam to join the dancers, but he kept shaking his head. It occurred to Henry that he'd never seen Adam dance or heard him sing, although he frequently talked about the music he enjoyed. The Comtesse looked elegant, as did Adam in one of his new suits. Henry and Eloise watched as a man claimed the Comtesse, and Adam took a seat at a table with Hume. The Comtesse was graceful and a very accomplished dancer, as was the man she danced with. Henry noted that Adam watched her the whole time, and when the dance was complete, the Comtesse immediately returned to sit near Adam. "I guess he really is the shiny new attraction," thought Henry, but apparently his tutor couldn't dance a lick.

At the next number, Eloise pulled Henry back to the floor and they became lost in each other's eyes and steps again. As they spun around with the other dancers, Henry spotted Hew slipping out a side door with the girl. As the dance finished, Henry and Eloise were warm and starting to perspire. "Perhaps we can step outside, where it's cooler?" suggested Henry, taking her elbow.

"Yes," said Eloise, closing her hand over his, "I'm quite flushed."

Henry led her through a side door, and they found themselves in a long, cool hall of marble, with large Roman columns marching down the corridor in even formation. He pulled Eloise into the shadow of one of the columns and took her in his arms, kissing her, and was overjoyed to find that she returned his kiss willingly. They kissed, and then kissed again and again. Her full lips were warm and soft, and her arms circled his neck. As they kissed, Henry's hands wandered to her waist, then crept up until the palms of his hands brushed the underside of her bosom.

"No, Henry, no," Eloise murmured, catching his hands and trapping them with both of hers.

"Oh Eloise," Henry whispered, kissing her again, but she still held both his hands with hers.

"No, Henry," she said more firmly, pulling back.

"Why?" he softly implored, loving the touch of her hands even as she restrained his.

"It would be awkward," she said firmly.

"How so? We are young, and it's so... natural," Henry breathed, "and you're so beautiful." He leaned in again, but Eloise disengaged one hand and planted it squarely against his breast and pushed him back gently but resolutely. She looked him in the eye.

"It would be awkward explaining your bastard child after *you* return to England," she said clearly, then added, "I like you Henry, but no."

Eloise stepped back and composed herself briefly, then tried to restore some formality to her voice. "Good night, Henry, I hope to see you at salon."

Henry stood dumbfounded but could find no response as her words were obviously true. He was keenly disappointed, seeing her radiant loveliness in the dim light, feeling the soft lingering impression of her lips on his, and given her obvious attraction to him. Eloise leaned in suddenly and gave him a swift kiss on the cheek, and then marched off proudly. Just before she left the hallway, she gave herself away by sneaking a quick look back at Henry, rooted to the spot and still watching her.

The next morning Henry sat at his breakfast table drinking coffee in the late mid-morning. Hew came downstairs, looking rumpled with his hair tousled, and sat down across from his brother.

"Morning," Henry said, while waving his arm for the attendant. "Coffee?" he ordered from across the room, and the attendant nodded.

"So how did it go last night with Eloise?" inquired Hew once he'd taken his first sip.

"A proper gentleman doesn't discuss such things Hew," scolded Henry.

"Oh bother," said Hew, "you can be discreet." He leaned forward eagerly and added, "Just be detailed as well."

Henry sighed and took a drink of his coffee before replying, "She spurned me, Hew."

"No!" said Hew, "she seemed to like dancing with you. What was your blunder?"

"No blunder," responded Henry, stung. "Eloise knows I'm going back to England. She doesn't want to be left with, well, consequences."

Hew held up his hand, palm out. "Yes, say no more. I understand. Sensible really." He sat there, sagely nodding his head, and then added, as a huge grin spread across his face, "Glad they're not all like that!"

Adam came down the stairs and saw them eating. Approaching their table, he asked, "Any interest in attending Comtesse Boufflers' salon this afternoon?"

"Er, not for me, Mr. Smith," stammered Hew, "I, ah, plan to read in the garden." Adam perked up with interest and Hew immediately saw his mistake.

"What are you reading? How are you doing on your assignments?" asked Adam.

"I can't lie to you, Mr. Smith," confessed Hew, "I plan to sit in the garden holding my head. Don't tell Cook or he'll put it in his letters."

"A late night, I see," nodded Adam, "My friend Ben Franklin would say, *early to bed and early to rise, makes a man healthy, wealthy, and wise.*"

"I'll ponder that wisdom today, with coffee," said Hew.

"I met Ben Franklin, Hew," said Henry, "He had lots of quips like that one."

"How about you, Henry?" asked Adam, "the Comtesse asked for you by name."

"Please send her my regards, Mr. Smith, I must take the day off today," he replied with a shake of his head.

"I see this isn't the time to discuss scholastics. Let me leave you with one more tip from Mr. Franklin, *lost time is never found again*," Adam said smugly. He let a long moment pass, then added, "So, see you at supper?"

Adam entered the foyer of the Palace d'Conti escorted by a servant. He was spotted immediately by Comtesse Boufflers, who detached herself from the throng and came to greet him. Her guests had their backs to the door, engrossed in something on the other side of the room. The Comtesse gave both her hands to Adam, and he felt a thrill as he took them into his own.

"Monsieur Smith, so glad to see you today," she smiled, overwhelming him yet again. She had a way of looking straight into his eyes, as if only he mattered in the whole world.

"Good day, Comtesse," is all Adam could manage in reply.

Hume filled the doorway behind them and called out his greetings as they turned to him. "Hello, hello, my dear Smith. Hello, Comtesse," he boomed. A few in the crowd turned to see who had arrived, but most stayed occupied.

Comtesse Boufflers hooked an arm in each Scot and proudly walked them across the room, saying, "Here I have the leading lights of Scotland. I hear you were both at Julie's?"

Hume stopped their march and explained, "Yes, Comtesse, but don't take offense. Quesnay and Turgot were there. The King even popped in for a moment."

"You can't fool me, David," the Comtesse admonished, "Julie Espinasse invites ladies to her salon. In fact, I've poached one." She turned just as Eloise approached them.

"Hello, Monsieur Smith, is Henry coming today?" asked Eloise plainly. Adam remembered the joy he'd seen in the young couple the night before, so it was hard to let her down.

"He sends his regards, but no, not today," Adam said, "A late night, it seems."

Eloise nodded, knowingly, and Adam blushed as he regretted his choice of words. She said, "Henry dances well; he's not as stiff as some of our English visitors."

"Greetings, Lady Eloise," said Hume, "Comtesse, you should invite more such ladies, your crowd would grow ever larger."

"Perhaps," nodded the Comtesse, but then she stage-whispered, "too much competition!" Eloise heard and laughed, evidently it would be a friendly competition if there was one. The four of them stood behind the rest of her guests, still with their backs turned. Comtesse Boufflers clapped her hands twice, sharply. "Everyone! Please make a path so I can introduce Mr. Smith and Mr. Hume!" she called out. The musical effect of her voice could be both authoritative and charming at the same time. Backs straightened, people turned, and an aisle formed leading to a diminutive but handsome man, about fifty, sitting in a chair. He rose as they approached; the man stood a bit over five feet tall and was utterly dwarfed by Hume.

"Jean-Jacques Rousseau, allow me to introduce my Scottish friends, David Hume and Adam Smith," she said in a clear voice, as the group of forty crowded close to hear.

"An honor to meet you Monsieur Smith, and you, Monsieur Hume," said Rousseau in a high, reedy voice, "I am familiar with your works."

"And we, yours, my dear Rousseau," said Hume graciously, "What a pleasure to meet the man behind the books."

Rousseau fidgeted nervously, unsettled by the size of Hume, and said, "Every artist wants to be applauded, I suppose. You have an interesting theory of sentiments, Mr. Smith."

"Thank you, Monsieur," replied Adam, "your thoughts on education are very thought-provoking."

"Hah!" Rousseau barked, making Adam jump slightly, "We compliment each other without revealing our judgements."

"Complicated subjects defy simple evaluation, no?" Adam responded, taken aback by Rousseau's manner.

"You hold that our happiness depends upon the opinions of others," said Rousseau in a tone that was part challenge, part accusation. The crowd behind leaned in at the prospect of verbal fireworks at the first meeting between the philosophers.

"We seek the approval of our fellows, yes," answered Adam calmly.

"Why should we build our happiness on the opinions of others, when we can find it in our own hearts?" asked the combative Frenchman, "The sociable man is capable of living *only* in the opinions of others and derives the sentiment of his own existence *solely* from their judgement."

"Solely?" asked Hume.

"Only?" remarked the Comtesse.

"I would answer, Monsieur Rousseau, that the lonely man is rarely happy. We are not self-contained, we need each other," said Adam.

"What a lovely sentiment, Monsieur Smith," said Comtesse Boufflers, in front of everyone.

Eloise added, "How can we find happiness in our hearts without the love of others?" The crowd all murmured their appreciation, impressed by the new guest.

Rousseau looked flustered, his hands fluttered, but then he composed himself to respond, with all eyes upon him, "Nature made me happy and good, and if I am otherwise, it is society's fault; the result of poor education and oppression."

"A wise man proportions his belief to the evidence," replied Hume, "No human institution will ever reach perfection, especially education."

"It's rare that women are educated at all," added Comtesse Boufflers.

"Only Scotland educates her peasants," said Hume, "So they can better read the Bible, of course," he added to a smattering of laughter; mocking religion had become fashionable in the Paris salons.

"I can assure you that we Scots are reading everything we can lay our hands on," said Adam, "with education, knowledge lies open to all." He hoped he could divert a discussion that was flirting with contention.

"What good would it be to possess the whole universe, if one were it's only survivor?" asked Rousseau rhetorically, and the crowd nodded as if the discussion had ended in agreement. Adam noted that for someone who forswore the opinions of others, Rousseau was keenly interested in the reactions of the guests to his words.

Comtesse Boufflers clapped her hands and announced, "a light luncheon is served, everyone! If you don't see what you like, ask."

As the group lined up to load their plates at the long serving table, Rousseau tried to be cordial, saying, "I'm famished. A feeble body makes a feeble mind."

"After you, Rousseau," said Hume genially, gesturing for Rousseau to go ahead of him, "It would be unseemly if the largest philosopher goes first."

"My appetite is as big as you are, Hume!" said the small man, suddenly upbeat, "Look! Oysters!"

Hume picked up a plate and eyed the sumptuous fare. "Self-denial is a monkish virtue," he observed dryly, taking a double helping of the aromatic cheese dish.

"Woe to him who has nothing left to desire!" replied Rousseau, smiling.

As Rousseau and Hume led the way down the buffet table, Comtesse Boufflers followed Adam and pointed out the best servings. "Do you like oysters, Mr. Smith?" she asked.

"Yes, please, Comtesse, a rare treat," replied Adam.

"Only when they're fresh, like these," the Comtesse replied, wrinkling her nose as if they were the opposite. She laughed, and Adam couldn't keep his eyes off her and on the food. She was so close, and paid him such gracious attention, that he was aware of little else. No one noticed his evident infatuation, as most of the other men were orbiting the newcomer, Eloise. Hume and Rousseau sequestered themselves at a table, absorbed in conversation as they ate.

As the Comtesse and Adam seated themselves at a small table, she indicated the crowd around Eloise and wryly said, "You see why I am judicious about who I invite."

"I wonder if Henry knows who he is missing today," said Adam, meaning Eloise and not the famous philosopher Rousseau.

"I suspect sweet Eloise asked to attend in the hopes of seeing your Duke Henry," she said, looking across the room at the popular girl, "How could I say no to her?"

"You have a kind heart, Comtesse," replied Adam, meaning for himself more than Eloise.

"Love is the great good in the world," she answered, catching Adam's eye and holding it, "We all naturally desire, not only to be loved, but to be lovely. To be worthy of love. Don't you agree, Monsieur Smith?"

Adam was struck dumb as he recognized his own words from his book, quoted back to him from this lovely French Comtesse, in her musical voice, woven seamlessly into their conversation. Adam fell head over heels in love at that moment, but not even he knew it fully. "You do me great honor, Comtesse, to quote from my book," Adam gulped awkwardly, a lump in his throat.

"I hope to translate it into French, Mr. Smith. You write beautifully, and with such lovely sentiments," she replied, smiling radiantly.

"I... can only say... that you are lovely yourself, Comtesse," blurted Adam, and he blushed furiously to her happy satisfaction.

That night Adam, Henry, Hew, and Cook sat at supper in the Parc Royale. Servants were just bringing their drinks when Hume arrived from the Embassy. "Greetings, fellow Scots," said Hume, "Do you have room for another?"

"We surely do, Hume," answered Adam. He was in a very good mood that evening, it was plainly evident to Henry and Hew. Servants brought Hume a chair and a glass of wine, and everyone moved over to make space for him.

"Henry, someone was looking for you today at Comtesse Boufflers' salon," announced Hume.

"Did you get their name?" asked Henry, interested but not suspecting.

"Eloise," said Adam, smiling. Hume and Henry both looked at Adam, Henry for information and Hume because Adam had stolen his thunder. "She was the star attraction," added Adam, thinking privately that no woman could top the dazzling Comtesse.

Henry flushed and said, "I can imagine."

"Eloise took my side in a discussion with Rousseau," continued Adam, "More than just a pretty face, I assure you."

Hume nodded his agreement and added, "But what a pretty face, as we can all certainly agree."

"Comtesse Boufflers is also a handsome woman, wouldn't you say Mr. Smith?" commented Henry in reply, and he was pleased to see the impact it had on his tutor. Adam flushed uncharacteristically and looked at his plate.

"Ah, er, certainly, she's a charming woman," he said at last.

Henry smiled hugely and said, "Oh, she has her charms all right!"

Hew piped up with, "You never told me all this chit-chat was with beautiful women. Perhaps I *will* go."

"Their beauty is the bait, Hew," said Hume, "Most of the fish are silly grown men who enjoy being flattered excessively. Me, for instance. But Eloise met the moment, I agree with Mr. Smith."

"Who is this Rousseau?" asked Henry.

"Jean-Jacques Rousseau is a famous philosopher from Geneva. His writings are quite liberal, and often meet with censure here in France," Adam answered, eager to divert the discussion away from his embarrassment over the Comtesse.

"You met this famous man today at the salon?" Henry asked.

"Yes, both Hume and I met him for the first time," Adam replied.

"Is it *your* censure that kept this famous Rousseau off our reading list?" asked Henry, pointedly.

"No, not censure," said Adam uncomfortably, "you can read whatever you wish."

"Mr. Smith and I are unsure of Rousseau's principles, you see," said Hume.

Henry raised his eyebrows and asked, "How so?"

"We have both read much of Rousseau," answered Hume, "and we wanted to meet him. We got our wish today. Adam jousted admirably with support from Eloise. I then had a long talk with Rousseau over oysters."

"I'm interested, Hume," said Adam.

"Rousseau is a paradox," observed Hume, "Sometimes his insight is rare and fine, and other times, well, shocking."

"Shocking? That sounds dramatic," said Hew.

"For instance," continued Hume, "Rousseau said, 'man is born free, but is everywhere in chains.' He seems to think that human society corrupts us humans, instead of the other way around."

"I like the idea that we're not born sinful; that man is naturally good," said Henry.

"It's a lovely thought," agreed Hume, "but I quibble with his view of human nature." Hume took a drink of wine and paused while food was set on the table. Over the clatter of utensils, Hume continued in a slightly louder voice, "His idea of our natural state is something like, 'happy man running naked through the garden."

"Like Adam and Eve!" said Henry, laughing.

"I have a thought," announced Hew. Everyone stopped and looked at him. "What, you think I've never had a thought enter my head?" he said, acting astonished.

"You've had a thought, Hew," answered his brother, "I'm waiting to hear the second one!" Everyone laughed, including Cook, who had otherwise remained silent. Hew pretended to punch Henry's arm.

"One day in school we spent a whole hour talking about something said by Thomas Hobbes, an ancient Scot," continued Hew, "Hobbes said, 'the life of man is solitary, poor, nasty, brutish, and short."

"That is exactly what he said, good for you, Hew," complimented Hume sincerely.

"That seems the opposite of happy naked man in the garden, don't you think?" concluded Hew.

"It is indeed, Hew," confirmed Adam, pleased by his student, "although Hume, I don't think Rousseau used the word *naked*.

Jean-Jacque believes that man in his natural state is better than man in society."

"The question is, why does he see society as *chains*?" said Hume, "I, personally, *love* society. That's just me. That's where we quibble. Human nature is the science of man; and yet its study has been most neglected. How else to explain such different views of mankind?"

"Rousseau's view seems more optimistic," responded Henry, "Hobbes' view of man is so dark."

"Thus, the charm of Rousseau," said Adam, "but is such optimism warranted?"

"Mankind in chains seems optimistic to you?" asked Hume with raised eyebrows, "Study history to discover the principles of human nature. Look to the evidence."

"I agree, we are born to society," nodded Adam, "there is no separating man from his fellows."

"Rousseau is fascinating, and I will continue to engage him," said Hume, "Truth springs from arguments between friends."

"Mr. Smith assigned us your history of England, Hume," said Henry, "Easy to read; you write so clearly."

"Why, thank you Henry!" beamed Hume, "My friend Mr. Smith is a great teacher, he assigns all the best books."

Henry said slyly, "But Hume, I missed the lesson on human nature buried in your History."

"For that, you must buy my first book, *A Treatise on Human Nature*," replied Hume, smiling broadly. His smile turned down, and with perfect comic timing he added, "No one else did!"

Everyone exploded with laughter, including Cook. Hume's personality was irresistible, his humor usually self-deprecating. After the laughter died, with Hume greatly pleased by his performance, Adam said, "As a student at Oxford, I was punished for having a copy of Hume's treatise. It was considered scandalous."

"Why scandalous?" asked Hew.

"Rather less religion than what the Oxford deans were comfortable with, I expect," answered Hume, "It's harder to avoid censure than to gain applause."

"Are you an atheist, Hume?" asked Henry, hoping the man would speak openly amongst friends. Cook stared at Hume, obviously interested in a conversation he did not join.

"I don't have enough faith to believe there is no God," replied Hume seriously, "Nothing exists without a cause; the original cause of the universe we call God."

CHAPTER 25

T HE KING AND CALAS *September 1765*
St. Jean helped Adam into his jacket and put the finishing touches on his appearance, as they stood before the mirror in the room at the Parc Royale. "I'm always surprised when I see myself in these colorful French outfits," Adam said, "we Scots are much more subdued."

"You look handsome, monsieur," demurred St. Jean, "When in Rome, do as the Romans do."

"That is fine insight, St. Jean," he replied, admiring his French look despite his natural Scottish rectitude.

"Come in," he called as a knock came at the door. Cook entered, ignoring St. Jean as usual.

"Mail for London, Mr. Smith?" said Cook, "I'll be sending a messenger today."

"Yes, Mr. Cook, please take that letter to Charles lying on the dresser," replied Adam, adjusting his wig.

Cook retrieved the letter and left without another word. Adam looked at St. Jean, who wore his typical neutral expression. "How are you and Cook getting along?" asked Adam.

"Fine, monsieur," St. Jean replied, remaining entirely neutral and thus giving Adam no clues.

"He seems dismissive with you," Adam probed.

"He believes me below his station," responded St. Jean simply.

"Do you believe that?" Adam pressed gently.

"It does not matter; I serve you monsieur," said St. Jean, unruffled.

"If Cook doesn't speak to you, how can you arrange, say, our carriages?" asked Adam, finally getting a slight reaction from his polished young servant.

"Monsieur Cook would not tell me whether he had already arranged transportation," said St. Jean, matter-of-factly. Adam could detect no bitterness in his tone.

"I see," he said through pursed lips.

• • • •

THE WEATHER WAS GETTING cold at Adderbury that late in the year, and Charles sat comfortably before a warm fire in the drawing room. He lit his pipe with a brand from the fire and blew a large plume of smoke into the room.

Frances entered, announcing, "Letters have arrived, Father." She ran to hug Charles, then handed him the bundle.

"Thank you dear," he said, looking them over, "tell Mother there are letters from France, will you?" Frances skipped out, and Charles returned to his armchair and opened all the letters with a penknife. Pulling two sheets from the thinnest envelope, he set the rest on the armchair side table. Caroline swept into the room, followed by Frances.

"Any news from Henry and Hew?" asked Frances hopefully.

"Frances, give us some time," scolded Caroline, "We'll tell you the news in due course. Give us some privacy." Disappointed, Frances walked out much slower than she'd come in.

"Letters from Smith and Cook, but none from the boys, I'm afraid," informed Charles.

"Again?" said Caroline, "You'd think Mr. Smith could get them to write more."

"I wish Smith would write more," said Charles, "He's so miserly with ink you'd think he was writing in his own blood. Look at this Caroline, just two thin sheets."

"What does he say? Are the boys well?" asked Caroline eagerly.

Charles scanned the letter quickly. "The boys are well, that's the first thing he says. They met the Ambassador…., danced at the Harvest Ball, saw the King again! He says it was brief, but every visit with the King is significant! Excellent! Here, Caroline, you read it."

Caroline took up the sheets, saying, "Not a single complaint from the boys, I'll say that for your Mr. Smith." Once she'd absorbed his brief letter she added, "I just wish they'd write more."

"And then there's Cook," sighed Charles as he opened the fat envelope and unfolded the many sheets within. "More detail than I could ever imagine."

Just outside the door Frances stood listening.

The following evening Charles arrived in London, and had the carriage drop him off at his London club instead of his rented house. He strode inside, tossing his cloak and hat to the valet as he grandly entered the well-appointed club room. The other patrons knew him well, and appreciated the entertainment he provided, even though his reputation was that of a blowhard. But he was a politically powerful man on the rise, so they paid him the attention he craved. Charles raised his hands in the center of the room and announced in a loud voice, "Gentlemen! I have news from France!"

"What? War again?" a wag called out, garnering a smattering of laughter.

"Henry has *again* met with the King of France!" said Charles proudly.

"Peace at last!" said the wag, raising a glass to a roar of laughter, including Charles. He pulled Adam's letter from his vest and waved it around as evidence, as the group gathered around to hear the embellished details.

On the far side of the room, in an armchair turned away from the group, sat Ben Franklin, the American colonial representative in London. It gave him satisfaction that the young man he'd met in the London bookstore was doing well, as was Ben's friend Adam. Both seemed as opposite Charles Townshend as could be imagined.

• • • •

IT WAS BLUSTERY OVERCOAT weather in Paris as Henry, Hew, and Adam rode a carriage to Madame Espinasse's salon. Watching the street scene from the window, Henry again found himself noticing the shoes of the various classes of people.

"So, this is the salon that invites women?" asked Hew.

"It's where I met Eloise," answered Henry.

"Don't get the wrong impression, Hew," cautioned Adam, "This is the most intellectual salon we've attended. Listen carefully and you'll learn much."

"Will Hume be there? He is quite humorous for an old man," asked Hew.

"Not today," Adam responded, "Hume has Embassy business. He'll soon return to England with Lord Hertford."

"I'll miss him. Will Eloise be there?" asked Hew, the boy with a thousand questions.

"I don't know, do you Henry?" said Adam.

Henry hesitated, then shrugged and said nothing. "So…, maybe this salon will just be… conversation?" asked Hew doubtfully.

Adam turned to Hew and said firmly, "Society and conversation are the best way to restore tranquility and preserve a happy temper, which is necessary for satisfaction and enjoyment. No man is happy alone, Hew." Adam resisted the temptation to wag his finger at the boy.

"Who said anything about being alone? Paris is full of interesting people," smirked Hew, looking at ladies as they passed outside the carriage window.

The boys climbed the narrow stairs to the salon, followed by Adam, shedding their overcoats as they went. The door was opened by Madame Espinasse herself, and a young woman guest took their coats.

"Greetings Mr. Smith, Duke Henry," said Madame Espinasse, "and who is this handsome youngster?"

"Madame, this is my brother, Hew Campbell Scott," introduced Henry, as behind his hostess he saw Eloise approaching. He stiffened as Madame Espinasse and Hew exchanged pleasantries, but greeted her formally, "Hello, Eloise." She looked radiant, elevating his heart rate.

"Hello, Henry, hello Mr. Smith," she said with a brief curtsey, "a pleasure to see you, Hew."

Hew bowed low and answered gallantly, "The pleasure is mine, Lady Eloise," causing Henry to roll his eyes. Several guests arrived behind the two women, including Quesnay and Turgot.

"Monsieur Smith, may we claim you?" asked Quesnay, "We have more questions."

"And I for you, Doctor," smiled Adam, going with them, calling back over his shoulder "Every man lives by exchanging!" Madame Espinasse followed them, leaving Henry and Hew alone with Eloise.

"Something to drink?" asked Eloise. The boys scanned the room and saw no servants at all.

"I'd love some claret," said Henry, "No servants today?"

"Madame dismisses them when there might be frank talk," replied Eloise.

"Who is Frank?" asked Hew.

Eloise laughed and explained, "Some of the guests are atheists. Sometimes the servants complain to their abbe, which can be awkward. So, Madame dismisses them to allow free expression."

The boys fell in behind Eloise as she led them to a table with food and drinks. Hew, star-struck by the elegant Eloise, whispered to Henry, "Oh you blundered, brother!"

She filled their glasses, then they joined the group listening to Adam, arriving in time to hear him say, "Commerce and manufactures can seldom flourish if there is not enough confidence in the justice of government."

"Justice for the traders, or justice for all?" asked Madame Espinasse.

"No society can be flourishing and happy when the greater part is poor and miserable," Adam replied, "nor as wealthy as it could be."

"How would we raise the level of justice, and thus the confidence to invest?" asked Turgot, pragmatically, "Whatever is right, may be done. We have only to decide, and then do it."

Henry felt a small touch on his elbow and turned to see Eloise beckon him away, so he followed her to the far side of the room. Alone, she said, "I missed you at Comtesse Boufflers salon."

Relief flooded Henry at her intimate manner and tone, and he said, "I heard you were the star of the show."

"Nonsense," she smiled, "Monsieur Smith was, as he is today. He is too modest to say so."

"Eloise, I hope I haven't offended you," said Henry earnestly.

"Just the opposite, Henry," she replied softly, "I like you. But I mean what I said."

"Yes," nodded Henry, but wanting to touch her even more.

They looked up from each other's eyes as the door opened with a knock on the opposite side of the room, and King Louis XV stepped in. "Greetings, everyone," he said as everyone scrambled to their feet at the unexpected visit. "Hello, Mr. Smith, is Duke Henry here?" asked the King, switching to good English. Everyone in the room could speak both languages well and understood his words perfectly.

Henry was rooted to the spot, and he shared a brief, wide-eyed look with Eloise as she pushed him, whispering urgently "Go!"

Henry strode across the room, and the guests parted for him. He bowed low before the King, "Your Majesty."

"I'm glad I caught you here," said the King in a conversational tone, "and you, Mr. Smith. Oh, hello Hew."

"Your Majesty," bowed Hew, awed that his first salon visit would feature his apparent pal, the King of France.

"I have an announcement to make," said King Louis XV, changing his tone entirely as everyone assembled before him, and he spoke now in French. The King paused for dramatic effect, and every face showed rapt attention. "The scribes are preparing my formal verdict in the case of Jean Calas of Toulouse." he intoned, pausing again. "I announce it here, first, because Duke Henry and Monsieur Smith, our esteemed guests, witnessed a great injustice in Toulouse. I am here to right that injustice. I have overturned the guilty verdict against the Toulouse merchant Jean Calas!" he finished theatrically, raising his hand with a flourish. The guests burst into applause.

Henry started at the news, then stepped forward and bowed low and exclaimed, "Your Majesty!"

"There's more," said the King, "I also restore the good standing of the surviving Calas family. They are disgraced no more. Since nothing can undo the pain this family suffered, or restore their good home, I grant them 36,000 livres as a token of our sympathy." Everyone applauded again, as public opinion had turned sharply against the Calas verdict. Voltaire's Treatise on Tolerance had changed minds in Paris.

King Louis XV raised his hand again, and the guests grew quiet, "For provoking religious hatred, I have revoked the lifetime tenure of the Toulouse Magistrate, David Beaudrigue. He is relieved permanently of this duty, as soon as my verdict reaches Toulouse!" The guests applaud once again, as most of the Parisian elite had little use for Catholic dogmatism in the distant provinces. King Louis XV was happy with their response and beamed with satisfaction.

"Thank you, Your Majesty," said Henry, "I feel a weight has lifted from my heart."

"May I add my appreciation for your great act of justice, Your Majesty," added Adam.

"Come, let's sit and have refreshment," said the King, "I'd like to speak to you two alone. Oh, and Hew, please join us." Madame Espinasse, sans servants, mobilized several of her guests, including Eloise, to move five large chairs into a circle by the window, as it appeared Dr. Quesnay would join the private group as well. The King sat, then Adam, Henry, Hew, and the Doctor, as Madame Espinasse and Eloise swiftly prepared a tray of delicacies to set before the King. Delivered, everyone withdrew to a respectable distance.

The King sampled a tidbit, and the small group watched him silently as he ate. "One thing about being King," he said, "everyone waits for me to start the conversation." Henry and Hew smiled at this, but waited for the King to start the conversation, which he did after taking a sip of claret. "Voltaire's treatise convinced me that an injustice had occurred. Then, being Voltaire, he went on and on about it. I think he included a complete *history* of injustice. Or so it seemed," he concluded, smiling at his little joke at Voltaire's expense. "Did you read it?" he asked them, and they all nodded.

"I found it quite compelling," the King added, then asked, "Did you?"

"Indeed, we did, Your Majesty," said Adam.

"Speaking here privately, is there anything you would like to add?" asked the King, revealing his real purpose for their little chat.

"Voltaire speaks for me in this instance," replied Adam, thinking less opinion the better course.

"And me, Your Majesty," said Henry, "I grew quite fond of Voltaire during our visit."

"Voltaire is a great man, and a great writer," agreed King Louis XV, "I wish he could live in Paris."

Adam and Henry feared to tread, but Hew rushed in, "Why can't Voltaire live in Paris, Your Majesty?"

"He goes too far," replied the King, "If only he could manage to offend fewer people, less often. Voltaire writes a sharp letter, and I have ten nobles demanding that I throw him in the Bastille. Perhaps it's best that he remains near Geneva."

Even Hew was sufficiently adroit to avoid asking the logical follow-on question, "*aren't you the King?*" Instead, he said, "I understand, Your Majesty."

"Speaking of Geneva," continued the King, "there is another writer I may ask to leave. Some of his publications are so shocking that it seems only a matter of time. I hear you met him, this Rousseau?"

"Hume and I met him recently, Your Majesty," confirmed Adam.

"What were your thoughts?" inquired the King.

With trepidation, Adam asked cautiously, "On his writing, or his person, Your Majesty?"

Louis XV smiled, realizing he'd asked Smith whether he agreed with works he had just described as shocking. "His person," he clarified, "What manner of man is he?"

"Brilliant but eccentric, was my impression, Your Majesty," said Adam, daring to speak frankly.

"I hear Voltaire hates Rousseau," replied the King, "Yet to me they seem like two peas in a pod. Both go too far; always trying to change the order of things." He paused, reflecting on what he had just announced, then contradicted himself, "But in the case of poor Jean Calas, Voltaire really did change things, didn't he?"

"Indeed, Your Majesty," intoned Quesnay, silent until that moment.

Jubilation reigned in their carriage as it got underway, returning them to the Parc Royale. "Justice, justice is done!" exclaimed Henry, clenching his fist but smiling widely.

"I like the King," said Hew, "as a person, I mean. He was so open with us."

"You were brash enough to ask, Hew!" laughed Henry, punching his brother in the arm.

"No man can fail to please if he has the courage to utter his real sentiments as he feels them, and *because* he feels them. The man who invites us into his heart exercises a type of hospitality more delightful than any other," said Adam, rather intensely. Both Henry and Hew were struck by his eloquence, and his unusual passion.

"I think that's why I enjoy Hume so much," said Henry.

"A perfect example," nodded Adam.

"The King of France made me happy," continued Henry, "I didn't expect that."

"Hatred and anger are poison to happiness," replied Adam, "A furious man is more likely to exasperate his friends than his enemies."

"It shouldn't take a King to make you happy, Henry," observed Hew, "You should take a lighter view of things." He paused, then laughed and added, "I certainly do!"

"I hardly look to kings for happiness," answered Henry, "Even kings can be unhappy."

"They often are, I'm sure," said Adam, "King Louis suffered at the death of his son. The rich are no happier than the poor in the things that really matter."

CHAPTER 26

E XPULSION OF ROUSSEAU *January 1766*
"The red one, monsieur?" asked St. Jean as Adam stood before his mirror in his room at the Parc Royale.

"No, perhaps the blue?" responded Adam. Every time he thought about wearing the red suit with gold embroidery, he felt like a clown. He was still getting used to the bright colors favored in France after a lifetime of wearing mostly black, brown, and gray in his native land.

"Do you think the neck is snug enough?" fretted Adam, "I don't want to be... improper."

"Too tight will be uncomfortable, monsieur," replied St. Jean in his calm, diplomatic style, and he made no move to adjust Adam's collar.

"I want to do as the Romans do, St. Jean," smiled Adam nervously, as he examined his assembled self in the full-length mirror. "Look at me, a frumpy Scot professor fussing over his appearance."

"Do you attend salon today?" inquired St. Jean.

"Yes," sighed Adam as he pondered himself in the mirror, "Comtesse Boufflers."

Two rooms down, Henry stood before his own mirror, attended by Cook, while Hew lounged in a chair watching.

"Does this color suit me?" Henry asked, although he'd worn the distinctive dark blue jacket many times before.

"It's fine, Henry," replied Cook, letting a hint of exasperation creep into his voice, "Would you like to change again?"

"My God, Henry, how do you know Eloise will even be there?" asked Hew.

"I don't," replied Henry, stung. "I just want to look my best."

"He looks fine, Cook, send him off," said Hew dismissively, waving his hand towards the door.

"Aren't you coming today?" Henry asked Hew.

"Not today," he replied with a smirk, "Good luck brother."

Fifteen minutes later, Henry entered the carriage and sat across from Adam. Simultaneously, both asked the other, "How do I look?" They were diverted from their nervousness when their carriage pulled up before the Palace, where Hume and Rousseau stood in the driveway by themselves, in animated discussion. Hume broke off as Adam and Henry approached.

"Greetings," said Hume, and Adam could see that his friend was trying to calm himself.

"Hello Hume. Good day to you, Rousseau," said Adam in reply.

"It is *not* a good day, thank you very much," snapped Rousseau, who was not making much effort to calm himself.

"Our dear Rousseau has been asked to leave France," explained Hume, causing Adam and Henry to exchange knowing looks. Henry let Adam reply.

"When, and by whom?" asked Adam.

"By the King himself! The King himself!" exclaimed Rousseau, waving his hands fretfully.

"Can you return to Geneva?" asked Henry, and then regretted it as the small man scowled.

"I am no longer welcome in my home country," Rousseau snapped, "and Voltaire hates me."

"Perhaps Prussia, or Vienna?" suggested Hume.

"Heaven forbid! No place that speaks German, no." Rousseau was adamant.

"I must leave for England this month," offered Hume, "perhaps you can travel with me?"

"What would I do in England? How would I support myself?" fretted Rousseau, clasping and unclasping his hands anxiously.

"You are a distinguished man of letters, Jean-Jacque," replied Hume optimistically, "You could find any manner of occupations in London."

"It is difficult to think nobly when one thinks only of earning a living," was Rousseau's haughty reply. Adam could see that the irascible Rousseau was trying Hume's patience, but his friend kept trying to placate him, nevertheless.

"Well," Hume pondered, "perhaps I could prevail upon our King to grant you a pension?"

"A pension?" mused Rousseau.

"I cannot guarantee the amount, but I'm sure it would keep you in paper, quills, wine," encouraged Hume. This alarmed Adam as Hume could not guarantee any pension, let alone quibble over the amount.

"Perhaps," said Rousseau, "but the pension must not be made public."

"Why is that?" asked Hume, trying to keep a level tone to his voice.

"People would think I wrote for the King, and not for myself," answered Rousseau, the man who ostensibly believed that happiness should not depend on the opinions of others.

Hume looked at Adam blankly, both were taken aback by Rousseau's churlishness. Henry seethed but said nothing, wondering why they were so attentive to the irritating little man. "Let's go inside and see what everyone else thinks," volunteered Henry, anxious to see Eloise.

"No!" insisted Rousseau, "not today!"

"Rest assured, Rousseau, we'll keep it to ourselves," said the diplomat, Hume, while getting nods of agreement from Adam and Henry. All were eager to end the driveway impasse, and Henry found himself in agreement with the King over the fate of the little rascal.

Hume stepped aside for Rousseau to enter first, followed by Adam and Henry, so that they entered in height order. Comtesse Boufflers spotted them immediately, backdropped by Hume's embassy uniform. "Greetings, greetings, young Duke!" she said to Henry as she approached, "You arrive in esteemed company today, three philosophers!"

"It's a pleasure, Comtesse," said Henry, "I deliver them to you." Despite her greeting, Henry noticed the first person she physically touched was Adam, when she took his arm. Henry spied Eloise standing by the punchbowl, so he detached himself from the group.

"The three of you are just in time," said the Comtesse with a note of excitement, "We are discussing the King and the affaire Calas." She led the group towards the bulk of her guests, who turned to welcome them. Hume and Rousseau went first, and she held Adam back a moment.

"You look splendid today, Mr. Smith," she said in a low tone, in English, "I was hoping to see you wear your red suit."

"You... look splendid too, Comtesse," stammered Adam, "I haven't quite the nerve to wear the red one yet."

"We'll have to find a suitable occasion, won't we?" she murmured as she gave him up to the group, where Hume and Rousseau were already holding court. Even seated, Hume dwarfed Rousseau, the effect amplified by the red Embassy uniform Hume wore. A seat was offered Adam, and he took it, although most of the guests remained standing, gathered close around the three eminent philosophers. Henry and Eloise joined them.

Hume was speaking, "When men are most sure and arrogant they are often mostly mistaken."

"Are you speaking of me, sir?" asked a perturbed Rousseau.

"Ah, no, I was speaking of the Toulouse magistrate who was fired," replied Hume with a wrinkle across his normally placid brow.

"Beaudrigue," prompted Henry.

"Yes, that was the name," continued Hume, "Liberty of thought is always fatal to priestly power."

"Beaudrigue was the magistrate, not a priest," observed Adam, a stickler for accuracy.

"When the church and state act together to kill a man, does that distinction really matter?" replied his friend rhetorically, and Henry nodded his agreement.

"God makes all things good; man meddles in them, and they become evil," said Rousseau in a sour tone.

"We are all fallen angels," replied Hume, "but I would not call mankind evil."

"Certainly not!" interjected Comtesse Boufflers brightly, "look at all these good people here!"

"We are judged by our actions," stated Rousseau, "To do, is to be."

Eloise spoke up in a clear voice, "Descartes said, 'I think, therefore I am.' Are we defined by our actions, or our thoughts?"

"Actions," answered Rousseau promptly, and Henry noticed his tone with Eloise was pleasant and almost friendly. "Thoughts are often jumbled and indistinct," continued the philosopher, "There are times when I am so unlike myself that I might be taken for someone else, of an entirely different character. It is as if my heart and brain did not belong to the same person."

"So how do you decide how to act?" asked Henry.

"People who know little are often great talkers," scowled Rousseau, making Henry's blood boil in an instant.

Adam recognized the flame in Henry's cheeks and said, "A fine question, Henry. We're defined by our *sentiments*; how we *think* about our feelings. Our sentiments help us decide how to act. So, it's not one or the other, but all three; we feel, we think, and then act."

"Hmmpf," snorted Rousseau, "Trust your heart rather than your head."

"Reason is a slave to the passions, for sure," offered Hume, "But somehow we manage enough reason to remain civilized."

"Civilization is a hopeless race to discover remedies for the evils it produces," scoffed Rousseau. A murmur swept the group at this dark and cynical comment from the supposedly optimistic philosopher. Comtesse Boufflers clapped her hands to divert the conversation.

"Everyone! Refreshments!" she called out, and the group moved towards the buffet. She and Eloise tied petite aprons on each other to the amusement of the guests, as the servants had been dismissed so they could speak freely. Seeing the two beautiful women act like servants, separated in age by nearly twenty years, made the male guests forget the civilized debate for more immediate entertainment.

Adam stood next to Henry as they were served by the Comtesse and Eloise, standing on the opposite side of the table. They had trouble taking their eyes off each other, best evidenced when Eloise missed Henry's plate entirely with a spoonful of fruit salad. They all laughed.

"My salon is second-best now that the King himself attends Madame Espinasse," said the Comtesse.

"The food is better here," observed Henry with a grin, "the servers are too. Thank you, Eloise," as she successfully hit his plate with her second volley of fruit.

"His Majesty sought out Henry by name," said Adam.

"So, the King was not there for the food," replied Eloise promptly, "He was seeking our distinguished English guests."

"Scottish," replied Adam, giving Henry a wink.

The following afternoon found Henry and Hew practicing with pistols behind the stable at the Parc Royale. Despite being in the heart of downtown Paris, the solid oak wall had long been used by guests to practice with pistols. A servant placed wine bottles on a post that stood before the bullet-pocked timbers as the boys took turns. An upturned barrel served as their worktable, holding ball, powder, wadding, and related tools for ease in reloading the flintlock handguns. The distance from the barrel to the target post was twenty feet.

Henry took careful aim and remembered what Monsieur Dumond had taught him at Ferney; feet even, tighten slowly on the trigger, fire on the exhale. He did all these things, but still missed. Hew took half as long aiming and hit the bottle dead center, exploding it into a thousand shards.

"I'm mortified," frowned Henry, "Outshot and outrun by my younger brother."

"I'm the second son," grinned Hew, "It must come natural."

The servant placed another wine bottle on the post. At the rate guests drank wine at the Parc Royale, there was an endless supply. The servant, no fool, scampered behind a foundation wall. At least these guests weren't drinking, he thought.

Henry finished loading his pistol and took a careful bead. His arm was straight, his eye saw the bottle at the end of his pistol barrel, the hammer cocked, his finger tightening smoothly on the trigger. He began his exhale.

"May I try?" said a musical voice behind them. Henry lowered the gun, and they turned to see Eloise, elegant in her riding habit.

"Sure," smiled Henry and he carefully eased the hammer down. He placed the gun on the barrel. "It's not cocked, so it's safe," he said.

"I can see that," said Eloise, as she picked up the gun and inspected it. She cocked it and inspected the flint. In one smooth motion she pointed it at the bottle and fired. The bottle exploded.

"Where did you learn to shoot like that?" marveled Hew.

"My uncle was an army officer during the war," she replied, "He taught me how to shoot."

"It looks like you practiced some," observed Henry admiringly.

"It's fun to shoot," she smiled, "My uncle told me something else I will always remember."

She held their rapt attention for a long moment while she reloaded the pistol with expert fingers. "He said that an army marches into battle as a unit, but it's every man for himself when they rape and pillage. They ravage in small bands, led by the boldest amongst them. My uncle said, 'Eloise, you've got one shot. Shoot the leader, it's your only chance.'"

"Heaven forbid that should happen to any woman," said Henry, shocked at her frank commentary.

"Especially if it's the *English* army," returned Eloise, "All armies rape and pillage."

"Touche, Eloise," said Hew, "Your uncle did you a service."

"I've gone him one better," she replied, raising the pistol at a new bottle. She held her arm for a long moment, and Henry swore he could see her exhale. She fired and the bottle exploded.

Eloise looked at them with a satisfied expression, "I have *two* pistols."

"Care for a contest, my lady?" inquired Hew.

"First person to miss pays the other an English pound?" countered Eloise calmly.

"Hew, forget what I said about gambling," said Henry.

"You're on Eloise!" exclaimed Hew happily, "Ladies first!"

"Such a gentleman," smirked Eloise, "you could win without shooting."

Once reloaded, Eloise drew a careful bead on the target. There was a long moment before she fired, knocking the neck cleanly off and leaving the bulk of the bottle standing on the post.

"A near miss!" said Hew, "but clearly, I must shoot." He waved off the servant and took aim at the remaining bottle, hitting it plumb center.

"I will have to earn my pound, it seems," said Eloise, reloading swiftly. Again, she took careful aim and again shot the neck off the bottle.

"What a coincidence!" exclaimed Hew.

"Was it?" wondered Henry.

A cloud passed over Hew's face. He aimed at what was left of her target. Henry saw his eyes flick to Eloise and then back to the bottle, then he fired. He missed, and Henry was delighted. "Bested at pistols by a French lass!" he exulted, then he put a consoling arm around Hew's chagrined shoulders. "Let's not mention this in our letters home."

"You've been writing letters?" asked Hew, then he dug in his pocket and produced a coin. He handed it to Eloise, saying formally, "One English pound."

"I will keep it always as a souvenir," she replied, holding the coin in both hands close to her breast, "So I may always remember the joy of this moment!" She walked away from them laughing over her shoulder, and they watched her go in frank admiration.

Hew's smile faded. "I hate that I must be a military man," he said somberly.

"You don't, Hew," said Henry, turning his brother to look him in the eye. "No one can make you join the Army."

"But then I get to thinking, *somebody* has to," continued Hew. He paused, looking at the ground for a long moment. Then he picked up the loaded pistol lying on the barrel. In one smooth motion he raised the gun, fired, and shattered the bottle.

"See? I'm a natural!" said Hew, his mood restored.

• • • •

ON A COLD MORNING IN January 1766, a freight wagon was loading Hume's trunks and baggage. A small carriage was parked behind it, awaiting their departure. Hume stood in his greatcoat, making sure the freighters were careful with his luggage. Rosseau's baggage was already aboard, and the small man stepped out of the Embassy looking dapper in his traveling clothes.

"My good Hume, when do we depart?" asked Rosseau.

"They are almost finished with the baggage," replied Hume, as he watched them lash the trunks securely to the wagon rails.

"So, I am driven from the Continent," sighed Rosseau, "a melancholy prospect."

"A sad punishment for simply speaking your mind," nodded Hume.

"I was not much afraid of punishment, I was only afraid of disgrace," said Rousseau.

"Such punishment *is* a disgrace," said Hume stoutly, "but you can speak your mind in England."

"Off to England, I envy you Hume!" called Adam from horseback, riding up with Henry and Hew. They dismounted, and servants took the reins.

"We return home from our Crusade," agreed a beaming Hume.

"For you," said Rousseau, "for me it's exile."

"I suspect you'll be well-received in London, Rousseau," said Adam.

"No advantages in this world are pure and unmixed, Jean-Jacque," advised Hume, "Leaving is such sweet sorrow, just like the Crusades."

"What was sweet about the Crusades, Hume?" asked a puzzled Henry, having absorbed considerable Crusader history while studying in Toulouse.

"Their *end*," replied Hume emphatically, "the Crusades are the biggest monument to human folly in any age or nation. But at last, they all went home."

"Oh, I'm losing my philosophers!" lamented Comtesse Boufflers, surprising them in a shawl and carrying a covered basket. She had walked up by herself unnoticed.

"Here is the sorrow part," cried out Hume, "we must leave our dear Comtesse!"

"I brought some bakery treats for your ride to the coast," she said, "and to say goodbye."

Rousseau bowed low and said, "Your hospitality has been gracious indeed, Comtesse."

"Thank you, Jean-Jacque," she replied, "I will miss you." She turned to Hume and flung both arms around him, even the one holding the basket. "And you, Hume, my big, lovable Scot!" Rousseau's look turned sour when he saw that the Comtesse made no move to hug him.

"Is Lord Hertford traveling with you?" asked Adam, looking dubiously at the small carriage.

"No, the Ambassador left yesterday," Hume replied, "The new ambassador arrives next week."

Adam followed with, "What will you do in London?"

"It appears I may be appointed Secretary of State for the Northern Division," answered Hume proudly, "It's rare for the historian to help make history, is it not?"

"The Northern Division includes Scotland?" asked Henry.

"Indeed, that's why I'm so qualified for the post!" exclaimed Hume, spreading his arms.

"Dispelling with the light of his reason the shadows in which his government envelopes him," said Rousseau sarcastically.

"I'm sure that's exactly what he'll do, Jean-Jacque," said Comtesse Boufflers firmly, "Hume will be great in government."

"People once accustomed to government masters are not in a condition to do without them," responded Rousseau petulantly.

"The English are free to speak their minds, Rousseau," spoke up Henry, "We complain about our government freely!"

"Everyone needs a master," responded Rousseau, "Men are sheep."

"I thought you said men were born free...?" Henry challenged.

"I do not know how to be clear to someone who does not want to be attentive," Rousseau barked, "You powder your wig while the people starve."

Henry bit his lip with anger, but a servant approached to say all was ready for their departure. Hume gestured for Rousseau to enter the carriage before him, "After you, monsieur."

Adam called out, "Safe travels Rousseau," but the little man did not respond as he climbed in.

"I don't envy your journey with that rascal," said Hew to Hume as they shook hands goodbye.

"I don't even wear a wig," said Henry as he did the same. He was going to miss the kindly Embassy Secretary, but the cynical Frenchman nettled him. He was glad to see him go.

Hume smiled at the boys and put a hand on the shoulder of each. "We are happy when circumstances suit our temper, but we are *excellent* when our temper suits any circumstance. We'll be fine, Master Hew."

The Comtesse rose on tiptoes to kiss his cheek, and he bent down to accommodate her with a smile. "I will miss you dearly, Comtesse, write often, will you?"

"Goodbye friend," said Adam, as he extended his hand, "I'll let you know when we plan our return to London."

"What, no hug?" said Hume with a grin, and grabbed Adam in a bear hug to the delight of the boys and the Comtesse. "Goodbye, Henry. Goodbye, Hew. Remember that the sweetest path of life leads through the avenues of learning." Hume turned and climbed gingerly into the small carriage and sat opposite Rousseau. The carriage groaned as it settled down on its suspension. Hume, ever conscious of his size, instinctively joked self-deprecatingly, "I bless the memory of Julius Caesar, for the esteem he had for fat men and his aversion to lean ones!"

"I am lean," said an unsmiling Rousseau, "What do you imply, Hume?"

The carriage followed the wagon and then Hume and Rousseau were gone. They would learn much later that Rousseau grew increasingly paranoid in London and blamed Hume, despite all the efforts the genial philosopher made on his behalf.

"My salon will seem empty without Hume," said the Comtesse putting her hand on Adam's arm, "Monsieur Smith, you are even more valuable to me now!"

CHAPTER 27

SPRINGTIME IN PARIS *April 1766*

The winter months passed slowly, especially without Hume, but neither Adam nor Henry noticed the weather as both were preoccupied with love.

Henry's growing infatuation with Eloise was understandable; he was young, handsome, and rich; she was beautiful, talented, and intelligent. The more she hesitated before Henry's amorous advances, the more irresistible she became to him. Once a week she would accompany him on his morning ride, and she'd see him in a salon perhaps twice more. They usually kept their physical distance, to avoid wags, but once in the stable shadows they'd kissed passionately, and she let him run his hands all over outside her clothes. They didn't touch for over a month after that, but when they did, again in the stable away from prying eyes, she'd loosened her vest, allowing his hand in, and he glimpsed the warm full left breast inside her blouse. Still, she had refused to go further, and Henry dreamed of that one tantalizing shadowy glimpse every night thereafter. Eloise was Catholic and went to Mass every Sunday, whereas Henry paid lip service to his Christianity. He respected her faith, even envied her, but to him, religion was more a social convention than it was a spiritual communion. Lurking deep behind his intense infatuation with Eloise was the certain knowledge that he could never take a French wife, which he hid from his consciousness whenever Eloise was with him, either in body or mind.

Hew, true to his carefree nature, found that the young French prostitutes were fresh and pretty, and they seemed to like his company. He visited them twice each week; more often and the expense might become obvious to Cook. They weren't

323

cold, cynical and transactional as he imagined most prostitutes must inevitably become, and the girls would ply him with wine and song. Never for a minute did Hew think of it as anything more than sex with servants, never did he ponder the tragedy of a young woman beginning a life of prostitution. Hew took life as it came and accepted the order of things, which of course favored rich young men such as himself.

Cook was aware of Hew's visits and left them out of his letters to Charles, pursuant to his instructions on such matters. Cook was late catching on to Eloise, noting her twice when she practiced with pistols with Henry and Hew, and once he saw her riding with Henry in the morning. Because Cook did not attend salon, he remained unaware of Henry's lovesickness until spring was well upon them. Even then he did not consider it serious enough to trouble Charles.

As they established residency at the Parc Royale with its many servants, Cook's tasks became much simpler. With his role reduced, Cook's focus turned to expense control. Paris was expensive compared with Toulouse, and while Henry did not gamble and Hew's expenses were minor, Cook took issue with Adam's spending. He fussed that he still didn't have a complete accounting of all his new French clothes. Cook lacked self-awareness to see that this petty concern was expanding to fill the time available to it, and his manner became increasingly brittle. Meanwhile, at Adderbury, an overjoyed Charles cared not a whit for their expenses given their smashing success with the King of France.

Cook was the very farthest thing from Adam's mind, as for the first time in his life, he was in love. Since his father, also named Adam Smith, had died before his birth, Adam had always known that he was all his mother Margaret would ever have. She was the daughter of John Douglas of Strathendry, a military man, as were most of his relatives. Adam grew up coddled and encouraged by his attentive mother and protected by her father and uncle. As his intellectual gifts became evident at Kirkaldy grade school, he'd progressed to Glasgow, and then to Oxford, but always knowing that he could never leave his mother alone.

Adam Smith threw himself into his duties at the University of Glasgow, moving his mother to live with him there in 1751. A full professor at age twenty-eight, Adam's work crowded out any thought of having a family. He met a young widow, Kate, with two small sons whose husband had been an army officer killed in the late war. Adam visited Kate late at night, often after spending the evening talking and drinking with ship captains and merchants in the Glasgow clubs. The widow was grateful for the financial support, and Adam needed the warm physical intimacy he missed otherwise. They kept their relationship secret, to avoid embarrassing both the University and her honor. As much as they appreciated the arrangement, and took comfort in it, both knew it was not love.

Two years later, in Paris in the springtime, Adam thought only of Comtesse Boufflers. Looking back, he'd fallen head over heels when the Comtesse quoted his book back to him, not as a memory exercise, but in the natural flow of their conversation. She had not only read his book but understood it! Adam had never imagined that a woman so beautiful could also be so intellectual, so fluent, and the attraction overwhelmed him at times. Yet despite his deep infatuation, even love, Adam Smith remained the reserved and proper Scottish gentleman he would always be. He considered a thousand stratagems to approach the Comtesse romantically, but his sense of propriety always forbade it. He would rather die than sully the reputation of Scotland, the University, or of Henry. And then there was the Prince to consider; only a woman as fabulous as the Comtesse could properly represent the rarified status of one of France's foremost officials. The emotional magnitude of his conundrum appalled him, especially when she smiled and put her hand on his arm. If ever there was proof that love is a sentiment, and not just a passion, it was embodied for Adam in the graceful form of Comtesse Boufflers.

The Comtesse loved Adam in return; not as a dashing professor, dangerous soldier, or lively dancer, but for the light he brought to her salon. Demand for her select invitations grew, and then redoubled, as Smith's reputation as a well-spoken and learned fellow spread throughout Paris. Monsieur Smith was gracious, always respectful, but most important to the Comtesse, always interesting. She knew he came most often to her salon because of her charms, so she stayed as close to him as propriety would allow. Adam had met the Prince d'Conti twice, once formally and once casually, pleasing the Prince that his Court could feature such a distinguished and popular guest. He showed not a trace of suspicion that the plain Scottish professor was madly in love with his mistress.

Adam and Henry continued to visit Madame Espinasse's salon regularly, where Eloise was a regular attendee, as she was no longer invited to the Palace salon. They both assumed it was envy, but Adam didn't hold it against the Comtesse. The discussion in the plain room of the Madame was much more intellectual than the elite flirting and posturing at the gilt Palace, so close to the Royal Court. This was odd, considering that King Louis XV would occasionally drop in on Madame's salon to visit the men he called 'his Thinkers': Quesnay, Turgot, and d'Alembert, yet almost never appeared at the Prince's salon hosted by the Comtesse. For several months, Adam Smith was the featured guest at both salons, and an occasional guest at others. He learned much from the French intellectuals, and they learned much from him. As Adam would often quip, "Man lives by exchanging!"

Comtesse Boufflers had long since given up asking Adam about the red suit of clothes she'd encouraged him to buy, accepting fashion defeat at the hands of the humble Scot. But as he had left her salon the previous week, she'd pulled him close and said, "I'm hosting a musical event next week, Monsieur Smith," then she whispered into his ear, "Your red suit will be perfect!" So, Adam resolved to wear it.

• • • •

"IT'S TIME TO GET READY for the concert, St. Jean," said Adam, standing in his underwear in front of his mirror.

"Which suit today, monsieur?" asked St. Jean, moving to the closet.

"The red one," said Adam, firmly.

St. Jean smiled broadly, unusual for him. He brought the elegant red suit with the elaborate gold trim to Adam, saying, "At last!"

"The Comtesse requested it," said Adam ruefully, "it's rather opposite my normal attire."

"It's a fine suit, monsieur," said St. Jean, helping Adam put on the coat as he stood before the mirror, doubtful yet undeniably resplendent. "She will be pleased," he said, still smiling. Adam suspected that his resolve to wear the red suit would have proved insufficient without the quiet support of his valet, St. Jean.

As Adam, Henry, and Hew stepped out of their carriage that afternoon at the Palace, servants conducted them to a different wing of the sprawling estate. They entered a vast room, with pale yellow walls thirty feet high, door and window arches extending almost to the lofty roof, and long rose-colored draperies. The room was flooded with light. High above their heads hung portraits, mostly of women, forming a silent gallery overlooking the festivities below. At one end of the room stood a piano, with a man tuning a cello and another a guitar behind it. They joined a crowd of about sixty, almost half of whom were women, as most of the regular salon attendees had today brought their wives. A few had even brought their dogs.

"Adam, you look magnificent!" greeted the Comtesse happily, seeing that he'd finally taken her ultimate sartorial advice. Adam flushed but noticed that his ostentatious dress fit in quite easily in the rarified company of the Palace.

"Thank you Comtesse," returned Adam as she gave him her hands, "I feel rather conspicuous today; I hope I'm not expected to perform!"

"You won't be mistaken for a court jester in this crowd," observed Henry with a grin.

"You don't know any good jokes anyway, Mr. Smith," said Hew, clapping him on the back and making the Comtesse laugh.

"No comedy required, Monsieur Smith," she assured him, "Perhaps you didn't tell them who helped choose this outfit?"

"I am in your debt, Comtesse," Adam replied, giving her a little bow.

"Today we'll hear a musical prodigy from Vienna," she announced, "Wolfgang Mozart; he's only ten years old!"

"How good can he be at age ten?" wondered Henry, remembering his struggles to learn the violin at Buckingham School for Boys around that age.

"He was remarkable at age seven, when he was last in Paris," she responded, "His father has him touring the salons of Europe. We'll see how he's progressed."

"Is the Prince d'Conti here today?" asked Adam, looking about the huge room.

"No," replied the Comtesse, "He saw Mozart last time and thought that was enough prodigy. Do you enjoy music Monsieur Smith?"

"Indeed, I do," said Adam, "Music is all virtue, and no vice."

"No Eloise?" asked Henry, looking about in vain.

"No, Henry," replied the Comtesse, taking him aside briefly before continuing, "The Prince took note of Eloise, so I quit inviting her." Adam, standing close by, heard and understood immediately, but Henry did not.

"Doesn't the Prince meet all your guests eventually?" he asked.

"This is awkward for me to say, Henry, but the Prince is always looking for his next mistress," she explained in a diplomatic tone. "He prefers them younger, like Eloise."

Henry flinched as if he'd been slapped, then said ruefully, "I understand, Comtesse, thank you for explaining. We are in your debt." Now it was his turn to give her a little bow, thankful to the Comtesse for protecting Eloise, and inflamed at the thought of her becoming just another plaything of the rich and powerful. As Comtesse Boufflers led Adam into the crowd of guests, Henry stood rooted, unexpectedly thinking of the girl Collette in Toulouse.

The Comtesse stood before the piano and clapped her hands for attention, which she gained easily. The audience stood about in small groups or sat at tables with cups and plates before them, sampling the sumptuous spread of delicacies. A dog barked, and everyone laughed.

"May I present Wolfgang Amadeus Mozart, age ten," she announced simply, then moved back to stand beside Adam. A small boy, elegantly dressed, entered the room followed by his father. Mozart appeared unruffled; he was not apprehensive about his surroundings or the elegant audience, as his father had been exhibiting him before the salons of Europe since he was five. The boy took his seat at the piano and launched cold into a frenetic series of notes at the high end of the scale. The audience, taken aback, recognized the virtuosity but many showed expressions of visible surprise as the young boy attacked the keyboard with such gusto. After about a minute of unrelenting music, Adam saw Mozart's father make a small gesture to his son, unmistakenly signaling to "tone it down." Mozart gave no sign he saw his father's gesture, but seamlessly transitioned into a melody so lovely that the women in the room all broke into broad smiles. Mozart's father smiled too at the sight of this, as the musicians behind the prodigy picked up their instruments and joined in his more conventional overture.

"He's grown a bit since last time," whispered the Comtesse to Adam. She was so close to him that her voluminous gown pushed up against him, and he was held between two exquisite forces, love and music. He felt her take his hand, hidden by the folds of her gown, and hold it as they stood listening.

"Oh, that is lovely!" said the Comtesse, referring to the music.

"Yes, lovely," agreed a spellbound Adam, looking at her.

Behind them, Hew nudged Henry and whispered, "The Professor's in love!" Henry smiled and nodded, happy for his tutor, although somewhat amazed that a woman like the Comtesse would be attracted to such a humble and unassuming man. Yet as he stood there, reflecting on Adam's happiness, he could understand her attraction. Adam knew his own mind, was gracious and patient with everyone, and was slow to take offense. There was much for a woman to like about Adam Smith, but not necessarily at first glance. Today, wearing his elegant red suit, Henry had to admit that Adam looked handsome, a man in his prime.

The young prodigy Mozart played flawlessly, overseen by his anxious father but not upstaged by him in any way. Mozart's father was the business end of his son's talent, but his avarice trained Mozart's gifts into a finely honed skill. Enchanted, none of the distinguished guests interrupted the boy as he played beautifully for an hour straight.

When at last Mozart took a break, Henry and Hew watched the Prince's house artist, Michel Barthelemy Ollivier, paint the elegant scene. The towering pale walls and room details were all done in advance, and the man was swiftly adding the particulars as they watched, fascinated by his skill. Mozart and his accompanying musicians were already apparent; Henry wondered if perhaps he'd painted the boy's head too small but said nothing. Hew grabbed his arm and pointed as Ollivier began painting a man in a red suit standing across the room. Looking up, the boys saw Adam speaking with the mathematician Jean d'Alembert in the very pose captured by the painter.

Mozart returned and played another hour, but the guests paid less attention as they ate and drank. Comtesse Boufflers stayed close to Adam, and she saw to it that his glass of claret was never empty. Henry noticed that Adam seemed happy to the point of giddiness and wondered whether it was alcohol or the intoxicating Comtesse. It was of course both, and Adam was a happy drunk on the rare occasions he drank to excess. Today, with the Comtesse attached to his arm, he was especially so.

As their carriage arrived to return them to the Parc Royale, crowded in with many other elegant coaches and their teams, the Comtesse held on to Adam. Hew climbed in, followed by Henry, and they turned to see if a tipsy Adam needed a helping hand.

"Henry, Adam should lie down for a moment," said the Comtesse, "I'll send him home in another carriage."

"Fine, Comtesse," said Henry, looking at Adam, "Mr. Smith?"

"I'll be along shortly," Adam replied, his voice a bit slurred, "A bit too much fun perhaps."

Hew wasn't fooled and waved to Adam with a huge grin, "Good night, Mr. Smith!"

After they'd gone, the Comtesse guided Adam through the Palace, following a young woman servant holding towels in one hand and a pail of hot water in the other. Adam's heart raced as they entered her plush boudoir. His throat was dry as she sat him down on her bed, and with help from the servant, helped him out of his coat and removed his shoes. The servant closed the heavy drapes, allowing only a dusky glow from the late day sun to suffuse the room.

"A glass of cool water," said the Comtesse to the servant girl; when she returned Adam gulped it thirstily. "Let me help you with that neckcloth," purred the Comtesse, sitting on the bed beside him and working it loose. She then unbuttoned his vest for him; he let her continue, pretending helplessness, delighted yet apprehensive as she undressed him.

"Isn't it lovely to lie down after a busy day?" remarked the Comtesse, as she pushed him into a lying position on the bed.

"It surely is," agreed Adam, "but I've been drunker than this in the Edinburgh pubs. I always made it home."

"But why bother?" she said, releasing the pins in her hair and letting it cascade down around her shoulders. She stood and walked behind a folding screen; in a moment he saw her gown draped over the top as she began to undress.

"Wouldn't the Prince be dismayed to know I'm lying on your bed?" asked Adam tentatively, like a man in a canoe approaching a cataract without a paddle.

"Not at all," she responded as another garment was flung over the screen, "I am his ornament, his caged bird. My success at salon burnishes his image at Court. He has younger mistresses, so he comes here seldom."

Adam swallowed hard as her bustier came next, although she was still hidden behind the screen. "Call me Adam.... Marie," he ventured, then asked, "Does the Prince ever ask you to, ah, entertain people, ah, here?" He finally got it out.

The Comtesse emerged from behind the screen, dressed only in a thin nightgown. Adam was utterly transfixed, her rounded form no longer bound by corsets and petticoats, as she walked slowly towards him.

"Do you mean my bedroom, Adam?" she asked seductively, her body silhouetted by the dim light coming through the drapes.

"I'm sorry, I just..." Adam stuttered, until she leaned over him and put a finger to his lips. Her breasts appeared invitingly in the shadow of her nightgown as it fell open before him.

"It's a fair question," she whispered, kissing his lips as he lay before her, "but no, he never asks such things. I am free to do as I wish."

"You are free but caged. A paradox," replied Adam, as she stood and moved to the drapes to darken the room still further. She knew he was watching, so she took her time lighting a candle. His blood raged at the sight of her walking back towards the bed, illuminated by the single flame. "If I could only be convinced.... that this is all right," he murmured.

The Comtesse kissed him again, warmly, and he responded. She began to unfasten his breeches.

"Oh, I'll convince you Adam," she said softly, blowing out the candle, pfft, and plunging the room into ecstasy.

· · · ·

EARLY THE FOLLOWING morning, Henry met Eloise in the stables of the Parc Royale. She wouldn't tell him where she lived, or much about herself other than she lived part of the year with her uncle near Nantes, and part of the year with her mother in Paris. Her father, also a military officer, had died of yellow fever in the West Indies. Radiant as usual in her riding habit, they walked their horses along the Paris streets, talking.

"We leave for Compiegne in a few days, hunting with the King," said Henry.

"You travel in the highest circles, Henry," she smiled, "It must be good to be you."

"I understand my advantages," replied Henry, "but my feelings are the same as anyone's."

"Your feelings, or your sentiments?" She smiled at him.

"I hear Mr. Smith in your question," he smiled back, "My feelings are the same as any man's; my sentiments are improved by his instruction."

"I can believe it," she nodded impishly, "I've seen a marked reduction in your natural haughtiness these past weeks."

Henry laughed and said, "I admit Charles chose wisely. I have great respect for Mr. Smith."

"He is star of the salons, especially with Hume and Rousseau gone to England," she replied.

"It's humbling to be a mere bystander to his eminence here in Paris, but it's well-deserved," said Henry, "The way he remains calm during a flurry of questions. I wish I could have taken his class in Glasgow."

Eloise wrinkled her brow at this. "A strange wish, seeing how he is your personal tutor. Your stepfather has your interest at heart."

"And his own, I'm quite sure," scoffed Henry, "Charles wants me to stand for Parliament."

"That is misfortune?" she queried, noting his tone, "It *is* good to be you, Henry."

Henry nodded as they plodded along slowly astride their mounts, and said, "My money makes me greater than my confidence, it seems."

Eloise reached out and caught his sleeve, and pulled their horses close abreast. She leaned over and gave him a long, full kiss in the middle of the street. Finally, she released him and said earnestly, "You are great Henry. Wherever you call home, you'll make it better."

A wave of affection swept over him, and he blurted out impulsively, "Come with me, Eloise!"

Surprised, Eloise looked at him for a long moment, then laughed. Henry looked hurt, misunderstanding.

"To each man his own country, Henry, and to each woman, hers," she said, looking deep into his eyes, their horses still stopped in the street. "I'm sure your family has already arranged a wife for you in England. I could never stand their fury were you to bring me home from France."

Henry was speechless, forlorn, but he knew that what she said was true. "I'll miss you while I'm in Compiegne," he said, "Will I see you when I return to Paris?"

Eloise looked at him tenderly, wistfully, and replied, "Perhaps, Henry."

CHAPTER 28

H UNTING WITH THE KING *June 1766*
It was quiet in the summertime forest, with just the occasional bird and the buzzing of insects disturbing the warm serenity. A young buck stepped onto an overgrown wagon track, head up, alert, nostrils quivering. Just as the animal's head dropped to begin grazing, the birds stopped. In the distance came the baying of hounds. The deer fled down the track; the baying grew louder as the dogs burst into view over a small rise, chasing the scent. Thirty seconds later the hounds were followed by thundering horses, as King Louis XV and his retinue pounded the track in pursuit, Henry and Hew near the van and the King riding regally in the middle of the group. The sounds faded, quiet almost restored, when laboring over the rise came two wagons with servants, food, and pavilions. Halting to give the horses a blow, they drank water and chatted amongst themselves. In the far distance they heard a gunshot. Snapping the reins, the drivers started the wagons rolling again in support of the King's recreation and comfort.

A mile ahead, in a dappled glade not far off the track, the King sat on his horse and watched the deer carcass being dressed. Two peasants did the messy work; their bounty was the guts in a burlap bag. The rest of the retinue stood their horses haphazardly or had dismounted. The King noticed Henry and waved him forward.

"Henry, did you see the shot?" asked the King when Henry rode up.

"No, your Majesty," Henry replied, "Did you make the kill?"

"Oh no," laughed the King, "I rarely make the kill anymore. The deer is just the excuse we use to ride pell-mell through forest like boys!"

Henry laughed with him, glimpsing the happy boy in the middle-aged King. "It's glorious, Your Majesty," he agreed.

"French kings have hunted these woods for a thousand years," said the King, "but if we rode like boys without a purpose the peasants would think their king mad. So, we'll eat venison tonight and prove our sanity!"

The wagons arrived and the servants began setting up a pavilion for the King's luncheon. Almost everyone dismounted, but the King remained on his horse talking to Henry. Three other men remained mounted just behind them, all equipped with sheathed swords and pistols.

"Thank you for inviting us, Your Majesty," said Henry, "What a beautiful forest."

The King's horse walked forward a few steps, and Henry nudged his horse alongside. After a moment, the three men mounted behind them moved forward as well. "It's bittersweet," said the King, "This is my first hunt since the death of my eldest son last year."

"My condolences, Your Majesty" said Henry gravely, bowing his head.

Again, the King stepped his horse forward a few steps, and Henry followed. Turning in his saddle, the King held up his hand to the three men behind them. "Give us space," he ordered. They glanced at each other uneasily but complied.

"They worry about me," explained the King to Henry.

"Here in your forest? Why?" asked Henry.

"Perhaps it's the armed Englishman riding next to me?" grinned the King, surprising Henry. He unconsciously put his hand on the gun slung in a long scabbard from his saddle and saw the three guards immediately put their hands to their weapons, ready to draw.

Laughing, the King put up his hand and said, "Stop! Henry, let's put the guns aside and have something to eat." Both dismounted and walked towards the pavilion, followed by the armed guards at a respectful distance. Much later, Henry would learn that a domestic servant named Damien had tried to stab King Louis XV in 1757, thus earning the distinction of being the last man drawn and quartered in the Kingdom of France.

Later that day, inside the palace at Compiegne, Adam and Quesnay sat at chess. Sunlight streamed through the tall windows, gilding the interior, drapes muffling the small echoes off the marble walls. Tapestries and paintings of the many hunts of yore adorned the hall. The men sat at a small table, dwarfed by the magnificent room, alone. Quesnay captured Adam's knight with his bishop. "When the King invited us to go hunting, I wondered if I'd be sleeping in a tent," observed Adam.

"This is nearly camping, compared to Versailles," returned Quesnay with a wry grin. Footsteps approached; a servant refilled their glasses with claret and left the bottle. "The chessboard is like a country; we are always trying to seize more land," said the elderly doctor. Adam moved his own bishop and captured a pawn. "And then hold on to it," continued Quesnay, "Property is everything."

"In the great chessboard of human society, every single piece has its own principle of motion," replied Adam.

"I see your point," said Quesnay, "I've seen some bishops go sideways!"

Adam laughed at this, and Quesnay was pleased with his joke. Adam responded, "Their motion can be altogether different than what the legislature might try to impose." He intentionally referred to the English 'legislature,' instead of 'the King,' although the latter was true in France.

Quesnay moved to take a pawn of his own, then replied, "Property gives security; without property the land would still be uncultivated."

"The property every man has in his own labor is the original foundation of all other property," answered Adam, taking Quesnay's queen with his own. The Frenchman frowned.

"We disagree on capital, then," he said, "I say capital is the land, and you say it's the labor."

In the distance doors banged open, and the King, followed by his retinue returning from the hunt, strode down the hall towards them. He stopped at the chess table, holding up his hands to keep Adam and Quesnay from jumping up to bow.

"Sit, sit, my geniuses!" said the King, "What a glorious day for hunting. Who's winning?"

"Monsieur Smith just dealt me a fatal blow, Your Majesty," responded Quesnay ruefully.

The King nodded sagely, examining the board, and observed with a wink at Adam, "The Scots are a crafty bunch." He turned and gestured to one of the men standing behind him. "Thanks to the marksmanship of Lieutenant Goulet here, a fine deer will grace our table!" Lieutenant Goulet stiffened with pride; his buff trousers splashed red with deer blood.

"Excellent, Your Majesty," said Quesnay, "Mr. Smith and I have already eaten."

"Your Majesty," asked Adam, "did Henry and Hew return with you?"

"I left them shooting at rabbits!" laughed the King, "Those are fine young men."

"Thank you, Your Majesty," Adam responded, immediately thinking that he'd be happy to report those words to Charles.

The King turned to continue down the hall, and the retinue turned to follow. But after three steps the King stopped abruptly, causing confusion in the group behind him. He turned back to Adam. "I understand the boys' father died young," he said, "Does their mother survive?"

"Indeed, Your Majesty," Adam answered, "Her name is Caroline."

"Tell Caroline that the King of France wishes her well for raising such fine sons," said the King.

Adam rose and bowed low, and said gratefully, "Your Majesty, I will." The King nodded, turned on his heel, and strode away down the hall, followed by his retinue.

Near dusk, Henry and Hew galloped into the stable yard, disheveled and sporting a brace of rabbits hung from their saddles. Dismounting, they turned the horses, the guns, the equipment, and the rabbits over to the stable hands, then strode towards the hall rumpled, tired, triumphant.

"It's good to know we could put meat on the table," said Hew.

"Nonsense," replied Henry, "We're hunting in the King's private reserve. Otherwise, the peasants would have all the rabbits."

"Why do you say that?" asked Hew.

"They're better hunters than us, brother," stated Henry.

"They don't have guns, Henry," replied Hew, shaking his head.

"Their snares and traps do less damage to the rabbit," said Henry, "Look, you have blood on your breeches."

Hew frowned, then replied, "Don't tell anyone that it was just a rabbit. We're fierce hunters."

The servants had already cleared much of the food when they saw the young English gentlemen arrive late. Two servants rushed several dishes back to the table and stood ready to assist Hew and Henry.

"The salad looks refreshing," said Henry, and the young male servant began dishing his plate.

"No rabbit food for me," said Hew, shaking his head, "I want to tear meat with my strong white teeth." He seized a chicken leg and tore off a big bite as a demonstration.

"You *are* fierce, Hew. Watch what you do with that poor chicken," smirked Henry, then he asked the server, "What is this orange sauce?" He noticed that the boy was pale and sweating profusely, even though the evening was cooling rapidly.

"French dressing, monsieur," replied the lad listlessly.

The next morning St. Jean walked a long marble hallway with a covered dish balanced on each hand. Rather than depend upon the King's servants for their personal service while in Compiegne, Cook and St. Jean had come along. Adam, rising much earlier than the boys, had instructed St. Jean to deliver breakfast to their door. He stood between the two doors, each on opposing sides of the hallway, and wondered how to knock while supporting both trays like a waiter. Cook appeared at his elbow and snapped, "Who told you to bring breakfast?"

"Monsieur Smith," replied St. Jean.

"Mr. Smith is in charge of their meals now?" asked Cook acidly, "Does he know how hard it is to get cooperation around here?"

One of the doors opened, and a rumpled Hew emerged, in breeches and wrinkled shirt. "I smell bacon," he said, and took one of the trays. "Perfect timing St. Jean!" he said over his shoulder as he disappeared back into his room.

This exasperated Cook even further, and he grabbed the second tray from St. Jean, saying brusquely, "Here, I'll take that."

"Oui, monsieur," replied the St. Jean, and then left quickly at the dismissive wave of Cook's hand. Cook took a moment to calm himself before knocking on Henry's door.

"Henry, I have your breakfast!" Cook called through the door, trying to take the irritation out of his voice.

"No breakfast, Cook," replied a muffled Henry without opening the door, "Sleeping in."

"I have crispy bacon," offered Cook, temptingly.

"Go away, Cook," replied Henry.

Cook stood there, alone in the hallway holding the covered plate. He took a deep breath, feeling defeated, then regained his composure and marched off with Henry's breakfast.

Later that morning, Adam sat reading in his room with a cup of tea. St. Jean was brushing one of Adam's suits as it hung on a hanger. There was a knock, and St. Jean opened it to reveal Cook.

"Would now be good time to discuss expenses, Mr. Smith?" said Cook, twisting his hands and revealing his anxiousness.

"Is there a concern?" asked Adam as Cook stepped into the room and St. Jean closed the door.

"I'm drafting my report to Mr. Townshend," he replied, "I don't have the items nor the total expenditure for your clothes." Cook gestured at the coat that St. Jean had resumed brushing.

"Mr. Cook, thank you for managing our accounts here in France," answered Adam calmly, "I am sure my expenses meet with Mr. Townshend's approval."

"I represent Mr. Townshend's interests here," replied Cook imperiously, "and I owe him a complete report."

"We are enjoying the King's hospitality here at Compiegne," answered Adam, remaining calm despite Cook's obvious agitation and his own growing irritation, "How could there be expenses?"

"My report includes Paris, where our expenses are substantial," replied Cook, gesturing at St. Jean, "Your man here just spends and spends as if money were free."

"Mr. Cook!" snapped Adam, making Cook jump, "St. Jean does what I ask him. If you have a concern, address it to me!"

Dismayed by Adam's sharpness, Cook paused, uncertain, as the response was so unexpected from the mild professor. He plunged ahead regardless, saying bitterly, "I'll tell him Professor Smith is too absent-minded to account for his funds!"

Adam stood and replied in a steely voice that neither servant had heard him use previously. "For eight years I was Chief Administrator for the University of Glasgow," he glowered, "I oversaw *all* the accounting. Tell Mr. Townshend whatever you wish, Mr. Cook." He walked to the door, opened it, and pointed to the hallway. "St. Jean, when we return to Paris, provide Mr. Cook a complete inventory of my wardrobe."

Cook accepted this as the best his excesses would allow, and replied in a brittle voice, "Thank you, Mr. Smith. Good day to you," as he stalked out.

Adam closed the door and looked at St. Jean. "What was all that about?"

"Monsieur Cook is frustrated," replied St. Jean, "He struggles to buy from the French."

"How so?" asked Adam.

"Trade is... relationships," explained St. Jean, "Monsieur Cook's English snobbery earns him higher prices and slower service. Or no service, just a shrug."

"Hmmm..., thank you for that confidence," said Adam, "Have you provided our expenses?"

"Oui, monsieur," St. Jean answered, "but in French. I am not good at writing the English."

"Your manner with Mr. Cook is admirable, St. Jean," said Adam after a moment's reflection, "I admit, your patience exceeds mine."

"Monsieur Cook is unfriendly, yes," offered St. Jean, "But he is honest. He serves the brothers, not himself. There is much to admire, despite his difficult manner."

"Spoken like a good Christian, St. Jean," said Adam. "Paper, ink, and quills if you please," he added after a pause. "I must write to Charles."

Later that day, Cook knocked again at Henry's door. Hearing nothing, he called through the door, "Henry, are you still in your room?"

"Come in, Cook," came Henry's muffled reply.

Henry sat up on his bed as Cook entered, looking pale, disheveled and damp.

"I wonder if I could trouble you for a moment," began Cook.

"For a moment," said Henry, "I'm not feeling my best today."

Cook held a sheaf of papers before him, saying, "I've written it all down if you'd prefer."

"No," Henry said bluntly, "In very few words, what?" He poured a glass of water from the pitcher at his bedside and drank thirstily. Cook did not appear to notice Henry's condition.

"Well, Mr. Smith and his new servant are not letting me do my job," said a petulant Cook.

Henry put his glass down and looked at Cook wearily. "In what possible way is that true?"

Cook let his indignation creep back into his tone, answering, "Mr. Townshend requires a full accounting of our expenditures. He was very pointed in that regard!"

"Yes. And?" asked Henry, hoping Cook would go away soon.

"They won't give me their expenses! They spite me intentionally!" exclaimed Cook.

"Spite you, Cook?" replied Henry disbelievingly.

"Their expenses are incomplete and are written in French!" said Cook.

Henry's face blanched, and he leaned over suddenly to vomit violently into the chamber pot.

• • • •

HOURS LATER, DUSK HAD fallen and Cook lit candles in Henry's room as Hew sat at his bedside. Adam knocked, and Cook admitted him and St. Jean. Cook pursed his lips but said nothing.

"He's burning up, Mr. Smith," said Hew anxiously.

Adam put his hand on Henry's forehead to feel the heat, and saw that Henry was unresponsive.

"He fell asleep a few minutes ago, rather suddenly," offered Hew.

"Henry?" said Adam but got no response. Hew shook Henry's arm gently and got only a low moan. Henry's eyes didn't open. Adam looked at Cook in alarm. "Have you called for the doctor?"

"Not yet," replied Cook, making no move to do so.

"Go fetch him, quickly!" said Adam sharply.

Cook snapped back, "You go fetch him, Mr. Smith, I'm not leaving Henry!"

"Cook, that's ridiculous," said Hew, "Run for the doctor."

"I'm not leaving Henry," replied Cook stubbornly, "The doctor won't come at this hour."

Adam looked at Cook a long moment, clenching his teeth but not wanting to alarm Hew. He turned to St. Jean and with effort controlled his voice. "I'll go for Doctor Quesnay. Please stay and help Henry, starting with fresh cold water and clean towels."

"Oui, monsieur," said St. Jean and he swiftly departed.

Adam put his hand on Hew's shoulder and tried to sound reassuring. "Dr. Quesnay is the best doctor in France, Hew," and then he left as quickly as St. Jean.

At midnight, Quesnay sat at Henry's bedside in the room lit by candlelight. Cook bathed Henry's forehead with a cold compress. St. Jean poured fresh water into Cook's bucket. Adam and Hew stood near the door, watching, deeply alarmed that Henry remained unresponsive. They watched as Quesnay picked up a scalpel and bled Henry's arm. St. Jean caught the blood in a cup.

"We'll take one cup now, and another in the morning," said Quesnay, wiping his hands.

"Finally, he's getting some treatment," said Cook, "Thank you doctor."

"Give him some cool tea, when he awakens," instructed Quesnay as he bandaged Henry's arm. Henry stirred, and everyone paused, looking at the patient and hoping he would wake up and reassure them. After a low moan, Henry lapsed back into unconsciousness. "I'll see him again in the morning," said Quesnay at the door, "Good night."

The room was quiet after he left, with everyone looking at Henry instead of each other. "Now what?" said Hew, lifting his eyes and looking at Adam.

"I propose we take turns sitting with him," said Adam, "Someone should be here if he wakes."

"I'm not leaving him," stated Cook with finality.

"Suit yourself, Mr. Cook, you take the first watch," replied Adam frostily, his tension spilling out after so many anxious hours. "Stay awake and keep his forehead cool."

Adam and Cook glared at each other. Hew touched Cook's arm and broke the stalemate. "I'll be right across the hall, Cook. Wake me."

"I'll send St. Jean back with some tea," said Adam, standing to leave the room. In a moment just Cook and Henry remained and Cook stood staring at the door angrily.

"Cook, what's going on?" said Henry weakly, causing Cook to spin around.

"Henry, you're awake!" Cook said excitedly.

"I've never felt worse," whispered Henry, "I think you should get the doctor."

"He was just here," said Cook, hesitating before adding, "While you were... sleeping."

"So that's why my arm hurts," replied Henry, before lapsing again into unconsciousness.

• • • •

TWO DAYS LATER, HEW sat nodding in the chair next to Henry's bed as he slept, so he didn't notice when Henry opened his eyes. "Hew" said Henry weakly.

"Henry!" exclaimed Hew, sitting up from his doze, "How are you brother?" He took Henry's hand in one of his.

"I feel so weak," said Henry, "Like my guts are in a wringer."

"Can I get you some water? Broth?" offered Hew.

"A drink, yes," replied Henry, trying to sit up but then spilling some of the water on his chest. He coughed and then lay back on his pillow and Hew mopped up the spill as best he could.

"Should I fetch Doctor Quesnay?" asked Hew.

"No, it hurts when he bleeds me," said Henry.

"It's for your own good, Henry," insisted Hew.

"Not now," replied Henry with a weak shake of his head.

"The King came by yesterday and asked how you were," said Hew brightly, trying to cheer him.

"What did you tell him?" asked Henry.

"That you wouldn't be hunting today," said Hew, trying to be lighthearted, "Maybe tomorrow."

Henry smiled weakly and tried to make a joke. "Maybe I have Rabbit Fever."

"Ah-hah, a sense of humor," grinned Hew, "a sure sign of recovery."

"I'm not so sure," replied Henry as his eyes closed again.

Hew watched his brother to see if he would continue, but it appeared as if he was sleeping again.

"Get well, Henry," whispered Hew, "Don't make *me* be the Third Duke of Buccleuch." There was no answer from his brother.

The next day, Adam and Quesnay sat again at chess, this time at a table near the doorway to Henry's room, which was closed. They whiled away the time, unwilling to go far from the patient. "Man is just another animal when you bleed them," observed Quesnay as he pondered the board.

"Is more bleeding always better?" asked Adam.

"Not at all," replied the King's physician, "the doctor's good judgment is vital."

"In England, a doctor certificate can be bought for as little as twelve pounds sterling," Adam said, adding, "No offense, Doctor."

"None taken" replied Quesnay, "We do the same when nobles buy a regiment for their pampered sons. War shows our animal side. There is always so much bleeding."

"Man is an animal that makes bargains; no other animal does this, no dog exchanges bones with another," replied Adam, trying to defend mankind's loftier aspects.

"I agree, Monsieur Smith," said the doctor, "Man is rational. Until we bleed, then we are just animals." Quesnay moved his piece, and said, "Check, Monsieur Smith."

"A bold move, my good doctor," mused Adam, examining the board. He moved a piece to escape check, then offered, "Hume would say, that reason is a slave to the passions."

"And what would you say, Monsieur Smith?" Quesnay asked, glancing up from his attack.

"That reason is a partner to our passions; as a man rides a horse," replied Adam, "I wrote a book on the subject."

"Touche," smiled Quesnay, "but our feelings cannot determine matters of state. Statesmen must use their heads, not their hearts.

"Our feelings tell us what we want; our reason, how to get them," parried Adam, "Statesmen cannot tell us what we want. He who would direct private people how to employ their capital, assumes an authority that could be trusted to no man whatsoever. Especially to a man with enough folly to presume himself fit to exercise it!"

Quesnay shook his head. "Men and their feelings come and go. If something is right, it should be done. Make it so!" He slapped the arm of his chair for emphasis, but accidentally hit the corner of the board. Several pieces were knocked to the floor. "Oh, my!" exclaimed the elderly doctor, "I've upset our game. Chess is like war, and war is all destruction."

Adam bent over and retrieved a broken piece, setting the fragments on the board. "Your king has lost his head," Adam observed dryly.

"Let's keep that to ourselves," answered Quesnay with just a hint of a smile, "We'll call this game a draw. Speaking of which, is it time to draw another cup from Henry?

CHAPTER 29

A THEISM *September 1766*

September sunlight streamed into the Adderbury drawing room as Charles dictated a letter to Frances, who served as his amanuensis. She sat at a table surrounded by papers and quills; he stood near the fireplace although it was too early in the season to need a fire for warmth.

"Furthermore," began Charles, then he stopped and put his chin in his hand. "No, make that, nevertheless..."

A servant appeared at the door. "Letters from France, sir."

Charles rifled through them, then said, "Frances, run and get your mother. Letters from Smith, and from Cook."

Frances left swiftly, calling for her mother, as Charles held the two letters, one in each hand. Cook's envelope was thick, and Smith's, as usual, was thin. He opened both with a pen knife, then pulled Smith's missive first and began to read. "A fever! A serious fever!" said Charles to himself as he read the alarming news, then he muttered with relief, "Better! Fever reduced..."

Caroline and Frances entered the room. "Any letters from the boys, Charles?" asked Caroline.

Charles looked up and said in a steady voice, "Smith says Henry is ill, and apparently it was serious. But he seems on the mend."

"No!" cried Caroline and her hand flew to her mouth in dismay. "Is he sure?"

"Only what I read here, Caroline," answered Charles, "Smith is miserly with his letters."

"Well, we must know!" exclaimed Caroline.

Charles read directly from Adam's letter to appease his distraught wife. "Today, Henry's fever was so moderate that they didn't even bleed him. When a French physician judges bleeding unnecessary, you may be sure the fever is not very violent."

"He still has a fever?" fretted Caroline.

"The King's own physician is attending Henry, a Dr. Quesnay," soothed Charles, "He is in good hands, Caroline." Calming his wife's upset helped settle his own anxiety at the disturbing news.

Caroline calmed herself, but Frances stood silent next to her with knotted hands and worried brow. Caroline extended her hand for Smith's letter once Charles turned to Cook's. "You'll like how that letter ends, Caroline," said Charles, pulling Cook's many pages from the envelope.

As Caroline finished the first page of Adam's letter, she set it down and Frances immediately picked it up. "Frances! Put that down!" commanded Caroline.

"Mother! How cruel!" exclaimed Frances with a frown.

"Let her read, Caroline," said Charles gently, and she relented with a nod. As Charles finished each page, he handed it to Caroline, who handed her finished pages to Frances.

"Oh dear," said Caroline, reading Smith's second page, "Cook has offended the Professor. Mr. Smith thinks him impertinent." A broad smile replaced the fretful look on Caroline's face as she continued reading.

"The King of Frances wishes me well, by name!" she said excitedly, "For raising two fine sons!"

"They were raised by wet nurses and boarding schools, Mother," said Frances, half to herself.

"Frances!" replied Caroline sharply, "Don't tarnish the finest compliment I have ever received! The King! Imagine!"

"A fine compliment indeed, my dear," said Charles, "I can hardly wait to tell the chaps at the club. But I expected too much of Cook."

"How so, dear?" asked Caroline.

"Cook is competent, but he's overmatched," Charles answered, "The length and tone of that letter proves it."

"If he's arguing with the Professor, I'd say he's overmatched," observed Caroline dryly, reading Cook's first page. She finished and handed it to Frances.

"My goodness, Cook is a strident, petty man!" exclaimed Frances.

"Frances, keep a civil tongue," clucked Caroline, but she didn't disagree.

• • • •

IT WAS MID-SEPTEMBER before a big coach and four arrived in front of the Parc Royale in Paris. Cook stepped out and held the door for a pale Henry, who climbed down slowly and grabbed Cook's arm briefly for support. Adam, Hew, and St. Jean followed.

"Mind the luggage, Cook," instructed Hew, "I'll see Henry to his room."

As Hew escorted his brother, Adam pulled Cook and St. Jean aside before they entered the hotel. "We've had a difficult time," said Adam, "Now that Henry has recovered, I suggest we put resentments behind us."

"Oui, monsieur," nodded St. Jean. Cook nodded but said nothing.

"We didn't quarrel about ourselves, we quarreled over Henry's welfare," said Adam. Cook nodded again but did not show evidence of agreement. Adam tried again. "So, we agree on our main priority, Henry's welfare," he ended lamely.

Cook finally relented, saying, "Yes, Mr. Smith. I apologize if I was overzealous in that regard."

Adam smiled, relieved. "Not at all, Mr. Cook, you are attentive to your duty. I'll tell Charles that when I write him next." Turning to his valet, Adam instructed, "St. Jean, please inventory my clothes in detail. I will translate the list for Mr. Cook."

"Thank you, Mr. Smith," Cook acknowledged as they entered the hotel. Adam followed last and almost patted Cook on the back but withdrew his hand with Cook none the wiser.

Two days later, Henry and Adam returned to Comtesse Boufflers salon at the Palace. She greeted them at the door, extending both hands to Adam. He blushed and took them, a bit awkwardly, to Henry's delight. "Adam! Henry! It's been so dull without you!" she said warmly.

Hew and Henry had discussed Adam's breakthrough with the Comtesse during his long convalescence, although Adam himself had said nothing whatsoever. His blush at seeing the Comtesse again proved it without a doubt, as well as her use of his first name. "I'm glad to return, Comtesse," answered Adam with a wide smile. "Henry has been ill, could we sit?"

"Of course!" answered the Comtesse, leading them to a pair of chairs. She went to fetch another for herself. Adam tried to assist, but only hindered her. "Thank you, Adam, I can manage," she smiled at him. "No servants today, as Baron d'Holbach is here."

Henry sank gratefully into his chair, and the Comtesse said to Adam, "Help me get a drink for Henry? Tea?"

"Yes, please," answered Henry.

Adam followed her to the table where she poured a glass of cold tea from a pitcher. He noticed that she wore a dainty apron. "Who is this Baron you mention?" asked Adam.

"Baron d'Holbach was born in Germany near the border but grew up here in Paris, she replied. "He is a firm atheist, but he is also a Farmer General, a tax collector, so he must keep it quiet. He is very powerful, but I've dismissed the servants, so they don't complain to the priests."

"So here, in your salon, he is openly atheist?" asked Adam.

"Yes, and he wants to talk to you!" smiled the Comtesse with satisfaction.

Carrying two glasses each, they returned to Henry. Sitting in one of the chairs opposite him was a distinguished man who rose at their approach. About the same age as Adam, and as tall as Henry, he projected an air of confident authority.

"Monsieur Smith, please meet Baron d'Holbach, of Grandval," introduced the Comtesse, "Baron, the illustrious Adam Smith."

"At last, we meet, Monsieur Smith," greeted the Baron, with a bow.

"The pleasure is mine, Baron," replied Adam with a brief bow, "I see you have met Henry."

"I took the liberty seeing the open chair," said the Baron, "An honor to meet such imminent Scotsmen." Henry started at this, but said nothing, accepting his drink from the Comtesse.

"Please sit down, Monsieur Smith," she invited, "I'll find another chair."

"No, Comtesse, please allow me," insisted Adam, until she relented and sat in his chair. Adam pushed another into the circle and sat, pleased with himself.

"Adam, er, Monsieur Smith," started the Comtesse, "the Baron just missed you. He arrived in Paris after you left for Compiegne with the King."

"I missed Hume as well," said d'Holbach, and so my first question is, are you an atheist like your friend Hume?" Adam and Henry were stunned by the blunt question, and they glanced at each other. Comtesse Boufflers sipped her drink, fascinated by what would come next.

"No, Baron, I'm not," replied Adam cordially, "But neither is Hume, I'm afraid. Hume is a skeptic, but not an atheist."

Baron d'Holbach bored in. "So, he lacks faith in his own convictions? We hear he is shunned in his own country as an infidel."

"Yes, sometimes," nodded Adam.

"How can a man be enlightened if he still believes in God?" asked the Baron, his tone civil but his words blunt.

"Hume is a skeptic about God, but not a denier," replied Adam, "There is a difference."

"And you, Monsieur Smith? What is your view of God?" asked the relentless Baron. There was no small talk with this man; Henry and the Comtesse waited eagerly for Adam's answer, which came after a moment's contemplation.

"I like how Voltaire put it during our recent visit," he began, "He told me, 'I cannot imagine how the clockwork of the universe can exist, without a clockmaker.' Hume says much the same thing, when he says, 'it's absurd to think the universe exists without a cause.'"

"I'm impressed, Monsieur Smith," said the Baron, "You quote your friends from memory." Henry and the Comtesse nodded, impressed as well.

"I like the term, Author of Nature," said Adam, "God exists, because Nature had a cause."

Baron d'Holbach considered this for a long moment. No one spoke, waiting for his response. A few of the Comtesse's other guests had drifted over, plates and cups in hand, to listen while standing behind the chairs. "Forgive me, Monsieur Smith, but that seems like sophistry," he said at last, "Nature exists, but why must we believe that there was always something before, something greater? It's enough that we have Man, and Nature, and these are first things. Not second things." Many of the listeners nodded in agreement, as by no means was Baron d'Holbach the only atheist in attendance.

Unexpectedly, Henry interjected, "I disagree with both of you." All eyes turned to him.

"I was recently very ill," he said, "I felt that I might die. God seemed very real to me then, more than ever before. I would say that God is not just the Creator; but that he lives on, in my heart. In our hearts. In our sentiments."

The Baron couldn't prevent a smirk from crossing his face, but he remained cordial. "Far be it from me to make light of your illness, Duke Henry," replied d'Holbach, "To each their own belief, of course. I would say that what you felt was not rational, but emotional."

"Yes," nodded Henry, "it was emotional. How does that lessen my experience of God? That he is not above our lives, or indifferent, but part of us?"

All the listeners, including Adam and Comtesse Boufflers, sat silent in rapt attention.

"Only that our reason is superior to our emotions," answered the Baron with confidence, "We must rule our emotions, or life becomes, as your own Thomas Hobbes put it, 'nasty, brutish, and short.' Without reason, we have war, violence, bloodshed."

"Baron," interjected the Comtesse, "may I observe that *with* reason, we just had seven years of war, violence, and bloodshed?"

"The follies of the recent war were caused by pride, by dogma, and by religious vain glory!" responded the Baron emphatically, "The very *opposite* of reason."

"Hume would say that all certainty is really just probability," said Adam, "That is the heart of scientific inquiry; we are always just a bit unsure, always a bit skeptical. Always asking more questions."

"Of course we can be sure, Monsieur Smith! Why would we doubt ourselves?" said the Baron, shaking his head, "Your view invites doubt and indecision. Man must act!" d'Holbach smacked his fist into his palm, showing his blood was rising.

"My heart is full of doubts, Baron, but not because I lack reason," replied the Comtesse sweetly.

"Forgive me, Baron, but if Reason replaced God, it would seem just as dogmatic, just as vulnerable to abuse. For bloodshed, even," said Adam, remaining calm.

"Nonsense," barked d'Holbach, "Men must have the power to do good, to do right. As reason dictates, not some priest."

"My sentiments include God because my heart does," said Henry.

"What a beautiful expression Henry!" smiled the Comtesse, "I agree."

"Such superstitions!" snorted the Baron, rising to his feet, "How can you call yourself enlightened?" Abruptly he rose and walked away towards the refreshments, followed by some of the listeners.

"Well!" said the Comtesse, breaking into a brilliant smile that drained tension from everyone, "I expected fireworks, and the Baron didn't disappoint!"

Adam put his hand on Henry's shoulder and caught his eye. "Well done, Henry. Well said."

"When you jump in its headfirst, Henry!" laughed the Comtesse, "Your timing was impeccable!"

A flush of gratitude warmed Henry's wan face. "Thank you, but I'm afraid I offended him."

"Such a rational man, the Baron, and a very generous one," she said, smiling, "but he has emotions like any other."

"Comtesse, have you heard from Eloise?" asked Henry, and his heart sank as she shook her head.

• • • •

THE VERY NEXT AFTERNOON, Henry followed Adam slowly up the stairs to Madame Espinasse's salon. He felt weak in everything he did, but knew he was on the mend. "Henry, I'm so glad to see you hale and healthy!" greeted Madame Espinasse as they entered. Tired from the stairs, he felt somewhat less than hale.

"Madame, have you heard from Eloise?" was Henry's first question, as Adam was pulled away by Quesnay and Turgot.

She paused, then took his elbow and pulled him aside. "Eloise is spending the winter in Nantes, with her uncle," she informed him gently.

"Did she leave a message?" he asked, crestfallen. Nantes was two days' ride from Paris in good weather.

She shook her head and said, "Not with me, Henry. Perhaps the short goodbyes are best."

"Perhaps... that's what she said when I asked if I'd see her again. Perhaps," Henry replied morosely, looking at the floor.

"She likes you, Henry, but Eloise knows her own mind," replied Madame Espinasse. She'd heard Eloise's tearful lament over her torn heart regarding Henry, but kept that in complete confidence.

"That's what makes her special," agreed Henry.

"Yes," she nodded, "Now, Henry, allow me to introduce my guest ...." She turned Henry and he found himself face to face with Baron d'Holbach.

"Baron, this is..." began Madame Espinasse.

"You again!" exclaimed the Baron.

"Yes sir," said Henry, surprised. Madame Espinasse was surprised as well; she hadn't heard they'd met the brash Baron the day before at the Comtesse's salon.

Baron d'Holbach smiled broadly and spread his arms, palms out. "I must apologize for yesterday, young Duke. I am ardent in my opinions, but I am a tolerant man. Forgive me." The apology was unexpected, surprising Henry again. The Baron spoke with such certainty that it seemed he would never apologize for anything.

"Of course, Baron, of course," Henry smiled in return, "No apologies needed. I enjoyed our conversation, er, despite our differences."

"Spoken like a future politician!" replied the Baron, clapping Henry on the back. "We keep a keen eye on your stepfather, Duke Henry. Charles Townshend might be Prime Minister one day. Your future seems bright, to say the least."

"I suspect Henry's future will shine just as brightly wherever he lands," added the Madame graciously, and Henry gave her a grateful look.

"I'll excuse myself," said the Baron, "as I have more questions for Monsieur Smith." He gave a short bow, which Henry returned with a smile, and then he was gone.

"Thanks for the kind words, Madame," said Henry, "Could you possibly pass a letter to Eloise?"

CHAPTER 30

HEW CAMPBELL SCOTT *October 1766*

Henry sat at the desk in his room at the Parc Royale, composing his letter to Eloise. Or trying to compose it; several crumpled efforts littered the floor around him. Late afternoon light came through the window as he pulled a fresh sheet and dipped his quill in ink. Just as the tip touched the page, a knock came at the door. "Henry?" called Hew.

"Come in," Henry responded, relieved by the diversion.

Hew stepped into the room, dressed to go out. Spying Henry's efforts with the quill, he asked, "Has Mr. Smith given you an assignment?"

"No, I'm writing a letter to Eloise," Henry sighed.

"Are you in love, brother?" asked Hew, with a smile.

"No. Yes. I can't be, not here in France." Henry rested his chin on his palm, elbow on the desk.

"Yes, here in France. Especially, here in France. Fewer prudes in France, I'd say," replied Hew.

"That's not what I mean," returned Henry.

"Less writing with my definition of love," returned Hew, who hated to touch pen to paper. "I heard Mr. Smith singing your praises about something you said at salon."

"What did he say?" asked Henry, examining the tip of his quill.

"I don't know, I couldn't really follow it," said Hew, "Just that it was well-timed and pleased the Comtesse."

"It was about God, Hew," said Henry, somberly. Hew noted a new gravity to his brother but was unsure whether it was due to his illness or Eloise.

360

"You are more serious than me," said Hew, putting his hand on Henry's shoulder, "You think about God and Love, and I think about Girls and Love."

Henry sighed. "Oh, I'm thinking about a girl all right."

"Have you asked Eloise to come to England?" asked Hew suddenly, with a flash of insight.

"Yes," replied Henry miserably, "I blurted it out. Don't you dare tell Charles or Mother."

"Mum's the word, brother," nodded Hew, "What did Eloise say?"

"No, of course," said Henry, chin still on palm, "She couldn't stand the ire of my family."

Hew nodded somberly. "Yes, there would be serious upset if you brought a French beauty home with you." They brooded together for a long moment. Hew brightened, and said, "But then, you'd be *home*, and have a *French beauty* with you!"

Henry laughed; his carefree brother always cheered him. He stood and stretched, then asked, "You're going out. Where?"

"A pint of ale at the tavern down the street," said Hew, "Join me?"

Henry lifted his coat from its hook and shrugged it on. "What would I do without you Hew?"

Hours later and much drunker, Hew navigated Henry towards a particular house a few blocks from the Parc Royale. "Come in with me, Henry, it will help you forget Eloise," said Hew.

Henry recognized the house but had never been inside. He was tempted to follow his brother, but Hew's mention of her name made him think of Eloise, and that decided it despite the alcohol. "No, you go, Hew, have fun," he said, pushing his brother towards the door. He returned to the Parc Royale alone, in the dark, thinking of Eloise and wrestling about what to say in his letter.

By the evening of the next day, Henry delivered his envelope to Madame Espinasse for delivery to Eloise. "*Perhaps, once I reach majority ...*" he'd written, but then he thrust those thoughts out of his head. The agony of composition was over; no use regretting a letter already sent.

• • • •

TWO WEEKS LATER HENRY and Hew entered the Parc Royale after a morning ride in the crisp October air. Cook was waiting for them in the common room. "Mr. Smith asks that you go directly to Comtesse Boufflers salon," directed Cook, "he is already there."

"Both of us?" asked Hew, as he didn't usually go with Henry and Adam to either salon.

"He said you in particular, Hew," said Cook.

"We'll change," agreed Henry, "Cook, have a carriage ready in twenty minutes?"

"Twenty minutes," nodded Cook, and he left to arrange it.

"Why now?" complained Hew, "I've mostly avoided the salons so far."

"You'll see," answered Henry, smiling. "I forgot it was today. Wear your best coat."

At the Palace, Comtesse Boufflers led them through a throng of attendees to the far side of the room, where a balding, middle-aged man sat on a stool before a canvas on an easel. An empty, elegant gilt chair sat opposite.

"Mother wants your portrait, Hew," informed Henry.

"Hew, Henry, may I introduce Jean-Baptiste Greuze?" said the Comtesse.

"A pleasure to meet you both," he replied graciously, "Monsieur Hew, please take a seat?"

"I suppose there is no getting out of this little trap you've sprung?" said Hew as he sat in the upholstered chair.

"None. I promised Mother," grinned Henry with folded arms.

"Greuze is the foremost painter in Paris," enthused the Comtesse, "His style is in vogue."

Greuze posed Hew so he faced the light of the window, elbow on the arm of the chair, one foot forward of the other but both planted firmly on the floor. "Henry, I'd hate to tremble and spoil this good man's aim," said Hew, "Can you fetch me a small claret?"

"Gladly brother," replied Henry, and looked at a servant to confirm that he'd heard the request. Henry held up two fingers and the man nodded.

Sipping his claret, Henry watched the painter work. Before they had arrived, Greuze had painted the background and had the chair itself sketched into position. Swiftly he added the basic lines of Hew's arms and legs, and progressively began filling in colors and preparing for later details. Adam and the Comtesse watched nearby, and Henry smiled at how close the Comtesse stood to his teacher.

Forty minutes after they arrived and were fully absorbed with Greuze's progress painting Hew, there was a commotion at the door. King Louis XV entered, followed by several ministers and a lad of about thirteen. The Comtesse immediately went to greet him, followed by Adam. The King rarely visited her salon, and she curtsied deep as she greeted him.

"Your Majesty! You grace us with your presence," she said.

"Thank you, Comtesse, I've come to see the Prince. He is expecting me," said the King. "I stopped by your salon, hoping to see young Duke Henry?"

"Right over here, Your Majesty," smiled the Comtesse, leading the way across the room followed by the King and his retinue, and then Adam. The rest of the guests crowded close, to hear what the King had to say to their English guests. "Hew is having his portrait made," she said, "and here is Henry."

Henry bowed low; Hew and Greuze jumped up and bowed low as well. "Do your best work, Greuze," said the King.

"I will do my very best, Your Majesty," replied Greuze with a smile, "Such a handsome subject."

Hew grinned widely at being called 'handsome' before King Louis XV, and the monarch turned to Henry. "Duke Henry, I understand you are fully recovered?" he asked solicitously.

"Yes, Your Majesty," Henry replied, "thanks for lending me your doctor."

"Quesnay serves me well," nodded the King, "A bit eager to take that extra cup of blood sometimes."

"All's well that ends well, Your Majesty," said Henry with a grin, pleased that the King would inquire about his health.

The King gathered the boy close with his arm and presented him to the young Englishmen. "Duke Henry, Hew, this is my grandson, Louis. Someday, he'll succeed me as King."

Henry and Hew bowed their greetings, and the young Louis bobbed impatiently but said only, "Monsieurs," before the King let him go and he ran off to find the refreshments.

"Just a boy, but he has a good head on his shoulders," said the King, looking after him. Henry knew the King had lost his own son, the boy's father, only the year before. Whether Kings bled blue or red mattered little; they suffered as anyone when their children died. Neither foresaw the awful fate of King Louis XVI, executed at the hands of the Revolution in 1793.

The Prince d'Conti entered the room and quickly found his way to the King. Adam noticed the Comtesse step away from him the instant she saw the Prince, who wore a white ermine cape and was dressed in such finery that he almost eclipsed the King himself. The King turned to watch Greuze work for a moment, making both the painter and Hew self-conscious. The Prince turned to Adam.

"I am honored to have such a scholar in my home, Monsieur Smith," he said cordially.

"We are honored by your hospitality," replied Adam, and then the Prince leaned in close and said in a low tone, not heard by those standing around.

"I trust you enjoy the company of the Comtesse?" leered the Prince with raised eyebrow, and Adam stiffened in understanding.

"She is very gracious," was all Adam could manage, crushed by the comment. His head said, "of course," but his heart wasn't listening as it sundered completely.

The King turned, and with only a nod to everyone he swept out of the room, followed by the Prince, the Ministers, and the Comtesse, without a backward glance. Adam stood dumbly beside Henry as they turned back to watch the painter.

"Not sparring with the intellectuals today, Mr. Smith?" asked Henry in a jovial tone, but he saw that Adam was lost in reverie.

"Huh?" said Adam, "Oh, perhaps, perhaps." His preoccupied look returned as he sipped his claret absently.

Henry saw he wasn't going to get much from him, so he turned back to Hew and said, "Try to look well-educated Hew, Mother should see she's getting her money's worth."

Hew smirked, "I only have one look, the dumb one. I depend on Monsieur Greuze to make me look smart."

"It's all in the eyes, monsieur," said Greuze, "Just the right spark, to please your mother."

"She's pretty hard to please," admitted Hew, smiling.

"What is her name?" the painter asked.

"Caroline Townshend," replied Hew, then he looked at Henry and said, "I'm hot. Henry, a cool refill?" He coughed, and perspiration had broken out on his forehead. Henry returned in a moment with the glass and Hew took a sip. "How long will this take?"

"Another hour," said Greuze, "The face and hands done today, and I can fill in the details later."

"I'm starting to feel a little unsteady," replied Hew.

• • • •

ONE WEEK LATER, ST. Jean carried a bucket of water quickly but carefully down the dark hallway at the Parc Royale, clean towels thrown over one shoulder. He rapped at Hew's door with his knuckle; it opened to reveal a candle-lit room with Adam, Cook, Henry, and Dr. Quesnay surrounding Hew as he lay on the bed with eyes closed. Quesnay was just cutting Hew's arm and catching the blood in a cup. "Watching that makes my arm hurt all over again," winced Henry.

"We must drain away the bad blood," said Quesnay.

"Does he have what I had?" asked Henry, concern etched on his face.

"I don't think so," answered the doctor, "Your fever fluctuated; Hew's is steady and high. Also, there is this." Quesnay lifted Hew's wet shirt to show a scarlet rash across his chest.

"St. Jean, pour a glass of water," said Adam, "Hew is burning up."

"Oui," said St. Jean, and dipped a glass into the bucket he'd just brought. In the candlelight the water was cloudy in the glass.

"Can we find cleaner water?" Adam asked.

"This is what the kitchen uses," said St. Jean.

"Perhaps some tea," advised Quesnay, "boiled water is less cloudy."

St. Jean nodded and left immediately, but he left the bucket. Cook dipped a towel into it and bathed Hew's forehead. Hew stirred at the cool contact, and everyone paused to see if he would awaken, but after muttering something incomprehensible, he lapsed back into his quiet but labored breathing. "What does the rash mean, Doctor," asked Cook, biting on his knuckle.

"Typhus, I suspect," was Quesnay's grim answer.

"Oh God!" Cook cried out, and Adam noticed that Cook had drawn blood on his hand with his teeth. St. Jean had been right about the man's motivations; irritating as Cook could be, he was loyal to the brothers.

"Your brother is young and healthy," said Quesnay to Henry with a frank look, "He may well survive. Have hope. I'll be back in the morning and bleed him again."

"Doesn't bleeding weaken the patient?" asked an anxious Adam.

"What else can we do?" shrugged Quesnay as he left.

"We must do everything we can!" exclaimed Cook to the door after it closed behind the doctor.

Early the next morning, Hew lay unchanged on the bed, a compress across his forehead. Cook was tilted back in a chair, head against the wall, asleep. Adam quietly entered, leaving the door ajar, and he checked Hew's pulse. He lifted the compress and felt his forehead.

"Cook," said Adam, but got only a small snort of a snore in response.

"Mr. Cook!" called Adam, bringing Cook's chair to the floor with a thump.

"Hmmpf! No change in his condition, Mr. Smith," said Cook, disoriented.

"I see that," said Adam kindly, "Why don't you get some rest? I'll stay until Quesnay arrives. Henry will be along shortly."

Hew stirred, and then raved loudly in his sleep. Adam and Cook froze, poised to respond if Hew regained consciousness. A long moment passed but he had lapsed back into silence. "Why don't you get some rest?" repeated Adam.

"Why don't you get the doctor?" exploded Cook with pent anguish, "He needs better care!" Henry appeared at the door, surprising Cook, who jumped.

"Does better care always mean draining blood?" Henry questioned.

"I share your concern," said Adam, "But I don't know what else to do. We know so little."

"Has Quesnay been here yet?" asked Henry.

"Not yet," said Adam, as Henry freshened the compress and laid it across Hew's damp brow.

"Cook, fetch more water," instructed Henry while looking at Hew, "Clean water." Cook plainly did not want to leave, instead looking at Adam as if he was the one who should fetch clean water.

"Cook! Clean water if you please!" said Henry sharply, causing Cook to grab the bucket and flee out the door. In the hall he nearly collided with Quesnay, followed by St. Jean with a pitcher and a stack of fresh towels. Cook lingered in the hallway as they entered the room.

"Any change?" asked Quesnay, pulling up a stool at Hew's bedside.

"I'm afraid not," replied Adam, "His fever is unrelenting."

Quesnay lifted Hew's shirt to inspect the rash, and then took his pulse carefully at the wrist. Henry bathed Hew's forehead with water from the pitcher. Cook looked on from the doorway, transfixed. "Cook!" barked Henry, "Are you back with the water?"

"On my way!" cried Cook and he fled down the hallway with the bucket.

"Henry," said Hew suddenly as his eyes opened, "I'm glad you're here."

"Hew!" cried Henry, grabbing his brother's hand and holding it in both of his. But Hew raved in delirium and lapsed back into unconsciousness. Henry looked at Adam grimly; both men were shaken.

"Let's take a cup," said Quesnay, "St. Jean, will you assist?" As the doctor laid his scalpel on Hew's arm, St. Jean stood at his elbow and readied the cup.

"Stop," ordered Henry, "Stop. Don't cut him again, Doctor."

Cook arrived back at the door with a full bucket, just in time to hear Henry stop the doctor. "Yes, yes, let the doctor help him!" objected Cook animatedly, slopping some of the water as he dropped the bucket to the floor.

"Cook!" commanded Henry in a steely voice, "I've decided. No more bleeding."

Quesnay looked at Henry, then at Adam, who nodded his deference to Henry. Quesnay withdrew his scalpel, and St. Jean straightened. A flame of color flushed Cook's pallid face, but he choked back whatever response he had.

Hew opened his eyes again, and said in a clear voice, "Henry, I...."

Henry grabbed Hew's hand and waited. "Yes, Hew?" he asked, but then as the moment lengthened, he realized in horror that Hew had died. His brother's open eyes looked at Henry as if he was about to tell him something, but that moment was gone forever, last words unsaid.

"Hew!" cried Henry in anguish, clutching his hand and burying his face in Hew's chest.

Cook cried out, "No!" and then burst into racking sobs that shook his thin frame. Tears flowed down Adam's cheeks while Quesnay bowed his head, dry-eyed, and closed his medical case. St. Jean took two steps backward to remove himself from the intimate group at the time of their greatest grief.

Finally, Henry raised his head, still clutching Hew's dead hand. His face was drawn and wet and his hair plastered his forehead. "We return to England at once," he ordered.

CHAPTER 31

H OME WITH HEW *October 1766*
St. Jean adjusted Adam's collar and neckcloth for the last time, standing before the mirror at the Parc Royale on the day of their departure. Then he held Adam's black Scottish frock coat as he put his arms in the familiar sleeves. "It feels right," mused Adam.

"Monsieur?" St. Jean lifted an eyebrow questioningly.

"My humble Scottish coat. That's the end of my fancy Paris outfits," explained Adam.

"You wore them well, monsieur," said St. Jean.

"Are my trunks loaded?" asked Adam.

"Oui, monsieur," nodded St. Jean.

"Then I would like to settle our arrangement, St. Jean," he said, "Hume recommended you highly, and now I know why."

Adam pulled three coins from his purse and gave them to St. Jean. "Here are your wages for the last week," he said, then counted out nine more. "And here is a bonus, St. Jean."

"Merci, Monsieur Smith," replied St. Jean, visibly surprised, "It has been my pleasure."

"You are not from here, St. Jean," observed Adam, broaching a topic he hadn't discussed during St. Jean's service to him, "How did you arrive in Paris, with such a flawless manner?"

St. Jean, whose task as valet was to remain in the background, thought for a moment before answering. "I was born in Dominica," he said, "My father was a French colonist, my mother, a Caribe. She sent me to Paris in my youth, to save me."

"Are they still there?" asked Adam.

"They are both dead, monsieur," replied St. Jean gravely.

"Your mother did well, St. Jean. I will honor her memory," said Adam, looking the young man in the eye, "You did well in difficult circumstances, and I thank you." Adam extended his hand and St. Jean shook it as tears filled his eyes. Adam's mention of his mother had finally pierced his formal reserve. "Oh, one more thing," said Adam, picking up a sealed envelope and handing it to St. Jean. "Here is a letter of recommendation, addressed to the incoming British ambassador. I have notified him separately, and he will be expecting you."

St. Jean bowed low to Adam. "Merci, Merci, Monsieur Smith," is all he could say.

"Merci to you, St. Jean, and Godspeed," said Adam.

Adam left the room for the last time and descended the stairs into the lobby, followed by St. Jean carrying his valise. His heart fluttered when he saw Comtesse Boufflers, wrapped in a shawl and waiting for him in the lobby. She was accompanied by a single maid who stood discreetly behind. As Adam approached the Comtesse extended her hands with a sad smile, and Adam took them in his own. "Comtesse," smiled Adam, "have you come to see me off?"

"I am so sorry for young Hew," said the Comtesse.

"A hard blow to take, a sad way to leave France," replied Adam, "I thank you for your hospitality."

"I will write to you, Adam," she said, and he was surprised to see a tear in her eye.

"You honor me, Marie," said Adam, feeling a lump rise in his throat. Comtesse Boufflers leaned in and kissed his cheek, making Adam blush as they were standing in the middle of the lobby. He didn't know what to say but was spared by a man approaching from the door. It was Jean-Baptiste Greuze, the painter.

"Monsieur Smith, have I missed the young Duke?" asked Greuze.

"No, we leave in a moment together," replied Adam, as Henry came down the stairs.

"My condolences, Monsieur Duke," bowed Greuze, "My portrait of your brother...."

"Yes, is it finished?" asked Henry, giving the man his attention but hiding his sorrow.

"Not quite, Monsieur. The face and hands, yes. I will finish the rest within the week," replied the artist, "May I ship it to you in London?"

Henry shook several gold coins from his purse and handed them to Greuze. "Is that sufficient?" asked Henry.

"Oui, Monsieur, oui," nodded Greuze vigorously as the coins disappeared into his pocket.

"Please ship it to Adderbury, near Oxford, to the attention of Caroline Townshend," replied Henry, "Package it well, monsieur."

"I can help with the shipping," volunteered the Comtesse, figuring she'd get to see the completed portrait that way.

Cook approached the group and said, "Everything is loaded and ready, Henry."

Adam realized there was no hope for a last moment of intimacy, so he bowed and said formally, "Comtesse Boufflers, I bid you adieu."

Henry bowed as well. "And I, Comtesse, your salon was my very favorite," he lied, as Eloise was usually at Madame Espinasse's.

"That is high praise indeed, Henry, merci," she replied with a gracious smile, "Please deliver Mr. Smith safe back to Scotland, and to his friend Hume."

Henry nodded and followed Cook out the door. Adam turned to follow Henry. "Adam, wait," he heard her say, and his heart fluttered again as he turned back. "A letter for Henry," she said, handing him an envelope. He took it with a pang that it wasn't for him, but he nodded as he left the Parc Royale for good.

In the courtyard a large coach and four waited, with the door open and Cook standing beside it. Behind the carriage two wagons stood, one for their baggage and the other carrying Hew's coffin. It was a cold, blustery day in late October, suitable for their dark journey to Calais.

Henry hesitated before the carriage, then turned to Cook and said, "I'll ride with Hew." He climbed up on the high seat beside the wagon driver transporting the coffin. Cook and Adam both nodded, understanding. Wordlessly, Adam handed the letter up to Henry, and then climbed into the carriage. Cook climbed in behind, closed the carriage door, and the sad caravan got underway. Comtesse Boufflers, Greuze, and St. Jean waved as they pulled out of the drive.

For several hours the caravan travelled the road from Paris. Henry, sitting on the hard, high seat of the wagon, turned the sealed envelope over and over in his hands. Written on the envelope in Eloise's elegant script was simply, 'Henry.' For hours he looked at his name, unable to open the letter and find her answer, now that it was too late. Hew's death had changed everything. Dark clouds scudded across the sky, matching his mood, and the wind whipped fitfully.

"The light will soon fail, monsieur," said the wagon driver, unexpectedly. Startled from his brooding reverie, Henry looked at the driver, a wiry, weathered man in his forties, who nodded at him kindly. The day's darkness was turning to dusk. The road passed through a stand of trees where the breeze was less, and Henry tore open the envelope and pulled out three sheets filled with Eloise's strong handwriting.

"Dearest Henry," the letter began, "I know my last word to you was, '*perhaps.*'

A lump rose in his throat, and he paused as his eyes filled with tears. The wagon emerged from the trees and approached a bridge over a stream. He forced his eyes to return to the page.

"I write to share my heart..." he read, and then, quick as a wink, a sudden gust of wind plucked the pages from his hand. He grabbed at them futilely, then with horror watched them tossed on the turbulent air before settling onto the slowly flowing waters of the stream. Mouth agape he watched them sink, lost forever. In his left hand he still held the envelope, with its single last word, 'Henry.'

The wagon driver pulled on the reins and stopped the horses, and the baggage wagon stopped on the bridge behind them. The driver turned to Henry with a contrite expression on his face, and said, "Sorry monsieur."

Crushed, Henry looked at him blankly, then turned and placed one hand on Hew's casket behind him. "I feel I've lost everything," he said, dumbly, as heavy drops of rain began to fall.

"Would you like to ride in the carriage, monsieur?" asked the driver, embarrassed to be sharing such a sad, poignant moment with the young English duke, and kicking himself for saying anything at all to the bereaved young man.

"No, I have my oilskins," answered Henry dully, pulling them from his bag and struggling into them as the rain steadily increased. He carefully tucked the empty envelope inside his coat. In a twinkling, the driver lashed a tarpaulin over Hew's coffin. Henry noticed that the man was missing the two outside fingers of his left hand; despite this, he was swift and competent with rope and knot.

The carriage had long disappeared into the gloom ahead as the two teams got the wagons underway. Henry was thankful for the hood on his oilskins, and for the rain, as his tears flowed and he felt like a silly boy riding the wagon with the Frenchman.

They traveled half an hour in silence before Henry spoke. "Merci for covering the casket," he said.

"Oui, monsieur," nodded the driver.

"What is your name?" asked Henry.

The driver looked at Henry sideways in the fading light, and as tough as the man had been in his difficult life, his heart went out to the heartsick youth. "Francois, monsieur," he said, and the corner of his mouth turned up. He never showed his teeth as he was missing several.

Henry recalled his first meeting with 'Francois' in Geneva and managed a wry smile. "I am Henry, and my brother here is Hew," he said, reaching back and patting the tarpaulin covering his brother. Unexpectedly, a broken sob escaped Henry, further embarrassing the Frenchman.

"I am sorry, monsieur," was all the driver could say. They traveled on, both embarrassed by the awkward situation they were in, but also affected by the deep melancholy that so often settles over those in the presence of the dead. After a few minutes, Henry tried to recover by renewing a normal conversation.

"How long have you been a wagon driver, Francois?" he asked, speaking over the splashing rain.

"Two years or so, ever since the War," said Francois.

"Were you a soldier?" followed Henry.

"A sailor, monsieur," he replied.

"Did you lose your fingers in battle?" asked Henry.

Francois lifted his left hand and contemplated his fate in the dim light before responding, "Battle with nature, not with men. We were hoisting the mainsail when it filled with a sudden gust. My fingers pinched off between the line and the spar." Francois snapped the fingers of his right hand, "Gone in a snap."

"Just like I lost my letter," reflected Henry.

"Oui, monsieur," nodded Francois.

"My apologies, Francois, for comparing my lost letter to your lost fingers," said Henry after an awkward moment.

"A broken heart hurts just as much, monsieur," replied the Frenchman.

Suddenly the wagon lurched to a stop, jerking the horses from their plodding rhythm. Jumping down, Francois and Henry saw that the right rear wheel had fallen through a hole in the collapsed roadbed. As they watched, the wagon settled even further, and Hew's casket strained at the lashings. Henry wondered if the whole wagon would disappear into the gaping declivity that had swallowed their wheel and imperiled the dignity of Hew's final journey. The baggage wagon driver climbed down and pulled a long pole from under his wagon, while Francois tumbled down a large wood block from his. Quickly they used the block as the fulcrum and positioned the pole under the axle to lever the wagon up out of the hole. The two drivers, off the road and three feet below the level of the wagon, put all their weight on the end of the pole. Henry watched from the road as the wagon groaned, but the wheel did not clear the hole.

Francois, straining, turned to Henry standing on the roadway and said, "Monsieur?" Henry belatedly realized that they needed his help. He slipped down the road embankment and fell flat in the mud but scrambled up and added his weight to the straining pole. Their combined weight lifted the wagon slowly up, but with all of them manning the pole how would they move the wagon?

Francois clicked his tongue twice and said, "Haw!" His faithful horses took several steps forward and stopped, and the pole slid off its block. But the wagon was on the firm roadway once again.

"Clever horses!" exclaimed Henry, grinning despite being covered in mud and streaming wet.

"They know me well," said Francois proudly, relieved that the incident, unpleasant as it had been, had interrupted the young duke's larger anguish.

Full dark had fallen, but far ahead there was a light. It turned out to be an inn, and they were grateful to see the carriage parked there. Cook, dressed in oilskins, stood out front holding a lantern as the wagons pulled to a stop. "Where have you been?" shouted Cook at Francois angrily, venting some of his alarm at finding the wagons were not close behind the carriage as night had fallen.

Henry drew back his hood and barked, "Cook, enough!" Cook bit his lip as Henry climbed down and gestured back up at the driver. "Cook, this is Francois." Cook glanced at the driver but said nothing. "Go with him and see to Hew," instructed Henry, "Secure his casket for the evening, and arrange for its transport to the boat tomorrow." His tone left no room for argument.

"Yes, Henry," Cook said, standing there.

"Climb up and go with him," repeated Henry, gesturing at the wagon step. Cook complied but said nothing as he took his seat next to Francois in the rain.

"Let's take proper care of this poor gentleman, Monsieur Cook," said the old sailor, snapping the reins and rolling the wagon towards the barn.

Henry turned and saw Adam standing in the lighted doorway of the inn. Adam said, "We were beginning to worry, Henry."

"We had a bit of wagon trouble," said Henry.

"I can see that," smiled Adam, nodding at Henry's muddy breeches and torn stockings as he pulled off his wet oilskins just inside the door. The powerful smell of hot food caught Henry's nostrils, and his hunger flared.

"They're just bringing beef and ale," said Adam, inviting Henry inside.

• • • •

EARLY IN THE MORNING two days later, Henry and Adam were rowed to the ship that would take them back to England. Cook rode in the barge that carried Hew's coffin, and another craft bore their trunks and baggage. Henry waved at the wagon driver Francois, who had finished helping load the boats. The Frenchman doffed his hat in somber reply, and then France was behind them.

The weather remained foul, and Adam huddled in his cloak in the stern as the men pulled on their oars. "I was very happy in France," he reflected, "but once I get back across this water, I think I shall never cross it again."

CHAPTER 32

SAD GREETINGS *November 1766*

After a swift but turbulent Channel crossing, Adam, Henry, and Cook were rowed ashore in Dover on a gray blustery afternoon. The boat ahead of them carried Hew, and the boat following, their baggage. As the first craft approached the quay, the choppy water caused a rough landing, drawing Henry's concern as they watched from the second boat. On the quay was a distinguished-looking man of about forty, standing alone in a topcoat and watching their approach.

As soon as their boat touched the quay, Henry leaped out and went to make sure Hew's casket was swung safely out of the first boat. Cook followed him, both completely ignoring the waiting man. Adam climbed out carefully and the gentleman stepped forward. "Mr. Smith, I presume?" he said cordially, in a rich Scot's brogue that warmed Adam's heart so much that he smiled broadly at the stranger.

"Indeed, sir," replied Adam.

"I am John Craigie, Advocate. I oversee the duke's estate in Scotland," he said formally, giving a small bow.

Adam returned his bow. "It's an honor to meet you, Mr. Craigie." Adam gestured towards Henry as he watched Hew's casket being hoisted safely onto the quay, "Please forgive Henry, losing his brother hurt him badly."

"Such a tragedy," Craigie replied, "I've come straight from his family at Adderbury. I was there when they received your letter." They watched as the third boat bumped into the quay, jarring their luggage but not worrying the skilled boat hands a whit as they nimbly secured the craft.

"I last saw Duke Henry at his father's funeral," said Craigie as they walked towards Henry and the casket, "He was just a wee laddie." He waited beside Adam until Henry noticed them and turned, then Craigie stuck out his hand and said, "Duke Henry, allow me to introduce myself. I am John Craigie."

"My Scottish superintendent?" asked Henry, shaking his hand, surprised that the man would be meeting them personally in Dover.

"Yes," replied Craigie, "I will take your brother directly to Dalkeith." He gestured to three teamsters who had approached, and they effortlessly hoisted Hew's casket onto their shoulders. Henry joined them and helped carry his brother to the waiting wagon. Craigie and Adam followed, while Cook oversaw the unloading of their luggage. Once Hew was safely aboard the stout wagon, Henry turned back to Craigie.

"Thank you, Mr. Craigie. I will ride with Hew," said Henry.

"I beg your pardon, Duke Henry," said Craigie, "I come from Adderbury and your mother. She is distraught and wants to see you right away."

Henry nodded silently for a few moments while they all stood at the rear wheel of the freight wagon in the damp wind. The moments stretched to a full fifteen seconds, but everyone waited patiently for his answer. "Yes, I see," he said finally, "Can we trust these men to carry Hew with dignity?"

"These men work for you, Duke Henry," Craigie replied, "I will accompany your brother as well. The carriage is ready to take you home." He indicated a fine coach and four waiting at the foot of the beach road.

"After so long in France, I'm not sure Adderbury is home," mused Henry, but only Adam caught his comment.

"Mr. Craigie, might I travel with you to Edinburgh?" asked Adam.

"Mr. Townshend wants you at Adderbury, Mr. Smith," answered Craigie, "Insisted, in fact."

"Please come with me, Mr. Smith," pleaded Henry, "I need your counsel."

"My mother misses me, but given the circumstances, I can only oblige," said Adam, "Carry on, Mr. Craigie."

Henry put his hand on Hew's casket and said, "Travel well, brother." Then he walked to the head of the wagon, where Craigie had just climbed up beside the driver. "Godspeed, Mr. Craigie. I will see you at Dalkeith around the first of September. We will have much to discuss."

"You were a mere boy when I last saw you, Duke Henry," replied Craigie, "We'll be ready for you in September." Henry stepped back, the driver cracked the reins, and the wagon lurched into motion.

Adam, Henry, and Cook walked towards the waiting carriage. Henry said, "Craigie seems like a good fellow," and Adam nodded. Turning to Cook, Henry directed, "Cook, why don't you ride with the driver?" His tone indicated it wasn't a question, but an order.

Cook looked at the darkening sky and felt a few scattered raindrops. "Er, yes, Henry, if you wish," he said, not understanding the strange order, but not wanting to argue with him about it. He turned up his collar and climbed awkwardly up to sit beside the driver. Adam and Henry climbed into the spacious carriage and their journey to Adderbury commenced as a rain squall swept in. Bouncing on the high seat, Cook cursed inwardly and struggled into the oilskins the driver offered him.

Adam and Henry were exhausted from the uncomfortable and cold crossing, still somewhat seasick, and the inside of the carriage was cold. They sat wrapped in their coats as the carriage splashed along.

"Your family must be in great sorrow," said Adam after a spell, "I wonder why Charles wants me to come along?"

"I don't know," said Henry, "maybe he doesn't trust me to maintain my composure."

"You have been very firm, Henry, in the face of such calamity," said Adam. "Too firm, perhaps. Let the tears come."

"They already have, Mr. Smith," Henry acknowledged, "I've never been one to blubber in public."

"Sometimes we keep too tight a rein on our horse. Let the beast run," advised Adam gently.

Henry nodded, but he remained dry-eyed as they splashed along the road from Dover. He didn't think about Cook's comfort at all, happy to have an opportunity to talk in confidence with Adam.

"I fear Charles already has a plan for me in Parliament," Henry began.

"I suspect you have many options available to you," replied Adam, seeing how Henry would soon inherit the largest landholding in lowland Scotland.

"I'll be blunt," replied Henry, "I must confront Charles over my estate, and my future."

"Confront?" said Adam, tentatively.

"Charles is a top minister to Pitt," said Henry, growing animated, "Someday he might be Prime Minister. I'm still just twenty."

"Do you suspect Charles will try to force you in some way?" asked Adam.

"I am my own man!" exclaimed Henry, and Adam saw he'd touched a nerve. "Charles married Mother for more than love. The Buccleuch estate is his power. He will not simply turn it over to me when I turn twenty-one."

"What do you fear he'll do?" Adam probed gently.

"I don't know," said Henry, "His letters are obsequious to a fault. That's what makes me suspicious. I think he wants to buy me a seat in Parliament to support his faction." He looked as if he would continue, but then fell silent.

"Do you?" prompted Adam.

"Do I what?" asked Henry.

"Support his faction in Parliament," said Adam.

"I have no idea!" exclaimed Henry, throwing up his hands, "Charles says what people want to hear, I don't know what he truly believes. I'm not sure I want to be in Parliament. I'm not sure I even want to live in England!"

A moment passed, then a slow smile spread across Adam's face. "Scotland is a bonny place!"

"I'll take your word for it," replied Henry with a wry smile. Although Adam hadn't offered him any specific advice, he felt better voicing his concerns to a sympathetic ear.

Riding atop the wet wagon, Cook could hear Henry's voice but not Adam's, though he couldn't make out any words over the wind, splashing wheels, and the rhythmic clop of the four-horse team. He knew now why he'd been banished from the carriage but had no way of knowing what Henry and Adam were talking about. He sat and stewed, cold and wet, and wondered.

• • • •

IN THE ADDERBURY DRAWING room two days later, Frances sat quill in hand, dressed in mourning black, waiting for Charles' next word. Charles stood in the middle of the room deep in thought, until finally he gave up. "Drat, my thought has vanished," he said, "Read back the last line, Frances."

Frances cleared her throat and read, "We defended America from the French and Indians, so it is only right that the Americans, as proper British subjects, should bear some of the expense."

"Hmmm, not 'some of the expense,'" mused Charles, "Change that to 'should bear the expense.' What do you think dear?"

"It depends on whether you want America to pay some of the expense, or all of the expense," replied Frances, matter-of-factly.

"Well, the more the better," Charles said, arguing with himself, "I must raise an American revenue! Write that, "We must raise an American revenue.""

Frances swiftly added the line. "Now, read the last two lines back to me," Charles instructed. Frances did so while Charles moved to peer over her shoulder.

"Put an exclamation after the word, 'revenue," he said, putting a hand on her shoulder. "You are the most patient amanuensis, my dear."

"I like writing your speeches Father, you never yell at me like Mother does," she smiled at him.

"Oh, she means well," answered Charles, "She yells at me too, Frances."

As if on cue, they heard Caroline's strident voice call out, "Charles! Where are you, Charles?" In a moment she appeared at the door of the drawing room, also dressed in mourning black. "Oh, there you are," she said, "When will Henry arrive? I'm growing anxious." The carriage was expected to arrive yesterday, and now it was already mid-afternoon.

"You know how the roads can be in November, dear," said Charles, trying to ease her worry.

"Frances, if you're done here, run along," Caroline instructed, "I must speak to Charles."

Charles nodded to his stepdaughter, and she left. Caroline waited just a moment before saying, "I want to discuss a suitable match for Henry."

"Dear, wait until he arrives, and we see how he is," protested Charles, "Not a word about it until a month of mourning has passed."

A servant appeared at the door and announced, "A crate has arrived from Paris. I have left it in the parlor."

Caroline, irritated by the interruption, snapped at the servant, "Can't you see we're busy? We don't have time for parcels just now." The servant departed, and Caroline turned her attention back to Charles.

"Henry is the most eligible young man in London," she said, "Scheming young women will have their hooks out. They will be lovely, they will be crafty, and not all will be reputable. Not all will be rich. Henry must marry for advantage, not, not..., *lust!*" She spat the last word contemptuously.

"There has to be a little lust, Caroline," replied Charles, smiling disarmingly, "How else will we have grandchildren?"

"Men are beasts!" said Caroline, not at all disarmed.

"Please, I'm trying to be lighthearted," said Charles, "Let's not be angry when Henry arrives." He reached out and touched his wife's arm, but she pulled away unmollified. There was little love or lust left in their marriage, and there had never been much to start with. "Let's welcome Henry home. He'll need our support," he pleaded.

Caroline took a deep breath and relaxed, softening her features as she nodded. "Yes, we'll greet Henry with grace and love. Time enough to find him a suitable wife."

"He will choose his own wife, Caroline," said Charles firmly, then added, "But we can have a hand in it, for sure."

The house servant reappeared, and Frances, who had been listening outside the door, slipped away undetected. "They have arrived!" announced the servant, causing Charles and Caroline to rush out the door. Frances followed along behind them as they entered the entry hall. The outside door swung open, revealing Henry framed in the doorway. Caroline flew to him with a hug.

"Oh, Henry!" is all she could say as she embraced him.

"Good to be home Mother," Henry said, returning her embrace with a wan smile. Adam and Cook entered behind Henry but stayed in the background during the family reunion.

"Safe and sound, safe and sound!" exclaimed Charles, "Home at last!" He shook Henry's hand while he was still hugging his mother. Caroline finally released him, and Frances ran in to hug her brother tight. Charles shook Adam's hand, but both were watching Henry.

"Henry, I missed you!" Frances said, voice muffled as she pressed her face into his coat with her arms wrapped around him.

"I missed you too, sister," Henry smiled, "You're bigger and prettier than when I left you!"

Frances burst into tears and looked up at her brother, who seemed taller than she remembered. "I miss Hew! You're the only brother I have left! We'll never see Hew again!" cried Frances.

"I miss him too, Frances, terribly," said Henry, "Every day. But when his portrait arrives, we'll have a picture to remember him by."

"Portrait?" said Charles and Caroline simultaneously.

"Hew sat for a portrait by Monsieur Greuze in Paris," said Henry, "He promised to ship it here."

Charles said excitedly, "The parcel from Paris! Where is it?"

Cook had already found the parcel and was unwrapping it. Henry shook his head, saying, "It couldn't have arrived here ahead of us." But when Cook opened the crate, the portrait of Hew emerged and he held it up for all to admire. It amazed Henry that the painting had beaten them home. Greuze had finished it on the day of their departure, and then the Comtesse had hired an express to ship it to Adderbury. It was a plain, touching portrait; due to the haste of completion it was bereft of many of Greuze's sentimental touches that typically adorned his paintings.

Caroline burst into tears and put both hands on the ornate frame and brought her head close to the canvas as if to touch her dead son. Cook stood awkwardly, holding the portrait, although his arms were growing tired. "A fine likeness, that," said Charles, with a lump in his throat.

"Oh Hew!" cried Frances, as Caroline stepped back. Cook lowered the portrait so that it rested on his toes, and Frances knelt before it in tears.

"Hew had such a joy for life," observed Adam quietly, "Everyone he met in France loved him."

Charles looked at Adam with sincere appreciation, and said, "Thank you, Mr. Smith."

"Yes, Mr. Smith," agreed Henry, turning towards him with eyes filling with tears. To the surprise of all, including himself, he impulsively hugged his teacher. "A finer tutor I cannot imagine, sir."

"I learned as much as you, Henry" said Adam, touched by his student's gesture.

Caroline had regained her composure, and she hooked an arm through Henry's. "Let's go to the parlor and catch up," said Caroline, and Frances attached herself to his other arm. "Cook, bring the painting along," Caroline ordered. Turning to the servant, she said, "Tea and biscuits in the parlor." Her instructions were the first words anyone had spoken to Cook, who carried the painting ahead of them down the hall and into the parlor, where Frances' writing desk was still littered with papers and quills.

CHAPTER 33

A USPICIOUS CONNECTIONS *November 1766*
The rain stopped that night, and by mid-afternoon the next day it was dry enough to venture out. Charles, Henry, and Adam emerged from the house bundled against the crisp weather, and Charles led them on a walk around the extensive estate.

Pointing to some new statuary, Charles said, "We've made a few improvements while you were gone, Henry. I hope you like them."

"At what cost?" asked Henry bluntly.

Charles was taken aback by his terse response, but he didn't let it ruffle him. "I don't have that figure at hand," he replied smoothly, "Adderbury will be yours, so we wanted it beautiful for you." Charles spread his arms expansively to encompass the entire estate.

Henry ignored his gesture and kept his eyes on Charles. "I met John Craigie at Dover," he said evenly, "Before I see him again at Dalkeith, I'd like to review the Buccleuch finances."

"Certainly," nodded Charles, "I'll have Craigie prepare a report."

"Good," said Henry, "but what expense for Adderbury? How much does Craigie send you each year? How much is re-invested in Scotland, versus gardens and statuary here?" Henry gestured towards a marble statue of a winged griffin that had appeared in his absence.

Charles felt under attack, unexpectedly so, and he glanced warily at Adam, wondering what was motivating Henry. "Let me assemble some figures for you, Henry," he answered calmly, "My head is full of Parliament and budgets right now."

Seeing an opportunity to divert the conversation, he turned to Adam and said, "That's where you come in, Mr. Smith. I need help with the national budget. Can you stay in London for a few months? Your country needs you." Having appealed to Adam's patriotism, he now shifted to the personal and implored, "I need you."

"Well, if you put it like that, I must say yes," replied Adam, taking a deep breath. His mother was counting the days until his return to Scotland, and he hated disappointing her. But Charles was Chancellor of the Exchequer, and this was an opportunity to see the government budgeting up close. Such an experience would be invaluable as he wrote his book about how nations grew wealthy, and how they didn't.

"Excellent! Wonderful!" Charles enthused, clapping Adam on the back. "We'll leave for London day after next."

"So soon?" asked Henry with a scowl, "We've only just arrived."

Charles beamed at him with a broad smile as he sprung his surprise. "You have an audience with King George on the tenth of November, Henry. We must prepare!"

• • • •

A WEEK LATER THEY FOLLOWED a servant through the ancient Guildhall, built on the site of an even more ancient Roman amphitheater. Their measured steps clicked on the stone floor. King George III, age 29, was holding his audience that day in an antechamber off the enormous central hall. Their appointment was eleven a.m., and they were precisely on time, dressed in the newest finery that the best London haberdasher could provide. Henry was resplendent in a deep blue coat with silver facings, snow-white cravat, neckcloth, and stockings, shiny black shoes with silver buckles. Clothes shopping is what Charles had meant when he said they must prepare to meet the King, and they'd spent days at it. The royal servant opened a door, stepped in ahead of them, and announced them to the unseen King inside.

"Charles Townshend, Chancellor of the Exchequer, and Henry Scott, Third Duke of Buccleuch," he said crisply, and they bowed low upon entering the presence of the King, who stood, nonchalant, on the far side of the room. Broad daylight streamed through the high windows, and Henry was struck by how young the King looked. Halfway across the room, Charles and Henry stopped to bow low again, according to the protocol. They bowed a third time as they reached him.

"Greetings, Chancellor," said King George III, conversationally.

"Your Majesty," returned Charles as they straightened, "may I present my stepson, Henry Scott, Third Duke of Buccleuch."

"Your Majesty," said Henry, trying to formulate a dignified but respectful tone and having no idea if he'd succeeded. In his throat his voice sounded like a squeak.

"Good to meet you, Duke Henry," said the King, giving him a slight smile. The King looked back to Charles. "So which stepson needs a regiment?"

"Er, that was Henry's younger brother, Your Majesty," answered Charles, embarrassed but too smooth to show it.

"Hew Campbell Scott, Your Majesty," volunteered Henry, voice returning to normal. "He died last month in France."

"Oh, how unfortunate," said King George, "My condolences to you both."

"Thank you, Your Majesty," responded Charles graciously.

"Chancellor, I hear that Pitt suffers from poor health," said the King.

"Yes, Your Majesty. The Earl of Chatham spends much of his time at Bath, hoping the waters will cure his gout. We communicate by letter," replied Charles, who always spoke clearly and well, but especially when speaking to the King.

"Oh yes," laughed the King, "I made Pitt an Earl. Forgive me if I still call him Pitt instead of Chatham."

"I still think of him as Pitt as well, Your Majesty," smiled Charles.

"So, Duke Henry, has Charles here found you a suitable seat in Parliament?" asked the King.

Shocked, Henry took an extra second to formulate his response, but he avoided glancing at Charles. "I... I... don't reach Majority until next September," he finally managed.

"Oh. Well. I'm sure you'll have your chance," replied the King, "I became King at your age. With a great title comes a great responsibility."

"Yes, Your Majesty," said Henry, relieved that perhaps he'd survived that topic of conversation.

"Tell me your impressions of King Louis?" asked the King.

"King Louis treated us with courtesy and respect," answered Henry, "We hunted with him at Compiegne."

"What were your observations about his person?" followed the King.

Henry was a little unnerved being interrogated by the King, but he said, "King Louis favored me with his conversation. I found him well-spoken, sensible and kind. Sad, as he'd just lost his son."

King George III put his hand on his chin and gazed at Henry, trying to see more than Henry could paint with his words. "Hmmm. Would you consider him a decisive person? Strong-willed?"

Charles waited for Henry's reply with bated breath, hoping the boy wouldn't editorialize with the King, which he knew from experience could be risky. "I have no observation on that matter," answered Henry, "He appears to trust his advisors."

The King smiled broadly for the first time and looked at Charles. "Where would a King be without his trusted advisors, eh Chancellor?"

A quarter hour later, Charles and Henry emerged from Guildhall exultant. "Trusted advisor, he called me!" said Charles happily, clapping Henry on the back.

"He spoke to us like normal people," grinned Henry, pleased by his encounter. To meet the British King seemed more auspicious than meeting a foreign King, even though he thought George III was a stiffer personality than the genial King Louis XV. Henry wondered that King George hadn't asked any questions about Jean Calas, Voltaire, and the overturned verdict.

"It's because of who you are, Henry," said Charles, "His Majesty knows his kingdom well, who is important, who is not." That answered his wonderment, as it was likely the King of Britain was less concerned with civil justice outside his own country.

"I have met two kings, and I am only twenty!" laughed Henry boyishly, as they waited for their carriage to jockey into position for them to board.

"Great things await you, Henry," enthused Charles, putting his hand on Henry's shoulder, "Parliament is just the first step."

"First, I must see my estates in Scotland," warned Henry, but his smile pulled his punch.

"Of course, of course," nodded Charles vigorously, "We'll have a grand banquet at Dalkeith on your birthday!"

"That's ten months from now, Charles," was Henry's wry reply, feeling this was perhaps the best moment he'd ever shared with his stepfather. Happy people are attractive, even Charles, who was happy indeed at the success of their royal audience, and it showed on his face.

Charles leaned in and said in a conspiratorial manner, "London is full of brides-to-be, Henry. You won't find their like in Edinburgh." He winked at Henry.

Their carriage stopped before them, the door opened, and Cook stepped out. On their way back to the hotel, Cook was silent, and Charles beamed at his protégé for a job very well done indeed. Henry looked out the window, thought of Eloise, and then remembered that first day he'd sailed the blue Mediterranean with Hew.

At that very moment, back at the hotel, Thomas Gainsborough was painting a young woman in the same alcove off the lobby where he'd painted Henry in 1764. Adam descended the stairs just as a tall man entered from the street. He was plainly dressed, and his steps were uncertain, a member of the serving class out of place in the fancy London hotel.

"Robert!" Adam called out, recognizing his former house servant.

"Mr. Smith!" replied Robert Reid, with a big smile as he strode to meet his former employer at the bottom of the stairs. Adam shook Robert's hand with both of his, and his smile of delight matched Robert's.

"I thought you'd be in Canada by now," said Adam.

"I'm off for Spithead tomorrow; my boat leaves in a week," replied Robert, excitedly, "Overheard the duke had returned to London. I'm glad I found you!"

"So, your plan remains the same?" asked Adam.

"Yes, I'm going to Quebec. Do you have a moment, Mr. Smith?" Robert asked, and Adam took his elbow and guided him to a sofa at the far side of the lobby.

"Any news about my dear Mother?" asked Adam as they seated themselves.

"Not for some months," answered Robert, "I delivered her to Kirkaldy safe and sound, and stayed with her until she hired suitable help. Then I returned to Glasgow to prepare." Robert glanced around to make sure he was unobserved, then pulled a small purse from his pocket. "Here's the money you lent me, Mr. Smith."

"That looks like the same purse I gave you nearly three years ago, Robert," observed Adam, surprised.

"Same purse, same coins, Mr. Smith," beamed Robert, "I haven't spent a farthing."

"You paid ship's fare on your own?" asked Adam, impressed.

"Not only that, but I've been able to afford some practice with my pistol," said Robert eagerly as he parted his coat to show the polished butt of his gun.

"Well, I hope you won't need that!" said Adam sincerely, though he said it while smiling.

"I can use it if I must, Mr. Smith," grinned Robert, then he grew serious and said, "I came to offer your money back."

"Why?" asked Adam.

"In case you had second thoughts, it's a generous loan," replied Robert firmly, who had wrestled with accepting Adam's generosity for three years and knew if he had a chance he'd offer it back.

"You are a good, honest fellow," said Adam, "and that money is right where it should be, in your pocket. Godspeed to you, Robert."

Robert nodded and returned the purse to his pocket gratefully, his mission of doubt completed. "Godspeed to you too, Mr. Smith. Are you off to Scotland?"

"Seeing you makes me homesick, Robert, but I have some work in London first," said Adam.

Robert nodded, then stood and stuck out his hand. "I won't keep you, Mr. Smith. I thank you for the loan, and the peace of mind."

Adam again took his hand in both of his and shook it warmly. "It's not a loan, Robert. Canada will be grateful to have you. Safe travels." With bittersweet feelings Adam watched as Robert walked out, and before the door closed behind him it was caught by Cook, who held it for the person behind him. To Adam's surprise, it was Frances.

"Ah, Mr. Smith," hailed Cook, "We've just arrived from Adderbury."

"Hello, Mr. Cook. Hello, Frances!" greeted Adam, "What brings you to London?"

"Father needs me as his amanuensis," said Frances, as her eyes strayed around the ornate lobby and the fashionable people moving through it. Frances rarely came to London, especially without her mother. Adam noticed that in their long absence in France, Henry's little sister had grown to a lovely young woman, but she still had her bubbly girlish personality.

"Does he need you full time?" asked Adam, "I write so slow it takes a week to pen my name!" Frances laughed, and Cook smiled, happy to be in London instead of Adderbury with Caroline.

In the alcove, Thomas Gainsborough lifted his brush and waited as his subject turned to watch the lobby through the fronds of a large potted plant. She watched as Adam greeted Cook and Frances, then turned back to the painter.

"Who is the Scottish gentleman?" she asked.

Gainsborough resumed his work as he answered. "That is Adam Smith, the Glasgow philosopher. Could you return to the pose, please?"

She did so, and then said, "I've heard of Adam Smith. What brings him to London?"

"He just returned from France, with his student, Henry Scott, the Duke of Buccleuch," replied Gainsborough, brush moving swiftly over the canvas, "I painted the duke's portrait before he left, almost three years ago."

"Who is the young lady with Adam Smith?" she asked.

"I don't know," answered the painter, "The man works for Charles Townshend, the Chancellor of the Exchequer." She turned again and saw Cook and Frances ascend the stairs and disappear.

"Everyone in London has heard of Charles Townshend," said the young woman, "He's considered the best speaker in Parliament. I have never seen him." She returned to her pose.

"You might, Townshend is staying in this hotel," said Gainsborough, working swiftly as his eyes flickered back and forth between the lovely young woman and his canvas. She was Elizabeth Montagu, twenty-two, daughter of a respected Earl and his wife, both anxious about who their headstrong daughter might find as a husband. She had already rejected two wealthy matches her parents had painstakingly arranged.

The door to the street opened, admitting Charles and Henry as they returned from their audience with King George III. Elizabeth turned again to peer through the fronds, and Gainsborough lifted his brush and waited patiently.

"Something tells me I'm looking at Charles Townshend right now," she observed.

"You are indeed," confirmed the painter, "and with him is Duke Henry."

Elizabeth watched as Charles and Henry stopped to talk to Adam, and saw a tall, distinguished man growing stout, standing beside a handsome young man with brown hair, almost as tall as Townshend, resplendent in dark blue, silver, and white. She had trouble taking her eyes off the elegant young duke.

Gainsborough, with a small smile on his face, observed from behind Elizabeth, "They say Henry Scott is the most eligible young man in London."

"Aye, but what *kind* of a man is he?" asked Elizabeth over her shoulder as she watched Henry disappear from the lobby.

"A very rich one, Miss Montagu," said Gainsborough, smiling again as he resumed painting now that Elizabeth had returned to her pose.

"But that doesn't mean he's a *good* man, does it? What else do you know about him?" she asked.

"He and his brother are charming young fellows; last I saw of them. I know he loves horses and rides most mornings," remarked the genial painter, his brush working quickly now that Elizabeth was again perfectly posed.

• • • •

THAT NIGHT TWO BROAD fireplaces blazed, warming the busy tavern as a maid threaded the tables with two mugs of beer in one hand and a bottle of wine in the other. Arriving at a long table along the far edge of the room, she set the mugs down in front of Henry and Cook, and poured wine for Charles, Adam, and Frances. Charles sat at the head of the table, with Frances on one hand and Adam on the other. Henry sat beside Frances, who was fashionably dressed and excited to be joining the men in a tavern for dinner.

"I'm so glad you're with us, Frances," said Henry, raising his glass.

"So am I," seconded Charles, "I warn you dear, I have many letters to write. They repealed the Stamp Act!"

"I'm ready to write, Father!" answered Frances, taking a careful sip of her wine.

"Is our task to replace the lost revenues?" Adam asked.

"What lost revenues?" snorted Charles, "The colonists rioted when we tried to collect it. We have the *right* to tax the colonies, surely, we do."

"Why would they riot over a modest tax?" Henry wondered.

"They'll pay trade tariffs, but not internal taxes," replied Charles, shaking his head.

"That's not much to riot about. Surely there's more to it," Henry persisted.

"No taxation without representation, they say," said Charles with a frown, "Ingrates! They should help pay for their own defense." Looking towards the door on the opposite end of the room, Charles spied two large men enter the tavern. He only saw the face of one, and recognized Ben Franklin.

"Hush! No more talk about America, Ben Franklin is here," Charles warned the table.

Spotting them, Franklin waved and made his way in their direction. He was followed by Hume.

"We're looking for the philosopher who was lost in France!" said Franklin jovially.

"And we've found him in fine company," added Hume, "Good to see you, Mr. Townshend. Mr. Smith, we simply couldn't wait to see you again."

"It's good to be back Hume," smiled a nodding Adam, "Ben."

"And who is this charming young lady?" asked Hume, radiating a smile down at Frances.

Henry stood and shook hands with Franklin, then said, "Hume, allow me to introduce my sister, Lady Frances Scott, of Adderbury, recently arrived in London."

Frances stood and gave Henry an appreciative glance for the adult introduction. She managed a brief curtsey in front of her chair, and the older men bowed as low as their stoutness allowed. Benign smiles adorned both Hume and Franklin, putting flustered Frances at ease. Charles beamed watching Frances enjoy the company. "It's indeed an honor, my lady," said Hume.

Franklin turned unexpectedly to Cook, who sat silently. "Allow me to make your acquaintance sir," he said, "I am Ben Franklin, American representative in London."

Cook stood abruptly at being addressed, bumping the table and slopping a bit of ale. "An honor to meet you, Mr. Franklin," he said finally, giving a short bow. Charles looked bemused at Cook's discomfiture.

"Cook here is my personal aide," he said dismissively, "He accompanied Frances from Adderbury."

Franklin didn't miss a beat, saying, "A more important task I can't imagine, Mr. Cook. Pleased to meet you." Charles smirked at Franklin's egalitarianism, but Cook nodded, pleased to be recognized by the friendly American.

"Join us, gentlemen, join us!" said Henry, indicating the empty chairs at the table.

"That would be presumptuous, we couldn't...," started Hume.

"Plenty of room, gentlemen," said Charles authoritatively, "Find chairs, the food's still coming."

A steaming platter of fried fish arrived, followed by a pot of chowder. Hume and Franklin needed no further urging and sat, and soon they were equipped with plates, mugs and ale. "We have much to discuss, Mr. Smith," said Hume, "but as intruders, we'll just eat and listen tonight."

"What brings you to London, my dear?" asked the grandfatherly Franklin of young Frances.

Charles answered, saying, "Frances is my indispensable amanuensis. Completely trustworthy, I might add." He gazed at his stepdaughter, and she blushed at the attention.

"Well, Frances, you are surrounded by luminaries but still the star of the table," observed Adam, smiling at the girl.

"Hume, I heard you are now Secretary of State?" asked Henry, recalling a comment from Charles in the carriage to Guildhall that day.

"Yes, for the Northern Division," confirmed Hume, "Lord Shelburne has the Southern."

"Northern covers Scotland, Southern deals with India and America?" asked Adam.

"Yes," smiled Hume, "So we can drink beer together in perfect propriety, Mr. Franklin."

Franklin laughed, clinked mugs with Hume, and took a pull on his ale. He sighed with satisfaction, wiped his mouth, and said, "Beer is proof that God loves us and wants us to be happy!" Everyone at the table laughed, including Cook who couldn't help himself. Hume and Franklin were both impossible men to dislike in person, although many abhorred Hume's religious skepticism.

"I've never tasted beer," volunteered Frances.

Eyebrows went up and all eyes turned to Charles. "By all means, dear, try a sip of Henry's," he approved. Frances took a bold gulp, made a face, then laughed; everyone joined her and took a drink of their own beverage.

"It's good to see you out of the house, Frances," said Henry.

"It's been a while since Mother has allowed me to go anywhere," said Frances. "Thanks for sending for me, Father." Turning to Cook, she added, "Thank you, Cook, I should have been frightened to make the trip alone."

"My honor, Lady Frances," nodded Cook, touched.

Charles ignored Cook and kept his attention on Frances. "I couldn't work without you, dear," he said, and Henry noted something odd, slightly maudlin, about Charles' tone that seemed unlike his normal brash manner. Henry thought he must have a soft spot for Frances, the last Scott child remaining at Adderbury after the brothers had decamped to France.

"Now Hume, now Franklin, let's enjoy our dinner without politics!" boomed Charles, his nature restored.

"Impossible!" said Hume, "but we'll try!"

CHAPTER 34

P OOP ON HIS BOOTS *November 1766*
Early the next morning Henry walked across the stable lot and entered the large barn behind the hotel, filled with horses in two rows of stalls. As he strode the aisle between the stalls, a forkful of wet manure landed suddenly at his feet. Henry stopped sharply in dismay and saw a young woman in a work dress and scarf mucking a stall occupied by a fine mare.

"Sorry sir!" she called out, glancing at him over her shoulder.

Henry noticed the girl's fine features and thought her pretty for a servant. "No harm," he said, letting his irritation die, "do you work here?"

"What does it look like I'm doing?" she answered tartly, still mostly turned away from him as she bent for another forkful.

Henry, taken aback, shrugged it off and said, "I forgot an apple for my horse." She tossed him two, one at a time, from a bag hanging in her stall. He caught them deftly. "Thanks," he said, and she gave him a brief smile over the back of her horse. He noticed her smooth skin and dainty nose, with dark eyes that sparkled.

"Which horse is yours, sir?" she asked, throwing a saddle blanket over the mare.

"The big bay stallion three stalls down," said Henry, "He sees me here, with apples." The stallion nickered at Henry impatiently. "Can you help me saddle my horse?" Henry asked.

"Yes," she said, "let me finish here first." She tossed the saddle onto the mare's back and cinched it snug. Henry could see she was experienced with horses. He didn't move, watching her, and absently took a bite of one of the apples.

"The cook can give you a better apple than that," she said, "That's a horse apple."

Henry grinned and took the few steps necessary to feed the apples to the bay. Opening the stall door, he led the big horse into the aisle. The horse nuzzled him for more apples, so Henry looked up and saw another in mid-air as she tossed it. He was quick enough to catch it without the embarrassment of it hitting his forehead. His horse was grateful. Henry swiftly threw the saddle blanket on, followed by the saddle.

"You look like you know what you're doing," she observed, and then noticed the dung streaked on his polished boots. "Sorry I got poop on your boots," she apologized with a smile.

Henry laughed, looked at his boots, and grinned back at her. "That's why I wear boots in barns." It was impossible to be irritated with such a pretty woman, even one mucking a horse stall.

Henry put his foot in the stirrup and mounted the bay. Looking down at the girl, he said, "My horse and I say thanks for the apples," and tossed her a schilling. She caught it as easily as he'd fielded the apples and put it in a pocket of her plain dress. She looked up at him, smiled, and her beauty shook him to the core despite her plain work garments. This was no mere stable girl.

"My name is Henry," he said, meeting her gaze and holding it.

"I'm Betsy," said Elizabeth Montagu, eyeing him bravely.

Henry nodded at the saddled horse and asked, "Who's riding the mare?"

"Me," she said, "I'm taking her out for exercise."

Henry nodded and let the bay take a few steps towards the barn door. He stopped and looked back at her. "Ride with me, Betsy."

She looked at him fetchingly, despite the dowdy scarf she wore, but then shook her head slowly. "Oh no, sir, not dressed like this," she demurred.

"It's a cool morning, you'll need a cloak," said Henry, "C'mon, ride with me." He knew his wealth and good looks made him attractive to girls of lower social orders, but he did not want to appear imperious or presumptuous. Still, she hesitated, so he added, "I'd rather not ride alone."

Elizabeth disappeared into the stall and emerged throwing a cloak over her shoulders. She mounted easily, riding like a man. Henry watched her, noting her natural grace, and noticing that the cloak she wore was a much finer garment than the work dress. Sitting the mare, she smiled at him, revealing attractive clean teeth.

"You have a smudge on your cheek," he said.

Elizabeth blushed and wiped blindly, he pointed, and then nodded when she'd found it. "Thanks," she smiled charmingly.

They walked their horses out of the barn, not riding too close to each other. "So, you like working with horses?" asked Henry.

"I love horses," she replied, "I suspect you do too."

"All my life," he said, "I groom them myself sometimes. We're all equal in the eyes of a horse."

"I'm not so sure," laughed Elizabeth, "Smart horses know when they have a royal arse in the saddle."

Henry laughed and asked, "Royal? How so?"

"Royals are fatter than most, smell better, but they rarely give their horse an apple," she replied.

"I like to think I smell as pleasant as any royal," grinned Henry, "Better than some, I expect."

"How would you know?" taunted Elizabeth with a smile, "Met any royals lately?"

Henry was about to tell her about meeting King George just the day before but thought it would sound pompous, so he bit his tongue. Instead, he said, "I hear there is a big difference between French and British royals in that regard."

"I'm a patriot," said Elizabeth archly, "I'm sure English royals smell like roses."

Henry laughed as they walked their horses into a park, and said, "Betsy, I don't think you work in that stable."

"No?" asked Elizabeth, but she couldn't keep a smile off her face.

"You are educated, your speech refined, and your fine cloak gives you away," said Henry, omitting the quality of her teeth as that would sound crass. "May I inquire as to your full name?"

"Just Betsy for now, Henry," she said, "My father favored me with an education, for which I am forever grateful. But I'm just a shopkeeper's daughter." She removed her scarf and shook out her lustrous brown hair, captivating him again with her beauty. "Shall we pick up the pace?" she asked, spurring her horse into a canter. He kicked the bay into an easy canter to match, and they rode across the park through the cold morning mist.

After they parted at the barn, promising to look for each other in the stable another day, Henry walked into the hotel whistling. Charles was in the lobby with Cook, who was helping him with his greatcoat. "There you are, Henry!" said Charles, "I'm off to Parliament. I thought you were coming with me?"

"I was?" asked Henry, mystified.

"I can't wait, but you can ride with Mr. Smith," instructed Charles, "I made arrangements for both of you to observe."

"You did?" asked Henry.

"Yes! Look your best, all eyes will be on you today," advised Charles, turning towards the door.

"They will?" wondered Henry.

Charles stopped his hasty departure mid-stride and turned back to Henry. "All of London knows of you, wonders about you. Especially what role you'll play in politics."

"It seems my education is over then," said Henry.

"No, you'll learn a lot from this," answered Charles, "Mr. Smith knows the particulars. Cook, help Henry."

Henry looked at Cook and said, "Can we start with a bite to eat?"

Charles was already at the door, but called back over his shoulder, "No time! And get that mud off your boots!" Then he was out and into his carriage, which departed swiftly.

Both Cook and Henry looked at his streaked boots, and Henry broke into a broad grin remembering how the dirt got there.

Later, Charles walked briskly down the hallway leading to Parliament, flanked by two aides. Charles was skimming a paper in his right hand but gave it to one aide as the other opened the large door. Charles stepped into the large room filled with the babble of talking members. The murmurs rose in pitch as everyone watched Charles as he stood to speak. Adam and Henry were just taking their seats in the gallery, next to Hume.

"Gentlemen!" Charles began and the members grew quiet to listen. "Time is short, our debt is great. This is our critical minute!" Charles raised his hand to punctuate his declaration. "We must raise revenue to pay our war debts. We must, at the same time, consolidate our emerging British Empire. We can do both, in America!"

Yays and nays erupted, and Henry had his first formal glimpse at the splendid speaking ability that made Charles Townshend famous in his own time, but largely forgotten later. "Our financial situation is dire, as we know," he continued, "In the meantime, America calls for all our talents, skill, discretion, and *firmness!*"

Another round of cheers and catcalls, as Henry began to see the political divisions that animated the different factions based on their opposition or favor of taxing the colonies. The failure of the Stamp Act had sent the members back to the drawing board regarding American taxation, but the unruly behavior of the colonies had inflamed many.

"I have heard asserted with great pleasure the *right* of our taxing America," boomed Charles, "*That* is not disputed." When Parliament repealed the Stamp Act, they also passed the Declaratory Act, confirming their right to tax the colonies. Henry noticed that Adam and Hume exchanged grave looks at this, but he wasn't sure what their opinions were regarding America.

Charles continued his oration, saying, "Will these Americans, children planted by our care, nourished by our indulgence, protected by our arms; will they contribute their mite to relieve us from our burden?" Charles held up a thumb and forefinger close together, illustrating his 'mite.'

There was another storm of agreement conflicting with a nearly equal number in opposition. A distinguished member with an eye patch stood for his turn to speak and was recognized. Isaac Barre, Vice-Treasurer of Ireland and a member of Parliament, lost his eye at the battle of Quebec in 1759, and despite his injury had witnessed the death of General Wolfe and the French surrender on the Plains of Abraham.

"Planted by your care?" questioned Barre, "No! English oppression planted them in America. Nourished by your indulgence? It's by your *neglect* that they have prospered! Protected by your arms? The Americans have nobly taken up arms in their own defense! Do you demand they pay in blood *and* treasure for English wars in America?"

Barre spoke forcefully and clearly in going up against Charles, and Henry saw Hume and Adam nodding slightly as he spoke. He also noticed members stealing glances at the gallery, wondering how he would react to the debate. Charles had been right about that.

Charles stood again and animatedly countered Barre. "*We* paid in blood! To defend *them*! My brother Roger, killed at Ticonderoga. My brother George accepted the surrender of Quebec after the heroic death of General Wolfe. *That* is sacrifice, gentlemen!"

A roar of approval followed, and then Barre stood and waited for quiet. He countered Charles by asking bluntly, "So we make our America policy over your dead brother?"

"How rude!" thundered Charles, "Roger gave his very life!"

"He was a soldier, as was I," replied Barre, "Soldiers do their duty; they make that sacrifice. I gave my right eye at Quebec!"

Another roar from the members, but Barre kept his feet and continued. "Taxing the Americans, these sons of Liberty, is the surest way to drive them from us. Look around! Do you see any Americans represented here?"

Charles stood to respond but turned down the bombast in favor of calm persuasion. "Our good judgment represents the Americans," he cajoled, "That's why this issue is so urgent. We are like parents with unruly children," Charles paused, then raised his voice back to bombast with his punchline, "By unruly, I first refer to those *rioting New Yorkers!*"

Bedlam erupted, the New York Stamp Act riots had inflamed all of Parliament and offended King George. After a minute Barre stood to speak again, but he had to wait another full minute before he could make himself heard.

"You would raise their taxes," Barre said, "You would replace their colonial legislatures with English tax collectors. Worst of all, you then demand a complete monopoly on their trade. No wonder your children are unruly!"

At Barre's mention of 'your children,' Henry noticed several members glance at him. He whispered to Adam, "I'm not unruly, am I?" Adam didn't answer but put his hand to his chin and pretended to contemplate the question, making Henry smile.

"Oh, come now, Mr. Barre," countered Charles, "We haven't even introduced our final bill. We'll have it prepared soon. I suggest we renew this discussion when we have the particulars." There was a murmur of approval at this, despite Charles' initial claim of urgency. Members stood to take a break, and the gallery stood as well.

Hume leaned close to Henry's ear, and said, "You see why Charles Townshend fancies himself the cleverest man in London."

"Charles was brilliant," admitted Henry, "but the one-eyed man matched him stroke for stroke."

"Isaac Barre," said Hume, "is from Ireland; so he knows how oppressive the English can be."

"Did he really lose his eye in battle?" asked Henry.

Hume nodded. "Shot in the face, yes. Fighting for England, more's the wonder."

Henry looked down on the members as they crowded around the door. He noticed Charles, surrounded by his allies, mocking Barre by holding one hand flat over his right eye while making a crying motion with the knuckle of his left in the other.

The next morning Henry bound down the stairs and made for the door, eager to see if Betsy would be in the barn again. As he pulled on his gloves, he saw Adam, wearing outdoor garb, move to intercept him. "Riding today?" Adam asked.

"Uh, yes," Henry replied, "are you heading out?"

"I was hoping to catch you," Adam replied, "I have something to discuss."

Henry gave up hope of avoiding Adam this morning. "Sure, let's ride," he answered, and soon they were walking through the barn where Henry had met Betsy the day before. He noticed her mare alone in her stall, but no sign of Betsy. An attendant arrived to assist Adam with a horse, and they began their ride on a calm but cold morning.

"Charles has asked for my assistance preparing tax revenue estimates," began Adam as they walked their horses side-by-side down the street.

"Sure," Henry nodded, "Who better to ask?"

"Thank you, but this places me... in a somewhat awkward position," said Adam.

"How so?" asked Henry.

"I fear Charles will ask my opinion on policy," replied Adam.

"Good, he should ask you," agreed Henry, wondering what this was about.

"I shall be blunt, Henry," said Adam, "Will the yearly pension Charles promised me depend upon my agreement with his colonial policy?"

Henry looked at Adam as if he'd been hit by a brick. He had not even considered such a thing yet could immediately see that Adam's concern was valid. Upon a moment's reflection, Henry made his decision. "Tell Charles whatever you please, Mr. Smith," he said firmly, "Your pension is safe with me."

"I appreciate that Henry," said Adam, relieved. "So, what is your opinion on colonial policy?"

"I was about to ask you the same thing," replied Henry, as the horses plodded along slowly.

"You saw Charles debate the point yesterday with Isaac Barre," said Adam.

"The one-eyed Irishman? I admit he had my sympathy yesterday," Henry responded.

"And today?" probed Adam.

"I don't know, Mr. Smith," said Henry, shrugging his shoulders, "As much as I've learned, I'm still just twenty. Please, tell me your thoughts."

"You know more than you think, Henry, but yes, I agree with Mr. Barre," said Adam.

"How about Hume?" Henry followed, "As Secretary of State, he's in the cabinet, right?"

"Of the Northern Division," cautioned Adam, "Colonial policy is with Shelburne."

"But if you all agree, can you convince Charles?" asked Henry.

"Perhaps," said Adam, nodding, but after they rode along for several seconds, he looked at Henry, shook his head and added, "Not a chance." Their conversation was so focused that Henry didn't see a woman rider coming in the opposite direction.

"Good morning, Henry!" called out Elizabeth from the back of her mare.

Henry stopped his horse abruptly. After a step or two, Adam reined in his horse as well. The three of them sat on their horses in the street, which at that moment was not too busy.

"Good morning, Betsy!" said Henry, smiling, "what a pleasure to see you again. May I present my good friend and tutor Mr. Adam Smith, of Glasgow."

"A pleasure to make your acquaintance, Mr. Smith," replied Elizabeth with a gracious smile.

"This is Betsy, who I met yesterday riding just as we are now," said Henry. Betsy was fashionably dressed, even though she was in coat, hat, and gloves. There was no smudge on her cheek today.

"A pleasure, my lady," replied Adam, bowing his head. Now he understood Henry's initial reluctance to ride with him this morning.

"Henry, you didn't tell me you had a famous friend," Elizabeth scolded with a disarming smile.

"Well, I didn't want to brag," smiled Henry back, "In Paris, Mr. Smith here was the star of the fashionable salons."

"Paris?" replied Elizabeth with raised eyebrow, "Why, there is another topic of discussion we missed."

"Perhaps a ride tomorrow, Betsy?" offered Henry.

"Ten o'clock sharp, or I ride off and leave you!" laughed Elizabeth, trotting off and throwing a dazzling smile back over her shoulder at Henry.

"I'll be there!" called out Henry, smitten to the core by the lovely girl. He made no move to resume their ride, lost in pleasant thought.

Finally, Adam cleared his throat and said, "Shall we continue?"

Henry looked at him blankly. "What was that?" he asked.

Adam gestured in front of them and started his horse. Henry snapped out of his spell and caught up. Adam resumed their discussion, smiling inwardly at Henry's evident infatuation with the pretty girl. "The Prime Minister suffers from gout and remains at Bath," he said, "That leaves the government largely in Charles' hands. Hume and I fear that he'll make mischief in America while Pitt is absent."

"Why is taxing America so wrong?" asked Henry, "Aren't they British subjects?"

Adam nodded, but said, "Without representation in Parliament, Henry. Most Americans are *there*, because they had so little opportunity *here*."

"They risk wild savages for opportunity? Without a government to protect them?" wondered Henry, looking askance at Adam.

Adam nodded soberly and they rode along for a minute or so before he gestured to a clutch of poorly dressed men and women in the street. When he responded, Henry could sense the heartfelt emotion running strong beneath Adam's normally placid demeanor. "We don't teach them, then we mock their ignorance," Adam said, "We pay them a pittance, then mock their poverty. We deny them opportunity, and then mock their hopeless despair. Is it any wonder they'll risk leaky ships, savages, and starvation for a desperate chance?"

They rode along for another minute, and Henry saw a fine carriage clatter past. A shoeless ragamuffin darted across the muddy street, despite the cold of November. "So, we shouldn't tax them?" Henry ventured, not sure what to make of Adam's soliloquy.

"Not without representation, Henry," Adam said, "I don't think the Americans will stand for it. We should be happy with them as trading partners."

"So, no to a tax, but yes to the trade monopoly?" followed Henry, trying to grasp the issue.

"Oh no, Henry, monopoly is the very opposite of free trade," replied Adam, shaking his head.

Henry sighed and said resignedly, "I'm just not ready for Parliament."

CHAPTER 35

A SHOPKEEPER'S DAUGHTER *November 1766* Henry entered the barn the next morning and closed the door behind him as it was raining hard and blowing. It was no day for a ride, he thought ruefully. He took off his fine cloak and shook it, droplets cascading even though it was a short run across the stable yard. His heart pounded, but not from the hastened steps in bad weather.

"Good morning, Henry," greeted Elizabeth, working a curry comb across her mare's back. She stepped out of the stall at his approach, dressed in the same drab work dress and scarf, but also a rather bulky sweater. Her face, however, was radiant.

"Hello Betsy," said Henry, his heart racing, "Yesterday's fine weather is gone."

"All weather is good for something," she said, "I'm brushing Intrepid."

"Intrepid?" asked Henry, smiling despite his best efforts to remain nonchalant, "That sounds like a stallion's name."

"Oh really?" responded Elizabeth, "What do you call your stallion then?"

"Saucy," grinned Henry, "I rode a horse in France named Saucy, and I fancied the name." He felt giddy in her company, foolish even; the very opposite of the aloof composure he'd imagined himself possessing.

Henry stroked Saucy and then led him out of his stall, looking up in time to see Elizabeth toss him an apple, which he caught and gave to his horse in one sweeping motion. He took up a curry comb and began to groom the animal and she continued combing Intrepid.

"Speak more of France, Henry," she said.

"I spent the last three years in France on my Grand Tour," said Henry, while combing Saucy's thick mane.

"With Mr. Smith the whole time?" she asked, glancing over the back of her horse as she combed the other side.

"Yes, he was my tutor," answered Henry, "a fine man and a fine teacher."

Elizabeth ducked under Intrepid's neck so there was no horse between her and Henry. "You had the personal instruction of a famous Glasgow professor, for three whole years, in France?"

"Yes, my brother and I," returned Henry, "We were fortunate."

She eyed him sardonically and said, "Fortunate doesn't begin to cover it, Henry." Then she bent to scrape a pebble from the horse's hoof with a small pick.

Henry fidgeted for a moment, wondering if he'd offended her. "Well, yes, I understand my position, Betsy. If you must know, I am Henry Scott, Third Duke of Buccleuch."

Elizabeth stood and faced him and gave him a dazzling smile; he was afraid she was about to mock him. She let three seconds pass and then said, "Everyone knows who you are, Henry."

Henry grinned uncontrollably, because there was not an ounce of contempt or sarcasm in her tone. "Even you?" he asked, feeling happy and foolish again.

Her smile was undiminished. "Yes, even me, I admit."

"So, you *deliberately* threw poop on my boots?" accused Henry, laughing and taking a step forward; she had somehow also closed the distance, and suddenly she was in his arms, and he was kissing her passionately. Relief and gratification flooded his every fiber as she kissed him back fiercely. Then it was over, and she was pushing him back.

"Oh my! Henry! Forgive me!" she gasped, lips parted, smile gone, but compounding her beauty tenfold in his eyes despite her dowdy clothes.

"Betsy, enough of this mystery! Tell me who you are!" urged Henry, reaching for her again, but she quickly put her horse between them again. She busied herself with her horse and avoided his gaze, but he could see her cheeks were flushed.

"No, Henry," she said as she bent to inspect Intrepid's left forelock. Henry ignored Saucy, who stood patiently behind him. Finally, she stood and addressed him over the back of her mare, so that only her face and scarf were visible. "I'm too proud to be your mistress, Henry. If I kiss you again, I'm afraid that's where it will lead."

"Then kiss me, Betsy!" exclaimed Henry, grinning uncontrollably, arms wide with palms up.

Elizabeth shook her head and said, "Pay attention to Saucy, Henry," and tossed him another apple. Distracted, he missed the toss entirely and it bounced off his chest and rolled on the straw floor. He bent to retrieve it, brushed the dirt off, and then fed it to his horse. Brushing the mare's tail, Elizabeth said in an offhand manner, "Don't students go on Tour to sow their oats, so to speak?"

"What? No!" said Henry, shocked by her frankness, "Well, yes, it's true *generally*," he admitted, "my stepfather calls it 'gallantry.'"

"I see," she said as she led Intrepid back into her stall. She emerged and met his eager gaze calmly. "I hate to be blunt, Henry," she said, "I like you; I admit it. But tell me this – how much money would it take for a family to marry into the noble house of Buccleuch? I doubt my poor father could afford the price."

"Money?" replied Henry indignantly, "I'll not let money decide. I'll marry who I want!"

She smiled cryptically and said, "We can remain friends, Henry, let cooler heads prevail." She stepped close, put her hand on his arm, and leaned in to kiss him swiftly on the mouth. Then she fled the barn, leaving Henry standing by his patient horse, bewitched.

Thirty minutes later, the elegant front door of the Montagu house, deep in tony London, opened to admit a wet Elizabeth. A maid emerged to take her cloak and scarf, and from the drawing room came the deep voice of her father. "Elizabeth?" he called.

"Yes, Father," she answered, unpinning her long brown hair and shaking it out over her sweater.

George Brudenell, until recently the 4th Earl of Cardigan, now the First Duke of Montagu, appeared in the doorway. A proud smile creased his face at the sight of Elizabeth. Brudenell was a brisk, competent man of great business intelligence, but rendered a sentimental softy by his lively daughter. "Your mother and I would like a word, dear," he said.

Elizabeth followed her father into the drawing room and gave her mother, Mary, Duchess of Montagu, a quick peck on the cheek as she sat on an upholstered divan. "Hello, Mother," she said perfunctorily.

"Such a nasty day for riding dear," said her mother, "I hope you weren't soaked."

"I just groomed Intrepid, Mother, I never left the barn," she replied truthfully.

"That's good, you look a little frumpy dear," replied Mary, patting the seat beside her. Elizabeth raised an eyebrow at this but sat down without reply.

"We'd like to discuss your marriage again, Elizabeth," said George, standing next to the blazing fireplace with one elbow resting on the mantle.

"My answer is the same, Father," said Elizabeth in a level tone, "I will marry for love."

"I know, I know, dear," nodded George, "We respect your wishes, we really do. But you've already spurned two good marriage proposals. You're almost twenty-three; your mother and I grow concerned."

"I didn't love them, Father, it's as simple as that," she answered in the same level tone.

"I understand, dear, I do," her father sympathized, but he didn't voice the words that came next to mind, *'but it's not at all simple.'*

"You don't want to become a spinster, do you?" asked her mother tartly.

"I'm not in spinster territory just yet, Mother," replied Elizabeth sourly.

"Here's the point, dear," continued George, stepping away from the fire as his stockings grew too hot for comfort. "I was recently speaking to a man very high up in the Chatham Administration. He has a son..."

"Stepson, George," interrupted Mary.

"Yes, stepson, recently returned from France," said George, nodding. Elizabeth stood and wandered away, towards the fire, so she could better manage her response. George paused, hoping she'd see the opportunity without further explanation from him.

"And?" prompted Elizabeth, back turned to them as she stood in front of the fireplace.

"It's Henry Scott, Third Duke of Buccleuch! A finer match could not be imagined!" blurted out Mary, too excited to wait for her husband.

"Yes, yes, Henry Scott," said George with a frown, "You stole my thunder, dear."

"I've seen him, Elizabeth, and he's so handsome!" continued Mary, enthused. "Please say you'll meet him!"

Elizabeth turned to face them, but didn't respond at once so her father added, "His stepfather is Charles Townshend, Chancellor of the Exchequer!"

She made them wait anxiously for her response, then said slowly, "So you like this duke's political connections?"

"No, no," said George, shaking his head, "As a politician, Townshend is totally feckless." An astute businessman, Brudenell knew bad government financial policy when he saw it. He also knew that position was everything, and this opportunity was rarified air indeed.

"Who gives a fig about politics?" exclaimed Mary, "Henry Scott is rich!"

Elizabeth frowned and shook her head disapprovingly. "Really Mother, love means more than good looks and money."

"Yes dear, of course" agreed Mary, nodding, "but surely it's possible that you *could* love a handsome, rich man?"

"But not *because* he's handsome and rich," insisted Elizabeth, "Or entitled." She hid the small smile that showed she had her own game afoot.

George took a deep breath and plunged ahead, declaring, "I had a chance, and I took it, dear. I've arranged a private meeting before the Christmas Ball."

"All arranged, is it?" said Elizabeth scornfully, but inside she was delighted, and resisted the urge to smile.

"Henry and his parents, yes," said George with a resolute nod, "It would cause me considerable embarrassment if I backed out now. I'm sorry if I've put you in a pickle, dear."

"Oh Elizabeth, please just meet him!" implored Mary, hands clasped as if in prayer.

"I'll meet him, Mother," Elizabeth agreed calmly, then she raised her chin and said archly, "Just don't be upset if I refuse him!"

At the same time Henry returned to his London hotel and ran up the stairs two at a time. Striding down the hall, he passed the door to Charles' room, which stood ajar.

"Henry!" called Charles as he glimpsed him pass.

Henry stopped and entered the room, closing the door behind him at the gesture Charles made by drawing a downward circle in the air with his finger. Frances sat at a desk inside the door, surrounded by paper, ink, and quills. "Hello, Henry," said Frances, "Do I have ink on my face?"

Henry smiled at his sister and shook his head.

"Your mother will be in London for the Christmas Ball," announced Charles.

"Good," nodded Henry, "is that all?"

"Henry, I've arranged a meeting for you," continued Charles.

"With whom?" said Henry, wondering who could top King George III.

"The Duke and Duchess of Montagu," Charles replied, then added after a pause, "and their daughter Elizabeth."

Understanding broke across Henry's face and he nodded slowly. "Matchmaking, I see. Charles, I insist on choosing my own bride. Marriage isn't just a, a, ... a financial contract."

"Sure it is, Henry! Of course it is!" Charles spread his arms. "It's a rare prize to marry into the noble estate of Buccleuch."

"How rare, in pounds sterling?" asked Henry sarcastically, remembering Betsy's question.

"The Duke of Montagu offers thirty thousand!" said Charles excitedly.

"You make it sound like he's selling his daughter," replied Henry with a frown.

"Oh Henry, please," said Charles, exasperated, "You know how the world works, that's why we sent you to France!"

Henry barked a short laugh, but he bit his tongue to stop a rude comment about gallantry, remembering Frances' handwriting on the letter he read on the canal path with Hew. Frances put her quill down and waited, sensing something was eminent. "I've fallen in love," announced Henry defiantly.

Charles was struck motionless with fear and sudden danger, and Frances drew in her breath. "With whom, Henry?" asked Charles, trying not to overreact.

"A shop-keeper's daughter," answered Henry levelly, looking Charles in the eye as his stepfather's normal poised reserve fell away in an instant.

"No! Is she with child?" exclaimed Charles, throwing up his hands in alarm.

"Father!" said Frances sharply.

"Frances, run along," commanded Charles, "leave everything as it lies."

"She can hear, let her stay," countered Henry. Charles nodded reluctantly, and Frances cautiously sat back down.

"Is she with child, Henry?" repeated Charles anxiously.

"Of course not, she's a lady!" replied Henry indignantly.

Charles expelled an audible sigh of relief, then said, "Thank God, this can all be mended."

"I don't want it mended, Charles," said Henry tersely.

Charles knew direct confrontation wouldn't win the day. He nodded and said, calmly, "I understand, Henry, you're a young man in a hurry. What is this young lady's name?"

"Betsy," replied Henry.

"Where did you meet Betsy?" asked Charles.

"In the horse barn," answered Henry.

Charles groaned and put his head in his hands. After a moment, he raised his head and plunged on. "Henry, it will embarrass me if you don't meet the duke and his daughter. She is reputed to be quite lovely."

"So, you haven't seen her," said Henry.

"No," admitted Charles.

"How do you know I'd even like her?" challenged Henry.

"You don't have to marry her if she repels you, Henry," said Charles, "I've arranged to meet just prior to the Christmas Ball. Dance this Elizabeth around the floor once or twice. Your mother and I would be very pleased."

"I'll meet her then," Henry scowled, "but no more matchmaking Charles. I must find out Betsy's last name."

"You don't even know who she is?" exploded Charles, "Henry, don't be gullible!" He sat down on a sofa and then glared at Henry and shook his finger at him. "She's a crafty young woman who would love to parlay her brief youthful beauty into a lifetime of luxury. At *your* misery and expense! Including her entire extended family! *Especially* the mothers-in-law!"

"Father!" scolded Frances, "Grandmother Argyll died just last year!"

"Yes, sorry Frances," apologized Charles hastily, "Grandmother was certainly an exception."

"Betsy's not a maid or a washer woman," said Henry indignantly, "She's educated, distinguished."

"Is she beautiful, Henry?" asked Frances.

"Very," said Henry, keeping his eyes on Charles.

"Oh Henry, they all are! They all are!" protested Charles, "Does she offer thirty thousand?"

"You sound like you've already spent it, Charles," said Henry.

"It would more than cover the improvements we've made at Adderbury," admitted Charles.

"We made? I wouldn't have chosen that ugly statuary," snapped Henry.

"Henry," countered Charles wearily, "Adderbury is for you, and your bride. Please don't marry below your station. It would be such a scandal."

"That's for me to decide," said Henry stubbornly.

"You'll grow to love whomever you marry, Henry," said Charles, "Look at your mother and I!" prompting Henry and Frances to glance dubiously at each other.

"I'd rather fall in love first, and then marry," replied Henry.

"Either way, you end up in love!" said Charles, brightening, "But with care, you can also get the thirty thousand!"

Exasperated, Henry stared at Charles, then turned on his heel abruptly and stormed out the door without another word. Charles shook his head, wondering how to manage the utter disaster of Henry falling in love in a barn, and knowing he'd bungled his first try.

To Frances, Henry falling in love was good news. She looked at Charles and said, "Father, may I go to the Christmas Ball?

REYNOLDS PAINTS FRANCES *December 1766* Henry stood in his breeches and shirt in his London room, sipping his tea and looking down at the traffic on the street below. Cloaked pedestrians hurried through the wet streets as it began to snow; large wet flakes that somehow made Henry glad to be home. Sitting on the edge of a chair, he pulled on his boots, finished his tea with a gulp, shrugged on his coat, and made his way downstairs to breakfast.

The hotel servant had just placed his meal before him when Cook descended the stairs and spotted him at his table. "Good morning," greeted Cook, "Do you need anything before I go?"

"I'm fine, where are you going Cook?" Henry mumbled with his mouth full of egg.

"Mr. Townshend is taking Frances shopping, and he asked that I attend them," Cook replied.

"Christmas shopping on a snowy day, sounds perfect," said Henry, and Cook departed with a nod. Henry thought Cook seemed almost happy this morning; he was probably glad to be home as well. Less than a minute later Frances came down the stairs and skipped over to Henry as he cut his sausage.

"Morning, Henry, I'm getting a new dress for the Christmas Ball!" she announced happily, grabbing a piece of toast from Henry's plate. Cook reappeared with her cloak, and she turned so he could drape it over her shoulders.

Charles followed her downstairs. He approached with a light step and a smile, hoping Henry harbored no ill feelings about their argument over Betsy three days before. "Good morning, Henry, Frances would love it if you came along...?" he said, raising his eyebrows hopefully.

Henry laughed and shook his head. "Dress shopping! I'll pass."

"I don't ever think I've seen her this happy," said Charles, looking at Frances as she waited with Cook by the door.

"The tailors will jump to attention with you there, Charles," said Henry, "Buy her the best."

"I intend to," nodded Charles, "My plan is to have the dress fitted before her mother arrives."

Henry nodded sagely at this, and Charles gave him a knowing wink as he left the hotel with Cook and Frances. Left alone, Henry suddenly recalled his lost friend James MacDonald, who had hailed him from across this very room before they'd sailed for France. The memory made him think of Hew, and how the two of them had always made him laugh. Henry felt his spirits drop, remembering.

As if on cue, the hotel door opened to admit David Hume, his greatcoat flecked with snow. He beamed when he saw Henry sitting alone at breakfast and strode over with a characteristic smile on his broad face. Hume was the perfect antidote to melancholy. "Henry! Good to see you lad," said Hume, pulling up a chair and perching on it, still in his greatcoat. He raised a questioning eyebrow as he helped himself to a piece of Henry's toast.

"What brings you out in the snow, Hume?" asked Henry after he'd swallowed his bite.

"Christmas!" said Hume brightly.

Henry laughed, as Hume's humor was infectious. "So even a religious skeptic enjoys Christmas?"

"Of course, Henry. The food alone makes it my very favorite holiday," said Hume, helping himself to another piece of toast.

"Happy Christmas to you then," nodded Henry, as he saw Adam approach from the stairs.

"Well, two of my favorite people sitting together!" smiled Adam.

Hume replied, "Don't you mean to say, 'my two favorite people' Adam?"

"Hume! You insult my dear mother," replied Adam, and they all laughed.

Hume stood and said, "We're off to discuss tax policy, Henry. Care to come along?"

"My second good offer this morning," Henry answered, shaking his head. "I regret I have more pressing engagements."

"Really?" said Hume in mock surprise, "More fun than helping calculate tax revenue?"

"Charles took Frances shopping today, so you're both safe," informed Henry.

"Plenty of work without him," responded Adam, "Come Hume, those numbers won't pluck themselves out of thin air." They waved at Henry as they left the warm hotel; when he resumed his breakfast, he found he had no toast.

Later that morning Henry went again to the horse barn, as he had every day since he last saw Betsy. The mare stood in her stall looking mournfully at Henry as he fed an apple to Saucy, so he gave one to Intrepid as well. He went to find the stable attendant, a middle-aged man missing his two front teeth, with a bushy mustache that attempted to hide that fact.

"Say fellow, has the lady been to see her mare today?" asked Henry.

"Yes, very early this morning," the man said, "weren't hardly light yet."

"Did she ride?" followed Henry.

"No sir," said the man, shaking his head, "I'm to look after the mare while she's gone."

"Gone? How long?" asked Henry with a sinking feeling.

"Beggin' your pardon, sir, but I'm not at liberty to say," he answered, "Keepin' the lady's confidence, ye see."

Henry stared at the man, frustrated, but the man looked back at him without intimidation. He had his mission, and he was sticking to it, and Henry found that he couldn't blame the man. He turned to leave without another word. After a few steps, he turned back to the attendant. "Thank you, for keeping the lady's confidence," Henry said, flipping him a schilling which the attendant caught with alacrity. "Some oats for my stallion, if you please."

"Yessir!" said the man, showing his missing teeth with a delighted smile.

• • • •

"COOK, WE'LL DROP YOU at the hotel," said Charles, as the carriage clattered over cobblestones on their return from the tailor. "Frances, we have another appointment."

"Should I change out of my new dress then?" asked Frances, who was so taken by her beautiful new clothes that she had insisted on wearing them out the door of the tailor's shop.

"On the contrary, my dear!" Charles beamed at her. "You'll want to look your very best."

Later, Frances sat poised and self-conscious on a stool in the studio of Joshua Reynolds, not used to being pretty but excited to have her portrait painted. Reynolds was in close competition with Gainsborough as the most popular portrait artist in London, although the two were friendly when they encountered each other in the clubs. Reynolds had previously painted Charles.

"Keep your chin up, Frances," instructed Reynolds in a kindly tone as he worked. Charles sat in a chair behind the artist, who wasn't as particular about being watched as was Gainsborough.

"I wonder what mother will think!" said Frances, complying by lifting her chin back to level.

"Of what, dear?" said Charles, who had been distracted for a moment.

"Me, having my portrait painted," replied Frances.

"We aren't telling her just yet," advised Charles, causing Reynold's eyes to flick, but he volunteered nothing.

"I can't show it to her?" asked Frances.

"It's her Christmas present, dear," answered Charles.

"What if she doesn't like it?" said Frances with alarm, imagining a ruined Christmas if Caroline criticized the picture.

"Of course she'll like it!" Charles reassured her, "How could she not?"

Charles sounded slightly patronizing, and unconvincing, uncharacteristically uncertain despite his reassurance. Frances felt uneasy. They both knew Caroline had a sharp tongue.

"Lady Frances, I will not fail to capture your beauty," said Reynolds; his kind smile calmed Frances' fears and she settled back into her pose. In her new dress, she hoped she'd look so pretty that even her mother would be pleased.

CHAPTER 37

THE CHRISTMAS BALL *December 1766*

Caroline Townshend swept into the hotel two days later, in the late afternoon, dressed in fur and followed by servants carrying luggage. Cook appeared, cutting off the hotel attendant.

"My lady, all is prepared. Let me show you to your suite," Cook said.

"Thank you, Cook," Caroline nodded, "Efficient as usual." Cook beamed at hearing the rare praise and led Caroline up the stairs. As they walked down the hall a door swung open and they saw Frances, with Charles standing in the background. Frances wore her writing apron which was smudged with ink, as Charles was dictating letters.

"Hello, Mother," greeted Frances.

"Oh, there you are, Frances," said Caroline, "making yourself useful I see."

"Indeed, she is dear," called out Charles from inside the room, so Caroline entered with Cook and the servants going past with the luggage.

"Where is Henry?" she asked.

"Out, not sure where exactly," answered Charles, hastening over to give his wife a peck on the cheek. Caroline bent and offered a cheek to Frances, who kissed it dutifully.

"Does he know about meeting the Montagus?" Caroline asked Charles.

"Yes, Henry agreed, at the Christmas Ball," confirmed Charles, nodding his head vigorously, eager to communicate good news.

"Mother, I have a new dress!" volunteered Frances, with a hopeful look on her face.

"Whatever for, Frances?" replied Caroline, "You have ink enough on the one you're wearing."

"For the Ball, Mother!" said Frances.

"Hmmpf, you shouldn't get your hopes up, Frances," replied Caroline with disdain.

"Surely you don't object to Frances going to the Christmas Ball?" asserted Charles, aghast.

"Of course not," said Caroline, "I just care about her feelings. Everyone will look their very best at the Ball. Frances will be plain by comparison."

"That's why we bought her a fine new dress," replied Charles, stating the obvious.

"Well, I hope you didn't spend too much," said Caroline, "There is only so much to work with."

Hearing this, Frances burst into tears and fled the room. Charles finally let his temper flare, outraged by his spiteful wife. "Caroline! She's your only daughter for God's sake!" he barked.

"Well, with looks like hers she'll just have to grow a thicker skin," replied Caroline archly, "Life will be full of disappointments much bigger than being a wallflower at the Christmas Ball."

Charles remained silent, glaring at Caroline, upset but not willing to carry it further.

"Now, tell me about the Montagu offer," she commanded, changing the subject.

"They offer thirty thousand pounds," answered Charles, trying to return his voice to its normal tone. "Montagu was only made a duke last year. Previously he was the Earl of Cardigan."

"Henry is the most eligible bachelor in London," said Caroline, "Surely we could do better?"

"Not likely," said Charles shaking his head, "Henry is stubborn; he won't marry the Montagu girl if he doesn't take to her, whatever the price."

"What is her name again?" Caroline asked.

"Elizabeth," he replied.

"Is she likely to attract Henry?" she queried.

"I don't know, I'm told she is quite lovely," Charles replied, kicking himself for not trying to at least lay eyes on the girl.

"I suppose we can live with thirty thousand," agreed Caroline.

Charles took a deep breath and plunged ahead. "Now Caroline, don't be alarmed," he cautioned, and he saw her eyebrows come up. "Henry told me that he's already in love with someone else."

Caroline immediately became very alarmed. "No! With whom? This is a disaster!" she nearly shouted, waving her hands in the air.

"He calls her Betsy," said Charles, motioning with his palms down as if to suppress Caroline's anxiety that way. "He met her in the horse barn; I have not seen her."

"You mean he's sleeping with the milk maid?" exclaimed Caroline.

"No, no, Caroline, settle down," said Charles, "They went riding together, is all. He claims she's educated."

"But not worth thirty thousand pounds, I'll wager!" Caroline waved a finger at her husband as if it was all his fault, "Probably some conniving hussy!"

"The less said, the better, Caroline," soothed Charles, "He's agreed to meet Elizabeth so let's hope for the best. Perhaps this Betsy is just a momentary flame."

Two nights later, Charles and Caroline stood in the hotel lobby in their finest clothes, anxious, with Cook attending them.

They looked up and saw Frances descending the stairs, followed by Henry. Frances wore her new dress, white with two shades of green trim, with traces of gold in the stitching. Two women were brought in to fix her hair, and Henry thought it entirely worthwhile as Frances' coiffure made her look grown up and elegant. She stepped slowly, self-consciously, afraid of tripping, as everyone in the lobby stopped to watch. Henry, handsome in his dark blue coat with silver facings, caught his share of admiring glances.

"Frances, you look lovely," said Charles, and everyone could see that he meant it.

"I'm impressed, Frances," nodded Caroline, reaching out to touch her daughter's shoulder, "You cleaned up well."

"Thank you, Father, thank you Mother," replied Frances, sincere in the first but finishing with a sardonic touch to her mother's faint praise.

"You are beautiful inside and out, sister," admired Henry.

Frances impulsively hugged her brother with both arms. "Thank you, Henry," she said, voice muffled by his coat.

"Don't muss your brother," Caroline laughed, flooding both Charles and Frances with relief at the sound. If Caroline was in a good mood the night would go better indeed. "Henry must look *resplendent*," she added, moving in to adjust his lapels as Frances let go.

"Cook, is the carriage here?" asked Charles over his shoulder.

"It just arrived," advised Cook, looking out the door.

"Good, we can't be late," said Charles, using his arms to shepherd the group out the door, "I promised Montagu that we'd introduce Henry and Elizabeth before the first dance."

Henry climbed in after Frances and settled into the carriage seat beside her. "Let's get this over with," he said, but he was smiling at the sight of his pretty sister on her way to her first

Ball. The conversation was light but pleasant during the ride; everyone's spirits rose with no sharp comments from Caroline, who almost seemed happy.

Arriving at the ballroom, Henry escorted Frances behind Charles and Caroline as they mounted the steps and entered the large foyer of the great hall. An attendant dressed in elegant livery approached, bowed, and said, "Mr. Townshend, Lady Townshend, the Duke of Montagu and his family await in the salon. Please follow me."

The four of them followed the attendant into the richly furnished salon, where the Duke and Duchess of Montagu stood to greet them. George Brudenell and Mary Montagu matched Charles and Caroline in their exquisite finery but did not exceed them. All were dressed flawlessly as nothing was quite as important as appearances in elite London.

"Lord Townshend, so glad to see you," said the Duke of Montagu, "This is my wife Mary, the Duchess of Montagu."

"Hello George," greeted Charles jovially, "A pleasure, Duchess. Allow me to introduce my wife, Lady Caroline Townshend."

George Brudenell, Duke of Montagu, bowed low to Caroline. "A great pleasure, Lady Townshend," he intoned, and kissed her proffered hand. Caroline beamed; this kind of society was what she lived for.

"And here is Henry Scott, Third Duke of Buccleuch," said Charles, putting a hand on Henry's shoulder.

Henry stepped forward to return Brudenell's bow. "An honor and a pleasure to make your introduction, sir," he said.

"And I, yours, Duke Henry," replied the Duke of Montagu, equal in title but a generation older in age. Who is this charming young lady?" asked Brudenell, smiling at Frances.

"May I present my sister, Lady Frances Scott," said Henry, bringing Frances forward with his hand on her shoulder. Frances curtsied properly, noted Caroline with satisfaction.

"A pleasure, young lady," said the elegant old duke, gallantly kissing Frances' hand.

There was a small pause, with just a hint of fidget as the Duke of Montagu scanned the doorway anxiously. "Our daughter Elizabeth will be here any moment," he said, tapping his toe. As they all looked towards the empty doorway, Brudenell continued, addressing Henry. "So, Henry, I understand you have been in France?"

"Yes, just back from nearly three years of study there," answered Henry as they all turned back to look at Duke George.

"Glad to have you back in England," Brudenell replied, making small talk as he continued to watch over Henry's shoulder for sign of his daughter. After an uncomfortable minute, a broad smile creased his lined face. "Ah, there you are Elizabeth!"

Everyone turned back to the door, which now framed an exquisite Elizabeth, standing in a long ivory gown that looked as if it were decorated with diamonds. Gone was the work dress and bulky sweater. No dowdy scarf covered her lustrous brown hair.

"Betsy!" exclaimed Henry, happy and relieved despite having fallen for her gambit. Henry took a few steps towards her, spreading his arms wide. "Betsy, short for Elizabeth! It never even occurred to me!" He was grinning ear to ear.

"Hello, Henry," said Elizabeth, smiling as she greeted him. She was literally sparkling as she walked, with more diamonds in the hair piled high upon her head. "I hope you aren't offended that I took charge of my own affairs," she said, extending her hands to Henry. He took them gratefully and kissed them.

They turned to face the group, all standing mystified at the turn of events. "Am I to understand...," began Charles tentatively.

"Yes. Charles, Mother, this is Betsy," said Henry, who couldn't stop smiling at the happy surprise.

"Well, that's a relief," said Caroline, dipping in curtsey to Elizabeth.

"Betsy?" puzzled the Duke of Montagu, "We haven't called her that since she was a little girl."

"So, they've already met?" asked the Duchess, still unsure of what had just happened.

"Yes, Mother," said Elizabeth, smiling, "I met Henry in the barn where I keep Intrepid."

"That's just splendid!" enthused Charles as his worries vanished.

"We're so pleased you're not the milk maid," said Caroline happily, prompting a puzzled look from the Duchess.

"And my sister, Lady Frances Scott," introduced Henry, pulling his sister forward to meet Elizabeth.

"I'm so glad to meet you, Betsy!" said Frances, matching Elizabeth's curtsy with her own.

"Betsy, er, Elizabeth, this is my stepfather, Charles Townshend," said Henry, making the formal introduction to a beaming Charles, who bowed low.

"How do you do, Chancellor," said Elizabeth, which pleased Charles even more, gratified that she knew who he was and the high office he held. His relief was palpable; Elizabeth was far more beautiful than the London rumor. The thirty thousand looked promising.

A bell rang, announcing the beginning of the dance. The group hastened to the door, with Henry and Elizabeth last to file out.

"A shopkeeper's daughter?" asked Henry.

"Father's shop is more of a... trading house," she replied with a smile, taking his arm in hers as they prepared to enter the ballroom. Frances entered, unescorted, just before them.

"Be ready, Henry," whispered Elizabeth.

"For what," asked Henry, looking sideways at her.

"Every eye upon us," she smiled as they entered the enormous ballroom, filled with the finest London socialites in their best holiday dress. As she predicted, Henry felt every face turn to watch them enter. Elizabeth's hand on his arm sent a shock of dismay through the heart of many watching ladies, as Henry was indeed the most eligible bachelor in London.

As they were the last to enter, they walked through the parted crowd towards the dance floor, where the first dance was forming up. The crowd melted away, and to Henry's stark dismay, he saw too late that they had stepped into the last starting position of the minuet, a difficult couples dance that he hadn't practiced since Geneva. In an instant he went from glowing pride at having Betsy on his arm, to an extreme alarm at having to perform in front of everyone. The music began, and his first steps were wrong, he knew. He sensed that she danced perfectly, so Henry concentrated on following her feet and keeping his body pointed the right way. He started to sweat at the keen embarrassment that flooded over him.

"Oh dear," said Caroline, watching from the sideline.

"No one notices he's out of step," whispered Charles in her ear.

"Except us?" she replied sarcastically, noticing that several other nearby spectators were commenting behind raised hands.

Henry plunged on, watching Elizabeth's feet. As he turned, he glimpsed Adam and Hume standing side by side. Adam gave him an encouraging thumbs up.

"Remind me to never try that," said Adam to his friend.

"Not a good dance for clumsy Scots," agreed Hume.

"I'll wait for the one where everyone skips along in a circle," said Adam, illustrating his point by scissoring two downward fingers in a walking motion.

On the dance floor, Henry began to recover his memory of the complicated dance. He glanced at Elizabeth's face, which remained perfectly poised despite her flush of alarm at his evident discomfiture. All she could do was continue dancing flawlessly and making it easy for him to see what she was doing. Halfway through the dance, Henry was catching on, slowly, painfully.

"Two years in France and he still can't dance the minuet?" asked Caroline, embarrassed.

"He's improving dear, watch," advised Charles.

I'd be petrified!" said Frances, standing at Charles' elbow.

As Henry and Elizabeth danced past, he glimpsed Frances on the sideline, clutching her hands under her chin with raised eyebrows, as if watching them was utterly suspenseful. Finally, mercifully, the dance ended, and a group dance began. Charles, Caroline, the Duke and Duchess of Montagu, and many others crowded the floor. A young man approached Frances, and she blushed and allowed herself to be escorted to the floor. Henry steered Elizabeth to the edge of the floor, where they could step off. They sought refreshments, with Henry burning with embarrassment over the spectacle he'd created. Elizabeth didn't know what to say. Both took glasses from the servant and stood side-by-side, watching the dancers.

"I danced the minuet last year, in Geneva," said Henry, finally. "I struggled then, too."

"It's a complicated step," ventured Elizabeth.

"Which you danced flawlessly," Henry noted.

"Mother loves music," she replied, nodding towards her parents as the swept past, "I was raised singing and dancing."

"I'm sorry I embarrassed you," said Henry, looking at her, struck again by her beauty in the elegant dress and coiffure. Her loveliness made his discomfort more acute; he *had* embarrassed her. How could anyone *not* watch her dance?

"Not at all, Henry," she said, giving him a smile, "Every girl here envies me."

At that moment, a dashing young man approached with a supercilious look on his face. "A dance, my lady?" he asked, extending his hand.

"No, thank you," replied Elizabeth.

"Well, if your toes get sore from being stepped on..." he said, giving Henry a smirk of contempt, but Elizabeth shook her head, and he moved off. Henry wanted to snarl at him but bit his tongue, recalling Adam's words that an angry man exasperates his friends more than his enemies. Yet he couldn't keep the anger he felt from coloring his next words to Elizabeth.

"Please, don't let me keep you," he said with a sweep of his arm, as if giving her permission to dance without him.

"Of course not, Henry," replied Elizabeth carefully, reassuringly, admiring him for not overreacting to the man's insult. She put her hand on his arm and left it there.

"Was my embarrassment part of your carefully laid plan?" asked Henry, immediately regretting his tone.

She turned him towards her and pulled him further from the dance floor. She stood to face him, standing as close to him as propriety allowed. "I contrived to meet you in the barn, Henry, yes. The rest is fortune."

"You knew your parents would try to match us?" asked Henry, as his beating heart slowed, and his hot sweat cooled.

"I thought it likely," she replied, "so I wanted to get the jump on them."

"With horse poop?" Henry asked, with a hint of a smile.

"Yes," she said softly, looking at him with dark, penetrating eyes. "If you were quick to anger, I'd know you weren't the man for me." She moved even closer, hoping to show that he'd passed her test.

On the other side of the dance floor, Charles and Caroline chatted with the Duke and Duchess. "George, did you know your daughter had already met Henry?" asked Charles, still relieved by the fortuitous turn of events.

"Not a clue. Not a single clue," answered Brudenell, shaking his head in disbelief.

"Elizabeth has a mind of her own," said the Duchess, "She's already spurned two good offers!"

"Certainly not a catch like the Duke of Buccleuch," observed Caroline with her chin lifted proudly. When she saw Mary react with surprise, Caroline quickly added, "Clever girl, that Elizabeth!"

The duke said stoutly, "Mary and I promised Elizabeth she could marry for love."

"Like I said, Elizabeth can be stubborn," added Mary, nodding her head for emphasis.

"Where did they go?" mused Caroline, unable to locate her son as she scanned the crowd.

In an adjacent salon, Henry and Elizabeth found a darkened alcove behind a large armoire. He kissed her passionately and she returned his ardor in equal measure. Embarrassment forgotten; Henry felt that this would be the finest dance he would ever attend. Elizabeth pressed against him, and his hands roamed across her back and then drifted lower.

In the ballroom, Caroline watched Frances dancing with enthusiasm, but somewhat clumsily. "We should have paid more for dance lessons," observed Caroline.

"Oh dear, she's having fun," protested Charles gently.

"Duchess, *your* daughter is a fine dancer," said Caroline to Mary, hoping to atone further for her intemperate comment.

"Thank you," Mary nodded, "We have a musical family."

Frances left the dance floor and rejoined them on the sidelines, breathless and warm. "My goodness, Frances, you should have practiced more!" said Caroline, loud enough for the group to hear. Frances' lip quivered, her mouth turned down, and then she fled into the crowd.

"Now Caroline, she was having fun," protested Charles, less gently, and with a pained look.

Behind the armoire, Henry was starting to work on the front lacings of Elizabeth's bodice. While kissing him, her hands came up to arrest his progress. They froze when they heard someone come into the darkened room and close the door. A sob told them it was Frances, who threw herself on a divan and sobbed into the upholstery. Henry and Elizabeth were trapped. She mouthed the words "I'll go," and pointed at herself. She tightened up her laces as Frances sobbed unconsolably. Reassembled, Elizabeth took a deep breath and stepped out from behind the closet. Frances, face buried in the arm of the divan, didn't see her.

Elizabeth sat and put her hand on Frances' shoulder as she sobbed. "Frances?" she said softly.

Frances sat bolt upright, saw Elizabeth, and then buried her face in the divan again and cried, "I'm so embarrassed!"

"Whatever for?" asked Elizabeth gently, while Henry began to cool behind the armoire, listening.

"I'm mortified," is all Frances could sob. Elizabeth touched Frances' shoulder again, and the girl sat up and tried to compose herself. "I'm blubbering like a little girl," she said, wiping her eyes.

"We all blubber sometimes, Frances," said Elizabeth, "Are you all right?"

"Mother…, oh, why do I even try?" Frances stifled another sob.

"Not having fun at the Ball?" asked Elizabeth gently, putting her arm around Frances as they sat side-by-side on the divan.

"I know I'm not the best dancer," replied Frances, sniffling. From somewhere in her dress, Elizabeth produced a snow-white handkerchief, and Frances blew her nose.

"Dancing isn't about being the best, it's about moving to the music and having fun," said Elizabeth.

"Mother made fun of my dancing," said Frances bluntly, as she recovered her senses. "In front of your parents, Elizabeth. Now I'm crying in front of you." Behind the armoire, Henry sympathized with his embarrassed sister and felt a flame of anger towards his callous mother.

"Don't give up, Frances," soothed Elizabeth, "Tell you what. Have Henry bring you to my house. I'll give you dancing lessons!"

CHAPTER 38

IGNATIUS SANCHO *January 1767*

Just past noon on a cold, calm, and cloudy day in early January, Henry and Frances left the hotel wrapped in scarves and overcoats and walked towards the waiting carriage. They sat side-by-side in the small two-horse buggy that conducted them towards the Montagu house.

"Elizabeth is so kind to teach me dance," said Frances.

"I could use lessons myself," admitted Henry, remembering his debacle with the minuet.

"She'd rather teach *you*," teased Frances playfully.

"I'm a bigger risk to her toes," agreed Henry.

"I can tell you like her, Henry," prompted Frances, hoping to hear more about Betsy. She'd heard the details about how Elizabeth had contrived to meet Henry and thought it the most clever, romantic ruse ever conceived.

"Yes, sister, I do," replied Henry, smiling at the thought. This would be their first visit to the Montagu house, and he'd fussed over his appearance in front of the hotel mirror.

"Will you marry her?" asked Frances, turning sideways on the bench seat to look at him directly, so as not to miss any facial giveaways if he didn't answer her in words.

"Too soon to know," said Henry, "It may be that besides beauty, dancing, and horsemanship that she has no talents at all."

"Don't forget kindness and elegant style," prompted Frances.

"Those are all fine qualities," Henry countered, "To be fair, now let's discuss her weaknesses."

Henry and Frances rode along for several seconds, smiling at each other.

"You go first, I can't think of any," said Frances.

"Me neither," admitted Henry, "She has me dazzled, Frances."

"I'm so excited!" said Frances, clapping her hands like the girl she was, "Wait until Mother sees me dance next time."

"Mother doesn't offer much approval, Frances," replied Henry seriously, "Don't pin your hopes on it."

"I know," nodded Frances somberly, "But she's the only mother we have."

They rode in silence for several minutes before Henry changed the subject by commenting, "Charles seems to be keeping you busy."

"Letter after letter," agreed Frances, "I'm learning so much about government."

"Have you formed any opinions of your own?" asked Henry.

"I think his American policy is frightful," replied Frances promptly.

"How so?" he asked, surprised by such a serious remark from his little sister.

"He sees America the same as our colonies in India," she replied primly, "There to be plundered, it seems."

"Plundered?" grinned Henry, "That's how you describe British trade policy?"

"No, that's how I would describe Father's trade policy," she replied tartly.

"My little sister is an expert on trade!" laughed Henry, and now it was his turn to clap his hands.

The carriage came to a stop. Frances peered out the fogged window and said, "We've arrived, I think. Let's become experts at dancing!"

They approached the door of a fine mansion on an affluent street, and Henry clacked the ornate door knocker three times.

Within ten seconds it opened to reveal a tall black man, a bit under forty, neatly attired in a black frock coat.

"Henry and Frances Scott, here to see Lady Elizabeth," announced Henry, and the man smiled.

"Yes, she is expecting you," he said cordially, "Please follow me."

Henry and Frances marveled that Montagu's butler was black, as there were few blacks anywhere in London at the time. Even more unusual was that he spoke without any trace of a foreign accent. They paused as a house servant took their coats, scarves, and hats. The butler led them down a long hallway, heels clicking rhythmically on the marble floor. They could hear someone playing the piano.

The butler stood aside, and they entered a large room, furnished around the edges but with a large open polished wood floor in the center, entirely without carpets or rugs. Elizabeth rose from the piano to greet them. "Welcome!" I see you've met Sancho," she smiled graciously, indicating the butler who'd followed them into the room. Elizabeth was dressed plainly, hair piled haphazardly on her head, but Henry thought she looked as beautiful as she did at the Christmas Ball.

Henry assumed from her introduction that the man she called Sancho was the head butler, similar in role to Cook. It was odd that she was introducing the butler; in the Townshend household Cook was rarely if ever introduced to guests. He nodded at the man, and said, "How do you do?"

Sancho bowed in answer, and Frances said, "Hello Elizabeth, hello Sancho," as if she were greeting two old friends. She curtsied, causing Sancho to smile, and Henry noted that he had excellent teeth. He sensed that the man was something more than just a house servant.

"Sancho will be helping today," said Elizabeth, and she examined the feet of her guests. "Frances, those shoes should do nicely. Henry, you wore boots to a dance lesson."

Henry looked at his immaculate boots and replied, "I wore boots to *Frances'* dance lesson."

Elizabeth put both hands on her hips, cocked her head and said, "Well, there seems to have been a misunderstanding!" She couldn't keep the smile off her face, and everyone laughed. "I suppose your boots will do, but this isn't barn dancing. Sancho, can you give us a minuet?"

To Henry's amazement, Sancho sat down at the piano and played scales up and down the keyboard to warm up. Then he began to expertly play a minuet.

"Frances let's start with you," said Elizabeth, motioning Frances into position beside her. "Feet like this, begin."

Henry watched closely and could see that his sister wasn't completely new to the complicated dance. After a few turns, Elizabeth held up her hand and Sancho stopped playing. She explained a few details to Frances, showing how to place her feet. Then her hand came down, and Sancho continued playing without losing his place in the music. After a while, Elizabeth beckoned Henry for his turn.

The Duchess of Montagu appeared in the doorway and said, "Dancing! How fun!"

Elizabeth and Henry stopped dancing, but she held on to his hand. "Mother, we need you," she said, "Can you spell Sancho on the piano?"

Mary Montagu happily took Sancho's place on the piano bench and began playing scales.

"Sancho, dance with Frances," instructed Elizabeth, "I'll dance with Henry. Mother, a minuet?"

Henry was further amazed as Sancho proved to be an elegant dancer, light on his feet and attentive to Frances' steps. Elizabeth had to remind him to watch his own feet and not Sancho's. As Frances grew more proficient, a smile spread across her face that replaced a furrowed brow of concentration. As Henry danced on, the steps he'd fumbled so egregiously at the Christmas Ball became natural to him. Elizabeth and Sancho were patient and observant teachers.

It was almost dark when they bundled into their coats and scarves and bid the Montagus and Sancho goodbye. In the carriage once more, Frances leaned back, happy and spent.

"Oh, I just love Elizabeth!" she exclaimed, "Did you know she could play the piano?"

"No, but somehow I'm not surprised," Henry replied, "everyone in that house seems gifted."

"She is so kind," said Frances, "She never mocks or ridicules."

"I felt quite ridiculous dancing with her at the Ball," remembered Henry with a pang of embarrassment.

"Oh, Henry! You can't hold that against her, can you?" protested Frances.

"I'm crazy about her, Frances," Henry replied, "Keep that to yourself for now."

"I'll keep your secret, now you keep one too, Henry," said Frances, "Don't tell Mother or Father about our dance lesson."

"Why is that a secret?" replied Henry, suspecting the answer.

"I don't want to hear Mother's cutting remarks," answered Frances plainly, "When the time is right, we'll show her. Wasn't Sancho amazing?"

"I'm more than amazed," nodded Henry emphatically, "It's odd to hear such clipped English spoken by a man who looks so exotic."

Charles caught them as they entered the hotel. "Where have you been?" he asked, but not waiting for an answer, he added, "We've been invited for supper at the Montagu's tomorrow night!"

· · · ·

THE NEXT EVENING CHARLES, Caroline, Henry, and Frances arrived at the Montagu's and gave their coats and hats to the liveried servants who greeted them. In a moment Ignatius Sancho entered the foyer. "Welcome, welcome, please follow me to the sitting room," he said in his pleasing baritone. Frances smiled at him, and he gave her a secret wink, which Caroline caught.

Caroline leaned close to Charles and whispered, "Did the servant just wink at Frances? How impertinent!"

In the sitting room, Adam and Hume rose to greet them. Both were nattily dressed, but Hume had avoided his bright red uniform. Elizabeth's parents rose at the same time. "Our guests have arrived," announced Sancho.

"Welcome to our home," said the Duke of Montagu formally, and the guests mingled as a servant brought everyone a glass of claret, each already filled and balanced on a tray. Henry immediately saw that Elizabeth wasn't there, but he greeted Hume and Adam warmly. The room was large and comfortable, with a piano in the corner. He noticed that it was not the same piano as they'd seen in the dance studio. 'More like a trading house,' she'd said; the Montagus were obviously well-to-do. Every room was richly furnished and spotlessly polished.

Elizabeth rushed in, holding sheets of music in both hands, elegantly dressed but with a spot of ink on her chin. "Hello, welcome," she said, smiling and slightly out of breath, and dipping a curtsey to Caroline and Charles despite having both hands occupied. The duchess tried to discreetly signal her daughter about the ink. Henry smiled and bowed but didn't say a thing.

Frances blurted out, "Oh Elizabeth, you have ink on your chin!" Elizabeth's hand flew to her face, inadvertently smearing the ink drop so the effect was magnified. Her expression was so comical that everyone laughed. "I get ink on my face too!" laughed Frances, causing Duke George to glance at Charles with a raised eyebrow.

"Frances is my amanuensis," explained Charles, "She has a fine, steady hand."

Elizabeth found a mirror and her face flushed crimson. "Please excuse me for a moment!" she gasped and fled the room.

Mary Montagu said, "Elizabeth has adapted some music we'd like to play before dinner. Please be seated."

Elizabeth reappeared, composed and with a clean chin, and placed fresh sheets of music in the stands. She picked up a violin that rested on the piano. The duchess sat at the piano, and Sancho surprised everyone still further by seating himself with a cello. "Sancho and I have adapted a tune that we hope you'll like," announced Elizabeth.

"Who is Sancho, dear?" asked Caroline.

"Oh, good gracious, my apologies," said Duke George, "Ignatius Sancho, my butler. He is also an accomplished musician." Then, to the surprise of Charles and Caroline, he said, "Ignatius, my apologies," calling him by his first name.

Sancho gave a small nod, but only said, "Shall we play?"

The duchess began on the piano, and then Sancho and Elizabeth entered with their strings. They played several bars flawlessly, and smiles appeared on the faces of their guests. After several minutes there was a tempo change where Sancho plucked the cello strings like a big bass guitar, delighting them all. Color returned to Elizabeth's cheeks as she saw that Henry couldn't take his eyes off her, with a broad smile fixed on his face. Frances was swaying to the music in her chair, causing Hume and Adam to sway as well. Charles and Caroline were pleased by the quality of the music, as they'd heard the very best orchestras in London and Oxford and knew a good performance when they heard it. The tune ended, and everyone stood as one, applauding.

Pleased, Mary stood and said, "Thank you, thank you. Now, let us proceed to the dining room."

Servants hovered in the background as everyone was seated at the long dining table in the ornate high-ceilinged dining room. The duke and duchess took the end places, with Elizabeth and Henry on either side of her father. Frances sat next to Elizabeth, and then Hume, and Caroline, who was to the left of Mary. To Mary's right sat Charles, across from his wife, then Adam, and surprisingly, last to be seated, was Sancho.

Caroline leaned towards the duchess and whispered, "Your butler joins you at table?"

"Oh yes," Mary replied, "Sancho joins us often. He is a very interesting person."

Charles raised his eyebrows at this and glanced at Caroline, but neither made any reply.

"We enjoyed your visit, Frances," said Elizabeth, "I'm glad you could return so soon."

"We had fun," replied Frances, glancing at Henry as they realized their secret was blown.

When Caroline turned to ask Frances what she meant, her view down the table was blocked by Hume. She asked anyway, "Frances? What is this?"

"When were you here?" added Charles, wondering what he'd missed.

"Yesterday," said Frances, "We were dancing."

Henry explained, "Mother, Elizabeth was gracious enough to offer us a dance lesson yesterday.

"Well, Lord knows the two of you need dance lessons!" remarked Caroline, intending to be light-hearted but it came out with an edge. Hume saw Frances flinch slightly, so he jumped in.

"Mr. Smith and I are plain Scots, and thus, poor dancers," said Hume, pretending a frown.

"Speak for yourself, Hume," replied Adam, "I can dance a drunken jig, on occasion."

Everyone laughed, including Caroline, restoring the happy atmosphere. Hume was ever the diplomat. The soup arrived, distracting everyone for a moment. Frances, feeling safe on the far side of Hume, asked, "Ignatius, how did you end up here in London?"

"Who's Ignatius?" asked Caroline, as she hadn't paid enough attention to his introduction. The duchess nodded her head towards Sancho.

"It's a long story, Lady Frances," Sancho replied, "I don't want to hog the conversation."

"Sancho, please tell them your tale," prompted Mary, "I'm sure they'll find it most interesting."

"And you tell it so well, Sancho," added the duke, nodding encouragement to his butler.

As everyone lifted their soup spoons, Sancho kept his hands in his lap and told his remarkable story. "I was born a slave," Sancho began, "to slave parents, on a ship sailing from Africa. They both died when I was two. Through a quirk of fate, someone sent me to England to be raised as a house servant. All this is what I was told, as I was too young to recall."

Mary Montagu added, "Sancho ended up in the home of the Greenwich sisters. My father would go there to study the Bible with them. That's when he first saw Sancho." She motioned with her hand for him to continue.

"The sisters were devout Christians," said Sancho, "but they did not believe in educating the servants. The duke taught me to read."

"Against the sisters' wishes?" asked Henry.

"Yes," he nodded, "They would loan me as a servant, and the duke would teach me."

"How noble!" exclaimed Frances.

"Tell them how you came to us," prompted Mary.

"Once I could read, I was no longer happy to be their servant," he continued, "I ran away. I came to the duke, and he hired me into his household. I am now a free man."

"How admirable of you," said Adam, looking at George.

"Oh, it wasn't me," replied George, holding up both hands in protest with one holding his spoon.

"It was my father, the Third Duke of Montagu," explained the duchess, "George here was the Earl of Cardigan when we married."

"I'm not a Scot at all," said George, "My family name is Brudenell."

"Since my father left no male heir," continued Mary, "the Montagu name would have expired otherwise. So, we petitioned the King to make George the First Duke of Montagu. But Sancho, please continue."

"Once I began work in this house, I learned many things," said Sancho, "Music, writing, dance."

"Sancho has been in our household since I was a little girl," added Elizabeth.

"I am married and have three children," said Sancho, and my wife's name is Anne. I save part of my wages, and soon I will buy a house, with a store. When I own property, I will vote. My goal is to be the first black Briton to vote in England!"

"An excellent goal indeed," said Hume, nodding.

"My goal is almost within reach," said Sancho, smiling, "It is no longer a dream."

"What is your dream now, Ignatius?" asked Frances.

Sancho was charmed by Frances' use of his first name. The corners of his mouth turned up, and his eyes twinkled. Then his face turned serious, and he said, "My dream is that slavery should be abolished, everywhere in the world."

The next course was served, and side conversations sprang up around the table as everyone ate. At one point Charles said emphatically, "I will not be the obedient instrument of any party. I can only act honestly and independently, and therefore, *wisely*."

"Couldn't one be honest, independent, and *wrong*?" countered Hume.

"Even the most educated might ignore the evidence to preserve the coherence of their ideas," added Adam, "Especially when the party demands it."

"You philosophers are impractical," Charles scoffed, "All that's needed is confident leadership and plain common sense!" He smacked his fist into his palm for emphasis.

At the other end of the table, the duke said to Henry, "Elizabeth has been riding horses since childhood. I'm not surprised that you met in a barn."

"I love horses too," said Henry, smiling across the table at Elizabeth, "A fortunate coincidence."

"Yes, fortunate," replied Elizabeth in a sly tone, remembering her careful plan, "I think we become good at what we love."

"Or do we love what we are good at?" countered Henry.

"Father loves my penmanship," volunteered Frances, "But after a few hours, I love it... less."

"I hope you grow to love dancing, Lady Frances," said Sancho.

"I think I shall, Ignatius," she replied with a smile.

Later, when everyone moved to the foyer to don their coats for departure, Elizabeth lingered behind and caught Henry's hand. She pulled him out of sight from the hallway, just inside the dining room door. Leaning close, she brushed his lips with hers, and whispered seductively, "Arrange a room where I can arrive unnoticed."

She was close, inviting, and Henry wanted to kiss her. But their families were just across the threshold, so he said in a low tone, "I'll send a messenger with the details."

Elizabeth gave him a conspiratorial smile. "Seal the envelope, Henry."

CHAPTER 39

A N AMERICAN REVENUE *January 1767*

Henry couldn't ask Cook to find him a confidential room, nor could he take anyone into his confidence over the matter. The gilt brocade on his elegant jackets would be noticed, so he would have to dress down. Where might he quietly buy presentable but not ostentatious clothes, when dress was how the various ranks of people designated themselves? Henry fretted over such details but managed to assemble his outfit by buying the articles separately; a plain frock coat at one place, a floppy hat at another, a respectable but drab vest at a third. He combed the London Courant for available rooms in the right neighborhoods; in other words, none of the ones he or Elizabeth frequented.

It was a whole week later that Henry knocked upon the door he'd chosen and greeted the middle-aged woman who opened it. He felt nervous, as if the woman would know immediately that he was an imposter looking for somewhere to hide something. "I'm here about the room?" inquired Henry pleasantly.

"Yes, yes, come in," said the woman, stepping back and opening the door.

Henry stepped inside and breathed a sigh of relief. The room was clean and dry, with good light from tall windows. The drapes were not dusty or moldy, and the sight of the large featherbed made his heart race. There was a vanity with a chair and mirror, a chest of drawers, two armchairs, and a tea table. The woman showed him the back door, with a staircase leading to the lane behind the stable.

"It's perfect, how much?" smiled Henry.

"One pound per month, in advance," said the woman.

"Does that include care for my horse, and clean bedding?" asked Henry, posing with chin in hand as if he was worried about the price. A man in his pretended position would take a one-pound expense seriously.

"Every time you use it," nodded the woman.

"Food and drink?" inquired Henry.

"Them'll be extra," she replied, pleased to see a smiling Henry already offering her a coin.

Fifteen minutes later, Henry mounted his horse and rode to the end of the lane. As he turned into the street, he heard someone call his name. "Why, Duke Henry! What brings you to my neighborhood?" Henry turned and saw Ben Franklin smiling as he crossed the street to greet him. Henry dismounted.

"Hello Mr. Franklin!" said Henry, "Is this your neighborhood?" He could see that Franklin had noticed his clothes.

"My rooms are one block over," said the American, "I'm just going to dinner; care to join me?"

"Thank you, but no," smiled Henry, "I'm off to have dinner with Charles at the Ministry."

"Dressed like that?" inquired Franklin, returning his smile.

"I'll change, of course," stammered Henry, "I was seeing about a horse," he added lamely.

"I understand Charles is working on the budget?" asked Franklin, making his own silent observations.

"Ah, the less said the better, I suppose," replied Henry, unsure of what he should tell the American Representative. "He is Chancellor of the Exchequer, so, generally, yes."

"Of course, my apologies, Henry," laughed Franklin, "I'll save my questions for when you're in Parliament."

"Parliament!" replied Henry, "One thing at a time!"

"Yes," nodded Franklin, eyes twinkling, "First you must court a lady. He that hasn't a wife is not yet a complete man."

Henry was brought up short by this, wondering what the wily Philadelphian had deduced. He opened his mouth and shut it again, unable to form any response at all. "Well, you should be off," smiled Franklin, "or you'll be late to dinner. Lost time is never found again!"

He turned and strolled down the street with a wave of his hand, and Henry mounted his horse. "Good to see you, Mr. Franklin," he called out, finally finding his voice.

Franklin turned and waited a moment until Henry had caught up with him. He looked up at the mounted Henry and held up his hand. "One more thing? You seem quite unlike Charles Townshend. Did he raise you?"

Henry did not expect such a question, but after a moment's hesitation saw no reason not to answer the kindly American. "Charles married Mother when I was nine," he said, "I was already at boarding school by then."

"That explains much," said Franklin, "Farewell, young duke!"

At that moment, in a government building in downtown London, Charles Townshend stood and began pacing. Lord Shelburne and Hume, the two Secretaries of State, sat at a long table with Adam. Hume took notes with quill in hand, the tabletop was strewn with sheets of figures with scrawled column headings.

"I promised the King that I would raise an American revenue," repeated Charles as he paced.

"I agree, Townshend," said Shelburne brusquely, "but it matters *how* we raise it. Too heavy-handed and we'll drive the Americans further away."

"We let the Americans collect our taxes and then act surprised when they send us so little," Charles replied, "*British* tax collectors must do the job."

"You'd render their colonial legislatures meaningless," objected Shelburne.

"In France, the tax collectors were everywhere the least popular men," added Adam.

"You too, Smith?" asked Charles, surprised, "I thought you were helping me!"

"The annual revenue you propose is only about forty thousand pounds," returned Adam calmly, "It seems far too little reward to take such risks."

"How about you, Hume?" asked Charles, "I'm sure you have an opinion."

Hume laid his quill down carefully before he responded, "I am an American in my principles, and wish we would let them alone to govern or misgovern themselves as they think proper."

"Well, no help from the Scots," said Charles, scowling as he continued to pace, "I'm happy you cover Scottish affairs and not American, Hume."

"Are the Americans not British subjects?" interjected Adam, "Why not offer them representation in Parliament?"

"Impractical!" exclaimed a frustrated Charles, "It takes weeks to cross the ocean. We represent the Americans. We defend them, we look out for them."

"And we tax them for it," observed Shelburne, "Isn't that the point of this meeting?"

A knock at the door was answered by Charles, who was closest, and Thomas Fitzmaurice, a young man of twenty and brother to Lord Shelburne, stepped inside. "I'm sorry to interrupt..." he began.

"Not at all, brother, come in," waved Shelburne as he got to his feet, and Adam stood too.

Thomas extended his hand to his former teacher, and Adam took it with a smile. "I heard you were here," smiled Thomas, "so good to see you, Mr. Smith."

"How are you, Thomas? You look fit, all grown up," said Adam, holding him at arm's length and inspecting him up and down.

"Educated, thanks to you, sir," he replied, "I'm starting with the Diplomatic staff."

"I recall young Fitzmaurice here, sitting in my kitchen, worrying about you, Lord Shelburne," said Adam, "the Battle of Minden, I believe."

This softened even the irascible Shelburne, and he looked at his brother gravely. "You were right to worry, Thomas," he said, "I saw terrible things that day. But it was victory."

"Testimony to the power of prayer," replied Thomas, "many of mine, for sure."

Adam looked at Charles and said, "I recall you met young Thomas during your visit to the University."

"That was nearly seven years ago," Charles observed, "but it's good to see you again, Thomas."

"And you sir," said Fitzmaurice, then he turned to see Henry behind him in the doorway, dressed in a brocade jacket with no hint of his clumsy disguise.

"Henry!" called out Charles, happy to see him but expecting him a half-hour earlier.

"Hello everyone," greeted Henry.

Adam put his hand on Thomas' shoulder and said, "Henry, may I introduce Thomas Fitzmaurice, brother of Lord Shelburne, and my former student in Glasgow."

Instead of a bow, and not waiting for Adam to introduce him, Henry stuck out his hand. "A pleasure to meet you, Thomas."

"And you sir," said Thomas, grasping his hand, grateful for the unexpected intimacy extended by a stranger in a time when only good friends shook hands.

"Thomas, this is Henry Scott, Third Duke of Buccleuch," continued Adam, "Also my former student."

"I will always be your student, Mr. Smith," said Henry.

"As will I, sir," agreed Thomas.

Charles observed the sincerity of Adam's students, unsure whether to be pleased with his choice of tutor seven years previous or alarmed at the evident devotion shown by his stepson to that very teacher. "Well, Mr. Smith, better evidence can't be imagined," Charles said in a jovial tone.

"Evidence?" asked Smith.

"That my choice in Henry's tutor was a wise one," Charles beamed, "Congratulations, sir."

"Thank you, Chancellor," nodded Adam gratefully, sensing there was something more behind the compliment than met his eye.

"I propose we all break for dinner at the club," said Shelburne.

"An excellent idea," agreed Hume, standing.

"Thomas and I can catch up," Adam nodded, but they could all see Charles hesitate.

"I invited Henry to dinner....," he began.

"Let's all go together, Charles," said Henry, unaware of why his stepfather had invited him in the first place.

"I have some family business to discuss," said Charles, looking at Henry and hoping he wouldn't ask what it was in front of everyone.

"All right…," Henry reluctantly agreed, showing obvious regret at not being part of such an auspicious dinner group. He nodded at Charles.

"Let's reconvene at three o'clock, gentlemen," said Charles, relieved.

Inside an eating house down the street, hot soup was served to Charles and Henry, who sat across from each other at the wooden table. Henry sniffed the steaming bowl appreciatively, tore a bit of bread, and dipped it. "Family business?" he prompted, then took a bite. The soup was so hot he had to suck in his breath to cool his mouth.

"First, Adderbury," said Charles, "Your mother and I will move to London once you marry. Adderbury is yours."

Henry was irritated that Charles offered him Buccleuch property as if it were a gift, but instead he said, "You promised me the cost of the improvements?"

"Working on that," said Charles dismissively, "but that leads to my next topic—Elizabeth Montagu."

"Yes?" Henry set down his spoon and eyed Charles warily.

"Your mother and I are pleased that you and Elizabeth seem to take to each other," Charles began, trying for a complimentary tone of voice.

"Things are going well, yes," agreed Henry cautiously, picking up his spoon again.

"Not to be too mercenary about it," said Charles, "but remember that the Duke of Montagu has promised a wedding gift of thirty thousand pounds."

"And?" prompted Henry, after waiting for Charles to continue. Charles had thought thirty thousand would speak for itself.

"That is slightly less than we'd hoped, but more than enough to cover the Adderbury improvements," said Charles, a tad defensive.

"So, you *do* know the costs," observed Henry coolly.

"I estimate we spent about twenty thousand," admitted Charles, trying to sound offhand.

"*We* spent," said Henry sardonically.

"Adderbury was running down, it needed refreshment," defended Charles, "We wanted it elegant and impressive, as a wedding gift to you, and to your bride."

"Who is 'we' again?" pressed Henry, knowing that it was Charles who was spending the money.

"Why, your mother and I!" Charles replied, acting shocked.

Henry took a bite of buttered bread while he waited for his soup to cool, but continued with his mouth full, "That's money already spent; the work is done."

"I borrowed the money from the Pay Office when I was Paymaster," admitted Charles.

"Well, that sounds ethical," Henry said sarcastically, "What am I involved in here?"

"Nothing, Henry, nothing at all," Charles hastened to reassure him, "It's a common practice, a perk of the Paymaster position."

"Free loans?" questioned Henry doubtfully, "So, if I marry Elizabeth, the Duke's money will pay off the Adderbury loans?" He meant it as an accusation, but Charles took it as confirmation.

"Exactly!" he nodded, "How is it going between you and Elizabeth?" he asked again.

The server refilled their glasses, and Henry took that moment to ponder his response. "Charles, don't count our courtship before it hatches," he said, "I won't marry for your financial advantage."

"My advantage?" replied Charles with raised eyebrow, "Didn't I say that Adderbury is yours? Caroline and I would rather live in London anyway." Henry shook his head in disbelief and glimpsed again what it was about his stepfather that made others cynical about him. Glib Charles was slippery as an eel.

"Whatever happens with Elizabeth *will not* be affected by your shenanigans," said Henry heatedly, slamming his spoon down audibly, rebelliously.

"I understand, Henry, I do," placated Charles, knowing when to make a strategic retreat, "Take your time with Elizabeth. Let love grow."

They both concentrated on their cooling soup for several minutes without exchanging a word. Henry seethed, unsure of what to do but knowing he had to do something, decide something. Would Charles let him run his own estate? It was his money that gave Charles his political power, and his stepfather would be reluctant to hand him the reins in September. He felt a wave of uncertainty—was he, at age twenty, even ready for that responsibility?

Then Charles said, "We're returning to Adderbury in two days; your mother wants to see you."

CHAPTER 40

L OVE IN THE AFTERNOON *February 1767*
Quill in hand, Henry labored over his love letter to Elizabeth. Dressed in breeches, shirt, and boots, he sat at his hotel room table, with his baggage packed for his return to Adderbury. As he wrote his excitement grew; he knew his visit home would be brief. With a slow deliberate hand, he finished with, *'I can't wait to see you, Henry.'* He folded the letter and sealed it carefully with sealing wax. Once cooled, he inserted it into an envelope and then sealed that as well. The fancy letter 'S' pressed deep into the red wax.

Two weeks later, Elizabeth rode hooded and cloaked down the lane towards the address Henry had given her. She dismounted and walked her horse towards the stable he'd mentioned. She was hailed by a man in a floppy hat and a low voice.

"Care for your horse, milady?" he said.

"Yes," said Elizabeth, noticing the man wore a rough wool workman's coat and that he was quite tall. She handed him the reins and followed him as he walked the horse into a stall. She entered behind him to check on the quality of hay and to reassure Intrepid about this new place. Behind her, the man drew a burlap curtain across the stall entrance, and she looked up just as he removed his hat to reveal Henry, his face breaking into a wide grin. "Henry!" she laughed and flew into his arms. They kissed, embraced, then kissed again.

"Come," he whispered close to her ear, "We'll use the back entrance. Keep your hood."

She raised her hood to cover her head, as it had fallen back during their greeting, and said, "Perhaps we should not go at the same time."

"Right," Henry nodded, "Watch where I go and follow in one minute."

"Go," nodded Elizabeth, concealing herself behind a post to watch him as he mounted the stairs. The clandestine nature of their long-awaited tryst heightened her nervous excitement. She waited thirty seconds, which seemed to her like thirty minutes, then drew her hooded cloak about her and skipped up the stairs and through the back door. Henry met her just inside, folding her into a long kiss while kicking the door shut with his foot. He pressed her back to the door, and they kissed for a full minute. Then she pushed him away gently so she could remove her cloak. She hung it on a rack next to his coat, and then turned to face him. She reached behind her head and removed the pins from her hair, which fell in lustrous waves down to her shoulders.

Facing him from about three feet away, she said, "First, we negotiate."

Henry remembered Charles' cautions about conniving women. "Negotiate?" he repeated warily.

"Business before pleasure," she said, trying to sound businesslike but her smile gave her away. "I must see what I'm getting into," she said seductively, pulling off her gloves. "Father has been negotiating my marriage for some time. You are the first suitor who I've found, well, suitable."

"That's good then," said Henry, not sure what she was up to.

"Yes," she replied, nodding, "The other two were entitled boors, with the added feature of being ugly. One was quite fat. But more important than looks – any husband of mine will be kind and slow to anger."

"Hence your barn strategy," grinned Henry.

"Yes, you pass every test," she smiled, "and now, the last one. I want to see you."

Henry took a big step towards her, and she swiftly took a similar step backwards to maintain their distance. "See me?" he asked, puzzled.

"Yes," she nodded, "please remove your shirt."

Henry grinned slowly and pulled his shirt over his head; thankful he'd arrived early and lit a warm fire. She nodded appreciatively, standing with arms folded, a small smile on her face. He felt self-conscious under her frank gaze.

"The reverse is true, what am I getting into?" he asked, unable to keep a grin off his face.

"Fair enough," said Elizabeth, and she removed her riding jacket. He stood bare chested, but she still wore her vest, blouse, and full skirt. She nodded at him with raised eyebrows and said, "Next?"

Henry pulled up a chair and removed his boots and stockings. He stood back up, clad only in his breeches. Elizabeth took a step closer and turned her back to him. "Remove that pin in my bustle," she commanded. Henry pulled the pin while Elizabeth undid a button, and then she stepped out of the full skirt, electrifying Henry. She still wore a cotton shift beneath as Henry reached for her impatiently. She took another step away.

"Not yet, Henry," she said temptingly. Although she was confident and in charge of their little game, Henry saw her tremble slightly. He removed his breeches, leaving him naked save his cotton undershorts. He covered himself with his folded hands as his excitement grew noticeable.

Elizabeth slowly unbuttoned her vest and took it off, hanging it on the back of the chair. He could see the full roundness of her breasts beneath the thin blouse as she turned back to him. The trembling was more pronounced now, and the confident smile faded with nervous anticipation. They stood facing each other, wordless, both knowing the moment had arrived. Henry gulped and removed his last article of clothing. He stood before her in complete nakedness, covering himself with his hands in embarrassed excitement. She drew it out as long as she could, which was about four seconds. Then she cried, "Oh Henry, you'll do!" and leaped into his arms.

Two hours later, night had nearly fallen, and the room was dark. Henry peeked out to see the dim form of Elizabeth throwing more wood on the fire. She lit a candle and carried it back to the bed, where she fixed it in a holder on the nightstand. As she bent to do this, Henry saw the outline of her breast through the diaphanous shirt that was her only remaining garment. His blood surged, and he pulled her to him yet again. Afterwards, he rolled onto his back and said, simply, expressively, "My God." In a moment she sat up and sat cross-legged on the bed beside him.

"Thank you for making my first time good, Henry," she said softly, "I've worried... about how it would be."

"How old are you, Elizabeth?" he asked.

"Twenty-three," she replied.

"I'm only twenty," Henry said, "How could you wait so long?"

"Because the available rich boys were unappealing," she said frankly, making him laugh.

"Not good enough to be your one true love?" he asked with a smile.

"Hardly," she said, then grew serious. "I don't want my life to just... happen to me. I can't imagine marrying someone I don't really love."

"That happens all the time," Henry observed, "I'm grateful... that you waited for me."

"I wouldn't risk a baby with just anyone," said Elizabeth.

"You just risked a baby with me," said Henry, propping himself on his elbow.

"Because you were slow to anger, Henry," she replied, leaning in to kiss him.

Hours later, only a candle stub remained when they awakened. They were hungry but decided against getting dressed. The fire had burned low, so they stayed snuggled under the covers.

"You seem very different than your parents," Elizabeth said, combing his tousled hair with her slim fingers.

"Well, yes," Henry agreed, "My actual father, Francis Scott, died when I was four. I remember his funeral, but not much about him. Charles married Mother when I was nine."

"I noticed that you call him Charles, but Frances calls him Father," she ventured.

"Frances, and... my brother Hew never knew our father," Henry answered, and she noticed his hesitation before he continued, "Charles is all they knew."

"I read about your brother before I ever saw you," she said, as Hew's death had made the London papers in the story about Henry's return to his native country.

"He got sick and died, rather suddenly," said Henry somberly, "That's when we returned to England."

"I'm so sorry, Henry," she said, holding his head close to hers, then kissing him.

"We were close, especially in France," Henry said, "Then there was James, my best friend from Eton, who died in my sight in Toulouse. That's when Charles sent Hew to join me. To cheer me up, which he did, admirably."

Elizabeth shuddered, causing her hair to fall over her face. "Died in your sight?" she was almost afraid to ask, as she pulled the strand aside so she could see him with both eyes.

"James fell through a hay loft floor while he was walking towards me," Henry said, a bit stiffly as he didn't want to cry in front of her, "Broke his neck."

"You lost your two best friends!" Elizabeth wanted to cry herself at the sad story. "Were you and your brother close in childhood?"

"Only after he came to Eton," Henry replied as the lump in his throat subsided, "We were in different boarding schools before that."

"When did you first go to boarding school?" she asked as he got up to throw more wood on the dying fire.

"I was around six, I imagine," said Henry over his shoulder, then he turned and walked back to her sitting on the bed. In the soft candlelight she looked supremely beautiful to him.

"So, your mother didn't raise you?" she asked, knowing that her own childhood owed much to her musically gifted mother and Mary's strong personality.

"Yes, of course...." Henry began, then changed direction. "Well, no, I guess not. She said she had a distaste for feeding babies. We were all suckled by wet nurses."

He rolled onto his back, and she lay back beside him, both staring up at the rafters. "My fondest memories of mother are actually of Mrs. Lewis, the boarding school cook," he continued, "She was always so kind to me. Her son was my best friend. She would treat us with a spoonful of pie filling, or cake batter." Henry smiled wistfully at the memory.

"What was your friend's name?" she asked.

"William," said Henry, "We used to hunt rats in the stable. We were friends the whole time I was there."

"How long was that?" queried Elizabeth, fascinated as his childhood unfolded before her.

"Oh, I don't know, maybe five years?" he replied.

"Where is William now?" she asked, silently wishing that her childhood had contained a true friend like Henry's William.

"Heaven knows," Henry shrugged, "He was a cook's son. He's probably apprenticed somewhere."

"Was the school here in London, or in Oxford?" she asked, a dim plan forming in her mind.

"In London, a block off Piccadilly Square," he returned, staring up at the rafters again. "Buckingham School for Boys."

Early the next morning, a hooded and cloaked Elizabeth walked Intrepid out of the lane and into the street, looking both ways before she did so. The outline of her handsome face was revealed, very briefly, to a nearby pedestrian unnoticed by Elizabeth as she rode away. Ben Franklin looked up and glimpsed Henry in the window, watching the girl leave. Neither of them saw Franklin, who smiled to himself and continued with his early morning stroll. He loved it when a hunch proved correct.

• • • •

IN THE DINING ROOM back at Adderbury that day, Charles, Caroline, and Frances sat at dinner. The dining room table seemed too big for just the three of them.

"I don't understand why Henry was so anxious to return to London," said Caroline, "He barely got here, and then off he went."

"I should have gone with him," said Charles, "I'll head back tomorrow."

"So soon?" Caroline complained, "You seem as impatient as Henry."

"Too much going on," replied Charles, taking a drink of his port, "India. America. Chatham's gout keeps him at Bath, so at the moment we're leaderless."

"Do you need me in London, Father?" asked Frances hopefully.

Charles looked at Frances affectionately, but he saw Caroline shaking her head. "Frances has already spent too much time in London," she declared.

"I won't argue the point," answered Charles, seeing his wife's mood, "But Frances has been very useful to me at work." He smiled benignly at Frances.

"Next we know you'll have her *employed*, for heaven's sake," snorted Caroline, "My daughter, the tradeswoman."

"I like writing Father's letters, Mother," Frances replied bravely.

"Of course," said Caroline contemptuously, "It makes you feel more important than you are."

Frances flinched as if slapped, then appeared resigned at her mother's continual denigration. Charles looked sympathetic but didn't challenge Caroline. He sighed and looked at his plate.

"When Henry marries," Caroline continued, "he'll have Adderbury. We will move to London. You'll have plenty of time to get ink all over yourself then."

"On that subject," interjected Charles, "I have a very good feeling about Elizabeth Montagu."

"Do you think she's worthy of Henry?" asked Caroline, "He's the most eligible bachelor in London, after all."

Charles shook his head, nettled by his wife's negativity. "How would you know that, Caroline? London is a big town."

"Size of the estate," she replied confidently, "plus, he's so handsome."

Frances set down her fork and asserted, "I think Henry will marry for love. And I think he has already fallen in love with Elizabeth."

Charles and Caroline gaped at her, with Caroline first to respond. "What do you know, Frances?"

"Yes, what have you learned?" seconded Charles.

Frances hesitated, not wanting to betray Henry's confidence. She stammered, "I, I, I, just love Elizabeth. I can't imagine Henry not loving her too."

Caroline said dismissively, "Silly sentimental girl."

"I'm not sure she's wrong, Caroline," said Charles optimistically, "I have a good feeling about the Montagu girl."

Later that afternoon, Charles composed a letter as Frances sat attentively at her writing desk.

"New letter, Frances," said Charles, "this one to Samuel Touchet, spelled T-O-U-C-H-E-T, Member of Parliament, Shaftesbury."

"Samuel Touchet, sounds French," commented Frances.

"He's not," said Charles, chin in hand as he thought of his first line. He looked at Frances and dictated, "Dear Sir, Salutations, etc. As previously discussed, by this letter I authorize you to invest 7000 pounds sterling in East India Company stock."

Frances wrote the words swiftly, pausing twice to dip her quill. She looked up expectantly. "Execute this purchase immediately and confirm at your earliest opportunity. Your humble servant, blah, blah."

Frances scribbled industriously, then looked up with a deadpan expression. "How do you spell 'blah,' Father?"

Charles laughed and moved to stand behind her, looking over her shoulder at the letter and placing a hand on her shoulder. "I'm glad you have a sense of humor, Frances. Despite your mother's sharp tongue. And such an elegant hand, I will miss you in London."

"I'll miss you too, Father," replied the girl, pleased by his compliment, "I like London; I feel lonely here at Adderbury."

"Me too, Frances," said Charles, with his hand still on her shoulder, "I feel lonely in a crowd, so to speak, when you are not with me." Frances noticed his hand and turned to glance at it as he squeezed her shoulder. He continued, musing, "Perhaps I'll renew the topic with Caroline…" He finally removed his hand and began to pace the room with his hands behind his back. Frances waited, assuming he would continue dictating letters.

Charles turned towards her suddenly and took a diamond ring off his little finger. He extended it to her, saying, "Here, Frances, I want you to have this ring."

Frances was surprised by this unusual gesture but did not extend her hand to take the ring. She could see by the size of the diamond that it was worth a small fortune. She said simply, "I can't take that, Father, what would I tell Mother?"

Charles stood frozen for a moment, still extending the ring. Finally, he thrust it back on his finger nervously and nodded. "Of course. Of course. You're right, Frances. Tell you what. I'll wear the ring, but it's yours from this moment onward."

Frances sat dumbfounded by his strange behavior, and finally replied, "Well, thank you Father." She was puzzled as to what had got into him, and more than a little disturbed by his manner.

"I'll think of you whenever I look at it," he mused, "But it's yours, Frances, it's yours."

Charles paced for a minute more, as Frances sat wordlessly, watching him. Finally, she asked, "Are there more letters to write?"

Charles came out of his reverie and looked at Frances for a long moment. Then he shook his head and said, "No, dear, not today."

CHAPTER 41

M ARRY ME, ELIZABETH *February 1767*

Henry stepped out of his London hotel, pulling on his gloves against the brisk temperature and squinting into the bright sun. The stable attendant appeared, leading Saucy, just as he'd arranged. Henry mounted easily and adjusted his coat. He tossed a penny to the paperboy. As he bent to take the paper, he heard a musical voice behind him say, "I like a well-read man!" It was Elizabeth, riding Intrepid, with a dazzling smile as they both turned to look at her. Her face was radiant but the rest of her was bundled against the cold.

"Elizabeth," greeted Henry, "Percy, here, keeps me well-informed for only one penny a day."

"You're a remarkable fellow then, Percy," said Elizabeth.

The tattered paperboy bowed and said gravely, "Thank ye, milady." She smiled at him, and Percy was sure he was looking at the most beautiful lady in London.

Henry and Elizabeth trotted down the street side-by-side, as the traffic was light. Henry felt exhilarated, as he did every time he saw her. People on the street looked up as they passed, noticing the fine clothes, splendid horses, and happy expressions of the handsome couple. "I'm tempted to call you Betsy," said Henry, smiling uncontrollably at being in her company on such a fine winter day.

"Not since I was a little girl has anyone called me Betsy," she smiled in return, "I wondered if you'd put two and two together."

"Where should we ride?" asked Henry.

"Oh, let's just wander in the sunshine," she replied, "Turn left just there."

They walked their horses through the sunlit streets, conversing. Henry found Elizabeth easy to talk to; she was open, observant, and intelligent. "Your mother taught you music?" he asked.

"Yes. Sancho and I learned together much of the time," she replied.

"He's an interesting character," said Henry, "and he sure can dance."

"Sancho is remarkable," she agreed. "When he first came to our household, I was about eight. I had never seen a black man, and he frightened me."

"He seems a member of the family now, though," observed Henry.

"Very much so," she nodded, "Sancho taught me to think of distant people as real individuals. Not just foreigners, or enemies." She pointed to a street and said, "Turn here."

"Who taught you how to ride?" he queried, eager to absorb every new tidbit about his love.

"My father, and from a young age too," she said, pointing out their next turn.

As they nosed their horses down a narrow lane, Henry recognized the lane behind his rented room. They'd approached from a completely different direction. "Hey, look where we are!" exclaimed Henry, beaming at her.

"Imagine that, Henry," she said impishly. He laughed as they dismounted at the stable entrance. They led their horses into their stalls, then plunged into each other's arms in a long, passionate kiss. Henry walked her backwards until they tumbled into an empty stall filled with fresh hay. She gave a giggle as he lay on top of her in the straw.

"Is someone there?" they heard a man call. From his voice they could tell it was likely a servant or stable attendant.

Henry stepped out of the stall, brushing straw off his breeches. "Yes, can you give some oats to these horses?" He pointed towards Intrepid and Saucy as they munched hay in their stalls.

"Yessir," the man said, catching the coin that Henry flipped to him. As the man turned to fill a bucket with oats, Henry rushed Elizabeth out of the stable and up the stairs. They were flushed and laughing as he opened the door, and they tumbled inside.

An hour later, Henry and Elizabeth snuggled close together, naked, under the heavy bedcovers as they hadn't bothered to light a fire before jumping into bed. Shafts of sunlight streamed through the cracks in the hastily drawn curtains. This, Henry felt, was love and happiness, so much so that he knew for sure that his happiness depended on love.

"Marry me, Elizabeth," he said suddenly, and without a doubt in his mind.

She rolled onto her side and nuzzled his ear. "Yes. Yes, Henry, yes!" Although she was whispering into his ear, her excitement and certainty flooded him with gratitude. She kissed him tenderly and long.

"I love you," he said, "I loved you when you were still just Betsy the tradesman's daughter."

"I love you too, Henry," she said, "I feel a great relief."

"We might have problems, though," warned Henry, in a mock seriousness.

"Problems?" she asked, with a lifted eyebrow.

"I've always been opposed to arranged marriages," he said, "but here I happily am, *arranged!*"

"It depends on who does the arranging, does it not?" was her pert reply.

"We might have even bigger problems," he said.

"Other than happy parents?" she asked, as they lay on their sides facing each other, with hands roaming under the covers.

"Catholic, or Protestant?" he asked, although he was sure he knew the answer already.

"Protestant," she replied promptly.

"Whig, or Tory?" he asked, raising an eyebrow to show that the questions were getting tougher.

"I see both sides," she replied diplomatically.

"No sitting on the fence, Betsy," said Henry, keeping his mock seriousness.

"Whig then," she answered, "and you?"

Henry rolled onto his back and said contemplatively, "Actually, I see both sides...." and laughed as she hit him in the face with her pillow.

• • • •

LATER THAT DAY AND several miles away, Charles sat in a room at the Ministry with his informal advisers, Adam Smith, David Hume, and Lord Shelburne. The table before them was strewn with papers scrawled with columns of numbers. As the light faded, servants entered to light the lamps.

"Gentlemen, let's call it a day," said Charles, "India will still be there tomorrow, will it not?"

"We need Chatham here," groused Shelburne, "Will he never leave Bath?"

"He did leave Bath, nearly a week ago," replied Charles, "I heard he only made it to Marlborough, too ill to travel further."

"A headless administration, for the moment," observed Hume.

"How ill is the Prime Minister?" asked Adam.

"Ill. Gout, as usual, but something worse, I expect," answered Charles glumly.

"He relies on us, and we can't agree on either India or America," said Shelburne.

"Let's begin again tomorrow, say ten?" Charles replied, standing. The others stood as well, and soon Charles was alone. A moment later, a door opened at the far end of the room, and a stout middle-aged man appeared. Samuel Touchet was a Member of Parliament for Shaftesbury, but also a speculative foreign trader in tobacco, spices, and slaves.

"Sorry to make you wait, Samuel," said Charles, waving him in.

"I was listening. They seem undecided. You seem undecided," said Touchet.

"Just as I intend," nodded Charles, "Did you buy the East India stock?"

"All seven thousand pounds, as agreed," replied the stout trader, nodding vigorously.

"The market thinks the government is about to cut ourselves into the Company's territorial revenues in India," said Charles, rubbing his hands together in glee, "There are calls to investigate the Company, and the stock price has plunged."

"Our plan is working perfectly," said Touchet with a smile, "I bought at the lowest price."

"When Parliament reconvenes, I'll switch positions," said Charles, "I'll suggest a modest annual renewal fee for the monopoly on the India trade. The stock will rise, and we will profit handsomely."

"I only wish we could have raised more cash to invest," lamented Touchet greedily.

"Liquidity is always a problem," nodded Charles, "Now, another subject."

"Yes?" said Touchet, leaning closer, knowing it paid to listen to Charles' ideas on any subject as the man was canny like a fox.

"How valuable might it be to someone, such as yourself, perhaps?" mused Charles with a glint in his eye, "to hold the monopoly for the American trade in *tea*?

• • • •

FEBRUARY WAS WELL-ADVANCED when Elizabeth, wearing her cloak and hood, stepped her mare into the street after another tryst with Henry. She waved a demure hand to him as he stood watching in the window. He turned to pull on his boots, and within fifteen minutes he walked Saucy into the street.

"Greetings, young duke!" called out Ben Franklin from behind him.

"Good morning, Mr. Franklin," said Henry, turning to look over his shoulder. He stopped Saucy until Franklin caught up with him.

"It's noon, Henry," smiled Franklin up at him, "I'm on my way to dinner. Join me?" At that moment Henry's stomach growled noticeably, as he and Elizabeth had stayed in bed all morning and ate no breakfast. Within a half hour, Henry and Franklin were served in a nearby tavern.

"I see a lot of you these days," said Franklin, buttering his bread, "Not complaining, mind you."

"I often ride this way," nodded Henry with his mouth full.

"I see a lot of Elizabeth Montagu as well," said Franklin, holding his buttered bread but smiling at Henry across the table.

Henry finished chewing and took a drink before responding, "So you are on to me."

"From the first Henry," nodded Franklin, "But take no alarm, your secret is safe with me."

"It's her reputation I'm concerned about," said Henry seriously, "We are engaged to be married."

"That is the rumor, yes," said Franklin, taking a big bite of his bread.

"Rumor, what?" asked Henry, alarmed. They had tried to be so careful.

"That you're to be married," replied Franklin, "Don't worry, your little love nest is safe yet."

"We haven't announced it just yet," said Henry.

"I have found," advised Franklin, "that men take note of the really beautiful women."

"Of course, that's nature," Henry replied, "What do you mean?"

"Elizabeth is very beautiful. Your secret won't last long, Henry," answered the American.

"You said our secret is safe with you...?" questioned Henry.

"Three can keep a secret if two of them are dead," replied Franklin, bluntly. "If I noticed," he shrugged, "others will."

"I'll find new rooms," mused Henry with trepidation, hoping he hadn't compromised Elizabeth.

"I don't mean to meddle, Henry," said Franklin, "I do mean to wish you and Elizabeth happiness and good luck."

"Thank you. You have the advantage of age," Henry said, "Do you have more advice?"

"I guess I don't mind being old," pondered Franklin philosophically, "as I do being fat and old!" Henry laughed, and they paused as the serving girl refilled their glasses from a pitcher. Franklin continued, "Wise men don't need advice; fools won't take it."

"I'm not wise yet, but neither am I foolish," protested Henry.

"Then of course I have advice for you!" smiled Franklin. Henry found it impossible not to like the kindly man, and Franklin certainly seemed as wise as he was witty.

"Keep your eyes wide open before marriage, half-shut afterwards," said Franklin with a twinkle in his eye.

"Are you saying she will lose her beauty?" challenged Henry with a grin.

"We all lose our beauty, Henry," Franklin answered soberly, "this advice cuts both ways. If you can bear your own faults, why not the faults of your wife?"

"What if we fall out of love over time?" asked Henry, "Must one of us always be at fault?"

"Where there is marriage without love, there will be love without marriage," replied Franklin.

"And my mother and her sister will gossip about it!" laughed Henry.

"Don't fight," Franklin continued, "Anger always has a reason, but seldom a good one."

"Sensible," nodded Henry, glad he was 'slow to anger,' as Elizabeth had put it.

"Here's my best advice of all," offered Franklin, "If you want to be loved, be lovable."

"That sounds like Adam Smith," observed Henry.

"Where do you think I got it from?" smiled Franklin. "Any word on your Parliament seat?"

"No," said Henry, shaking his head emphatically, "I forbid Charles from even discussing it until I return from Scotland."

"At your Majority?" asked Franklin.

"Yes, in September," Henry confirmed.

"When you become officially wise and responsible," nodded Franklin, buttering bread.

"In theory," Henry shrugged, "It's hard to feel wise when I can't make up my own mind."

"That job is never done," said Franklin, "The job of deciding is always with us. When you finish changing, you're finished."

Henry nodded slowly and took another bite as he absorbed this profundity. "I know my heart about Elizabeth," he said, "but I'm not sure about Parliament."

"There are three things extremely hard," Franklin replied in his kindly manner, "diamonds, steel, and to know one's self. Who has deceived thee as often as thyself?"

"I'll always have doubts if I lie to myself," Henry agreed, "but I have decisions to make right now. Charles just assumes that I'll take the seat he arranges for me."

"Your worth to the world is determined by subtracting your bad habits from the good ones," advised Franklin sagely, "No one is perfect; we do the best we can."

"Now you talk like Voltaire!" replied Henry.

"Where do you think I got it from?" answered Franklin with a laugh, before asking seriously, "Do you feel obligated to do as Townshend says?"

"Not directly, no," replied Henry, somewhat defensively, "I'm my own man. But you've heard him talk. I think Charles could sugar-coat lemons and make us think them candy."

"Words may show a man's wit, but actions his meaning," replied Franklin, "Never confuse motion with action. Well done is always better than well said."

"Yet look where his smooth words have landed him," countered Henry, "A step or two from Prime Minister, if you can imagine."

"Perhaps," nodded Franklin, wiping his mouth with his napkin, "but remember that it's the worst wheel of the cart that makes the most noise. They don't call Charles Townshend the 'Splendid Shuttlecock' for nothing!"

* * * *

ON THE LAST DAY OF February, the Montagu's hosted a fancy supper in their London home. The meal was well-underway and both conversation and claret flowed; arranged around the elaborate table were the Duke and Duchess of Montagu, Elizabeth, Ignatius Sancho, Adam, Hume, Henry, Charles, Caroline, and Frances. When the final course was done, servants brought champagne glasses for everyone.

Henry stood and tapped his glass with a spoon. All eyes turned to him, and the room grew quiet.

"Mother, Frances, thanks for coming to London so quickly," Henry began, "I have an announcement to make." Frances knew what was coming and she smiled at Elizabeth, who gave her a secret smile back. "Elizabeth has graciously accepted my offer of marriage," declared a beaming Henry.

Everyone broke into cheers and stood as one, with Hume raising his glass the highest because he was the tallest. Hume began a round of toasts that emptied the champagne glasses twice, keeping the servants busy as each guest and the hosts took turns offering congratulations to the happy couple. After dinner, everyone retired to upholstered chairs in the drawing room. The drinking continued until all hearts were glad, even Caroline's.

Charles and Duke George stood near the fireplace where they could talk between themselves. "How soon can you ready the thirty thousand?" asked Charles in a businesslike tone that belied the many toasts he'd drunk.

"A few months, I'm afraid," replied Brudenell, "The problem is liquidity. I propose a May wedding."

"No sooner?" replied Charles with a small frown, "Hmmm, I suppose it can't be helped. But it's good to see them both so happy." They gazed with contentment across the room, where Henry and Elizabeth were holding hands as they talked with Adam and Hume.

"I never thought anyone could please Elizabeth; now just look at her!" beamed her father with a warm glow as he gazed at his lively daughter. He was happy to pay the thirty thousand.

CHAPTER 42

BUCKINGHAM SCHOOL FOR BOYS *March 1767* At the end of a long shadowy hallway was a door, and beyond the door someone knocked. There was no response. After a moment there was a second knock, and then a middle-aged woman in an apron and kitchen hat bustled down the hall and opened the door. In the street beyond stood Elizabeth and Ignatius Sancho. The woman was startled at the sight of the tall, well-dressed black man, as there were so few in London. "Can I help you?" said the woman, surprised by the unexpected pair.

"My name is Elizabeth Montagu, and this is my butler Ignatius. I'm looking for Mrs. Lewis?" said Elizabeth politely.

The woman was surprised to hear her name, and her hand flew to her chest. "Me?"

"Are you the school cook?" asked Elizabeth.

"I am indeed," she replied, "Has someone got sick?"

"Oh, heavens no! I'm here about Henry Scott," Elizabeth smiled reassuringly, realizing what an unexpected visit this must be for the woman.

"Duke Henry! Oh my, I hope he's not dead?" exclaimed Mrs. Lewis.

"No, no, nothing like that," Elizabeth said, "I'm his betrothed, I'd like to talk to you."

"Mrs. Lewis? Who is it?" called a prim woman who appeared at the far end of the hallway.

"Just giving some directions madam," called Mrs. Lewis over her shoulder. Turning back to Elizabeth, she said, "Follow me to the kitchen where we can chat. Imagine, Henry's getting married!" Soon they were seated in an immaculate kitchen on the first floor of Buckingham School for Boys, where Mrs. Lewis was still the school cook. A delicious baking smell came from the large oven as she set teacups in front of her guests.

"You are too kind, madam," said Sancho, and Mrs. Lewis was surprised by his cultured English without a trace of foreign accent.

"Thank you, Mrs. Lewis," said Elizabeth as she raised her cup and took a small sip of the hot tea, "Henry has fond memories of you, and your son William."

"Well bless his heart," smiled Mrs. Lewis, "Henry and William were such good friends."

"Where is William now?" asked Elizabeth.

Suddenly Mrs. Lewis jumped up and put baking mitts on both her hands. She opened the oven door and removed a tray of biscuits, flooding the kitchen with their mouth-watering smell. As she raised the large tray, she saw that the oven top was occupied by a saucepan and a teakettle. Sancho saw the dilemma immediately and swiftly removed both. Mrs. Lewis set the tray down with relief and looked up at Sancho.

"Thankee, thankee, we don't want biscuits on the floor!" she smiled.

"They smell so heavenly, I would dive headlong to save a single biscuit," replied Sancho gravely.

"Just like the boys!" she said, pleased with the courtly butler, "Ignatius, is it? You'd be surprised how much good behavior can be bought with a single warm biscuit!"

Mrs. Lewis placed two biscuits each on the tea saucers in front of Elizabeth and Sancho. "Mmmm, thank you," said Elizabeth, taking a bite. "About William?"

"Oh yes, William was best pals with Duke Henry. Must have been, oh, five years that Henry lived here. I haven't seen him for nearly ten," she replied, putting a third biscuit on Sancho's plate as he picked up his second. Elizabeth was still nibbling on her first and finding it delightful.

"Grateful, madam," mumbled Sancho, with his mouth full.

"And where is William now?" asked Elizabeth.

"Apprenticed to Mr. Tottham in the leather trade, just down the street," replied the kindly woman.

An hour later, Elizabeth and Sancho approached Tottham's Leather Goods, which was open in the front but warmed by a large fire deep inside the shop. They saw a large man seated at a workbench near the fire, focused on his work with his broad back to them. He was surrounded by leather goods, finished and in process, and the tanning smell of fresh leather was as pleasant in its own way as Mrs. Lewis' biscuits. Sancho carried a small sack that Mrs. Lewis had given him upon their departure from her warm kitchen.

"Hello?" called Elizabeth, seeing no one in the shop but the workman. He didn't hear her, so she stepped deeper inside and called louder, "Pardon me?"

The man, startled, jumped up and turned to face them. "Oh! You surprised me!" he said, and Elizabeth saw a tall young man, taller than Henry, with muscular arms and a mass of tousled blond hair stuffed under a leather cap. He wore a work apron, his fingers were stained with tannin, and his handsome face wore a puzzled expression. Elegant upper-class women rarely visited any leather shop, and Sancho was beyond his experience entirely.

"I'm sorry," said Elizabeth politely, "I'm looking for William Lewis?"

"You found him," said the young man, "I'm William."

• • • •

TEN DAYS LATER AND several miles from Tottham's Leather Goods, Charles stood to address Parliament. Adam, Hume, and

Lord Shelburne sat in the gallery with Henry. Most of the MPs were in attendance, including Samuel Touchet, as they were all interested in the India question. Chatham's administration, of which Charles Townshend was the head finance minister as Chancellor of the Exchequer, wanted more investigation and control of the British East India Company, which held the official monopoly over the Indian trade. Chatham had also favored the recent repeal of the American Stamp Act, which had caused such colonial upset, especially in New York. "I rise to address the Members, and regret to inform you that Chatham remains too ill to attend," Charles began, "However, we've been in touch with him and understand his views on the various subjects at hand. We speak for Chatham."

Shelburne leaned towards Hume, although Adam sat between them, and whispered loud enough for the four of them to hear, "When did he last hear from Chatham? It's been two weeks since I've had a word." None of them could answer his question, and Hume just shrugged.

"First, the India question," said Charles in his mellifluous baritone, "With all that is before us in these turbulent times, we must simplify our approach. Our colonies in India are halfway around the globe. Investigating Company management, and regulating their trade, is too much for us to manage here in London. We are too distant to meddle in the daily affairs of the trade. Thus, we propose a simple, yet substantial, charter fee for the India monopoly, and let the Company handle it from there."

A loud murmur swept through the Members, as they saw immediately that it was a near reversal of Chatham's previous position. Opposition members were pleasantly surprised; Chatham's party members showed visible chagrin, even anger.

"The Splendid Shuttlecock strikes again," muttered Hume, loud enough for them to hear.

"Not a word to me! Not a word!" sputtered Shelburne angrily, "And I'm responsible for India!"

"We'll submit a bill to that effect shortly, once we negotiate the charter fee," said Charles briskly. Numerous messengers consulted with various members before hastening out the door. Charles' reversal would move the markets, and the quicker traders would profit. "Next, the Americas," continued Charles after taking a drink of water.

"Now what, for God's sake," said Shelburne, not caring who heard him.

"Our budget includes only 42,000 pounds in tax from America, which is a light touch indeed considering the recent insolence from New York. These duties will come from various luxuries, including tea. Our bill will include some administrative changes as well," said Charles, who then abruptly took a seat. There were murmurs again, but no one stood to object.

"Administrative changes?" questioned Adam.

"Look out, Shelburne!" said Hume openly.

"Does he mean the changes we all opposed?" demanded Shelburne angrily, but they were in the gallery and had no right to address Parliament from there.

"Did Charles just reverse course for the whole Administration?" asked Henry, noting with alarm their disturbed response to Charles' words.

Three heads turned to him in unison and said, "Yes!"

• • • •

THREE DAYS LATER, HENRY sat with Adam at breakfast in their London hotel. At his elbow was a folded copy of the London Courant. "Should I stand for Parliament, Mr. Smith?" asked Henry suddenly, "After watching Charles the other day I don't know what to think."

"I can't answer that question for you, Henry," replied Adam carefully, "You're back from France, you've found your bride, so what you do from here is up to you."

"I always assumed I'd live in London, or Adderbury," Henry mused, "and find some public position to occupy myself. Now that time is here, and I'm clueless."

"Not clueless, Henry," smiled Adam, "I just spent three years giving you a clue."

"I'm grateful," nodded Henry with a wry smile, "Despite all I've learned, I'm just not sure I want to stand for Parliament."

"Most would find your dilemma envious, Henry," said Adam, taking a sip of tea.

"After watching Parliament, and Charles...," he said, slowly shaking his head, "I thought it was more high-minded, more..., well, noble. All the philosophy you taught me...," he trailed off.

"All the philosophy I had you read," corrected Adam gently, "I'm not Socrates or Aristotle."

"Sure," nodded Henry, "but when Charles can be so fickle, I'm wondering if philosophy is more hindrance than help in politics."

"Philosophy should inspire politics, but they are not the same thing," replied Adam, "Philosophy is the study of principle; politics is the compromise between competing principles."

"Isn't it wrong to compromise your principles?" responded Henry, taking a bite of toast.

"Name one thing in human affairs where only one principle applies," said Adam, "There are always trade-offs; two sides to every coin. Principle is black and white. Politics are shades of gray, as different principles are weighed against each other by their advocates."

"So, I have to choose which principles are sacred, and then choose when to compromise them?" questioned Henry, "Maybe

I should skip Parliament and become a farmer. It seems more honest."

"Farmers have to compromise too, Henry," replied Adam. "The first thing is to know yourself. Only then can you step outside yourself; to see things as others see them."

"The Impartial Spectator, from your book," nodded Henry.

"Indeed," said Adam, pleased. "The hard part is honest self-awareness; knowing how you feel and what you want. Knowing your own heart is the start of wisdom."

Frances bounced downstairs and saw them at their table. "Good morning!" she said, "Am I too late to join you?"

"Not at all, please sit down," smiled Henry and he waved at a servant while pointing at Frances.

"I hope I'm not interrupting," she said, taking a seat, "I'm writing more letters for Father today."

"A good amanuensis is worth their weight in gold, Frances," Adam observed.

"I sure learn a lot about composition," she replied as the servant brought her a plate and utensils and filled her glass. "Father is very eloquent." Another servant appeared with a tray of eggs, ham, and toast.

Henry glanced at his newspaper and was startled, saying, "My God, shares in the East India Company are up twelve percent in two days!"

"Since Charles addressed Parliament?" asked Adam.

"Oh, Father will be so pleased!" said Frances brightly.

"How so?" asked Henry.

"He invested seven thousand pounds in East India stock just last week," she replied happily. Henry and Adam gaped at each other, and Frances looked puzzled as she saw that her words had an unintended effect.

"How do you know this, Frances?" asked Henry carefully, putting down his fork.

"I copied a letter from Father telling Samuel Touchet to buy the shares," she said uncertainly, as Henry and Adam's faces fell even further. An awkward silence ensued. "Perhaps I shouldn't have told you...," she ventured, uncertain.

"No, ah, there's no problem, Frances," Henry stammered, "Just surprise, is all."

"I don't talk about Father's letters with anyone else, Henry," Frances reassured him, thinking that perhaps their shocked expressions were due to her breaking confidence with Charles.

"That's probably best," nodded Henry, and Adam remained silent.

Reassured, Frances took a bite of her breakfast before changing the subject. "Don't forget our dance lesson at the Montagu's. We leave at two o'clock."

Later that day, Frances sat at her writing table in the hotel room Charles had rented as his London office. She wore an apron smudged with ink as Charles stood over her shoulder and watched her write his last lines. He recited the words out loud, "your obedient servant... yes."

A knock revealed Henry in the doorway. "May I interrupt?"

"Perfect timing, that letter's done," said Charles, "What do you need, Henry?"

"Now that I'm engaged, I want, well, I *need* that financial review we've discussed," he replied, "Adderbury, and my Scottish estates."

"Sure, sure, whatever you need," said Charles, waving a hand and turning back to Frances, who was blowing gently on her last lines to dry the ink.

"Tomorrow, then," insisted Henry.

Charles took a deep breath and looked at Henry, seeing he wasn't going to be put off easily. "That's very soon, Henry, I don't have everything put together yet," Charles replied carefully.

"This isn't my first request," said Henry, "Let's set a time, tomorrow, for you to tell me what you know. I'd like Mother there as well."

A long moment passed as they stared at each other, then Charles nodded slowly and said, "Very well, I'll consult your mother, and we'll find an hour tomorrow."

Henry slowly nodded in return, and then turned to Frances and brightened his expression as he pointed at her. "Two o'clock!" he said, and then turned on his heel and left.

"What's at two?" asked Charles, keeping his tone level although Henry had ruffled his feathers.

"Dancing!" replied Frances eagerly. Outside the door, Henry had paused to listen.

"Next letter, Frances?" said Charles, hoping to get back to business.

She readied a fresh sheet, dipped her quill, and said, "Ready."

"This one is to…, oh, drat," said Charles, putting his chin in his hand. "No more letters today, Frances, go and fetch your mother, will you?" Before Frances could get out the door, Henry had hastened away so she did not see him lurking.

Promptly at two in the afternoon, Henry and Frances knocked on Montagu's door. Soon they were on the dance floor, paired with Elizabeth and Sancho, while the duchess sat at the piano playing a minuet. The dancers moved gracefully through the delicate steps, showing their recent practice. The duchess finished the piece and clapped. "That looked lovely everyone!"

"Lady Frances, I think you've got it!" said Sancho.

"So do you, Henry," whispered Elizabeth seductively into his ear.

"I love my teacher," Henry replied, "but this dance was designed to be difficult."

"Yes, the minuet demonstrates refinement, and culture," she agreed, turning his complaint aside.

"So *that's* why it comes so hard to me," said Henry sardonically.

"You are much better than before, Henry," said Frances optimistically.

"Thanks for that humiliating compliment, dear sister," he replied with a grin, "But for that Christmas dance disaster I would be off hunting or something, instead of dancing the minuet."

He smiled at Elizabeth, who was the real reason he was spending his afternoon dancing. She turned to the duchess and said, "One more time, Mother?"

At that moment a servant appeared in the doorway to the dance studio, and announced, "Your guest has arrived, milady."

"Excellent!" exclaimed Elizabeth, and she followed the servant out the door without further explanation. They all stood and waited, and presently she returned leading William, dressed in his best clothes and wringing his cap in his big hands.

"May I present Master William Lewis," she said, and was delighted to see Henry start and stare in amazement at his childhood friend.

"William, it's you!" exclaimed Henry, striding forward to shake his hand with a wide smile on his face.

"Hiya Henry, you look well," said William with a grin.

"As do you! Look at the size of you, man!" said Henry, finally releasing his hand. "I forget myself. William, this is my sister, Lady Frances Scott."

Frances curtsied, flustering William, who bowed awkwardly and said, "How do you do, milady."

"It's a pleasure to meet you, William," responded Frances, smiling up at him.

"Hiya Sancho," greeted William.

"Good to see you again, William," replied Sancho with a nod.

"And this is my mother, the Duchess of Montagu," introduced Elizabeth as Mary stood, and William bowed again.

"Hello William, I'm glad you could come," said the duchess graciously. "Sancho, stay here and help entertain our guests. I'll go see the cook about dinner. You can all stay, I hope?"

"Yes, thanks," answered William, "Mother sends her regrets, she has to feed the students."

As the duchess went to see about dinner, Henry turned to Elizabeth and said, "You invited Mrs. Lewis as well?" She smiled and nodded, pleased to see the success of her venture.

"How is Mrs. Lewis?" asked Henry, "I remember your mother fondly, William."

"Well, me too," said William, "What son doesn't love his mum? She's fine and dandy, thanks for asking, and sends her love."

"William, we were just practicing some dance steps," said Elizabeth, pointing to a chair near the piano, "Would you care to be our audience?"

"Sure," he said, and sat in the chair.

"Sancho, you will have to provide the music I'm afraid," said Elizabeth.

"I'll be in the audience with William," said Frances, dragging another chair near his and sitting down beside him. He looked at her gratefully, but uneasily, as he was unused to pretty girls in fancy homes.

Sancho began the same minuet, and they watched Henry and Elizabeth repeat their dance without evident miscue. At the end, Frances clapped enthusiastically, and William joined her.

"Excellent!" she exclaimed, "What do you think, William?"

"Sancho can sure play that piano!" William replied, making Frances laugh.

"Yes, he is good," she said, "but how about the dancers? Henry is getting so smooth!"

"That sure is a dainty dance," William said, "What do you call that?"

"It's the minuet," informed Elizabeth, "do you dance, William?"

"I sure do, I love music," replied William, "but it's a lot different than that!"

"Can you show us?" asked Elizabeth, gesturing towards the dance floor.

William stood, but instead of showing them a dance he picked up a violin from its stand near the piano. He tested the bow briefly by drawing it across the strings, as everyone watched in surprise. "Here it goes, Sancho," he said, "If you get the hang of it, join in." With that, William began to fiddle a jig, with considerable expertise, and the music was upbeat and infectious. Soon Sancho began picking out complimentary chords on the piano, and Frances began clapping along. In a moment, Henry and Elizabeth joined Frances, and their clapping formed the beat. His jig was much more fun than the careful minuet, and smiles lit everyone's face. After two minutes of this, William stopped, beaming and flushed with his reception in such an elegant home.

"What a surprise! You play so well, William," exclaimed Elizabeth.

"You have talent, William!" added Henry.

"Oh, that was wonderful!" said Frances, and William smiled at the compliment, as Frances was utterly sincere and without a trace of guile. She smiled back at him.

"Sancho, you have skills," said William simply, nodding to the butler.

"As do you, William," replied Sancho, "I hope this is just the start of our musical collaborations."

Ninety minutes later, they all sat for an early supper in the Montagu dining room, joined by the duke. William was uncertain about the cutlery and fancy surroundings, but everyone was so friendly that his nervousness wore off quickly.

After the soup was served, the duchess started the conversation by asking, "So, William, what were you thinking when Elizabeth and Sancho approached you?"

"I figured she wanted a fancy custom saddle with all the trimmings," William replied.

"You're in the leather trade?" inquired the duke.

"Apprenticed, in my fifth year sir," nodded William, reaching for a piece of buttered bread.

"How do you like that?" asked the duke, politely, knowing very little about the leather trade other than as an international cargo.

"How do I like apprenticing?" replied William, "I call it two years of training and five years a slave, begging your pardon, sir." A surprised look appeared on the duke's face at this.

"I think he was asking if you enjoy working with leather," said the duchess with a smile.

William flushed with embarrassment but plunged ahead. "Oh, yes sir, it's gratifying to make something well. To please the customer with something from my own hands."

"When did you find time to learn the fiddle?" asked Henry.

"You should know, Henry," said William, "I was raised in a boarding school. I got an education, Mum saw to it, on the side, so to speak. I remember listening to the teachers with you."

Henry looked at his childhood friend in amazement; he did not remember William attending classes with him. "I remember chasing rats in the rain," he said.

"I remember that too!" said William, breaking into a broad smile, "The headmaster wanted to show you to some rich people, and you were a muddy mess!"

"Yes," nodded Henry, smiling at the memory, "I was their best advertisement. They'd parade me out to meet parents who were considering Buckingham for their children. It was embarrassing."

"Your story is impressive," added Elizabeth, "Your mother is impressive."

"Her biscuits are especially impressive," added Sancho in agreement.

"Any prospects for marriage, William?" asked the duchess, looking at the handsome young man with frank admiration. Frances pricked up her ears but tried not to show that she was interested.

"No, milady," he answered, the smile fading from his face, "I'm apprenticed two more years."

The duchess had little understanding of apprenticeships, as they fell outside her range of experience and none of her friends talked about tradesmen other than complaining about poor workmanship. She plunged on, good naturedly, asking, "Do you have your eye on some lady?"

"She married and has a child with someone else now," William replied, the smile gone from his face as the painful memory returned, "She couldn't wait seven years."

There was an awkward pause at this. Elizabeth asked, "In two years, you'll be accepted into the guild?"

"I'll be *eligible* for the guild," William corrected, "If they decide there are too many leather workers, I may have to wait."

"That seems an uncertain prospect," observed Henry, "What is the future of the leather trade?"

"The need is there, but there's not much cash money," he replied, "No one has enough to place a large order."

"It's a problem of liquidity," nodded the duke in sage agreement.

"I'm sorry you lost your love, William," said Frances.

CHAPTER 43

THE LETTER TO CRAIGIE *April 1767*

Cook helped Charles into his coat before the mirror in his hotel suite, as Caroline sat nearby. Henry was due to arrive in ten minutes, and they were apprehensive. "Your blue coat is being cleaned; I'll have it back this afternoon," said Cook, brushing the shoulders of the red one that Charles had just put on.

"Good," said Charles absently, "That's one of my favorites."

"Oh Charles, I'm afraid Henry will be cross with us," fretted Caroline.

"Tut-tut, Caroline," he reassured her, "He's old enough to understand complicated finances. Let me explain it to him."

"When he sees the cash balance..." she worried, "Cook, leave us now."

"Yes, ma'am," Cook demurred, stepping out of the room.

"We have less than two thousand pounds ready money, Charles," she whispered once he was gone, "Thank goodness the Duke of Montagu is paying for the Wedding Ball!"

"Now, now, Caroline," he soothed, "You fail to appreciate the wonders of credit." Charles adjusted his wig in the mirror, then peered closely at his forty-two-year-old face. "Plus, some investments of mine have recently done quite well. It's not like we're impoverished."

"Impoverished? That's the very last word I expected to hear today," said Henry, surprising them by his sudden appearance in the doorway. Both Charles and Caroline were flustered, wondering what he'd heard.

"There you are, Henry," gushed Caroline, "My, you look splendid. Healthy. Happy."

"But impoverished?" Henry asked, raising his eyebrows.

"Of course not, Henry, that was just a figure of speech," said Charles, making a palms-down motion with his hands as if to calm his stepson down.

"That's what I'm afraid of Charles," Henry said, "Figures of speech, but no real figures. I'd like some actual numbers."

"I don't have the numbers drawn up for you," protested Charles, keeping his tone calm, "We only spoke about it yesterday."

"No, we spoke about it at Adderbury," responded Henry, prickling at Charles' placating manner.

"Henry, be reasonable," replied Charles, adding a hint of steel to his tone, "As Chancellor of the Exchequer, duty calls. Personal things must be set aside, while I address urgent matters of State."

"In September, I will reach majority, Charles," pressed Henry, "I marry Elizabeth in May. When do you propose to tell me what I have?"

"Soon, soon, Henry," reassured Charles, turning back to the mirror for a final look.

"Henry, be patient," added Caroline, "Why are you so concerned?"

Henry exploded in anger; anger long suppressed and thus vented at high pressure. "I'm concerned!" he shouted, and both Charles and Caroline physically recoiled at the unexpected outburst from their normally reserved son. "Yes, I'm concerned! Charles borrows money from the Pay Office to buy statues for Adderbury. He needs the Montagu wedding gift to pay it off. What other debts do I have?" Henry felt himself shaking with anger, but somewhere deep inside he was thankful that his words came out cleanly. He glared at Charles and ignored his mother.

"Henry, that kind of loan happens all the time," replied Charles smoothly, as he was no stranger to verbal conflict. "I am the main finance officer for the entire British government. You doubt my ability to manage credit?"

"Don't patronize me, Charles!" snapped Henry, "How encumbered is Adderbury? How many of your loans are secured by my Scottish estates?"

Charles paced the room twice before responding as calmly as he could make himself appear, "Few, Henry, only a few. You are the largest landowner in lowland Scotland. And lowland Scotland is the productive part of Scotland. You needn't worry about money, for God's sake."

Henry turned to his mother while pointing his finger at Charles, and said, "And then he proceeds to patronize me."

"Patronize? That is exactly true Henry," replied Charles stoutly.

"Who manages our accounts in Scotland?" asked Henry.

"Mr. Craigie," Charles replied.

"Where is his last report?" followed Henry.

"I'm not sure exactly," Charles dissembled, "Caroline, do you know?"

"I don't worry my head about finances," she said dismissively, "I wouldn't even know what his report looked like."

Henry controlled his anger with a visible effort, then said in a brittle tone, "I must conclude that you are deliberately hiding the details from me. I will write Mr. Craigie myself and ask him."

"Henry, don't be rash," objected Charles, "We aren't hiding anything. You have a huge estate; it's complicated."

"Complicated!" Henry exploded again, his frustration boiling over, "Is it as complicated as your speculations in East India stock?"

Charles stiffened as if slapped, wondering how Henry knew about his machinations with Samuel Touchet. "Now, where would you hear a thing like that?" evaded Charles.

Henry checked himself, not wanting to betray Frances, saying instead, "Sitting in the gallery at Parliament, when you reversed Administration policy on India."

Charles scoffed, "That's just idle speculation from Smith and Hume. Impractical philosophers."

"Don't forget Lord Shelburne," snapped Henry with steel of his own.

"Henry, I will not be the obedient instrument of any set of men," Charles said tersely, aware that he was skating on thin ice.

"So, you will betray them all equally?" said Henry, glaring at him.

"Henry! Really!" protested Caroline from her chair.

"Now, Caroline, Henry is upset," soothed Charles, but his words had the opposite effect on Henry.

"Don't patronize me!" he shouted, startling Cook, who stood listening unseen outside the door, "I'm upset for a damn good reason! I've half a mind to run for Parliament to oppose you!"

There was a long tense silence as the four of them waited for someone to say something. Finally, Charles gathered himself and said as calmly as he could, "Henry, your worries are groundless, and I will prove that to you. You have nothing to think of but your health. You have secured the world and added the friendship of the best characters to the most ample advantage of birth and fortune. You have everything."

Henry took a deep breath and let it out slowly before saying, in a firm but calm tone, "I don't believe you, Charles. I will write to Craigie." He turned on his heel and left so swiftly that Cook barely had time to avoid detection as he slipped into a neighboring room.

After a long ride on Saucy to clear his mind and collect his thoughts, Henry returned to his room and removed his boots and jacket. He sat at his desk and penned a careful letter to Dalkeith, avoiding any hint of animosity between himself and Charles. He signed it simply, 'Henry' and sealed the letter with red wax. He wrote, 'John Craigie, Dalkeith, Scotland,' on the envelope, then sealed the flap with another red 'S.' Barefoot, he padded to the door and called for Cook. Presently Cook appeared in the hall. "Yes, Henry?"

Henry waved the letter at him from the doorway. "Can you post this for Dalkeith straight away?"

"Certainly," nodded Cook, taking the letter, and disappearing down the hall. He descended the stairs into the hotel lobby, where Charles hailed him as he neared the door.

"Cook, where are you off to?" asked Charles.

"To post a letter," Cook replied, "Do you have anything for the post?"

"Yes, but I'll post them at Parliament," Charles responded, "That will save a day. Give me that and I'll send it with the others."

Cook hesitated, but there was nothing to do but surrender Henry's letter to Charles, who looked at the addressee and then tucked the envelope into an inner coat pocket.

• • • •

SEVERAL DAYS LATER, Henry met Elizabeth for a ride on a sunny April afternoon. Eventually they arrived at Tottham's Leather Goods near Piccadilly Square, where they greeted William. He was showing them some fine saddle work he had done, when Mr. Tottham appeared.

"William, do you have a customer?" inquired Tottham from across the shop, concerned that William wasn't at his workbench, but seeing opportunity in the wealthy couple he spoke to.

William hesitated, then replied, "Yes, Mr. Tottham."

"How can I help you sir, my lady," asked the leather merchant in his most unctuous manner. He was an oily man, literally, as he wore his hair plastered to his head and it shone in the afternoon sun. His large nose, weak chin, and thin face made him resemble a chicken.

"Actually, I'm interested in your man William here," Henry replied.

"Yes, William does fine work, as you can see," said Tottham, "He is apprenticed to me."

"This is fine work indeed," Henry replied, laying a hand on the ornate saddle, "You have a valuable man. I am well-equipped for leather goods at the moment, as is the lady here."

Elizabeth nodded pleasantly at the man, but let Henry do the talking. A shrewd expression showed on Tottham's face as he responded, "If you are looking to hire him, he is bound to me for two more years."

"I understand," nodded Henry, "I'd like to borrow him, as a musician. I'll pay you for his time."

This brought the man up short, and he turned to William with a puzzled expression and said, "A musician? William?"

"I play the fiddle, Mr. Tottham," he explained.

"Henry and I are to be married," added Elizabeth, "We would like William to play at our wedding. We'll need him for rehearsals, fittings, whatnot."

"If William agrees, of course," added Henry.

"I'm honored," William said, then asked, "What's a fitting?"

Tottham was clearly impressed with Elizabeth, but his financial interests came first. "Well, not so fast," he said, "We have orders, I need William's work here in the shop."

"Did I mention that I'll pay for his time?" replied Henry, winning the argument by taking out his purse and giving the miserly man a handsome down payment.

· · · ·

TEN DAYS LATER FOUND Elizabeth, her mother, Sancho, and William poring over sheets of music scattered over the top of the Montagu piano in the early afternoon. A servant escorted Henry and Frances into the room. Elizabeth looked up and said excitedly, "Henry! Sancho has created a dance; I'd like to try it."

"Sancho is going to dance for us?" Henry asked, misunderstanding.

"No silly," laughed Elizabeth, "We are going to dance the steps he has prepared for us."

"We're working out the music just now," added William, "Let's give it a try."

The duchess remained at the keys, and William picked up the violin. The piece started with a plaintive, simple series of notes on the piano, joined after the first measure by William's violin. Sancho, Henry, and Frances listened to the charming melody completely through, enchanted. Then Sancho began showing them his dance steps as Frances took a seat near William. Despite the focus Elizabeth and Henry gave to learning the dance, they both noted that Frances kept looking at William as he sawed easily with his horse-hair bow.

After a few times through, Elizabeth asked, "Frances, can you keep the beat with rhythm sticks?" and Frances nodded uncertainly. Elizabeth dug two polished sticks from a box behind the piano and showed Frances how to use them. After a few turns through the composition, it was evident that Frances could keep the beat, and she was delighted to participate. Henry found that the rhythmic clack of the sticks made it easier to keep time with Elizabeth, and he could concentrate on learning the steps themselves. After two hours, they felt confident enough to commit to the innovative dance, and the music William and Sancho had composed, as their wedding dance. Henry's embarrassment over the Christmas Ball faded as his confidence grew, aided as it was by Elizabeth's soft hand in his as she danced effortlessly by his side. The melody was so infectious that he found himself humming it on the carriage ride home with Frances after supper.

Two days later, at mid-morning, Henry and Elizabeth knocked again at the door of Buckingham School for Boys. Behind them stood Cook and William. This time the door was opened by the prim headmistress. "Good morning," greeted Elizabeth, smiling, "We are here for Mrs. Lewis."

"Oh, there must be some mistake," said the headmistress, "We can't do without Mrs. Lewis. Who will feed the boys?"

At that moment, Mrs. Lewis appeared in the hallway behind the headmistress, wearing a shawl but looking apprehensive.

"We have that covered," replied Elizabeth, and Cook snapped his fingers. Four servants appeared from behind the carriage, each carrying two big baskets of food. The headmistress stood aside in amazement as Cook led them confidently into the hallway.

"Directions to the kitchen?" he asked courteously.

Mrs. Lewis led them inside to show them the place, while Elizabeth and Henry chatted with the headmistress, who knew William well and obviously liked him. She was quickly won over to the day's adventure, so that when Mrs. Lewis reappeared the headmistress assured her that she could go. This greatly eased the mind of Mrs. Lewis, and she smiled in excitement as she climbed into the big carriage with Cook's attentive assistance.

Soon they were in the richly appointed tailor's shop, being attended by several of the tailor's assistants as they guided Mrs. Lewis and William through the various fabrics, colors, and styles. William emerged from the fitting room dressed in a fine suit of clothes. Elizabeth smiled and clapped her hands at the transformation of the strapping leatherworker.

"So, this is what 'fitting' means," said William sheepishly, "Like fitting harness to a horse."

"You look perfect, William," Elizabeth laughed, "You are a clothes horse."

"Thank you, I think," replied the self-conscious William, "I feel like a peacock."

"A peacock is a handsome bird," smiled Henry, enjoying his friend's reaction and agreeing with Elizabeth that he looked splendid.

"A bird that struts about making a god-awful noise," said William with a grin.

"We can't begin to pay for these things, milady," protested Mrs. Lewis, looking dramatically improved herself in a fine dress and accoutrements, her neat gray hair tucked under a fashionable hat. "We'll keep 'em clean, though. William, no fighting in your nice clothes."

"You and William are part of our wedding, Mrs. Lewis," responded Elizabeth, putting a reassuring hand on the woman's shoulder. "The clothes are yours, with our compliments."

"Invited to your wedding! This is all so unexpected," said Mrs. Lewis, overwhelmed by the experience, "We never thought we'd see you again, Duke Henry."

"I owe that to Elizabeth," smiled Henry, "I'm glad she found you."

"I can't remember my last day off from cooking," she exclaimed, "Look how fancy we are, William!" and she did a matronly pirouette that made everyone laugh, even the tailor.

"Fancy, yes, but this isn't who I am, Henry," said William, eyeing his friend seriously.

"I know," Henry grinned, "thanks for putting up with us."

The next day, Henry was in the hall, passing Charles' office, and heard his mother inside as the door was ajar. He knocked and stepped inside, pushing the door wider. Charles and Caroline sat inside, and Cook sat sideways at Frances' writing desk, his long shanks unable to fit beneath the desk. He wasn't writing anything anyway.

"Oh, there you are, Henry, we were just discussing your wedding," said Caroline.

"That's what I want to discuss," said Henry in an authoritative tone, "We'll be married on the second of May, at the Montagu's."

"That's impossible," dismissed Caroline with a wave of her hand, "your Aunt Mary won't be back from France by then."

"Elizabeth's brother is in Italy, and will miss it as well," answered Henry briskly, "We've decided on a small wedding, with our Wedding Ball ten days later."

"The duke will have the thirty thousand by then?" asked Charles, as that was his first thought.

"I don't know," said Henry dismissively, "May 2 and May 12 are the dates. Is Frances here?"

"She's in her room," said Cook, standing and slipping out the door.

"All this was decided without consulting your mother?" huffed Caroline.

"Yes, I'm letting Elizabeth decide everything," he responded firmly.

"That's as it should be, dear," said Charles, still thinking about the money.

Frances entered the room, followed by Cook, just as Henry said, "The wedding will be very small, just our immediate families."

"I'm so glad, Henry, I love Elizabeth," said Frances, giving her brother a hug and eliciting a small smile from Henry's stern demeanor.

"So, Henry, how many guests are we allowed?" asked Caroline, sounding aggrieved.

"To the Ball, as many as you like," he answered promptly, "To the wedding, none, Mother."

"Let it go, Caroline, they've decided just family," offered Charles, trying to gain some credit with his prickly stepson.

"I have three other guests, and Elizabeth will as well," said Henry, "I'll invite Smith and Hume."

"And who is the third?" asked Charles, hoping it wasn't Lord Shelburne, who was very cranky with him right then.

Henry turned to look at Cook, who stood unobtrusively in the corner. "I'd like Cook, here, to attend," he said. Cook's jaw dropped, his mouth opened and closed twice, but no words came out. He was flabbergasted. "Cook, you're a bit of a fuss budget, but we couldn't have done without you in France," said Henry, "I'd like you to be there."

Cook suddenly burst into tears, gasped "Thank you!" and then covered his face with his hands to muffle an uncontrollable sob. He looked at Henry, tried to speak and failed, and then fled. There was a shocked silence in the room.

"I think that was a yes, I'm not sure," ventured Henry after a moment.

"You touched him, Henry, that was remarkable," said Charles, looking at Henry in a new light.

"Is he crying because he wants to go, or because he doesn't?" asked Caroline, nonplussed at the strange reaction from their long-time butler.

"Oh, Cook wants to go, Mother, the poor man," said Frances.

"One more thing," said Henry, recovering the thread of his thought, "Between the wedding and the Ball, we'll honeymoon. At Adderbury, alone."

"Certainly," agreed Charles readily, "We'll stay in London. I'm sure she'll love Adderbury."

"Will you want Cook there as well?" asked Caroline.

"Not on my honeymoon, no," said Henry, wondering if his mother was being sarcastic.

"No servants at all?" she followed, innocently.

"Be sensible, Mother," said Henry, frowning, "We'll need the kitchen staff, and housekeeping."

An hour later, Henry pulled on his boots in his room as a knock came at the door, admitting Cook. "I'm going out," said Henry, "Help me with the finishing touches?"

Cook seemed relieved that he'd been called for a routine task. Helping Henry into his coat, he said, "Henry, I'm sorry about my outburst earlier. I'm honored by your invitation."

"You have a good heart, Cook," nodded Henry, looking at himself in the mirror as Cook adjusted his sleeves at the wrists.

"I try to be godly," said Cook, "but I'm... human," he said at last. "Working in this household, watching you grow up, you and Hew....," he trailed off, unable to express himself.

"We've been through a lot together, Cook," said Henry, looking him in the eye.

"Indeed," nodded Cook, and Henry could see that the man was choking up again. Cook took a deep breath, stepped back, and pretended to review Henry's immaculate appearance. "Have you heard from Mr. Craigie?" he asked, trying to sound offhand.

"Not yet," Henry replied, "I heard Craigie is a punctual man."

"He is, usually," observed Cook. Something in his expression caught Henry's attention.

"Out with it, Cook," demanded Henry, "Did you mail my letter?"

"Charles took it from me," Cook admitted, "He said he'd mail it with some of his letters."

Henry looked at Cook blankly, absorbing the implications. "Do you know if he mailed it?"

"I don't know, Henry," said Cook, "I'd think Mr. Craigie would have responded by now."

Henry removed his jacket and said, "Paper and ink, Cook."

CHAPTER 44

THE WEDDING *May 2, 1767*

Three weeks flew by, filled with dance lessons, invitations, clothes shopping, and three delightful trysts with Elizabeth in Henry's rented room. Their wedding dance became part of them; Henry found himself humming the tune and imagining the steps at all hours of the day. At times he'd feel a surge of trepidation, knowing that he'd have to perform before hundreds of guests at their Wedding Ball. Elizabeth's effortless dancing gave him confidence, but he also had a keen fear of embarrassing her. His amazement at the talents of William and Sancho grew with each lesson.

Prying William away from Mr. Tottham became an irritation, as the man increasingly resisted giving him up. Henry was sure it was an act intended to get more money, which he grudgingly paid, knowing all the while the man was extorting him. It was worth it; watching William play the violin with Sancho made Henry wonder if the world was being deprived of William's true abilities by condemning him to a life making saddles, belts, and harnesses. He wondered the same thing about Ignatius Sancho, an even more remarkable example of latent talent.

Each week he ate supper with Adam and Hume, once joined by the irascible Lord Shelburne, and once by Ben Franklin. Although Charles was cautious with Franklin, considering him something akin to an American spy, Henry found him humorous and insightful. Hume and Franklin were a delight together, their witty repartee would keep Adam and Henry in stitches. Once Henry had blown soup through his nose at a funny quip from Hume, which caused them all to roar with laughter. Adam was his rock; he always felt reassured spending time with his former tutor. If Henry was grateful to Charles for anything, it was his choice of Adam Smith as his tutor. Smith was popular in London, although less lionized than he'd been at the Parisian salons.

· · · ·

DAYLIGHT WAS FADING to dusk on May 1, the day before his wedding, and Henry sat pensively at the writing table in his room. He had no doubts about Elizabeth, none, but many doubts about his future. A knock, and Cook entered.

"A letter, Henry," he said simply, handing it to him. He turned to leave.

"Stay, it's from Craigie," ordered Henry, so Cook stood just inside the door and waited as Henry opened the envelope and unfolded the several pages inside. Henry began to read, and Cook to fidget, as the moments stretched to minutes. Henry turned to the second page.

"I thought, being the night before your wedding, you'd be out having a drink with your friends or something," Cook said, as Henry pored over page two.

Henry looked up briefly, then continued reading with a curt, "Hew and James died in France."

"I'm sorry, Henry," said Cook, abashed.

"Don't be," said Henry absently, "Wait," as he continued to focus on Craigie's missive. The third and fourth pages were columns of numbers, and Henry pored over these for some minutes while Cook stood nervously by the door. He felt he was complicit in a conspiracy against Charles, his employer, but it was Henry, so he stood quietly. The skullduggery made him shift anxiously from one foot to the other. Finally, Henry looked up at him, his expression tense but controlled, and said, "Tomorrow is my wedding day, and then our honeymoon at Adderbury. We return to London the day before the Wedding Ball."

Cook listened without responding, expecting more. Henry shook the letter at him and said sternly, "Not a word about his until after the Ball, Cook."

"I promise," nodded Cook.

"You can go now," said Henry, looking again at the final page with the financial totals. Cook put his hand on the doorknob but lingered. Henry looked up and asked, "Something else?"

"Charles' desk at Adderbury… the top drawer sticks a little, but it's not really locked," said Cook with a neutral expression.

"What does he keep there?" asked Henry.

"Financial things, I expect," said Cook as he slipped out the door.

• • • •

THE SECOND OF MAY DAWNED bright and clear, a good omen, thought Henry, as he stood at his hotel window sipping tea. That was his last calm moment before he was swept into the whirlwind of preparation, his bath, his hair, his clothes. Once again, and for the last time, he declined his mother's request that he wear a traditional wig. Then the swirl of servants subsided, they all boarded an ornate coach and six, complete with liveried drivers and footmen, and they were off to the Montagu's.

As they stepped out of the coach, careful not to muss their finery, the Duke of Montagu emerged to greet them. "Welcome, welcome! What a wonderful day it is!" exclaimed the duke, spreading his arms and smiling ear to ear. He turned and led the group inside and into the main drawing room where the ceremony would be held. Adam, Hume, William, and Mrs. Lewis rose to greet them, and soon they were joined by Sancho and his wife, a plump, well-dressed woman with a huge smile and warm manner. "Charles, Caroline, may I introduce Anne, wife of Ignatius," introduced the duke, and she curtsied deep.

"It's an honor to meet you both," said Anne.

"Pleased, I'm sure," replied Caroline, somewhat aloof as she thought it odd that they were being introduced to the servants.

"Anne, it's a pleasure," said Charles pleasantly, "Good to see you again, Sancho." Charles considered Brudenell's apparent elevation of his household servants to family members as just another of his eccentricities.

The duke repeated the process with "Mrs. Margaret Lewis, and her son, William." When everyone was introduced, they mingled. Caroline pulled Charles aside and whispered, "Am I to understand they've invited their servants as wedding guests?"

"The Duke and Duchess are odd in that way," answered Charles in a low tone, "Just go along with it, Caroline, and don't make it a distraction."

"Did you see the rough hands on that boy, William?" said Caroline, "And his mother's? They must be the washerwoman and the stable boy."

"Now I see why Henry wanted Cook here," Charles replied, but he knew what was important and what wasn't, so he was not as alarmed as his wife. Servants made sure everyone had a full glass of champagne, and Charles caught Brudenell near the fireplace. "Has the money come through?"

"I'll have it ready in one week more, Charles," replied George, "I couldn't ask Elizabeth to delay from the date they chose."

"Of course not," nodded Charles in agreement, "The whole thirty thousand, in one week?"

"Assuredly," nodded the duke.

Henry pulled Adam aside on the opposite side of the room, and said, "I lost my brother and best friend in France."

Adam nodded, as he'd been there for both tragic events. "I wish Hew and James could see you today, Henry," is all he could think of to say.

"I feel closer to you than anyone, Mr. Smith," said Henry plainly, "I would be honored if you would stand as my witness."

"The honor is all mine, Henry," Adam replied warmly, as Henry pulled a small box out of his pocket and took out a plain gold band. He dropped it into Adam's open palm.

"Give it back to me when I turn to you in the ceremony," said Henry, and then impulsively he hugged his tutor. For the rest of Adam's life, he remained close to Henry Scott, the bonds built through adversity and learning in France endured until the philosopher died in 1790, twenty-three years later.

The pastor arrived, so Henry went to be introduced. The Duchess of Montagu swept into the room, looking almost regal in her elaborate dress, hair piled high atop her head and held in place with diamond stickpins. After meeting the pastor, Mary Montagu pulled Sancho aside, and said, "Now Sancho, you are not the butler today. You and Anne are Elizabeth's wedding guests. Let the others serve today."

"It's an honor, duchess," replied Sancho gravely, then with a smile added, "I will try to keep my habits in check."

"I am so happy for Elizabeth, duchess," said Anne, "Such a kind and happy heart she has."

"I'll miss her dearly," said Mary, "Yet I'm so happy with the man she chose."

Henry kept his eye on the door, expecting Elizabeth. Caroline collected him for a brief conference with the pastor, with all four parents listening closely as the cleric outlined the order of the ceremony. Adam and Hume stood by Mrs. Lewis and William, soon joined by Frances and Cook. Frances looked older and quite sophisticated in her elegant gown and elaborate hair, impressing everyone with her maturity and grace. Cook looked positively dapper, with his hair combed carefully and a fine black suit that fitted him perfectly. Hume turned to Mrs. Lewis and politely asked, "You knew Henry when he was a schoolboy?"

"I'm head cook at Buckingham School for Boys," replied Mrs. Lewis brightly, "We met Henry when he was seven or so." She was unabashed, not sure why she'd been invited but happy to be there, however it had come about.

"I'm glad Henry has a school chum here today," said Adam, with feeling.

"This is all a bolt from the blue," said William, "I never thought I'd be wearing fancy clothes."

"You look the perfect gentleman, William," said Frances, keeping her frank admiration under wraps as best she could.

"Mrs. Lewis, we both knew Henry as a schoolboy," said Cook, unexpectedly, as he'd been silent until then. "We have that in common." She nodded at him and smiled; thus encouraged, he continued, "May I inquire about Mr. Lewis?"

"He was a sergeant in the British Army, killed at the Battle of Minden eight years ago," she replied matter-of-factly, the tragic blow softened by time.

"My condolences, good lady," said Cook graciously.

Across the room, the pastor's instructions delivered, Caroline pulled Henry aside and gave a slight nod to where William stood talking to Frances. "Who is that man?" she asked pointedly.

"That's William, my childhood friend from the boarding school," he replied, "Mrs. Lewis is his mother, the school cook." He smiled at the sight of Cook chatting with Mrs. Lewis; it seemed such an odd combination, but he was not sure why that would be.

"Just as I suspected," griped Caroline in a low tone, "Servants!"

"No, friends," replied Henry bluntly, the smile leaving his face. "Elizabeth sought them out and invited them. One of the many reasons I love her, Mother."

Caroline softened at his romantic comment, saying, "I approve of your bride, of course. She has a fine family name." But then her face became stern as she pointed discreetly at Frances, who was still talking to William. "But you keep an eye on that, Henry. Frances cannot, *will not*, marry a tradesman." As they watched, they saw a servant approach Frances, speak briefly, and then lead Frances from the drawing room.

In her bed chambers, Elizabeth and two maids finalized her wedding ensemble. The servant stood aside as Frances entered the room, as the final makeup touches were being applied. Elizabeth said, "Frances! Please come in. You look lovely today, so mature!"

"You are so beautiful, Elizabeth, especially today," Frances replied, in awe.

Elizabeth motioned for the maids to leave, then turned to Frances and extended both her hands. Frances took them in hers, as Elizabeth said, "I have a favor to ask of you, Frances."

"Yes!" said Frances impishly, making Elizabeth laugh.

"You are too kind," she smiled, "I have many society friends, but few intimate ones. So, I invited them to the Ball, but not the wedding. I know we haven't known each other long, but would you stand as my witness today?"

Frances' mouth flew open in surprise, but she quickly recovered and composed a dignified answer. "Oh Elizabeth, that is such an honor. I'll try to act elegant."

"You look elegant, Frances, beautiful in fact," said Elizabeth, still holding Frances' hands in hers, "I'm going to love having you for a sister."

Henry knew Elizabeth was beautiful, both dressed and undressed, but he was stunned when Elizabeth appeared in the doorway of the drawing room. Her simple white gown sparkled as if it had jewels sewn into the very fabric. More sparkles appeared in her hair, piled high and swept off her neck, revealing the exquisite form of her oval face and the luminosity of her flawless skin. Everyone in the room knew Elizabeth and had seen her many times both casual and formal, yet all gaped at the vision of Elizabeth looking her very best. Her parents swelled with pride, Henry's heart fluttered with giddy excitement, and Frances flushed with joy at being part of something so momentous and fine. The only person who wasn't gaping at Elizabeth was William, who kept glancing at Frances.

George Brudenell extended his elbow to his daughter and walked her proudly through the short column of guests to meet Henry, standing before the pastor. On Henry's side were Adam, then Caroline, Charles, Hume, and Cook. On the bride's side stood Frances, then the Duchess and Duke, Mrs. Lewis, William, Anne and Sancho. In a blur of ceremony they took their vows, and Henry turned to Adam for the ring. Placing it on Elizabeth's finger, they kissed, and it was official. Elizabeth was now the Duchess, wife of Henry Scott, Third Duke of Buccleuch.

Chapter 45

HONEYMOON AT ADDERBURY *May 1767*
The sun shone brilliantly on the morning of May 3, 1767, as Henry stepped into the street outside his hotel. He was dressed well for their ride to Adderbury, and the carriage clattered into position as he stood there.

"Percy!" he shouted, and the paperboy ran towards him, dodging a freight wagon as he crossed the street.

Percy offered a paper with one hand while catching Henry's penny with the other. Henry had never seen Percy drop any of the coins he flipped to him; it was as if Percy's hand was magnetic, and the penny made of iron. Henry glanced at the paper in the warm sunshine, opening it to see the wedding announcement Charles had placed with the Courant.

At that moment Elizabeth appeared, dressed for travel, and Henry was again dazzled by his lovely wife. Cook emerged in time to hold the carriage door for them as they boarded. The driver snapped the reins, and the horses began the long pull to Adderbury.

Inside the carriage as it rocked through the London streets, Elizabeth pulled closed the window shades, removed her hat, undid the pins that held her hair, and teased it out so it fell fetchingly over her shoulders. She hiked up her skirts and knelt on the cushions of Henry's seat, straddling him in his lap as she gave him a long, tender kiss. "I waited so long for my handsome Duke, now I can't get enough of him," she purred, beginning to unlace her blouse.

A half hour later, a flock of sheep clogged a bridge over a stream, and the driver halted the carriage. As they waited, the driver turned to his assistant with a broad grin and pointed behind them. They were at a complete stop, but the carriage was still rocking.

. . . .

IN CHARLES' HOTEL OFFICE, he stood with his chin in his hand, pondering his next line. Frances sat attentively at her writing desk, wearing her apron, but since the wedding Charles saw Frances as a woman and no longer a child. He found it difficult to take his eyes off her as she finished his last line. She looked up to see Charles staring at her, which made her feel slightly uncomfortable. Charles averted his eyes and continued with the letter.

"Each colony will be assigned an agent of the Crown, who is responsible for the collection of these duties and their prompt remission to the British Government," he dictated, as Frances penned the lines. "Frances, I meant to tell you that you looked very grown up at Henry's wedding," Charles interrupted himself. "I was so proud of you."

"Thank you, Father," Frances replied, "I love Elizabeth; I couldn't believe she asked me to stand with her."

"Why couldn't you believe it, honey?" Charles asked in a maudlin tone that caused France to hesitate. He had never called her 'honey' before either.

"Mother calls me dull and clumsy and plain," she replied.

"Well, Mother is wrong about that," said Charles resolutely. He mastered himself and continued with the letter. "The Crown Agent will be independent, and not subject to oversight by the Colonial legislatures," he dictated as Frances resumed with her quill.

"*Not* subject to oversight?" asked Frances.

"Yes, not subject," said Charles, "read it back to me."

As Frances read it back, Charles reached behind the desk and pulled out a medium-sized portrait frame. He rested it on his desk and turned it towards Frances, saying, "I wanted to show you this." It was the portrait of Frances by Joshua Reynolds.

Frances put her quill down and looked long at the portrait without saying anything. She rose and crossed the room to inspect it closely. She was surprised by how good it was, proud even, yet disturbed that Charles had kept it secret for so long. She had wondered when it wasn't brought up at Christmas, but then had forgotten all about it.

"Has Mother seen it?" she asked tentatively, as Charles came around the desk and put his arm around her shoulders as they gazed at the painting.

"No... I couldn't bear to show it to her," admitted Charles.

"Why, Father?" asked Frances, feeling uncomfortable that Charles continued to hold her close as they stood looking at the secret picture.

"I love this painting," explained Charles, haltingly, "as I love you, Frances. I just... couldn't stand the thought of her criticizing it."

Frances was silent for a long moment, wishing Charles would remove his arm. "She would criticize it," she finally agreed.

"I fear that. Yes," said Charles, nodding.

"How long have you had it?" she asked, her concerns about his touch growing to acute discomfort as he kept her pressed close to his side. Her discomfort trebled as his fingertips brushed her breast through her apron, although she couldn't tell if it was deliberate.

"Some time now," he said, "I just had to show it to you. It is so wonderful." Finally, he released her, and she returned immediately to the relative security of her writing desk. She eyed him warily as he put the portrait back behind his desk, face turned towards the wall.

He walked across the room and approached her desk. He pulled the diamond ring off his finger and extended it to her, pleading in an odd voice, "Frances, take this ring. Please."

Frances rose to her feet as he came to a stop in front of her, holding the ring in his palm. "If you can't show Mother my portrait, how could I ever take that ring?" she asked in a resolute voice, though she trembled. Charles didn't answer, and she saw that his hand shook so much that the ring almost danced in his palm. Frances untied her apron, draped it over her writing chair, and calmly walked out of the room. Charles, standing alone with the ring still extended, began to shake uncontrollably. He put the ring on his finger, sat down at his desk, put his head in his hands, and sobbed. Frances, with tears streaming down her face, walked the hallway to her room. She was finding that being a woman was much more difficult than she had ever dreamed.

• • • •

ADDERBURY WAS EMPTY, as Henry had changed his mind and given all the servants a holiday. He and Elizabeth were alone in the enormous house, and in mid-morning they sat cross-legged in bed eating bread, butter, cheese, and apples from a tray that sat between them on the rumpled bed. Elizabeth wore only a light shift, and Henry was bare-chested.

"Today, we leave the bedroom and inspect the estate," said Elizabeth.

"One more day in the bedroom?" offered Henry hopefully before she fed him a slice of apple.

"Men are weak and easily distracted," said Elizabeth with a smile.

"Why put our clothes on if we're just going to take them off again?" pondered Henry.

Elizabeth swung her legs off the bed and stood, tousled and fetching in her shift. "Then let's tour the house without getting dressed," she said.

Henry hopped out of bed, dressed in pajama bottoms, and said, "What? You'll walk naked through the ancestral family home?"

She laughed and said, "Nearly naked, but not quite. You dismissed *all* the servants?"

"I did, that's why we eat in bed," he said, pointing to the tray and the crumbs on the bedcovers.

They wandered through the large house, almost warm in early May but they had neglected fires entirely. He almost turned back for a shirt, but then noticed the effect on Elizabeth's nipples beneath the thin fabric and followed her happily, chill or no. He opened a door and said, "This is Charles' office." He hesitated when he saw the desk, and she noticed.

"What?" she asked, but he shook his head and closed the door again.

"Oh, nothing," he said, and they moved into the large drawing room, where hung Greuze's portrait of Hew, next to Gainsborough's painting of Henry. "My brother, Hew," is all he said. Elizabeth moved close and wrapped both arms around him, and they stood there for a full minute before resuming their tour. Seeing the portrait of Henry's dead brother brought the family tragedy into clear focus, and she saw a tear in Henry's eye. He surreptitiously brushed it away.

Later in the afternoon they ventured out to walk the Adderbury grounds, dressed informally and holding hands. They stopped beside one of the new statues Charles had installed.

"Interesting," she commented, "Did you have a hand in selecting this one?"

"Er, no," Henry smirked, "For a man who attends church as seldom as Charles, he sure has a taste for angel wings."

Elizabeth nodded her agreement, saying, "This *is* the third angel we've seen."

"Oh, it gets better," said Henry, "Up ahead we see a winged Griffin."

"No winged devils, I hope?" she said facetiously.

"No, the devil is in London presently," he mused.

"Your relationship with Charles seems... a bit strained," she ventured.

Henry turned towards her and took both her hands in his. "Until you, I felt my whole life was already planned. Tour France, come home, enter Parliament, live here or in London. Now, with you, I find...," he trailed off.

"That anything is possible?" she suggested to finish his thought.

"Yes. Exactly. We can do what we want, live where we want. Mother and Charles expect us to live here, at Adderbury, but we don't have to," he said, growing animated.

"Adderbury is lovely, Henry," she said as they resumed their walk, "With luck, someone will buy a few of these statues from us."

Henry laughed, relaxing in the presence of her good humor, and kissed her. "This is where I'd come on holidays from school. Otherwise, I've never really considered Adderbury as home. Isn't that odd?"

"Your real home is Buckingham School for Boys?" She smiled and put her arm around his waist.

"No," he grinned back at her, "But after spending so much time in boarding schools, and then France, I feel... unattached. Perhaps we should buy our own house in London?"

Elizabeth entwined her soft fingers with Henry's as they walked along. "I don't care where we live as long as I'm with you."

Much later, at dusk, Henry swung his feet off the bed after another romp, leaving Elizabeth sleeping. He put on trousers and shrugged a loose shirt over his head, then padded silently out of the room. Entering Charles' office, he sat in the desk chair and tested the top drawer. It didn't open, so he jiggled it and just as Cook had said, it opened suddenly. He took the papers from inside and laid them on the desktop, careful to leave them in the same order as he'd found them. In the fading light, he read the first few pages.

"Damn!" he exclaimed as their import became apparent. As the light failed, he rose and brought two candles back to the desk. Since there were no fires lit, he took some moments to kindle a small blaze to light the tapers. Placing them on the desktop, he continued to peruse Charles' papers. Absorbed, he jumped when the door opened to reveal Elizabeth, a robe wrapped around her in the cooling house. She held a candle of her own.

"What's so serious, love?" she asked gently, seeing the mass of papers in front of him.

"Charles is up to no good, he has investments all over the place," said Henry.

"I'd think it odd if he didn't," she replied, perching on the edge of the desk, "He's the Chancellor of the Exchequer, is he not?"

"Speculations secured by real estate," said Henry, "Trading on his political influence, it appears."

"I still don't follow, Henry," said Elizabeth, tilting her head in puzzlement.

"He's made risky investments secured by our real estate, Elizabeth," Henry replied, "Adderbury, in particular. No wonder he wants to give it to me."

"Will Adderbury have to be sold?" asked Elizabeth with eyebrows raised in concern.

"Not if his bets pay off, I suppose," he said, "but Charles has been hiding the finances from me."

"Charles is your legal guardian?" she asked.

"He is," Henry replied glumly, "I signed the papers when I was thirteen. I suspect that I've been unfortunate in my choice of guardian."

"How can a thirteen-year-old boy choose anything?" Elizabeth tugged on his hand. "Come, worry about this later."

Henry placed the pages back in the drawer, careful to leave them looking the same as he'd found them, and then closed the drawer. He rose and took Elizabeth into his arms. "Everything is planned for me, a life of ease, of comfort... and of debt, politics, intrigue. For all I learned with Mr. Smith in France, I feel totally unprepared."

"Good problems to have, Henry," she said softly.

"What do you mean?" he asked, unsure if she meant the debt, the politics, or the intrigue.

"Everyone should be so lucky; to have the many problems that come with a large, beautiful estate," she admonished gently. She pulled his head down and kissed him, and he knew she was right.

"I know my birth was fortunate," he nodded as he pulled her close to him.

"As was mine," she said, "Come, let's walk through our dance steps. Just three days till the Ball." As she pulled him out of the office, he grabbed the candlesticks but failed to notice that he dripped wax on the desk.

"With no music?" he protested, following her into the broad hallway.

"I miss Frances and her rhythm sticks," said Elizabeth, "I'll count the beats, one, two, three..." Once the tune filled their imaginations, their many repetitions took over and they danced their Wedding Dance, flawlessly, alone, silently, by candlelight.

CHAPTER 46

T HE WEDDING BALL *May 1767*
Henry and Elizabeth spent the night of May 11 in the London hotel. They woke early, and then didn't see each other for many hours as each was enveloped by separate groups of servants, maids, and valets, who bathed, groomed, powdered, coiffed, and dressed them in different rooms. To Frances' delight, Elizabeth had them give her the same pampered treatment. They all glowed by the end of it, and Henry felt he needed a nap.

Henry chose a dark blue coat, with a snow-white shirt, collars, and cuffs. A colorful band sparkled across the black background of his vest from his shoulder to his hip. The facings and buttons of his coat and vest were pure silver. As always, he would not wear a powdered wig. Instead, his longish brown hair was swept back in a short ponytail bound with a silver bow. His shoes and leather shone with black polish, and his stockings and breeches were buff. He would omit a hat of any kind, as it was a warm day in May, and they'd be dancing.

Elizabeth wore a relatively simple short sleeved white gown trimmed in dark green, with her dark brown hair swept up off her neck and held in place with diamond pins that sparkled as if she wore a crown. The necklace and earrings were made of green tourmaline that perfectly matched the trim of her dress. Her liquid brown eyes caught highlights of green, giving a woodland cast to the completed ensemble but without an actual leaf in sight.

Frances stared in rapt amazement at Elizabeth, despite being giddy with her own sky-blue dress with white lace trim, and her hair fashionably styled. Elizabeth looked at Frances, ready to debut on the social stage of elite London and saw a beautiful grown woman.

It was early evening but still broad daylight when Charles, Caroline, Frances, and Cook boarded their handsome coach and six in front of the hotel. Charles had fretted about using the coach, thinking it perhaps too plain for such a grand occasion. Henry dissuaded him from renting something even finer, and gave two reasons: one, their coach was excellent, with the team of horses all matched blacks; and two, that his hostlers, drivers, footmen, and other servants would be denied their chance to shine. The 'plain' coach was buffed to a high sheen, and every servant was dressed in matching new livery. Even though none of them would attend the Ball, this was their night too.

The Townshend coach was good enough to serve, but they rented the fancy open-top carriage that would carry Henry and Elizabeth. It was pulled by two white geldings, each sporting tall, feathered plumes atop their heads and harness that sparkled with silver trim. The carriage's body was painted ivory, the polished wheels jet-black. As the coach departed, the wedding carriage replaced it in front of the hotel. The vehicle was too small for footmen, but the pair of liveried drivers were immaculate in dark gray coats with white and silver facings.

Elizabeth faced Henry alone in the lobby. Neither could see a flaw in the other, either in character or dress. "Are you ready?" asked Elizabeth.

"As ready as I can be," he smiled, "If I blunder, it's just a hundred friends watching."

"You don't know my mother," she said, "while we were making love, *she* was planning this Ball."

"I'm grateful to her," he said, "but I've not a clue about the details other than our dance. Will there be ceremony?"

"A few announcements, nothing formal or we'd have been drilled on it," she answered, lifting a hand to smooth Henry's hair but deciding it was already perfect. "A Ball is for dancing, and for showing off, and my mother loves both!"

Once seated in the open carriage, Elizabeth placed a top hat on top of Henry's head, promising, "Just for the ride," so he let it remain. Pulling away, they both waved at Percy, standing with his bundle of papers and his mouth agape. The boy responded by waving and cheering as his customer Henry was carried along on his wave of good fortune.

After a ride of only two miles, they arrived at the wedding venue in downtown London. They waited as the coach ahead of them disgorged Charles, Caroline, Cook, and Frances. Henry was shocked at the size of the crowd lining the broad marble steps into the massive building, it was a thousand people or more. The spectators gawked at the well-dressed attendees ascending the carpeted steps, and they formed a broad aisle enforced by ceremonial guards in their bright red coats and tall black hats. At the top of the stair Henry spotted the backs of Adam and Hume as they entered the hall.

A servant opened the carriage door, Henry stepped out and turned to give his hand to Elizabeth as she floated regally to the pavement. The huge crowd got a good look at them and burst into sustained and vocal applause. There was no lack of resentment and envy in the spectators as they watched the elite parade their wealth before them, but they gave beauty its due when they saw it. The applause rippled, redoubled, and then trebled as Henry walked his bride slowly up the steps, and everyone got a better look. Henry found the public applause enormously gratifying, and by Elizabeth's radiant cheeks, she did too. They glowed at the public approval; though much of it was because the idle rich were rarely this attractive.

Passing the threshold, Henry was overwhelmed by the layers of guests, below them on the ballroom floor, even with them on the mezzanine, and above them along the balcony rail of the second floor. The ceiling of the ballroom was thus three stories high, giving a dazzling impression of vast space. The hall was filled with glittering guests, attired in their very best, watching for the bride and groom to make their grand entrance. They burst into sustained polite applause as Henry and Elizabeth stood side by side, holding hands with their right hands and waving with the left, at the top of the interior stairs that led to the ballroom floor. Henry felt like he was on stage, and he was, but standing next to Elizabeth he felt overjoyed instead of intimidated or self-conscious. She deserved this and was worthy of it. "Your mother invited half of London!" said Henry as they waved.

"She must have scaled back her original plan," replied Elizabeth, breaking into a dazzling smile that caused the cheering to redouble.

Charles and Caroline closed on Henry's left, and the Duke and Duchess of Montagu closed on their daughter's right. As the proud parents joined them in the spotlight, Henry noticed Sancho and William at their places with the orchestra. On the mezzanine rail he first spotted Hume, prominent in his red Embassy uniform, and next to him stood Adam, waving enthusiastically. He spotted Lord Shelburne on the other side of Hume, not waving but also not scowling, which was an improvement over his normal expression. Beside Shelburne was a beaming Ben Franklin.

The Duchess of Montagu stepped forward and raised her hand, and all grew quiet. Mary Montagu loved music and the theater, and she had perfect stage presence. She said in a loud, clear voice, "Thank you all for joining our celebration! I am proud to say my daughter Elizabeth Montagu is now Mrs. Henry Scott, the Duchess of Buccleuch!"

The crowd applauded, and Mary allowed ten seconds before raising her hand again. "To start the Ball, the duke and his bride will perform their wedding dance. This is an original composition of our special guest, Mr. Ignatius Sancho, at the piano." She gestured towards the orchestra and Sancho rose and bowed elegantly. A murmur swept the crowd, not in animosity but amazement at seeing such a distinguished black man, a novelty in London. "Ignatius is accompanied by Mr. William Lewis on violin. Mr. Lewis is a childhood friend of the duke." William rose and bowed, creditably in Henry's estimation. In his fine new clothes William was undeniably handsome. At the edge of the mezzanine balcony, Frances couldn't take her eyes off him.

Elizabeth placed her hand on Henry's arm, and they descended to the ballroom level. The crowd ringed the dance floor as the couple took their positions in the center. William put his chin to the violin and picked up his bow, and Sancho lifted his hands, ready for Duchess Mary as she raised her hand to signal for the music to begin.

"All stand for His Majesty King George the Third!" called the King's Messenger, who had appeared suddenly at the top of the stairs behind them. All eyes turned as King George, flanked by two attendants, appeared beside the Messenger, who then stepped back.

The twenty-nine-year-old King absorbed the eager attention for several seconds before announcing, in a loud and commanding voice, "I heard this was the best party in town!" and broke into a broad smile. The guests, including Henry and Elizabeth, burst into applause and laughter. The Wedding Ball of the Buccleuch/Montagu marriage was truly the place to be, the social event of the year. The King's presence proved it. The guests applauded themselves for being in such august company.

King George turned to the parents, who had quickly reassembled next to the King on top of the stairs, while Henry and Elizabeth kept their ready positions on the dance floor. Both ladies curtsied; Charles and Brudenell bowed low.

"Duchess of Montagu, Lady Dalkeith, may I first congratulate the mothers of this fine couple," intoned the King.

"Thank you, Your Majesty," they both said, virtually in unison.

"Montagu, Charles, congratulations," nodded the King, having a practical business relationship with both, but especially Charles. The King shook his finger at Charles in mock severity, but smiled as he said, "Not a single word of politics tonight!"

"I wouldn't think of it, Your Majesty," laughed Charles, pleased with the King's easy familiarity in front of everyone.

The King descended the stairs and stood in front of Henry and Elizabeth. She curtsied gracefully, and Henry bowed. Then the King said formally, "Congratulations to the bride and groom!" to more applause. He looked Elizabeth up and down, and when the applause receded, he said to her, "My spies certainly brought me good information."

"Spies, Your Majesty?" said Elizabeth with a charming smile.

"I asked them to find the most beautiful woman in all of London," the King replied in a voice all could hear, "They directed me here." When the applause quieted, he turned to Henry and said, "My compliments to the Duke of Buccleuch. Well done, Henry." Touched, Henry bowed again.

"I won't interrupt further!" announced the King, raising one hand and sweeping the room as if to include everyone in his gesture. "May the dancing begin!" Pleased with himself, the young King mounted the stairs to stand by the proud parents.

The orchestra picked up their instruments again. Henry and Elizabeth resumed their positions in the center of the floor.

"No pressure, now," smiled Elizabeth.

"Everyone is looking at you anyway," replied Henry.

In front of the orchestra, Ignatius said, "Are you ready William?"

William grinned broadly and said, "In the leather business, we call this taking the bull by the horns. Start us off, Sancho."

Ignatius Sancho, born a slave and orphaned in the West Indies at the age of two, began the first clear notes on the piano, and then William, fifth-year leatherwork apprentice, joined with the plaintive sound of his violin. On the dance floor, Henry imagined he was practicing by candlelight, and they flowed into the innovative steps Sancho had taught them. The King, the parents, and the guests watched and listened, as both the dance and music were unlike anything they had ever heard. Original, yet compelling on the first listen, and they watched transfixed as Henry and Elizabeth performed. Many of them remembered Henry's debacle at the Christmas Ball and wondered. There was no false note, no false step. The orchestra joined in, the music swelled, and the couple danced as one. Finally, it ended, and the watching guests burst into sustained applause.

"That was exquisite!" enthused King George, "The music, the dance..., Duchess, tell me."

Mary Montagu pointed to where Ignatius sat smiling at the piano, relieved that everyone had played flawlessly, and proudly said, "Our butler, the amazing Ignatius Sancho!"

Across the hall, on the mezzanine balcony, a servant appeared next to Hume with a tray and four glasses. Still under the spell of the music, they accepted full glasses from the man. The servant stood aside, took the bottle in his hand, put the tray under his arm, and waited.

"To the lovely couple," toasted Hume, raising his glass, and everyone drained the toast in a gulp. The servant promptly refilled each glass with the bottle.

"Well now, there's a likely lad," said Franklin appreciatively, nodding at the servant, and fished in his pocket for a coin.

"The Duchess insisted, no tips," said the servant resolutely, shaking his head.

The four men looked at each other, and said in unison, "To the Duchess!" and drained their glasses in laughter. The servant smiled at their good humor and didn't notice that Adam slipped a schilling into his pocket.

On the dance floor, a minuet started with Henry and Elizabeth in the lead position. Henry felt so confident that he looked at Elizabeth's eyes instead of her feet, and said, "Does the King of England attend all your mother's dance parties?"

"Only when we aren't at war with France," smiled Elizabeth, spinning around and looking over her shoulder at him.

"Seldom, then," said Henry, taking a turn of his own but never losing step or eye contact.

When that dance ended, Henry and Elizabeth retired to the edge of the dance floor and watched the group dance begin. Among the spectators lined up on the far side of the dancers, Henry spied a natty Cook bring a glass to Mrs. Lewis, handsome in the dress she wore to the wedding. They clinked glasses and drank, and Cook actually smiled. She touched his arm with her hand and Henry saw Cook jump slightly as if she were electric. Elizabeth touched his hand and pointed to the dance floor, where William and Frances were dancing with big smiles on their faces. With a shock of his own Henry saw again that Frances was no longer a child, and that she and William made an attractive couple.

Caroline appeared beside him and grabbed his elbow. She hissed in his ear, "Henry, I asked you to keep an eye on that!" and her eyes showed she meant Frances as she danced happily with William, holding both his big hands in hers.

"Yes Mother," Henry said, catching her eye as he admonished, "But this is our Wedding Ball. Don't spoil their fun." Caroline pursed her lips and disappeared into the crowd.

"Frankly, I think they look charming together," observed Elizabeth mischievously.

"Look at Frances," is all Henry said, his smile returning at his sister's evident bliss. Cook danced past with Mrs. Lewis, and Henry observed that the pinched look that Cook often wore was entirely absent.

Caroline appeared at Charles' elbow. "Frances is dancing with that servant boy!" she complained, clutching his arm.

Charles had been watching Frances with strong emotion, but he collared his feelings enough to tell Caroline, "That servant boy is a fine musician, and quite the fair dancer as well."

"She *will not* sully her reputation with that man!" Caroline said sharply, loud enough to cause Charles to look about in case they'd been overheard despite the music.

"Of course not, dear," he soothed, "But for God's sake, don't spoil her fun tonight!"

"That's what Henry said!" she huffed, "You two are in league against me!" Caroline stormed off, and Charles shook his head. Then, like a magnet, his gaze sought Frances in her pretty blue dress, but he couldn't find her as the dance ended and people milled about.

William led Frances to the orchestra, where Sancho was still playing the piano. He gave Frances her rhythm sticks, and he lifted the violin. They had practiced a tune that William suggested, with an upbeat melody. Frances sat next to him and kept time with her sticks, William's fiddle began to wail, and Sancho played double-time on the piano. It was infectious, and since it was adapted from a country dance, everyone thought they knew it and thronged onto the dance floor. Hume danced by with a large stout woman, and everyone gave them room. Adam danced, smiling, with a woman Henry didn't recognize, then Franklin took a turn with Mrs. Lewis. Cook danced with an elderly woman who was delighted that she had a dance left in her. A young man danced past with an attractive girl; Henry belatedly recognized Thomas Fitzmaurice, Adam's former student. Everyone danced to William's country dance, except Charles, Caroline, and the dour Shelburne. At least so it seemed to Henry as he swirled the floor with his lovely Elizabeth, her soft hand placed perfectly in his.

As the dance ended, the flushed guests thronged the punch bowls and mingled while the orchestra played gentle background music. Sancho, William, and Frances found a punchbowl at the back of the room that wasn't surrounded by parched and perspiring guests. Everyone chattered enthusiastically about the music; few had such fun at other such Balls. Usually, they were for social posing and not uninhibited dancing joy.

Sancho returned to the orchestra as the crowd, refreshed and rested, moved back to the dance floor. William and Frances lingered by the punch bowl with their cups. Three young men approached, aristocratic in bearing as were most of the young men in attendance. Frances and William moved away so they could step up. As the first took up a glass for the server to fill, he turned and leered at Frances and said to his accomplices, "I hear some girls lose their innocence at their sister's wedding. They're envious of what their sister's getting."

William overheard the remark, and asked the man calmly, "What did you say?"

The young aristocrat sneered at William and said, "What's it to you, fiddler? Look at his hands! He's a bloody servant!" They weren't intimidated by William's size, because they did not respect his class. Frances saw William's right hand form a big fist, though it was still down by his waist. She clutched at it with both hands, afraid of what William might do, and at the same moment the insolent man saw the fist as well.

"Threaten me and I'll have you flogged!" he flared in righteous indignation.

"Ignore him, William!" implored Frances. Remaining calm, William turned towards Frances and said gently, "No?"

"No William, he's not worth it," she said, shaking her head and looking him in the eye.

"Ha, he hides behind her skirts," jeered the unfortunate man.

William kept his head turned, looking at Frances with a tender expression. Lightening quick, without looking, he hit the man in the nose with a straight left jab. The man fell back, partially caught by his friends, but as he collapsed, they all ended up sprawled on the floor. Before any could rise, Frances had escaped with William's right hand still firmly in hers as she pulled him away. There was no pursuit once the aggrieved party understood that he'd insulted Frances Scott, sister of the duke and stepdaughter of the Chancellor. The crowd danced on; the fracas unnoticed.

After several more dances, Henry and Elizabeth mounted the stairs, waved to all amidst increasingly drunken applause, and then made their formal exit. The fancy carriage pulled away and the guests returned to the dance floor, as the Ball would last for another hour. Henry pulled Elizabeth close and covered their laps with a wool blanket to ward off the evening chill. Spent, she put her head on his shoulder and closed her eyes, murmuring, "That was lovely."

Later, the family coach departed with Charles, Caroline, and Frances. Cook was missing. It was very dark inside, with only stray light coming from a half-moon in the clear sky, and the lanterns that illuminated the doors of the buildings they passed. A full minute passed in silence.

"You must care little about your reputation, Frances," snapped Caroline, "Or your family's reputation, for God's sake!" A momentary stray beam showed a drawn and angry face; Frances hoped hers would remain in darkness.

"Oh Caroline, don't start," said Charles, his face in shadow so his pained expression didn't show.

"You will *not* see that boy again!" Caroline nearly shouted.

A bit of light showed Frances sitting stony faced, and Charles' heart broke for her. In a steely voice, Frances said, "This was the best night of my life, Mother. You will not take it from me!" surprising them both and shocking them into a momentary silence.

"Just so, Frances," spat Caroline bitterly into the dark, "The best night of your life is *someone else's wedding!*"

CHAPTER 47

FRANCES' PORTRAIT *May 1767*
Late morning of the following day found Henry and Elizabeth still in bed, sleeping, exhausted by the swirl of events culminating in their Wedding Ball. The bottle of wine they'd shared upon their return lay empty on the floor, and the chair draped with their finery lay upturned on its back. Henry opened his eyes and surveyed the wreckage in the dim light that slipped through the drawn drapes. He watched Elizabeth just as she opened her eyes. She sat up and looked at him.

"First things first," said Elizabeth, putting her bare feet on the floor.

"Which is?" he asked, rubbing his eyes.

"First, I pee," she replied, rising in her rumpled shift and scampering behind a screen at the far end of the room. Henry heard a distant tinkle in the chamber pot. She returned as Henry stood.

"Second, I pee," he said, disappearing behind the screen. She heard a strong, steady stream.

"Men pee like horses," she observed dryly as he returned to the bed and reached for his breeches.

"Especially when they drink like fish," he returned, ruefully eyeing the empty bottle on the floor. He rubbed his hand over his face, then ran his fingers through his tangled hair. "What's the third thing? Coffee, tea, bath?"

Elizabeth sat cross-legged on the bed, tousled but still fetching in the eyes of her new husband, and said, "Life is full of decisions."

An hour later both were presentable, and they descended the stairs, looking for food. Thomas Gainsborough was in his nook in the hotel lobby, and they saw with surprise that his subject was Ignatius Sancho. "Elizabeth!" Ignatius called out, waving his hand and turning his head, causing the painter to lift his brush until he resumed his pose.

"Why Sancho, you're up early after being the star of the party last night," greeted Elizabeth.

"I had great fun," replied Sancho with a smile, "But Elizabeth, it's past noon." She raised her eyebrows at this, as she never slept that late, but Gainsborough nodded his confirmation.

Henry missed that exchange, causing the painter and his subject to smile when he said, "Good morning, Sancho, good morning, Mr. Gainsborough."

"And you, sir," nodded Gainsborough, "I hear congratulations are in order."

"Yes, thank you," Henry replied, "When I saw your portrait of Elizabeth, I knew she was the girl for me!" She smiled and pulled him close by his arm, pleased.

"Her real beauty can't be captured in a painting, not even mine," said the painter graciously.

"That's really all the flattery a girl can take in one day, thank you very much!" said Elizabeth, rewarding them with her radiant smile.

"Just drumming up business," laughed Gainsborough, "How about a portrait of the two of you?"

"Not today, we're famished," she replied, "Sit still, Sancho, Mr. Gainsborough is the best painter in London."

"You are too kind, Duchess," replied the painter, resuming with his brush, "Joshua Reynolds might have something to say about that!"

Breakfast was nearly finished when Frances approached their table. "Good morning," she said, but they both noticed the strained tone in her voice, and she was not smiling.

"Sit and join us, Frances," invited Elizabeth, and Frances perched on the edge of a chair.

"I don't want to disturb you," said Frances.

"Nonsense, sister, toast?" offered Henry, but she shook her head. "What's on your mind?" he followed, seeing her anxious expression.

"Can I show you something when you finish eating?" Frances asked, and Elizabeth could see by her demeanor that it was important.

"We are just finishing," said Elizabeth, "Do you want both of us?"

Frances clutched her hands and looked back and forth at each of them, then replied quietly, "Yes, follow me upstairs."

In the hallway, Frances produced a key and unlocked the door to Charles' office. Once inside, Frances closed the door behind them. "You have a key to Charles' office?" asked Henry.

"He gave it to me," said Frances as she walked behind the desk and lifted the portrait. She turned the painting so that it faced them and rested it on the desk.

"That's lovely, Frances!" exclaimed Elizabeth in genuine admiration, and Frances gave a small smile of gratification that quickly disappeared.

"It's wonderful," agreed Henry, "When was this done?"

"Months ago," said Frances flatly, "Charles took me to Mr. Reynolds, instead of Mr. Gainsborough."

"Months!" said a shocked Henry, "Why haven't we seen it?"

"That's what bothers me, Henry," replied Frances, "Father showed it to me, then put it back behind the desk. He won't show it to Mother."

"But why? It captures you beautifully," said Elizabeth.

"He said he couldn't bear to hear Mother criticize it," Frances replied in a small, forlorn voice.

Henry and Elizabeth shared a concerned glance, and Henry admitted, "I can see his point."

"Then why have it painted in the first place?" countered Frances, her mouth turning down.

Henry stepped forward and put his hand on top of the picture frame, standing next to it as he addressed his distraught sister. "Tell you what. Mother returns to Adderbury tomorrow. Let me show it to her, alone, before she goes."

Elizabeth was nodding, but Frances' hands flew to her mouth in horror. "No Henry!" is all she could say. Frances sat down in the chair behind the desk. Henry looked at Elizabeth, both wondering at her dramatic reaction if Caroline's criticism was indeed the primary concern.

"Why, Frances?" asked Henry, putting a hand on Frances' shoulder and alarmed to feel tension wracking the girl.

"I..., I..., don't think he wants her to see it," Frances choked out at last.

"She's critical, yes," said Henry earnestly, growing concerned by his sister's evident anguish, "Let's get that out of the way, because *everyone* should see this picture."

Frances burst into tears and buried her face in her hands. Elizabeth divined a larger darkness and laid a gentle hand on Frances' sobbing shoulders.

"Has he been.... inappropriate?" she asked in a quiet voice, bending low to bring her mouth close to Frances' ear.

Frances uncovered her tear-stained face and stared at Elizabeth with wide eyes, but then burst back into tears and returned her face to her the palms of her hands. In a muffled voice, Frances cried, "He wants to give me his ring!" Elizabeth looked at a puzzled Henry and motioned with her eyes for him to leave the room.

Dread flooded through Henry as he complied, still not understanding what could be wrong with Frances but knowing it was something very serious. What was that about a ring? Closing the door behind him he stood in the hall, uncertain, deciding finally to guard the door in case Charles or Cook should come at such an inopportune time.

Fifteen minutes later the door opened, and Elizabeth and Frances emerged. Frances had regained her composure, but neither wanted to tell Henry what had transpired. It wasn't until later that night that Elizabeth told him her suspicions. Henry was overwhelmed with anger and revulsion, followed by more anger, so much so that Elizabeth worried about him. Strong emotions ran their course, as they must, and by midnight Henry was forming a plan.

At ten the next morning, Henry sat writing in his hotel suite. He finished the letter, blew on it gently to dry the ink, and then folded it carefully and inserted it into an envelope. He lit a candle, melted the red wax, and pressed his signet ring into the cooling seal. On the envelope he carefully wrote, 'John Craigie, Dalkeith,' then added, 'Scotland.' There was a knock on the door.

"Enter," said Henry, getting to his feet.

Cook stepped inside. "You called?"

Henry extended the envelope to him, saying, "Send this letter to Craigie by the fastest possible post." Cook took the envelope, but Henry held on to the end of it and caught Cook's eye.

"Don't give it to Charles this time," Henry instructed seriously, but then gave Cook a wry grin.

Cook nodded deprecatingly, remembering the last time. "It will go out today, Henry."

"Not a word to anyone, Cook," warned Henry.

"Yes, Henry," replied the butler, "I mean, no, not a word."

Cook departed with the letter, and Henry stood in front of the mirror for nearly a minute, pondering his reflection. He combed his tousled hair, then went to the chair and lifted his coat. Indecisive, he stood holding his coat in his hand, and then finally draped it on the back of the chair. He'd do this informally, in his shirt sleeves.

Charles and Caroline were in his office when Henry knocked on the door, then entered.

"Henry, I can't find Frances," said Caroline, "I'm ready to leave for Adderbury."

"Frances isn't going to Adderbury today, Mother," said Henry, trying to appear casual.

"Of course she is! Charles and I were just discussing that," she said dismissively.

"Caroline, I merely suggested that she could stay here to help with my letters," said Charles.

"Frances is at the Montagu's with Elizabeth," informed Henry.

"She *knew* I wanted to leave today!" barked Caroline, irritated.

"If Frances wants to stay in London, she should stay," said Henry flatly.

"You two are in league against me!" cried Caroline, "You know I hate to travel alone."

"Mother, you sound as if you are going alone on horseback," chastised Henry, "Take as many attendants as you wish."

Caroline went to the door and called sharply, "Cook!"

"I sent him on an errand, Mother," said Henry, "What do you need?"

"To fetch Frances from the Montagu's," Caroline snapped.

"No, Frances is a guest there," replied Henry, remaining calm, "Elizabeth invited her. She'll stay as long as she likes."

Caroline glared at Henry, with Charles standing uncomfortably near the desk. He said, "Caroline, be sensible. Frances can stay. When she returns, I'll send her to Adderbury with Cook."

Henry turned on Charles and said tersely, "Charles, Frances is not your clerk. She has more important things to do than scribble your letters."

Charles was wordless for once, and Caroline said accusingly, "Like what? Is Frances seeing that boy, William?"

"William is apprenticed, Mother, he works long hours every day," replied Henry with a steely tone, "That's what you hate about him, remember?"

Charles and Caroline were both unsettled by Henry's assertiveness. Caroline pursed her lips, and asked, "So what, may I ask, is Frances doing at the Montagu's?"

"Singing," said Henry, "Frances has discovered a love of music, and Elizabeth is teaching her."

Caroline didn't answer and looked at Charles questioningly. He shrugged his shoulders as if to say, "Who knew?"

"I'm glad I caught you together," Henry continued, "Elizabeth is tired of living here in the hotel. I, naturally, am reluctant to live with her parents. Appearances, you know." Henry paused, seeing he had their complete attention. "I'd like to buy a house here in London, right away. I suppose I'll need five thousand pounds, ready cash."

Caroline and Charles exchanged an alarmed glance before Charles replied, asking in a reasonable tone, "Why by a house before you know which borough you'll represent in Parliament?"

"We can always buy a second house, if it comes to that," Henry answered, giving the nail another firm whack with his rhetorical hammer.

"Oh Henry, don't be impulsive," said Caroline, "Remember, you'll have Adderbury."

"Oxford is not London, Mother," Henry replied dismissively, then added, "I've already put out inquiries of suitable homes. When can the cash be readied?"

Charles took a deep breath before answering, "You see, Henry, it's a problem of liquidity. Inquiries, did you say?"

"How much cash could I have, say, in one week?" asked Henry bluntly, knowing he had them right where he wanted.

After another long pause, Charles admitted, "About twelve hundred pounds, more or less."

Henry let another long moment transpire, then said, "Now we're getting somewhere. An actual number. Where is the thirty thousand from the Montagu's?"

"It went to pay for the Adderbury improvements, as we discussed," said Charles.

"If I recall the vague twenty thousand estimate you provided, that leaves ten thousand, enough for two houses," calculated Henry.

"I was optimistic about that," admitted Charles meekly.

"So, the fabulous House of Buccleuch can muster a mere twelve hundred pounds ready money?" asked Henry, looking at his parents each in turn.

"Well, I'll leave the money matters to you two," said Caroline, rising and heading towards the door. "I'm going to Adderbury." As she left, she turned back and reminded Charles, "Send Frances along with Cook."

"We certainly will, Caroline, fair travels to you," said Charles, leaving him alone with Henry.

Henry stepped behind Charles' desk and raised the portrait of Frances. Setting it on the desk, he was unsettled to see the fearful expression on his stepfather's face. "Frances showed this to me," said Henry neutrally.

"I..., I couldn't bear to show that to your mother," Charles said, looking down at his shoes, unable to meet Henry's eye.

"Why not?" asked Henry.

"Because I think it's beautiful," replied Charles.

"It is beautiful," Henry agreed, "Why must you hide it?"

"I didn't want to hear your mother's criticism," said Charles.

"That I can understand," nodded Henry, "but did you consider how Frances would feel? Putting her portrait face to the wall? Hiding it?"

Charles hung his head, defeated. "You're right, I'll apologize. When is she coming back?"

Henry waited until Charles raised his head and met his gaze. "I don't know," he said, "I have to decide how to break the bad news to Elizabeth."

"Bad news?" asked Charles.

"That we can't afford a house, Charles," Henry snapped at him.

"You are very wealthy, make no mistake, Henry," reassured Charles, "It's just a problem of liquidity. Idle capital makes no returns, your money is fully invested."

"So, sell one," said Henry bluntly, "I need five thousand pounds."

"Sell one, what?" wondered Charles.

"Sell one of your investments," repeated Henry.

Later that day, Sancho opened the front door at Henry's knock. A servant took charge of Saucy, and Henry followed Sancho inside, where Elizabeth and Frances stood near the piano. Elizabeth stepped forward to kiss her husband. Sancho lifted an eyebrow and tilted his head towards the piano, wondering if they'd continue playing music. "No, Sancho, we'll take a break." Elizabeth said, and Sancho slipped out.

"We've been dying to hear how it went," Elizabeth said, clutching Henry's elbow.

"I was afraid Father would send Cook to get me!" said Frances breathlessly.

"Actually, that was Mother's idea," said Henry, "She wants you back at Adderbury. She's afraid of William."

Frances said, "Oh," in a small voice, then took a seat on the piano bench.

"So, they bought the singing lessons?" asked Elizabeth.

"Completely," nodded Henry, "Mostly, because it's a darn good idea."

"I know!" said Elizabeth, "That's what we've been doing. We warble while we wait."

"You should have seen Charles' face when I demanded money to buy a house," said Henry, grinning, "Panic!"

"Did he argue about it?" she asked apprehensively.

"He said it was a problem of liquidity," Henry answered, "I told him to sell an investment."

"Do you think he suspects what you know?" Elizabeth asked.

"Suspects what?" said Frances.

"I don't think he suspected before, but he might now," said Henry, answering Elizabeth, "I ruffled his feathers, for sure." He stepped to Frances and put his hand on her shoulder as she looked up at him. "Financial things, Frances. And I challenged him about your portrait."

Frances' hands flew to her mouth. "Challenged him?" she asked weakly.

"That he would put your portrait to the wall," said Henry stoutly.

"You were right to challenge him," agreed Elizabeth, but then contritely added, "I'm sorry Frances, I shouldn't interfere."

"Not at all, Elizabeth, let's carry on with the plan," Frances replied bravely, "But there is one more problem."

"Problem?" prompted Henry, after sharing an uncertain glance with his wife.

Frances looked at them sheepishly, then said simply, "William."

CHAPTER 48

TAXING THE AMERICANS *May 1767*

Samuel Touchet sat in his office near the Ministry, supervising several clerks who scribbled industriously at a long table, preparing copies of the revenue bill that would bear Charles Townshend's name when he introduced it in Parliament. A knock, and a clerk rose to admit the bill's namesake. "Ah, there you are, Townshend," greeted Touchet, "We're nearly done."

"Too late for last-minute changes?" asked Charles hopefully, taking a seat across the desk from the MP. They leaned forward so the clerks couldn't hear their words.

Touchet shook his head and said emphatically, "Yes! The last minute was two days ago, when my clerks started copying the final bill." Touchet waved his hand at the busy scribes.

"I had a few thoughts, but I suppose the bill is fine as it is," agreed Charles reluctantly.

"Don't let the perfect be the enemy of the good," said Touchet.

"That sounds familiar...?" questioned Charles with raised eyebrows.

"I quote the French writer, Voltaire," answered Touchet.

"Henry and Smith met Voltaire in Geneva," said Charles, "Henry was impressed with him."

"Speaking of Smith," Touchet asked, "have your advisors come around to your views on the American colonies?"

"No," Charles said flatly, "Smith, Hume, and Shelburne are all against the plan."

"And Chatham?" asked the shrewd Touchet.

"I'm not sure Chatham will survive his illness," replied Charles.

"He is still Prime Minister, Townshend," warned Touchet, "Any chance of his showing up in Parliament and wrecking our plans?"

"None," said Charles, "He remains at the Marlborough estate near Oxford. I have someone watching in case he leaves."

"Chatham is one person who can scuttle the Act," said Touchet, "Lord Shelburne is the other."

"No one likes Shelburne," Charles scoffed, "Even if he objects, we can still win the day."

"When will you go for the final vote?" asked the portly merchant, lighting his pipe and blowing a cloud of smoke into the room.

"Tomorrow, late in the day," Charles leaned forward in his chair, rubbing his hands, "Only about fifty members will be in attendance. I hope to advance the bill without controversy."

Touchet puffed his pipe and shook his head. "Isaac Barre will object for sure."

"Barre is out of town!" exulted Charles, "That's why tomorrow is a good day. Now, another subject. I need five thousand pounds, right away."

"What?" Touchet sat up straight in his chair. "If we're to corner the American tea trade, we'll need more investment, not less."

"Agreed," nodded Charles, "But Henry wants to buy a house in London. Have you sold the East India stock?"

"Yes, but it's been reinvested," responded Touchet, "as we discussed, Charles, this is no time for half measures."

"Imagine my difficulty, Samuel," countered Charles, "How do I tell the rich young duke that he lacks the funds to buy a simple residence?"

• • • •

THE STAGE WAS SET, and late in the afternoon on the following day, Charles Townshend rose to address Parliament. As expected, the chamber was about half-full, and the gallery was nearly empty. No Smith, no Hume, no Shelburne, no Isaac Barre, thought Charles with satisfaction.

"I rise to address the Revenue Bill for America," announced Charles, "Regretfully, Lord Chatham remains ill. But the business of Parliament must continue." His eyes scanned the room and saw that Touchet met his gaze. "We have a need for American revenues," continued Charles, "as we've discussed many times. Our war debts remain. We must re-assert our authority over the American colonies, as the lamentable riots in New York so amply proved." He paused for a sip of water from a crystal glass on the table beside him.

"Our bill adds forty-two thousand in revenue, per year, to the Crown. These revenues will come from duties on paint, on lead, on ink, and on tea. Collectively, and humbly, we can call these duties the Townshend Acts." A cynical murmur swept the attending MPs, as neither party thought Charles Townshend humble. "This is *sure revenue*, not just requests of the colonial legislatures," added Charles, pointedly, "We know that our requests are not often or honestly met. This Act creates a Board of Trade, made up of appointed Crown administrators, who will live in the colonies and collect the duties directly."

A young member stood to be recognized. Edmund Burke was a new Member of Parliament who, like Barre, was a native Irishman. Charles knew him to be a Whig, and the personal secretary for former Prime Minister Rockingham, but otherwise knew little about the man.

Burke said, "Chancellor, it appears that you are repeating the very policy that failed under the last Administration."

"That's why Crown agents must collect the duties, Mr. Burke," countered Charles.

"Those who don't know history are destined to repeat it," said Burke, "The Stamp Act was repealed less than a year ago, have you already forgotten?"

"Not at all," said Charles, "this time we'll act with firmness. We must show the Americans that they are proper British subjects."

"British subjects have representation in Parliament," replied Burke, "Did I miss that in your Bill? I believe our *patience* will achieve more than force."

"We need the revenue now," insisted Charles, "All American revenues must be promptly collected, in full." A murmur of agreement swept the hall, encouraging Charles.

"More easily said than done," Burke countered, "I support American taxation; I don't support making their legislatures useless. Bad laws are the worst form of tyranny."

"This is a good law," said Charles firmly, "By making the collection of duties more consistent, it will foster free trade with the colonies."

"Free trade is not based on utility, but on justice," said Burke stoutly, "That's why oppressive taxation leads to smuggling; they feel the tax is unjust."

"Are you suggesting that the Americans be exempt from British law? You condone their smuggling?" said Charles, going on the offensive.

"Not at all," responded Burke, "I object to your use of the words, 'free trade,' when what you mean is, 'Crown monopoly.'"

"We all understand what this law intends, Mr. Burke," said Charles condescendingly, "You quibble with words."

"A very great part of the mischiefs that vex the world arise from words," responded the Irishman with a hint of heat creeping into his voice. "Your great error is not knowing where to stop; you'd lose all we have gained by an insatiable pursuit of more." His voice rising, Burke finished with, "The Americans will say no! They already said no!"

Charles waved his hand dismissively. "We've discussed these issues before. It's getting late, let's put this to a vote and get home to our families."

A Member shouted to second the motion, and the Parliamentarian rose and said in a loud voice, "All in favor raise your hands, aye!" Counting the hands carefully, he then announced, "The motion passes. The Townshend Acts will go to the King for final approval."

· · · ·

AN HOUR LATER HENRY entered the hotel and spotted Cook. "Any mail?" he asked.

"Yes," Cook nodded, and left. He reappeared quickly with several envelopes. "None from Dalkeith, I'm afraid," he said as he handed them to Henry.

"This one is in a woman's hand," said Henry tearing it open, "No return address." He shook out the letter and grinned. "It's from Craigie. Clever fellow, he had a woman address the envelope." Henry read the letter quickly with Cook standing by expectantly. When he finished, he caught Cook's eye and said in a low tone, "Cook, can you deliver Frances' trunk to the Montagu's?

"Of course, Henry," nodded Cook.

"Without Charles knowing?" he asked, holding Cook's gaze with a keen intensity that made Cook uneasy.

"Should I also bring her portrait?" asked Cook.

"So, you know about that too," Henry observed, nodding his head. Not much got by Cook.

"Yes. I worry about her," said Cook tersely.

Henry grabbed him by the elbow and steered him into a corner for more privacy. "Tell me what you know, Cook," he said urgently.

Cook said, "I don't think it's good that Frances continue as his amanuensis."

"Because?" queried Henry.

"Because she is innocent and affectionate, and Charles is weak," replied Cook promptly, but with a strained voice.

Henry looked long at Cook, knowing he was going to have to trust him. "We're taking Frances to Scotland. I need your help."

Just then Adam entered and spotted them in the corner. He hastened over.

"Mr. Smith," greeted Cook, stepping away from his close consultation with Henry.

"Good evening, Mr. Cook," replied Adam with a nod, "Hello, Henry, I'm glad I've caught you."

"Caught me?" asked Henry, struggling to shift gears quickly from the importance of what he was discussing with Cook.

"You must join me for supper," Adam said, reaching for his arm to draw him away, "Charles just taxed the Americans."

Adam led him to a waiting carriage that dropped them at a tavern in downtown London. Winding their way through the supper crowd to a table at the back, they found Hume, Franklin, Lord Shelburne, and his younger brother, Thomas Fitzmaurice. They all had drinks before them, and a platter of bread and butter, but the meal had yet to be served. After they found seats, and full glasses were set before Adam and Henry, Lord Shelburne rose to make a toast.

"To young Duke Henry, his health, his future, his happiness," said Shelburne, raising his glass.

Surprised at the noble gesture from the unexpected source, Henry replied, "Thank you, Lord Shelburne, those are kind words indeed."

"I don't want you to take it personal, but I'm about to abuse your stepfather severely," followed Shelburne, provoking a bitter laugh around the table. This supper was a wake of sorts, for the loss of a sensible American policy at the hands of Charles Townshend.

"Mr. Smith filled me in," nodded Henry, "I understand Charles passed his American tax?"

Shelburne slapped the tabletop with his palm, and everyone instinctively reached to steady their drinks. "Without saying a word to us!" he railed, "Without Chatham! Townshend reversed the considered judgment of the Administration he supposedly represents, including Hume and me. Now *we* must deal with the results, as Townshend counts his precious revenue!"

With a deadpan expression Hume said, "I applaud your calm and considered demeanor, Lord Shelburne," making everyone laugh and breaking the tension. Even Shelburne had to laugh, which was rare at the best of times. Hume shifted his gaze to Henry, and added, "Luckily I am Northern Secretary, and won't have to deal with the mess Charles has made."

"How is Chatham?" asked Adam, "Has he rendered an opinion, even from his bed?"

"No," scoffed Shelburne, "I don't think he is even informed, nor does he ask to be. The mice play while the cat's away."

"More like a rat than a mouse, my friend," said Franklin, "I'm at a loss how to explain this back home. There will be hell to pay."

"The famous Franklin at a loss for words? I won't believe it!" said Hume.

"When words do come, they won't be pretty," said Franklin seriously.

"We'll be ruined," lamented Shelburne, who as the Southern Division Secretary was responsible for colonial policy. "And it will be on my watch," he added gloomily, "Thomas, pass the bread."

"My friend, there is a great deal of ruin in a nation," agreed Adam, nodding.

"If Chatham can't continue, what likelihood that the King will ask Townshend to form a government?" asked Franklin.

"Charles as Prime Minister? Heaven forbid!" said Shelburne angrily, "Even our young King can't be that mad."

"What if he asks you, brother?" interjected Thomas, who had been quiet until then. William Petty, Lord Shelburne, looked sharply at his younger brother at his conjecture, but he wouldn't become Prime Minister until 1781, just in time for the British surrender at Yorktown. Everyone paused at Thomas' question, pondering the chances of the handful of politicians who might be acceptable to King George. At that moment Edmund Burke approached the table.

"Forgive me, Lord Shelburne," Burke said, "I was told I might find you here."

"Join us, Mr. Burke," invited Shelburne, "I hear you were the only opposition to Townshend's smooth move."

"Feeble opposition, in the end," nodded Burke, "The Americans will see this as much worse than the Stamp Act."

"I agree, young fellow," said Franklin, "If riots ended the Stamp Act, how can we expect anything but riots now?"

Shelburne brought his palm down onto the table with a loud slap, causing everyone to reach for their glasses again. "Do you know what's worse? That wheedling bastard will blame me for the rioting. I'm Secretary for Colonial Affairs!" He nodded at Henry and added, "No offense."

"None taken, sir," smiled Henry, who then turned to Burke. "I'm Henry Scott, Third Duke of Buccleuch."

"Edmund Burke, MP for Wendover," nodded Burke, "a pleasure to meet you sir."

"Mr. Burke is more than a politician, Henry," advised Hume, "He wrote a very pretty treatise on the sublime."

"Thank you, Hume," acknowledged Burke, "Now, I consider myself a good Whig," he said, taking a glass from a waiter, "But there I was, debating another Whig, and finding myself outnumbered!" A wry laugh at this, as Burke was an engaging, pleasant fellow with an open manner. "If this is Whiggery, it's enough to make me consider the Tories!" he joked.

"Don't be rash young man!" said Shelburne, laughing again despite his outrage. At that moment servers brought supper, interrupting the conversation as they set to the meal of pork and vegetables, washed down with plenty of ale and claret.

Hume turned to Burke and asked, "How did it feel speaking alone in a losing cause?"

Burke set down his fork, took a sip of claret, and pondered the question for a moment before saying, "Nobody makes a greater mistake than he who does nothing because he can only do a little. This won't be the last debate on America, I assure you."

"I appreciate your optimism, especially today," remarked Adam, "All our advice to Townshend was for naught."

"Burke shook his head. "Not so, Mr. Smith. The only thing necessary for the triumph of evil is for good men to do nothing. The war is worth fighting even when a battle doesn't go our way."

Adam and Henry shared a carriage back to the hotel, long after dark so they only saw each other in snatches of moonlight. Both were a little drunk, but not to the point of slurring their words.

"I'm leaving for Scotland soon, Henry," said Adam, "Going back to see my mother in Kirkaldy."

"Will I see you at Dalkeith for my birthday, Mr. Smith? September second," Henry asked.

"I wouldn't miss it," nodded Adam, although his face was in shadow, "Only a day's journey from Kirkaldy to Dalkeith."

"Unless the pubs of Edinburgh delay you?" joked Henry.

"Then I'll leave early," Adam smiled, "Edinburgh is a temptation when Hume is there, less so when he's working in London. I'll miss Hume."

"Hume and Franklin seem oddly similar to me," observed Henry, "Not in looks, of course, but in age, outlook, and manner."

"Both Hume and Franklin are great literary talents; both are wasting their lives dabbling in politics," said Adam, the claret loosening his tongue.

"They are good people," agreed Henry, "We need them dabbling or evil might triumph. Mr. Burke makes sense."

"Yes," said Adam, "My part in the fight against evil is to write another book."

"On Justice?" Henry asked, as Adam had mentioned his hope of one day writing a book on jurisprudence.

"That comes later," Adam replied, "First, I want to finish my book on the wealth of nations."

"So, not back to Glasgow, to the University?" Henry inquired, recognizing that Adam had given up his position to take the job as his tutor.

"No, I'm going home to live with Mother," said Adam, "And to write. But I'll see you in September."

"I've seen you every day, for nearly four years, Mr. Smith," said Henry, "I'll miss your advice."

"Surely you'll survive without me until September?" smiled Adam in the dark.

"I have questions right now," Henry replied, "I'm questioning Parliament, although even the King assumes that's where I'll be. Above all, I question Charles."

"Never complain of that which it is at all times in your power to rid yourself," Adam advised, "You can decide. You don't even have to live in London."

"Yes..., I suppose. I'm the duke, after all," replied Henry slowly.

"You're talking to a Scotsman, a true Scotsman who's finally heading home. Wait until you see your estates, Henry. We'll talk more in September."

CHAPTER 49

ESCAPE TO SCOTLAND *June 1767*

A young male amanuensis sat at Frances' writing desk in Charles office. Charles stood near the window, hand on his chin. "Furthermore..., no, make that, in addition...," he broke off, looking distractedly out the window at the street scene below, where carriages came and went, pedestrians strolled, and vendors plied their trade. "Oh, that's enough for today," he said finally, "Are you available tomorrow, same time?"

"Yes sir, same time," said the clerk, rising and slipping out the door, leaving the writing materials where they were. Once he was gone, Charles sat at his desk and lifted Frances' portrait and set it before him. He gazed at it for a minute, then returned it to its place on the floor, facing the wall.

"Cook!" he called out loudly, and in a moment, his butler appeared at the door. "Go fetch Frances from the Montagu's," instructed Charles firmly.

"Right now?" inquired Cook.

"As soon as you can have a carriage brought around," nodded Charles.

Cook left promptly, but then stood in the corridor pondering his situation. Charles' instructions would advance the plan's timing. He went to Frances' room and saw her trunk standing near the mirror, mostly packed. Cook collected her combs, a sweater, and a few other items and put them in the trunk, then he closed the lid and fastened the latch. He left swiftly and found the hotel head of staff downstairs. "A coach and four, right away, for the duke's account," ordered Cook.

"Right away," said the man, and nodded to the valet standing nearby, who left.

"Have someone fetch the trunk of the young lady, Frances Scott, from her room. Have it loaded on the coach in the barn, before bringing it around front," Cook instructed. He loved being back in England, where his instructions were obeyed promptly.

"Give me ten minutes, Mr. Cook," said the man, who spun on his heel and left.

Cook took the hotel stairs two at a time and poked his head inside Charles' office. Charles hastily put Frances' portrait away when he saw his butler. "Coach is on its way," informed Cook briskly, "Did you intend to come along?"

Charles seemed almost frightened at the prospect of collecting Frances in person. "No, no, I'll stay right here," he said, "but hurry, Cook." Minutes later, Charles watched Cook board the coach and depart, failing to notice Frances' trunk strapped to the back.

• • • •

AT THAT VERY MOMENT, Henry and Elizabeth dismounted in front of Buckingham School for Boys and led their horses around to the kitchen entrance. Mrs. Lewis was pleasantly surprised to see them at her door. "Henry! Elizabeth! Do come in!" she said, and they stepped into the kitchen where again they were assailed by the enticing aroma of baking. "Just making more biscuits," she said, "How is Ignatius, Elizabeth?"

"Fine, Mrs. Lewis, and he sends his regards," replied Elizabeth, perching on a stool.

"If you can wait, you can take some home to him," smiled the cook, charmed by anyone who loved her efforts.

"He would love that," said Elizabeth, "We're on a mission that starts here, Mrs. Lewis."

The cook stopped her bustling and looked at Elizabeth. "A mission?"

"We want William to come to Scotland with us," said Henry.

"What does William say?" asked his mother.

"We wanted to ask you first, Mrs. Lewis," said Elizabeth, "We'll be gone for several months."

"Bless your heart, dear," replied the cook, "You two showed up and our whole lives turned upside down! In a good way, mind you, seeing the King even! Heavens!" Henry and Elizabeth laughed, but Mrs. Lewis gave them a serious look, and said, "William is a man; he'll decide for himself. You go ask him, and I'll abide his answer."

Fifteen minutes later, they dismounted in front of Tottham's. William came out to greet them, wiping his hands on a rag and dressed in his work clothes, looking very much like the first day Elizabeth had seen him. "Henry, Elizabeth! What brings you here?" he greeted them with a grin.

"We have a proposition for you," said Elizabeth brightly.

"We're going to Scotland and want you to join us," added Henry.

William fixed them with a level gaze and said, "You're kidding. I can't go to Scotland; I have two more years on my apprenticeship."

As if to underscore his words, Tottham appeared from the back of the shop and called, "A customer, William?"

"No, it's Henry and Elizabeth," he replied, stepping sideways to clear the view for his master.

"Fine," Tottham replied tartly, "Remember that harness must be done by today!"

"Just finishing it, Mr. Tottham," nodded William, then he turned back to his friends. "I'm touched, really. My whole life seems different since you came back. Frances, your wedding, playing music, seeing the King!"

"In that order of importance, I imagine?" Henry inquired, smiling.

"Oh, well...," William blushed, but shook his head. "No. I have two more years. I can't waste the five I've already spent."

"You can't get your position back?" Henry pressed, "I expect we'll return in October."

"Not likely," said William, "I'd be left without a trade, and no prospects for a wife."

"Surely leather work is needed in Scotland? You won't waste your talents, William," said Henry.

"There are guilds in Scotland, Henry," responded William, "I'm sure they'd be happy to accept an Englishman."

"Yes! I'm sure they would!" agreed Henry, nodding his head and looking at Elizabeth.

"I detect a note of sarcasm," advised Elizabeth, shaking hers, and William gave her a wry grin of confirmation as Henry frowned.

"Your offer means the world to me, Henry," said William, looking at his friend with a grateful eye, "but I must stay."

Henry extended his hand, which William took in his strong grip. "I'll visit when we return," he said, finally taking no for the answer. As they turned away, the Townshend coach pulled up in front of the shop. Cook popped out and held the door for Frances, who stepped down looking every inch an English lady. Frances was surprised to see her brother and Elizabeth at Tottham's.

"Oh, what are you doing here?" she said, flustered.

"I'd ask the same of you, Frances," replied Elizabeth, "We were saying goodbye to William."

"Without me?" asked Frances with arched eyebrows, as William stepped forward, twisting his cap in his hands.

"We asked him to go with us, but he's apprenticed," said Henry, "Two more years."

Frances ignored her brother and looked up at the tall blond leatherworker. "William, I would like you to go to Scotland with us."

Tottham reappeared and called out, "William, that harness won't finish itself!"

William gave no response to Tottham, looking at Frances as she held his gaze. He looked at Henry and said, "I can be ready in an hour. I'll have to tell Mum goodbye."

Frances broke into a big smile, and bounced on her toes in pleasure, but she remained ladylike and said, "I'm pleased you can join us, Mr. Lewis," causing him to grin ear to ear.

"We'll meet you at the school," said Henry, smiling, "her biscuits should be ready." He called over Frances' shoulder, "Come Cook, bring the coach!"

"Hold on there, do I understand that William is leaving?" said Tottham with a frown.

"Mr. Tottham," said Henry formally, turning to address the man, "I would like to buy this saddle. I understand William made it?"

Yes, a fine piece of work," replied Tottham, "I require twenty-five pounds for it."

"Done," agreed Henry emphatically, "I'd like William to deliver it to Buckingham School for Boys in one hour." He pulled twenty pounds from his pocket, which was all he had with him, and asked Cook to provide the final five.

Tottham took the money, but then turned to William and hissed, "You'll lose *everything*. You'll never do leather work anywhere in London!"

"I understand, Mr. Tottham," returned William placidly, resigning himself to the consequences of his impulsive decision but not regretting it.

An hour later Henry, Elizabeth, Frances, and Cook were seated around Mrs. Lewis' kitchen table, a plate of fragrant biscuits on a plate before them. Everyone except the cook was eating one. William entered, flushed by his flurry of activity, saying, "Done! My bag and the saddle are on the coach."

"Have a biscuit, William, you won't see the like again for some months!" said his mum, hugging her son tight as he grabbed one and took a big bite.

"I'll miss you Mum," he replied, mouth full, "and your biscuits."

"You can take biscuits with you, but your mother stays here," replied Mrs. Lewis with a tear in her eye and a lump in her throat.

"Cook, did you get Frances' trunk?" asked Henry, once Cook told him how Charles had hastened their timetable by asking him to fetch Frances.

"It's on the coach, Henry, with your luggage," replied Cook, "Charles was at his desk, so I couldn't get the painting." Cook was in fine spirits, part of a great adventure, with his bravery bolstered by the presence of Mrs. Lewis.

"Painting?" asked Frances, looking at Henry for an explanation.

"Your portrait, sister," Henry confirmed, "I thought we'd take it with us."

"Tell me again your plan, now that it's suddenly underway," said Elizabeth.

"First, to your place to say goodbye and pick up your things," replied Henry, "Then to the hotel to pick up the painting. Third, we have lodging tonight after an hour or two on the road."

"Then I'll pack some food for you," said Mrs. Lewis, who began bustling about her kitchen.

"Do you think it wise?" asked Elizabeth doubtfully, "We might run into Charles at the hotel."

"Yes, that's part of the plan," nodded Henry.

"I thought you were going to leave him a letter? Avoid a confrontation?" Elizabeth wondered.

"Yes, that's part of the plan," agreed Henry, mouth full of his second biscuit.

"I can't talk to Father right now, Henry!" Frances burst out; her fingers intertwined so that her plea resembled a prayer.

Henry smiled at her. "You won't Frances, you'll already be on your way to Scotland."

As the group rose to leave, Cook pulled Henry aside and whispered in his ear, "Any chance of me keeping my job after all this?"

"Yes Cook," nodded Henry, smiling at the earnest butler, "That's part of the plan."

Two hours later, at the Montagu's, Cook fretted that Charles would be growing anxious for his return with Frances. He doubted that Charles would come himself, but he might suspect something was afoot. Elizabeth had already begun packing for the trip, so it was a quick process to get all the luggage loaded on the Montagu wagon. The Duke and Duchess of Montagu assembled in the driveway with Sancho and his wife, Anne, who held their baby. Servants scurried about loading the wagon and tying a tarp over the various trunks and bags. Then they tied the reins of Intrepid and Saucy to the back. The coach stood in front of the wagon with the door open.

"What a lovely baby!" said Frances to Anne as they said their goodbyes, "What is her name?"

"Elizabeth," smiled Anne, as her baby grabbed Frances' finger in her chubby fist.

"We will miss you all," said Sancho in his rich baritone, "Especially the music."

"I hope we can play again, Sancho," said William, shaking the musician's hand.

"You have a talent, William, do not forget it," Sancho replied, then turned to accept a hug from Elizabeth. "We'll see you before the snow flies," she said, releasing him. She was the first to climb into the coach, followed by Frances, and then Cook. William climbed up on the big wagon next to the driver, and Henry tossed him a wide-brimmed floppy hat.

"Hide behind this," instructed Henry, "and don't look up when we get to the hotel. Charles may be watching from his window." William nodded as he donned the hat, and Henry climbed into the coach and closed the door. He waved the wagon to go first, and they all waved goodbye from the windows as they pulled away. Elizabeth felt a pang of regret as her childhood home disappeared, but it was quickly overwhelmed by the excitement of their clandestine departure and the lure of a new adventure, a new husband, a new life, and a new country.

On the way, Henry and Cook huddled in close consultation. When the wagon pulled up in front of the hotel, Charles was watching but since he was looking for the coach, he paid no attention to it. He barely noticed the two drivers idling on the high seat, certainly not the one whose face and blond locks were hidden behind the brim of a floppy hat. Cook appeared suddenly in the doorway, surprising Charles. "Frances was out with Elizabeth," he said, "but I found Henry. He'll be up shortly."

"Oh," said a startled Charles, "I was watching for the coach."

"It's in back," said Cook, turning crisply and departing before Charles could ask more questions.

In less than a minute Henry replaced Cook in Charles' doorway. "Cook said he found you at the Montagu's," was all Charles could think of saying.

"Yes, we're going back soon," nodded Henry briskly, stepping into the room. "I promised the Duchess that she could see Frances' portrait."

Charles' mouth opened, but there was a long pause before he spoke. "Is the Duchess here?"

"No, I'll take the portrait to her," said Henry, standing in front of Charles' desk expectantly.

"Right now?" Charles hesitated.

"We came back for it. As you might expect, the Duchess has grown quite fond of Frances," Henry said, looking at Charles with a strange intensity.

"Well, who wouldn't?" said Charles with a weak attempt at a smile. There was something bold, almost peculiar, about Henry, but perhaps it was just his own reluctance to part with the painting. Reaching for the portrait, he handed it slowly and carefully to Henry. "Take good care of it, Henry."

"I will, Charles," he replied, holding the portrait up so they could both enjoy it. Instead, Charles felt a sudden sense of panic, which he hid.

"Bring it right back," said Charles.

"This should end up at Adderbury, next to Hew's portrait from France," replied Henry.

"Of course, Henry, that's exactly where it will go," Charles nodded, but Henry had already turned heel for the door and was gone. He sat weakly in his office chair and leaned his face in his hands, elbows on the desk. Three silent minutes passed before he stood and looked out his window to see the coach pull up and Henry step out of the hotel, carrying Frances' portrait.

"Did you see Henry?" asked Cook from the door, surprising Charles again.

"Yes, I see him now," answered Charles, gesturing to the window. "Aren't you going with him?"

"He said he didn't need me," said Cook, shaking his head, a neutral expression on his face as befits a quality butler. At Charles' nod, he vanished again.

Charles watched Henry get in the coach, which appeared to be empty, and wondered how long Henry and Frances would stay at the Montagu's. The coach pulled away and was gone. A few minutes passed before Cook reappeared in the doorway, waving an envelope. "Henry left you this letter," he said, placing it on the desk before departing. Charles noticed the ornate letter 'S' stamped in thick red sealing wax.

CHAPTER 50

T WO ROOMS AT THE INN *June 1767*
Only minutes had passed but they had crossed a threshold as the coach pulled away from the London hotel. Dalkeith, not Adderbury, was their destination; Henry again felt a rushing sensation as if he was going over a waterfall in a canoe. He smiled at Elizabeth and Frances, still huddled together on the opposite seat to avoid detection from above. The painting sat on the seat next to him, facing outwards. "I just went up and asked him for it," said Henry, proud of himself.

"No questions?" asked Frances, as she scooted over to give them some room now that they were a block away from the hotel.

"I said I was taking it to show Elizabeth's mother," Henry explained, "And we will show it to her... eventually. By way of Scotland. I didn't tell a single lie."

"Come now, Henry, you were utterly false with him," smiled Elizabeth, "Not that I disagree."

"Lies by omission are less flagrant," grinned Henry.

The coach followed the wagon out of London and into more rural districts. It was a fine day in June, and William in his floppy hat joked with the wagon driver as they drove the coach through farmland bursting green in the early days of summer. William thought it was a fine adventure indeed, but if anyone was plunging down a waterfall in a canoe, it was him.

Frances contemplated her portrait sitting opposite on the seat next to Henry, and observed, "It's odd to look at a picture of myself. Like looking into a mirror, only the picture is nicer."

They all agreed that Joshua Reynolds had performed admirably, though Elizabeth said, "No mere painting can capture your sparkle, Frances."

"That's kind of you," she returned, "but looking at myself makes me... unsettled."

"How so?" asked Elizabeth, turning in her seat to look at the girl.

"It's indulgent to stare endlessly into a mirror," said Frances.

"Of course," nodded Elizabeth, "But the important mirrors are the faces of those we talk to. Their expressions guide us, tell us how we look."

"Mr. Smith talks about that very thing in his book," agreed Henry, "We read people's approval or disapproval in how they respond to us. We adjust accordingly."

"That is interesting," said Frances, "Just the same, I don't like staring at myself. Can you turn it towards the cushion, Henry?"

"No, Frances, I won't," said Henry shaking his head but looking at her with a kind expression, "That's what Charles did, and I took him to task." He smiled at Frances, then added, "But we should protect it for the trip." He pulled a traveling robe from under the seat and wrapped the painting in it.

"Here, we'll set it next to Frances," said Elizabeth, deftly switching places with the bundle so she now sat beside her husband. She laced her fingers through his and snuggled close to him.

"Good," said Frances, "I'd rather look at you than me."

Henry pondered his sister and said, "When I left for France, you were just an awkward girl. Now look at you, Frances, you've grown beautifully."

"I still feel like plain old Frances inside," she returned, folding her hands in her lap. Half a minute lapsed in silence, then she added, "Father won't send Cook after us, will he?"

"No, rest easy," said Henry, "I explained in the letter."

"But he doesn't know William is with us," said Frances, "unless you told him in the letter?"

"No, no, of course not," said Henry uneasily, "I said I want you with me when I first see Scotland." He paused to see if this eased her fears, but couldn't tell by Frances' blank expression, so he continued, "I told him we left immediately to avoid buying a house in London." Frances still looked at him, and her silence caused him to add, "And we didn't tell him because we wanted to avoid argument."

For several minutes they rode in silence as the long summer shadows lengthened across the waving fields of grass. Frances gave a Mona Lisa smile and said, "I'm glad we're going to Scotland, Henry."

An hour later they tumbled out at the first inn of the journey. Cook had sent a letter ahead, but only to assure accommodation for the first night. They'd be on their own for the rest of the week's journey to Dalkeith, which lay just south of Edinburgh. The proprietor bustled out to greet them, wiping his hands on his apron.

"Well, this is where we miss Cook," said Henry to no one in particular.

"Good evening, milord, how can I help you?" said the man, as he waved a hostler towards the wagon that had stopped just in front of the coach. William was climbing down from the high seat and Elizabeth saw Frances eye him nervously.

"I need three rooms for the night, plus dinner for my party here," said Henry, "My man Cook sent an inquiry?"

"Yes, yes, we were expecting you," nodded the man, "but there are only two rooms, milord. I hope that will serve?"

Henry looked at Elizabeth in consternation, as William joined them. "You and William can share a room, and I'll sleep with Frances," said Elizabeth decisively.

"I can sleep in the barn with the wagon driver," offered William.

"Nonsense, William," said Henry, turning to address the innkeeper, "Sir, two rooms will be fine."

Despite the gayety of their supper conversation, over the course of their evening meal Henry's apprehension grew. He loved seeing Frances happy; her close relationship with Elizabeth warmed his heart. Nor did he doubt for one minute the wisdom of taking her out of the oppressive situation at home, whether Adderbury or London. Henry was grateful for William; having lost his two closest friends it was a relief to find an old one. But as Henry watched Frances with William, he knew he'd lit a powder keg.

Later, by candlelight, Henry and William prepared for bed in their small room. Donning their night shirts, William's strapping physique made Henry feel slightly self-conscious; a life of physical work hardened the body. Both were keenly aware of the difference in the quality of their clothing but said nothing. "I'm glad you're here with us," said Henry, climbing into bed and pulling the light cover up to his chin.

"Glad to be here," nodded William as he tested the bed by sitting on it. "Scared, but glad."

"Quite a leap, for all of us, really," said Henry, looking at the ceiling as William lay down on his bed, which was barely long enough to accommodate his tall frame.

"Can I ask a question?" asked William after Henry blew out the candle, plunging the room into darkness. "Why all the secrecy around Frances?"

Henry was glad of the darkness, as he hadn't prepared for such an obvious question. "Just timing, really," he faltered, "I'm not legally Duke until my birthday."

"Her mother is her guardian?" asked William.

"Yes," Henry nodded unseen in the dark, "We felt that Frances would benefit from a vacation, from her mother if you must know."

"Her mother is at Adderbury?" William asked.

"Yes," Henry admitted, "but I didn't want to argue with Charles about it."

"She seems a bit afraid of her mother," observed William.

"Her mother is certainly afraid of you," quipped Henry, regretting it instantly.

"I saw that in her eyes," agreed William, "She'll be angry if she knows I'm here."

"I must confess, I was so grateful that Elizabeth sought you out, that you came to our wedding, and your mum, but..." the words came in a torrent, but then Henry stalled. William remained silent, waiting for him to finish his thought. "I feel bad that you gave up your apprenticeship, William. I was only thinking of Frances."

"I was thinking of Frances too," said William in the dark.

"You make her happy, William, Elizabeth says so, we both see it," said Henry, "We're happy for both of you, but..."

"But there's a catch," said William.

"Yes," Henry agreed resignedly, "The laws of inheritance."

In the next room Elizabeth and Frances lay in their beds in the dark, talking just as Henry and William were. "Oh Elizabeth," gushed Frances, "I'm mad about William!"

"I know," sighed Elizabeth.

"I should be thinking about what Mother and Father will say about all this," Frances admitted, catching the tone of Elizabeth's sigh in the dark.

"Plenty of time for that, Frances, let's not second-guess ourselves," reassured Elizabeth.

"Of course not, I'm ever so grateful to you and Henry," responded Frances.

"We bought a bit of time," said Elizabeth, who needed reassurance herself.

"Can William ride in the coach with us tomorrow?" asked Frances, undeterred about the future when the object of her affection lay on the other side of the bedroom wall.

"Perhaps.... Frances, we've acted hastily," responded Elizabeth, "We are glad William came with us, but we must consider your reputation."

"Unmarried people can ride in coaches together, Elizabeth," replied Frances.

Elizabeth laughed, and said, "But not *alone* in coaches, Frances!" remembering her honeymoon ride with Henry.

"Elizabeth!" said Frances, shocked at the implication, "But you'll be there too."

"What if Henry and I want to ride our horses?" countered Elizabeth, "Could we trust you alone in the coach?"

In the darkness Frances blushed, but then blurted, "Oh Elizabeth, I've never been kissed!"

"It's not kissing that I'm worried about Frances," warned Elizabeth, "It's what kissing leads to, and the laws of inheritance."

Early the next morning, Henry, Elizabeth, and Frances stood with steaming cups of tea, while William waited outside for the wagon and coach to pull into position. William was wearing the fine suit they'd bought him for the wedding, which made Henry feel better about appearances, although the essential problem remained. Frances sipped her tea and watched William through the window.

"Henry, a moment?" said Elizabeth, pulling Henry by the elbow, "Excuse us, Frances." She pulled him through a door, saying, "We have a problem..."

Out of sight, Henry took her in his arms and kissed her. "I have a problem...," he murmured as he kissed her again affectionately.

Elizabeth returned his kiss, then pushed him to arm's length. "Frances wants William to ride in the coach with us."

"That's best," nodded Henry, "Let's talk to them both, sensibly."

"Let's then," began Elizabeth, but was interrupted by Henry kissing her again.

"A week sleeping apart!" he muttered, pressing her to him with a hand on her lower back as he kissed her. She returned his kiss passionately, and Henry backed through another door in case they were surprised by his sister. On the other side of the door, Frances startled them anyway as there she was, kissing William.

"Oh!" said a surprised Frances, stepping back, her cheeks flushed scarlet, as were William's.

"Well! Young people in love!" said Elizabeth, the first to recover, and then she hastily added, "Shall we go?" They followed her out the door and straight into the coach, which the driver had positioned in front of the inn. Elizabeth climbed in first, then Frances, but Henry hesitated.

"Ride with us today, William," he invited, stopping his friend who was turning towards the wagon. William caught his eye, hesitated, then boarded the coach without saying anything. Henry followed him; Frances and Elizabeth sat embarrassed on one cushion, and the men sat opposite, facing them.

"I had the cook prepare some food, so we could get an early start," said Elizabeth, reaching into a basket that sat on the seat between her and Frances. She passed out buttered rolls, cheese, and boiled eggs as everyone eagerly welcomed the distraction.

Mouths full, they avoided discussing the kissing episode; after they finished, they rode along making small conversation.

After two hours, they stopped to relieve themselves near a vacant roadside barn. Henry and William used one side of the shabby structure, while Elizabeth and Frances used the opposite.

"Elizabeth says men pee like horses," said Henry.

William smiled at this, but then turned serious and said, "Sorry about this morning, Henry. I heard you last night, but then, there she was."

"It's only natural William, she likes you," Henry responded, "but it's still a problem."

"When she came into my arms, I couldn't refuse her," said William.

"She came to you?" asked Henry, raising his eyebrows.

"Yes," nodded William, "for the life of me, I couldn't say no. I love your sister!"

On the far side of the barn, Frances said, "I'm sorry Elizabeth, I heard what you said last night."

"Yet there you were...," admonished Elizabeth gently.

"When I told you that I'd never been kissed, I knew... I knew... that my first kiss had to be with William!" admitted Frances, blushing again.

"So, my careful speech about caution had the very *opposite* effect?" asked Elizabeth, bemused.

"I suppose.... I know it's not fair," Frances replied as they came around the corner of the barn at the same time William and Henry did, "But just *look* at him!" She smiled at William as they climbed into the coach again, but this time she contrived to sit beside him. Henry sat next to Elizabeth, who unconsciously entwined her fingers with his. Seeing this, Frances shifted towards William and looked at his hands, wishing she could do the same. William looked at her, then at Henry and Elizabeth, with a serious look on his face.

"Henry, perhaps you could repeat what you told me last night," said William.

Henry paused, again unprepared, but then slowly nodded and said, "Yes, yes, that's a good idea," wishing he could be as brave as his friend.

"In the leather trade, it's called taking the bull by the horns," said William, trying to be lighthearted despite his nervousness.

Henry laughed, relieving his tension. If William could face this odd situation, then so could he. "I, we, well, William and I ... he began haltingly, "discussed the laws of inheritance. The duties and responsibilities that come with a title of nobility." He could see Frances stiffen, fearing what he'd say next. "What it means to be a duke," he finished firmly.

"Your duke-ly duties?" joked Frances, causing Henry to smile, albeit somewhat painfully.

"Specifically, Frances, the laws," he replied, "the duty the law imposes." He saw her face grow serious and she settled back into the seat beside William. "Per law," Henry continued, "as the eldest son, I become duke and inherit the Buccleuch estates. And the responsibility to care for all the people who live there."

"You haven't met a single one, Henry," Frances reminded him.

"True, it's more likely they take care of him," interjected Elizabeth, "but that's not his point."

"My title to the land is a matter of law, not preference," said Henry, "My older brother died at age four, so this fell to me."

"Yes, *you* Henry. Why am I bound by all this?" complained Frances, "Why can't I be happy and choose who I wish?"

"You weren't there when Hew died," answered Henry somberly, bringing his sister up short. "He died within days of falling ill. I almost died as well. It matters who inherits, Frances."

"Let me jump in, Henry," said Elizabeth, noting the tears welling in Frances' eyes, "My own family is an example. My grandfather had no male heir, only Mother. The House of Montagu would have ended, had she not married Father. The King intervened to transfer the title to him, but that was only possible because Mother was an heir."

"The entire responsibility falls to you and me, Frances, the last remaining heirs to the Buccleuch estate," added Henry.

"Why couldn't William be like your father?" asked Frances with a frown and causing William to shift his position uneasily.

"Because wives yield to their husbands, Frances, under law," replied Elizabeth, "My father was the Earl of Cardigan before the King made him Duke of Montagu."

"That's why Mother is so afraid of William," added Henry.

William turned to Frances and told her gently, "I'll never be welcome with your parents."

Frances frowned, her lower lip quivered, and then she burst into a sob and hid her face in her hands. William took one of her hands in his and held it; after a moment Frances threw both arms around him and buried her face in his chest. William's lip quivered as well, as did Elizabeth; only a heart of stone could stay unmoved.

"I'm sorry, Frances," said Henry, "I'm sorry for you too, William."

William put his arms around Frances and let her cry for a full minute. Putting a brave face on things, he said, "Well, let's call this a vacation then. We'll have a good time while it lasts." Frances looked at him with tear-stained cheeks, then burst into tears again and returned her face to the comfort of his strong embrace. Henry knew that William was stronger than him in more ways than mere muscles.

CHAPTER 51

SCOTLAND AT LAST *June 1767*

Charles returned to Adderbury without Frances, accompanied only by Cook. It was a warm summer day, so he shrugged off his coat and removed his neckcloth and removed an envelope from the inside pocket. The red seal was broken, it was the letter from Henry. Cook took his coat and disappeared. "Caroline?" Charles called, but there was no response. The house was very quiet. He walked to the end of the hall and called again, "Caroline?"

"She's out for the day," said Cook, reappearing after checking in with the serving staff. "Can I get you anything?"

Charles shook his head and Cook left again. The quiet resumed. Charles wandered aimlessly through the first floor, and found himself in the great drawing room, gazing at the portraits of Henry and Hew. Late afternoon sun slanted through gaps in the tall curtains. Charles' lonely footsteps echoed on the polished wood floor until he reached his office. He sat down in his desk chair with a sigh.

"A big empty house," he muttered to himself. A beam of sunlight shone across the desk, revealing several spots of hardened wax. Absently he flaked them off with his thumbnail. A thought occurred to him, a puzzled look crossed his face, and he straightened in his chair. Jerking the drawer open, he stared at the papers inside. He placed his hand on them but did not remove any; they all appeared as he remembered. His body deflated with another long sigh; he put his elbow on the desk and rested his chin in his hand. A full minute passed, with nary a sound. Finally, Charles leaned back in the chair, shook Henry's letter out of the envelope, and began to read it once again. It would be a long, lonely evening no matter when Caroline returned.

• • • •

THE FOLLOWING MORNING, as the Scotts assembled to board their coach, William approached from the wagon. Dressed in his good clothes, he retained his workmanlike approach.

"The wagon driver drank himself a headache last night, asked if I could drive awhile," he informed them. Henry wasn't sure if this was an excuse to avoid the embarrassment of the day before; he glanced at Elizabeth, who shrugged. William climbed to the wagon seat and waited while the normal driver slowly took his place beside him. Henry saw the man slump in the seat, head in hands, which irritated Henry but at least it implied that William wasn't embarrassed to ride in the coach with them.

The coach driver muttered an apology, nodding at the slumped wagon driver, as he took his place and picked up the reins. Henry and Elizabeth boarded, then watched Frances linger in the door until she caught William's eye, and she waved. Satisfied, she sat across from them with a smile.

"Wait!" said Elizabeth suddenly, and she stepped down from the coach and ran up to the wagon. She called up to William, "Stop in Northampton." He nodded, and she returned to her seat in the coach. They spent the next two hours traveling through a perfect day in early June, with the fields bursting green, livestock grazing contentedly, and children running after the fancy coach as they passed through the hamlets and villages.

In Northampton, Elizabeth found a tailor who could provide traveling clothes for all of them. Their London attire was becoming increasingly ostentatious; she outfitted everyone in muted blues, greens, and greys, and made sure they all had a light wool cloak and cap.

As William appeared in his new clothes, Frances said, "You look fine indeed, William, Elizabeth has an eye for this."

"I can't afford this suit, Henry," said William, pleased by Frances' compliment but embarrassed by the fitting.

"No one expects you to," said Elizabeth brightly, "this is my purchase. People talk; we must keep up appearances. During our journey, you can be Mr. William Lewis, musician."

"Do musicians make much money?" asked William, looking hopeful.

Henry and Elizabeth looked at each other, shaking their heads. "Not usually, no."

"This is the second suit of clothes you've bought me," stated William bluntly.

"Take them, William," said Henry, "In our case, the musician is worth a great deal."

After a brief dinner, they approached the wagon and coach in their new clothes. The wagon driver was sound asleep, sprawled across the tarpaulin covering their luggage.

"Looks like I'm still driving then," said William.

"Nonsense," said Henry with a frown, "Roust that fellow and put him to work."

"It's a fine summer day," said William, "Frances, would you ride beside me on the wagon?"

A smile spread across Frances' face, and she replied in mock formality, "I'd love to, Mr. Lewis!"

William helped her clamber up to the high bench seat, and quickly folded a traveling robe to act as a cushion. The wagon got underway, the coach following, with Henry and Elizabeth sitting beside each other in the forward-looking seat. They watched

Frances ride the wagon beside William, laughing and smiling the whole time, with the wagon driver asleep behind them.

Alone in the coach, Henry kissed Elizabeth, first gently and then passionately. His hands began to roam. "No, Henry," she said, holding both his hands in hers, "I know it's tempting, but we're not on our honeymoon."

"What does that have to do with it?" asked Henry, leaning in, handcuffed, to kiss her again.

"I think the carriage drivers knew what we were up to," returned Elizabeth with a wicked smile, "I saw it in their smirking expressions when we arrived at Adderbury."

"Worse things could be imagined," laughed Henry.

"We must set a good example, we're still in a predicament," said Elizabeth, growing serious.

"Isn't it odd how we all felt better once William wore better clothes?" observed Henry.

"William is clearly superior to the average Lord, Duke, or Earl," Elizabeth opined, "He makes our social pretensions seem silly."

Henry nodded soberly, and she released his hands as he sat back and said, "I felt ridiculous yesterday, saying, how the law favored me and not him. And it covers Frances, but not him."

"The law protects property from conniving gallants who would woo lonely, homely rich girls," said Elizabeth in a matter-of-fact voice.

"Acute analysis, dear," replied Henry, reaching for her, "but no one is safe from a gallant *duke*." He kissed her again. She returned his kiss warmly.

"Just months ago, we were in their exact situation," she said, "We flew into each other's arms."

"I knew you weren't a stable girl by then," he breathed, while kissing her forehead, her cheeks, her mouth.

"You didn't think I was marriage material, did you?" asked Elizabeth, pulling away slightly.

Henry let her go and sat back. Slowly he nodded his agreement, and said, "I see your point."

"Now the shoe is on the other foot," Elizabeth said primly.

"Not really," Henry shook his head, "Men don't get pregnant."

"Agreed," she nodded, "nor does their reputation suffer as hers would."

They rode along for another ten minutes, watching Frances have the time of her life riding the wagon with William. Henry had never seen her so happy; despite their dilemma it was impossible to deny that there was good in all this.

"I might have a solution, but I won't know for months," said Elizabeth, out of the blue.

"Solution?" asked Henry, turning to look at her.

"I might be pregnant, Henry," she said, smiling at him.

Henry's great fortune wasn't his land or his money, it was that he had no doubts, none whatsoever, about Elizabeth as his wife. He hugged her close and whispered, "That's wonderful!" breathlessly in her ear. They rocked along in the swaying coach, holding each other, happy. It was at this grand moment that Henry felt the awesome responsibility of being a father, a duke, a landowner. Both exciting and frightening, immense in scope yet so personal in feeling, ready or not, Henry approached Scotland with a full heart.

"We've been trying hard enough," she smiled at him, as they finally pulled apart and Henry looked about for a bottle of wine to celebrate.

"Not lately," he winked at her, moving in for another kiss.

"If it's a boy, does that let Frances off the hook... inheritance wise?" asked Elizabeth.

Henry took a moment to ponder this, then nodded, "It just might!" Then his face deflated, and he added, "But not in time. We wouldn't be sure until the baby passed its first years." It was a sad fact that in 1767, a third of all babies didn't survive infancy.

Elizabeth nodded and then put her finger to her lips and said, "Secrecy, Henry, I'm not sure." For a minute they watched through the coach window at Frances talking happily with William in the summer sun, her unbound hair streaming behind her, gesturing with her hands to punctuate her words. "I worry about Frances and William in the meantime," she said.

"I'm starting to think we can trust William to be honorable," said Henry, admiring his friend's steadfast and sensible nature.

"Don't take this wrong, dear, but it's your sister I worry about," said Elizabeth frankly.

"I feel like her father, guarding her innocence," replied Henry with a wry expression.

"Her stepfather failed notably in that regard," returned Elizabeth soberly, "She needs you."

That night Henry again asked for two rooms; he hated to sleep apart from his wife, but he was thinking about Frances' reputation. The next two days they traveled north, with William in the coach much of the time. With new clothes, William's working man image changed to more closely resemble the duke and duchess he accompanied. After some gentle advice from Elizabeth, Frances was a model of decorum. Henry was struck by how her girlish mannerisms were fast becoming womanly charms; he could see what William admired in his sister.

Two days' travel took them through Leicester, to Stoke-on-Trent, through Manchester, and into northern England. The weather remained good; roads dry but often too rough to make good time. The agricultural prosperity of England was everywhere apparent; the fields were lush, the cattle fat, the chickens many. This far north, workers in the fields stopped and stared at the elegant coach as it passed. Even the big wagon drew some admiring glances, painted glossy black with white trim instead of the rough wood of the farmers' wagons. Saucy and Intrepid always caused remarks, as the farmers had a good eye for livestock and horses of that quality were rare.

They arrived one evening in the town of Carlisle, just south of the Scottish border and a bit southeast of the Solway Firth. They crossed a river on an ancient stone bridge and thought it fitting when told they'd just crossed the Eden River. Was this the Promised Land? As the Scottish border approached, Henry wondered if he would discover his fate, his destiny, when he reached his ancestral home. Then he shook his head, bemused, and imagined that the French atheists would say ideas like Fate and Eden were signs of residual bigotry and were thus just superstitious myths. Henry wasn't so sure, but he felt he was on the road to find out.

That evening they rode horseback to see the ruins of the ancient wall of the Roman Emperor Hadrian, built to defend against the fierce predecessors of the modern Scots, the Caledonians, well over a thousand years before. They thought it scenic but unimpressive, plundered as it had been for building materials over hundreds of intervening years. As the late sun set over a golden landscape, they ate their last English supper and quaffed their last English ale looking over the high-water mark of the ancient Romans in England. Henry noted that the Romans had stopped just short of Scotland; should he?

Underway from Carlisle for an hour the next morning, Henry spied through the open coach window a pair of mounted horsemen waiting beside a large rock far ahead. The long straightaway allowed a slowly developing view of the waiting men, as it took several minutes for the plodding team to travel the distance. He could see that both men held themselves well, both had sturdy mounts, both horses were brown, and the men had their heads turned towards the advancing coach. Soon Henry identified John Craigie astride the foremost horse, who at that moment held up his hand for the driver to stop. They stopped with the coach abreast of the riders.

"Good day to you, Duke Henry," greeted Craigie through the window, his Scottish brogue reminding Henry immediately of Adam.

"Hello, Mr. Craigie," said Henry, "Took me a moment to recognize you."

"Welcome to Scotland," returned Craigie, with something of a smile hidden behind his bushy moustache. He dismounted, as his companion did, so Henry opened the door, and they all tumbled out into the warm morning sunshine. The rock turned out to be the border marker; Henry stood on Scottish soil for the first time. It felt no different, it was the same as the ground on the south side of the marker. It was Craigie's voice that marked their crossing.

"A pleasure to see you again, Lady Frances," said Craigie, giving a small bow to Frances, who promptly curtsied.

"And you, Mr. Craigie," she replied with a smile, giving no hint that they'd last met on the day of the terrible letter about Hew, at Adderbury, the prior October. Craigie remembered the poor girl as mostly tear-stained and distraught; now here she was, a charming young lady standing in June sunshine. Henry introduced his wife to Craigie.

"A great honor, Duchess Elizabeth," Craigie bowed, pleasing Elizabeth by using the title she was just getting used to having. Craigie could only imagine the splash this beautiful duchess would make at Dalkeith.

"The pleasure is mine, sir," replied Elizabeth, "May I introduce Mr. William Lewis, of London?" As they were greeting each other the wagon pulled up behind the coach.

"I'd be honored to escort you through your estates, Duke Henry," offered Craigie.

"I'd like that very much Mr. Craigie," said Henry, "And who is this fellow?" gesturing towards Craigie's companion, a smallish man of about forty years, clean shaven and respectably dressed.

"Forgive me, this is Mr. Oglivie, the Supervisor over your south estates," introduced Craigie.

"It's an honor to meet you all, Your Grace," said Oglivie, respectfully, and Henry was struck not only by another Scottish accent but by his use of the title, 'Your Grace.'

"How far until we cross into my property?" inquired Henry.

"Your property starts right here," said Craigie, pointing at their feet, "At the border. We'll stop for the night in Langholm, about five miles further on."

"Let's ride horseback," suggested Elizabeth with girlish enthusiasm, grabbing her husband's arm.

"Excellent, yes," Henry nodded, looking at the wagon driver, who understood and climbed down to release Saucy and Intrepid.

"William, will you drive the wagon again?" asked Frances, "I love the view from the high seat."

"Sure," he nodded, "This is my first visit to Scotland."

"Mine too!" said Frances and Henry at the same time, making everyone laugh. It was the laugh that made their border crossing auspicious.

They started off two abreast, with Henry and Craigie in the lead, and Elizabeth and Ogilvie following. The wagon came next, with William and Frances grinning on the high seat, followed by the empty coach with the two drivers. The wagon driver made as if to ride inside; the coach driver laughed and shook his head as the man resignedly took his place beside him. Oglivie thought he'd died and gone to heaven, riding next to the most beautiful woman he'd ever seen personally, and was too intimidated to say much.

"Mr. Craigie," called out Frances, "will we reach Dalkeith tomorrow?"

"Day after tomorrow, perhaps" he called back, not wanting to commit the young duke to a fast pace, and thus a fast look at his vast holdings. As it was, they would only see what was on the direct route north.

William shook his head in wonder at this, understanding at a blow what put Henry in a separate class of beings. "Three days to travel across his own land!" he mused, but Frances missed it as she waved back at Craigie. She was in no mood for this journey to end, with William, she felt it was the best adventure of her young life.

Word traveled quickly, and before long people came out of their houses and fields to line the road to watch them pass. They looked much like the people of northern England, though poorer, thought Henry. Riding at the head of the procession with John Craigie, Henry felt slightly pompous and ridiculous, like a returning emperor instead of the twenty-year-old Englishman that he was. He was glad that he'd insisted they wear their traveling clothes that morning, as they'd have seemed even more ridiculous in their fancy London clothes. The Scots were decidedly humbler in their appearance than the English, and the muted colors of their clothing matched that fact. Again, Henry thought of Adam, and the fancy red suit he'd been so reluctant to wear in Paris. Now he could see why; Adam Smith was raised a plain Scot and would remain one until the day he died.

"Do they expect me to greet them all?" Henry asked Craigie as the number of people increased, appearing at the end of every lane and clustered in the hamlets.

"Not at all," replied Craigie, "They just want to pay their respects. And take your measure."

"Take my measure?" asked Henry, wondering if he should have worn fancier clothes after all.

"No Duke of Buccleuch has lived in Scotland during any of their lifetimes," Craigie said, "This might be their only chance to see what their duke looks like."

"Well, I hope I look presentable," answered Henry, "We've been traveling some days now."

"Not just your clothes, Henry," advised Craigie, "Even a humble eye can see keenly. Your tenants are poor, but they are educated."

"Really? How many?" Henry assumed poor Scotland could afford less education, not more.

"Nearly all," replied Craigie proudly, "Scotland is the first country to try to educate everyone."

"I'd heard word of that, and wondered why," said Henry, feeling ignorant about his patrimony. When Adam had told him about education in Scotland, while they were in Toulouse, it had seemed too distant to concern him. It was hard for him to imagine what other people knew, or didn't know, when they made their decisions, but he recalled with a shudder the bloodthirsty mob at the execution of Jean Calas.

"A shortage of priests willing to live in cold, poor Scotland, that's why," snorted Craigie.

"What do priests have to do with literacy?" asked Henry, imagining the opposite would be true.

"Without enough priests, the Kirk thought folks should read the Bible on their own," replied Craigie, "That was the start of it. Now we read everything we can lay hands on."

CHAPTER 52

M EET THE ARMSTRONGS *June 1767*
It was just past noon when they rolled into the village of Langholm. An ancient castle loomed on the hillside above, but Craigie stopped his horse before the humble Langholm Inn. "Langholm Castle has stood vacant for some forty years," he informed them, "No one can afford the upkeep." As everyone dismounted, a thickset bearded man of about forty emerged from the inn, a broad smile on his face.

"Your Grace, may I present Colin Armstrong, the proprietor," said Ogilvie, as the Southern Estate Supervisor, he knew the man best.

"Good to meet you, Mr. Armstrong," said Henry, watching the man bow.

Straightening, Colin said, "My great honor, Your Grace, let me know your every need." He had the jovial expression and manner of a man suited for hospitality. Craigie made the rest of the introductions standing before the inn door.

"I'm sure the ladies are tired from their journey," said Henry, although early in the day they needed to relieve themselves.

"Ann, show them their rooms!" called Armstrong, and a woman emerged to guide Frances and Elizabeth inside.

"How many rooms do you have, Colin?" asked Craigie.

"Six, and you have them all," replied the man promptly, "Settle in while the missus fixes dinner."

"No guests in the middle of summer?" asked Henry, wondering how the man survived if true.

"There were, but I asked them to leave!" replied Colin with a wide grin.

"Asked them to leave?" wondered Henry, "Why?"

"Not every day the duke comes through!" said Colin, gesturing them inside the inn, where they found a small sitting room adjoining the dining room, and a long table being set by two servants. Despite the low ceiling and humble furniture, the room seemed bright as all the curtains were pulled back from the windows, filling the room with sunlight.

Thirty minutes later they were all seated around the inn table, including Colin Armstrong, who'd put on a vest and coat for the occasion. Two women waited on them, but none wore livery of any sort. When everyone's glasses were full, Craigie stood and raised his glass.

"A toast to Duke Henry Scott, on the occasion of his first visit to Scotland," he said formally, and everyone raised their glasses and drank. Ogilvie added a, "hear, hear," to second his superior. Everyone looked at Henry for a response.

He stood slowly, wondering what memorable line he might utter that would properly meet the moment. He raised his glass, and everyone did likewise.

"To Scotland!" is all he could think to say, but he did so in a ringing tone.

Ogilvie and Colin Armstrong jumped to their feet with a cheer, surprising Henry and making Craigie smile beneath his moustache. Everyone stood and repeated the toast in unison, "To Scotland!" and Henry noted the harmonious blend of English and Scot inflections. They all laughed, and Henry considered how rare it must be for a Scot to hear an Englishman toast his country, for an Englishman he must seem to them.

After they'd all finished a bowl of mutton stew, Craigie settled back and lit his pipe. "There's good news, and bad news," he said, "The good news is we have the duke and his bride two months earlier than expected. The bad news is the condition of the house at Dalkeith."

"We must camp in tents?" joked Henry.

"I prefer 'pavilions,' said Elizabeth, "How bad is it, Mr. Craigie?"

"Other than one wing, no one's lived in the house for many years," Craigie said as he exhaled a plume of tobacco smoke, "I have men working on it, but it takes time."

"We need to see it anyway," said Henry optimistically, "We'll cross each bridge as they come."

"Speaking of bridges," said Oglivie, "there are some pressing maintenance issues..."

Craigie grabbed Ogilvie's arm with his hand to interrupt. "Plenty of time to discuss business later, Mr. Oglivie."

"Yes, of course, pardon me," retreated Ogilvie, seeing that Craigie had some other concern.

"Mr. Lewis, is it?" asked Craigie, to William's surprise.

"Aye," he responded, swallowing his last bite of mutton.

"Friend of the family, Mr. Lewis?" Craigie asked pleasantly, but directly.

"Childhood friend of Henry, sir," William replied.

"He's also a friend who plays violin," added Elizabeth, "William played at our Wedding Ball."

"Music, that's a fine talent," nodded Craigie, "What do you do for a living, then, Mr. Lewis?"

William hesitated, and saw that Frances was watching him with wide eyes. "I'm... looking for opportunities in the leather trade," he said finally.

"Ah, now you're talking!" responded Craigie, taking the pipe out of his mouth, "Glasgow is booming with leather goods. Americans send up their tobacco, and we send the ships back full of saddles and the like."

"The Americans love good Scottish craftsmanship," added Ogilvie.

"Is there a leather worker's guild in Glasgow?" asked William, trying to keep the hopeful tone from his inquiry.

"Oh, sure, and in Edinburgh," said Craigie, "Can't escape the guilds anywhere."

It dawned on Henry what Craigie's concern with William might be, so he said, "William and I attended the same boarding school when we were boys. You can speak freely in front of him."

Craigie shared a look with Ogilvie, who raised his eyebrows as if to say, "Can we discuss business now?" "Well then," said Craigie, the bridge over the River Esk needs some repair. I'll show it to you when we're finished here."

"Excellent, I count on you gentlemen giving me your frank opinions," declared Henry, turning towards the proprietor as he did so. "Colin, for example."

Surprised, Colin looked around the table before he responded tactfully, "Things are quite good, Your Grace, quite good."

"Glad to hear it," responded Henry, "What would make it perfect?"

"Well now, outside of Jesus perfection's not possible," replied Armstrong, "Perfection be the enemy of the good."

Henry gave the innkeeper an odd look, and said, "I've heard those words before, Colin."

"The French writer, Voltaire," said Armstrong, pleased with himself.

"My compliments on your learning," Henry replied with an appreciative nod of his head.

Encouraged, Colin Armstrong leaned in towards his Duke, raised his index finger for emphasis, and said with a conspiratorial air, "Let me tell you of a *real serious problem*, Your Grace. A lack of good books in Langholm!"

They spent the afternoon walking through the village and inspecting the condition of the ancient bridge that spanned the River Esk. A crowd of villagers gathered throughout the day, so that the evening was spent meeting the humble tradesmen, farmers, and sheep owners who lived there. Colin Armstrong, being the first of his tenants Henry had met, managed the throng so that each got a chance to greet their young Duke. There was nothing shy about Colin Armstrong, his manner, though sometimes brusque, was always kind. The long summer evening was pleasant, so Henry, Elizabeth, and Frances held court outside in the town square until the light failed.

Henry noted that Craigie and Ogilvie kept a low profile, and that the residents didn't seem intimidated by them. Henry was relieved, as he'd worried that Charles had administered his estates with hired tyrants. That fear vanished over the course of the evening, just as Ogilvie and Craigie were similarly reassured that Henry wasn't dictatorial either. They all understood that the world hardly lacked tyrants, and that they came in many forms.

In the narrow hallway as they sought their beds, Henry caught William's arm, and whispered, "Change of plans tonight, we have three rooms between us." William looked at him quizzically in the light of the candlestick he held. "You and Frances each have your own room," Henry elaborated, "Elizabeth and I will share the other."

"Sure, say no more," smiled William, nodding.

Henry kept his hold on William's sleeve. "If Frances comes to your room, don't let her in."

William's face showed conflicted surprise, but then he nodded slowly in agreement. "I'll do my best." He looked Henry in the eye and added seriously, "Trust that I won't go to her."

"I do, William," reassured Henry, "My first night in Scotland... should be with my wife."

William nodded soberly, but then the corner of his mouth curled upward. "Sensible," he said.

Henry found Elizabeth already in the room when he entered and closed the door behind him. Turning towards her, he said, "I think we can trust...," but was cut off by her urgent kiss. She was mostly naked and was pulling off his coat. His lips left hers only long enough to blow out the candle.

The next morning brought continued good weather; Henry and Elizabeth knew they were seeing their estates in the best possible light. As the expedition assembled before the inn, they rode out ahead on Saucy and Intrepid, with Henry dressed in just a shirt as no coat was needed. This left Frances and William alone inside the coach, but they sat on opposite sides and all the windows remained open. With a glance at each other, Henry and Elizabeth thought it was worth the risk and galloped off. They crossed the river and loped along a long stone fence line that marked the beginning of the first farm. They slowed their horses to a walk.

"Your land is beautiful, Henry," said Elizabeth.

"Our land, dear," he answered, reaching out to touch fingertips as they rode abreast. "It seems strange to see it for the first time." He swept his arm along the green horizon, "So much of it!" he added, with feeling.

"Let's see it faster!" called Elizabeth, putting her heels to Intrepid and racing ahead. Soon Henry caught up on Saucy, and they let their horses run, laughing all the while. Elizabeth shook out her long brown hair and it streamed in the wind. Two miles swept past in a blur of summer joy, shedding worries as they went. Finally, they slowed their racing mounts. Far ahead, they could see a figure waiting near the lane in front of a small farmhouse. They approached to see a man in his thirties, average height, brawny of arm but lean of hip, and dressed like a farmer.

"Good morning!" called Henry, as they approached.

"A fine morning, indeed," returned the man, and Henry again noted the Scottish accent. "Have you seen the Duke?"

"Which duke is that?" asked Henry, bemused.

"Henry Scott, Third Duke of Buccleuch," said the man promptly, "His carriage is rumored the finest in all Scotland, don't want to miss it."

"Seeing the carriage, or the Duke?" asked Henry, and he could see the farmer's startled expression as he saw Elizabeth. With her thick brown hair framing her flushed face, Elizabeth was more than he'd seen.

"Both," he said, "My name's Armstrong."

Dismounting, Henry extended his hand to the man, who took it without hesitation. "I'm Henry Scott, and this is my wife, the Duchess Elizabeth."

Farmer Armstrong bowed low, and said, "Beggin' your pardon, Your Grace."

"Are you related to the innkeeper?" asked Henry, smiling.

"Colin's my cousin," replied the man, "Long ago, Langholm was the seat of the Clan Armstrong. Lots of us sprinkled about. You can call me Neil."

"Neil Armstrong," said Elizabeth, "Is this your family?" A woman with two small children stood shyly in the doorway of the small, thatched cottage.

"Yes!" beamed Neil, "Come in, come in!" He waved at them to follow and headed in ahead of them. Henry and Elizabeth exchanged glances, shrugged, and followed him through the door. Henry had to duck to clear the threshold. Inside was a living room with a fireplace, clean but sparsely furnished. The windows were few, so it was dim.

"Martha, this is Duke Henry Scott, and the Duchess Elizabeth," Neil said to his wife, who was clearly awed to have such nobility in their humble dwelling. Martha dipped and mumbled a quiet greeting, too quiet for Henry to catch. Elizabeth bent to the children, both barefoot in the summer, a boy of about seven and a younger girl.

"I am Elizabeth, who are you?" she asked the boy, who stood close to his mother's side.

"Neil," he answered solemnly.

"This is Mary, milady," said Martha, as the girl buried her face in the folds of her mother's dress.

"Look here, Your Grace, my prize possessions," said the senior Neil Armstrong, pointing at a shelf that held three books.

Henry leaned close, and in the light from a small window read the spines of the worn volumes. "The Bible, Plutarch's Lives, and Mandeville's Fable of the Bees," read Henry, "Have you read these, Neil?"

"Oh yes, many times," he replied eagerly, "I'm not sure about the bees, though."

"How so?" asked Henry, remembering that Adam had assigned Mandeville's fable in Toulouse. All he could recall was that he found it excessively cynical.

"Mandeville holds that private vices create public benefits," replied Armstrong, "That our greed, our gluttony, create business to satisfy our desires. What do you think, Your Grace?"

Henry looked at the man blankly, utterly confounded to be asked such a deep question in the poor home of a tenant farmer. He looked at Elizabeth with raised eyebrows, but she simply folded her arms and smiled at him, waiting to see what he would answer. "It seems... that many small wrongs could never make a large right," said Henry at last, desperately trying to remember the book's arguments.

Neil Armstrong smacked his thigh with his hand in delight. "Exactly!" he exclaimed, "My thoughts exactly! And look about ye, gluttony don't describe our situation at all."

"You are remarkable, Neil," said Elizabeth simply.

Flustered by the direct praise of the beautiful young Duchess, he stammered before finding his voice. "Ah, it's nothing, Duchess. Stewart, two farms over, has four books. He says it makes him one quarter smarter than me!"

Henry and Elizabeth both laughed, and Henry said, "I've read Plutarch, do you have an opinion?"

"Opinion?" the delighted man replied, "I've got a million of 'em!" He laughed and smacked his thigh again, and young Mary smiled at her Papa's joy from behind Martha's skirts. "For one," he continued eagerly, "Alexander the Great wasn't so great. More butcher than hero, me thinks. Not so civilized as us poor Scots."

At that moment the coach stopped out front. Craigie and Oglivie dismounted their horses, exchanging worried looks at what Armstrong might have told the Duke. Elizabeth stepped outside, followed by Henry and Neil.

"How long have you been a tenant?" asked Henry.

"All my life, and my father before," Armstrong answered, pointing at the ground, "Right here."

"What was his name?" Henry asked.

"Neil," replied the farmer.

"Do you suppose your son might leave one day?" Henry asked as they stepped out into the sunshine, and with a nod towards Martha and her children. "Walk outside your footsteps?"

Armstrong gave a dismissive snort and looked sideways at Henry with a grin. "He'd sooner walk on the moon!"

They left Neil Armstrong waving at his gate, impressed. Craigie and Henry rode in the front, with Ogilvie close behind.

Elizabeth joined Frances and William in the coach, tying Intrepid to the back of the wagon. "Did Armstrong mention his leaky roof?" Craigie asked, after they'd gone a mile.

"No," Henry said, "Does he complain of it?"

"Constantly!" volunteered Ogilvie, and a look of consternation crossed Craigie's face.

"He does mention it, yes," confirmed Craigie.

"Why doesn't he just fix it?" Henry asked.

"The estate provides his house, as part of the tenant agreement," informed Craigie.

"So, you are supposed to fix it?" Henry asked, "I mean, we are?" He thought of the very plain house they provided the Armstrongs.

"Yes," admitted Craigie, "but if we fix his roof, we'll have to fix them all."

"His is not the only leaky house?" asked Henry with raised eyebrows.

"Far from it!" said Ogilvie, drawing a stern glance from Craigie.

"Best if we wait," advised Craigie, "I can present the finances more thoroughly at Dalkeith."

As they progressed, and the day advanced, people lined the road to see the duke. Flocks of sheep pressed close to the road, tended by their shepherds. At one point the whole flock was in the road, blocking their advance. "My apologies for the delay," said Craigie, as the coach and wagon stopped behind them. "I asked them to have their sheep near the road when you pass by."

"Why?" asked Henry, puzzled.

"So you can see the wealth of your land, Your Grace," admitted Craigie, embarrassed that his careful planning had instead blocked their progress.

Sitting astride Saucy, Henry noticed a boy and his mother sitting on the low stone fence that bordered the road. He dismounted and strode over to them; it was disconcerting to see their fright at being approached. He could see that both were poor, their clothes ragged, but the boy's hair was combed. With a pang, Henry noticed that the boy was shoeless, and he instinctively knew it wasn't because of summer.

"Good day to you," he smiled, trying to put them at their ease. The boy looked at him boldly, without a hint of shyness, and said, "G'day milord." The woman just nodded, too timid to attempt a response.

"I am Henry, the Duke of Buccleuch," he said pleasantly, "What are your names?"

"Mrs. Telford, Your Grace," said the woman, finding her voice, "This be my son, Thomas."

"A pleasure to make your acquaintance," Henry nodded, looking at the boy to include him. "Where is Mr. Telford today?"

"Dead in his grave, milord," said the boy plainly, and the woman nodded. "I tend sheep to help Mum," added the lad, whose keen eyes missed nothing as they took in Henry, the horses, and the expensive vehicles.

"Like to get him apprenticed as a stone mason, Your Grace," the woman blurted out, grasping the desperate chance that Henry presented.

"I'll make note," nodded Henry, not wanting to make promises before he knew the scope of the problem. "A pleasure to meet you, Mrs. Telford, and you, Thomas." The boy grinned and waved, and for some reason Henry felt a flood of gratification. The people, even the poorest, didn't seem hostile. The boy's confident manner boded well for the future; if the poorest had hope then all was possible. Henry wouldn't forget the widow Telford or her bold son Thomas; the precocious lad, ten years old in 1767, would get his stone mason apprentice in Langholm and eventually rise to become the greatest civil engineer in British history.

From the idled coach, Elizabeth watched her husband speaking to the woman and her son. She couldn't hear a word, of course, but knew that she'd married the right man. She would never have guessed that Henry, just a few years earlier, was often rude to servants if he chanced to notice them at all. His Grand Tour had taught him something.

William, looking out the window in the other direction, saw a family of sheepherders waving, and he waved back. "They're all waiting to see the Duke," he observed.

"It makes me feel like royalty, somehow," said Frances, waving from the window as she sat opposite William.

"You are royalty," he said simply.

"Bosh, William, I'm just Father's clerk," said Frances dismissively, but blushing at the way William looked at her.

"Technically, he's right Frances," said Elizabeth, turning from watching Henry. "Titles of Nobility exist because of royal decree. Dukes, Earls, and Lords are all agents of the King."

"That's not how it feels to me," said Frances, shaking her head, "Royalty means the Royals; and attending King's Court. Mother and Aunt Mary Coke love playing cards at Court."

"How many poor Scots can even imagine King's Court?" asked Elizabeth, watching as the boy waved goodbye to Henry.

"I couldn't have imagined it, at least before your Wedding Ball," said William.

The coach lurched into motion again, and for a moment it seemed as if they were passing through a sea of sheep. "This reminds me of the Prodigal Son; the Return of the Duke!" observed Elizabeth grandly, waving at the Telfords.

"Except we've never been here before," said Frances with a smirk.

"And we all talk like Londoners," added William, winking at Frances.

CHAPTER 53

T WO YOUNG LOVERS *June 1767*
As the afternoon progressed, more people lined the
road to see the rare sight of a Duke of Buccleuch visiting
Scotland. From Langholm word traveled quickly that the duke
and his entourage had actually talked to the citizens, setting the
countryside abuzz. Two miles from the village of Hawick, people
began to follow the coach and wagon, and as they pulled into the
main street, they saw that a large crowd had already filled the
town square. The crowd closed around the coach and wagon,
stopping forward progress.

"Back up!" called Ogilvie, "Give us space!" He succeeded
enough to allow the riders to dismount, including Henry, still
coatless as it was a warm day. The coach door opened, and
William climbed out; he held the door as Elizabeth and Frances
emerged. A murmur swept the crowd at the sight of the two
young ladies, dressed impressively in their London finery, and
the crowd took a further step back to allow room.

Craigie hooked Henry's arm and led him through the crowd
and up the stone steps of the church facing the square. From the
top step, Craigie announced in a loud voice, "May I present His
Grace, Henry Scott, Third Duke of Buccleuch!" Polite applause
rippled through the crowd, but it was not overly enthusiastic as
Henry was just a handsome young man in his shirtsleeves. They
waited expectantly, and Craigie motioned to Henry as if to say,
"the floor is yours."

Henry looked out over the sea of faces and saw attentive,
intelligent eyes upon him. The people were clean and presentable
for the most part, but Henry noted most of their clothes were
old and worn. He cleared his voice but found he had nothing
prepared to say. "Greetings..., ah, good people of Hawick," he

said lamely, and knew he'd only have one chance to make a good first impression. He saw Elizabeth and Frances standing by the coach, with William, watching him.

"Allow me to introduce my wife, Duchess Elizabeth," said Henry in a loud voice, pointing towards the coach, and then beckoned her forward. "And my sister, Lady Frances Scott," he added. The crowd parted respectfully as the women made their way towards Henry, and then up the steps to stand beside him. As Elizabeth and Frances turned to wave, the whole crowd saw them clearly and gave a roar of approval. Henry beamed; his wife flushed, and Frances grinned uncontrollably. For thirty seconds the applause continued unabated; the women made a much greater impression than Henry ever could. Seeing the Duke was a curiosity; Elizabeth and Frances were real attractions. The women in the crowd absorbed every detail about their dress, their hair, and their mannerisms while the men just gaped.

When the cheering subsided, Henry said, "We hope to meet you all over the next few months, while we're here."

"Don't crowd them, everyone," announced Ogilvie, whom the people saw often and knew well, "Let them find their rooms and eat supper." A disappointed murmur followed as Ogilvie began to lead them down the steps towards the inn across the square.

"When can we ask 'em things, Ogilvie?" shouted a tall man in the crowd.

"Let them get settled first!" Ogilvie replied in a loud voice, his arms resembled a swimmer's breaststroke as he cleared a path through the throng.

"Settled at Dalkeith!" called Craigie, who followed, "Don't pester His Grace with your problems, we're just passing through today."

Henry stopped and looked at the tall man, and raised his voice to say, "I'll hear you in good time." Raising his voice even louder, he called out, "I'll hear all of you!"

The tall man nodded, and replied, "On your way back to London?"

Henry paused, noting the assumption that he'd continue to live in England. "I should think much sooner," he answered, but his words sounded unconvincing even to himself.

"But not before we get him settled at Dalkeith," said Craigie, and they managed to squeeze through the door of the inn, where Ogilvie was greeted by the proprietor. The main room of the large tavern was mostly empty, save the crowd that began to funnel inside behind them. The proprietor led them across the tavern and into a separate dining room and closed the door behind them for privacy.

"Where's William?" asked Frances as they were seated around a long dining table. A servant began filling glasses with a pitcher of ale, and another brought two bottles of wine.

"We'd like to discuss estate finances," said Craigie into her ear, and she nodded her understanding. Still, she immediately went to the door and looked out, but the tavern was already full of townsfolk, and she failed to spot William.

On the far side of the tavern, William saw Frances looking and waved to her, but he could see that she'd failed to locate him. His heart sank as he saw her close the door, so he wedged close to one end of the bar and signaled the barkeep, "Ale?"

Behind the bar the man noted the English accent and asked, "You here with the Duke?"

"Yes," nodded William, taking a drink from the cup the man handed him and sliding him a coin.

"What do yer do for him?" asked the barkeep; in his new clothes William was better dressed than most, but they could tell that he wasn't nobility. William never felt so English.

"Duke Henry and I were childhood friends," he answered, drawing the attention of several of the men crowded close to the bar. The room was packed, and the din made it hard to hear anyone more than a few feet away.

"Interesting," said the barkeep, and William saw the man glance at his big hands wrapped around his cup of ale. "What do you do?"

William decided to come clean and not put on airs. "Apprenticed in the leather trade," he said.

Another man nodded appreciatively, but a second inquired, "Not looking to practice here?"

"Perhaps, I suppose," William answered hopefully, "depending on how it is here."

"Plenty of good Scots in the leather trade," returned the man, "Don't suppose we need any English ones." Several of the patrons nodded their agreement with this, but none seemed hostile towards William. It was just the way of things; guilds were everywhere.

"I was advised to look in Glasgow," said William tentatively.

"Same situation in Glasgow," observed another man, taking a drink of his ale and leaving his mustache frosted with foam.

"I'm just here for the celebration then," said William, thinking that the less he said, the better.

"Don't be hasty, friend," replied the barkeep helpfully, "Perhaps you've another skill?"

"Can ye farm?" said the first patron, and William shook his head ruefully. There was no farm anywhere near Piccadilly Square.

"Can ye shear a sheep?" asked another man.

"I've never sheared a sheep," said William, shaking his head again.

"Can you fish?" asked the second man.

"No, never fished either," said William.

"Well English," said the barkeep, putting both palms on the bar, "What *can* you do?"

In the private room, Craigie was discussing estate affairs as they were served supper, telling Henry, "It's a problem of liquidity. Vast land, little cash; no cash, no land improvements."

"And without land improvements we can't increase the yield," said Henry to confirm he understood. "Tell me, what percent of the annual harvest is re-invested?" Elizabeth and Ogilvie listened closely, but Frances seemed distracted.

"A pittance," Craigie replied sorrowfully, "two percent in the best of years. Much of it goes to pay the debt." He paused meaningfully and caught Henry's eye before adding, "The rest goes to Adderbury."

Unexpectedly, Frances asked, "Does that harvest number include wool?" Everyone turned to look at her.

"Yes, Lady Frances," replied Craigie.

"And wool is about one third of total estate income?" Frances inquired.

"Yes, Lady Frances," nodded Craigie, sharing a surprised glance with Ogilvie.

"And the yield per acre for sheep grazing is less than half that of farming?" continued Frances, as the whole table now gaped at her.

"Far less than half," returned Craigie, "You have a good understanding of the estate, my Lady."

"Very sophisticated," added Ogilvie, impressed.

"Many of Father's letters to you were in my hand, Mr. Craigie," explained Frances, "I've been his amanuensis for some time."

Henry saw Craigie and Ogilvie exchange another uneasy glance before Craigie looked back to Frances. "Forgive me, Lady Frances, but I must ask if you disagree with my summary of the estate?"

"Not at all," reassured Frances, "I only know what Father put in his letters. I must admit I always thought the estates were… a fountain of money, I suppose. Now I see that it's real people, raising real sheep."

"You are wise beyond your years, milady," said Ogilvie in frank admiration.

"You continue to impress, Frances," smiled Elizabeth.

"Thank you for the compliments," replied Frances, "I have one final question – is any of the grazing land suitable for farming?"

"A fine question," replied Craigie, "It comes right back to land improvements, the need to put some of the profit back into the land. Field drainage, enclosures to keep the sheep out of the plantings, such things."

"Instead of going to Adderbury," nodded Henry, "I hear you, Mr. Craigie."

In the tavern beyond the closed door, someone struck up a lively tune on a violin. They stopped talking to listen to the music, rising above the muffled sound of shouts and stamping feet.

"That's a wicked violin," observed Elizabeth, "Who plays so well in Hawick?"

"William!" said Frances suddenly, rising swiftly and opening the door. A flood of sound poured through the doorway, and then Frances disappeared into the crowded tavern.

Henry stood and said, "Wait for us. Don't let them take my plate!" He followed Frances out the door, followed by Elizabeth, and was immediately engulfed by the crowd of shouting, stamping, and dancing Hawickians. He held Elizabeth's hand as he guided her through the packed tavern until they could see William playing the violin with a huge smile on his face. Accompanied by a local percussionist, the upbeat tune was infectious, and they could see Frances arrive close to William, beaming and clapping in time with the music. William finished with a flourish, to enthusiastic applause, and he grinned happily at Frances.

Late that night, Henry and Elizabeth lay side by side in their bed, utterly spent from their wild tavern dancing and their lovemaking afterwards. William's violin had made their visit to Hawick the stuff of legend. The Duke and Duchess danced with the plain folk, and what a Duchess!

"Frances loves William," said Elizabeth.

"William loves her, I'm sure," agreed Henry.

"In every world but ours, they could be together," lamented Elizabeth in a low tone.

"It's impossible," said Henry, shaking his head, "I'm glad we can trust William."

On the other side of the wall, William stood stripped to the waist at the washstand, washing his face, hands, and chest in the light of a single candle. He heard a small tap on his door; he opened it a crack and Frances quickly slipped inside, wrapped in a shawl over her night dress. Her light brown hair was tousled and undone, falling over her shoulders.

"Frances!" said William, surprised, as she came immediately into his arms and lifted her lips to his. He crushed her to his bare chest and returned her kiss with passion as she let the shawl slip to the floor. His hands told him she was naked beneath the light shift she wore.

"I love you, William!" gasped Frances, then she kissed him again and pressed close, trembling at his touch.

"Oh, you shouldn't be here!" William exclaimed, but kept his voice a rough whisper knowing the walls wouldn't hold it otherwise. He pushed her to arm's length.

"You want me to go?" panted Frances, incredulous, bewildered and fearing rejection.

"Hell no, I want you to stay!" exclaimed William, pulling her close and crushing his lips to hers.

On the other side of the wall, Henry and Elizabeth lay on their backs in inky darkness. "Frances looked so happy watching William play, it's romantic."

Henry said, "Musicians sure can woo women. Music must be naturally romantic."

"They make a beautiful couple, Henry, admit it," came her low voice from the dark.

"In a perfect world, yes," he whispered, "But that's not the one we live in." He let several seconds go by before adding, "I sure hope we can trust William."

Elizabeth could hear something going on outside their room but couldn't identify it. Perhaps some rowdy townsfolk were still drinking in the tavern.

Beyond the wall, William pushed Frances away with a hoarse whisper, "*We can't!*"

Tears sprang into her eyes, and she pleaded, "I want to! With you, William!" Frances was shaking with the memory of his body against hers. "I came to you...," she trailed off.

"I'll remember this my whole life, Frances," swore William earnestly, desperately, fearing she'd be unable to bear the rejection and be angry with him.

Frances stepped away, put her hand on the door and turned. "Shouldn't love be more important, than..., than..., *silly rules?*"

"They'd find a way to throw me in jail, Frances, and you'd be humiliated," he whispered from the center of the room, holding his shirt in his hands to hide his body's excitement.

Frances remembered her shawl on the floor and wrapped it around her. She silently opened the door as tears streamed down her cheeks.

"I love you terribly, Frances," cried William in an anguished whisper as she fled the room.

Coach and wagon awaited in the town square as Henry and Elizabeth stepped out of the inn the next morning into bright sunshine. The town of Hawick glistened with the morning dew, and several people stood about hoping for a glimpse of the Duchess, and the Duke. They cut splendid figures, as this morning they were both dressed in elegant London clothes. They expected to arrive at Dalkeith later that day and wanted to play the part to the fullest. Craigie and Oglivie followed them outside, and the morning was so pleasant it was difficult to be in low spirits.

"It's a lovely Scottish morning," observed Craigie with a satisfied look, pleased also with the memory of the Duke and Duchess dancing up a storm in the Hawick tavern the night before.

"Indeed, it is, Mr. Craigie," nodded Elizabeth charmingly, cracking the man's reserve so that his bushy mustache couldn't hide his smile. The Duke was handsome, but the Duchess was dazzling.

"I must take leave of you," said Ogilvie, "I return to Langholm this morning. It's been a great honor to meet Your Grace, and his lovely Duchess." He bowed low, as dazzled by the Duchess as Craigie was.

"You'll be at Dalkeith for my birthday, won't you Mr. Ogilvie?" asked Henry.

"If that's an invitation I am honored indeed, Your Grace," said Ogilvie, unable to control the happy grin that spread across his face.

"It is, we'll look for you then," returned Henry, "Safe travels, Mr. Ogilvie."

"If you ride with me, I can continue my property narration," said Craigie, "Dalkeith by suppertime, I expect."

"Elizabeth, ride with us?" Henry asked, but he saw the small shake of her head.

"I'll start in the carriage," said Elizabeth, who was nearly sure about the baby but kept it quiet.

William emerged from the inn just in time to open the door for Elizabeth to step up and in. Holding the coach door, he looked to see Frances march out of the inn. Her arms were crossed, and her lips were pressed in a straight line that matched her determined walk.

As Frances put her foot on the coach step, she said tersely to William, "I'd like to talk to Elizabeth, in confidence."

"I'll ride the wagon then," William nodded stoically, closing the door after her.

Henry observed this from a distance and was puzzled. Mounting his horse, he saw William climb up beside the wagon driver. Townsfolk waved as they got underway, with Henry and Craigie on horseback leading the caravan. Henry waved back, but noticed many of the waves were directed behind him. Finally, he saw one man wave and make like a fiddle; Henry turned in his saddle in time to see William returning the wave. Musicians are popular everywhere, he mused enviously.

"Forgive me, Henry," said Craigie in a low voice, "but is William your friend, or your sister's?"

"Both, why?" answered Henry warily.

"They seem very... aware of each other," Craigie replied.

"You are observant, Mr. Craigie," said Henry guardedly.

"William sure can play the fiddle. Big strapping lad, as well," observed Craigie.

"Yes. Do you have a point?" said Henry bluntly.

"Do you suppose they might marry?" Craigie was blunt in his reply.

Henry shifted in the saddle, uncomfortable. "They like each other well enough," he nodded, "but William is not a property owner."

"Ahh, now I see the dilemma," Craigie replied, "I'll keep my comments to myself then."

"The less said, the better," agreed Henry, catching Craigie's eye.

Craigie held his gaze. "Agreed. But if I can see it, so will others."

Henry nodded but did not reply, considering how Adam had given him that same advice in Toulouse, and Ben Franklin in London. Now, Craigie in Scotland. Their every public move would be *observed*. The men rode several minutes in silence before Craigie began pointing out tenants, their farms, their homes, the improvements made and those dearly needed. Henry listened, questioned, and waved at the people who lived on his vast estate as they thronged the roadside to watch their Duke and Duchess pass.

CHAPTER 54

D ALKEITH *July 1767*
     Crossing the Teviot on an ancient stone bridge just outside Hawick, Craigie led Henry at a brisk pace through the warm morning, waving at the tenant families and children who waited to see them pass. The coach kept up with the riders, but soon the wagon fell behind. Henry worried about disappointing the spectators by riding too fast, but he quickly saw that the faster they rode, the more the people cheered. The elegant coach speeding along made a far greater impression than the slow plodding of a dignified walk. The *idea* of a duke was all they had, and the crisp, purposeful passage of his entourage met their expectations.

They stopped for a brief picnic dinner on the banks of the River Tweed. The wagon was just catching up as the coach was preparing to resume, so Frances was spared having to interact with William. She spent the entire morning confiding in Elizabeth, weeping on her shoulder on two occasions. After midday, she sat looking dreamily at the passing countryside through the open coach windows and waving at the shepherds and children who became less frequent as the day wore on. Elizabeth napped through much of the warm afternoon, lulled by the swaying coach as it rocked along.

Late in the day they climbed a long grade and turned into a long, straight lane lined with trees. It continued up a moderate incline until they emerged onto the lawn of Dalkeith House. It stood, massive and handsome in the early evening light, on the edge of a steep hill. At the foot of the ancient glacis wound a ribbon of trees marking the River Esk. Henry first saw his ancestral home in lovely light, and it moved him. At the same

621

time, he noticed that what appeared to be 'lawns' were fields cropped close by cattle.

They rode into the carriage circle before the huge house, built in 1702 on the site of the earlier Dalkeith Manor. Four stories of yellow stone towered above them, with the entrance of the main building recessed into a courtyard. Chimneys bristled from the peaked rooftops; it would take an army of servants to keep heat in all the rooms. No smoke issued from any chimney in the warm, quiet evening as they dismounted. The coach pulled in behind them, the tired team of black horses blowing foam from their flaring nostrils, their flanks covered in sweat. A few chickens wandered across the driveway as Elizabeth, Frances, Henry, and Craigie stood before the massive stone pile.

"Welcome to Dalkeith, the ancestral home," said Craigie.

Henry was unsettled by the quiet and lack of any kind of greeting. He felt that his arrival was a momentous occasion but realized that it was mostly his emotions that were momentous. They were early, very early, due to their unexpected departure from London. Still, Dalkeith, impressive as it was, hardly appeared to be the epicenter of his vast estate. Voltaire's advice occurred to him, that he should 'visit Scotland and see what your heart tells you.'

"When did the last duke stop living here?" he asked.

"Hundred years or so," Craigie replied, then deadpanned, "I wasn't here then." He grinned at them beneath his mustache, a rare joke from a serious man who was glad to be home.

Craigie led them to the large double front doors and opened only one half of the door. They passed through and stood inside a large entry foyer, with a tall ornate ceiling and marble floor. The room was largely unfurnished, with no carpets, swept but not polished, and evidently used as a passage towards the hallway on their left. Another hallway led right, but all they glimpsed was a large shadowy room with several pieces of furniture draped in dusty canvas, and all the drapes drawn closed.

"Margaret, where are you dear?" called Craigie, to no response. "Wait here a moment," he said, and he disappeared down the left-hand hallway. Henry, Elizabeth, and Frances stood uncertainly in the large room, utterly silent. There was nothing about the big empty room that felt like home. Several large portraits, dulled by dust, hung above their heads, unsmiling men and a few women wearing ancient dress or armor. Henry pondered them as if they were ghosts; he had no idea who any of them were.

The door opened, and William peeked inside. "May I?" he said.

Henry beckoned him. "Come in, the view so far is mostly dust." He saw Frances stiffen and she avoided looking at William by stepping away to examine one of the portraits.

"Found her!" announced Craigie, reappearing from the lefthand hallway, "Come," he beckoned, "watch your step."

They followed him past an open door to a big kitchen that showed signs of current use, down the marble hallway adorned with more old portraits. Craigie opened a door into a room where a middle-aged woman in an apron held a paint brush in her hand. Two other painters were busy painting the opposite wall but stopped with the arrival of visitors. "Oh, here so soon?" said the woman, smiling and brushing a strand of hair that had escaped from under her work scarf.

"Your Grace, Duchess Elizabeth, may I present my wife, Margaret," said Craigie, formally, despite the very informal nature of their meeting.

"Beg your pardon, Your Grace, Duchess," said Margaret brightly with no sign of embarrassment, "We're getting your house into shape!"

Henry looked at Elizabeth; neither of them expected to see the wife of the estate administrator painting the walls. Behind him, William stood beside Frances just outside the door, both keenly aware of each other but neither offering a word. "You see the effect of your letter, Henry," said an upbeat Craigie, "All hands on deck, so to speak."

"We need more hands then," said Henry, "Can we get more help now that our ship has come in?"

"Easily," Craigie reassured, then added, "Thankfully!" He exchanged a glance with his wife, and then turned back to Henry and said, "Expensively," with a rueful nod.

"How so?" asked Henry.

"Summertime is peak farming," Craigie replied, "I can send to Edinburgh for labor, but it will be a few days."

"Please send to Edinburgh, Mr. Craigie," said Elizabeth, smiling, "but let's not interrupt the farming. We can raise pavilions if need be."

"Pavilions?" asked Craigie, missing her jest, "Do you mean tents? We'd have to send to Edinburgh for those too."

"Then by all means send to Edinburgh," seconded Henry with a laugh. They left Margaret Craigie at her work and returned to the hall.

Craigie leaned close to Henry and whispered, "Cash is king in Scotland. Do you have any?"

"Will a hundred pounds suffice?" asked Henry, trying to remember how much money they'd brought with them.

Relief flooded Craigie's face at this; one hundred pounds cash money was a fortune in Scotland. "Yes, yes, I'm grateful," he replied, nodding.

"This is for the estate, is it not?" said Henry, unnerved by the man's reaction at the mention of a mere hundred pounds.

"I'm glad you see it that way, Duke Henry," returned Craigie, "Most of the cash goes to Adderbury."

After a picnic supper the tired travelers went to bed, but the wagon and coach drivers drank and sang in the barn long into the night. William joined them, even though Henry had shown him a room in the house specifically for his use.

Elizabeth sat cross-legged on their bed in her night shift, brushing her long hair by candlelight. Through the open window drifted snatches of the drivers' drunken song. Henry entered, holding a candle in a small candlestick. He cast about for a place to put the candle down, as the room had only the bed, a chair, and a small night table.

"Set it here," said Elizabeth, clearing a space on the tabletop amongst her brushes and combs.

Henry sat on the chair and removed his boots by the light of the two flames. "Our first night at Dalkeith but it feels like another inn," he sighed.

"A bit rustic," agreed Elizabeth, "but I'm glad we're here, Henry." She brought a finger to her lips and whispered, "Frances is in the next room."

Henry nodded and returned in a low voice, "Odd that William insisted on sleeping in the barn."

"I think the jug played a part in that," said Elizabeth.

"When he started drinking, I started worrying," admitted Henry, shucking his stockings and removing his breeches. He stood next to the bed in his shirt and undershorts.

"Rest easy, husband," said Elizabeth, "William passed the test last night."

"What? Tell!" exclaimed Henry in a hoarse whisper, causing Elizabeth to caution him with another finger to the lips.

"I pledged Frances my confidence," said Elizabeth as Henry climbed into bed beside her.

"Don't tease me, love," urged Henry, "Tell!"

"Frances went to his room, and William turned her away," whispered Elizabeth, her mouth close to Henry's ear. "Last night."

Henry gave an audible sigh of relief and with feeling whispered, "Strong fellow! Good heart!"

"Yes, William was an oak," nodded Elizabeth, "but the dilemma endures."

"Frances seems upset," observed Henry.

"To put it mildly," she agreed, "Imagine, brother, the disaster to your dear sister."

"William's fortitude is *not* a disaster," replied Henry stoutly, "It's our saving grace."

Elizabeth frowned at him. "You are thick as a post, Henry. Frances offers herself to the first man she loves, and he... *turns her away!*"

"Yes, thank God!" nodded Henry eagerly.

She shook her head, exasperated at his density, and leaned over to blow out both candles. As they lay back in bed, they could hear the distant singing, which was growing more disjointed as the drinking progressed, often interrupted by raucous laughter. They listened to these happy sounds for a minute in the dark, until their eyes adjusted from candle to moonlight.

"Enough about your sister's virginity," whispered Elizabeth, "I'm pregnant, Henry!"

When Henry's eyes opened early the next morning, he briefly wondered where he was. He turned to see that Elizabeth was still sleeping, lying on her side facing away from him. Her breathing was smooth and even, and he remembered her news with a rush of happiness and satisfaction. He swung his bare feet to the floor and began to quietly dress.

He was pulling his breeches over his stockings when she rolled over and looked at him sleepily. "Time to get up?"

"Sleep, love, I like to ride early in the morning," whispered Henry.

"Me too," she said, sitting up, "Would you rather ride alone?"

"Join me," encouraged Henry, and she stood in her nightdress.

She looked at the dress she'd worn yesterday, hanging on a hook behind the door. "My riding clothes are in my trunk."

"Do you know where they put it?" asked Henry; without any of their personal servants they were somewhat unmoored.

"No clue," she answered, "I don't want to wake the house."

"No," he agreed, "Let me look about."

He slipped out the door, and Elizabeth used the opportunity to use the chamber pot. In a few minutes Henry returned, holding clothes draped over his arm.

"I found some servants' clothes in a closet," he said, "these are smallest in size."

She looked at the trousers, shirt, belt, and suspenders, and gave a little laugh. Standing, she stepped into the trousers and stuffed her nightdress inside. She sniffed the shirt to make sure it was clean, then shrugged it on over her shift. She put on the belt and Henry helped her fasten the suspenders. Dressed, she put a hand on her hip and asked, "No hat?"

Henry laughed and hugged her tight and kissed her. She put her finger to her lips and cautioned him, "Quiet!" and wriggled out of his grasp. Slipping on her shoes, they stepped into the hall. As they passed the kitchen door, they could see two women inside preparing to bake bread. Passing through the empty foyer, they stepped out into their first dawn at Dalkeith.

William was sleeping in a pile of hay, and the two drivers snored soundly nearby. Henry and Elizabeth saddled the horses as quietly as they could. They mounted once they'd walked the horses to the front driveway.

"Wait," said Henry, remembering.

"What?" Elizabeth looked at him quizzically.

Henry thought that even dressed as a man, no one would ever miss his wife's beauty. "Should you be riding, in your condition?"

"Do you mean dressed like this?" she smiled at him fetchingly, tousled hair framing her face.

"No, silly," he laughed, "the baby."

"I won't show a bump for a while, Henry," she replied, "A little morning ride is just the thing."

They rode down the path that switch-backed down the hill and crossed the River Esk on a charming stone bridge. They could see peasants already beginning work in the fields. The scene was bucolic, the soft morning light illuminating Henry's patrimony to the finest possible effect. He thought of hiring a landscape painter to capture its beauty, and perhaps supplement the dusty old portraits.

Circling the hill crowned by the Dalkeith house, they came upon the family burial vault located in the center of a grove of trees in a small hollow. They dismounted and stood before the stone marked, 'Hew Campbell Scott,' in elegant script, freshly engraved. Elizabeth put both her arms around Henry as he stood for several minutes with head bowed. He didn't cry, but he remembered the debt he owed Craigie for managing Hew's proper burial. They remounted and returned to the house.

As they rode into the courtyard, the front door opened, and Craigie emerged. "Ah, there you are!" he said, hastening towards them.

"It's a fine morning, Mr. Craigie," replied Henry stepping down from Saucy, "What news?"

Craigie noticed Elizabeth's clothes as she dismounted. "Did we misplace your trunk, Duchess?"

She laughed and said, "We snuck out without disturbing anyone. I'm sure my trunk is near."

Craigie nodded, but said, "The locals know you've arrived. You'll be having visitors soon."

Elizabeth raised an eyebrow at this, and asked, "Where might I find my trunk, then?"

"Margaret is just inside, Duchess," Craigie replied, "She'll know." They would find over the next few weeks that Margaret Craigie was a marvel of administrative efficiency; Henry's cash had taken the paintbrush from her hand and liberated her management skills to full effect. Elizabeth sauntered off in her man clothes, and Henry and Craigie watched her disappear inside.

"It's a fine land," said Henry, holding the reins of both horses.

"I've always thought so," agreed Craigie, who then yelled, "Bob!"

An older man appeared around the edge of the house, dressed in the plain clothes of a hostler or outdoor servant. He walked with a peculiar rolling gait, and he eyed Henry up and down. Bob had been at Dalkeith for many years, but this was his first look at the Duke of Buccleuch.

"See to His Grace's horses," said Craigie, and Bob took the reins from Henry and led both horses towards the barn. His mouth said nothing, but his eyes missed nothing.

"What's the next step?" asked Henry as they turned towards the house.

"Cash is king," said Craigie briskly, "Help is arriving, mostly household help at first, but then workmen will come who can make repairs. Who should direct them?" he asked as he held the door for Henry.

"Elizabeth," was his firm reply, "but she'll take suggestions from you and Margaret, I'm sure."

As Henry entered the empty foyer, a flood of light nearly blinded him coming from the large drawing room to his right. All the tall drapes had been pulled back and bright morning sunlight filled the unused room. Dust motes flew thick, backlit by the strong rays, creating a magical effect that made him sneeze, suddenly and violently, three times.

"Sorry about the state of the house," Craigie said, "We thought we'd have more time."

"I understand," said Henry, wiping his nose with his handkerchief, "Thanks for the quick reply to my letter."

Craigie nodded as they stood illuminated in the dust-filled drawing room. "We have much to discuss, but first, we'll see to your comfort."

"Mr. Craigie, Elizabeth and I found Hew this morning," said Henry, "I must thank you again for taking care of his last journey."

"It was an honor, Your Grace," nodded Craigie somberly, thinking back those many months to a more difficult time for both. Henry's poise that morning in Dover had reassured Craigie considerably; he'd feared a spoiled child who took after his unreliable stepfather. The success or failure of Craigie's estate administration critically depended on how the young Duke would behave after his impending Majority.

Frances appeared in the doorway of the drawing room, took one step into the bright light and had to put a hand to her forehead to shade her eyes.

"Good morning, Frances!" called Henry brightly, hoping she'd shaken her upset.

"Good morning," replied Frances, but giving no hint as to her mood.

"That reminds me," said Henry, turning to Craigie, "Do you have writing materials?"

"Certainly," he nodded, "Right now?"

"Yes, I'd like to send a letter to Mr. Smith," Henry nodded vigorously, and Craigie left swiftly.

"Do I remind you of letters, Henry?" asked Frances, raising her eyebrows at him.

"Today you do, yes," nodded Henry, smiling at her. He was gratified to see her give him a small smile in return.

"Let me write it for you," she offered, "Do you think Mr. Smith will recognize my hand?"

"I'm not sure, Frances, but I'd be honored," Henry replied, further relieved that his sister didn't seem angry. He walked over to a large piece of covered furniture and seized a corner of the dusty canvas. Turning his head away, he pulled it away with a flourish and a cloud of dust.

"Just what I was looking for!" exclaimed Henry, and then he sneezed again. For lying beneath was a huge, ornately carved wooden desk. It appeared centuries old.

Craigie returned with the writing supplies and deposited them on the desk. He admired the old wood for a moment as Henry pulled up a chair for Frances. She immediately began setting up the writing materials and prepared a quill.

"I'll go see about breakfast," said Craigie, moving towards the door.

"Can you send someone with a spot of tea?" asked Henry automatically, and Craigie had nodded and was gone before Henry caught himself. He missed Cook; here he was treating his Estate Administrator as his house servant. He winced but said nothing.

"I'm ready," said Frances, inked quill in hand.

"Dear Mr. Smith," Henry began, "I hope this letter finds you well."

Frances' quill scratched across the page quickly, and she looked up.

"We arrived at Dalkeith yesterday, much sooner than expected," continued Henry. He peered over her shoulder and observed her clear, even penmanship marching horizontally across the page. "Please join us at your earliest convenience. Bring several copies of your book."

Frances was just finishing the letter when there was an authoritative knock on the door. Henry walked through the foyer and opened it to reveal a tall clergyman in a black frock coat. His walking stick was poised to rap again when he saw Henry. The man had a ruddy complexion and a prominent nose, which he managed to look down despite being just a bit taller than Henry. The man exuded moral authority and a certain supercilious air.

"Good day, sir, I'm Henry Scott," greeted Henry, stepping back to invite the man in.

"Your Grace, I am honored to meet you," said the clergyman, "I am Reverend Alexander Carlyle of Inveresk. I heard you'd arrived."

"A pleasure to meet you Reverend," replied Henry politely.

"The Duke answers his own door?" asked Carlyle dubiously, looking down his nose again.

"Today he does," Henry nodded, "We're just getting organized."

Frances entered the foyer from the drawing room, drawing Carlyle's immediate interest. "May I present my sister, Lady Frances Scott," introduced Henry, and he could see the minister was impressed when she curtsied and said, "Welcome to our home, Reverend Carlyle." His whole demeanor visibly softened.

"Thank you, Lady Frances," he said, "You make this dusty old room seem bright and new."

Frances smiled at the compliment and said, "The dust will be gone in a twinkle, I assure you."

"How long might you stay at Dalkeith?" ventured Carlyle, but didn't get an answer as Elizabeth, properly dressed, swept into the room.

"This is my wife, Duchess Elizabeth Montagu Scott," said Henry, "Elizabeth, this is Reverend Carlyle of, of, ..."

"Inveresk," finished Carlyle, doubly impressed by Elizabeth, and giving her a bow, "It's an exquisite honor to make your acquaintance, Duchess."

"Welcome, Reverend," she said as she curtsied, "Can I get you some refreshment?"

"No, thank you," he responded graciously, then looked at Henry and said in a low voice, "Have you no servants at all?"

"Why hello, Reverend," said Margaret Craigie warmly, as she entered from the direction of the kitchen, followed by her husband, "You're just in time for tea!"

"Please, everyone, let's sit in the kitchen," invited Craigie, pointing them out of the sunlit drawing room and getting them seated around the long table. It was a decidedly informal reception, but there were two teen girls helping Margaret and they quickly had tea in front of all of them. Carlyle smiled when asked about sugar and held up two fingers. Soon there were fragrant biscuits as well.

"Your Grace," Carlyle began, "what was your impression of France?"

Henry noted the distinguished clergyman's use of the honorific, and again was uncomfortable with it, especially coming from a religious authority. He was a duke, not a deity.

He replied, "Reverend Carlyle, please call me Duke, or Duke Henry."

"Thank you... Duke Henry," nodded the Reverend, pleased.

"I have mixed impressions," said Henry, taking up his question, "France is poorer than England, despite having much better farmland. The Catholicism of Toulouse was at complete odds with the atheism we encountered in Paris."

Carlyle nodded slowly, and Henry expected a follow-on question about religion. Instead, Carlyle asked, "How did you find your tutor, Mr. Smith?" His tone was even, his pronunciation clear, and despite his Scots accent, it was evident that Alexander Carlyle was an accomplished orator.

"A more decent, cordial, and learned man I can't imagine," replied Henry, "I was fortunate that Charles chose him."

"We all thought it an odd choice," said Carlyle, "What do you think of his book, his theory of sentiments?"

Henry sensed he was being tested, but said honestly, "At first I was intimidated; now I consider it the best book ever written." Carlyle's eyebrows shot up questioningly, so Henry hastily added, "After the Bible, of course."

Carlyle smiled, draining tension from everyone around the table who listened carefully as the Reverend probed the young Duke. "His book has merit," he acknowledged, "Not enough God in it, though. Smith is too close to that infidel Hume."

"Reverend, I know we've just met," spoke up Elizabeth pleasantly, "but I know that particular infidel. Mr. Hume is a gracious, kind, and accomplished man. We all love him."

Rather than be offended, Carlyle seemed pleased by Elizabeth's firm defense of Hume. "I yield the point willingly, Duchess, in fact, I agree." He reached for a second biscuit as the first was just crumbs on his saucer. "Hume is amiable, too amiable, which makes his doctrines all the more insidious."

"While in London, Elizabeth and I met Ben Franklin, the American Representative," interjected Frances, alertly diverting the subject away from Hume.

Carlyle was pleased to be diverted, something about Frances' pert manner seemed to charm the man. "And your thoughts, my Lady?" he asked, giving her his full attention while taking a small bite of his biscuit.

"He is humorous and kind," said Frances, looking at Elizabeth for agreement and finding it.

"Humorous, but with such depth behind the twinkle," added Elizabeth, "Friendly and able; I'm sure Mr. Franklin serves the Americans well."

Craigie spoke up, adding, "Reverend Carlyle has met Ben Franklin. He also met Charles Townshend when he visited in 1759."

"What was your impression of Charles, Reverend?" asked Henry.

Carlyle put his biscuit down and raised both hands theatrically, loving an audience and always ready to perform. "Like a meteor, Charles dazzled for a moment, but the brilliancy soon faded away, and left no very strong impression." He ended with his hands coming down and his voice trailing away, so that they all laughed.

"Reverend, you have a way with words," laughed Craigie, who had his own concerns about Charles. "Townshend went from here to Glasgow to hire Mr. Smith, some eight years ago now."

"Why did you think Mr. Smith an odd choice, Reverend?" asked Henry.

"A more absent man in company I never knew!" proclaimed Carlyle, "But he obviously had a quality student, Your Grace, er, Duke Henry."

"On Henry's quality we can all agree," said Frances with a smile, seeing another opportunity to be diplomatic. She didn't agree with the Reverend about Mr. Smith whatsoever, as he was a most observant man.

Carlyle set his teacup carefully on his saucer and rose to his feet. "It's wonderful to meet you, Duke, Duchess, and Lady Frances," he intoned, "Welcome to Scotland, and to your estates. Will I see you all in church?"

"Now, now, Reverend," said Margaret, "Let them move in first. We'll see you soon."

Henry stood, and everyone followed suit. "We are pleased by your visit, Reverend Carlyle. I hope you will attend my birthday party in September?"

Carlyle nodded, pleased. "Invitation accepted, good day to you all." He turned on his heel and left the room, followed by Margaret to see him out.

She returned just they had all resumed their seats, and said, "Just like the man! But he's a good minister; well-regarded by everyone. I can tell he likes you."

"Mr. Craigie, how many people live on Buccleuch land, all told?" asked Henry abruptly.

"More than a thousand souls, Henry," replied Craigie, "In your care financially; in the Reverend's care spiritually."

"Come, John," admonished his wife, putting her hand on his shoulder, "They are mostly in *your* care. You are the manager here."

"Hear, hear," said Elizabeth, and Henry nodded his agreement. Craigie looked at his wife with affection.

"My John is appreciated, by me, by everyone," said Margaret, "Now, time to tour the house! The balance of the morning was spent exploring the vast mansion, opening rooms that had been shuttered for many years, viewing old paintings, and opening dusty drapes to let the light back in after long absence. Only a tiny portion of the house was currently in use as the Craigie's residence. Henry could tell by Craigie's manner that he assumed Henry would never see these rooms again, once he returned to London after his birthday.

CHAPTER 55

HENRY DUNDAS, SOLICITOR *July 1767*

Charles sat at his desk in his office at Adderbury, with Caroline perched on a nearby chair. A blank page sat before him, inkpot to his right, as he took quill in hand. In the upper right corner, he wrote the date: July 4, 1767. He left the quill tip too long on the paper, resulting in a large ink spot that obscured the last digit. He sighed and pulled out a fresh sheet.

"I miss Frances," he muttered, "it's been some time since I put pen to paper."

"Ask if William went with them," ordered Caroline, "First thing you say, Charles."

"Now Caroline, would you like to write the letter?" he asked, extending the quill towards her.

"Of course not, it must come from the man in the family," she replied tartly, "You must be stern."

"I think a carrot is the better approach, dear," said Charles.

"Carrots? You write, I'll tell you what to say," replied Caroline dismissively.

"Seems like a distinction without a difference," he replied, shaking his head.

"Rise to the occasion, Charles!" Caroline snapped, "Their secret escape to Scotland is all about that grasping commoner. He's after the family jewels, for God's sake! Do something!"

"Caroline, dear," soothed Charles, "It's just young love gone astray. This William fellow wooed young Frances with his violin. You know musicians."

"Start writing and I'll tell you what to change," she said, sitting back in the upholstered chair.

"Yes dear," he said resignedly, and dipped his quill in the ink.

• • • •

TEN DAYS LATER, HENRY and Elizabeth sat side by side in the big drawing room with the ornate desk. They were examining a detailed map of the estate as workmen came and went. The restoration of one wing of the mansion was well underway, and the interior of the house showed significant improvement under the direction, mostly, of Elizabeth and Margaret Craigie.

"A walking path along here, I think," she said, pointing to the map while Henry nodded.

Bob appeared at the door, waving an envelope. "A letter, Your Grace!"

Henry gestured him in and took the letter from the man. Bob had a wobbly walk from a long-ago leg injury, but his manner was comical because he always had an optimistic outlook no matter the weather. Henry smiled at his back as he departed.

"Charles," he said to Elizabeth, looking at the seal. The drawing room was too busy for sufficient privacy, so they walked outside and strolled down the long lane between the columns of tall trees. Henry broke the seal and removed three sheets from the envelope.

"July 4," he read, "Ten days ago. Dear Henry." He examined the page, and then the other two, and turned to Elizabeth. "This is in Charles' own hand, no clerk, him to me."

"Do you want to read it privately?" she offered, but he shook his head.

"This affects us both," he said, and returned to the first page and began reading as they walked slowly down the lane in dappled sunlight. "I hope this finds you well at Dalkeith," Henry read, "Look for us there by the first of September to help celebrate your big day."

"That's cutting it a bit close," observed Elizabeth.

"No rush, frankly," replied Henry, and he continued reading, "Your sudden departure from London surprised us. We can only assume that you indulged Frances' desire to go along. Your mother and I, despite our ruffled feathers, agree that perhaps this vacation will be good for Frances. If you could be so gracious to confirm our understanding by the earliest post, it would ease your mother's mind considerably. Especially, reassure her that the young musician, William, did not go with you to Scotland. She has it in her head that it might explain the secretive way you left us." Henry interrupted his narration to share a long look with Elizabeth. How would he answer this letter, or would he? He turned to the second page.

· · · ·

TEN DAYS EARLIER, CHARLES said, "See? A softer touch is better."

Caroline scowled and said, "That man William is a greedy pirate with an eye on our fortune. Stating that fact clearly is not inappropriate, Charles. He's taking advantage of naïve young Frances."

"She may be naïve, but she has fine penmanship," said Charles ruefully as he made another ink spot at the start of his second page. He cut a new quill, took a fresh sheet, and pondered his next words.

"Is that all you're going to say?" asked Caroline impatiently.

"About William, yes," returned Charles firmly, "I must warn Henry about Craigie."

"Mr. Craigie always sends the money," said Caroline, "He is not the problem, Charles."

"Henry takes control of the entire estate on September 2, Caroline," Charles replied with an edge to his voice. "I suggest that fact is at least as important as Frances' love life."

Caroline jumped to her feet in anger and shouted, "I'm shocked! Shocked! You worry more about money than your daughter's chastity!"

"Oh, for heaven's sake, Caroline," said Charles, exasperated, "Has it ever occurred to you that Frances has a mind of her own? That she just wants to be happy?"

"Happy?" screeched Caroline, "Happy? What does *happy* have to do with it? What about *our* happiness, for God's sake?" She glared at Charles and then stormed out of the room.

Charles sighed and propped his chin on both hands on the desk, staring at the page before him.

• • • •

TEN DAYS LATER, HENRY resumed reading Charles' letter as they walked slowly down the Dalkeith lane. "In my experience, John Craigie is a reliable man and able administrator. He is, however, somewhat given to alarmism. Don't let him raise your fears. All the roofs are not leaking."

Henry looked at his wife and asked, "What is your impression of Craigie?"

"Reliable, able, yes," she agreed, "He seems honest. The tenants we met don't seem to fear him."

"Good point," Henry nodded, "He isn't a tyrant. Do you think he exaggerates?"

"We can visit some tenants when it's raining, I suppose," she suggested.

Henry resumed reading. "Some think all caution useless; others think all confidence is dangerous. I wish to take the middle way, so should you. Hold with firmness the freedom of your own judgment, and the command of your conduct, as that is the first requisite to both real greatness and true satisfaction. Let each man have the rank he can fill, and no more."

"Rank he can fill?" asked Elizabeth with a puzzled frown, "Is he talking about Craigie, or William?

"I'm not sure," Henry said, "I think he's saying, 'play both ends against the middle.' Typical Charles."

• • • •

CHARLES FINALLY FINISHED the letter, blew carefully to ensure the ink was dry, and then carefully folded the pages in thirds. He slipped it into an envelope, dripped sealing wax on the flap, and pressed his signet ring into the seal. "Cook!" he shouted, disturbing the silence.

"Yes?" replied Cook, coming to the door in seconds.

"A letter, to go out immediately," instructed Charles, holding it extended in his hand as he remained seated at the desk.

"How timely," observed Cook, taking it from him, "I was just about to accompany Lady Dalkeith to London."

"To London? Right now?" asked Charles, thinking that Caroline must really be angry.

"Yes, she wishes to play cards at Court with her sister Mary Coke," replied Cook, pretending he was none the wiser about her being upset.

"Right away, Cook," said Charles resignedly, returning his chin to his hands, elbows propped on the desk. Soon he was all alone in the big house, save the servants.

• • • •

HENRY AND ELIZABETH turned to walk back towards the house, and Henry returned the letter to its envelope and then to his pocket.

"All in all, that's a good letter," said Elizabeth, "Frances can stay until September."

"He's nervous about Craigie," said Henry, "Charles knows I'm discovering all the things that he hid from me."

"Wonderful though William may be, we all agree that it was a mistake to invite him," said Elizabeth bluntly, "How should you answer Charles?" Before Henry could answer, she put a hand on his arm and pointed with the other. In the distance they could see Frances walking slowly with William, on another path, clearly conversing but not holding hands. "Speaking of..."

"Their love seems so reasonable, but it isn't," said Henry.

"Is it reasonable to indulge our passions?" she asked rhetorically.

"Within reason, of course," smiled Henry.

"As the Duke, you represent the very rules that keep them apart," observed Elizabeth, and the remark stung Henry. Before he could respond she was pointing again, this time at the far end of the lane behind them, where a carriage behind a two-horse team approached at a trot. Standing aside, the polished carriage pulled abreast of them and stopped. A handsome man, well-dressed and accompanied by a lady sitting on the far side, smiled out at them.

"Good day to you!" greeted the man through the carriage window, "Have I found the Duke of Buccleuch?"

"You have indeed," Henry replied, "How can I help you?"

"I'm Henry Dundas, Solicitor of Scotland," the man replied, "We're from Edinburgh, come to make introduction. Are you coming or going?"

Henry remembered Adam asking the same question that last morning with Voltaire. He smiled as he replied, "Please proceed sir, we'll meet you at the house," pointing politely up the lane. The man smiled, tipped his hat to Elizabeth, and the carriage rolled on.

"Should I have introduced you through the carriage window?" wondered Henry, but Elizabeth laughed and shook her head.

"We'll meet them soon enough!" she said as she hooked her arm in his and they followed the carriage up their lane. Arriving at the driveway five minutes later, they encountered Bob leading the couple back out of the house.

"Your man showed us the facilities," greeted Dundas, "It's a long ride from Edinburgh." A young woman of Frances' age stepped up beside him. "And this is my wife, Elizabeth."

"Well, that's just remarkable," said Henry, "I am Henry Scott, and this is my wife, *Elizabeth!*"

Elizabeth Dundas burst into laughter and clapped her hands. "A pair of pairs! How delightful!" she exclaimed with a childlike exuberance, bouncing on her toes. She seemed very young.

"A coincidence indeed," agreed Dundas with a broad smile, "I take it as a good sign."

"It's an honor to meet you both," said Elizabeth, "My family name is Montagu, we are recently wed in London."

"What brings the Solicitor to visit?" asked Henry, oblivious that they were still standing in the courtyard.

"Your presence, Duke Henry," replied Dundas, "I am the man who will certify your Majority."

"Then, you and Elizabeth must also attend Henry's birthday party," invited Elizabeth, "September second."

"We accept with great pleasure," nodded Dundas, and then Henry led them into the house behind a group of workmen carrying buckets of paint.

In the distance, Frances and William saw the carriage arrive, the occupants meet Henry and Elizabeth, and then go inside the house. The couple continued their slow walk along the path, William pacing with his hands behind his back, Frances with her fingers laced in front of her. The path entered a glade of trees, concealing them from the house.

"William, about Hawick...," began Frances tentatively. She came to a stop and turned to look up at him.

"I'm glad you came to me, Frances," he said immediately, as he'd agonized over what he should say if she ever asked him, deciding that his very first words must be to reassure her.

"I am too," she said gratefully, and extended her hand. He took it in his with a flood of relief. "I'm mortified," she continued, "but glad anyway. Doesn't that seem strange?"

"Our love sure seems right to me," William blurted, "Even though we all pretend it's wrong. Even you and I, Frances."

They continued walking, very slowly, through the dappled shade of the friendly glade, hand in hand. "You are strong, stronger than me," said Frances softly, and despite the obvious physical truth, she wasn't talking about muscles.

He stopped her again, before they left the trees, and took both of her hands in his and faced her. "If we can't marry, I can't stay here," he said plainly, sorrowfully.

"Well, don't we all plan to go back to London?" asked Frances, hoping his words weren't as final as they sounded.

"I've no place, here or there," he replied, keeping hold of her hands.

"William, Henry is the Duke. I'm sure he can find a place for you," she replied, trying to sound optimistic.

"Henry is kind; he was kind when we were boys, and I was just the cook's son. The other boys weren't." said William, "But I can't be his servant."

"Don't look at it that way!" said Frances plaintively, looking up at him and moving closer, "He will find you employment."

"It would be torture to see you marry another, Frances," he said simply, and saw her eyes fill with tears. She threw her arms around his neck and hugged him close. He put his arms around her and hugged her back, feeling her body tremble against him.

"I want to marry you, William!" she sobbed into his shirt.

He lifted her wet face and kissed her. "I love you," he said tenderly, "But your mother will never accept me. We can't change the rules."

"Rules!" wailed Frances, tears renewed, "Keeping us from love! It's unnatural!" She didn't let him go, so he didn't either. He kissed her again, and then again, and finally pulled away and took her hand in his. They resumed their slow walk, with Frances drying her eyes with a lace handkerchief.

"Too many rules," agreed William somberly, head down, "But that's why I have to go."

Inside the newly renovated drawing room, a servant served tea to Dundas and his young wife as they sat across a low table from Henry and Elizabeth. Margaret Craigie entered with a plate of warm biscuits; she placed them on the table and turned to leave.

"Margaret, can you find your husband?" asked Henry, "Then join us if you can." Pleased by this, Margaret bustled off to collect John.

"John Craigie is a good man," volunteered Dundas, "You can believe what he tells you."

"Between the two of you, I hope to get an objective view of the situation here," Henry explained.

"I think Craigie will agree what the problem is, Your Grace," replied Dundas, "Charles Townshend has bled your estate dry to support you in England."

Henry and Elizabeth were shocked into silence at this, causing Elizabeth Dundas to look at her husband quizzically. She did not typically listen to her husband's business details but could readily see the effect of his words on their hosts. "Sorry to be so blunt," said Dundas when they offered him no ready answer, "Ah, here's John."

Margaret and John Craigie entered the room, and he dragged a chair over and seated his wife courteously before fetching a second chair for himself. "Good to see you Dundas, Elizabeth," he nodded as he sat down. He knew the Solicitor well.

"Craigie," asked Dundas, keeping an eye on Henry, "What do you think about Townshend?"

Instead of answering the dangerous question, Craigie addressed himself to Henry and said, "Don't worry, Dundas here knows all about the estate. It's a good portion of Scotland, after all."

"I know the yields of the farms," Dundas hastily added, "I do not know your family finances."

"Thank you for clarifying that," said Henry slowly, "as Solicitor, do you have concerns?"

"I have many concerns," nodded Dundas, "I rank them by importance, so I can address them one by one. As regards the Buccleuch estates, I have one *main* concern." He lifted his right hand, index finger poised just above his head and paused for dramatic effect. He wasn't the government's lawyer for nothing, Dundas could put on a show equal even to Charles Townshend.

"Which is?" prompted Elizabeth when his dramatic pause seemed overlong.

"Leave some capital in Scotland, for God's sake!" finished Dundas pointedly.

"Hear, hear!" said Craigie, almost rising to his feet, but then he sank sheepishly back into his chair, embarrassed by his intemperate enthusiasm. "I will, of course, faithfully execute your instructions, Your Grace," he added humbly.

"Enough with the 'Your Grace,' said Henry abruptly, "As long as we're not in public, call me Duke Henry."

Dundas smiled; he liked this young Duke who was only a few years younger than himself. "We Scots are blunt of speech, perhaps a bit rude in our manner," he said, "But we are Scots, through and through. Your estates could yield half again as much if you invest properly. Invest here, in Scotland!"

"What is your second concern?" prompted Elizabeth, but the Solicitor was too savvy to push too far, too fast. His other complaints all stemmed from the first.

Dundas lifted his eyebrows and asked brightly, "Have you seen Edinburgh yet?"

A week later, with the weather remaining fine, they took the coach to Edinburgh to meet Dundas, taking William, Frances, and Craigie with them. With his wife, Dundas led them on a tour of Edinburgh Castle. They walked the Royal Mile, which encompassed most of the town's business center. Everywhere they went, Dundas met people he knew and introduced the Scotts. Henry and Elizabeth concluded that Dundas was respected and popular, and that his pretty wife loved the social aspects of her husband's blossoming career, but not the intellectual part. Tired from hiking up the hill to the castle gate, they found a tavern and soon had glasses before them.

Dundas stood and raised his glass of claret, "A toast to Duke Henry!" he said, and everyone raised their glasses.

"To the Duke's wife!" toasted Henry, grinning at Elizabeth.

Somebody on the far side of the crowded room took up a violin, and William perked up at the sound. Frances, careful to sit across from him and not next to him for appearances sake, smiled at his reaction.

"William!" called Dundas from the opposite end of the table.

"Sir?" said William, startled, as he'd tried to keep a low profile all day.

"How do you find Scotland?" asked Dundas.

"Impressed," nodded William, "Thanks for including me."

"We were about to nickname you, 'Will B. Silent," joked Dundas, "Elizabeth tells me you are a whiz with the fiddle. Speak!"

Frances looked at William nervously as he put his glass down and prepared to answer. First, he looked at Elizabeth and said, "That is a fine compliment, thank you," before raising his eyes to meet the brash lawyer's. "My English accent doesn't go over so well, I'm afraid."

"My apologizes," said Dundas, smiling with a dip of his head, "What you say is unfortunately true." He circled his finger to include everyone at the table and added, "Not all, of course."

"William played beautifully at the Wedding Ball," volunteered Frances proudly.

"Attended by King George the Third himself, I might add!" said Elizabeth, smiling at William.

"You played for the King of England?" asked Elizabeth Dundas, incredulous, looking anew at the quiet Englishman.

"Well, I was playing for Henry and Elizabeth," William replied, "It was their wedding. Then the King showed up and said it was the best party in town!" Everyone laughed, reassuring William and thus, Frances.

"What academy taught you?" asked Elizabeth Dundas.

Without a beat of hesitation, William answered, "Buckingham School for Boys, milady."

In the background, the violin music stopped. Elizabeth stood and said, "William, let's see if they'll let us play!"

Delighted by the prospect, Dundas stood and said, "I'll ask for you!" Looking at William, he grinned and added, "They might say no to the English!"

Soon William and Elizabeth both had violins in their hands, and the tavern patrons all turned to listen. William began with a familiar upbeat tune, and Elizabeth joined. The crowd clapped in appreciation when they heard the quality of the music, and of course, the rare quality of the three lovely young women. Soon they had everyone stomping to the tune, and Dundas began dancing with his wife, who flowered at all the attention. Henry danced with Frances, and many of the patrons joined in, dancing however they could raise their heels to the catchy music. Their informal debut into Edinburgh society was thus a rousing success.

Chapter 56

P ROPERTY WHICH EVERY MAN HAS *August 1767*
Elizabeth rose from her bath and her Scottish maid Flora helped her into a thick robe. As she did so, Elizabeth saw that Flora noticed the small bump, the beginnings of a baby.

"Not a word, mind you," said Elizabeth, catching the girl's eye.

"It's a blessing, Duchess," replied Flora with a nod, "I'm happy for you."

"Thank you, Flora. Promise me your confidence. Not a word, not even your mother," she said, trying to be firm without being stern.

"I promise," smiled Flora, making a key gesture with her fingers as if locking her mouth shut.

"An heir to the House of Buccleuch is big news, as you might imagine," Elizabeth explained, as she sat before the mirror in her robe and began to brush her wet hair.

Henry appeared at the door, poked his head inside and asked, "May I intrude?"

"You are always welcome, husband," replied Elizabeth, talking to his reflection in her mirror as her back was towards the door. Henry entered and pulled up a chair next to his wife, who said, "You may go now, Flora." The maid nodded and slipped out the door.

"Ready for a difficult conversation?" asked Henry as Elizabeth continued brushing. She gave him one eye and he announced the difficult subject, "William."

"And thus, Frances," she replied, pursing her lips in the mirror as she tamed her wet hair.

"I need your thoughts," said Henry, nodding, his head close to hers.

"On what can be done?" she said, anticipating his thoughts.

"We lured William into an impossible situation," he said, shaking his head regretfully.

"Frances lured him," Elizabeth said flatly, "They love each other, Henry."

Henry saw that most of her left breast was showing through the gap in her robe. "What chance have our feeble brains when our hearts are so inflamed?" he murmured, leaning closer and kissing her ear.

"You wax poetic husband," she said, primly adjusting her robe, "but you don't solve the problem."

"If William feels about Frances as I do about you..." he said, kissing her ear, her cheek.

"I'm amazed they haven't done it already," said Elizabeth bluntly, making Henry sit bolt upright. But then he nodded, knowing how much he'd worried about that very thing.

"William is mocking us," he said.

"Mocking? I don't see that," she said, putting down her brush and turning towards him. "He is a gentleman."

Henry nodded and sat back in his chair. "He is tall, well-formed, musical. Educated. Diligent, reliable, amiable." He ticked off each virtue by opening a finger of his closed right hand, then used his left as William's virtues mounted. "He mocks the whole idea that some class of elites, such as us, are naturally superior and should rule society and government."

"Says the Duke," smiled Elizabeth, putting her hands on his knees.

"I know, I'm the one who's supposed to be naturally superior," Henry nodded, "Yet William is. Perversely, he's the one who is not good enough to marry my sister. Who, by the way, is mad about him."

"William is *not* your typical commoner," she replied, keeping her hands on his knees, "and he has a duke's education. Mrs. Lewis did well by her son. This is a peculiar case. You and William, two unique individuals, do not represent the whole system of hereditary property."

"Sure we do," disagreed Henry promptly, "and he did not attend Eton. But what do we do about him? Unique, non-typical, William?"

"Let me talk to Frances, privately," said Elizabeth, not having an answer but settling on the next step. She took up the brush again.

"Yes, get her thoughts," agreed Henry, "and soon." He leaned in and nuzzled her ear. "There's another problem," he whispered, his hand slipping into the robe that had fallen open again.

"Problem? One I can help with?" she said coyly, lips turning upwards.

"We're falling in love with Scotland," he murmured as she put down the brush and let his hand explore, "but the Scots aren't so fond of the pillaging English. Can you help with that?"

She turned her face to him and kissed him. "We're both Scots, they know that. They love us."

"Scots with English accents, they hate us doubly," he softly disagreed, pulling the robe off her shoulders and kissing her again and again.

· · · ·

MID-AFTERNOON A WEEK later, Henry brushed Saucy in the barn, feeding him carrots and kissing the big horse on his nose. Elizabeth entered and gave a carrot to Intrepid, who nickered at the sight of her. "You're up late," Henry observed, as she'd slept very late that day even though the weather remained fine.

"My body is telling me to rest," she said, kissing Intrepid as Henry had kissed his stallion.

"It's a glorious day, do you care to ride?" asked Henry, but she shook her head.

"I could, but I find myself reluctant," she said, "Protective, maybe."

"That seems natural," he agreed, secretly pleased as he felt protective too.

"With all your efforts, I'm surprised I don't have three or four babies in there," she smirked.

"One at a time, dear!" he said, and laughed. He returned Saucy to his stall, and they left the barn, Elizabeth linking her arm in his as they stepped into the warm August sunshine. They emerged in front of the house as a carriage pulled into the courtyard. The door opened, and Adam Smith stepped down and stretched, both arms extended high over his head.

"Mr. Smith!" exclaimed Henry, "So good to see you." Henry turned and called back over his shoulder, "Bob!"

Bob appeared almost at once, his peculiar rolling gait was comical, but it conveyed him at deceptive speed. He quickly helped the carriage driver unload Adam's trunk.

"Hello Henry! Hello, Duchess!" greeted Adam with a broad smile of genuine pleasure at the sight of them, "So, this is Dalkeith," he added, looking at the huge house that still showed some signs of its previous neglect.

"Good to see you, Mr. Smith," returned Elizabeth warmly, offering him her hands which he took in both of his while he bowed low.

"We're renovating, Mr. Smith," said Henry, "But we have a room all ready for you." He nodded to Bob, confirming the man knew where Adam's trunk should go.

Margaret emerged from the house and said, "Oh, this must be Mr. Smith!"

She smiled and grabbed Adam by the elbow and steered him for the door, saying, "Come, Mr. Smith, let's get you settled."

Henry laughed at her efficient informality, and called out, "You're in good hands, Mr. Smith! We'll wait for you in the drawing room."

As Margaret and Adam disappeared into the house, another servant appeared to help Bob with the trunk. As Bob waited for him to approach, Henry asked him, "How did you get that peculiar walk, Bob?"

"Falling from the mainmast of a British man 'o war," replied Bob with a grin, and then he rolled off bearing Adam's trunk to his room while Henry and Elizabeth gaped at each other.

An hour later, Adam, Henry, and Elizabeth sat at tea in the newly refurbished right-side drawing room, long abandoned but now the center of activity in their rekindled Dalkeith. Margaret arrived from the kitchen with a plate of warm biscuits, and Adam happily took two. She sat to join them and poured herself a cup of tea. By this time, everyone, including the just-arrived Adam, knew that Margaret was the head of the Dalkeith household.

"These biscuits are divine, Mrs. Craigie," Adam proclaimed as he finished his first bite.

"Do they compare to English biscuits, Mr. Smith?" she replied, gratified by his sincere praise.

"Favorably," Adam mumbled, his mouth full of his second bite.

"I have cake in the oven," said Margaret, rising to leave, "I'll leave you to catch up."

"Cake!" smiled Adam, "Things just keep getting better."

"Is everything well at home, Mr. Smith?" asked Elizabeth, finishing her first nibble and putting the biscuit on her saucer.

"My mother is well in Kirkaldy," nodded Adam, "and I'm working on a book I began in France."

"A book about why some countries are rich, and others poor," said Henry, remembering several discussions on the subject with his tutor.

"Yes," smiled Adam, remembering their talks as well, "An inquiry into the wealth of nations, and what makes them so."

"If it's as successful as your first book, you'll go down in history, Mr. Smith," said Elizabeth.

Adam gave her one of his famous smiles; the charm of this plain-spoken man was that he could give people his undivided attention, and then warm them to the bone with his genuine, empathetic smile. Only the envious or dogmatic could find fault with his person; for the same reason his students always spoke highly of him. When Adam Smith left the University of Glasgow rather abruptly in December 1763, his students refused his refund of the balance of their tuition. If he *didn't* give his undivided attention, it was because he was focused on other thoughts, which made boring or bombastic people consider him absent in their company. "One can only hope," he said at last, charming Elizabeth and being utterly charmed in return.

"You are just in time to help us with a vexing problem," said Henry, missing all this.

"Farm improvements?" asked Adam, thinking his former student's head must be spinning as he learned the economics of his vast estate.

"That's less vexing," said Henry, "It's about my friend William. He and Frances are in love with each other."

Adam understood the implication immediately. "They can't marry across the ranks?"

"Exactly," said Henry, "It seems so hurtful to come between them, but we can't see a solution."

Adam nodded slowly, reflecting, for almost a minute before responding slowly, "This disposition to admire the rich and despise the poor, though necessary to maintain the order of society, is at the same time the greatest corruption of our moral sentiments."

Henry nodded gravely and Elizabeth asked, "Why is it necessary, Adam?"

Adam started just a fraction at her use of his first name, which was very rare, such was his gravitas in company. But he didn't hesitate in his response, "To protect the property of the few against the desires of the many. The indignation of the poor, through want and envy, would cause them to invade the possessions of others."

"And we'd end up with lives nasty, brutish, and short," said Elizabeth in agreement.

"You've read Thomas Hobbes," smiled Adam in admiration.

"She's much more than a pretty face," volunteered Henry, looking at his wife with love.

"I can see that," said Adam, then he continued, "Whenever there is great property, there is great inequality. Our entire social order is based on land."

"Not so different than France, really," Henry observed.

"Not much," agreed Adam, "the property which every man has in his own labor is the most sacred and inviolable. Labor, not land, is the original foundation of all other property."

"We discussed this in France," said Henry, explaining to Elizabeth, "Adam believes the farmer is more important than the farm."

"It would seem that both are necessary," Elizabeth replied.

"Indeed, Elizabeth," nodded Adam, "Two sides of the same coin."

"A coin is a good metaphor for your book about money," suggested Henry.

"Remember that money is not wealth, Henry," replied Adam, "Money facilitates, but never creates. Only human labor creates and produces. The land lies in its natural state without us."

"Is that why you call labor sacred?" asked Elizabeth, as he was always so reticent to discuss his religious beliefs that she wondered about his use of the word.

"Exactly why," said Adam, pleased. "Every person should have the liberty to choose their own work; create their own future, acquire property, pursue their success. In this way, we are all but one of the multitude, in no respect better than any other."

"But that's not the world we live in," said Henry.

"No," agreed Adam, "Guilds restrict labor; the nobility restricts land. Men like William pay the price."

They heard happy voices in the foyer; an instant later William and Frances entered the drawing room. "Mr. Smith! So glad to see you again!" Frances flew to Adam and gave him a hug, which embarrassed him a bit and pleased him enormously.

She released him and Adam extended his hand to William, the object of their recent discussion, and said, "Mr. Lewis, welcome to Scotland."

"It's a bonny place, Mr. Smith!" laughed William, adopting the local slang.

"Ah-ha, bonny indeed!" laughed Adam, "We're already making a proper Scot of him!"

He sensed that his last comment had reminded everyone of their predicament, so he added, "For as long as you're here, William, you are an honorary Scot."

"Now if only we could lose these English accents," mused Henry with a smirk.

"Perhaps we could wear the tartan!" offered Frances brightly, "We'd look like proper Scots."

"No, that would make you look like proper Highlanders," laughed Adam, "You'd scare folks!"

"We're off to the kitchen for a bite to eat," said Frances, "See you at supper!" and the young couple left. Elizabeth found herself wishing that Frances and Williams could at least hold hands, but they did not.

In the void left by their departure, the three sat looking at each other. "So," said Henry after a moment, "No ideas how to solve our problem?"

"Sadly, not a clue," returned Adam, shaking his head.

• • • •

TWO DAYS LATER, ADAM joined Henry and Craigie for a long ride through the estate, through the ripened fields turning gold before harvest. Elizabeth would have joined them but for the baby, which remained a secret as Flora was true to her promise. The riders paused at the crest of a stone bridge spanning a stream.

"What river is this?" asked Henry.

"The southern fork of the River Esk, which drains Dalkeith," informed Craigie.

Henry pointed towards a bucolic scene of sheep grazing in the lush riverside meadows. "Sheep turning grass into wool, I love it," he laughed, but saw that Craigie frowned instead.

"Well, Henry," he began slowly, so slowly that Henry said, impatiently, "Out with it, John."

"With proper drainage and enclosure, that meadow would grow grain," Craigie explained, "The sheep should graze the rocky hillsides. Then you'd have both grain *and* wool."

"There are rocks aplenty for fences," observed Henry, "Ditching is simple labor. It's just a matter of effort, you don't need money for that."

"Labor is capital," reminded Adam, "When farmers build fences they aren't farming. It's the same cost no matter how it's paid."

"And the tenant leases are too short," added Craigie, "Fences and drainage are improvements that pay off over years. It's not their land, and they know it."

"Bosh," said Henry, "That Armstrong fellow told me his family was generations on that land."

"Langholm is the ancient seat of the Armstrong clan," returned Craigie, trying to remain diplomatic, "Your estate came... much later."

Henry saw Adam looking at him, as if wondering what he had missed during all their time in France. "I feel sheepish about my sheep," he said, smiling, and thus reassured Adam and Craigie. Everyone knew the land did not belong to the tenants, so asking them to work extra would always be an imposition on their already difficult lives. Yet, they saw many fences during their ride, although often they were old and needed repair.

"You have hundreds of tenants, with hundreds of farms," Craigie reminded him, "with houses and barns," he added as they started their horses again, knowing that it wouldn't always be dry summer, and many roofs leaked.

Late in the day, the shadows stretched across the golden fields as they rode into the yard of Neil Armstrong's farm. He emerged from his small house, his wife and children beside him.

"Neil Armstrong, if I recall!" said Henry as they dismounted. It was obvious that Adam was very sore from their long day on horseback.

"Thankee for remembering, Your Grace," said Armstrong.

May I introduce my Glasgow tutor, Mr. Adam Smith," said Henry, as Adam limped over to meet Neil Armstrong. "Mr. Smith brought a gift for you," he added, smiling at his friend.

Adam removed a package wrapped in plain brown paper from one of his saddlebags and handed the parcel to the man without further ado. Armstrong unwrapped it hastily as his family looked on in growing excitement. It was a brand-new copy of Adam's *Theory of Moral Sentiments*.

"I've heard of this book!" said Armstrong excitedly, although his children seemed a bit disappointed. "It's for me? Why?"

"Henry asked me to bring it to you," replied Adam, simply.

"Next to my Bible, this is the finest gift I ever got," exclaimed Armstrong with a wide grin.

"Next to the Bible, this is the finest book I've ever read, Armstrong," said Henry, "Read it and you'll be smarter than that man Stewart."

"You giving Stewart one too?" asked Armstrong immediately.

"Not today, rest assured," laughed Henry, "Does your cousin Colin have room for us tonight?"

"Do you have a book for him?" Armstrong asked again with raised eyebrows.

"Yes, yes we do," nodded Henry as Adam patted his other saddlebag.

CHAPTER 57

WILD INDIANS IN AMERICA *August 1767*
The congregation was mostly assembled in the stout church at Inveresk as Reverend Alexander Carlyle, already standing in the pulpit, reviewed the notes of his sermon. He looked up as a murmur swept those already seated; Henry and Elizabeth stood momentarily in the broad doorway. Dressed in their finest, they created a sensation, or perhaps a spectacle, as they entered the church, followed by Frances, and then William. John and Margaret Craigie were next, and Carlyle waited as they found seats in the middle of the congregation. He noted with satisfaction that the young Duke didn't immediately command the front row. Several people moved to allow them to sit together.

Carlyle cleared his voice, a signal to begin, and all fell silent. "Peace be to you, and may God hold you all in the palm of His hand," he said, his stentorian Scot voice filling the chapel. He noticed that everyone was trying to sneak peeks at the Duke and Duchess, which was difficult for those seated in front. Carlyle yielded to the situation. "We are joined today by distinguished visitors," he intoned, "May I present Henry Scott, Third Duke of Buccleuch, and Elizabeth, Duchess of Buccleuch. Your Grace, Duchess, would you stand?"

Both stood as one, and the congregation swiveled so all heads faced them. There hadn't been a Duke in the church in over twenty years. Even more remarkable, especially to the women, was the elegant Elizabeth, and to a lesser extent, Frances. The details of their dress, hair, and manner were absorbed hungrily, food for a thousand female imaginations. Henry felt both proud yet pompous; there was something ridiculous about "ranks," as he and Elizabeth stood with heads held high.

"Thank you, Reverend Carlyle, for inviting us," said Elizabeth in a clear, gracious voice, and something of a sigh was audible. Elizabeth was beyond their experience; something they could barely imagine appearing suddenly before them, like an apparition. Henry and Elizabeth sat, and it was with reluctance that the congregation gave their attention back to Reverend Carlyle.

In the pulpit, Carlyle pushed the pages of his sermon aside. He opened his bible instead. "I read from the Book of Luke," Carlyle intoned, with a final glance down at Henry before bowing his head to read, "I arise and go to my father, and I will say to him, 'Father, I have sinned against heaven and before you. I am no longer worthy to be called your son. Treat me as one of your hired servants. And he arose and went to his father."

The congregation was silent, recognizing the verse and wondering where their pastor was taking it. Did it mean the Duke was coming back to Scotland to stay? Or that he was a sinner?

"But while he was still a long way off," continued Carlyle, reading with head bowed, "his father saw him and felt compassion, and ran and embraced him and kissed him. And the son said to him, 'Father, I have sinned against heaven and earth and before you. I am no longer worthy to be called your son."

Had he sinned? Henry wasn't sure the parable applied, but as Duke, he knew he represented more than just himself.

Carlyle looked up and scanned the congregation, which remained silent. Every eye was upon him, he held them in the palm of his hand. He continued reading, "The father said to his servants, 'Bring quickly the best robe, and put it on him, and put a ring on his hand, and shoes on his feet. And bring the fatted calf and kill it and let us eat and celebrate. For this my son was dead, and is alive again; he was lost, and is found."

Carlyle closed the Bible and caught Henry's eye from the pulpit and held it, giving him a slight nod. Elizabeth slipped her hand into Henry's. "We are pleased to receive you at Inveresk, Your Grace," said Carlyle, "We hope we will see you often. Now, I'll proceed with my sermon."

After the service, Reverend Carlyle stood at the door as his flock filed out. Henry and Elizabeth remained until last, with the Craigies, William, and Frances, but as they emerged, they saw that the entire congregation stood waiting in the courtyard to watch them leave. Behind the crowd Henry could see their glossy black coach, standing out among the humble wagons, buggies, and farm carts.

"I know this is your first visit to Scotland, Your Grace," said Carlyle, "but I couldn't resist reading that passage. We haven't seen a Duke here since your grandfather."

"It feels appropriate, Reverend," said Henry, "thanks for not reading the next passage in the story of the prodigal son."

"About the older brother?" asked Elizabeth.

"Yes," Henry nodded, "the resentful one."

The congregation parted to allow them a narrow aisle down the church steps and across the courtyard to their awaiting coach. Their footmen attended to the doors in proper order, and they boarded while everyone watched. As the coach pulled away, Frances waved out the window. They were celebrities, glamorous novelties, but also a portent of changing times ahead.

At dusk that night, Henry sat at a small desk in their temporary room at Dalkeith, reading a letter. He lit a candle as the light failed, and a knock came on the door. "Henry? Can we talk?" said William, his low voice muffled through the door.

Henry admitted his childhood friend. "Sure, I want to talk to you as well."

"You first then," said William, sitting in a straight-backed chair.

"No, I can tell you came for a reason," said Henry.

William nodded, took a deep breath, and said, "Frances." Henry sat in his chair looking at him, but when he didn't say anything, William continued, "I have an idea."

Henry raised his eyebrows, listening, but still offered no words.

"But first," said William, taking another deep breath before plunging on, "Is there any chance of me marrying Frances?"

Henry blanched, but there it was, the reason he'd been avoiding William for the past several days. He looked frankly at William and took a deep breath of his own. "I don't think so, William," he said at last, "It would cause heartache in the end, and I fear..."

William raised his hand to cut him off. "I understand," he said, "My whole life changed because of you, because of Elizabeth."

"It's not that I don't think you are good enough for my sister," Henry said, "You are, William."

This brought William up short, and a lump formed in his throat. "That means a lot, Henry," he said finally, but then added, "If we can't marry then I must go."

"I feel bad that you gave up your apprenticeship," said Henry, "I feel responsible somehow."

"I was free to choose," said William, "I chose to spend time with Frances. I wouldn't change a thing." He paused, keeping Henry's eye, then added, "So I'm going to America."

Henry was shocked, his mouth opened, closed, and then opened again as he found his voice. "America? You mean sail across the ocean?"

"That's what I mean," nodded William.

"Courage, William, that takes courage!" Henry exclaimed, clapping a hand on William's shoulder. "Are you sure?"

"Yes," said William, "I was hoping you could help me."

"I'll help however I can," said Henry, his mind in a whirl, "With regret at losing you, of course. Have you told this to Frances?"

"Not yet," William replied, "Could you lend me passage to New York, or Philadelphia?"

"Not lend, William, give," nodded Henry, "What else do you need?"

"A good set of leather-working tools, so I'll have my trade when I arrive," William said promptly, having thought long on the subject.

"Absolutely, can you get them in Edinburgh?" asked Henry.

"Yes," William nodded, "I'd like to make these arrangements quietly."

"Are you going to tell Frances at all?" Henry asked bluntly.

William paused, looking at Henry and then away, then back again. "I want to ask Frances to go with me," he blurted out.

"No!" said Henry shocked, "No! Have you already?"

William's face showed his disappointment at Henry's response, but he'd expected it. "Not a word, I wanted to ask you first."

Henry looked at his friend for a moment, shaking his head, then he admitted, "I'm afraid that she'll say yes."

"I hope she says yes," replied William, eagerly.

"No!" said Henry, springing to his feet and pacing the room. "I'd miss her terribly."

"I'll miss her terribly," said William, "But I can't stay here."

"I'm sure I could find you a place...," started Henry, but William held up his hand.

"Not if I can't marry Frances, Henry," responded William with finality.

Henry paced back and forth, fretting and thinking. "I'll buy the tools, pay your way to London, buy ship's fare," he agreed, but then looked at William and pleaded, "But don't ask Frances, you would separate her from all she has, all she knows."

William stood, nodding soberly, and said, "I wanted to ask you first. I owe you that."

Henry nodded, aware that his friend was not promising him anything regarding his sister. "When you have your tools, we'll call a carriage to return you to London."

"That's kind of you, Henry," said William, and he turned towards the door. Pausing, he added, "If I had it to do again, I would." He slipped out the door, closing it carefully behind him.

Henry resumed his pacing but was stopped by his reflection in the mirror. Staring at himself, he said, "Perhaps it's for the best." There was a tap at the door, and Elizabeth came in.

"Were you just talking with William?" she asked.

"He's going to America," Henry told her, "I agreed to help him."

Elizabeth was as surprised by this as he had been, and she took a moment before asking, "Did he ask Frances to go with him?"

"He asked me if he could, I told him no," recounted Henry.

"Are you worried she'll go anyway?" she asked carefully.

"Hell yes! What do you think?" Henry blurted, then quickly regretted his outburst.

"She might," returned Elizabeth calmly, "Shouldn't it be her decision?"

"Frances is so young, so naïve!" worried Henry, wringing his hands as the enormity of the situation continued to grow within him.

"She's eighteen, Henry," said Elizabeth calmly, "Don't be fooled by her girlish enthusiasm. She's wise beyond her years."

"Do you think William will ask her to go, despite my opposition?" asked Henry.

"I think it likely," she nodded, "Honorable for him to ask you first."

"Even though I'm against it?" Henry asked.

"You are not her father, Henry," she replied firmly, "He loves Frances, and she loves him. What would you do?"

"The gulf is too great," Henry sighed, "I can't put myself in William's shoes."

"Nor Frances' shoes," Elizabeth said, "How will she be when Charles and your mother arrive?"

Henry had no answer, so they blew out the candle and climbed into bed. Elizabeth snuggled against him and was soon asleep. Henry lay awake for an hour, thinking through the ramifications of William's bold decision, and how he should feel about Frances. He drifted off at last, and dreamed he was on a small ship in a vast ocean, lost.

Just after breakfast the next morning, Henry and Elizabeth sat in the drawing room discussing the guest list for Henry's impending Majority. Craigie appeared at the door.

"Is there a carriage that can take William to Edinburgh today?" called Henry.

"That can be arranged," nodded Craigie, "What does he need in Edinburgh?"

"Tools," replied Henry shortly, "The sooner they start, the better."

"I'll send Bob with him," said Craigie.

"Any word on when Charles will arrive?" asked Henry, worried that they might catch William at Dalkeith but not admitting that to Craigie.

"Not a word," replied Craigie, shaking his head, "That means they haven't made the Scottish border yet. I have a fast rider watching for them."

"Very well," nodded Henry, "A question for you. Should we invite a few tenants to the party, perhaps the Armstrongs?"

"With all due respect," said Craigie, "please don't."

"Why?" asked Henry.

"For the same reason your sister can't marry William," he said frankly, startling them both.

"Explain, Mr. Craigie," ordered Henry warily, wondering why his superintendent would skate onto thin ice.

"When I visit a tenant," said Craigie, "they usually complain about their house. Now they ask when they'll get their book like the Armstrongs did. Some lines shouldn't be crossed, Duke Henry. You create expectations that can't be filled."

Henry and Elizabeth looked at each other, and slowly nodded in agreement. Henry could see the sense in Craigie's words, and belatedly, he could also appreciate the risk the man took to make his point. They wouldn't invite any tenants to the party.

Craigie didn't wait for a response, saying curtly, "I'll see to the cart," as he left the room. Less than a minute after his departure, Frances entered.

"Good morning, have either of you seen William?" she asked.

"Not since last night, sister," said Henry, "He's going shopping in Edinburgh today."

Frances raised her eyebrows quizzically, but then decided to say nothing. She lingered for a moment as they watched her, then she spun on her heel and left with only a nod.

"I sense momentous events draw near," said Elizabeth.

"I'm sorry William has to leave before my birthday," sighed Henry.

"I'm sorry William has to leave, period," agreed Elizabeth.

Next it was Adam who appeared in the drawing room doorway. "I'm off for a short ride, care to join me?" he asked.

"Hello Mr. Smith, not for me today," said Elizabeth.

"I'll join you, Adam," said Henry, and soon Elizabeth was alone in the drawing room.

A half-hour later, Henry and Adam walked their horses down the shady lane. "Any word on when your parents arrive?" Adam inquired.

"Not yet," replied Henry, "Craigie says they're not to the border yet or he'd know."

"Are you ready to take charge, Henry?" Adam asked plainly, seeing there was something on the young Duke's mind.

"I think so," he began tentatively, "I'm concerned about their arrival. We left London on the sly because of William."

"How will they react, seeing him here?" Adam inquired gently, dipping his head to avoid a low-hanging branch.

"He's going to America, Adam," said Henry, "Keep it close."

Adam raised his eyebrows. "That's a surprise, but understandable. My former servant Robert went to Canada. Will Frances go with him?"

Henry looked at him in exasperation, and said fervently, "I sure hope not." They rode along, slower than their normal pace, for several minutes before Henry asked, "Can I ask you something else?"

"Certainly," replied Adam.

"When we left London, we didn't tell any falsehoods to Charles or Mother, but we didn't tell them our plan either. Do you consider that lying?"

"The prudent man is always sincere," advised Adam, "but not always frank and open. He never tells anything but the truth, but he does not always tell the whole truth. You are not bound to tell all you know to everyone."

"Elizabeth and I have been pondering that," Henry said, "Here's something else – should we let William ask Frances to go to America with him?"

"That may be out of your control," said Adam, "William and Frances might decide for themselves."

"That's what Elizabeth thinks," nodded Henry, "She said I should put myself in William's shoes and see from his point of view."

"The first thing you have to know is yourself," was Adam's reply.

"But it's William I'm wondering about," replied Henry, puzzled.

"You are trying to decide how *you* should feel about William," corrected Adam, "And about Frances."

"So, I'm just being selfish?" Henry asked with a wrinkled brow.

"When our feelings are almost always so selfish," said Adam, "how comes it that our active principles should often be so generous and noble?"

"I do care about William," Henry agreed, "and Frances."

"Is William resolved to live free, fearless, and independent?" Adam asked.

"That sounds like him," said Henry.

"Then William should go to America," smiled Adam, kicking his horse into a canter.

· · · ·

IT WAS A QUIET AND sultry afternoon the next day as Frances walked by herself through the gardens, watching the hired gardeners restoring the flowerbeds and trimming the shrubbery.

"Frances!" called William, and she turned to see him hastening towards her. A smile spread across her face as he got close. "I have something to tell you," he said, "Can we walk?"

They walked side by side, but not holding hands because of the gardeners. "Mother and Father will be upset when they arrive," started Frances, voicing a concern that grew daily as Henry's Majority approached.

"Don't worry," said William, "I'm leaving tomorrow."

Frances stopped abruptly and turned to him. Her voice trembled. "Leaving?"

"I'm going to America, Frances," he said. Her lower lip trembled, her eyes moistened, and then she threw her arms around him and burst into tears. "Oh no!" she sobbed into his chest.

"Yes, it's best," he whispered, hugging her tight, a lump forming in his throat.

"There are wild Indians in America!" she wailed, not caring what the gardeners might think.

"Only on the frontier, Frances," he replied earnestly, "Places like Ohio."

"Such a long voyage! I'll never see you again," she cried.

William gently disengaged and looked at her tear-stained face. "Come with me, Frances!" he urged fiercely, squeezing her arms in his big hands.

"Go with you?" said Frances in a small voice.

"Yes!" said William with enthusiasm, "There are no guilds in America, no dukes, lords, or earls. We can make our own way. I'll take care of you, Frances."

She looked at him for a long moment, then threw her arms around him again and pulled him close. "Oh, I love you, William," she sobbed into his chest, and they stayed that way for a full minute, the gardeners no longer even in their awareness.

"Come with me, love," he said gently.

"How can I leave my family, my country?" she asked, "If I cross the ocean I'll never return."

"We'll start a new life there, Frances!" said William with hope, "I bought tools in Edinburgh yesterday. I should say, Henry bought me tools."

"Henry knows you're going?" asked Frances, her cheeks wet so that strands of her hair stuck to them. She brushed them back absently.

"Yes," William nodded.

"What did he say," asked Frances.

"He said he'd help me," he responded.

"Did he mean, help *us*?" she persisted.

"He didn't want me to ask you," William admitted, "He loves you too much. But if there's even the slightest chance of us being together..."

Frances pulled him close again and they stood that way for several minutes. From an upstairs window of the Dalkeith mansion, Elizabeth watched, wondered, and worried. Finally, William and Frances walked on, and this time they were holding hands.

Chapter 58

A TRI-CORNER HAT *August 1767*
Caroline appeared in the doorway of Charles' Adderbury office, dressed in short sleeves as the days had been so warm. "Are you all packed, husband?" she asked brightly, "We leave tomorrow morning."

Charles put down the letter he was reading, pushed back his chair, and got to his feet. He felt a disturbing twinge in his lower abdomen, and it took him a moment to straighten with a grimace.

"I think so, dear," he replied, then raised his voice and yelled, "Cook!"

Cook appeared behind Caroline in the doorway. "Am I packed for Scotland?" Charles asked.

"Your trunk is ready," replied Cook, "only your personal bag is left."

Charles sat down heavily, wincing again, so that Caroline noticed and asked, "Are you not feeling well?"

"I'm sure it's just gas," he replied, shaking his head. "It's nothing."

"Well, perhaps you should lie down," advised his wife, "We have to be there by his birthday."

She left him sitting at his desk, where Charles remained for several minutes holding his head in his hands. Finally, he pulled an envelope from a drawer and dipped a quill in ink. He carefully wrote 'Frances' on the envelope, then pulled the diamond ring from his finger. Placing the ring inside, he sealed it with his signet ring and put it in another drawer. Charles sighed and returned his head to his hands, where he remained for half an hour.

• • • •

MILES NORTH THAT EVENING, William was in his Dalkeith room, carefully packaging his new tools for safe transport. He was barefoot, in breeches and an open shirt, and a large trunk stood packed and ready in the middle of the room, which was illuminated by a single candle. His new suit hung nearby, pressed and ready. His face was somber but wore a determined expression as he fitted the tools into the trunk and closed the lid. As he latched it, a gentle tap came on his door. He opened it and Frances slipped inside, dressed in her night shift with a shawl wrapped around her shoulders. She came into his arms and lifted her face to be kissed, and he readily obliged.

For a minute he crushed Frances' body to his and kissed her again and again. Finally, he pushed her to arm's length and said, "I must know."

She investigated his desperate, determined face with love, but said firmly, "I can't go with you to America, William."

His face fell, his chin dropped, and he said, "You shouldn't have come, love. It's torture to hold you... to feel you."

Frances stepped closer to him and put her palms on his broad chest. "I've just found a new country here in Scotland," she said, "I won't leave my brother."

"Even when he returns to Adderbury?" asked William, fighting back his despair but trying to maintain his composure for her sake. His hands slipped around her waist and his fingers rested in the small of her back.

"Oh, I'm sure...," Frances said uncertainly, "but now that I've seen Scotland, I feel it's part of me. That I'm part of something much bigger than myself." She stood on tiptoes to kiss him again, moving her arms to encircle his neck. He pressed his body to hers and felt it tremble as they kissed.

Frances stepped back and let the shawl slip from her shoulders. She pulled at the bow that secured the neck of her short summer nightdress and let the front fall open to reveal much of her breasts. She looked at him without embarrassment and said, "It has to be you, William, my first love." She stepped forward back into his arms, kissing him again and again as his hands roamed hungrily over her body. He lifted her in his strong arms and carried her to bed, her nervousness overcome by the flame of their long-suppressed passion.

Much later, they lay close together on the bed, side by side, with the room dimly illuminated by moonlight through the open curtain. The candle had long since expired. "You're wonderful, William," whispered Frances, nervousness long gone.

"I will always love you," he whispered.

"I love you," Frances answered, rolling over and putting one hand on his chest. "Will you write to me?"

"I will," he promised, "Here or at Adderbury?"

"Adderbury, to start," she replied, "Where in America?"

"Wherever the ship goes, I suspect, perhaps New York," he said, uncertain.

"Tell me all about it," she said, throwing an arm around him and snuggling close. They whispered for another hour until William drifted off to sleep. Quietly Frances rose and wrapped her shawl over her disheveled night dress. She bent over the sleeping William and gently kissed his cheek, then, dry-eyed, she slipped towards the door. As she closed it carefully behind her, she heard him whisper, "God bless you, Frances."

The moon was almost down, and the last pale light shone dimly into the room, as William lay on his back with tears streaming silently down his face.

Frances woke an hour past dawn the next morning and stretched languidly as she blissfully remembered the experience of William's body. She felt different, womanly, but then her eyes went wide, and she jumped out of bed. Wrapping her shoulders in the shawl, she went to the window that looked out over the front courtyard. She carefully parted the curtain and peeked out.

A carriage and two-horse team waited in the driveway, the driver sitting idly as he waited. She watched as servants emerged with William's trunk and secured it to the back of the small vehicle. Then Henry and William came out, followed by Elizabeth, and she stepped back from the window in case they looked up and noticed her.

William was dressed smartly in his suit, and he sported a handsome new tri-corner hat. She watched Henry extend his hand, and William take it, shaking solemnly. Elizabeth carried a violin case, which she handed to William as they stood by the open carriage door. He opened it, and Frances glimpsed the fine instrument before he carefully closed the case and put it inside the carriage. He turned to them with a grateful look, and Elizabeth threw her arms around him and hugged him. Releasing Elizabeth, William turned back to Henry only to be hugged again, which made him look embarrassed. Frances laughed out loud from behind her window, but a lump formed in her throat as she watched their goodbyes.

William put one foot on the carriage step as Henry and Elizabeth stepped back. At that moment, he turned and looked directly at Frances standing in the second-floor window. He blew her a kiss, doffed his new hat to her, and climbed inside. The carriage rolled away as Henry and Elizabeth waved, and Frances stood bawling at her window. Her precious William was gone, gone to America. Frances watched as the carriage rolled out of sight, then she threw herself on the bed and no one saw her till noon.

Late that afternoon, Elizabeth found Frances wandering slowly in the garden. She stopped to smell a flower, then turned with a start as she heard Elizabeth's footsteps. "How are you feeling, Frances?" she asked, and was relieved when Frances gave her a small smile.

"I'm at peace with it, Elizabeth," replied Frances, her voice level and calm.

"You can confide in me," said Elizabeth, "I won't tell Henry."

Frances looked at her, wondering what she suspected. "I understand why he went," she replied after a moment, "But I worry about him. It was nice that you gave him a violin."

"That was Henry's idea," said Elizabeth, "He also gave him one hundred pounds cash money. He nearly wrestled William to get him to take it. Rest assured; William will step off that boat in America looking every inch the fine English gentleman."

"He looked handsome this morning," Frances said wistfully as she smelled a different flower. Then she turned back to Elizabeth and declared, "There are two reasons why I couldn't go to America with him. One, I am a Scott, and I belong here with Henry. But I'm not sure that's the main reason."

"What is?" prompted Elizabeth after a long pause, when Frances didn't continue.

"Fear!" laughed Frances suddenly, "Fear of the ocean. Fear of wild Indians!"

CHAPTER 59

MAJORITY *September 2, 1767*

Just past dawn, Elizabeth sat in front of her mirror, brushing her hair. The house was quiet, and Henry slept on the bed behind her. In the reflection she watched his eyes open, and then prop himself upon an elbow and look at her. She gave him a bemused smile, without turning, and without pausing her brush. An early sunbeam pushed a tentative shaft of light past the closed curtain. At last, it was the second of September.

"Happy Birthday, Duke Henry," she said to his tousled reflection, and saw his smile. She watched as he disappeared behind the screen and used the chamber pot, and then he returned to the bed, dressed only in his shorts. As he sat and reached for his breeches, she turned to look at him directly. "Would you like your present now, or later?" she asked.

He grinned at his fetching wife, with her lustrous brown hair brushed down and falling over her shoulders. She was his greatest gift and would be for all his years. "Now, please," he said.

Elizabeth rose and walked slowly towards him, hitching up her night dress a little bit with each step. He could just detect the baby bump beneath the thin fabric, and thought it added immeasurably to her great beauty. She came into his arms, kissed him long, and then pushed him back on the bed and climbed on top of him.

Afterwards, Henry flopped back on the bed, spent, and sighed, "Oh wife you are good to me."

Elizabeth sat cross-legged on the bed, ravishing, brushing her hair after Henry's hands had mussed it again. "Still no Charles or Caroline," she observed.

Henry had expected them for several days, and when each day ended with no sign, he felt relieved. "I never replied to Charles' letter," he mused, "Maybe they feared the worst."

"Terrible things," nodded Elizabeth, "Like their daughter falling in love with a wonderful man?"

"Yes," Henry replied, "They feared that exactly. Frankly, so did I. William's resolve was remarkable."

"Unbelievable, almost," she replied casually, looking away.

Henry detected something in her tone. "What do you know, wife?"

"I know nothing," she said innocently, continuing with her brush.

"But you suspect?" he pursued, sitting up beside her and bringing his face close to hers.

"Have you noticed a change in Frances since William left?" she asked.

"I... thought she took his departure rather well," said Henry, uncertain, aware that he might have missed something.

"There is a certain... maturity in her look," Elizabeth said, putting her brush down and looking frankly at her husband.

"Oh God, you mean after all that?" Henry said, clapping a hand to his forehead in disbelief.

"It's just my intuition, nothing more" cautioned Elizabeth, "You can't confront her with it. No questions, Henry."

"If there's a baby?" he returned, wondering at that moment, somewhat oddly, what Reverend Carlyle would think if the Scotts brought scandal with them to Scotland.

"We'll cross that bridge when we come to it," said Elizabeth simply, "If she comes to it."

Henry placed his hand on Elizabeth's bump and gently leaned his forehead against hers. "Speaking of baby...," she murmured, running her fingers through his unbrushed hair.

"Should we announce?" Henry asked, knowing the bump would soon show through her clothes and there would be no hiding her joy.

"God no," she responded crisply, "Don't mix patrimonies, one Duke at a time!"

An hour later, Henry, Elizabeth, Frances, Adam, and the Craigies sat at breakfast. They were well served; Margaret didn't have to do anything. The servants were happy as they wore fresh white breeches, shirts, and stockings, and black shoes with silver buckles. Each wore a smart dark blue vest with silver embroidery; the women's outfits were similar, with white dresses and blue vests. Since it was late summer, Elizabeth had skipped coats entirely, saving much time, money, and fitting. The servants were pleased to be in livery at all, especially since they'd been told the new clothes were theirs to keep.

"No word from Charles, Henry," said John Craigie, "Looks like you're on your own today."

"Can we certify my Majority without him? Without Mother?" Henry asked.

"I believe so…," Craigie responded slowly, "We'll ask Dundas when he gets here. Either way, I advise that it's too late to delay the party. Most of your guests are already on their way."

"What is the guest count, John?" asked Elizabeth.

"We kept it to fifty," Craigie answered, "With some effort, mind you. No tenants, as we discussed."

"Mr. Smith, if you need any letters written while we're here, I can help," volunteered Frances, making Henry wonder if she was thinking of Charles' impending arrival.

"A wonderful offer, Frances," replied Adam with a smile, then, turning to Henry, he asked, "When will you return to London?"

"I suppose it depends on when, or if, Charles and Mother are coming," said Henry, "What do you say, Elizabeth?"

"I'm in no rush as long as it's before winter," she replied, and at that moment Bob appeared in the kitchen doorway.

"Carriage in the lane!" Bob called out and disappeared.

Henry looked at Craigie, as it was not yet nine o'clock. "Dundas?" he wondered.

"I don't expect him for an hour or so," said Craigie, wiping his mouth with a napkin as he rose.

They all followed Craigie outside and into the courtyard, where far down the lane a carriage approached. Margaret quickly assembled the liveried servants in ranks on either side of the door, to make an impressive greeting for the long-expected Townshends. Henry stood before the door, flanked by Elizabeth and Frances. Adam and the Craigies stood on either side of the Scotts.

"Are you ready for this, Frances?" asked Henry in a low tone.

"As ready as I'll ever be," she replied with a serene small smile, reassuring her brother with her nonchalance.

Henry looked at the servants in their crisp livery, standing proudly at attention as the carriage approached up the long lane. He saw Bob, dressed exactly how he always was, with no fresh white clothes or blue vest.

"Bob, no fancy uniform for you today?" Henry called out.

A huge grin split the man's homely face, and he gestured to himself with a sweeping motion of his hands, "How can I improve on all this?" he returned, making everyone laugh and breaking the tension.

The carriage rolled briskly into the courtyard and came to a stop between the ranks of attentive staff. The door opened, and Cook stepped out; he was taken aback by the formal reception arrayed before him, with him at the center of attention. He didn't smile or hesitate; he straightened himself and said in a dignified, clear voice, "Charles is dead!" and all smiles were swept away in an instant.

A half hour later, Cook sat at the kitchen table surrounded by the Scotts, Craigies, and Adam Smith. Breakfast had been cleared away, but a plate was put before Cook as he gratefully drank a cup of coffee. He'd been long on the road, but he ignored the food. Taking a letter from his pocket, he gave it to Henry. "From your mother, Henry," he said, and as Henry read the single page, Cook picked up a piece of toast and took a small bite, then another, bigger one.

"It's in Mother's hand," announced Henry, raising his head, "A sudden illness, less than three days. She wants us to return as soon as possible."

"Did she mention his will?" asked Cook, mouth full as he discovered how hungry he really was.

"No, what of it?" asked Henry.

Cook swallowed, took a drink of coffee, and then said, "There isn't one."

Craigie groaned out loud, causing everyone to look at him, and his cheeks flushed. "Apologies," he said, "I have a bad feeling about this. I'm sorry for your loss, Duke Henry, Frances."

Frances had remained quiet, but at Craigie's mention of her name she burst into tears. Elizabeth moved to put her arm around the sobbing girl, but Frances moved instead to embrace Cook. She sobbed into his chest as one gangly hand awkwardly patted Frances on her back. Cook's lower lip began to tremble, and then he gave a big sob, and tears flowed down his cheeks. The attentive butler, so reserved, so competent, so prickly in attitude, loved the Buccleuch children from long association. With the death of Charles, Cook's entire world was spinning apart. Everyone stood watching Frances and Cook embrace, sobbing, and they were touched. Yet everyone in the room instinctively knew it wasn't because they'd loved Charles.

Bob reappeared in the doorway. "Another carriage in the lane!"

Cook started to respond, letting go of Frances, but Henry put his hand on his shoulder. "You are not on duty today, Cook. You're my honored guest. God bless you man."

There were two carriages in the lane, the first one bore Henry and Elizabeth Dundas, and the second delivered Reverend Alexander Carlyle. Margaret Craigie ushered them into the drawing room, where Henry, Elizabeth, Frances, and Adam rose to greet them.

"Tea, coffee?" inquired Margaret, and saw Elizabeth Dundas shake her head.

"Coffee would be splendid," nodded Henry Dundas, who preferred the rare beverage to tea.

"Just tea for me, Margaret," replied Carlyle primly, as he was known to rail in the pulpit against extravagances like coffee. The Reverend immediately sensed the strained atmosphere in the room, as did Dundas. "Is everything well today?" Carlyle asked Craigie.

"Well, no, not everything Reverend," he replied, "You should hear it from Henry."

"Are we still on for the signing?" asked Dundas.

"You tell me," said Henry, "Charles Townshend is dead." A stunned silence ensued. Charles Townshend was famous, even in Scotland, and the news was sobering no matter what opinion they each had of him.

"My condolences to you all," said Dundas, bowing his head gravely.

"Oh, that's terrible," said Elizabeth Dundas, "What an awful birthday present."

"God rest his soul," intoned Carlyle, "I remember him from his visit in 1759."

Surprised as they were, everyone in the room was calm and dry-eyed about it, including Frances, who had recovered.

"Do we need Mother, or my Guardian, to certify my Majority?" asked Henry of Dundas.

Dundas slowly shook his head, and then confirmed, "No, we don't. All we must do is witness that you are of sound mind and body, capable of taking responsibility for your estate." He gestured at Carlyle, who stood regally with hands clasped behind his back. "I brought Reverend Carlyle as the official witness. He is a disinterested party, you see."

"Not that I am disinterested in the noble House of Buccleuch," Carlyle added hastily, "It means that I am not in your direct employ."

"I welcome your witness, Reverend," said Henry, "Perhaps we can move to the desk?"

Everyone assembled around the ancient desk that Henry had uncovered the day they'd first arrived at Dalkeith. The ornate carvings had been dusted and polished, making it a suitable vessel for the event. Henry gestured for Dundas to sit in the upholstered chair, and everyone else arranged around the desk.

Henry spied Cook at the doorway by himself, and waved him in. "Cook, join us," he called, and was rewarded with a grateful look as the butler stood behind Frances, looking over her shoulder.

Dundas was thus the only one seated when he said formally, "As Solicitor of Scotland, I, Henry Dundas, ask Henry Scott, Third Duke of Buccleuch, if he is of sound mind and body on this day of Majority, September second, 1767?"

"I am," said Henry simply.

Carlyle was shaking his head, and Dundas, seeing him, looked sheepish.

"Whoops," he said, "You're supposed to raise your right hand, and then say, 'so help you God."

Henry smiled and raised his hand. "I am, so help me God."

"Reverend Alexander Carlyle of Inveresk, as duly appointed Witness, do you agree and attest that Henry Scott, Third Duke of Buccleuch, is of sound mind and body and capable of meeting his title and the responsibilities thereof?" Dundas intoned.

Carlyle, a dramatist by nature and by calling, let a long pause develop while he stood silent, as if his approval might be in doubt. He looked down his long nose at the young duke, then nodded gravely and said, "I do so witness."

Dundas signed the document as Solicitor, then gave the quill to Carlyle, who dipped it and signed elegantly in a bold script. Then Henry signed, and it was done. He felt Elizabeth's hand on his shoulder, and he turned and hugged her, then Frances. Amidst the chorus of congratulations, Elizabeth pulled Henry away.

"Allow me a moment with my husband," she said graciously, taking his hand and leading him out of the room. Slipping into an anteroom she embraced him and kissed him. "Congratulations, Duke Henry," she said, before kissing him again.

"What a shock about Charles," said Henry without letting her go.

"How do you feel?" she whispered, looking for evidence in his eyes.

"Forgive me, but I feel... *relief!*" he said, "Shocked at first, then relieved. It sounds terrible, but I felt like I was being swept towards a life I didn't choose."

"Like, Parliament?" she asked, wondering how far this would go, how their lives might change.

"We can do whatever we want!" he said excitedly, his reaction to the news of his stepfather's death anything but grief. Henry felt liberated, unburdened, free; that it came at the expense of his stepfather's life added drama to his situation, but not anguish.

"You're a monster," smiled Elizabeth, "but you're *my* monster, and I love you."

Just past noon, the carriages from Edinburgh began to arrive and disgorge the well-dressed guests. The servants bustled about, managing the carriages and the many horses, getting drinks for everyone, and directing people to the facilities after their long rides. They congregated in the large, refurbished drawing room, where long tables had been set up. Henry and Elizabeth, dressed in their finest, established themselves near the tall windows. Carlyle stood beside them and soon a receiving line formed, ever replenished by the arriving carriages. Carlyle introduced each guest, they exchanged a few words, then they were released into the drawing room where they were quickly supplied with champagne.

John and Margaret Craigie stood near the wall with Adam, watching the receiving line. The Craigies were dressed in their best finery, impressing Adam who had decided against wearing one of his fancy French suits. Instead, he wore his standard black frock coat, a snow-white neckcloth, and his freshly powdered wig. "Henry turned out a fine man, Mr. Smith, my compliments to you," said Craigie with a nod to the professor.

"With a beautiful wife," added Margaret.

"Henry was fine when I first met him," said Adam, "My Scot's brogue scared him some."

"I wish they didn't have to go back to England," said Margaret, "Life is so much more exciting since they arrived."

"He seems a steady lad," observed Craigie, watching Henry shake hands with the Chancellor of Edinburgh University, "Not shy, but not arrogant either."

"Their steadiness gives them natural grace," agreed Margaret, as she watched from afar as Elizabeth charmed the chancellor.

"In the ordinary situations of life," observed Adam, "a well-disposed mind may be equally calm, equally cheerful, and equally contented."

"Aye," said Craigie, "but this is no ordinary life, Mr. Smith."

On the other side of the drawing room, Frances stood beside Cook, watching the guests mingle.

"Thank you for bringing the news all the way to Scotland, Cook," she said.

"I'm sorry it was bad news, Frances," he replied, "May I say, you seem to be taking it well."

"I'd say the same to you," she answered, "but weren't we bawling on each other's shoulders a moment ago?"

"Just so, Frances, just so," nodded Cook, "But now we're composed, just in time for all this fancy company."

"Were Father here, he'd be taking all the attention from Henry," said Frances.

"Yes," Cook replied, "But for all his faults, he loved you dearly."

"I know," said Frances.

Henry Dundas and his wife joined Craigie and Adam, all holding glasses of champagne, but Margaret had moved off to talk to other guests. Elizabeth Dundas said, "You have become quite famous, Mr. Smith. Why have you never taken a wife?"

Adam, surprised by her question, paused then said, "I am a beau only in my books, I'm afraid."

"Speaking of books, I hear you're writing another?" inquired Dundas.

"Yes, a book on Tax and Revenue," replied Adam, "The Wealth of Nations, so to speak."

"No offense, but that sounds frightfully dull," observed Elizabeth Dundas. She knew Adam was famous, but had little interest in anything other than titles, social standing, and the related gossip.

"Not in Mr. Smith's hands, I'll wager," said Craigie, "The subject of money is always a sure people pleaser."

"Any thought of writing a book about Justice?" asked Dundas, "Your lectures on that topic are famous throughout Scotland."

"They are?" asked his wife, and Adam smiled inwardly as Dundas had been less than ten years old when he'd delivered those lectures in Edinburgh in 1750. He saw that Dundas was well-read and knew his city.

"I hope to, Mr. Dundas," Adam replied with a nod at his compliment, "All that's necessary for a successful country are secure borders, low taxes, and a tolerable sense of justice."

"Well-said, Mr. Smith," Dundas replied, "As an Advocate, I am in the justice business!"

"Society might exist without kindness," returned Adam, "but injustice must utterly destroy it."

The guests had all arrived, the reception line emptied, and soon Alexander Carlyle joined their group with a glass in his hand. "I must say, Mr. Smith, that our worst fears about you were wrong," said the clergyman.

"Fears?" asked Adam.

"When Townshend appointed you Henry's tutor, we all thought it a peculiar choice."

"Peculiar?" wondered Adam.

"A closeted academic is not exactly a man of the world, is he?" asked Carlyle rhetorically, "But Duke Henry has turned out well despite all that."

"Despite?" said Adam.

"Now, now, Reverend," interposed Craigie, "Henry shows a remarkable grasp of estate affairs, and I'm sure the professor had a hand in that."

Elizabeth Dundas had wandered off to find more interesting conversation, so Dundas leaned in and asked, "How will Henry's majority affect the estate, Craigie?"

"He can't possibly be much worse, can he?" shrugged Craigie, "Don't mean to speak ill of the dead, God rest his soul."

"He'll be off to London and that's the last we'll see of him," sniffed Carlyle, watching the young duke mingle on the far side of the drawing room.

A servant rang a bell, threw his shoulders back, and announced, "Please be seated for dinner."

The long tables were set up parallel to each other and connected at one end by the shorter head table, where sat Henry, Elizabeth, Frances, John and Margaret Craigie, and Adam Smith. Next to Adam, at the first position on the long table, sat Cook. On the other side, Carlyle occupied the first position, sitting next to Margaret Craigie. The rest of the guests sat along the long tables that stretched the length of the drawing room. The curtains had been tied back, and bright September sunshine filled the space.

When everyone was seated and had their glasses refreshed, Henry stood. He didn't need to tap a glass for attention, as he saw all heads turn towards him. "Thank you all for coming to my birthday," he said in a loud, clear voice, "Today, I reach Majority and assume control of the Buccleuch estates." Everyone clapped, politely, briefly, and then Henry said, "First, may I ask Reverend Carlyle to lead us in prayer."

Carlyle, pleased by this, rose imperially to his feet and held up his open hands. "Lord, bless these guests, Duke Henry and his family, Dalkeith Estate, and all Scotland. Favor the Duke's return to his ancestral lands, where his brothers and father are buried, and where his future is bound with ours. Let us enjoy in your grace the fair and bountiful land you have provided. Amen." Carlyle gave Henry a piercing glance, then sat down.

Henry wondered what he'd meant about 'futures bound with ours,' but said simply, "Thank you, Reverend." All eyes turned back to him. "This is my first visit to Scotland," he admitted, "I very much wish that I'd come sooner."

Henry paused to collect himself, seeing only the blank faces of people he'd just met. The supportive eyes of his family were on each side of him, so he couldn't see their faces. "My prepared remarks are useless, because of terrible news we received this morning, delivered by Charles' Townshend's chief of staff, Mr. Cook."

Henry gestured towards Cook, and then waved for him to stand. Cook did so, abashed by the sudden recognition. He gave a little bow, and quickly resumed his seat.

"Charles Townshend died last week," announced Henry, and the guests who hadn't heard gasped. Townshend was famous throughout the United Kingdom.

"My mother, Caroline, remains in Oxford attending to his funeral," he said, "So, nothing but tumult this morning."

Henry paused again, measuring the reaction, but all he could see were polite, attentive faces. "Life goes on," he continued, "In the two months we've been in Scotland, I've learned much. John Craigie, Estate Administer, and William Ogilvie, South Estates Manager, please stand."

Both rose briefly to their feet and nodded as Henry led a round of applause. The guests knew Craigie; he was the solid note of continuity against the unexpected changes that the young Duke might bring. "These men will continue to administer the estate as before," reassured Henry, and an approving murmur swept the guests. Continuity seemed good to them; changes brought risk.

"You might know that I returned to London last fall, on the death of my younger brother, Hew Campbell Scott," he continued, "I spent over two years traveling with Adam Smith, former Professor of Moral Philosophy at the University of Glasgow. Mr. Smith, please stand."

Adam stood, but did not bow, as Henry added, "Mr. Smith is a very famous Scot, known throughout France." At this the guests clapped much more enthusiastically, not for the Professor so much as for famous Scots. Adam looked pleased nevertheless as he resumed his seat.

"He made me read many difficult books," said Henry, "His, for example." Laughter swept the room, and Henry looked directly at Adam and added, "A finer Scotsman has never walked the land, Mr. Smith," to renewed applause. Reverend Carlyle frowned; he thought the finest Scotsman should be a more religious man.

"The plan was to come here for my Majority, then return to London," Henry said, "where all the Buccleuch dukes have lived for some hundred years now." The room grew very quiet, as absentee nobility was a sensitive topic in Scotland. "As I've visited the farms, attended church services, talked to the people, I've fallen in love with Scotland."

At the far end of the long table a male guest added loudly, "You haven't been here in the winter!" and got a big laugh, including from Henry.

"You're right, I still have much to learn about Scotland," Henry nodded, "Despite my English accent, I am a Scot. My wife Elizabeth is a Montagu, so she's a Scot too." There was a round of applause at the mention of Elizabeth, her reputation had spread to Edinburgh, and this was their first look at the Duchess. To hear that she was a Scot was a real pleasure for most.

"So, as *Scots*," continued Henry in a resolute voice, "we plan to live here, at Dalkeith."

His proud announcement was greeted by complete silence as they absorbed the momentous news. Everyone wanted Scottish nobility to pay more attention to their native lands; now that one intended to do so, they worried about the change that might bring. As the silence extended, Henry lamely added, "We just decided this morning," and sat down. He was gratified that Elizabeth slipped her hand into his. The silence was ominous.

Dundas slowly rose and raised his glass. "A Scottish duke living in Scotland, imagine that!" he said jovially, but no one raised their glass, and the uneasy silence continued. Disappointed, Dundas resumed his seat.

Alexander Carlyle stood and straightened himself to his full height. He waited until all eyes were upon him, then he rendered his judgment. "I, for one, welcome the news," he intoned, "It's long overdue. Living amongst his own people, the Duke can't help but share our interest." Carlyle paused, eyes sweeping the room to ensure he held their attention. "Attending church in his own community," he said, his voice rising. "Tending his own lands, raising his own sheep!" Carlyle raised his hands dramatically, "Raising his children here! How refreshing! How wonderful!" Raising his glass high above his head, he fairly shouted, "A toast to Henry Scott, Third Duke of Buccleuch!"

The crowd rose to their feet as one, lifted their glasses, and replied, "To Duke Henry, hooray!" drank, and then, resumed their seats. Carlyle gestured towards Henry and yielded the floor. He'd done his part; he hoped the young Duke was grateful.

Henry stood again, wondering what he should say next, pleased with the ringing endorsement from Reverend Carlyle but finding him a hard act to follow. He thought of his English accent and remembered his first toast after crossing the border near Langholm. At his beckon, Elizabeth stood and clasped his free hand, raising her glass in the other. Henry smiled at her, raised his glass, and said in a loud voice, "*To Scotland!*"

THE END

NOTES ON HISTORICAL ACCURACY

Henry Scott, Third Duke of Buccleuch is a dramatization of a true story. All the essential events happened, and almost all the characters are real people, doing the things that made them famous in their time, and in history. Where applicable, their actual words are incorporated into the dialogue. To avoid turning a drama into a reference work, no footnotes are used in the text. The historical references are confined to the attached bibliography. Deviations from the known history are few, and they are intended to enhance the interest of the true story, not change it in any fundamental way.

Two of the main characters, William and Eloise, are invented. The character of William allows the story to highlight class differences (Adam Smith's 'ranks'), in employment, marriage, and society. Eloise provides a romantic interest for Henry in France beyond 'sowing his wild oats;' her presence avoids the inadvertent denigration of the sexual ethics of French women generally. (While we don't know for sure that Adam Smith slept with Comtesse Boufflers, it seems quite possible based on a letter she wrote to Hume after he returned to London with Rousseau.)

Many of the servants are invented, as they are usually lost to history, although Cook, Ignatius Sancho, Robert Reid, and St. Jean were all real people who served in the roles described. Ignatius Sancho is a remarkable person in history, and he really was the butler in the Montagu household during Elizabeth's childhood. He was also a noted musician and choreographer, and more than worthy of his own story.

The sad tale of Jean Calas is true, including Voltaire's Treatise on Tolerance and the King's reversal of the Toulouse verdict in 1765. However, his execution occurred two years before Henry and Adam's visit, so they did not witness his death. Nor did they consult with King Louis XV about the case. A drama that unfolded over four years is here shortened by half.

James MacDonald of Sleat died in Rome of illness in 1764; his death in Toulouse is a dramatic fiction. James accompanied Henry to Paris, and then visited him in Toulouse, as described.

Adam Smith's personal papers were burned at his direction by his friends, Joseph Black and James Hutton, in the days preceding his death in 1790. Accordingly, little is known about Smith's personal life, including his love life. The liberties taken regarding his personality are consistent with the person captured by his various biographers; the idea that Smith was an 'absent-minded professor' is supported only by a few recorded anecdotes of people who did not know him well. Brilliant teachers and lecturers are rarely absent-minded people; we know so little about Smith that it's easy to give excessive weight to minor incidents recorded mostly by hearsay.

Smith's first biographer, his former student Dugald Stewart, reported that Smith gave away most of his wealth, anonymously. As a human being, Adam Smith was the very opposite of the greedy capitalist caricature.

From letters Henry Scott wrote in his old age, his love for Elizabeth was lifelong. Although their first child, George, didn't survive his first year, they had many children and raised them at Dalkeith. Frances also remained in Scotland, eventually marrying the Duke of Douglas and raising several children. Much of the biographical information about Frances, including the allusion to Charles Townshend's inappropriate behavior, come from a memoire written by a close friend, Louisa Stuart, intended for Frances' daughter after her mother's death in 1817.

Rarely do so many influential figures in history coincide; even more remarkable is how well the adventures of Henry Scott illustrate the rise of the modern liberal order, particularly as they foreshadowed the American and French Revolutions at the end of the eighteenth century.

BIBLIOGRAPHY

How Adam Smith Can Change Your Life Russ Roberts
Penguin Group USA 2014 253 pages
Life of Adam Smith John Rae
Augustus M. Kelley, NJ 1895 / 1965 449 pages
The Theory of Moral Sentiments Adam Smith
Henry G. Bohn, NY 1790 / 1853 538 pages
The Wealth of Nations Adam Smith
Arlington House, NY 1776 / 1965 1020 pages
Adam Smith As Student and Professor W. R. Scott
Jackson & Son, Glasgow 1937 445 pages
Adam Smith, An Enlightened Life Nicholas Phillipson
Yale University Press, CT 2010 346 pages
The Life of Adam Smith Ian Simpson Ross
Clarendon Press, Oxford 1995 495 pages
Lectures on Jurisprudence Adam Smith
Oxford University Press 1982 610 pages
Adam Smith In His Time & Ours Jerry Z. Muller
Princeton University Press 1993 272 pages

• • • •

ADAM SMITH'S LOST LEGACY Gavin Kennedy
Palgrave Macmillan, NY 2005 285 pages
Adam Smith & the Scotland of His Day C.R. Fay
Cambridge University Press 1956 174 pages
Adam Smith Francis W. Hirst
Macmillan & Co, London 1904 240 pages
Adam Smith E.G. West
Arlington House, NY 1969 221 pages
Adam Smith in Toulouse and Occitania Alain Alcouffe
Palgrave Macmillan, NY 2020 312 pages
On The Wealth of Nations P.J. O'Rourke

Atlantic Monthly Press, NY 2007 242 pages

Our Great Purpose Ryan Patrick Hanley
Princeton Univ. Press, NJ 2019 156 pages

The Infidel and the Professor Dennis C. Rasmussen
Princeton Univ. Press, NJ 2017 316 pages

The Third Duke of Buccleuch & Adam Smith Brian Bonnyman
Edinburgh Univ. Press 2014 218 pages

The Life of David Hume Ernest Campbell Mossner
Thomas Nelson & Sons 1954 683 pages

How the Scots Invented the Modern World Arthur Herman
Three Rivers Press, NY 2001 472 pages

The Calas Affair David D. Bien
Princeton Univ. Press 1960 199 pages

The Townshend Moment Patrick Griffin
Yale University Press 2017 355 pages

Charles Townshend Namier & Brooke
Macmillan & Co. NY 1964 198 pages

Memoire of Frances, Lady Douglas Louisa Stuart
Scottish Academic Press 1985 106 pages

Letters & Journals of Lady Mary Coke Mary Coke
Kingsmead Reprints, Bath 1896 / 1970 247 pages

Educating an Eighteenth-Century Duke Ian Simpson Ross
Scottish Academic Press 1974 20 pages

The Righteous Mind Jonathan Haidt
Random House, NY 2012 500 pages

A Conflict of Visions Thomas Sowell
Basic Books, NY 2007 329 pages

Humanomics Vernon Smith, Bart Wilson
Cambridge University Press 2019 216 pages

On Crimes and Punishments Cesare Beccaria
Bobbs-Merrill Co., NY 1764 / 1963 99 pages
The Wit & Wisdom of Benjamin Franklin Ben Franklin
Barnes & Noble Books, NY 1995 86 pages
The Life of Voltaire, Vol 1 & 2 S.G. Tallentyre
Putnam/Smith Elder, NY 1903 730 pages
The Friends of Voltaire S.G. Tallentyre
Smith Elder & Co., London 1906 303 pages
Autobiography of Dr. Alexander Carlyle Alexander Carlyle
T.N. Foulis, Edinburgh 1910 615 pages
Websites
ADAM SMITH AT DOWNING STREET, 1766–7 - Scott - 1935 - The Economic History Review - Wiley Online Library[1]
"Adam Smith and the Contesse de Boufflers" by Mary Margaret Stewart (sc.edu)[2]
Adam Smith's Moral and Political Philosophy (Stanford Encyclopedia of Philosophy)[3]
Charles Townshend, 1725-1767, (historyhome.co.uk)[4]
TOWNSHEND, Hon. Charles (1725-67), of Adderbury, Oxon. | History of Parliament Online[5]
Adam Smith's Lectures on Rhetoric and Belles Lettres (sc.edu)[6]

---

1.   https://onlinelibrary.wiley.com/doi/abs/10.1111/j.1468-0289.1935.tb00886.x

2.   https://scholarcommons.sc.edu/ssl/vol7/iss3/7/

3.   https://plato.stanford.edu/entries/smith-moral-political/

4.   http://historyhome.co.uk/people/townshen.htm

5.   https://www.historyofparliamentonline.org/volume/1754-1790/member/townshend-hon-charles-1725-67

6.   https://scholarcommons.sc.edu/cgi/viewcontent.cgi?article=1721&context=ssl

From Benjamin Franklin to Mary Stevenson, 14 September 1767 (archives.gov)[7]

From Benjamin Franklin to Lord Kames, 25 February 1767 (archives.gov)[8]

Turgot: The Man Who First Put Laissez-Faire Into Action - Foundation for Economic Education (fee.org)[9]

Programme – Program – Colbert de Castlehill en son temps[10]

Tolerance (earlymoderntexts.com)[11]

08 | March | 2015 | Micheline's Blog (michelinewalker.com)[12]

The Paris Review - The Gruesome Case That Made Voltaire a Crusader for the Innocent[13]

Previous Exhibitions | Boughton House[14]

Isaac Barré: Advocate for Americans in the House of Commons - Journal of the American Revolution (allthingsliberty.com)[15]

Ignatius Sancho (1729-1780) – British Literature to 1800 (pressbooks.pub)[16]

---

7.   https://founders.archives.gov/?q=Volume%3AFranklin-01-14&s=1511311112&r=152

8.   https://founders.archives.gov/?q=Volume%3AFranklin-01-14&s=1511311112&r=32

9.   https://fee.org/articles/turgot-the-man-who-first-put-laissez-faire-into-action/

10.   https://colbertdecastlehill.com/programme/

11.   https://earlymoderntexts.com/assets/pdfs/voltaire1763.pdf

12.   https://michelinewalker.com/2015/03/08/

13.   https://www.theparisreview.org/blog/2015/03/13/broken-on-the-wheel/

14.   https://www.boughtonhouse.co.uk/the-english-versailles/previous-exhibitions/

15.   https://allthingsliberty.com/2015/08/isaac-barre-advocate-for-americans-in-the-house-of-commons/

16.   https://ohiostate.pressbooks.pub/engl2201/chapter/ignatius-sancho/

About the Author

A life-long resident of Washington State, Tim Hurlocker is an avowed history geek. He lives with his wife Suzanne overlooking Puget Sound, the most beautiful place on earth. His goal is to illustrate and promote the foremost figure of the Enlightenment, the Scottish philosopher Adam Smith.